Jewish Living

Jewish Living

A Guide to Contemporary
Reform Practice

by
Mark Washofsky

UAHC Press   New York

Library of Congress Cataloging-in-Publication Data
Washofsky, Mark
Jewish living: a guide to contemporary reform practice / by Mark Washofsky
p. cm.
Includes bibliographical references (p.)
ISBN 0-8074-0702-X (pbk.)
1. Reform Judaism—North America—Customs and practices. 2. Jewish law—Reform
Judaism. I. Title.

BM197.W37 2000
296.8'341—dc21
00-033770

Contents

Preface

Diversity.

There is no better or more accurate word to summarize the state of religious practice in today's North American Reform movement. Each Reform congregation or community charts its own course in Jewish living. Each makes its own decisions as to how it shall worship, how it shall organize and conduct its business, how it shall celebrate Shabbat and the festivals, and how it shall mark the important moments in the life cycle of its members. No one community's decisions are binding upon any other; neither the movement nor its rabbis attempt to enforce a uniform standard of religious observance among Reform congregations. Each community, rather, exercises independence in matters of practice. Diversity in approaches to observance is the inevitable result of the autonomy that each congregation enjoys. One cannot, therefore, identify a single standard, a single way of performing any ritual or ethical practice, as *the* correct standard for Reform Jews everywhere. This book, at any rate, does not try to accomplish that impossible task.

At the same time, however, Reform congregations and communities strive to ensure that their religious practices are unmistakably *Jewish* in style and substance. Though free to make their own decisions unencumbered by outside authority, Reform Jews do not define their Judaism as an all-new religion, lacking any real connection to Jewish tradition. On the contrary: Reform Judaism has tended to see itself as part and parcel with that tradition, a modern development of it and not a radical break with it. It is for this reason that, despite all the diversity and difference in detail, the general patterns of Reform Jewish practice—worship, Shabbat and festival observance, the ceremonies that mark the important events of the life cycle, and all the rest—follow the lines set down in the texts and sources of the rabbinic heritage. It is for this reason, too, that Reform Judaism has developed a literature of practice, a body of writings that explain Reform Jewish religious observance in light of the rules, principles, and methods of thinking that Jews have utilized for nearly two millennia to construct the form and content of their religious lives. The term the tradition uses to denote these rules, principles, and methods of thinking is *halakhah*, and the writings that embody them are called the halakhic literature. It is the Reform Jewish version of these writings, the compendia, responsa, and guides to religious practice composed over the years by Reform Jewish scholars, that I have in mind when I speak of "Reform *halakhah*." The authors of this literature do not regard themselves as legislators or judges; they do not seek to impose a particular standard of observance upon individuals or communities. Their goal, instead, is to explore and to nurture the enduring connection between Reform approaches to Jewish life and the halakhic tradition from which those approaches have developed. Reform *halakhah* is the literary product of rabbis and thinkers committed to the proposition that Reform religious practice is a form of authentic *Jewish* practice and that it therefore ought to be expressed in the language in which Jews have historically asserted and debated their responses to God's call.

This book offers an account of their work.

I owe debts of gratitude to so many people that the brief thanks I can express here hardly does them justice. Yet try I must. I begin with my colleagues on the faculty of the Hebrew Union College–Jewish Institute of Religion. They have created a community of scholarship in which I most truly feel at home. My students over the years, many of whom are now my fellow rabbis, have encouraged my learning by means of their questions and challenges, their discussions and arguments. *Harbeh lamadeti mirabotai...* (*B. Ta'anit* 7a).

Three of my teachers deserve special mention, both for the Torah they have taught me and the example that their life's work has set. I was never fortunate enough to meet Rabbi Solomon B. Freehof, let alone study at his feet, but every page of this book is testimony to his lasting influence. Although he did not create the genre of writing called "Reform responsa," he shaped it, breathed life into it, and set its agenda for generations to come. To those of us who work in the field, and indeed to all who read and learn from his writings, he is *harav hamuvhak*, our teacher *par excellence*. Rabbi Walter Jacob, his successor as chair of the Responsa Committee of the Central Conference of American Rabbis, serves to this day as my model of the scholarly rabbi, a teacher and pastor whose immense learning, deep humility, and gentle good humor leave a powerful impression upon all those who know him. Rabbi W. Gunther Plaut, my immediate predecessor as chair of the committee, also brings luster to the Reform rabbinate by dint of his scholarship, which he pursues—as he pursues all things—with boundless energy.

My perspective on many of the issues in this book has been shaped as well by conversation, discussion, and argument with any number of individuals. I am deeply grateful to them all, and at the risk of omitting names that ought to be included, I list them here: Rabbi Howard Apothaker, Rabbi Richard Block, Rabbi Ilene Bogosian, Robin Elkin, Rabbi Joan Friedman, Harvey Gordon, Dru Greenwood, Rabbi Yoel Kahn, Rabbi Peter Knobel, Cantor Sharon Kohn, Rabbi Audrey Korotkin, Rabbi Ruth Langer, Rabbi Dow Marmur, Rabbi Rachel Mikva, Rabbi John Moscowitz, Rabbi Stephen Passamaneck, Rabbi Richard Rheins, Rabbi Jeffrey Salkin, Rabbi Daniel Schiff, Barbara Shuman, Rabbi Arnold Jacob Wolf, and Rabbi Moshe Zemer.

Aron Hirt-Manheimer headed the UAHC Press at the time this project began. He, in fact, suggested that I undertake the project. Kenneth Gesser of the Press has shepherded the book through the publication maze. My editor, the indefatigable Bonny Fetterman, whipped the manuscript from a loosely constructed pulp into the actual book you hold in your hands. I am deeply indebted as well to Debra Hirsch Corman, expert proofreader, whose careful and sensitive attention rescued this text from many mistakes. The text owes its existence, in very large part, to them. For this reason, I would love to blame them for any and all errors found therein. Alas, I cannot; that responsibility rests with me.

I close with a special note of thanks to my wife, Connie, and my daughter, Michal, without whom none of this would ever have come to be.

Note:
The *Haftarah* portions for holiday readings suggested in this book are based on citations from Hoffman, *Gates of Understanding*. Other texts may list alternative *Haftarah* portions.

Introduction

This is a book about Reform Jewish religious observance. It is an attempt to describe the Reform Jewish movement of North America and its approach to religious life: its practices of public and private prayer; the organization of its synagogues; its celebration of the Sabbath, festivals, and special moments in the life cycle; the means by which one enters its religious community; its instruction concerning issues of medical ethics; its relationship to the non-Jewish world and to the wider Jewish community; and its teachings as to how we might sanctify the world in our daily conduct.

This is also a book about *halakhah*, Jewish law. It refers frequently to the sacred texts from which *halakhah* is derived, the Bible and the Talmud, along with the many commentaries, legal compendia, and rabbinic responsa written through the ages to explore those texts, resolve their difficulties, and apply their words to an ever-changing reality. This book is about the connections between Reform Jewish observance and the sources of Jewish law, and ultimately about the ways in which Reform Jewish religious life draws its definition and content from its ongoing relationship with the *halakhah*.

Rabbinic Judaism and Jewish Law

Judaism, as we know and understand it today, is a *rabbinic* creation. Jewish religion, in virtually every form we encounter it, is the product of a circle of thinkers and scholars called "the Rabbis" or "the Sages," who flourished during the first five centuries of the Common Era, which we therefore designate as "the Rabbinic Period." True, the origins of Judaism are much earlier than the Rabbinic Period; the Bible is the founding document of Judaism, and parts of it precede the rabbinic literature by more than a thousand years. But the ancient Israelite religion of the Bible is not yet "Judaism," certainly not the Judaism that we would recognize. It is the Rabbis who interpreted the biblical text for us and who turned it quite literally into a Jewish book. This is the case with the *aggadah*, the narrative or "story" aspect of Judaism. The Rabbis expanded upon the biblical tales, told stories *about* the Bible's stories, and created an inexhaustible treasury of literature that has served us ever since as material for thought, discussion, and debate over Jewish theology and religious values. It is even more the case with the *halakhah*, which deals with the forms of Jewish religious behavior. The Rabbis took biblical religion, replete with sacrifices, purity rituals, and agricultural festivals, and translated it into the institutions we identify as *Jewish*: prayer, the observance of Shabbat and festivals, aspects of Jewish home and family life, and all the rest. Without *halakhah*, the religion we call Judaism would never have come into being.

The Rabbis differed from their contemporaries primarily in their definition of "Torah." All Jews at the time believed that God had revealed the Torah to Moses at Sinai and that this Torah comprised the basic law of the holy community of Israel. The Rabbis, however, contended that in addition to the "Written Torah" (*torah shebikhetav*), a term that designates the Bible in general and the Five Books of Moses in particular, they possessed a set of materials referred to as "Oral Torah" (*torah shebe 'al peh*), a collection of laws and teachings that extend, expound, and supplement the biblical *mitzvot*. How the Rabbis viewed the precise relationship between these two "Torahs" is a matter of debate among historians today, but they clearly held that both of them, the Oral as well as the Written Torah, originated in the single act of revelation at Sinai and that together they define the covenant between Israel and its God.

The Rabbis of the first two centuries of the Common Era, who are called *tannaim*, expressed the Oral Torah in two distinct literary forms. One of these is *midrash*, a term meaning "interpretation" or "investigation." It presents the *halakhah*—that is, the laws and insights of the Oral Torah—as though it is derived directly from the analysis of the text of the Written Torah. The second form is called *mishnah*, a word that means "repetition." A *mishnah* is a statement of Oral Torah that does not require a verse of Scripture as a "prooftext"; it stands on its own and is learned, as it were, through repetition, rather than in the form of a commentary upon a written text. The relationship between these two methods of study is also a subject of scholarly controversy. Eventually, the product of these kinds of learning was written down in the form of books which bear their names: *midrash* came to refer to the collections of ancient rabbinic midrashic exposition of Scripture, while *mishnah* described particular collections of statements of oral Torah (*mishnayot*), edited by individual sages who taught them to their students.

Today, the word *mishnah* is best known as the title of one such literary collection, that attributed to Rabbi Judah ha-Nasi (about 200 C.E.). This collection soon supplanted all other such collections as the basic study-text in the rabbinic academies of Palestine and Babylonia. For this reason, it is called "the" Mishnah or "our" Mishnah, and its editor, Judah ha-Nasi, is referred to in later literature simply as "Rabbi," without need of further qualification. The content of the Mishnah is arranged generally by subject matter into six major orders (*sedarim*), each of which is divided into tractates (*masekhtot*). Rabbi was quite selective in determining what went into his Mishnah. From all the texts created by the *tannaim* he chose but a small fraction, leaving the rest out. For this reason, his work appears to be a legal code of the Oral Torah, one which includes the teachings he favored while omitting those he regarded as incorrect.

Unlike most legal codes, however, Rabbi's Mishnah cites many individual opinions which dissent from the majority, or the accepted understanding of the law. We are not certain why it does so. We do know that, over the course of its intensive study, the Oral Torah became the subject of numerous disagreements among the *tannaim*, so much so that, by Rabbi's time, dispute (*machloket*) had become a characteristic feature of rabbinic learning. Rabbi may very well have found it impossible to try to restate the Oral Torah without acknowledging the deep and widespread disagreements among its sages. We might put it this way: if there is no such thing as rabbinic Judaism without the Oral Torah, there is no such thing as Oral Torah without *machloket*, argument and debate.

> Why are the words of the individual sage mentioned along with those of the majority (who disagree with him)? After all, is not the *halakhah* decided according to the majority opinion? Because a court may some day be persuaded that the opinion of the individual sage is the better one and declare the *halakhah* in accordance with him. (*M. Eduyot* 1:5)

The scholars who studied the Mishnah in the academies of Babylonia and Palestine are called *amoraim*. They produced a great deal of textual material of their own, which took the name *talmud* (literally, "study"). The word *talmud*, like *mishnah* and *midrash*, eventually became a proper noun, the title of particular collections of this learning, so that today we can refer to the Babylonian Talmud and the Palestinian Talmud (or Talmud Yerushalmi). The Talmuds, which in sheer size dwarf the Mishnah many times over, are organized according to the Mishnah's orders and tractates, and this makes them appear to be commentaries to that earlier work. But they are much more than that. Talmudic literature discusses extensively not only the Mishnah but many of the texts of the *tannaim* that Rabbi excluded from it. In addition, it treats many legal subjects that are not, strictly speaking, part of the Oral Torah. These include institutions established by enactments (*takkanot*) or decrees *(gezeirot)* of the ancient Rabbis as well as practices that originated in the custom (*minhag*) of the community. The Talmuds, especially the Talmud of Babylonia, also contain a good deal of *aggadah*: commentary on biblical narratives, stories about biblical figures and earlier rabbinic sages, and speculations concerning physical reality and human nature. In short, anything that was of interest to the Rabbis winds up in the Talmud, which in turn became a kind of encyclopedia of the rabbinic mind.

As books of law, the Talmuds differ greatly from the Mishnah in style and approach. The Mishnah states its rules in a straightforward manner, usually not supporting them with Scriptural references or other argumentation. The Talmuds (and this is especially true of the Babylonian Talmud) are dialectical: their predominant form is debate, in which propositions are raised, attacked, refuted, and modified through the give-and-take of argument and counter-argument. The talmudic method of Torah study emphasizes a fact we all know, that there are at least two sides to every interesting question. More often than not, the Talmud does not usually conclude its arguments with the clear declaration that one answer or the other is the "correct" one to the question posed. It often leaves us with the impression that both sides are "correct," that either position can be supported as a reasonable, plausible interpretation of the principles or the text under discussion. The Talmuds, therefore, unlike the Mishnah, cannot be called "codes" of law. They are study-texts, whose goal is to help the reader think through a problem or a question as the talmudic editors would rather than to serve as an authoritative statement of the law.

Yet over the course of time, the Babylonian Talmud (also called the Bavli or the Gemara) came to be accepted as just such an authoritative statement. All declarations of the *halakhah* had to be supported by evidence and arguments drawn from this Talmud. That this happened is due in no small measure to the efforts of the scholars known as *geonim*, the heads of the renowned rabbinical academies in Babylonia from the seventh through the eleventh centuries of the Common Era. Located in Baghdad, the political and commercial seat of an Arabic empire, which stretched at its height from Persia to the Pyrenees, these academies maintained close contact with Jewish communities living in Muslim lands and, to a lesser extent, those living in Christian Europe. The *geonim* achieved an exalted standing as teachers and scholars in the eyes of rabbinic Jews everywhere. Individuals and communities would send their questions on difficult or disputed issues of *halakhah* to Baghdad and the *geonim* would respond with answers based upon texts and interpretations derived from their Talmud. Ultimately, these academies went into decline. By that time, rabbinic Jews accustomed to seeking their law in the Babylonian Talmud had begun to develop local rabbinical schools and intellectual traditions that enabled them to study the Talmud on their own.

The study of Talmud, a process that concentrated the attention of the rabbinic mind for nearly fifteen hundred years, has produced a huge literature consisting of three major forms, all of which originate with the *geonim*: *commentaries* to the Talmud and to related rabbinic works, which seek to explain these texts, resolve their internal contradictions, and derive new ideas from them; *codes* and *compendia*, books of law which present the halakhic rulings of the rabbis in accordance with some pattern of organization; and *responsa*, rabbinic answers to actual questions concerning Jewish legal and religious practice.

This last group deserves special mention. The responsa literature is the largest single genre of rabbinic writing of any kind; we know of over three thousand volumes of responsa containing more than 300,000 individual answers *(teshuvot)*. Each responsum is the answer of a recognized authority to a particular question *(she'elah)* submitted for judgment. Along with the answer, the responsum almost always contains the author's reasoning, the arguments he uses to justify *this* decision, rather than others that could plausibly be considered, as the best interpretation of the legal sources. Responsa are of immense importance to us as we study the history of Jewish law. They show us how the *halakhah* has developed over the centuries, case-by-case and step-by-step, quite literally in *response* to new questions, challenges, and uncertainties that previous generations had not resolved or even addressed. Responsa also afford us vivid examples of the rabbinic mind at work. In each responsum, we enter the rabbi's study, as it were, to watch an act of literary creation. We see the scholar take old texts and translate them into new statements of meaning, apply them to issues to which they have never before spoken, derive new understandings from words which have never been understood precisely in this way before. In each responsum, we listen to a rabbinic speech, a kind of legal sermon in which the rabbi formulates an argument that he hopes will persuade his intended readership to view the world of Torah and *halakhah* in *this* way as opposed to some other way.

This process affords us an important insight into the nature of Jewish law. In searching for a single idea which expresses the nature of *halakhah,* however imperfectly, we might well settle upon the word *conversation.* Jewish law is a dialogue among scholars, a discourse over the meaning of our sacred texts. In pursuing this age-old discourse, rabbis constantly rearrange the texts into new structures of meaning in order to respond to the challenges of the Jewish present and future. Like the printed page of the Talmud, which encompasses texts, commentaries, and commentaries-upon-commentaries that span fifteen centuries of rabbinic thought, *halakhah* is an arena of discussion in which the generations converse with one another, forward and backward in time, in a never-ending argument. The argument never ends because there are few answers to questions of Jewish law which are so clearly and obviously "right" as to preclude objection and criticism. It never ends because there are no short-cuts in Jewish law; there is no way to arrive at the answers one seeks except by way of the path of conversation. To determine the "correct" answers to questions of Torah is not a matter of rules and formulae, for *halakhah* knows of no automatic indices which can distinguish the right from the wrong interpretations. "Correct" answers emerge out of the process of argument that fills the Talmud and all the books written to explain it. They are tentative conclusions whose rightness is based upon the ability of one school of thought to persuade the community of rabbinic scholars that its point of view represents the best understanding of Torah and of God's demands upon us. To engage in *halakhah*, therefore, is to take one's part in the discourse of the generations, to add one's own voice to the chorus of conversation and argument that has for nearly two millennia been the form and substance of Jewish law.

Reform Judaism and the Halakhah

The Reform movement, over the two centuries of its history, has taken an active participating role in this conversation. It has always concerned itself with matters of *halakhah*, and the language of *halakhah* has always served as its means of religious expression. In the formative period of Reform Judaism, in both Europe and America, Reform scholars and thinkers sought to explain and justify in halakhic terms the innovations they introduced into Jewish religious observance. They did this out of their conviction that this "new" Judaism was a direct continuation of the rabbinic religion that was the common heritage of all Jews. Thus they wrote responsa which attempted to demonstrate that their innovations in Jewish ritual, such as prayer in the vernacular, the use of instrumental music at services, and the placing of the *bimah* at the front rather than in the center of the sanctuary, were entirely consistent with Jewish law.

This Reform halakhic literature waned after several decades. Many reformers sought to explain their position in terms of the forces of historical development rather than through the dialectics of talmudic argument and found responsa ill-suited to their purpose. Others, the so-called "radical reformers," who saw their religion as a revolutionary new phenomenon in Judaism, broke sharply with the rabbinic-halakhic heritage. This was especially true in the United States, where Reform Judaism developed in a most radical direction. Yet halakhic language never disappeared from Reform Jewish speech, nor were subjects of halakhic importance dropped from the movement's agenda. The *Yearbooks* of the Central Conference of American Rabbis (CCAR), which began to appear during the height of the "radical" period in 1890, contain numerous lectures, papers, and debates devoted to questions of ritual observance in which halakhic literature plays a central role.

In recent decades, moreover, North American Reform has turned away from radicalism and toward a renewed interest in religious observance, an interest marked by the appearance of such guides to ritual practice as *A Guide for Reform Jews* by Frederic Doppelt and David Polish (1957) and *Liberal Judaism at Home* by Morrison D. Bial (1971). While these were works of individual scholars, during the 1970s and 1980s the CCAR itself, through the agency of its Committee on Reform Jewish Practice, published comprehensive guides to religious observance, which were and are widely distributed among North American Reform congregations. *A Shabbat Manual* (1972), *Gates of Mitzvah* (1979), *Gates of the Seasons* (1983), and *Gates of Shabbat* (1991) describe the central elements of Jewish observance as interpreted by Reform Judaism, and all of them draw deeply upon the literature of Talmud and *halakhah*. The editions of the CCAR *Rabbi's Manual* and the two volumes of *Gates of Understanding*, the commentaries to the prayer-books currently published by the CCAR, offer explanations of Reform practice in life-cycle ceremonies and in liturgy that are replete with references to the Talmud, codes, and responsa literature. Perhaps the most systematic and ambitious of all these works is Solomon B. Freehof's classic *Reform Jewish Practice in Its Rabbinic Background*, which attempts to "describe present-day Reform Jewish practices and the traditional rabbinic laws from which they are derived." And then there are the responsa, hundreds of decisions and opinions on questions of Jewish practice issued by the Responsa Committee of the CCAR, which has existed since 1906, and by individual Reform rabbis, most notably Solomon B. Freehof, the author of eight volumes of responsa. These essays and decisions, taken together, constitute the largest single body of Reform Jewish thinking on matters of observance and practice. And like the responsa literature in general, Reform responsa are essentially *halakhic* documents: they speak in halakhic terms, cite halakhic sources, and reach their conclusions through a process that students of halakhic literature would find quite familiar.

How do we explain this record of writing, this continuing attachment to *halakhah* and its literature in a "non-halakhic" movement which has rejected the authority of Jewish law? The only reasonable answer is that this rejection was never as drastic as it may have seemed. Reform Judaism may indeed have dispensed with the "rule of law," the notion that every religious question must be submitted to rabbis for authoritative judgment, but it did not discard the law itself, the substance of halakhic observance as it has come down to us. That substance can be seen quite clearly in the concrete religious life of Reform Judaism. The forms of our religious practice are all based upon "traditional" Jewish models, which are *rabbinic* and *halakhic* in nature. Consider for a moment some of the more prominent features of Reform observance. When we gather in our synagogues to worship, we recite a liturgy whose fundamental elements—the recitation of the *Shema*, the *Tefillah*, the reading of the Torah, benedictions recited at various occasions—are described and defined for us in the Mishnah and the Talmud. When we celebrate our holy days—when we kindle the Sabbath and *yom tov* candles, say *Kiddush*, and eat the festive meal; when we conduct our Pesach Seder; when we build and sit in the *sukkah*, when we take the *lulav* and *etrog*; when we hear the *shofar* on Rosh Hashanah and fast on Yom Kippur; when we joyfully observe Simchat Torah, Chanukah, and Purim—we are performing ritual acts rooted in the halakhic sources, rituals constructed out of sketchy or even non-existent biblical references. Then there are the ceremonies of the life cycle, the ways in which we mark such important moments as birth, marriage, and death. Some of these rituals are mentioned in the Bible, but we must turn to the halakhic literature to learn about them in detail. The very stuff of our religious life as Reform Jews, in other words, is halakhic. The ways we pray, celebrate, commemorate, and mourn, even in our liberal and modern style, are modes of sacred action that we have inherited from the rabbinic legal tradition. And it is to that tradition, to the Talmud and to the codes, the commentaries, and the responsa that we must turn if we wish to know this heritage and understand ourselves as Jews.

The reformers certainly created a new approach to Judaism which reflected a modern outlook on the world. Yet no matter how innovative or "radical" they may have been, they never created a brand new religion. Neither do we Reform Jews today define our religion as separate and distinct from the rabbinic Jewish heritage. Rather, Reform Judaism has always strived for a recognizably *Jewish* approach to religious life. And the standard by which we measure "Jewishness" is not one of our own creation but one that links our religious experience to that of other Jews. Reform Judaism cannot be understood without reference to the rabbinic tradition from which it emerged and which continues to serve it as a source of inspiration, definition, and structure. Moreover, this tradition within which we define our Jewishness is a fundamentally halakhic one. It is in the literature of *halakhah* that the tradition speaks most directly and clearly to matters of ritual and ethical behavior and works out its answers to the eternal question: what precisely does God, our Partner in covenant, want us to *do*? To the extent that Judaism expresses its highest commitments through deed, through actions intended to sanctify our world and ourselves, then the language of *halakhah*, the language of its religious practice, *is* the language of Torah. If we Reform Jews regard ourselves as students of Torah and our religious practices as part of that tradition, then we, too, must continue to take part in the conversation of *halakhah*, learning and speaking the language in which the tradition creates our practices, gives them shape, and bequeaths them to us.

On Reform Responsa

Halakhah is therefore a heritage that belongs to us as it belongs to all Israel. Its continued vitality in Reform Judaism links us to the religious expressions of other Jews, uniting us with them as part of a community whose history spans many countries and many generations. This does not mean, however, that rabbinic law and its literature function for us in exactly the same way as they function for other Jews. Just as we have our own particular experience as a modern Jewish religious movement, so do we have our own unique approach to *halakhah* which emerges from that experience.

Let us look for a moment at Reform responsa, our own version of the "questions and answers" literature that rabbis have been composing for centuries. In some important respects, Reform responsa are quite similar to those of other rabbis. They are, as we noted, halakhic documents, learned answers to questions Jews ask, written in the mode of traditional Jewish legal reasoning. Yet Reform responsa differ from other rabbinic responsa in significant ways. Some of the more obvious and important differences can be listed here.

First and foremost, Reform responsa are not "authoritative": the answers they reach are in no way binding or obligatory upon those who ask the questions, upon other Reform Jews, or upon the movement as a whole. Our responsa do not claim this sort of authority because, however important it may be to the definition of our religious practice, we do not regard *halakhah* as a process which yields mandatory conclusions. In Reform Judaism, religious decisions are arrived at by individuals or communities who take into account all the factors that seem relevant to them and then choose accordingly. Decisions are not imposed upon individuals or communities "from the outside," whether by rabbis or lay leaders. Thus, our responsa writers have always described their work as "advisory," emphasizing the right of its readers to reject or to modify the answers as they see fit.

To say that our responsa are not "authoritative" does not mean, of course, that we are neutral or impartial as to the decisions our people ultimately reach. Far from it: the very purpose of a responsum is to recommend a particular decision to the consideration of the person or persons who ask the question. As noted above, a responsum is essentially an *argument*, a reasoned attempt to justify one particular course of action, out of two or more plausible alternatives, as the best possible reading of the Jewish legal tradition on the issue at hand. A responsum takes sides, presenting an interpretation and advocating its acceptance. Like any true argument, it seeks to win its point through persuasion, and it can persuade its intended audience only by appealing to those texts, ideas, and principles which that audience, a particular Jewish community, accepts as standards of religious truth and value. A Reform responsum is just this sort of argument, directed at a particular audience: Reform Jews committed to listening for the voice of Jewish tradition and to applying its message to the religious issues before them. It is an invitation to the members of that audience, its partners in religious conversation, to accept the understanding of Torah and Jewish responsibility that its author or authors set forth. It is an attempt at persuasion, not an act of power or authority. This, we believe, is what the responsa literature at its best has always been.

A second feature that distinguishes our responsa from most others is our definition of the "right" answer to a question. Our responsa, like others, search for that answer in the halakhic literature; for all the reasons we have stated, we are deeply interested in what the *halakhah* has to say. We do not, however, identify *halakhah* as a set of crystallized rules or as the consensus opinion held among today's Orthodox rabbis. We see *halakhah* as a discourse, an ongoing conversation through which we arrive at an understanding, however tentative, of what God and Torah require of us. As far as we are concerned, this conversation cannot be brought to a premature end by some formal declaration that "*this* is the law; all conflicting answers are wrong." We hold, rather, that a minority opinion in the halakhic literature, a view abandoned long ago by most rabbis, or a new reading of the old texts may offer a more persuasive interpretation of Jewish tradition to us today than does the "accepted" halakhic ruling. We therefore assert our right of independence in halakhic judgment, to reach decisions *in the name of Jewish law* which, though they depart from the "Orthodox" position, make the best Jewish religious sense to us. In so doing, we follow the opinion, held by the some of the greatest teachers of Jewish law, that the "correct" halakhic ruling is not determined by the weight of precedent or by "what all the other rabbis say," but by the individual scholar's careful and honest evaluation of the sources.

A third difference lies in our history as a liberal Jewish religious community. Our experience has led us to see that Torah, if it is to serve us as a sure source of religious truth, cannot exist in the absence of certain essential moral and ethical commitments. These commitments are discussed and elaborated in the great theological statements issued by our movement and in the writings of our prominent religious thinkers. They operate in a concrete way in our responsa literature as underlying assumptions which govern our work and direct our conclusions. Among these, we can cite the following examples:

1. Reform Judaism is committed to gender equality. Our history teaches us that the ancient distinctions between the ritual roles of men and women are no longer justifiable on religious, moral, or social grounds. We reject any and all such distinctions in our responsa process.

2. Reform Judaism affirms the moral equality of all humankind. The Bible and the rabbinic literature sometimes seem to restrict the field of their moral concern to the people of Israel, suggesting that the "neighbor," "fellow," or "brother" to whom one bears true ethical responsibility is a Jew and *not* a Gentile. At least, that is what some Jews understand our sources to be saying. We, on the other hand, do not share in this narrow-minded view of Torah. We are moved rather by those passages in our traditional texts which call upon us to regard all human beings as children of God, entitled to justice, righteousness, and compassion from us. Distinctions between Jews and non-Jews are appropriate in the area of ritual behavior, for it is by means of these rituals that we express our exclusively Jewish identity. We reject them as most inappropriate, however, in the arena of moral conduct. Thus, Reform responsa hold that the standards of ethical behavior which our tradition demands of us apply to our dealings with Gentiles as well as Jews.

3. We are open to the possibility and the desirability of religious innovation and creativity. We do not believe that existing forms of ritual observance are necessarily the only "correct" forms of observance from a Jewish perspective. We believe that the tradition permits us to adopt new ritual and ceremonial expressions which serve our religious consciousness better than those we have inherited from the past. Permission to innovate, to be sure, is not an invitation to anarchy. Our responsa literature will call upon us to innovate in accordance with the basic guidelines by which the tradition defines and structures our worship and other rituals. Our responsa will also remind us that traditional observances, precisely because they are well-established, define us as a religious community, speak to us from the depths of our people's historical experience, and therefore make a powerful claim upon our allegiance. Yet while we should innovate carefully and respectfully, and while we should not abandon the standards of traditional practice without good reason, our responsa will not say "no" to new ideas merely because they are new or because they depart from familiar forms of practice.

4. Finally, while our responsa seek to uphold traditional halakhic approaches whenever fitting, we reserve to ourselves the right to decide when they do not fit. When even the most liberal interpretations of the texts and sources yield answers that conflict with our moral and religious commitments as liberal Jews, we will modify or reject those interpretations in favor of others that better reflect our religious mind and heart.

About This Book

This volume seeks to summarize Reform *halakhah*, to describe and to define the religious practice of North American Reform Judaism as set forth in the halakhic literature of the movement. Much of this literature consists of Reform responsa, particularly the decisions of the Responsa Committee of the CCAR written as answers to individual inquiries submitted by rabbis and lay persons. These responsa are published in the volumes *American Reform Responsa* and *Contemporary American Reform Responsa* edited by Walter Jacob, and *Teshuvot for the Nineties* edited by W. Gunther Plaut and Mark Washofsky. The collected responsa of Rabbi Solomon B. Freehof and Rabbi Walter Jacob also serve as vital sources for our Reform halakhic thought.

This book also relies heavily upon the following works: the guide-books to Jewish observance published by the CCAR, especially those which have appeared under the auspices of its Committee on Reform Jewish Practice; the prayer books, the *Passover Haggadah*, and other publications of the CCAR's Committee on Liturgy, along with the recognized commentaries to these works; the most recent CCAR *Rabbi's Manual* and its accompanying "Historical and Halachic Notes"; and resolutions and reports adopted by the CCAR as official statements of its position on religious matters.

One of the most important of these sources is Solomon Freehof's two-volume *Reform Jewish Practice*, a book which serves in some important ways as the model for this one. In his introduction to that work, Rabbi Freehof notes that he most certainly did not intend to write an authoritative statement of law, a Reform version of the *Shulchan Arukh*, but rather a description of the practices of Reform Judaism as these have developed within the context of the rabbinic tradition. That is the intent of this book as well. And though in some respects this volume aims at a more comprehensive treatment of its subject matter than that which Rabbi Freehof provided, its debt to him cannot be overstated. Rabbi Freehof is the *rav muvhak*, the teacher *par excellence* of all of us who approach the work of Reform *halakhah*. We are eternally indebted to him. The books, essays, and responsa we write are the tribute we pay to the example his scholarship sets for us.

The text is divided into nine general subject areas of religious observance, each of which is further divided by individual topics. The Notes that appear at the end of the volume serve several purposes. First, they cite those passages in Reform halakhic literature from which the text draws its conclusions, allowing the reader to consult the original sources for what may be a more complete explanation or argument. Second, the Notes provide the traditional rabbinic sources—the Bible and the Talmud, the codes and the responsa—upon which our practices are based and from which they have developed. Third, the Notes offer extended discussion and analysis of particular issues, especially those aspects of Reform observance that diverge from the "standard" *halakhah* or that reflect particular Reform interpretations of Jewish law.

The intention of the Notes is to help place Reform Jewish observance in its wider context, as a development of and a variation upon the rabbinic and halakhic tradition. The point is that, along with our penchant for creativity, innovation, and freedom of religious choice, there is a deep and profound connection that binds the forms of our religious life to those which have defined Jewish religious life throughout the ages. It is a connection that gives shape and substance to the essential *Jewishness* of our practice, even when it differs from that of other Jews. These differences do not for the most part result from our rejection of *halakhah* itself. Instead, they reflect our conviction that there are other—and often better—interpretations and applications of its teachings and that it is our right and our duty as Jews to build our own religious practice upon these alternatives. We remain, in other words, inside the rabbinic circle, part of the rabbinic family; we insist that our voice also be heard in the ancient conversation and in the ongoing argument over the meaning of Torah.

1

The Worship Service

Reform Judaism and Jewish Prayer

You shall serve Adonai your God. (Exod. 23:25)

And it shall be that, if you hearken to My commandments which I command you this day, to love Adonai your God, to serve God with all your heart and with all your soul . . . (Deut. 11:13)

What is this "service of the heart" (*avodah shebalev*)? It is prayer. (*B. Ta'anit* 2a)

To call Jewish prayer a "service of the heart" is to define it as an act that is at once both formal and spontaneous, ritually-structured and emotionally-charged. Prayer is a *service*, a ceremonial devotion to God, that is *heartfelt*, expressing the mind and soul of the worshiper.

Jewish prayer has always embraced these two fundamental components. It is first of all a *mitzvah*, a duty we owe to God as God's servants, a required rather than a purely voluntary act. The Hebrew term for the prayer service, *avodah*, is the same term used to identify the service of sacrifice offered to God in the ancient Temple. Like the sacrifices, which were ritual practices defined by precise guidelines and procedures, traditional Jewish prayer is a fixed liturgy whose schedule, contours, and content are prescribed in minute detail by religious law (*halakhah*) and custom (*minhag*). Like the Temple service, Jewish prayer is largely a public, communal matter. Our liturgy is written in the plural voice, declaring that we are a collective body, expressing the yearnings of the Jewish people as a whole rather than those of a particular individual. Yet if the liturgy is a *service*, it is supposed to be a service *of the heart*. Jewish prayer, in its original intent, was to be a direct and immediate expression of what we feel. A fixed liturgy can work at cross-purposes with this intent. If, through rote repetition, the words of the prayer book become stilted and stale, if they do not spring from the soul, then our liturgy has lost an element that it can scarcely do without. It is not a "service of the heart." In the truest sense, it is no longer *Jewish* prayer.

These two demands, corresponding to the ritual and the personal aspects of prayer, stand in some tension with each other. In the words of Rabbi Jakob J. Petuchowski, Jewish prayer is founded upon "the apparently contradictory claims of *keva* (fixed times and fixed liturgy) and *kavanah* (inwardness and spontaneity). Yet traditional Judaism affirms both principles." The history of Jewish liturgy is an account of the attempts by sages and communities to find the proper balance between these goals. One way to do it was to make room for personal prayer alongside the established text. Following the recitation of the fixed prayers, worshipers would offer *tachanunim* ("supplications") which conveyed their own thoughts and petitions to God. Another solution was found in the *piyyutim*, poetic compositions that accompanied and sometimes supplanted the regular prayers on Shabbat and festivals. The *piyyutim*, which usually developed the theme of the day or of its Torah reading, invigorated the liturgy with new words and imagery and enabled the congregation to transcend the routine.

Reform worship, like other Jewish liturgies, strives for a proper balance between these two basic components. The early nineteenth-century pioneers of the Reform movement accomplished this goal, on the one hand, by shortening the service, principally by removing the *piyyutim* from the prayer book. These complex and linguistically dense poems had always been difficult to comprehend. They were now, to all but the most learned worshipers, a tedious exercise that served only to lengthen the service and to destroy the very *kavanah* that they were originally written to instill. At the same time, the reformers added new compositions to the prayer book, usually in the vernacular but sometimes in Hebrew as well. The goal of this "creative" liturgical activity was the same as that which had once led to the writing of the *piyyutim*: to restore the sense of sincerity and inwardness to Jewish prayer and make it a more moving religious experience for the worshiper. In this spirit, Reform liturgists worked to transform the set order of prayer into that most essentially Jewish kind of worship: a service of the heart. The reformers sought not to change the nature of Jewish prayer so much as to reaffirm its original intention, for as we read in the Mishnah, "when prayer becomes a fixed thing [*keva*] it is not a true supplication."

Innovative liturgy has become a hallmark of Reform Jewish worship. While this has been true for many years, today's technological advances permit congregations to produce new and special services with dazzling speed and frequency. Even the North American movement's fixed liturgy, *Gates of Prayer*, contains numerous alternative services for weekdays and Shabbat, each with its own discernible theme and approach. Given this daunting liturgical creativity, it may seem pointless to speak of a unified Reform prayer "rite" or *minhag*. Yet while Reform worship pursues *kavanah* with great energy, it also remains vitally concerned with *keva*, fixed forms of prayer. This concern is conveyed most notably by the prayer book itself. *Gates of Prayer*, like all Jewish prayer books, is a *siddur*, an "order" of service marked by a certain liturgical structure. This structure consists of texts and patterns of observance established by the ancient Sages, the Rabbis of the Mishnah and Talmud, and subsequently modified through centuries of rabbinic legal discussion and popular practice. It is through this liturgical structure, the words on the page and the manner in which they are spoken, that the Jewish people has traditionally organized its historical experience and asserted its identity as a religious people. The Reform *siddur*, as the movement's official liturgical statement, is the attempt by the organized body of North American Reform Judaism to express its understanding of itself as a community of believing and worshiping Jews. Although congregations may modify the prayer book service or depart from it altogether, it is precisely in its fixed liturgy—its *avodah*, its *keva*—that Reform Judaism offers its most carefully considered religious self-portrait, along with its answer to the question: what do we mean by "the service of the heart"?

The Structure of the Liturgy

While the services in *Gates of Prayer* vary in text and content, they all follow a fairly set liturgical structure.

1. *The Evening Service (Ma'ariv or Arvit)*

   Introductory Prayers and Readings. A selection of biblical verses and other texts which help put the worshiper in the proper frame of mind for prayer.

Keri'at Shema (The Recitation of the Shema) is introduced by the invocation *Barekhu*, "Bless God, who is to be blessed," and its congregational response *Barukh Adonai*, "Blessed is God, . . . " The *Shema* is not a "prayer" (*tefillah*), but a recitation (*keri'ah*) of Torah verses which declare God's unity, God's sovereignty, and our acceptance of the religious duties that proceed from God's existence and rule. In the Reform rite, the *Shema* consists of Deuteronomy 6:4–9 and Numbers 15:40–41. The congregational response *Barukh shem kavod*, "Blessed is the glorious kingdom," is usually recited aloud. The *Shema* is preceded by the recitation of two benedictions. The first of these praises God as Creator of light and the world; the second praises God who has given the Torah to Israel in love. Following the *Shema* are two other benedictions. The first, *Ge'ulah*, which contains the well-known passages *Mi khamokha* and *Adonai yimlokh* from the Song at the Sea (Exod. 15), recounts God's acts of redemption in our history; the second, *Hashkivenu*, acknowledges God as our protector. It is customary in most Reform congregations to stand during the recitation of the *Shema*.

Chatzi Kaddish ("Half Kaddish"). The *Kaddish* probably originated in talmudic times as a brief prayer of consolation and messianic hope with which preachers concluded their sermons. Later, it became a feature of the liturgy. *Chatzi Kaddish*, consisting of three paragraphs, is traditionally recited at the conclusion of the Torah reading and of various segments of the service. It serves here to distinguish between the recitation of the *Shema*, which Jewish law holds to be a required act, and the evening *Tefillah*, which is theoretically a non-obligatory prayer.

The Tefillah. Tefillah means "prayer" in general, but the word also refers to a specific prayer, the prayer *par excellence*, the means by which the Jew fulfills the Toraitic commandment to serve God with the heart. It originally consisted of eighteen benedictions (*berakhot*); hence it is often called the *Shemoneh Esreh* ("eighteen") even though a nineteenth benediction was later added. On weekdays, the first three of these are devoted to the praise of God; the intermediate twelve (later, thirteen) are petitions for individual and community needs; and the last three give thanks to God and ask God to accept our prayer. On Shabbat and festivals (Passover, Shavuot,

Sukkot/Shemini Atzeret, Rosh Hashanah, and Yom Kippur), the nineteen benedictions are reduced to seven. Since it is considered inappropriate to petition on these days for our everyday needs, the place of the intermediate benedictions is given to the *berakhah* of *Kedushat Hayom*, the sanctification of that particular day. For weekdays, *Gates of Prayer* offers a "standard" *Tefillah* of eighteen benedictions as well as several alternatives. For Shabbat and festivals, *Gates of Prayer* follows the traditional format of seven benedictions. The evening *Tefillah* is recited aloud by the congregation.

Concluding Prayers. These include the *Kiddush* on Shabbat and festivals, *Aleinu,* and the *Mourner's Kaddish.*

2. *The Morning Service (Shacharit)*

Introductory Prayers and Readings. These may include the traditional *Birkhot Hashachar* (morning benedictions), which cover a wide variety of personal physical and spiritual needs, and *Pesukei Dezimra* (poems of praise), the recitation of Psalms and other biblical passages which prepare the worshiper for prayer.

The Recitation of the Shema (Keri'at Shema), the same as for the evening service, with the exception that only one benediction (concerning redemption) is recited following the verses of the *Shema* itself.

The *Tefillah,* essentially the same as for the evening service, except that the *Kedushah,* the "Sanctification," is recited during the third benediction. It consists of Isaiah 6:3, Ezekiel 3:12, Deuteronomy 6:4 (on Shabbat and festivals), and Psalm 146:10 placed together in a poetic setting. On the three pilgrimage festivals (Pesach, Shavuot, and Sukkot/Shemini Atzeret), *chol hamo'ed* (the intermediate days of Pesach and Sukkot), Chanukah, Rosh Chodesh, and Yom Ha'atzma'ut, the *Tefillah* concludes with the recitation of *Hallel,* Psalms 113–18.

The Reading of the Torah (*Keri'at Hatorah*), on Mondays, Thursdays, Shabbat, festivals, and Rosh Chodesh. The *Haftarah,* a selection from the Prophets or Writings, is read on Shabbat and festivals.

Concluding Prayers: Aleinu, Mourner's Kaddish, Benediction.

3. *The Afternoon Service* (*Minchah*)

The "*Ashrei*," Psalm 145 introduced by Psalms 84:5 and 144:15.

Readings for Shabbat and festivals.

Chatzi Kaddish.

The *Tefillah*, essentially the same as for *Shacharit*.

On Shabbat, the reading of the Torah is traditionally the first section (*aliyah*) of the portion for the following Shabbat.

Concluding Prayers: Aleinu, Mourner's Kaddish, Benediction.

Kippah, Tallit, Tefillin

> Speak to the Israelite people and instruct them to make for themselves fringes on the corners of their garments throughout the ages . . . That shall be your fringe; look at it and recall all of God's commandments. (Num. 15:38–39)

> Bind [these words] as a sign upon your hand and let them serve as a symbol on your forehead. (Deut. 6:8)

On Traditional Observance. For many years, one of the most characteristic features of American Reform Jewish worship was that it did not "look Jewish." When assembled in their synagogues, Reform Jews by and large did not cover their heads with a hat or a skullcap (called a *kippah* or a *yarmulke*), nor did they don the *tallit* (prayer shawl) and *tefillin* (phylacteries). In Europe, to be sure, most Reform Jews continued to wear *kippah* and *tallit*, even as some Reform thinkers called for the abandonment of these observances as outmoded vestiges of a bygone age. In the United States, however, their absence became synonymous with Reform practice. In 1963 it could be stated without controversy that in Reform temples "the congregation and the rabbi worship with uncovered head." The *tallit* was reduced to a ceremonial object worn by rabbis while leading services. *Tefillin* virtually disappeared. Today, by contrast, these trends have been reversed. An increasing number of American Reform Jews wear the *kippah* and the *tallit*, and some have even begun to observe the practice of *tefillin*. There are indeed few more visible signs of a "return to tradition" within the American Reform synagogue than the reappearance of these items of "Jewish religious apparel."

How do we explain these developments, the rejection of these symbols and their subsequent recovery? Although an adequate answer to that question would require a much more detailed look at Reform Jewish history than can be attempted here, it would surely point to the shifting tides of culture and outlook in which Reform Judaism developed during the past two centuries. The movement came of age in an era characterized by a generally negative attitude toward traditional ritual practice, an age when liberal religious discourse was dominated by the great themes of reason, science, and aesthetics. During this period, enlightened believers were taught that the moral teachings of Judaism were infinitely more significant than its ritual practices. The former were the "essence" of our faith; the latter were its ceremonial trappings, externals which at best may serve to protect the "essence" but which at worst can distort the message of Judaism and divert our spiritual attention away from the things that truly matter. Proceeding from this starting point, Reform thinkers understandably dismissed much of traditional ceremonial law and custom as "totemism," "fetishism," and "talismans," remnants of primitive cults totally out of line with the progressive outlook of a modern religion. The classic expression of this attitude is undoubtedly contained in the Pittsburgh Platform, adopted by an assembly of Reform rabbis in 1885, which served for many years as the authoritative summary of American Reform doctrine:

> We recognize in the Mosaic legislation a system of training the Jewish people for its mission during its national life in Palestine, and to-day we accept as binding only the moral laws, and maintain only such ceremonies as elevate and sanctify our lives, but reject all such as are not adapted to the views and habits of modern civilization.

> We hold that all such Mosaic and rabbinical laws as regulate diet, priestly purity and dress originated in ages and under the influence of ideas altogether foreign to our present mental and spiritual state. They fail to impress the modern Jew with a spirit of priestly holiness; their observance in our days is apt rather to obstruct than to further modern spiritual elevation.

Jewish tradition, in other words, had ceased to be self-justifying. No longer was it sufficient to defend a religious practice on the grounds that it was old. To survive in this era, a custom or observance would have to prove its meaningfulness before the bar of an enlightened and elevated "modern civilization."

By the middle of the twentieth century, matters had substantially changed. A new generation of Reform rabbis pressed for a new statement of religious doctrine. The Columbus Platform, adopted by the Central Conference of American Rabbis (CCAR) in 1937, reflected the theological stance of this new generation. Defining Judaism as "the historical religious experience of the Jewish people," it abandoned much of the rationalism of its predecessor and portrayed Jewish faith in more overtly traditional terminology. Where the Pittsburgh document had written off the bulk of the "Mosaic legislation" as irrelevant to modern religious life, its successor could declare that

> Judaism as a way of life requires in addition to its moral and spiritual demands, the preservation of the Sabbath, festivals and Holy Days, the retention and development of such customs, symbols and ceremonies as possess inspirational value, the cultivation of distinctive forms of religious art and music and the use of Hebrew, together with the vernacular, in our worship and instruction.

If the Columbus Platform did not entirely reverse Pittsburgh on this point—ritual must still be "inspirational" to justify its preservation—the rejectionist tone of the earlier platform had disappeared. Traditional Jewish ritual had now been accepted as a legitimate aspect of religious life even for the progressive, modern Jew. This theme was amplified in the CCAR's Centenary Perspective of 1976:

> Judaism emphasizes action rather than creed as the primary expression of a religious life . . . The past century has taught us that the claims made upon us may begin with our ethical obligations but they extend to many other aspects of Jewish living, including: creating a Jewish home centered on family devotion; private prayer and public worship; daily religious observance; keeping the Sabbath and the holy days; celebrating the major events of life . . . and other activities which promote the survival of the Jewish people and enhance its existence.

These later platforms speak as they do, of course, because the rabbinical bodies that issued them no longer shared the negative attitude toward traditional observance of the Pittsburgh rabbis of 1885. History, in other words, has led us to reconsider and even to reverse some of the decisions on religious practice made by past generations of Reform Jews. This most certainly does not mean that we reject the heritage of our movement, let alone that we have somehow turned our backs upon

Reform Judaism in favor of a "return to Orthodoxy." It means rather that we in our time have developed a way of thinking and talking about Reform Judaism that differs in some important respects from that of our forebears. Reform Judaism has always recognized the tendency of Jewish practice to change over time in response to its environment. In the past, this quality of adaptation has led to the abandonment of traditional observances which are no longer found to be meaningful as well as to the creation of new rituals to reflect the aspirations of our time and place. We have championed this process of change as a positive good, a sign of Judaism's responsiveness to the needs of each generation. We have cited it in order to justify and defend on historical Judaic grounds our own efforts toward religious reform. Our predecessors may well have understood "change" as a one-way street, a progressive movement away from a religion steeped in ritual toward a more rational and enlightened conception of faith. In our own day, however,

> we willingly move also in the other direction as history and the mood of our people re-emphasize older customs . . . Nothing would, therefore, hinder us as Reform Jews from readopting customs once omitted if a new generation finds them meaningful and useful in its practice of Judaism. We have always understood that such customs, when adopted by us, do not represent a divine enactment. In other words, we are willing to change in both directions.

Many Reform Jews and their congregations have in fact chosen to restore rituals that previous generations had eliminated. Such changes have made it customary to speak of a "return to tradition" in Reform Jewish life. Yet this "return" is more than just the tendency to choose traditional over non-traditional approaches to practice. It also signifies a sharp change in the religious discourse of the Reform movement, that is, in the way that Reform Jews talk about issues of faith and observance. The rhetoric of modernism has given way to that of religious and spiritual meaning. Reform Jews today base their religious choices not so much upon appeals to reason, science, and aesthetics, as upon the language of religious and spiritual meaning. "Meaning," as we know, can spring from any number of sources, and one of the most important of these is tradition. True, the fact that a particular practice is "traditional" does not guarantee that a Reform Jew will find it meaningful. Still, an observance can be meaningful simply *because* it is traditional, because it evokes the religious experience of the Jewish people through the ages, and because we find strength in our identification with that experience.

The "return to tradition" means that, when confronting questions over specific religious practices, Reform Jews are more likely today than before to ask: "Is it *Jewish*? Does it fit within the broad contours of Jewish tradition as we understand it?" For this reason, appeals to tradition are more common and more acceptable in Reform Jewish discourse now than in generations past.

Kippah. As noted above, praying with uncovered head was the rule for many years in American Reform synagogues. This rule, at odds with traditional Jewish custom, was evidently based on the prevailing standards of honor and respect in the general culture which dictated that one remove one's hat when inside a building and during solemn occasions such as worship. In 1928, Rabbi Jacob Z. Lauterbach, a professor at the Hebrew Union College and chair of the CCAR Responsa Committee, wrote a richly-detailed study in defense of the Reform practice, declaring that "there is no law in the Bible or Talmud prescribing the covering of the head for men when entering a sanctuary, when participating in the religious service, or when performing any religious ceremony." The practice of covering the head is not based upon any explicit statement in Jewish legal sources; it "is merely a custom, a *minhag*, that first appeared among the Jews in Babylon" during the rabbinic period (roughly, from the beginning of the Common Era to 500 C.E.). In Palestine, by contrast, the sources indicate that "people would not hesitate entering a synagogue, reading from the Torah, and participating in the religious service with uncovered head." This difference in custom made its way to medieval Europe: in Spain, which tended to follow the Babylonian practices, authorities required that the head be covered during prayer, while in France and Germany, which were more influenced by Palestinian ritual traditions, there is some evidence that Jews would pray bareheaded. Although by the thirteenth century the northern Europeans (Ashkenazim) had begun to adopt the Spanish (Sefardic) custom, later authorities in central and eastern Europe continued to write that the prohibition against worshiping bareheaded "has no foundation in the Talmud." As one of them remarked (in Lauterbach's translation): "There is no prohibition whatever against praying with uncovered head, but as a matter of propriety it would seem to be good manners to cover one's head when standing in the presence of great men, and also during the religious service." From all of this, Lauterbach concluded that the custom of praying with covered head "is merely a matter of social propriety and decorum"; since in our own culture it is considered "good manners" to remove the hat as a sign of respect, there can be no objection to praying bareheaded. He writes:

> Although in the last century the question of "hat on or hat off" was the subject of heated disputes . . . we should know better now and be more tolerant and more liberal towards one another. We should realize that this matter is but a detail of custom and should not be made the issue between Orthodox and Reform. It is a detail that is not worth fighting about. It should not separate Jew from Jew.

One may quibble over Lauterbach's interpretation of a number of his sources. Some of them do not say precisely what he tells us that they say, and this tends to weaken his argument somewhat. His central point is certainly correct: Jewish law makes no absolute requirement that one cover the head to pray, to study Torah, or to participate in other religious acts. On the other hand, his conclusion—that covering the head "is merely a custom, a *minhag*"; "merely a matter of social propriety"— hardly reflects what is at stake in this issue, for surely he was aware there is no such thing as "mere" custom in Judaism. Much of Jewish ritual practice is based upon custom rather than upon Toraitic commandment or rabbinic decree, yet the tradition does not regard it as unimportant or irrelevant for that. As the old Ashkenazic saying puts it, "the custom of our ancestors is Torah." Jews have always related to their customs with intensity and seriousness. Fierce debates in Jewish religious life are as likely to take place over matters of "mere" custom as they are over issues of Torah law and theological doctrine. This is no less true of Reform Judaism. Disputes over *this* particular custom at times took center stage in a number of synagogues. This was because it was widely held that bareheaded worship was an essential sign of Reform identity; just as traditionalists asserted that one was not a "good Jew" if one prayed bareheaded, many liberals believed that one could not be a "good Reform Jew" and wear a hat or *kippah* during prayer. Lauterbach may be right in pleading that the *kippah* is "not worth fighting about," but the fact is that Reform Jews *did* fight about it, raucously, for years. Many congregations went so far as to prohibit the wearing of headcovering during worship. Were the issue as marginal and unimportant as Lauterbach described it, such rules would never have been made.

Nor does Lauterbach's argument speak to the religious concerns of many contemporary Reform Jews, who no longer find spiritual meaning in worship conducted in accordance with a certain notion of decorum and solemnity, that is, a style that conforms to Western standards of propriety and "good manners." This is not to say that these Reform Jews are indifferent to "good manners" or that they have turned their backs on modern culture. It is rather that they are apt to discover a more profound sort of meaning in precisely the kind of traditional worship experience which previous generations rejected. These Jews have come full circle; they want a religious service that "looks" and "feels" Jewish, one that draws deeply upon traditional forms of worship and religious life. It is no surprise that the *kippah* has reemerged in the Reform synagogue. Though it may not be an absolute requirement of Jewish law, it can serve those who wear it as an unmistakable sign of the tradition with which they seek to identify.

Other Reform Jews continue to regard the *kippah* either as irrelevant to their religious experience or reject it as a reminder of a style of observance that the movement has long since left behind. Today, therefore, many choose to wear a *kippah* during worship and study, while others do not. According to Reform doctrine, neither choice is necessarily the better one; both are legitimate exercises of the personal religious autonomy that the movement holds dear. But if the movement is officially neutral on the choice, this does not mean that the issue is a trivial one, not worthy of careful thought. To wear or not to wear the *kippah* is no simple, flip-the-coin choice of "hat on or hat off." Indeed, because it partakes deeply of the realm of symbolism, because it can serve as a concrete expression of the way in which an individual approaches Jewish prayer and Jewish life, the decision to wear the *kippah* or not to wear it can be the most serious kind of religious decision a Reform Jew can make. For those concerned about building strong and vital religious communities, the challenge is to create the kind of atmosphere in which individuals can make these decisions freely, without being subjected to the sort of pressure that says: "there is only one right answer for a good Reform Jew."

Tallit and Tefillin. Gates of Prayer offers the appropriate benediction "for those who wear the *tallit*":

> *Barukh atah Adonai Eloheinu melekh ha'olam asher kideshanu bemitzvotav vetzivanu lehitatef batzitzit.*

> Blessed are You, Adonai our God, Sovereign of the universe, who hallows us through the *mitzvot* and commands us to wrap ourselves in the fringed *tallit*.

The blessing is recited while standing, immediately prior to donning the *tallit*. Then, holding the *tallit* directly in front of you with both hands, let your right hand bring the corner of the garment around your back to the right shoulder. If the *tallit* is large enough to cover the head and most of the body, it is customary to wrap the head completely with its right side, so that the *tzitzit* (the long fringes on the *tallit*'s corners) of that side lie across the back while the left-side fringes remain in place. It is then draped across the shoulders, two *tzitzit* in front and two in the back, so that "one is surrounded by *mitzvot*."

The observance of *tzitzit* pertains to the daylight hours. The *tallit* is therefore worn by worshipers during the morning service and not at night. The major exception to this rule is the night of Yom Kippur (*Kol Nidrei*), when it is customary to wear white as a symbol of the purity of our repentance. In addition, it has become customary for participants in the Torah service and for those who lead services even at night to wear the *tallit*, and this is the practice in many Reform congregations.

Women wear the *tallit* on the same occasions that men do; the *tallit* is not a specifically "male" garment. In traditional practice, women do not wear the *tallit*. This is because the observance of *tzitzit* is a positive commandment (*mitzvat 'aseh*, a commandment to perform an act, as opposed to *mitzvat lo ta'aseh*, a prohibition against an act) which pertains to a particular time (daylight), and women are said to be exempt from all such obligations. "Exempt" means that, technically, women are not forbidden to wear *tzitzit* if they so choose. In practice, however, it was considered a sign of arrogance and an unsuitable display of piety for women to perform this *mitzvah*, and "we do not allow women to wear the *tallit*." Reform Judaism rejects the logic which draws any ritual distinctions between women and men, and with regard to this particular ritual we certainly do not think it arrogant for any Jew to choose to wear the *tallit* at its appropriate time.

Gates of Prayer also provides the benedictions "for those who wear *tefillin*." After donning the *tallit,* fix the tefillah shel yad (the box for the arm) upon the bicep of your weaker arm (i.e., the left arm of a right-handed person, and the right arm of a left-handed person) and recite:

Barukh atah Adonai Eloheinu melekh ha'olam asher kideshanu bemitzvotav vetzivanu lehaniach tefillin.

Blessed are You, Adonai our God, Sovereign of the universe, who hallows us through the *mitzvot* and commands us to wear *tefillin*.

Tighten the loop around the upper arm and then wrap the *retzu'ah* (the strap) seven times around the arm between the elbow and the wrist. Place the *tefillah shel rosh* (the headpiece) upon the head at a point slightly above the original hairline. Then say:

> *Barukh atah Adonai Eloheinu melekh ha'olam asher kideshanu bemitzvotav vetzivanu 'al mitzvat tefillin.*

> . . . and commands us concerning the *mitzvah* of *tefillin.*

> *Barukh shem kevod malkhuto le'olam va'ed.*

> Blessed is God's glorious realm forever.

The straps of the *shel rosh* should extend downward in front of you. At this point, wrap the *retzu'ah* of the *shel yad* three times around your middle finger, twice below the knuckle, once around the middle joint, and recite Hosea 2:21–22 ("I will betroth you to Me forever . . . "). Wrap the remainder around the palm, with the end of the strap snugly tucked in.

The *tefillin* are square-shaped leather boxes containing parchments upon which are written the following sections of the Torah: Exodus 13:1–10; Exodus 13:11–16; Deuteronomy 6:4–9 (*Shema* and *ve'ahavta*); and Deuteronomy 11:13–21. Each of these sections mentions the "sign," "symbol," or "memorial" that one is to place upon the hand or the forehead, references that tradition interprets as *tefillin.* Taken together, they call to mind many of the foundations of Jewish faith: God's unity, sovereignty over our lives, and mighty works of redemption in Jewish history. Thus, the wearing of the *tefillin* upon the head and on the arm in the direction of the heart can be understood as a concrete demonstration of our resolve to direct both head and heart toward the service of God. The *shel rosh* contains four compartments; each of the Torah sections is written on a separate piece of parchment and is inserted into one of the compartments. For the *shel yad,* which is made up of a single compartment, the Torah sections are written on a single piece of parchment.

Tefillin are not worn at night. Nor are they worn on Shabbat and festivals, that is, the first and last days of Pesach, the first day of Sukkot, Shemini Atzeret/Simchat Torah, and Shavuot. The reason is that *tefillin* are referred to as "a *sign* upon the hand" (Deut. 6:8) while Shabbat and festivals are themselves a sign of the eternal covenant between God and

Israel; since these special days are filled with visible evidence of our relationship to God, we need not display another sign upon our hands and heads. There is a dispute concerning *chol hamo'ed*, the intermediate days of Pesach and Sukkot. Some say that these days are themselves visible "signs" of the covenant, in that we eat *matzah* or dwell in the *sukkah* and therefore, *tefillin* should not be worn. Others say that since the Torah does not prohibit work on the intermediate days, they are not "signs" and we should put on *tefillin*. The Sefardic rite follows the first of these positions, while many Ashkenazim adopt the latter.

Prayer in the Vernacular

From its early days in Europe, the Reform movement conducted much of its worship service in the native language of the congregation. The use of the vernacular, to be sure, was not unprecedented in Jewish liturgical practice. But public worship, particularly the recitation of the *Shema* and the *Tefillah*, had been conducted in Hebrew from time immemorial. The substitution of translations for these and other sections of the liturgy therefore marked a radical break with ancestral custom. For this reason, vernacular prayer quickly became one of the sharpest points of contention between the reformers and their opponents.

The reformers defended their innovation on grounds of religious principle and of *halakhah*. As a matter of principle, the change to vernacular prayer seemed an obvious necessity. If prayer is to be a service of the heart, it seemed only natural that the liturgy be performed in a language that the worshipers understood and in which they could express their innermost thoughts and feelings. This was true, it was argued, not only for those worshipers unlearned in Hebrew, but also for those who had studied it, because a second language, no matter how well one knows it, remains an acquired, artificial mode of speech. As for the *halakhah*, the reformers noted that the Talmud and the halakhic literature explicitly permit one to recite the *Shema* and the *Tefillah* "in any language" and that according to some authorities it is preferable to pray in a language one understands if one does not know Hebrew. In the view of the reformers, the legal sources reinforced the basic conviction that the essence of prayer is understanding. One must know what one is reading; one must be able to say what one means to say before

God. To require that people pray in a language they do not know is to defeat the very purpose of worship.

The Orthodox critique of vernacular prayer took several lines of attack. First of all, the reformers were criticized for abandoning ancestral *minhag*, or custom. As we saw in our discussion of the *kippah*, custom is a potent force in the shaping of Jewish practice. This was always true, but the new "Orthodox" Judaism which rose in response to the Reform movement went much farther than did previous generations in its devotion to *minhag*. In the Orthodox view, all of the tradition, custom no less than the law of the Torah or the decree of the talmudic rabbis, possessed an equal measure of authority. All of the tradition was to be regarded as sacred and had to be preserved in its entirety. Since public prayer had long been conducted in Hebrew, that practice was a sanctified *minhag* which could not be altered, even if formal Jewish law allows prayer to be recited in the vernacular. Second, it was argued that the reformers wished to pray in the vernacular tongue because that is how their Gentile neighbors conducted their worship services. As such, this violated the biblical prohibition against adopting "the statutes of the nations," of imitating Gentile religious practices. This argument fails, however, because halakhic authorities have generally restricted this rule to those practices adopted *solely* out of a desire to imitate the Gentiles; "practices which reflect legitimate purposes . . . are not covered by the prohibition." Reform Jews believe that the use of the vernacular strengthens the worship experience and thus counts as a "legitimate purpose." Finally, opponents of reform noted that both the *Shema* and the *Tefillah* are texts whose wording is fixed by biblical or rabbinic authors. To render them into any other language requires a translation of the ultimate precision, one that captures the exact sense of the original Hebrew. This, by definition, is impossible, since every language is unique in its nuances, character, and shades of meaning. A translation of the prayer cannot substitute for the prayer itself. If the *halakhah* apparently permits one to recite the *Shema* or *Tefillah* in any language, this must apply only to unusual or emergency situations as, for example, when one needs to pray but does not have a prayer book at hand. But surely this permit cannot apply to the worship service of a congregation; such worship must consist of the recitation of the actual prayer texts in their original Hebrew language. The reformers responded that however imaginative and intriguing this argument might be, the halakhic sources contain no trace of it. In this case, perhaps ironically, the Orthodox utilized a "creative" interpretation of the talmudic texts in order to defend traditional practice, while the reformers justified their innovation with a more conservative reading of those texts, whose plain sense permits the worshiper to pray in any language.

While the early reformers introduced the practice of vernacular prayer, Hebrew never totally disappeared from Reform liturgy. The last several decades, in fact, have witnessed a reverse trend. The "return to tradition" and the acceptance of Zionism within the movement have combined to spark something of a Hebrew renaissance in the synagogue. In part, this renaissance reflects the movement's commitment to Hebrew as a medium of Jewish expression. Thus, "it is a *mitzvah* to learn and teach the Hebrew language." In terms of quantity, the amount of Hebrew used in the worship services of North American Reform congregations has dramatically increased. In terms of quality, the structure and content of *Gates of Prayer* reveal a deep commitment to the importance of the Hebrew language in the liturgy of the movement. The prayer book's "bilateral symmetry"—Hebrew as well as English title, Hebrew as well as English subtitles, the availability of a "Hebrew binding" (a book opening from the right cover rather than from the left)—along with its wide-ranging selection of Hebrew sources suggests that the book's Hebrew sources "have as much claim to our attention as do the English translations and paraphrases." Hebrew has thus attained the status of equal partnership with the vernacular as a language of Reform Jewish worship. If Hebrew prayer texts were once viewed as a hindrance to spiritual devotion, today's Reform Jews find in the Hebrew language a source of religious strength, an essential expression of identity for a generation that wishes to affirm its Jewishness in its experience of public prayer.

Music

Like vernacular prayer, the use of instrumental music at worship services was one of the first innovations introduced by the European reformers in the early nineteenth century. And like vernacular prayer, this reform touched off a storm of opposition from the rabbinic leaders of what would become "Orthodox Judaism." Their opposition centered around three key elements. First, *halakhah* forbids the playing of musical instruments on Shabbat and festivals. Second, even on weekdays we do not allow instrumental music into synagogue worship, for music is an expression of gladness while we are still in mourning over the destruction of the Temple. Third, since the musical instrument of choice was almost invariably the organ, which was a prominent feature of Christian worship, its introduction violated the biblical prohibition against imitating Gentile religious practices. The reformers rejected the halakhic argument, and they noted that even for those who (unlike Reform Jews) still mourn for the Temple, Jewish law permits the use of musical instruments "for purposes of *mitzvah* such as the celebration of a wedding." And what greater *mitzvah* is there than prayer? Instrumental accompaniment, they declared, would help greatly to beautify and dignify the worship service and to intensify the *kavanah* (devotion) of the worshipers. The Orthodox objections certainly did not dissuade the reformers from pursuing their course, "and in the meantime instrumental and vocal music have become a permanent part of Reform Jewish worship."

Jewish liturgical music stems from many sources, both sacred and secular, highbrow and popular. Often, we can trace the origin of a familiar synagogue melody to the folk music tradition of a surrounding culture. The melody becomes "Jewish" due to its many years of association with Jewish ritual use, an association which survives long after the song's non-Jewish roots have been forgotten. It is therefore no surprise that the synagogue music of Reform Judaism reflects many influences: the heritage of Eastern European musical styles followed by all Ashkenazic communities, the music of nineteenth-century Germany, American and Israeli popular music, the music of the annual Israeli "Chassidic Festival," and other styles. But liturgy is art as well as history; Reform synagogue ritual, in its music as well as its prayer-texts, is the product of conscious choices made by Reform communities that both work within the liturgical tradition and attempt to expand upon it. A community will decide to accept certain styles of music for its services while rejecting others, just as it accepts and rejects various approaches to liturgy and observance. A piece of music will be regarded as inappropriate when it is seen as destructive of the mood of sanctity we seek to establish in our worship. At other times, music that originates in nonreligious popular culture may be deemed acceptable for use when the community finds that it successfully serves its Jewish liturgical purpose. Such decisions are by their nature matters of judgment, and like all matters of judgment they can be contested and controversial. Yet given our desire to create a proper mood for prayer, these are judgments that we must make. The task is to make them carefully and responsibly, with a reverence for musical tradition that is balanced by an openness to innovation.

Much Jewish liturgical music shares common roots with the sacred music of other faiths. A piece of music is therefore not rejected for synagogue use simply because it borrows from motifs found in non-Jewish religious music. Nor does the fact that a song is written by a non-Jewish composer automatically render it unacceptable for Jewish worship. However, a musical selection firmly identified with another religion—for example, a Christian hymn—should indeed be rejected, both because it falls under the traditional prohibition of imitating Gentile religious practices and because there are ample resources of Jewish music which we can and ought to use in its place.

The Minyan

I will be sanctified *in the midst of* the people of Israel. (Lev. 22:32)

Judaism places great emphasis upon the value of public prayer. While the individual is entitled and encouraged to turn to God at all times, the tradition teaches the importance of communal worship (*tefillah betzibur*), of joining one's prayer to that of a congregation. And though the law permits one to say the *Tefillah* privately, one is traditionally encouraged to do so at the same time that the congregation recites its prayers. The most striking sign of this emphasis is the rule that certain sections of the liturgy are not to be recited privately by the individual worshiper. These sections are referred to as "matters of sanctification" (*devarim shebekedushah*). They include the *Kedushah*, the *Kaddish*, the reader's repetition of the *Tefillah*, *Barekhu*, and the reading of the Torah and the *Haftarah*. None of these can be recited without a congregation, that is, a *minyan* (quorum) of ten adult Jews (under traditional *halakhah*, ten adult Jewish *males*).

The requirement of a *minyan* is consistent with the idea that Jewish prayer is a "service of the heart" that combines fixed and formal elements with spontaneous, private ones. The formal "service" aspect of prayer is evident in the fact that the Rabbis modeled the structure of Jewish liturgy along the lines of the service in the ancient Temple. This is reflected not only in the schedule of the statutory prayers (*tefillot*), which follows the order of sacrifices and other ritual activities at the Temple, but also in the *public* nature of the worship service. The Temple was preeminently a public domain, where the daily and festival offerings were performed in the name of all Israel and where the Jews worshiped God not only as a collection of individuals but as *Israel*, a single and unique people. In a similar way, the Rabbis ordained that the "Temple-like" aspects of our own prayer service, those which involve the sanctification of God's Name, be recited only in the presence of a congregation. Likewise, just as Moses and Ezra expounded the Torah in the presence of all Israel, the reading of the Torah should take place in a public setting. They thus achieved a balance between the individual and the public aspects of prayer. While the individual may pray alone, it is only *"in the midst of* the people of Israel" that God can be declared holy. One may worship at any place and at any time, but worship is truly complete only when it is offered by a congregation, which serves as a "Temple-in-miniature," a microcosm of the single, united Jewish *public*.

If the "congregation" is said to symbolize Israel as a collective body, why is the minimum number for a congregation set at ten? The Rabbis derive this requirement through a rather forced midrashic reading of three Torah verses. The rule may in fact originate in an ancient conception of the number ten as the smallest significant division of an entire community. But whatever its origin, the rule exists and is a major factor in determining whether and which prayers can be recited at a synagogue service. According to tradition, one who is obligated to perform a particular religious duty may join together with others to help them perform that duty. Thus, only males aged thirteen and up could form a *minyan*, since only adult males are enjoined to fulfill positive time-bound obligations such as public prayer. In Reform tradition, adult women join to make up the *minyan*. While this expansion of the "public" theoretically makes it easier to assemble a *minyan* for services, there are many times when it remains a serious challenge, particularly on weekdays. In smaller communities it is often difficult to insure a *minyan* even on Shabbat and festivals. The failure to secure a *minyan* means that those who do attend the synagogue are unable to recite *Kedushah*, to hear the Torah reading, and to say *Kaddish*.

For centuries, Jewish communities and their rabbis have struggled with the question: may these rituals ever be performed in the presence of fewer than ten worshipers? While rabbinic authorities never abandoned the traditional insistence upon the *minyan*, in their concern for congregational life they sought to interpret that requirement so as to make it easier to secure the minimum quorum for public prayer. An old Palestinian tradition fixed the minimum number for a *minyan* at seven or even six men. Some authorities ruled it permissible to count a child or a woman as the tenth person when nine adult males are present. These ideas were ultimately rejected. One idea that did survive, though, was the decision that once a *minyan* has assembled, the congregation may complete the section of the service that it has begun even if some of its members should leave, provided that at least six (the majority of a *minyan*) remain. It was also decided that a *minyan* need not consist of ten people who have not yet prayed. Those who have already fulfilled their obligation may help make up a *minyan* on behalf of others. The history of rabbinic thinking on the *minyan*, in other words, is the record of a search for a liturgical compromise. While the authorities left the *minyan* requirement in place, they applied it broadly and liberally to allow many who otherwise could not recite the full liturgy to constitute themselves as a congregation.

The Reform discussions of *minyan* are marked by similar efforts to achieve the right balance between the public and private sides of Jewish prayer. It is true that, unlike the earlier rabbis, they display a readiness to do away with the *minyan* requirement if necessary. Yet Reform responsa express a certain ambivalence and unease over this solution. An exceedingly brief responsum from 1936, for example, declares that the importance of synagogue worship is such that services ought to be conducted even with fewer than ten persons present "in accordance with the . . . old Palestinian custom." Nonetheless, "every attempt should be made to have a full *minyan*." In 1963, Rabbi Solomon B. Freehof permitted the recitation of the *Kaddish Derabbanan*, the *Kaddish* said upon conclusion of the study of a passage of rabbinic literature, by an individual who cannot attend congregational worship. He took pains, however, to emphasize the importance of public worship in Jewish tradition. He worried, too, that allowing individuals to recite *Kaddish* alone would weaken one of the most powerful motivations for attending synagogue services. In 1992, Rabbi Walter Jacob addressed the question: "May we conduct a service at home with less than a *minyan*?" Surveying the rabbinic attempts to relax the strict ten-person requirement, he concluded that in most communities we should simply make every effort to assemble a *minyan*, "if it is at all possible"; thus, while not ruling against the recitation of *Kaddish* and other prayers without the presence of a congregation, Rabbi Jacob clearly placed the emphasis upon the *minyan* requirement. In 1993, the Responsa Committee again permitted the saying of *Kaddish* in the presence of fewer than ten persons. At the same time as stressing the essential Jewish value of public worship, it suggested a variety of alternatives in the event that a *minyan* cannot be secured. The Torah might be read from a printed book; the *Kaddish* might be recited in English, or substituted by another suitable reading; the mourner might stand alone to say the *Kaddish* rather than have all assembled recite it, as is the prevalent Reform custom. Such suggestions would create a system by which the presence or the absence of a *minyan* would be formally noted. This is important, the responsum argues, because there is a distinction to be made between public and private worship. This distinction remains valid because liberal Jews, too, recognize that the proper setting for a number of religious acts and experiences is a public one and that they ought to be carried out in the presence of a community. While the "rule of ten is frequently overlooked and disregarded" in large and small communities alike, and while "we are and have been lenient" in this as well as other ritual matters, "the idea of the *minyan*," in the Committee's view, "deserves renewed attention in Reform Judaism."

Non-Jewish Participation in the Worship Service

As for the foreigners who attach themselves to God, to serve God and to love the name of Adonai . . . all who keep the Sabbath and do not profane it, and who hold fast to My covenant, I will bring them to My sacred mount and let them rejoice in My house of prayer. Their burnt offerings and sacrifices shall be welcome on My altar; For My house shall be called a house of prayer for all peoples. (Isa. 56:6–7)

Speak to the whole Israelite community and say to them: you shall be holy, for I, Adonai your God, am holy. (Lev. 19:2)

Reform Judaism has long championed the doctrine of universalism. From its earliest days the movement has emphasized the ethical content of Jewish teaching, particularly as it is expressed in the stirring words of the biblical prophets whose call for moral conduct and social reform exalts universal human values that are not specifically Jewish in nature.

The insight that the "essence of Judaism" is the ethical message addressed to all humankind, along with Reform's liberal temperament, its
devotion to a religion of reason, its general openness to modern culture
and its accommodation to the life style of the surrounding society, has
led to a certain blurring of the traditional religious distinctions between
Jews and Gentiles. This can be seen in the opportunities afforded to non-
Jews for participation in Reform Jewish worship services. Non-Jews are,
for example, invited both to visit and to pray in Reform synagogues. Reform Jews frequently take part along with Gentiles in interfaith worship
services, which are often held in synagogues. "Furthermore, we have invited non-Jews, including ministers and priests, to address our congregations during our public services." To some extent, these activities
reflect the concept expressed in the Pittsburgh Platform that "we consider ourselves no longer a nation, but a religious community," and
therefore those with whom we share common religious commitments
need not be excluded from our services on the grounds of national identity. In Reform practice, therefore, the synagogue has become more than
ever a true "house of prayer for all peoples."

The willingness to embrace the non-Jew within the confines of Jewish
religious life, of course, has never been without limits. Judaism has
never abandoned its belief that Israel is a distinct and separate community, set apart from all others in its history and destiny. It is the fate of
Israel to become "a kingdom of priests and a holy nation" (Exod. 19:6).
The great Holiness Code of the nineteenth chapter of Leviticus, which
includes such sublime moral precepts as "you shall love your neighbor
as yourself" (19:18), is a speech intended for "the people of Israel."
Many of the prophets do direct their words to Israel alone, exhorting
them to be faithful to the ritual as well as the ethical components of
their covenant with God. Even Isaiah couches his broadly liberal offer
of acceptance to those Gentiles who observe the Sabbath—a specifically
Jewish ritual obligation—and uphold God's covenant. In Reform
thought, too, the conception of the Jews as a *people*, an organic community defined by a common history and a shared national identity,
never disappeared. It is found in both the Columbus Platform of 1937
and the Centenary Perspective of 1976, and its existence was crucial in
the Reform movement's eventual acceptance of the Zionist idea. As a
religious matter, the essential distinction between Jews and non-Jews
remains a vital element in the movement's discussions over mixed marriage, conversion, and its stance toward non-Jewish religious obser-

vances and customs. The fact remains that Reform Judaism, like Judaism in general, is a religion marked by particularistic Jewish elements along with universal "human" ones. The question, as always, is one of boundaries: At what point does Jewish ritual life become an exclusively or primarily Jewish affair, so that a non-Jew, though welcome to attend, may not participate on an equal footing unless he or she converts to Judaism?

The drawing of these boundaries has become more complicated due to the profound demographic changes that have taken place within North American Jewry in recent years. The increasing incidence of mixed marriage has brought a considerable number of non-Jews into the Jewish community. These non-Jewish family members often feel a strong emotional and material attachment to the synagogue. They may attend and take part in a full range of its activities: services, study groups, social programs, fundraising events. The non-Jewish family members can become an integral part of the community, to the extent that their position is similar to that of the *ger toshav*, the "resident alien" of ancient times. As such, it is no surprise that they may desire to participate, fully and publicly, in the community's worship. Their children are enrolled in the religious school, and frequently it is the non-Jewish parent who sees to it that the children get to their lessons. It is again no surprise that a non-Jewish parent wants to be included in the religious ceremonies that accompany such family celebrations as Bar and Bat Mitzvah or that their Jewish relatives seek to have them included. In this new social reality, "boundaries" become ambiguous and much harder to draw. It might be argued that it is inappropriate for a liberal and pluralistic movement such as Reform Judaism to insist upon those boundaries. Indeed, it might even seem hypocritical for a Reform congregation to accept non-Jewish family members into the synagogue community, allowing them to take part in communal life and requiring them to give financial support to its institutions, and yet denying them the opportunity to participate as equals in its religious services.

Reform responsa have nonetheless insisted that the lines be drawn. The synagogue is emphatically a *Jewish* institution. Its prayer services are not only opportunities for personal spiritual reflection but public occasions in which the Jewish community affirms its Jewish identity and renews its adherence to the covenant between God and Israel. There is a valid distinction to be made between the Jewish people, members of that historical covenant community who bear its identity and its sense of destiny, and all others. One may enter that community by birth, or one may choose to enter it through conversion; one does not enter it by marriage. To say that a non-Jew who has not formally adopted Judaism may be granted a full and equal role in the public religious life of a Jewish community is to say that the concepts of peoplehood, covenant, and historical identity do not, in the end, really matter very much, or that it it makes no substantial religious difference whether one is a Jew or a non-Jew. Reform responsa have refused to go so far. At the same time, the responsa have not overlooked the new demographic reality within Reform congregations. They have rather sought to determine the ways in which non-Jews might be included in religious services while yet preserving the essentially Jewish character of those ceremonies.

The line drawn in the responsa is based on that which distinguishes public from private worship. A non-Jew does not take leadership roles in specifically Jewish rituals in public worship. "Public," in this sense, refers to worship by a congregation (*tefillah betzibur*). It is roughly the same as *tefillat chovah*, "obligatory prayer," those liturgical forms that, like the daily sacrifices of old, symbolize the public, corporate aspect of Jewish worship. It includes all those elements of the liturgy customarily led by the worship leader (the *sheliach tzibur*, the "emissary of the congregation") such as the recitation of the *Shema* and the *Tefillah*, and rituals that traditionally require a *minyan,* such as the reading of the Torah and the recitation of *Kaddish*. It includes as well any ritual act over which a benediction is recited, since these acts are considered *mitzvot,* a Jew's obligations to God, and tend to be specifically Jewish in nature. Under this definition, a non-Jew does not perform any of the following "public" rituals:

1. *Leadership of services.* A non-Jew does not serve as *sheliach tzibur,* the "reader" of the service. The *sheliach tzibur* is a member of the community that he or she represents, one of those who is "obligated" to recite the prayer that he or she leads. While Reform congregations have long employed Gentile soloists and choristers to sing sections of the liturgy traditionally associated with "public worship," they do not fulfill the role of *sheliach tzibur.*

2. *The Torah Service.* The non-Jew does not take an active part in the rituals surrounding the reading of the Torah. These include the *aliyot* (the blessings recited before and after the reading of a Torah portion), such honors as *hagbahah* and *gelilah* (raising and dressing the Torah

scroll following the reading), opening the ark, and carrying the Torah in the processional to the reading desk. Participation in the Torah service is one of the most potent symbols of inclusion in the Jewish community, a ritual act which demonstrates that one affirms one's place in the covenant between God and Israel. Gentiles may well support the religious education of their Jewish family members, particularly their children, but Torah itself is a Jewish experience. To learn and to teach Torah is both a privilege and a responsibility for Jews, for Torah is the means by which Israel expresses its sense of self, its understanding of its God, and its conception of its destiny as a people. A non-Jew, no matter how supportive, does not share that privilege and responsibility so long as he or she chooses to remain formally outside the Jewish community.

3. Benedictions. It is inappropriate for non-Jews to recite benedictions (*berakhot*) associated with public religious ceremonies. This is true of *birkhot mitzvot*, blessings said before the performance of a ritual act, such as the lighting of the Shabbat candles. The formula of these benedictions contains the words *asher kideshanu bemitzvotav vetzivanu*, "who has sanctified us through the *mitzvot* and commanded us to . . ." Although the concept of "commandment" is a much-debated one in Reform Judaism, these words do declare that the one who is performing this act is a member of the religious community that expresses its relationship to God through rituals such as this. Nor should a non-Jew recite for the community the *birkhot nehenin*, benedictions such as *Hamotzi* before a communal dinner or a *se'udat mitzvah*, a meal connected with a religious event. Here, too, the public nature of these occasions makes it inappropriate for one who has chosen to remain outside the people of Israel to recite on the community's behalf words that affirm the community's Jewish religious identity.

Conversely, a non-Jew may participate in a public service in the following ways:

1. Through anything which does not require a specific statement (e.g., accompanying a child to the *bimah* at a Bar/Bat Mitzvah; serving as a member of a wedding party or as a pallbearer);

2. Through the recitation of special prayers at non-liturgical community-wide services, commemorations, and celebrations;

3. Through the recitation of special prayers, outside of the major liturgical ones, at family occasions such as Bar/Bat Mitzvah;

4. By delivering an address to the congregation if invited to do so.

These standards enable the non-Jew to participate in the service in a way that reflects his or her attachment to the congregation while at the same time helping the congregation preserve its integrity as a Jewish religious community.

The Reading of the Torah

Moses decreed that Israel should read the Torah at Sabbaths and festivals, at the new month and on the intermediate days of festivals. Ezra decreed that Israel should read the Torah on Mondays and Thursdays and on Shabbat afternoon. (*Y. Megillah* 4:1, 75a; *Soferim* 10:1)

History. Historians do not take literally the Rabbis' claim that the practice of reading the Torah in public began with Moses. For that matter, even though Ezra is said to have read the "scroll of the Torah of Moses" to the assembled people of Israel on Rosh Hashanah (Neh. 8:1–8), the Bible does not support the tradition that ascribes the origin of the three weekly readings to him. It is more likely that this institution developed in stages over many generations. Yet the attribution of the practice to two of Israel's greatest teachers (and, in another text, to "the prophets and the elders") testifies both to its antiquity and its importance in Jewish liturgy. Following the recitation of the *Shema*, in which Israel declares its acceptance of God's rule, and the *Tefillah*, by which this nation of priests performs its "service of the heart," the reading of the Torah fortifies the Jew to face life's challenges. "Let all who thirst come for water" (Isa. 55:1); as water refreshes the soul of the desert traveler, so Torah restores life to those who must wander through a wilderness of the spirit.

Torah Readings. Following the ancient Babylonian practice which is now universal, the Torah is divided into fifty-four sections (each one called a *sidra* or *parashat hashevu‘a*). These are read (one and sometimes two) every Shabbat, allowing the Torah to be completed within one year. Reform congregations customarily read a segment of the weekly portion rather than the entire *sidra*. The reading at the *Minchah* (afternoon) service on Shabbat as well as that for the *Shacharit* (morning) service on Monday and Thursday mornings is traditionally the first segment of the *sidra* for the following Shabbat. Reform congregations may also read the Torah at the Friday night service.

On festivals and Rosh Chodesh (new month), Reform congregations read from the portions traditionally assigned to each holiday. There are some exceptions to this rule. Reform practice does not observe the second day of a festival and changes the Torah reading accordingly, and during the intermediate days of Sukkot, other readings are substituted for the traditional selections from Numbers 29:17ff. Reform congregations generally dispense with the reading from a second Torah scroll (*maftir*) on festival days, on the intermediate days of Pesach, on the "special" Sabbaths, on Chanukah, and on Rosh Chodesh when it occurs on Shabbat. (For the Torah readings for festivals and other special times, see Chapter Three, "Sabbath and Holiday Observance," the sections relating to each special day.)

Aliyot. The honor of being called to the Torah is termed an *aliyah*, literally "going up," since from ancient days the Torah was read in public from a raised platform; one therefore "ascends to the Torah." Originally, the *oleh*, the person called to the Torah, would actually read from the text. By the early Middle Ages the degree of Hebrew literacy had declined to the point that most congregations appointed a special reader (*ba'al korei* or *ba'al keri'ah*) to perform this *mitzvah*. However, the earlier structure was maintained in that each *oleh* was theoretically regarded as the "reader," while the one who actually read the text was seen as his agent or representative. Thus, it is still customary for the *oleh* (m) or *olah* (f) to follow the reading with the *ba'al korei* and to recite in an undertone the words of the text.

At one time, it could be said that "in Reform congregations, the custom of calling people up to recite the blessings over the Torah has generally dropped out." Indeed, the prayer book compiled by Rabbi Isaac Mayer Wise expressly provides that "the sections from the Pentateuch are read in a style agreeable to modern delivery and without calling any person to it. The minister and the officers of the congregation have to do all the *mitzvot* connected therewith." But as one recent responsum has noted, this tendency had the unfortunate effect of removing the Torah reading from the people. Moreover, today's Reform congregations place a much greater emphasis than ever before upon active congregational participation in the worship service. Thus, many Reform synagogues have restored the practice of "calling people up" to the Torah for *aliyot*.

Reform congregations divide the Torah reading into one or several *aliyot*. The number may or may not correspond with the traditional component of three "readers" (*olim*) on weekdays, Chanukah, and Purim; four on Rosh Chodesh and the intermediate days of festivals; five on festivals and Rosh Hashanah when these occur on a weekday; six on Yom Kippur when it occurs on a weekday; and seven on Shabbat. Tradition requires that for each *oleh/ah* a portion of no less than three verses be read and that the entire reading consist of at least ten verses.

The *oleh/ah* is traditionally called to the Torah by his or her Hebrew name, though this is not an absolute requirement. Blessings are recited by each *oleh/ah* before and after the reading. While these blessings may be said in the vernacular, it is customary in Reform congregations to read them in Hebrew.

The procedure for the *berakhot* is as follows. The *oleh/ah* grasps the closed scroll by its two handles (*atzei chayim*, literally, "trees of life") and opens it. The reader shows him/her the verse from which the next section commences. If wearing a *tallit*, the *oleh/ah* may touch that spot with the *tallit*'s fringe and then kiss the fringe. (Others may use a prayer book for this purpose.) He or she then recites the blessing before the reading, beginning with the phrase *Barekhu*, "Praise God, to whom our praise is due." The congregation responds *Barukh Adonai hamevorakh*, "Praise God, to whom our praise is due now and forever"; the *oleh/ah* repeats this response, in order to demonstrate that he/she, too, is a member of the congregation, before finishing the blessing. During the reading, the *oleh/ah* keeps the right hand on the right *eitz* (handle). Following the reading, the *oleh/ah* "kisses the scroll" as before, grasps both handles, closes the scroll, and recites the "blessing after the reading."

Who May Be Called to the Torah? Reform Judaism has abolished the custom of calling persons to the Torah in order of priestly status: first the *Kohen* (priest; one who traces his ancestry to the family of Aaron), followed by the *Levi* (Levite; one who descends from the tribe of Levi but is not of the family of Aaron), and then the *Yisrael* (any Jew who is not a Levite). This order of priority in being called to the Torah is problematic even under traditional Jewish law, and some leading halakhic authorities have suggested that the *Kohen* does not enjoy the absolute right to read first. The practice, at any rate, is certainly indefensible in a movement dedicated to the religious equality of all Jews and which does not anticipate the rebuilding of the Temple.

Any Jewish adult may be called to the Torah. It is customary not to call children until they have reached the age of Bar or Bat Mitzvah. The congregation may refuse to call an "unworthy" person, someone of notorious reputation, to the Torah. Similarly, a congregation is within its rights to deny the privilege of an *aliyah* to individuals who refuse to meet their financial obligations to the synagogue. Such a denial might be considered a modern-day equivalent of the "ban" or excommunication once practiced by Jewish communities as a means of enforcing their rules and standards of conduct. On the other hand, the tradition urges that we take steps to include the sinner within the community, so that he or she may be encouraged along the path of repentance. Therefore, the extreme measure of exclusion from the Torah service should be employed most sparingly and only as a last resort.

Individual Prayer and Blessings

> Rabbi Yochanan said: Would that a person could go on praying all day long! (*B. Berakhot* 21a)

Our public worship service, as we have seen, is patterned after the order of sacrifices in the ancient Temple, and for good reason: we come before God in prayer as a *people*, rehearsing our identity as a community, just as our ancestors rendered their service to God as a community through these public offerings. As individuals, however, we may find the need to extend our prayers beyond the scope of the fixed liturgy. We may have other things we want to say to God, and we may want to say them at times of the day that do not correspond to the times of public prayer. We may wish, in Rabbi Yochanan's words, "to pray all day long." Jewish tradition acknowledges this need and provides for it in various ways. First, it extends the model of the ancient sacrifices to additional prayer opportunities. In the days of the Temple, individuals brought their free-will offerings on a variety of occasions; today, therefore, an individual may recite a personal *tefillah* (prayer) in addition to the public *Tefillah*. This voluntary prayer is called *tefillat nedavah*. Like the voluntary sacrifice of old, this prayer must be brought according to "the rules," the formal structure of benedictions that govern the public *Tefillah*. In order to make it personal and voluntary, however, the worshiper must add to this prayer new elements of his or her own creation. The second traditional opportunity for personal prayer is found during the weekday morning and afternoon services. Immediately following the recitation of the *Tefillah*, individuals may offer *tachanunim*, prayers of supplication which express their own personal desires before God. Then too, our prayer books contain a wealth of material for the benefit of individuals who seek to mark the important experiences of their lives. The traditional *siddur* will contain, besides the fixed liturgy for weekdays, Shabbat, and festivals and for the customary life-cycle observances, prayers of thanksgiving after childbirth, for a boy on the occasion of his Bar Mitzvah, for a traveler before embarking upon a journey, during illness and for recovery from illness, for a home service prior to a funeral, and other significant personal events.

Reform Judaism continues and greatly expands upon this tradition of innovation. Its prayer books, notably *On the Doorposts of Your House ('Al Mezuzot Beitekha)*, provide liturgies for many significant moments in human life, texts that are but a small sampling of such prayers composed by Reform Jewish individuals and groups. By its nature, much of this liturgical creativity is ephemeral; a prayer or service may be recited once and then forgotten. But much of it will "take root among our people and become part of our people's sacred times." In any event, the work of creative liturgy in Reform Judaism partakes of the tendency of Jewish prayer in all generations to assist worshipers who wish to "praise God at every moment" (Ps. 34:2) and to turn to God in the privacy of their personal lives as well as in the assemblies of the house of Israel.

Birkat Hamazon (Grace after Meals)

> You shall eat and be satisfied and praise Adonai your God for the good land which God has given you. (Deut. 8:10)

Jewish prayer knows of many *berakhot*, "blessings" or "benedictions," the liturgical formula that begins with the words *Barukh atah Adonai*, "Blessed are You, Adonai." These *berakhot*, according to tradition, were ordained by the ancient Rabbis as a means of reminding a person at all times of God's presence in the world and of helping one achieve proper spiritual intention (*kavanah*) in a variety of situations. They are classified according to function and occasion. *Birkhot hatefilot*, for example, are the "liturgical benedictions," blessings recited as part of the *Shema*, the *Tefillah*, and other major components of the worship service. *Birkhot hamitzvot* are the blessings recited over such ritual acts as lighting Shabbat candles, sitting for a meal in the *sukkah*, and fixing a *me-*

zuzah to a doorpost. We say *birkhot hoda'ah*, "blessings of thanksgiving," upon recovery from an illness and in gratitude for other evidences of God's goodness toward us. The *birkhot nehenin* are blessings we recite when deriving enjoyment from God's creation, upon eating, drinking, or smelling a pleasing fragrance. The *Birkat Hamazon*, or "Grace after Meals," falls into this latter category. Unlike the other "blessings of enjoyment," however, this blessing is recited *after* rather than before a meal. Moreover, unlike all the other blessings, *Birkat Hamazon* is not held to be "rabbinic" in origin. It is ordained, we are told, by the Torah itself in the verse from Deuteronomy cited at the beginning of this section: "You shall eat and be satisfied" and *then* "praise Adonai your God" by reciting grace.

Birkat Hamazon is recited after one has eaten bread made of any of the "five grains": wheat, barley, rye, oats, and spelt. It is composed of four benedictions:

Birkat hazan, which begins with a *Barukh atah* formula and concludes *Barukh atah Adonai, hazan et hakol*, "Blessed are You, Adonai, who provides food to all."

Birkat ha'aretz, which concludes *Barukh atah Adonai, 'al ha'aretz ve'al hamazon*, "Blessed are You, Adonai, for the land and for its sustenance." The "land" is specifically the land of Israel; thus, the text must mention the "delightful, good, and bountiful land" which God gave to our ancestors. Tradition also requires that one include in this benediction praise for God as Maker of the covenant *(berit)* and as Teacher of Torah. Since the theme of this benediction is thanksgiving for the gifts which God has bestowed upon Israel, it includes *'al hanissim*, texts recited on Chanukah and Purim which express gratitude "for the miracles" that God wrought for "our ancestors in ancient times at this season."

Birkat boneh yerushalayim, which concludes *Barukh atah Adonai, boneh berachamav yerushalayim amen,* "Blessed are You, Adonai; in compassion You rebuild Jerusalem. Amen." Since it was King David who made Jerusalem his capital and sanctified it as the center of the Jewish world, tradition requires that one mention *malkhut beit david*, the Davidic dynasty, in the text of this benediction. It also includes inserts for Shabbat *(retzeh)* and for festivals and Rosh Chodesh (*ya'aleh veyavo*).

Birkat hatov vehametiv, "the God of goodness who is good to all." Tradition recounts that this blessing was added by the Rabbis as a memorial to the slain defenders of Beitar, the last Jewish stronghold to fall to the Romans during the revolt of Bar Kochba (2nd century C.E.). This blessing expresses Israel's messianic hope; hence, it is appropriate to include within it supplications (*harachaman*, "O merciful one") that God bless one's home, family, and the Jewish people.

When three or more persons eat together, one of them recites the *zimmun*, an "invitation" to each other to join together to praise God (*rabbotai/chaverai nevareikh*, "Let us say grace"). The leader calls upon the company: *nevareikh she'akhalnu mishelo*, "Let us praise the One from whose bounty we have partaken." When the company numbers ten or more, the formula is embellished: *nevareikh Eloheinu . . .* , "Let us bless *our God* from whose bounty we have partaken."

The Reform movement has produced a variety of "abbreviated" forms of the *Birkat Hamazon*. This was done to remove redundancies from the text, to excise sections that may no longer be relevant to Reform Jews, and generally to produce a version of the grace which, owing to its brevity, was more likely to be utilized. Today, with a broader knowledge of Hebrew among the community, it is certainly appropriate to recite the full text.

Other blessings are recited after eating food other than bread. For any food other than bread that is made of the "five grains" (wheat, barley, rye, oats, spelt), the blessing is *Berakhah achat me'ein shalosh*, a single benediction containing the essence of the benedictions of the *Birkat Hamazon*. This *berakhah* is said as well after eating any of the produce "with which the land of Israel is blessed": grapes, figs, pomegranates, olives, dates, wheat, and barley (Deut. 8:8). A very short blessing, *borei nefashot rabot*, "Creator of all life," is recited after eating all other foods.

Other Blessings

> Whoever enjoys any of the goodness of this world without first saying a blessing has stolen from God, as it is written [Ps. 24:1]: "The earth and all its fullness belong to God." (*B. Berakhot* 35a)

The following blessings are recited before eating or drinking:

> *Barukh atah Adonai Eloheinu melekh ha'olam . . .*
> Blessed are You, Adonai our God, Sovereign of the universe . . .

bread

hamotzi lechem min ha'aretz.
who brings forth bread from the earth.

wine or grape juice

borei peri hagafen.
Creator of the fruit of the vine.

cooked foods other than bread made from the "five grains"

borei minei mezonot.
Creator of many kinds of food.

fruits that grow on trees

borei peri ha'eitz.
Creator of the fruit of the tree.

fruits and vegetables that grow in the soil

borei peri ha'adamah.
Creator of the fruit of the earth.

other foods

shehakol nihyeh bidevaro.
by whose word everything comes into being.

When foods are combined or cooked together, a *berakhah* recited over the "more important" one suffices for the entire meal.

The following are some of the other *birkhot nehenin*, blessings recited when enjoying the works of God's creation.

On the pleasant aroma of flowers, herbs, and grasses

borei isvei besamim.
who has created the fragrant grasses.

On the pleasant aroma of trees and shrubs

borei atzei besamim.
who has created the fragrant trees.

On the pleasant aroma of spices

borei minei besamim.
who has created the various spices.

The following are some of the *birkhot hoda'ah*, blessings of thanks to God:

On a joyous occasion

shehechiyanu vekiyimanu vehigiyanu lazman hazeh.
who has given us life, sustained us, and permitted us to reach this season.

On hearing good news for oneself or for others

hatov vehametiv.
the God of goodness who bestows good things.

On a sad occasion

dayan ha'emet.
the True Judge.

On recovery from illness or escape from serious danger

hagomel lechayavim tovot, shegemalani kol tov.
who bestows goodness even upon the undeserving, who has bestowed goodness upon me.

If recited at a public worship service, the assembly responds:

Mi shegemolkha kol tov hu yigmolkha kol tov selah.
May the One who has bestowed goodness upon you continue to favor you with all that is good.

On seeing lightning, comets, and other natural wonders

oseh ma'aseh bereshit.
who has created all things.

2

The Congregation

The Synagogue

> Any community consisting of at least ten Jews is obligated to set aside a structure where people may enter to pray at the appropriate times. This place is called a synagogue. (Maimonides, *Yad, Tefillah* 11:1)

In ancient times, those who assembled at the Temple in Jerusalem for the daily and festival offerings did so as the representatives of the entire community of Israel. The *kohanim* (priests) who performed the service of sacrifice, the Levites who assisted them and accompanied them with song, and the Israelites who stood in reverent witness to the proceedings were regarded as a microcosm of the people as a whole; their worship was not their own private offering, but the service of all Jews everywhere. Today, the Temple's function has been inherited by the community of prayer. Tradition teaches that when ten Jews—the minimum requirement for a "community"—gather for worship, they stand for Israel as a whole. The nature of their worship is transformed. As an individual, one recites one's own prayers; as part of a *minyan* (quorum of ten), one prays the prayer of all Israel. Even the humblest congregation is the present-day equivalent of those who sanctified God's name in the ancient Temple.

It stands to reason, therefore, that if even the smallest community is Israel in miniature, then surely that community must establish for itself a synagogue. The synagogue, we are taught, is a *sanctuary* in miniature. Just as the people of Israel in the wilderness were commanded to "build Me a sanctuary, that I might dwell among them" (Exod. 25:8), so must any community that aspires to *be* Israel create for itself a place of worship to symbolize God's presence within their midst, a structure which might, like that ancient holy place, serve to transform an aggregation of individuals into the congregation of Israel.

Membership

An adult of the Jewish faith may become a member of a synagogue upon the acceptance of his or her application by the congregation's board of trustees.

The synagogue is a Jewish institution. Its purpose is "to promote the enduring and fundamental principles of Judaism and to ensure the continuity of the Jewish people." It is therefore inappropriate for those who are not Jewish to enjoy formal membership in a congregation. According to Rabbi Solomon B. Freehof:

> Jewish congregations consist of Jews by birth or conversion. All who wish to come into Judaism are welcome. No sincere applicant for conversion will be rejected. But we cannot allow the transformation of a Jewish congregation so that it ceases to be the family . . . of Israel. Our people and our faith are one, joined in a covenant with God.

That is to say, to become a member of the synagogue one must first be a member of the Jewish people. That membership is open to all, especially to the non-Jews in our midst, through the process of conversion. Those who choose *not* to become Jewish, who for whatever reason determine to remain outside the people of Israel, bear none of the responsibilities and exercise none of the rights that flow from our understanding of Jewish peoplehood. We respect their decision as a sincere one, and we draw the proper and logical conclusions from their choice not to join us.

In the case of a mixed-married couple, membership and voting rights are vested in the Jewish spouse. The non-Jewish spouse may attend religious, educational, and social activities and share in the fellowship of the congregation. He or she may not, however, serve as an officer in the congregation or in its auxiliary organizations such as the Sisterhood, the Brotherhood, or youth groups, or serve as chairperson of a committee. The non-Jewish spouse does not vote at congregational or committee meetings. He or she may serve as a non-voting member of committees devoted to broad communal purposes but should not serve on committees that deal with matters involving Jewish knowledge or synagogue religious policy.

Membership privileges are not extended to Jews who have converted to another faith or belong to such sects as "Jews for Jesus," "Messianic Jews," and the like.

Unmarried Jewish couples may join the congregation as individual members. While the synagogue should refrain from publicly condoning their lifestyle, it should do everything to encourage them to participate in community life and to provide a Jewish education for their children.

A congregation is entitled to withhold membership from any Jew for sufficient cause. A criminal or a morally disreputable person may be denied membership in the synagogue. Similarly, a congregation may expel a current member for such cause. This is the functional equivalent of the *cherem* or *nidui* (ban or excommunication) that during premodern times served as a principal tool for enforcing communal discipline. Just as the ban was hedged by a number of procedural safeguards, however, so should the power of expulsion or exclusion be limited. For example, an individual should be informed that his or her membership or application for membership is under challenge and be given the opportunity to respond before a decision is made. Just as excommunication ordinarily lasted for only thirty days, an individual denied or stripped of membership in the synagogue should also have the right to apply for reinstatement after a reasonable time. Moreover, in former times there were communal punishments of lesser severity and shorter duration than the ban; today's congregation should provide for a preliminary punishment, a temporary suspension of membership, that might render total expulsion unnecessary. In any event, these measures should be taken only as a last resort. Congregations should seek to *include* rather than to exclude Jews from membership. As one responsum puts it: "Much more, it would seem, could be accomplished by bringing the Jew of ill repute under the influence of the synagogue and its teachings."

A synagogue may restrict its religious services to its members, provided that those services are not denied to the poor. The community must provide for the burial of all Jewish dead, but it is entitled to charge the deceased's family or estate for the service.

Governance

The Establishment of a Congregation. Our tradition recognizes the right of any group of Jews to establish a synagogue. At the same time, those who would form a new synagogue ought to consider the effect of their actions upon the existing congregations in the community, particularly when the membership of a new congregation would be made up primarily of those who withdraw from older ones. Some authorities, in fact, go so far as to forbid the formation of a new congregation when the loss of members would seriously undermine the stability and solvency of an existing synagogue. On the other hand, there are times when the founding of new synagogues is unavoidable: for example, when strife and contention among the members of a congregation is so grievous that it interferes with the spirit of devotion at prayer (*kavanah*), it is best that those who dissent from the majority form a new congregation. Reform responsa accordingly uphold the right of any group of Jews to form a new congregation when this course will best serve their religious needs. This is especially true in large cities where several congregations are already established and where the formation of new synagogues would not likely cause serious harm to the existing ones. The situation in smaller communities may well differ. In general, a careful adherence to the rules and procedures of the Union of American Hebrew Congregations and the Code of Ethics of the Central Conference of American Rabbis can help to minimize any friction with existing congregations.

Congregational Size. Some congregations seek to limit the size of their membership, citing a variety of justifications. Jewish tradition, however, tends to encourage large numbers of worshipers to come to synagogue. We are told that "a numerous people is the glory of a king" (Prov. 14:28); the Sages infer from this verse that it is better to pray in public than in private and that it is more meritorious to join one's prayers to those of a large assembly. Tradition does recognize some exceptions to this rule, but it maintains its general preference for larger congregations. Reform responsa have held that it is improper for congregations to place limits or "caps" upon the size of their membership. While the arguments for such a cap are weighty ones, the advantages perceived in a smaller congregation (such as the need to provide adequate space for all worshipers or the desire to achieve an intimate worship experience) can be achieved by other means short of turning away Jews who wish to join the synagogue. There is another concern as well: what some regard as a need for intimacy will be perceived by others as exclusiveness. A synagogue is not a country club, a private refuge for a small circle of members, but a public institution that serves as a place of prayer and Torah study for all those who seek them.

Congregational Officers. The Torah tells us that Jethro advised his son-in-law, Moses, to appoint officers to help him lead and govern the

Israelite community. These officers were to be "capable men who fear God, trustworthy men who spurn ill-gotten gain" (Exod. 18:21). We thus learn two primary qualifications for leadership in the Jewish community: 1) the capacity to perform the tasks of the position with wisdom and efficiency, and 2) moral probity, a personal record that is free of taint and suspicion. These are, of course, high and exacting standards that are not easily realized. Not everyone can be entrusted with the great responsibilities of serving the community. The ethical challenges that confront the officeholder are particularly serious, to the point that some have suggested that leadership positions be reserved for the wealthy, for only they can be counted on to resist the temptation to curry favor with the powerful. Though our democratic temperament leads us to reject this suggestion, we continue to hold our officials accountable to the highest ideals of our tradition. Just as the *sheliach tzibur*, the person who leads the congregation in prayer, should be an individual of blameless character, the *gabai tzedakah*, the person who administers communal funds, should be "well-known" and "trustworthy." The *gabai* must be scrupulously honest in fulfilling the duties of office and must take care not to give even the appearance of improper conduct.

We do not expect perfection from ourselves or from our representatives. We can, however, legitimately expect that those who lead us and administer our communal treasuries will lead lives that reasonably approximate the moral standards set by our tradition. Therefore, a person whose reputation clearly runs counter to these standards ought not to be chosen for office. A synagogue officer or board member who has handled the duties of office in an unethical manner should be removed from that position. When an officer or board member has committed grievous ethical misconduct in his or her private life, that individual should be persuaded to resign, and the congregation may withhold all synagogue honors, such as *aliyot* to the Torah, from that person until he or she steps down. These penalties are subject to three important limitations. First, the congregation, with the guidance of its rabbi, must endeavor to establish the facts of the case beyond reasonable dispute. A person should not be penalized or removed from office on grounds of mere suspicion. Second, the inquiry must be conducted with the greatest possible discretion; the prohibition against *lashon hara* (gossip and slander) protects the guilty as well as the innocent. While the congregation needs to discover the truth of the case, it should avoid the public spreading of rumors and innuendo—even if these turn out to be true—

that harm the reputation of the individual in question. And third, if removed from office, the officer or board member must be given the opportunity for *teshuvah*, to repent for the wrongdoing. Our tradition recognizes sincere repentance as evidence of the transformation of one's moral character. It is up to the congregation to determine whether the individual's repentance is sufficiently sincere to merit restoration to office.

Finance

Dues. The Torah prescribes two means by which the Israelites shall pay for the sanctuary that they are to erect as a dwelling place for God. The actual construction of the sanctuary was to be financed by a free-will offering, accepted "from every one whose heart so moves him" (Exod. 25:2). An additional, obligatory contribution was demanded to fund the expenses involved with the Temple service. This was a poll-tax, a payment of one-half shekel by every Israelite, rich or poor (Exod. 30:11–16). Later tradition adopted and modified these methods of fundraising in order to pay for the "small sanctuary" called the synagogue. The community, which continued to accept free-will offerings (*nedavot*), was also empowered to levy taxes upon its members to finance the synagogue. These taxes might be levied upon each person (*lefi nefashot*), so that all members would contribute an equal amount, or according to wealth (*lefi mamon*), so that the wealthier citizens would pay more. Halakhic authorities have long disagreed as to the preferred funding strategy. Some rule that all taxes collected for synagogue construction and operation should be assessed according to the wealth of the community's members. Others maintain that while this method suffices for the building of a synagogue, certain regular expenses must be met through a combination of contributions laid equally upon each member and those assessed according to wealth. Still others hold that since the synagogue benefits all members of the community, each person must contribute a minimum amount decreed upon all; expenses not covered by this sum are then met by contributions assessed according to wealth. Reform congregations use a combination of these methods to finance the construction and operation of the synagogue "and are thus in accordance with the main spirit of the law."

Assessment of Dues. Dues and other obligations set according to wealth are based upon the financial means of the household and not upon the income of individual members. Should the spouse who earns the greater income resign his or her membership, the other spouse is not entitled to individual membership at a reduced rate. Just as a family provides for all its other needs *as* a family, out of its combined income, so should synagogue obligations be determined by the standard of living of the entire household.

Collection of Dues. Dues and other synagogue assessments are considered legal obligations under Jewish law. One must fulfill these obligations even should one leave the community; "the resignation of any member shall not relieve him/her from payment of any obligation due to the congregation at the time of resignation." It is up to the synagogue to decide whether to attempt to collect delinquent dues and pledges through the civil courts. Jewish law traditionally discourages the resort to non-Jewish legal authorities, but the purpose of this prohibition was to preserve the autonomy of the Jewish legal system, that is, to insure the authority of Jewish courts to adjudicate disputes between Jews. In our time, when the Jewish community possesses no legal power over its members, it is more than doubtful whether this prohibition applies. Moreover, it has always been permitted to resort to Gentile authorities to secure justice when the opposing litigant refuses to appear before or accept the judgment of the Jewish court. This appeal, when authorized by the Jewish court itself, renders the civil court our agent in the enforcement of Jewish law and thereby serves to reinforce the integrity of the Jewish legal system. However, the spirit of Jewish tradition generally opposes the intervention of outside authorities into Jewish communal affairs as a *chilul hashem*, an embarrassment to the community's reputation in the eyes of the outside world. The synagogue must weigh the benefit of collecting a debt owed to it against its emotional cost, expressed in the "general feeling in the Jewish community that the disputes should never have been brought to the courts."

Gifts and Donations. Members and non-members frequently make gifts of money, ritual implements, or other property to the synagogue. Must the congregation restrict the use of these funds and objects to the purposes intended by their donors? The answer depends largely upon whether a valid contract exists under civil law. If so, then Jewish tradition, invoking the talmudic principle *dina demalkhuta dina* ("the law of the land is the applicable law") would hold that the contract must be honored. If no valid civil contract exists, then Jewish law grants the congregation a broad though not unlimited discretion over the use of gifts.

In particular, the tradition teaches that all synagogue funds and property may be directed away from their present or intended use toward a more sacred religious purpose but *not* toward one of lesser sanctity. As the Rabbis saw it, a goal was more or less "sacred" depending upon its proximity to the *mitzvah* of Torah study (*talmud torah*), which is said to be equal in importance to all the other commandments combined. Thus, a synagogue building may be sold to purchase ritual implements used in connection with the reading of the Torah; these implements may be sold to purchase sacred books; and the books may be sold to purchase a Torah scroll. But this does not work in reverse: a Torah scroll may not be sold to purchase an ark, since the ark is of lesser sanctity than the scroll. On this basis, halakhic authorities have concluded that any existing synagogue funds—including gifts and donations—devoted to specific purposes may be redirected to support *talmud torah*, which we might define as Jewish education. The same is true with ritual objects. Even if "the donor's name has not been forgotten"—for example, if there is a plaque or inscription affixed to the object—the congregation may sell that object and use its proceeds for a religious purpose (*devar mitzvah*). If the donor's name has indeed been "forgotten," the community may use those funds for any purpose it wishes.

The making of necessary or desired improvements on a synagogue building, so that the congregation may worship in a more suitable or beautiful structure, qualifies as a "religious purpose." The synagogue may therefore offer donors the opportunity to dedicate sections of a renovated building, even though the existing building and its contents were previously dedicated and bear the name of a donor. Similarly, some adjustments in religious ritual can be justified in the name of creating a more pleasing worship experience. A congregation, for example, is permitted to discontinue the reading of the names on its *Kaddish* or *Yizkor* (memorial) list, even if monetary donations had been made in order that the names be read in perpetuity, if it determines that this custom leads to an unnecessary lengthening of the liturgy. Clearly, discretion should be used with caution in these cases. In Jewish tradition, matters such as this are frequently resolved by resort to local custom, or *minhag*. If it is the custom that a gift may never be redirected from the purpose originally intended, then we might say that the gift was made on this condition and that the synagogue has obligated itself to respect the donor's wishes. Moreover, should a community utilize its legal power to change the terms of a donation too frequently, the long-term results might well be detrimental. One of the reasons why persons are permitted to inscribe their names upon objects they donate to the synagogue, says one prominent authority, is that we wish to take note of their good deed and to encourage them and others to make further donations. If donors realize that the purpose for which they make their gift might one day be changed without their consent, they may be deterred from making gifts in the future.

To summarize: the synagogue has the power to decide how to use the gifts it receives, particularly in order to fund a purpose of higher sanctity than that for which the gift was given, even if that purpose conflicts with the intentions of the original donor. This power, though, should be exercised carefully and with wisdom.

Donations from Disreputable Persons. An individual who donates to the synagogue is entitled, according to tradition, to be remembered for that gift, either in the form of an inscription or by the association of his or her name with the purpose of the donation, as in the case of a memorial or scholarship fund. But what if the donor is a criminal or a person of notorious moral reputation? May the congregation accept the gift? And is it required to acknowledge the donor's name? According to the Talmud, sinners are permitted to make gifts to the Temple in order "that they may be encouraged to repent of their evil." Gifts may not be accepted, however, from persons who repeatedly transgress the prohibitions against idolatry or against violating of Shabbat, for one who commits these sins is considered as though he has rejected the entire Torah and thereby excludes himself from the holy community. Some later authorities extend this reasoning to gifts made to synagogues: ritual use should not be made of any object associated with these individuals, nor should they be provided with an opportunity to "cleanse themselves" without first repenting of their sin. Others reject this analogy, declaring that the prohibition applies only to offerings at the ancient Temple but not to donations to synagogues and other worthy causes in our own day.

On this matter, Reform responsa advise that congregations may accept the donation but may not bestow honor upon the donor. We may accept the gift inasmuch as it is a *mitzvah* for a Jew to support Jewish causes and to contribute to *tzedakah*, and we wish to encourage the fulfillment of this religious duty. But we do not allow an evildoer to utilize a gift to the synagogue as a means of purchasing a good name that is undeserved until such time as he or she does *teshuvah*, repents and atones for his or her sin. The name of such a person should not be acknowledged on a plaque or tablet, nor should a synagogue fund be named for him or her.

Fundraising. In addition to dues and donations, synagogues utilize a variety of methods to raise needed funds. Some of these methods raise questions of propriety. The practice of selling tickets for High Holiday services, for example, strikes many as a particularly tasteless demand that the Jew be required to "pay before you can pray." Congregations are encouraged to avoid this device. Other means may be available to insure that Jews who use congregational services contribute their fair share to the maintenance of the synagogue. The fact remains, however, that each and every Jew *does* bear the responsibility to support the synagogue according to his or her means. Therefore, if no other system is feasible, it is acceptable for the congregation to sell High Holiday tickets, provided that those who cannot afford the price of the tickets are not excluded from services.

Reform responsa frown upon the custom of selling various ritual honors, such as *aliyot* to the Torah and *maftir* (the reading of the *Haftarah*). They similarly caution synagogues to stay clear of "kickback" arrangements, in which the congregation receives a fee in return for utilizing the services of a particular business, such as a catering firm.

Gambling. Synagogues should not resort to the use of lotteries, casino nights, and bingo games as a means of fundraising on a regular basis.

Jewish tradition is ambivalent concerning the propriety of gambling. Rabbinic law explicitly disqualifies the professional gambler as a witness in court, since his frivolous life style, which contributes nothing toward the betterment of the world, encourages dishonesty. Moreover, the history of Jewish communities throughout the medieval and modern periods is filled with efforts to control or outlaw gambling by means of communal ordinance. Yet these efforts were usually unsuccessful, and gambling remained a widespread and popular activity in which even some notable rabbis took part. Some prominent halakhic scholars went so far as to permit poor persons to sell their Torah scrolls by lottery as a means of raising funds to support their families, to provide for the marriage of their children and other basic needs. It is therefore inaccurate to say in an absolute sense that "Judaism prohibits gambling."

Nonetheless, it is just as inaccurate to say that "Judaism *encourages* gambling" or that it looks with equanimity upon synagogues supporting themselves in this way. While Jewish law accepts human frailty, the spirit of the tradition, as we interpret it, urges congregations to resist the temptation to use gambling as a regular means of financial support. That message is especially urgent today, given our awareness of compulsive gambling as a disease and of the horrendous damage it wreaks upon individuals, families, and entire communities.

The Synagogue and the Unaffiliated

Jewish tradition requires that communities establish synagogues and empowers them to raise the necessary funds to support them. The congregation sets the level of obligatory contributions to the synagogue, to *tzedakah,* and to other worthy causes and enforces its decisions, if necessary, by legal means. In pre-modern times, when the Jewish community was a self-governing legal entity within the larger non-Jewish society, these means included the attachment of wages and property. The recalcitrant community member who refused to pay could also be punished through excommunication (*cherem* and *nidui*). The legal status of the Jewish community is dramatically different today. The community no longer possesses legal autonomy and the power to enforce its decisions. The power to tax now rests exclusively with the government. Religious and ethnic association is viewed as a purely private matter, one of conscience. Thus, many Jews avail themselves of the freedom *not* to associate with the community, choosing not to join a synagogue. Those Jews who do belong to synagogues consequently must pay a higher sum in dues and contributions than would be the case if all the Jews belonged. Since unaffiliated Jews will utilize the services of the synagogue and its professionals from time to time, synagogue members protest that they are subsidizing these services on behalf of those who refuse to contribute to them.

What, precisely, is our responsibility as an institution toward Jews who choose not to belong to a synagogue? We must certainly reach out to them in friendship, doing all that we can to convince them to join us. The adult Jew, however, is a responsible person, capable of making informed choices, rather than merely the product of an environment that devalues religion. The unaffiliated Jew is unaffiliated by *choice*; he or she has made a conscious decision not to belong, and should thus be expected to accept the logical consequences of that decision. These consequences imply that the unaffiliated have a duty to contribute toward the maintenance of the synagogue whenever they seek to use it: to attend High Holiday services, to educate their children, or to engage the services of a rabbi for a life-cycle ceremony. The synagogue may set the level of the required contribution at that normally required for membership; that is to say, the individual must become a member of the synagogue in order to utilize the services that its members provide through their dues. As a matter of policy, of course, these demands may be waived if the synagogue believes that a lenient approach would encourage the unaffiliated to join and to remain in the congregation. And in any event, those whose financial circumstances are difficult are permitted to join at a reduced rate, since no Jew should be denied access to Jewish institutions due to inability to pay. As a matter of principle, however, those who can afford to but choose not to contribute to the synagogue have no right to demand religious services.

The Community and the Apostate

What should be our approach toward the person who abandons Judaism for another religion? The answer to this question involves two factors, each of which is complex in its own right: the attitude of Jewish tradition toward the apostate, and the self-understanding of Reform Judaism as a movement defined by tolerance and a respect for personal religious autonomy.

One way of summarizing the attitude of the tradition toward apostasy is to say that "once a Jew, always a Jew." The Talmud, the fundamental source of rabbinic Jewish law and lore, does not recognize the possibility that a Jew might "convert" to another religion and thereby cease to be counted among the people of Israel. The covenant between God and Israel is seen as a contract binding for all time upon the descendants of those who stood at Sinai, so that it is impossible according to Jewish law to totally sever the bonds that link the individual Jew to the Jewish people. Even though one has committed the most grievous transgressions against the Torah and is to be punished on that account, the texts refer to him as *yisrael mumar* or *yisrael meshumad*: an apostate *Jew*, a member (if not in good standing) of the Jewish collective.

The rise of Christianity and Islam posed a sharp challenge to this way of thinking. Unlike pagan religions, which permitted and even encouraged the individual to worship the gods of his or her own people alongside other deities, these new monotheistic faiths resembled Judaism in their demand for religious exclusivity from the believer. A pagan need not abandon his "old" religion; he simply adds new gods to it. One who becomes a Christian or a Muslim, however, "converts" to an entirely new way of religious life and renounces all other gods. If the talmudic apostate remained somehow within the fold and was regarded a Jew, albeit a sinful one, the convert to Christianity or Islam entirely removes himself or herself from Jewry. The question was naturally raised: is the person who has "gone over" to an entirely separate and distinct religious community still a Jew in any real sense of the term? In the popular imagination, certainly, one who "converted out" was considered no longer Jewish; the separation was total and complete. To a limited extent, the Rabbis followed the popular perception. For example, some authorities ruled that a convert to another religion ceases to be the "son" of his Jewish father and thus loses all inheritance rights. Others suggested that we no longer recognize his marriage as valid, so that his wife may remarry without having to receive a divorce from him. Ultimately, though, the Rabbis did not accept the notion that a Jew could legitimately "convert out" of Jewry. They taught that Israel was not merely a "church" composed of like-minded believers, but a people. Jewish identity was an historical fact, the non-transferable inheritance of every person who, by birth or by choice, became a member of that people. A Jew might indeed declare affiliation with another religion and even join that community through baptism or similar formal act. Yet alien sacraments possessed no legality under the *halakhah*; the Rabbis indignantly rejected the idea that by undergoing such a procedure a Jew could successfully efface the reality of his or her Jewishness. As the medieval halakhic authorities put it, in a classic reinterpretation of a talmudic text: "A Jew, even though he sins, remains a Jew."

This conception did not in any way imply a tolerant attitude toward apostates themselves. Though in theory they remained formally Jewish, apostates in reality were excluded from communal life. They were not counted in the *minyan*; they were not relied upon to give testimony in court; they were not buried among the other Jewish dead. At times, this exclusion was accompanied by a formal excommunication. The gates of repentance, of course, were always open, so that the apostate could return to Judaism. Until that time, however, the apostate remained separate and apart, shunned by other Jews, who regarded his or her apostasy as the ultimate act of social betrayal.

Reform Judaism's attitude toward the non-Jewish world differs from that of the halakhic tradition. The liberal culture of the modern age has made it possible for Reform Jews to look upon most other religions as comrades in the struggle for human betterment and social justice rather than chiefly as enemies and sinister threats to Jewish survival. That same liberal culture, moreover, has led recent Reform thinkers to emphasize the importance of personal religious autonomy in the definition of legitimate Jewish belief. That is, the power to decide between "right" and "wrong" answers in the search for religious truth rests predominantly in the hands of the individual Jew. In this view of religious life, it is difficult to support the notion that there exists some form of religious authority, whether in the form of tradition or of a formal institution, that could legitimately place limits upon personal religious choice. Through this commitment to individual religious freedom, Reform implies its acceptance of the widest possible variety of religious ideas. "Reform Judaism," declares the Centenary Perspective, the most recent statement of principles adopted by the North American movement, "does more than tolerate diversity; it engenders it . . . We stand open to any position thoughtfully and conscientiously advocated in the spirit of Reform Jewish beliefs."

Given its encouragement of diversity and dissent, one might think that Reform Judaism recognizes no "limits" whatsoever in religious choice. And given that contemporary attitudes toward other religions are not nearly so hostile as those that once prevailed, one might think as well that even should a Jew choose to adopt another faith, that choice is potentially legitimate so long as it is "advocated in the spirit" of a religious movement that champions freedom of choice. These conclusions, however, would be wrong. Reform Judaism has always concerned itself with the drawing of lines and boundaries that define the movement's beliefs and practices, setting it apart from other approaches to Judaism and insuring its distinctiveness from non-Jewish religions as well. It could hardly be otherwise. No coherent religious community can long exist without a sense of cohesiveness, of common commitments, of definition—in short, without some means of differentiating those ideas with which the community can live from those with which it cannot. Religious autonomy is never unlimited, for even the most liberal and tolerant religious movement must proceed from some basic understanding, shared at least in broad outline by the members of the movement, of what it is and is not about. To quote again from the Centenary Perspective: "In all our diversity we perceive a certain unity and we shall not allow our differences in some particulars to obscure what binds us together."

But how does a liberal religious movement determine just what it is that "binds us together"? How does it go about declaring certain choices and options invalid and thereby setting limits upon the autonomy of the individual? These determinations are not generally established by rabbinic pronouncements or resolutions adopted by official bodies. To the extent that they exist, the "lines and limits" of Reform Judaism emerge from the ongoing discussion carried out among that community of people who call themselves Reform Jews and who recognize each other as Reform Jews. It is through this discussion, a sometimes passionate argument that takes place, as it were, "within the family," that Reform Jews of diverse opinions have been able to identify the "certain unity" that "binds us together." This unity may consist of core affirmations which form a sort of religious consensus among those people who associate with the Reform movement. One who dissents from any or all of these affirmations is not necessarily wrong or in error; the concept of heresy is absent from even the most polemical writings of Reform thinkers. But the fact that Reform Judaism is willing to tolerate a wide spectrum of dissenting opinions, some which are regarded as extreme, does not alter the reality that even this most liberal religious enterprise has never recognized the absolute right of the individual to make any conceivable religious choice and to call it "Reform Judaism." The definition of Reform Judaism, in other words, has always been emphatically a *community* as well as an individual matter.

One article of belief that has always united Reform Jews is the conviction that a Jew who adopts another religion is no longer a member of the Jewish religious community. No responsible spokesperson of

Reform Judaism during the past two centuries has ever declared apostasy to be a legitimate exercise of Jewish religious autonomy. From the inception of the Reform movement in Europe, its advocates worried over the specter of mass apostasy. They feared that unless the faith of their ancestors were presented in a form that reflected modern sensibilities, Jews seeking entry into modern society would find Christianity, especially its more liberal denominations, more attractive than Judaism. The prevention of apostasy served as one of the justifications of religious reform. Stringent opposition to apostasy has been common to the leaders and thinkers of the movement, including the most radical, to this day. This means that the very subject of apostasy remains a live and relevant one in Reform Jewish thought and discourse.

This conclusion raises another question: granted that even in a liberal movement there is such a thing as apostasy, who, exactly, *is* an apostate? What counts as apostasy, especially in light of the particular challenges facing Jewish religion on the contemporary scene? Reform tradition generally defines apostasy as a Jew's abandonment of Judaism *and* adoption of another religion. We would therefore not label atheists or thoroughly secularized Jews as "apostates," for while they have renounced the faith of Israel they have not adopted another religion. We would, of course, regard as apostates those Jews who "convert out." This definition, however, arguably excludes the many Jews who claim to be influenced by the ways of the great Eastern religions: Buddhism, Hinduism, Taoism, and others. One does not "convert" to these traditions, which, unlike Christianity and Islam, do not demand that a Jew abandon Judaism in order to become involved with them. Is one who follows the teachings and practices of these religions to be considered an apostate? For that matter, such groups as "Messianic Judaism" and "Jews for Jesus" claim that a Jew who adopts their doctrine, a fundamentalist Christian theology encased within numerous Jewish ritual practices, does not renounce his or her Jewishness at all. They claim that their religion is simply a better, truer form of Judaism that allows its adherents to become "completed" or "fulfilled" Jews. Should we consider these persons, who insist that "we are Jews who follow Jesus," as apostates? Or are they simply Jews whose religious opinions dissent from those of the mainstream community? These questions pose a difficulty for Reform Jews, who themselves are regularly branded as apostates by Jews on the extreme religious right. How can we, who demand the right to dissent from established tradition and to define our own

Judaism, deny these rights to other Jews? Yet no matter how difficult the questions, answers must be found, so long as Reform Judaism continues to understand itself as a coherent religious movement, one which defines itself by what it believes and by what it does *not* believe, and one which does not accept *all* religious doctrines and practices as equally valid or legitimate. Those answers will be the product of the ongoing discussion among Reform Jews as to what constitutes the definition of Reform Jewish belief. What follows is a summary of that discussion as it is reflected in Reform responsa literature.

The Attitude Toward the Apostate. Following the rabbinic tradition, Reform Judaism does not reject the apostate entirely. The Jew, whether by birth or by choice, who converts to another religion remains a Jew in our eyes. We do not approach this individual with open anger, since we wish to encourage the apostate and the family of the apostate to reclaim their proper place in the Jewish community. Indeed, as Rabbi Solomon B. Freehof writes, "the door is always open for their return." However, the fact that this person has consciously and openly renounced even the most nominal attachment to Judaism means that he or she forfeits many of the rights and privileges to which a Jew is entitled. The apostate is not accepted as a member of a synagogue and is not allowed positions of leadership within the Jewish community. While permitted and even encouraged to enter the synagogue to pray, he or she may not ascend the *bimah*, be called to the Torah, serve as a reader in worship services, or address the congregation. To allow this person to participate in public worship in a leadership role would imply falsely that we condone the apostate's renunciation of Judaism, that we are neutral toward it, or that we consider it somehow a legitimate Jewish religious choice. On the other hand, while apostates may not join a congregation, their children may enroll in our religious schools. The children should not be penalized for their parents' actions, and we wish to do whatever we can to raise them as Jews. In addition, the apostate may be buried in a Jewish cemetery, inasmuch as we are required to bury all Jewish dead, including those deemed to be sinners.

Hebrew Christians, Messianic Jews, and Jews for Jesus. The various "Jewish Christian" groups, whose theology is centered upon the figure of Jesus but whose worship and religious observance are characterized by numerous practices adopted from Jewish tradition, pose a special problem. Unlike the established Christian churches, these groups present their religion as a form of Judaism. Moreover, while most other Christian denominations no longer actively seek to proselytize the Jews, "Jewish Christian" sects often approach Jews with aggressive missionary zeal. Their doctrine seems aimed primarily at Jews in search of spiritual fulfillment yet reluctant to abandon their Jewish heritage or to convert in a formal way to Christianity. "You need not change your religion to join us," they say, "for our faith is truly Judaism at its best, a Judaism fulfilled by the acceptance of Jesus, the 'Jewish messiah.'" As a community which has been the target of so much conversionary activity over the centuries, we resent this tactic; we find this deceptive message to be confusing and dangerous to our people.

For the sake of clarity, therefore, we should state in no uncertain terms that the religion of these "Jewish Christian" groups is *not* Judaism but Christianity and that a Jew who adopts their doctrine becomes an apostate. We should do everything in our power to correct the misapprehensions they preach and to maintain a strict separation from them. "Jewish Christians" should not be accorded membership in the congregation or treated in any way which makes them appear as though they are part of the Jewish community. We should refrain from officiating at marriages involving them, and we may refuse to bury them in our cemeteries. We should offer no support to their religious activities. Our synagogue gift shops, for example, may refuse to sell religious implements to them. Should refusal to serve them be construed as a violation of civil law, the staff of the gift shop may attempt to discourage members of these groups from purchasing Jewish religious articles.

The Returning Apostate. Unlike proselytes to Judaism, who undergo a ritual of conversion to mark their entry into the covenant, repentant apostates do not in theory require such a rite. They never leave the covenant; a Jew who sins, even to the point of apostasy, remains a Jew. Thus, say some authorities, no formal conversion-like ceremony ought to be required of apostates who seek to return to the Jewish community. Such a requirement would give the false impression that during their apostasy they had forfeited their Jewish status. Instead, we should do all that we can to reach out to these individuals and to draw them back in with love and friendship.

This opinion, however, is far from unanimous in the tradition. Other authorities demand that the repentant apostate undertake ritual immersion and declare their acceptance of Judaism in the presence of a rabbinic court. While those who hold this view acknowledge that neither the immersion nor the declaration is required under Jewish law, they reason that *some* ritual notice must be taken of a moment that, in point of spiritual fact if not in legal theory, signifies a dramatic change in this Jew's religious identity.

Reform responsa, in general, take the lenient approach, in the hope that we may allow those who wish to return to do so without embarrassment. There are times, on the other hand, when a more stringent standard is appropriate. One such case involved a born Jew who converted to Christianity, became ordained as a minister, and subsequently returned to the Jewish faith. In that instance, the Responsa Committee felt that more should be required of a person who not only affiliated with another religious community but actually served as one of its leaders. The Committee suggested that this person be asked to make a specific statement of *chaverut* (affiliation with the Jewish people and acceptance of Judaism) in the presence of three persons serving as judges of a *beit din*, a Jewish court. In the final analysis, the decision to apply such a requirement to returning apostates must be made on a case-by-case basis by the local rabbi and community.

The Synagogue Building and Its Contents

Synagogues must not be treated disrespectfully. (*B. Megillah* 28a)

The synagogue, like the Temple of old, is not an ordinary building; we do not treat it as we would any other. It is a holy place, set apart from common, secular use, a place that is to be used in pursuit of its own inherent purposes. Reform thinking on this subject, as with others, seeks to understand the requirement of reverence toward the synagogue in terms of the traditional texts that define it and also in light of contemporary circumstances and sensibilities.

The Synagogue Building: Consecration. For centuries, it has been customary to hold a service of dedication upon the inauguration of a new synagogue. We say "customary," because the Talmud and the great halakhic codes make no mention of a requirement that a building be ritually "dedicated" or "consecrated" for use as a synagogue. The building becomes a holy place, not as a result of some special ceremony, but from the moment that it is first *used* as a synagogue: that is, once people have assembled in it to pray. Prior to that time, the structure is not truly a sacred space. On the other hand, the money raised for synagogue construction and the materials purchased with it do possess a level of sanctity, and the tradition places severe limitations upon the power of the community to divert either the monies or the materials to other purposes. Thus, a synagogue building under construction, though not yet fully a synagogue, must be treated with all proper respect.

Sale. Jewish tradition permits the sale of a synagogue, so long as the proceeds of the sale are put toward an appropriate religious purpose. If the sale enjoys the full legal approval of the community, the proceeds may be put toward any purpose the community wishes. Originally, this sanction applied only to a synagogue in a small village or hamlet, where it could be presumed that the local residents were the only people who assembled there to pray. The members of the congregation were thus considered the sole owners of the place and accordingly had the right to sell it. A synagogue in a large city, however, could not be sold, since visitors from other communities regularly traveled to the city and would enter it to worship. Consecrated to serving the religious needs of outsiders as well as of the local congregation, the large-city synagogue was regarded in a real sense as the property of the entire Jewish people. All Jews everywhere, even those who did not contribute toward its building and upkeep, were its owners, and their consent was required in order to sell the building. Since it was clearly impossible to attain the consent of all these "owners," in practice a large-city synagogue could never be sold. During the last several centuries, halakhic authorities have largely erased this distinction. Faced with the reality that a large-city congregation, no less than one in a smaller community, will at times need to move or to build a new synagogue in a more favorable location, rabbinic opinion today generally upholds the right of its members to sell the existing building.

Just as Jewish law demands no formal consecration for a synagogue, so is there no requirement for a ceremony of deconsecration in order to sell the building for any secular or non-Jewish purpose. Again, the synagogue building is holy not because of some special ceremony but because the congregation uses it as a place of prayer; its sanctity therefore departs from the moment that it ceases to serve as a synagogue.

The synagogue building may be sold to any interested buyer for virtually any purpose. The building may therefore be sold to a Christian congregation for use as a church. At the same time, the spirit of the tradition would argue that a synagogue building not be sold to any individual or group which would use it for purposes inimical to our sense of moral propriety or Jewish interest.

Sharing a Building with Others. Some small congregations, unable to build or purchase a synagogue building of their own, will rent space in other structures in order to hold their services. Congregations should not, however, assemble regularly in non-Jewish houses of worship, nor should they join with non-Jewish congregations to purchase a building to be used for both groups. It is true that Jewish law permits a congregation to purchase a non-Jewish place of worship and to convert it into a synagogue. It is also true that Reform Judaism does not regard Christianity and Islam, the major non-Jewish religions with which we come into contact, as forms of idolatry, and that therefore many of the traditional objections to conducting our prayer services in their houses of worship or in proximity to their religious symbols would not apply. To do so on a regular basis, however, would sow confusion among members of both communities, tending "to declare publicly that these two forms of worship are not particularly different from each other." In these times of increased assimilation and the blurring in the popular mind of the real and important distinctions between the various religious traditions, Jewish congregations, which exist to promote the distinctiveness of Jewish religion, ought to seek their own distinct quarters, however humble they may be.

A congregation may allow a university to rent space in the synagogue in order to hold classes, provided that these classes do not meet in the sanctuary and that every effort is made to insure that classes are not held on Shabbat or festivals. A congregation may allow a Christian church to rent or borrow its facilities on a temporary basis for worship services. It is preferable, however, that no Christian symbols be brought into the synagogue.

Architecture and Landscaping. Synagogue buildings may be constructed according to a variety of architectural styles and landscaped with trees, lawns, and flowers. There is no requirement in Jewish tradition that the synagogue or its grounds assume a particular "look" or pattern. Despite this fact, some halakhic authorities in the nineteenth century ruled that it was forbidden to build synagogues according to new architectural styles and to plant trees in their courtyards. They took these stringent positions essentially in opposition to Reform Judaism. Those who sought to "modernize" their synagogue buildings or to make them more aesthetically pleasing tended to be associated with the movement for religious reform, and traditionalists suspected that their real motivation was a desire to imitate Gentile religious practice. The response from some Orthodox authorities, on this issue as on others, was an all-out defense of the traditional way of doing things. As in other cases, however, the "tradition," when studied thoroughly, did not support this negative view. Other Orthodox scholars insisted that there is no prohibition either against the planting of trees or the adoption of new and differing architectural styles. Indeed, a look to history informs us that Jewish houses of worship over the centuries have been constructed in a variety of styles. Synagogue architecture is determined not so much by *halakhah* but by the influence of artistic trends prevalent in the surrounding culture.

Even in the absence of explicit prohibitions, however, certain considerations ought to be taken into account. For example, those traditional authorities who are lenient on the subject of synagogue architectural styles condition their rulings on the presumption that the synagogue building and grounds are not designed consciously and openly in imitation of Gentile religious practice. This value should guide our thinking to some extent. Thus, if local churches tend to assume a certain architectural style, the Jewish community might want to design its synagogue so as to distinguish it as a *Jewish* house of worship. "Richly equipped as the synagogue is with adequate and satisfying symbols of its own, it stands to profit little from . . . glaring imitation of the church."

There is also the issue of access to the synagogue for the physically disabled. Such access must be provided, not only to comply with legal requirements where they exist, but also because our understanding of the Jewish tradition demands no less.

The Sanctuary: Orientation. Jews traditionally face in the direction of Jerusalem when reciting the *Tefillah*, the statutory prayer for weekdays and holidays. In Europe and in North America, that direction has been interpreted as east; it has therefore become customary to place the ark against the eastern wall of the sanctuary, so that worshipers face eastward when they rise to recite the prayer. Reform synagogues should, wherever possible, be constructed so that the sanctuary's ark rests upon the wall that faces Jerusalem, so as to express our spiritual unity with the Jewish people throughout history and our love for Jerusalem and Israel. Nonetheless, the fact that a sanctuary faces in a direction other than toward Jerusalem does not render it unfit for congregational worship. In such a case, we can rely upon the talmudic insight that "the Divine Presence is everywhere" and conclude that it is the worshiper's spiritual orientation, rather than the physical one, that counts. In a synagogue whose sanctuary faces in a different direction, therefore, the worshiper need not turn away from the ark so as to pray toward Jerusalem.

In Reform synagogues the desk or table from which the Torah is read is situated at the front of the sanctuary, facing the congregation. This pattern differs from traditional sources, which specify that the reading desk be placed in the middle of the sanctuary. From the early days of the Reform movement in Europe, the suggestion that the reading desk be moved to the front of the sanctuary aroused much opposition from traditionalists, who saw in these efforts a violation of sacred custom and a desire to imitate the architecture of Christian churches whose altars and pulpits are situated in the front of the sanctuary. The reformers denied that this was their motivation; they were more interested, they said, in maximizing the seating space in their synagogues. And they could cite weighty halakhic opinion to the effect that the location of the reading desk is a matter not of law but of practicality, one that differs with "time and place" and the requirements of the community.

The Torah Scroll

The Scribe (Sofer). Near the end of the book of Deuteronomy (31:19), God commands the people of Israel to "write down the words of this poem." Rabbinic tradition interprets this instruction as a requirement that every Jew write a Torah scroll (*sefer torah*). The purpose of this commandment, say the commentators, is two-fold: to insure the availability of Torah scrolls for study by the largest possible audience of learners, and to inspire the individual who writes the scroll with reverence for God and for God's teachings, "which are more precious to us than gold." One may fulfill this requirement by personally writing a scroll or, if one is not learned in the scribal arts, by hiring a scribe (*sofer*) to do the work. Indeed, even if one writes (or commissions the writing of) even one letter of a Torah scroll, it is considered as though that individual has personally received the Torah at Sinai. Some congregations commission the writing of a *sefer torah* as a way of enabling their members to take part in this meritorious act.

The *sofer* or scribe who writes Torah scrolls and the texts for *tefillin* and *mezuzot* is a Jew carefully trained in the technical requirements of the craft. The rules governing the writing of a sacred text are precise and meticulous; the *sofer* therefore must not write from memory but rather follow a correctly-written copy. The *sofer* is also distinguished by exceptional personal piety, since he must concentrate upon the meaning of the Divine Name whenever it occurs in the text. In addition, the *sofer* is traditionally a male, although we would hold on grounds of Jewish law and Reform principle that a woman is also qualified to serve as a scribe. We look forward to the time when the Reform movement succeeds in training its own scribes (*soferim*), male and female, in the writing of sacred texts.

Scrolls Fit and Unfit for Use. The Torah scroll used for public reading must be ritually fit (*kasher*). It is handwritten on parchment made from the specially treated skin of animals which in Temple times were suitable as sacrificial offerings. Its text is written and arranged according to precise rules, and as we have seen, the scribe (*sofer*) who writes a Torah must be a Jew who is faithful to the teachings inscribed in it. A Torah scroll which does not conform to these guidelines is called *pasul*, ritually unfit. Though a *pasul* scroll may be used for study and teaching, it is not to be read as part of a formal public worship service. Indeed, some (though not all) authorities require that a *pasul* Torah scroll be removed from the ark in order to avoid its accidental use. If it does not possess a *kasher* scroll, a congregation may find it necessary to conduct the reading from a printed text (*chumash*) or even from a scroll that is *pasul*. This is permitted, but since a reading from a *pasul* scroll is not a formal and proper "reading of the Torah," the customary benedictions should be omitted.

The Honor Due to the Torah Scroll. A Torah scroll is treated with the utmost reverence. During the service it is customary to rise and face the Torah when it is taken from and returned to the ark and when it is carried in a processional. One removes the Torah from the ark and takes it from another person with one's right arm, though during the processional one may carry it with either arm. It is not necessary to stand during the Torah reading, when the scroll rests upon the reading desk. If the Torah scroll is dropped, it is customary in some communities that the person who dropped it should either fast or give to *tzedakah* (charity or other communal need). It is customary to stand while the ark containing a Torah scroll is open, although according to *halakhah* this may not be necessary. Some authorities advise against the custom of displaying Torah scrolls, such as those rescued from the Holocaust, in glass museum cases. Others say that this practice is a way of rendering honor to the Torah and should be permitted. There is general agreement that a Torah scroll may be brought to a hospital or even to a jail to allow Jews in those institutions to hear the Torah reading. The general practice, however, is the reverse: the congregation should come to the Torah rather than have the scroll brought to them. The scroll should not be moved from the synagogue in the absence of a compelling purpose. For example, the scroll should not be moved to accommodate a private family service, such as Bar or Bat Mitzvah, that could and should be held in the synagogue.

It is forbidden to burn or destroy sacred texts which contain the name of God. This prohibition does *not* apply to impermanent writing, such as that on a computer screen, nor does it mean that one is forbidden to erase tape recordings which contain God's name. When a Torah scroll has become worn or *pasul* beyond the point of correction, it is either stored away or buried in a cemetery, preferably next to a Torah scholar. This rule has been extended to apply to all Hebrew books, and this fact accounts for the well-known practice of having a *genizah*, a storage place for old books, in many synagogues. A *pasul* Torah scroll may be divided up into the five component books of the Torah for purposes of study.

Sale and Ownership of the Torah Scroll. An individual who owns a Torah scroll is forbidden, in general, to sell it. The use of the Torah as an object of profit and commerce is seen as an insult to the honor due to the scroll. There are, however, some important exceptions to this rule. One may sell a Torah scroll in order to raise funds to marry, to ransom captives, and to study Torah. For this reason, it is certainly permitted for an individual to sell a *sefer torah* to a synagogue where it will be used for public reading or to a private buyer if the proceeds are put toward Jewish education. It is also permitted to use the Torah scroll as a means of fundraising for synagogues and Jewish education, for example, in a "Torah-writing project" where congregants donate specified sums toward the writing of letters or words in a scroll.

Individuals will frequently place their own Torah scrolls in the ark of their synagogue. This is certainly proper, since to read the *sefer torah* in public is to render it the highest form of honor. Such an arrangement can be a source of contention, however, when the owners or their heirs seek the return of the scrolls. Congregations may consider the original transaction as an outright gift rather than a loan, regarding themselves as the now-rightful owners. In the absence of documentary evidence, this dispute can be resolved in one of two ways. If there is a well-established custom in the community for individuals to lend their Torah scrolls to synagogues, the claim of the original owners or heirs should be taken with the utmost seriousness and the synagogue bears the burden of proof. If, however, no such custom is established or well-attested in local practice, we follow the rule that once a *sefer torah* has been placed in the ark, dressed in its mantle, and read in public, it has become sanctified for public use. From that time on, the synagogue is presumed to be its rightful owner, and those who argue otherwise must provide evidence to substantiate their claim.

Decorations. The various ornaments which adorn the Torah scroll—the mantle (*mitpachat*), the crown (*keter* or *atarah*), the breastplate (*choshen*), the "pomegranates" (*rimonim*) that fit over the wooden rollers (*atzei chayim*)—are considered "holy implements" or "appurtenances of the sacred" (*tashmishei kedushah*). This gives them a certain degree of sanctity. Like the Torah scroll itself, when they have outlived their usefulness they must be put in a special storage place (*genizah*) rather than thrown away. Some rule that money derived from the sale of these objects must be put toward the purchase of objects of greater sanctity, such as a Torah scroll; others permit the use of the funds for a variety of communal purposes.

Ritual Implements and Sanctuary Furnishings

Graven Images. Many synagogue sanctuaries feature considerable ornamentation around the ark, the *bimah*, and the reading desk. This may include carved or embroidered representations of animals (particularly lions) and Jewish religious symbols. In addition, many sanctuaries are decorated with stained glass windows upon which are displayed artistic renditions of plants, animals, and even human figures. This is hardly a modern innovation. Ancient synagogues unearthed in Beit Alfa and elsewhere in the land of Israel possessed stone floors decorated in elaborate mosaic patterns depicting human figures, the signs of the zodiac, and other designs. Yet it is difficult to square this practice with the prohibition, included in the Ten Commandments (Exod. 20:4), which declares: "You shall not make for yourself a graven image nor any likeness of that which is in the heavens above or on the earth below or in the water beneath the earth." Given the plain sense of this verse, how have Jews been able to justify the custom of decorating their synagogues with elaborate artistic imagery?

The legal literature on this subject is long, complex, and, not surprisingly, replete with conflicting opinions. Those who permit the placement of "images" and "likenesses" in synagogues argue that, inasmuch as these images are not used in pagan worship, there is no reason to prohibit them. While some authorities worry that the use of these images would create the impression that those in attendance are worshiping them as idols, others write that no such suspicion applies to the synagogue, where it is obvious that we worship the God of Israel. Not all rabbinic scholars, to be sure, were so lenient. And indeed, it might be argued that many of those who rule permissively do so "after the fact," more out of a desire to defend the Jews of their communities from the charge of violating one of the Ten Commandments than out of enthusiastic acceptance of the custom. Although the tradition is far from unanimous on the side of the affirmative, we can trace a considerable history of rabbinic approval of artistic imagery in the synagogue.

Reform Jews might add that, in this instance, custom (*minhag*) has determined the *halakhah*. In our view, the long history of synagogue art testifies to the fact that the Jewish people have decided that the use of artistic imagery to decorate the synagogue violates neither the letter nor the spirit of the prohibition against making graven images. More than that: we would argue that this heritage of creativity in wood, stone, paint, and precious metal is a positive good. It is clear to us that our people have chosen this method to accomplish the goal of *hiddur mitzvah*, the requirement that we "adorn the commandments" and make our worship of God aesthetically pleasing as well as spiritually fulfilling.

This value, of course, can be taken to unreasonable extremes. When adornment and decoration are too elaborate, they may no longer serve their intended purpose; when they are too expensive, they become an oppressive burden upon the community. Yet the fact remains that the aesthetic function has always been and remains a powerful consideration in the design of our houses of worship. If art and artistry speak to the soul, it is fitting that we use them to speak to God.

The Ark. The *aron kodesh*, the ark in which a congregation's Torah scrolls repose on a permanent basis, is classified as a *tashmish kedushah*, an "appurtenance of the sacred." This means, of course, that it must be treated with the utmost respect and that there are limits placed upon the purposes for which it may be used. On the other hand, there is a qualitative distinction between the ark with which we are familiar and the *teivah* or *heikhal*, the "box" mentioned in the rabbinic sources. The latter was a container for a single *sefer torah* which enabled the scroll to be carried outside to the public square for services on festivals and fast days. It was functionally equivalent to the *tik*, the ornamental wooden or metal case in which the Torah scroll rests according to Sefardic custom. Our ark, by contrast, resembles a bookcase, a structure in which texts are placed for safekeeping. As such, its sanctity is of a lesser degree than that of the mantle, the wimpel, and the other "appurtenances." Therefore, while the respect we owe to it demands that an ark which is no longer usable ought to be placed in a *genizah* (storage) rather than simply thrown away, it is permissible to sell the ark or to convert it for use as a bookcase to hold Jewish texts.

The Menorah. Upon the *bimah* of many synagogues stands a seven-branched *menorah* (lamp) reminiscent of the candelabrum, which stood in the ancient Temple (Exod. 25:31–40). One occasionally hears that this decoration violates the traditional prohibition against replicating the Temple's ritual implements. However, that prohibition applies only to exact copies. *Menorot* which consist of more or fewer than seven branches, which are made of materials other than metal, or which operate on electricity are not exact copies and are thus perfectly acceptable.

National Flags. Many congregations place flags upon their *bimah*, both the national flag and the flag of the state of Israel. This is not to say that the flag is a religious symbol, worthy of worship. It rather declares our acceptance of the responsibilities of citizenship and our love for Israel. As these are religiously legitimate devotions, it is proper to express them by placing flags upon the *bimah* or elsewhere in the synagogue. It is, however, not *necessary* to do so. Our loyalty to our country and our concern for Israel are obvious even in the absence of the flags. Moreover, we reject any and all rhetoric which equates "God and Country." While such expressions may not, strictly speaking, qualify as idolatry, they connote for us some of the most disturbing cultural tendencies of our time: chauvinism, racial and ethnic hatred, and rank oppression. If we truly believe that God alone is worthy of our worship, we ought to avoid language which, rightly or wrongly, suggests otherwise.

Proper and Improper Use of the Synagogue

The passage cited at the beginning of this section declares that "synagogues must not be treated disrespectfully." What exactly does this mean? How do we distinguish between "respectful" and "disrespectful" use of the synagogue? Which activities are improper to hold within its confines? Is there a difference between the sanctuary and the other parts of the synagogue building in this regard? These questions cannot be answered with total precision. "All such matters," notes Rabbi Solomon B. Freehof, "are necessarily vague." The definition of propriety is determined largely by *minhag*, the religious custom of the people, the standards of morality and taste that prevail within a particular community. As these standards will differ from place to place, so will the specific answers to all of these questions. Any declaration that a particular use of the synagogue is proper or improper is therefore a matter of judgment. This is *not* to say that it is a whim or that it is arbitrarily imposed upon the community by those who happen to be in power. A "judgment," in the sense used here, is a decision which is *justified*, argued for and explained according to the values that define us as a religious community. And it is a judgment that must be rendered. As long as we take our synagogues seriously as places of sanctity, as structures devoted to the sacred acts of prayer and religious celebration, then we will stand fast in our determination that they be treated as such. We will, no doubt, always disagree among ourselves over the precise definition of the standards of propriety. But when they are worked out through the ongoing discussion and debate that emerge from the give-

and-take of Jewish community life, these standards are truly the product of a religious decision, a reflection of ourselves and of our most deeply-held convictions about what it means to assemble in a holy place.

Non-religious Activities. The tradition forbids activities classified as "levity" and "idle chatter" from taking place in a synagogue. It is not clear that this prohibition applies in our time to any and all events not of a purely religious nature. Reform responsa have endorsed the holding of lectures on general subjects and concerts of "good" music in the synagogue; to us, these are not "hilarity" but sources of "cultural satisfaction." On the other hand, "sensual" or "riotous" music, or programs whose content might be considered to "border on what is inappropriate"—whatever these terms mean on the contemporary cultural scene—are an affront to the holiness of the sanctuary. Moreover, when events of a non-religious nature are held on the *bimah* and in the presence of the ark, it is appropriate to take steps that emphasize the sanctity of the place. These might include the recitation of psalms and prayers before or during the presentation and the placement of a screen in front of the ark as a symbolic distinction between the holiness of the sanctuary and the secular activity occurring within its confines.

Weddings and Other Celebrations. Weddings may be conducted in the sanctuary, although not before the open ark. Some traditional authorities fear that wedding ceremonies may lead to the kind of frivolity that is forbidden in a synagogue sanctuary. We do not share this concern; indeed, we believe that the sanctuary is a most appropriate environment for the consecration of a marriage. Nor does contemporary Reform practice oppose loud and raucous celebrations of such holidays as Purim and Simchat Torah within the sanctuary. Problems arise, however, with respect to secular celebrations, parties which have no connection to any Jewish ritual purpose. For example, some congregations organize New Year's Eve parties on their premises, especially when the night of December 31 coincides with Shabbat. While this may be a laudable effort to encourage synagogue attendance on an evening otherwise devoted to wild festivities, the party should not be held in the sanctuary. Festivities of a secular nature should take place in the social hall or some other suitable locale. Moreover, the celebration should reflect, through its tenor and through the content of its program, the fact that it is taking place in a synagogue or is being sponsored by a Jewish congregation.

Gambling. While Reform Judaism frowns upon gambling as a means of fundraising, there is no objection to the playing of "sociable games" of cards and chance in the synagogue's social hall.

Smoking. It is appropriate and desirable for a synagogue to ban smoking on its premises.

The Rabbi

The word "rabbi" first appears in the literature of the Tanaitic or Mishnaic period (the first two centuries of the Common Era). As a religious title, it denotes a "master" who imparts to one or several *talmidim*, pupils or disciples, his knowledge of Torah, both the Written Torah or Scripture and the Oral Torah, the law (*halakhah*) and commentaries which expanded upon the Written Torah and were considered its authorized interpretation. It was the possession and study of this Oral Torah that distinguished the rabbis and their followers from other Jewish sects of the time. The Oral Torah was ultimately redacted into written texts, such as the Talmud and the Midrash, which preserved the deliberations of generations of rabbis. These texts subsequently became the basis for the organization of Jewish life. The Jewish community was defined by its adherence to "Rabbinic Judaism," by its determination to construct its religion and culture according to the Torah as it is understood in rabbinic literature. The rabbi, henceforth, was that sage whose knowledge of those texts rendered him capable of teaching and interpreting them. It was the rabbi who declared the meaning of Torah for his community and who raised up disciples to insure that the study and teaching of Torah would continue into the next generation.

The rabbinate was not a priesthood. The title "rabbi" conferred upon its bearer no special sacramental powers or authority. Any adult Jewish male who possessed the rudimentary knowledge and skills could lead the worship service, read from the Torah, serve as a judge in a legal dispute, and officiate at weddings, funerals, and other life-cycle events. If the rabbi enjoyed a special status, this was due solely to his prestige as a scholar of the texts, a prestige that encouraged—but did not always require—his community to submit their questions to him and to agree to conduct itself according to his answers. Nor was the rabbinate, at first, a profession in the usual sense of the term. The sage did not usually earn his living as a rabbi. Indeed, the very idea of a professional rabbinate seems to run counter to the teachings of Jewish tradition: to learn and to teach Torah is, after all, a *mitzvah*, a religious obligation incumbent upon every Jew, and one should not have to be paid to perform a *mitzvah*. Eventually, however, medieval Jewish communities recognized that the need to insure the services of a rabbi to teach Torah and to serve as a legal authority required that some form of compensation be offered to him. Since then, it has become the norm for the community to pay a salary and other benefits to its rabbi.

Today's rabbinate is in every respect a profession. The rabbi generally works a full-time job that requires long and specialized training and the mastery of a body of textual knowledge and practical skills. This is especially true of the congregational rabbi, who serves the community as preacher, teacher, counselor, administrator, and officiant at religious services. The term "professional" applies as well to the growing number of rabbis who occupy non-congregational positions. College professors of Jewish studies, military chaplains, Hillel directors, and executives in Jewish communal agencies all perform functions long associated with the rabbinate. Like all other professions, the rabbinate has developed its own standards of conduct for its members. In addition, as the teacher *par excellence* of Judaism, the rabbi is expected to exemplify the highest ideals of learning, religious devotion, and moral probity proclaimed by the Jewish tradition.

The North American Reform rabbinate has expressed itself frequently on these issues, in resolutions of the Central Conference of American Rabbis (CCAR), in Reform responsa, and in the CCAR's *Code of Ethics for Rabbis*. The following is a brief summary of the idea of the rabbi as presented in those sources.

Ordination. Rabbis today customarily receive their title from a rabbinical seminary or a *yeshivah*, a traditional academy of talmudic learning. Upon the successful completion of his or (in the more liberal branches of Judaism) her course of study, the student receives "ordination," a declaration that the student is qualified to serve as a rabbi in the Jewish community in accordance with the understanding of Judaism maintained by that school.

The ordination practiced today should not be confused with *semikhah*, the ordination described in the talmudic sources. That ritual, in which an ordained scholar laid his hands upon his student, granted its recipient all the power and authority of the biblical judge (*shofet*). The institution of *semikhah*, which could be awarded only by ordained scholars and only in the land of Israel, has long since come to an end. Today's "ordination" is but a symbolic representation of the ancient ritual. It confers no power upon its recipient, but rather attests that he or she is sufficiently knowledgeable to interpret Torah for the community and does so with the permission of his or her teachers. Unlike the *semikhah* of old, this permission need not be awarded in a special place and by some official licensing body. No institution is empowered to compel the community to accept as rabbis only those individuals who have received an "approved" ordination. Today's ordination may be granted by any rabbi to any student. As a matter of strict Jewish law, moreover, there is no requirement that a person be ordained in order to function as a rabbi on the contemporary scene. It is for the community to determine whether a particular teacher of Torah, ordained or not, is qualified to serve them as a rabbi.

Still, if ordination is not demanded by Jewish law, it is nonetheless required in Jewish practice. For centuries, Jewish communities have demanded some evidence of a candidate's readiness to perform the rabbinic function. The process we know as ordination, though not equivalent to the original *semikhah*, came into being in response to this demand, as a declaration by a teacher or a group of teachers that a student has successfully completed the course of study which that particular community regards as necessary and sufficient to qualify one as a rabbi. In the Reform Jewish community, it is customary to recognize as "rabbis" only those individuals who have completed the prescribed course of study at the Hebrew Union College–Jewish Institute of Religion or other comparable institution. It is at such a school that the student is exposed to a diverse and distinguished faculty, a suitable curriculum of Jewish studies, a decent library, and a variety of supervised fieldwork opportunities. It is through this means that the community has chosen to determine that a candidate has, in traditional language, *higi'a lehora'ah*, reached a level of competence that permits him or her to serve as a rabbi. For this reason, Reform Judaism discourages the practice of "private ordination," in which a particular rabbi or group of rabbis ordain a candidate who has not successfully completed the course of study at a recognized rabbinical school. Moreover, persons who have received rabbinic certification from lowly-regarded rabbinical schools or from schools with which we are unfamiliar are not to be accorded the title "rabbi" in our communities. Private ordination and ordination from lowly-regarded schools are destructive to the process by which our community has chosen to insure a rabbinate that adheres to the highest intellectual and professional standards.

Duties and Prerogatives. Jewish law does not demand that communal worship or life-cycle ceremonies be performed by an ordained rabbi. Worship services are led by a *sheliach tzibur*, the "representative of the congregation," not necessarily a rabbi. The rituals associated with circumcision, baby-namings, Bar or Bat mitzvah, weddings, and funerals may all be performed without a rabbi's participation. The rabbi, it should be remembered, is a teacher, an expounder of Jewish tradition, and a judge of issues of Jewish law and practice; he or she is not a priest. Prayer services and life-cycle rituals are not "sacraments" which must be administered by an ordained cleric to be religiously effective. They are rather, in the traditional Jewish understanding, *mitzvot*, commandments incumbent upon all Jews. As such, any member of the community, so long as he or she is not otherwise disqualified, may lead them.

Nonetheless, Jewish communities have since medieval times found it prudent to restrict officiation at weddings and certain other ceremonies to ordained rabbis in general and to the rabbi of the community in particular. This was done in part to protect the income of the increasingly professional rabbinate, which depended largely upon the fees received for performing weddings and other legal acts. Moreover, a rabbi's participation in the procedures of marriage and divorce could insure a proper degree of competent supervision over what are, under *halakhah*, complex legal institutions. Errors in the execution of marriage and divorce law could result in embarrassing and even tragic consequences; a rabbi's presence at the wedding was testimony that this marriage satisfied the requirements of Jewish law. For at least the last six centuries, it has become customary in virtually all Jewish communities for weddings to be performed by the rabbi or by an officiant (*mesader kiddushin*) appointed by the rabbi or operating with rabbinic permission.

In Reform Jewish practice, "the performing of marriages is professionally, technically, and spiritually the exclusive function of the rabbi." Wedding ceremonies are performed by a rabbi or by a qualified officiant, such as a cantor or a knowledgeable layperson, designated by a rabbi. Insistence upon rabbinic officiation, for us no less than for other Jewish communities, provides the best guarantee that all aspects of the wedding, including its liturgy, its procedure, and the pre-nuptial counseling which frequently accompanies it, will meet the highest standards. With regard to other life-cycle ceremonies and to worship services, we do not find in Reform tradition an explicit requirement for a rabbi's participation. Here again, however, custom has its say. These events and rituals pertain to the religious policy of the synagogue, and religious policy, in Reform tradition as in Jewish practice generally, lies within the area of rabbinic competence. Hence, although such a service is "valid" if led by someone other than a rabbi, it should be composed and conducted with the advice and consultation of the rabbi of the congregation.

Rabbinic Jurisdiction. The rabbi of the congregation is the *mara de'atra*, the rabbinic authority for that congregation. In Reform Judaism, the definition and precise boundaries of rabbinic authority are fluid, always open to discussion. This must surely be the case in a movement dedicated both to the principle of personal religious autonomy and to the obligations that flow from a commitment to Jewish life and faith. In spite of this ambiguity, however, certain affirmations as to the rabbi's authority have attained the status of consensus in Reform congregational practice. Every rabbi surely exercises those powers without which the office of rabbi would be essentially an empty and meaningless one. The rabbi of the congregation, for example, enjoys freedom of the pulpit. This entails not only the right to preach and to interpret Judaism as he or she understands it, but also a considerable degree of rabbinic preeminence in that synagogue. "Preeminence" means that the rabbi of the congregation is empowered to determine the standards of religious practice and policy binding upon the congregation's other religious professionals. It implies as well that a "guest" rabbi should occupy a colleague's pulpit, officiate in the synagogue, or speak at a function of the congregation or of one of its auxiliaries only at the invitation of the congregation's rabbi. On the other hand, there are some clear limits to the rabbi's local preeminence. The rabbi of a congregation may not prohibit a colleague from officiating at a life-cycle ceremony for a member of that congregation when this ceremony is not held in the rabbi's synagogue. The colleague, however, should officiate only after consultation with the rabbi of that congregation. Moreover, the rabbi's relationships with the other rabbis and religious professionals of the congregation must be characterized by an attitude of respect, harmony, and solicitude.

Rabbinic Fees and Salaries. We have already seen that the tradition gradually accepted the necessity of a professional rabbinate and the need to compensate rabbis for serving the community. Originally, this compensation was structured largely on the basis of fees received by the rabbi in return for the performance of weddings and other services. Later, the custom arose for the community to pay a fixed salary to the rabbi from its treasury. In many communities today, where the rabbi receives a salary, it is considered improper for him or her to demand a fee for the performance of any ceremony on behalf of a member of that community. This is the case in North American Reform Judaism, where the rabbi's status as a professional, full-time spiritual leader of the congregation means that its members "have a right to rabbinic services in time of need for life-cycle rites and pastoral functions, provided that performance of such services shall not be contrary to the convictions of that rabbi." A rabbi should therefore set no fee for the performance of rabbinic services for members of his or her congregations. On the other hand, when approached for services by individuals unaffiliated with the congregation, the rabbi is entitled to an honorarium, so long as this is not excessive and is not required in advance. In general, the rabbi must take care to avoid all appearances of commercialism in the services he or she renders to the congregation and the wider community.

The Cantor

The office of cantor, or *chazan*, developed from the position of *chazan hakenesset*, a term which in talmudic literature designates a public functionary who performed a variety of tasks. The *chazan* seems to have been a paid employee of the community. He was the caretaker and administrator of the synagogue and often lived in the synagogue building. He supervised the worship service, particularly the activities surrounding the Torah reading, and at times served as the regular Torah reader. He often functioned as the teacher of young children, as a scribe who wrote legal documents, and even as the preacher (*darshan*). In many communities, the *chazan* took on the responsibility of leading public worship, to the point that the titles of *chazan* and *sheliach tzibur* ("the emissary of the community" who serves as the "reader" of the worship service) have become largely interchangeable. Today's cantor most closely resembles the *chazan* of old in this sense, as a leader of worship.

Jewish tradition speaks at some length of the qualifications required of the *sheliach tzibur,* particularly one who serves in that capacity on a permanent basis. The worship leader should be a person who is morally upright, free of sin and the suspicion of sin, who possesses a humble yet pleasing personality, a good voice, and a knowledge of Hebrew sufficient to recite the prayers with fluency. In the event that no one can be found who is blessed with all these qualities, the community may choose as its cantor one who exceeds in "wisdom and good deeds." That is to say, though the word "cantor" implies that the one who fills this position be distinguished by vocal ability, the tradition does not rank musical talent at the top of its list of priorities. On the contrary: if the choice is between one who is musically gifted but ignorant of Torah and Hebrew and another who does not have a pleasant voice but understands the words he recites from the prayer book, the latter candidate is to be favored.

The position of cantor exists today in a large and growing number of Reform congregations. As *chazan*, he or she performs any number of ritual and pedagogical tasks within the synagogue and the community. To insure that its *chazanim* possess the requisite Jewish knowledge, especially knowledge of Jewish music, and professional skills needed for this important work, the Reform movement has established a School of Sacred Music at the Hebrew Union College–Jewish Institute of Religion (HUC-JIR) for the training of cantors. While many congregations retain the services of "cantors" who are not formally trained as such, it is highly desirable that a cantor be invested (ordained) as graduates of HUC-JIR or a comparable program of education. In this way, the Reform community can best insure that its liturgical specialists reflect its highest ideals of Torah learning and professional competence.

3

Sabbath and Holiday Observance

Shabbat

God blessed the seventh day and sanctified it. (Gen. 2:3)

Remember [*zakhor*] the Sabbath day to keep it holy. (Exod. 20:8)

Observe [*shamor*] the Sabbath day to keep it holy. (Deut. 5:12)

If you refrain from trampling the Sabbath, from pursuing your affairs on My holy day; if you call the Sabbath "delight" [*oneg*], God's holy day "honored" [*mekhubad*]; and if you honor it and go not your own ways, nor look to your affairs, nor strike bargains; then you can delight in God. (Isa. 58:13–14)

Shabbat Observance and Reform Judaism. The Jewish Sabbath has been called an "island of holy time in a sea of secular activity." This is a powerful and apt metaphor, but it remains a metaphor, an inexact comparison. Unlike a true island, which is formed by an act of nature, Shabbat is a human construction. It becomes holy in our lives as a result of our own creative endeavor. According to our tradition, we sanctify Shabbat by means of actions that correspond to four separate *mitzvot*. We *remember* the Sabbath through our liturgy, by the words we say and sing that distinguish this day from all others. We *observe* the Sabbath by refraining from doing "work" on that day. And we *honor* and *delight in* the Sabbath through the foods we eat, the clothes we wear, and the special ends to which we devote the hours of the day that would otherwise be given over to work and the pursuit of material gain. In fulfilling these *mitzvot*, tradition teaches that we build a fence in time, setting

Shabbat apart from the other days so that we may experience a kind of life that is wholly different, a "foretaste of the World-to-Come." It is an exercise in "the art of living as it expresses itself through Shabbat."

How do Reform Jews experience Shabbat? As with every other aspect of Jewish religious life, Reform thought on the subject of Sabbath observance is the product of a long and continuing process of historical development. The one constant feature of this process has been change. Each generation of Reform Jews has arrived at its own conception or conceptions of the nature of Shabbat and of its meaning in our lives. The same shall undoubtedly be true for generations yet to come. This book attempts to summarize the current state of Reform Jewish thinking about the observance of Shabbat, particularly as this thinking is expressed in Reform responsa and in the movement's major works devoted to the subject: *A Shabbat Manual, Gates of the Seasons*, and *Shaarei Shabbat (Gates of Shabbat)*. These books have emerged out of an effort by the Central Conference of American Rabbis to "create old/new opportunities for Jewish living." That effort reflected an increasingly positive appraisal of the role of religious discipline in Reform Jewish life and the conviction that "the recovery of Shabbat observance" is an item of pressing significance on the Reform Jewish agenda. While the idea of *mitzvah*, of commandment, is deeply problematic in Reform theology, these writings hold that a life of Jewish authenticity—a pattern of living composed of acts that "a Jew ought to do in response to God and to the tradition of our people"—is "inexorably bound up with Shabbat observance." Put differently, no matter how "Reform" our Judaism, it would be Jewishly unthinkable without the *mitzvot* of Shabbat.

Shabbat at Home

Preparation. It is a *mitzvah* to prepare for Shabbat. By "preparation," the Rabbis meant those activities which of necessity must be carried out before Shabbat arrives, activities which help to make the day a special one and to create an atmosphere of serenity and Shabbat peace. These include: cleaning the house and adorning it with flowers, setting the table, and shopping for and cooking the meal. The Sabbath is a particularly appropriate opportunity to fulfill the *mitzvah* of *hakhnasat orechim*, welcoming guests into our homes, especially newcomers in the community and others who are alone. The final moments before the beginning of Shabbat are an especially appropriate time for the giving of *tzedakah* (donations to the needy).

Kindling the Shabbat Lights (Hadlakat Hanerot). It is a *mitzvah* to begin the observance of Shabbat with the lighting of candles. The Rabbis ordained this practice as a means of fulfilling the requirements of *kavod* and *oneg*, to honor and delight in the Sabbath, so that we welcome the Shabbat and eat our meal in an atmosphere of festivity, peace, and light. For this reason, the Shabbat candles should be large enough to insure that they will continue to burn until the meal is over. It also marks the formal beginning of Shabbat, after which none of the activities defined as "work" (*melakhah*) may be performed.

In traditional Judaism, the *mitzvah* of lighting the candles is considered the special responsibility of women, since they tended to be at home preparing the meal for the onset of Shabbat. Nonetheless, men are also required to light the candles and to recite the appropriate blessing if no woman is present to perform the *mitzvah*.

When does Shabbat begin? Technically, Shabbat starts at the onset of "night" on Friday, but precisely when does that moment occur? The uncertainties over this question led to the establishment of a requirement "to add from the weekday to the holy day," that is, to begin Shabbat sometime before nightfall on Friday and to end it sometime after nightfall on Saturday. How *much* to add is the subject of a long and involved rabbinic dispute; thus, the times listed in Jewish calendars for candle-lighting and for the end of Shabbat depend largely upon local custom. The most widespread practice in traditional communities is to light the candles at approximately eighteen minutes before sunset on Friday and to end Shabbat at about one hour after sunset on Saturday.

According to the rabbinic sources, we light *one* Shabbat lamp (*ner*). The widespread custom, however, is to kindle two lamps or candles, one corresponding to *zakhor*, "*remember* the Sabbath day" (Exod. 20:8), and the other to *shamor*, "*observe* the Sabbath day" (Deut. 5:12). It is customary in some communities to light more than two lamps or candles; some families kindle a light for each member of the household. The one who kindles the Shabbat lights recites the following blessing:

> *Barukh atah Adonai Eloheinu melekh ha'olam asher kideshanu bemitzvotav vetzivanu lehadlik ner shel shabbat.*

Blessed are You, Adonai our God, Sovereign of the universe, who hallows us through the *mitzvot* and commands us to kindle the light of Shabbat.

Most blessings are recited immediately before the performance of the act to which they apply. The kindling of the Shabbat candles is a major exception to this rule. The problem is that as soon as one recites the *berakhah* (blessing), it is considered as though Shabbat has begun for that person; from that moment on, it is traditionally forbidden to kindle a fire. Thus, the candles must be lit before the blessing is pronounced. However, since the rule requires the blessing be said *prior* to the act, one places one's hands between the eyes and the candles as a kind of screen to "hide" the flame. At the conclusion of the blessing, one removes one's hands, now revealing the flame, as if the benediction preceded the kindling.

Blessing the Children. It is a *mitzvah* for parents to bless their children at the Shabbat table each week. This blessing precedes the recitation of *Kiddush.*

Kiddush. It is a *mitzvah* to recite *Kiddush* at the beginning of the Shabbat meal. This fulfills the requirement to "remember (*zakhor*) the Sabbath day to keep it holy" (Exod. 20:8): we remember the Sabbath by *sanctifying* it, by reciting a blessing which sets it apart and distinguishes it from the six days of labor. The word *kiddush* means, in fact, "sanctification." As God sanctifies the Sabbath in the heavens, so do we declare it a holy day here on earth, in our homes and in our lives.

Kiddush is recited over a cup of wine. It therefore consists of two blessings (*berakhot*). The first, *borei peri hagafen*, is the benediction we say before drinking wine; the second, longer paragraph, which concludes *mekadesh hashabbat*, "Blessed are You, Adonai, who sanctifies the Sabbath," is the *Kiddush* proper, the actual sanctification of the Sabbath day. One drinks from the wine cup at the conclusion of this second benediction. It is important to note that, by itself, *borei peri hagafen* is not the *Kiddush*; *both* blessings must be said. While the *Kiddush* should ideally be recited in Hebrew, it is entirely permissible to say it in the vernacular. In addition, prior to *borei peri hagafen*, it is customary to recite the verses of Genesis 1:31 (from *vayehi erev*, "it was evening and it was morning") through 2:3, which recount God's sanctification of the seventh day at the completion of the work of Creation. (For the *Kiddush* and accompanying readings, see *Gates of Shabbat*, 24–26.)

The proper place for the recitation of *Kiddush* is at the dinner table. For this reason, many traditional authorities require that we recite it while seated, to emphasize that we are gathered at the Shabbat table for our meal, although others permit or even recommend the recitation of *Kiddush* while standing. The *Kiddush* recited in synagogue is not a substitute for the performance of this *mitzvah* at home.

Since wine is traditionally associated with joy, the Rabbis decreed that the sanctification of Shabbat, a day of delight (*oneg*), be recited over wine. The term "wine" refers to grape wine or unfermented grape juice, beverages over which we recite the blessing *borei peri hagafen*. In some communities there is a preference to use red wine for *Kiddush*, though white wine is perfectly acceptable. If no wine is available, or if one cannot drink wine or grape juice for medical reasons, *Kiddush* may be recited over the bread at the Shabbat table. In this case, one would recite the verses Genesis 1:31–2:3, the blessing *Hamotzi*, and then the paragraph that sanctifies the Sabbath, after which one would break or cut the bread, eat from it, and continue with the meal.

Just as we sanctify Shabbat by reciting *Kiddush* at the Friday evening meal, so do we recite a *Kiddush* to begin the noon meal on Saturday. This *Kiddush* consists of an introductory paragraph, usually *Veshameru* (Exod. 31:16–17) and an excerpt from the Ten Commandments (the second half of Exod. 20:11), followed by the blessing over wine. Frequently, beverages other than wine are used for the Shabbat morning *Kiddush*; if so, the blessing recited is *shehakol nihyah bidevaro*. This ritual, called euphemistically *Kiddusha Rabbah*, "the great *Kiddush*," is customarily recited in synagogue after the Shabbat morning service.

Hamotzi. It is a *mitzvah* to say *Hamotzi*, the blessing over bread, usually *challah*, at the Shabbat meal. Jewish tradition specifies that this blessing be said over two loaves, preferably unbroken and unsliced, as a reminder of the double portion of *manna* (*lechem mishneh*) that fell to earth each Friday to feed the Israelites during their desert wanderings following the Exodus from Egypt. The loaves are placed on the table before *Kiddush* and covered with a cloth while the *Kiddush* is recited. In some homes, *Hamotzi* is preceded by a ritual washing of the hands, symbolizing the state of ritual purity in which the priests, during Temple times, would eat their food. The washing is accomplished by means of a *keli*, a cup or some other container with which one pours water two or three times over each hand. Immediately before drying the hands, one recites the blessing:

Barukh atah Adonai Eloheinu melekh ha'olam asher kideshanu bemitzvotav vetzivanu 'al netilat yadayim.

Blessed are You, Adonai our God, Sovereign of the universe, who hallows us through the *mitzvot* and commands us to wash our hands.

After the recitation of *Hamotzi*, salt is often sprinkled over the bread after it has been cut or pulled apart and before it is distributed to those at the table. This too hearkens back to the sacrifices of old, which were consumed with salt. Both the washing of the hands and the sprinkling of the salt express the idea that our table is a kind of altar: the act of eating, surrounded by blessings and priestly rituals, becomes a religious rather than a purely physical act.

The Shabbat Table. The *mitzvah* of *oneg shabbat*, to "delight in the Sabbath," is fulfilled in part through the festive quality of the meal. Special foods and beverages are served, and *zemirot* (Shabbat songs) are sung. Even our conversation should be different from that of the rest of the week. The Rabbis interpret the verse Isaiah 58:13 as an instruction that "your speech on Shabbat should not resemble your weekday speech." This means that we should strive to speak of significant matters such as the weekly Torah portion or issues of concern to the Jewish people, topics that increase our sensitivity to Jewish and human values, rather than devote our conversation to business or to "idle talk" and gossip.

Birkat Hamazon. It is a *mitzvah* to conclude the Shabbat meal with the Grace after Meals. Since we eat bread at our meal, the appropriate *berakhah* is *Birkat Hamazon*, which includes a special paragraph for Shabbat in its third component benediction.

Shabbat Day. The Shabbat midday meal, like the meal of *layl shabbat* (Friday night), has a festive character. It is preceded by a brief *Kiddush* over wine and by the recitation of *Hamotzi* over *challah*, marked by the proper Shabbat atmosphere and conversation, accompanied with *zemirot* and concluded with *Birkat Hamazon*. It is customary in some households to eat *se'udah shelishit*, a formal "third feast" on Shabbat afternoon. There is no *Kiddush* at this meal, but *Hamotzi* over *challah,* Shabbat songs, and *Birkat Hamazon* are recited.

The Conclusion of Shabbat: Havdalah. It is a *mitzvah* to recite *Havdalah,* the blessing which marks the distinction between holy and ordinary time, between the departing Sabbath and the beginning of the work week. The ritual encompasses four *berakhot*:

1. *The blessing over wine* (*borei peri hagafen*). Like *Kiddush, Havdalah* is recited over a cup of wine. If one has no wine, one may substitute another beverage (except for water) and recite the blessing *shehakol niheyah bidevaro.*

2. *The blessing over spices.* The leader of the service holds up a box or a vessel containing spices and says:

> *Barukh atah Adonai Eloheinu melekh ha'olam borei minei vesamim.*

> Blessed are You, Adonai our God, Sovereign of the universe, who creates varieties of fragrant spices.

The leader then smells the spices and passes them on so that all assembled may enjoy their fragrance.

The use of spices at *Havdalah* may stem from the ancient custom of bringing fragrant spices on burning coals into the room at the end of a meal. Since the act of burning spices violates the prohibition against work (*melakhah*), it signifies the end of Shabbat. Another explanation is that the spices help to cheer us up as Shabbat departs, to compensate for the loss of the "additional soul" (*neshamah yeteirah*) which dwells within each Jew on the Sabbath.

3. *The blessing over fire.* The leader of the service holds up a lighted *Havdalah* candle, one containing multiple wicks, and says:

> *Barukh atah Adonai Eloheinu melekh ha'olam borei me'orei ha'esh.*

> Blessed are You, Adonai our God, Sovereign of the universe, Creator of the lights of the fire.

Those present cup their hands and extend them palms up toward the candle.

The practice of reciting a blessing over fire at the end of Shabbat may also reflect the practice, mentioned above, of burning fragrant spices at the conclusion of a meal. Another explanation, based upon rabbinic legend, is that God created fire at the conclusion of the first Shabbat. A candle with multiple wicks is preferred; special *Havdalah* candles are braided for this purpose. The reason is that fire is composed of "lights" of various colors; the use of multiple wicks assures that "lights," rather than mere "light," will be present. The blessing, therefore, says *me'orei ha'esh*, "the *lights* of the fire," rather than *me'or ha'esh*, "the *light* of the fire."

4. *The Havdalah benediction.* This blessing praises God "who separates between the holy and the ordinary," meaning Shabbat and the other days of the week. The leader drinks from the wine in the cup, and the candle is extinguished in the remaining wine.

In addition to the *berakhot*, it is customary to introduce the service with the recitation of biblical verses that express the hope for God's deliverance and salvation. Similarly, it is customary to conclude the service with songs that express Israel's longing for messianic redemption. Since Shabbat is considered a foretaste of the World-to-Come, we are sad at its departure. Yet we mix our sadness with a declaration of our faith in the coming of the "never-ending Shabbat," a time when "the world will be perfected under [God's] unchallenged will."

Shabbat in the Synagogue

Gates of Prayer, the *siddur* of the North American Reform movement, offers ten different services for Shabbat night and six for Shabbat morning. As with the weekday prayer ritual, it is therefore difficult to speak of a single "rite" or unified liturgy; nonetheless, the services share a core liturgical structure. It may be useful to compare this account of the Shabbat liturgy with that of the weekday services in Chapter 1.

1. *The Evening Service (Ma'ariv or Arvit)*

Lighting of the Candles (Hadlakat Hanerot). A member of the congregation kindles the lights of Shabbat and then recites the appropriate blessing. It is not necessary for the congregation to stand for the lighting of the candles.

Most Reform congregations begin their Friday evening services after dinner time and hence, for most of the year, long after nightfall. In some congregations, the lights are kindled prior to the onset of Shabbat and the service begins with a recitation of the blessing only.

Kabbalat Shabbat (*Welcoming the Sabbath*), consists of psalms, songs, and readings which introduce and set the mood for the holy day. *Gates of Prayer*'s Service I (118–27) follows the order of *Kabbalat Shabbat* in the traditional *siddur*, including the poem (*piyyut*) *Lekha Dodi*.

Chatzi Kaddish; recitation of the Shema (*Keri'at Shema*). This rubric follows the order of the weekday evening liturgy, except that the second benediction following the Shema, *Hashkivenu* (*Gates of Prayer*, 133), ends with an expanded form of the concluding blessing. In addition, most congregations sing *Veshameru*, Exodus 31:16–17, following *Hashkivenu*.

The Tefillah (*Prayer*). Like its weekday counterpart, the Shabbat *Tefillah* begins with three benedictions that praise God and concludes with three which express our acknowledgment of God's goodness and our yearning for peace. On Shabbat, the thirteen intermediate benedictions give way to a single *berakhah*, consisting of several paragraphs, called *Kedushat Hayom* ("sanctification of the day"), which declares our recognition of and thanks for the holiness of Shabbat. The evening *Tefillah* may be followed with the *me'ein sheva*, a brief poem that recapitulates the themes of the seven blessings of the *Tefillah*.

Keri'at Hatorah (*The Reading of the Torah*). Some congregations read from the Torah on Friday nights.

Concluding Prayers. These consist of the recitation of *Aleinu* and the *Mourner's Kaddish*, as on weekdays. In addition, the congregation recites *Kiddush*. This custom originated at the time when the synagogue served as a lodging place for travelers. Since they took their meals in the synagogue, it was appropriate for them to say *Kiddush* there. The custom continues today, long after the synagogue has ceased to serve as a hostel. The reason for retaining the congregational *Kiddush*, according to some authorities, is so that those who do not know the blessing may hear and learn it. The goal, of course, is that all should say *Kiddush* over the meal at home; as noted above, the recitation of *Kiddush* in synagogue is not a substitute for its recitation at home. Some congregations, notably those in the land of Israel, do not say *Kiddush* in the synagogue at all.

2. *The Morning Service* (*Shacharit*). This service follows the pattern outlined in Chapter 1 for the weekday *Shacharit*: introductory prayers and readings (which may be more extensive on Shabbat), *Chatzi Kaddish*, the recitation of the *Shema* (*Keri'at Shema*), the *Tefillah* (which has the same structure as the evening Shabbat *Tefillah*), the reading of Torah and *Haftarah*, and concluding prayers.

3. *The Afternoon Service* (*Minchah*). See the discussion of the *Minchah* service in Chapter 1, p. 6.

Shabbat Prohibitions

On Menuchah. The Sabbath is a day of "rest" (*menuchah*). The requirement that we rest on Shabbat is explained by the Torah according to two broad themes. First, God "rested" from the work of creation on the seventh day; therefore, we rest on that day to acknowledge God as the Creator of the universe. Second, we rest on Shabbat as a reminder of the Exodus from Egypt, our redemption from slavery. Our rest, a dignity not granted to slaves, reminds us that we are in bondage to no human master; we therefore acknowledge God's liberating power in our lives and in the history of our people. An intrinsic feature of *menuchah* is the prohibition against doing any manner of work (*melakhah*), a prohibition which the Torah mentions no less than six times. The Torah never defines the concept of "work" in precise terms. That task is accomplished by the Rabbis of the talmudic tradition, who enumerate thirty-nine general categories (*avot*) of *melakhah*, each of which is divided into numerous sub-categories (*toledot*).

The Rabbis are careful to insist that these categories are not their own invention. The definition of "work," they claim, is derived from the Torah itself, though at times they concede that the Scriptural basis for many of these rules is sketchy at best. One of the biblical verses which prohibits *melakhah* on Shabbat occurs immediately prior to Moses' instructions to the people on the construction of the desert tabernacle. From this fact, declares one *midrash*, we learn that the Torah defines "work" as any and all creative activities necessary for the building of that shrine. This teaches us that Shabbat takes precedence even over the

construction of the holiest of structures and therefore, too, over virtually every sort of productive human endeavor. Over the centuries, the
details pertaining to these categories have been expanded to include
activities that were certainly never contemplated by the authors of the
biblical and early rabbinic sources. In addition, the Rabbis enacted
numerous rules of their own—"fences around the Torah"—which forbid a host of activities that, while not technically defined as "work,"
seemed in their eyes to merit prohibition as safeguards of the holiness
of Shabbat. This system has been studied, commented upon, and developed through the centuries, and it constitutes today a massive and
complex subject in the curriculum of Jewish law.

Reform Attitudes. Reform Judaism also holds that Shabbat is a day of
rest and that work should be avoided. It takes with the utmost seriousness the tradition's requirement that Shabbat be a day of "rest," set apart
from all others not only through ritual activity but also through the
abstention from "work," those weekday activities which interfere with
the establishment of "an island of holiness in time." At the same time,
Reform Judaism has departed from the strict traditional definitions of
"rest" and "work" because it does not believe that these represent the
final word on Jewish practice. Just as the rabbinic Sages developed their
definitions on the basis of understandings rooted in their own environment, so do contemporary Jews continue to arrive at conceptions of
menuchah and *melakhah* that reflect the needs of their own time, place,
and circumstances. As adherents of a movement that cherishes religious
freedom, Reform Jews will respond to the demands of Shabbat in many
different ways. For this reason, the observance of Shabbat in Reform
Judaism—the definition of "rest" and "work"—will vary widely from
person to person and from community to community.

At the same time, the freedom to create new forms of Sabbath observance is accompanied by an important caveat. As *Gates of the Seasons*
puts it: "In creating a contemporary approach to Shabbat, Reform Jews
do not function in a vacuum. Although we may depart from ancient
practices, we live with a sense of responsibility to the continuum of
Jewish experience." When the Reform Jew considers a question of
Shabbat observance, he or she should begin with a thoughtful and careful consideration of traditional styles and standards, seeking "to maintain as much as possible our connections with the best of the Jewish
past." Our creativity is restrained and guided by our desire to express

our religious identity through observances that reflect and affirm the heritage we share in common with Jews around the world and through many centuries.

Reform responsa and other writings on Shabbat observance have sought to strike this balance between autonomy and tradition, between the freedom to innovate and the commitment to an idea of Shabbat that is unmistakably Jewish in its form and content. The following are suggested standards of observance that have emerged from this effort.

Personal Activities. The individual is encouraged to choose from among a variety of responses to the holiness of Shabbat. One may avoid engaging in any kind of "creative" activity, actions which involve the manipulation of the world around us, as an acknowledgment that the universe is not our creation but God's. On Shabbat, we leave creation as it is; we disengage ourselves from the material world in order to focus upon the "inner world" of self, family, and friends. This approach might involve the observance of a number of the traditional prohibitions concerning Shabbat activity. We might abstain from driving, the use of money, the telephone, the computer, and the like, so that we might devote ourselves to prayer, study, conversation, and other pursuits that have long been associated with the Jewish Sabbath.

Alternately, one may observe Shabbat as a day of freedom from devotion to necessity. That is, one may decide to engage in any number of activities which, though traditionally forbidden on the Sabbath, are done *likhevod Shabbat*, in *honor* of the Sabbath. One might not drive to the mall to shop, for example, but might drive to a museum and pay the price of admission, because one considers a visit to a museum an act that refreshes the soul. Or one might look upon Shabbat as a day to be devoted to such endeavors, including "creative" ones, as affirm our sense of human freedom, just as the Torah understands Shabbat as a memorial to our liberation from Egyptian bondage.

What unifies these alternatives is the conception that Shabbat is a day that is not to be treated as any other. It is not merely a day off; it is rather an expanse of time that is holy, different in quality and essence from all other days, consecrated both to God and to us for the purpose of our fulfillment as Jews. Reform Jews may seek that fulfillment in different ways, but they will find it only when they commit themselves with the utmost seriousness to the Jewish responsibility to observe (*shamor*) the Sabbath day.

The Congregation. Synagogues should refrain from conducting regular business on Shabbat. Jewish tradition allows a community to hold a business meeting on Shabbat, especially if the meeting is devoted to urgent public business or to important *mitzvot* such as *tzedakah*. This permit, however, reflects a time when Shabbat may have been the only day available for individuals to gather to discuss communal affairs. This is no longer the case, and given that "we have sought in every way to enhance Shabbat and the spirit of rest," it is inappropriate in the absence of an emergency situation to schedule a congregational business meeting on Shabbat.

Congregational fundraising projects, particularly if they involve the actual business transactions or the handling of money, should not be carried out on Shabbat. Similarly, *tzedakah* projects which involve activities normally considered to be "work" should not take place on that day. It is true that Reform Judaism regards *tzedakah* and social action as a central *mitzvah* in the life of our people. Yet the Sabbath is for us more than just a day off or even a day on which we are entitled to do all manner of good deeds. On the contrary: Shabbat is itself a *mitzvah*, defined by its own particular observances, a *mitzvah* that makes a legitimate demand upon our attention. Thus, unless the *tzedakah* activity involves an emergency, life-threatening situation, it should be scheduled on another day. Other congregational activities should be structured so as to emphasize the distinction between Shabbat and all other days. For example, while the synagogue gift shop ought to be closed on the Sabbath, the needs of the community may require that it operate before and after services. In such a case, while the shop may be opened for browsing, no business transactions should be completed. Delivery of and payment for goods can take place at the end of Shabbat.

Synagogue Employees. Non-Jewish employees of the synagogue may perform their normal duties on Shabbat. Contract employees, such as caterers preparing for Bar or Bat Mitzvah celebrations, may work in the synagogue on Shabbat.

Life-Cycle Ceremonies. Many important ritual events in the lives of individuals do not take place on Shabbat. Some life-cycle ceremonies, by contrast, may be held on Shabbat, while others *must* take place on that day.

Weddings. Weddings are not scheduled on Shabbat. The creation of a marriage is also the formation of a legal contract which establishes certain rights and obligations between the spouses, and Jewish tradition prohibits the initiating of legal agreements on the Sabbath. Moreover, the scheduling of weddings on Shabbat conflicts with our goal of honoring Shabbat as a holy day on which we do not carry out many of the activities that are and can be performed on other days. Since other days are available for weddings, they should not be allowed to conflict with Shabbat. If unavoidable final preparations must be made on Shabbat for a Saturday night wedding, care should be taken to preserve the spirit of the Sabbath.

Funerals. Funerals are not held on Shabbat. Those observing the seven-day mourning period (*shivah*) also observe Shabbat, both at home, with *Kiddush* and a Sabbath meal, and by attending synagogue services.

Circumcision (Berit Milah). The Torah (Lev. 12:3) requires that a Jewish boy be circumcised on the eighth day after birth. This applies even if the eighth day is a Sabbath, a festival, or Yom Kippur. If a boy is born on Shabbat, his ritual circumcision (*berit milah*) is performed on the following Shabbat. In no other case, however, does a circumcision take place on Shabbat, because there is no requirement that it be done precisely on that day. For example, if an infant's circumcision has been delayed for medical reasons beyond the eighth day of his life, it should not be performed on Shabbat. Similarly, if a conversion ritual involves circumcision or the taking of a drop of blood, that procedure should not occur on Shabbat.

Rosh Chodesh and the Jewish Calendar

God said to Moses and Aaron in the land of Egypt: This month [*chodesh*] shall mark for you the beginning of the months; it shall be the first of the months of the year for you. (Exod. 12:1–2)

Moses did not know how to determine the beginning of the month until God pointed it out to him: "*This* month shall mark for you . . . "; that is, "when the new moon [*chodesh*] appears in this manner, declare the beginning of the month." (*B. Menachot* 29a)

You shall observe the Feast of Unleavened Bread . . . at a set time in the month of Aviv, for in it you went forth from Egypt. (Exod. 23:15)

The Calendar. The Jewish calendar is lunisolar, reckoned by calculations based upon both the moon and the sun. It is *lunar* in that the year is usually composed of twelve months determined by the cycle of the moon's revolution around the earth. It is *solar* in that adjustments are made in it to insure that the annual festivals occur in the same season (early spring, late spring, early fall) every year.

The month begins with the appearance of the new moon (Rosh Chodesh). The ancient Rabbis understood Exodus 12:1–2 as requiring that the new month be determined by eyewitness testimony: just as God "pointed out" the appearance of the new moon to Moses and Aaron, so must witnesses declare before the judges of the Sanhedrin, the Great Court in Jerusalem, who stood in place of Moses and Aaron, that they had seen that form in the heavens. The judges did not accept this testimony naively. From their study of astronomy, a science well known to the peoples of the ancient Near East, the judges knew that the new moon of a particular month would appear at a certain position and a certain angle in the sky. They also knew that the duration of the moon's cycle is twenty-nine and one-half days and that the new moon would be seen either on the thirtieth or thirty-first day following the previous Rosh Chodesh. If the witnesses placed the new moon on an acceptable date and in its proper point in the sky, the Court would declare the month "sanctified" from the day on which the new moon was spotted. If no witnesses arrived to testify to the new moon on the thirtieth day of the month, the court would by process of elimination declare the following day to be Rosh Chodesh.

While eyewitness testimony was a legal and ritual requirement, therefore, the Sages knew how to determine the calendar by means of astronomical and mathematical calculations. Following the destruction of the Temple and the disappearance of the Great Court, the eyewitness procedure was abandoned, and these formulae became the exclusive means by which the Jewish calendar was set. There were a number of disputes over the precise details of the formulae, but these were resolved by the tenth century. The result is a calendar that has been virtually uniform throughout the Jewish world ever since.

The Months. The months of the Jewish year are as follows:

Month	Occurs	Days	Can Begin On
Tishri	Sept–Oct	30	M, T, Th, Shabbat
Cheshvan	Oct–Nov	29–30	M, W, Th, Shabbat
Kislev	Nov–Dec	29–30	all except Shabbat
Tevet	Dec–Jan	29	S, M, T, W, F
Shevat	Jan–Feb	30	M, T, W, Th, Shabbat
Adar	Feb–Mar	29	M, W, F, Shabbat
Nisan	Mar–Apr	30	S, T, Th, Shabbat
Iyar	Apr–May	29	M, T, Th, Shabbat
Sivan	May–June	30	S, T, W, F
Tamuz	Jun–Jul	29	S, T, Th, F
Av	Jul–Aug	30	M, W, F, Shabbat
Elul	Aug–Sept	29	S, M, W, F

In a leap year, an extra month is added: Adar I consists of 30 days and begins on Sunday, Wednesday, Thursday, or Shabbat; Adar II consists of 29 days and begins on Monday, Wednesday, Friday, or Shabbat.

This system begins with the fact, mentioned above, that the moon completes its revolution of the earth in twenty-nine and one-half days. Twelve lunar months should therefore total 354 days. Since a month cannot begin in the middle of the day, the calendar achieves this number by requiring that half the months of the year consist of thirty days while the other six months consist of twenty-nine days. A month that contains thirty days is called *malei*, "full," while one that contains twenty-nine days is called *chaser*, "defective." When a month lasts for thirty days, the Rosh Chodesh for the following month is traditionally observed for two days; the first day of Rosh Chodesh is actually the thirtieth day of the preceding month. (Rosh Hashanah, which is traditionally observed for two days, is an exception to this rule.)

Reform congregations generally observe Rosh Chodesh for one day, on the first day of the Hebrew month.

Two months—Cheshvan and Kislev—may consist of either twenty-nine or thirty days. This variation allows an adjustment to the calendar which insures that the following Rosh Hashanah will occur on Monday, Tuesday, Thursday, or Shabbat. This calendrical "fix" is essential in order to avoid the unacceptable complications in Jewish ritual life which would result were Rosh Hashanah to fall on Sunday, Wednesday, or Friday.

The Year. The lunar calendar of 354 days "lags behind" the 365-day solar year. Were no adjustments made to remedy this deficiency, the Hebrew months would begin eleven days earlier on the solar calendar each year. Over time, the Jewish festivals—for example, Passover—would fall in all four seasons. The problem here is that the Torah requires that Passover be observed in the month of "Aviv," that is, during the spring. Therefore, at regular intervals an extra month is added to the Jewish calendar to compensate for the days that would otherwise be "lost" against the solar year. This "leap month" is always Adar II (*Adar Sheni*). When a "leap month" is added, the holidays and observances of the month of Adar (Purim, Shushan Purim, the "special Sabbaths") take place during Adar II.

In ancient days, the decision to add an extra month rested in the hands of the Great Court in the land of Israel. The judges would assemble during the winter to determine whether the coming Passover would fall too "early" in the year, during the winter rather than in the spring. They would consider whether the grains and fruits that normally appear during Nisan would not blossom or ripen by that time, or if the winter rains would not cease by then. If they made this determination, they would add a month at the conclusion of Adar to delay Nisan (and Passover) until the spring. With the disappearance of the Great Court, the process of "intercalation" (the adding of an extra month of Adar) is, like the determination of Rosh Chodesh, left to mathematical formulae that have come to be accepted throughout the Jewish world. That procedure is based upon a cycle of nineteen years, during which a second Adar is added in the following years: 3, 6, 8, 11, 14, 16, and 19.

The Liturgy of Rosh Chodesh. Rosh Chodesh is marked in the Reform synagogue worship as follows:

1. The blessing of the new month (*Birkat Hachodesh*; *Gates of Prayer*, 453) may be recited following the *Haftarah* on the Shabbat which precedes Rosh Chodesh. This custom serves as a memorial of the days when the new month was decreed in the Temple in Jerusalem.

2. The passage "Be mindful of Your people" (*ya'aleh veyavo*; *Gates of Prayer*, 43, 67, 137, 310) is inserted into the weekday *Tefillah* and into the Grace after Meals (*Birkat Hamazon*).

3. The *Hallel* (*Gates of Prayer*, 525–30), consisting of Psalms 113–18, is recited in abbreviated form, following the *Tefillah* and preceding the reading from the Torah. It is customary to begin the *Hallel* with the following blessing:

> *Barukh atah Adonai Eloheinu melekh ha'olam asher kideshanu bemitzvotav vetzivanu likro et hahallel.*

> Blessed are You, Adonai our God, Sovereign of the universe, who hallows us through the *mitzvot* and commands us to recite the *Hallel*.

4. The Torah is read. The traditional reading for Rosh Chodesh is Numbers 28:1–15, divided into four *aliyot*. In Reform practice, where there may be but one person called to the Torah, the passage read is Numbers 28:11–15.

Women and Rosh Chodesh. It is not forbidden to do work (*melakhah*) on Rosh Chodesh. According to an ancient tradition, however, some women do abstain from work on that day. One legend explains that God granted Rosh Chodesh as a special observance for women as a reward for their refusal to donate their jewelry toward the making of the Golden Calf in the wilderness (Exod. 32). This does not mean that Rosh Chodesh is a "women's holiday," any more than the other festivals are "men's holidays." Indeed, Rosh Chodesh stands as a reminder to all Jews of the rhythm of the Jewish calendar. Still, many Jewish women have chosen to revive the ancient tradition, to interpret and to observe Rosh Chodesh as a day which bears a particular significance for them.

The Pilgrimage Festivals

> Three times a year you shall hold a festival for Me. You shall observe the Feast of Unleavened Bread, eating unleavened bread for seven days as I have commanded you, at the set time in the month of Aviv, for in it you went forth from Egypt; . . . and the Feast of the Harvest, of the first fruits of your work, of what you sow in the field; and the Feast of Ingathering at the end of the year when you gather in your produce from the field. Three times a year, all your males shall appear before God, the Sovereign. (Exod. 23:14–17)

> You shall rejoice in your festival. (Deut. 16:14)

One is obligated to see to it that one's household and children rejoice on the festival. (*B. Pesachim* 109a)

The first day shall be for you a sacred occasion; you shall not do your daily work. (Leviticus 23:7)

The Festivals. Aside from Shabbat, which is observed each week, and Rosh Chodesh, which falls every month, the Jewish calendar is replete with celebrations which occur once a year. Among these are the *chagim*, the three "pilgrimage festivals" of Pesach, Shavuot, and Sukkot, so-called because in ancient times all Israelite males were required to appear at the Temple in Jerusalem and to offer special sacrifices at those seasons of the year. The *mitzvah* of pilgrimage distinguished these festivals from other biblical holy days such as Rosh Hashanah and Yom Kippur. The *chagim* also differ from other observances in that they are agricultural celebrations, each of them marking a particular point in the harvest cycle in the land of Israel. Each one also memorializes an historical event, corresponding to a significant moment in biblical Israel's journey from slavery to freedom: Pesach, the liberation from Egyptian bondage; Shavuot, the receiving of the Torah; and Sukkot, the years of wandering through the wilderness on the way to the promised land.

Each of these great festivals is unique, recognized by rituals and observances entirely its own. Still, they share certain features which distinguish them from the other holy days. These are based upon the two biblical *mitzvot—simchah*, rejoicing, and *shevitah*, abstention from work.

Simchah. It is a *mitzvah* to rejoice on the festival day. The tradition understands this *simchah* not simply as an emotional state but as a call to action: we are required to spend time on the festival day in activities normally associated with joy. As the Talmud understands it, this implies an equal division of the day: half of it belongs to God, half to us. We therefore divide our time between prayer and study on the one hand and festivity on the other.

Originally, this notion of festivity was connected to the Temple in Jerusalem. Individuals and families would bring a special sacrifice, the *chagigah*, and consume it in the Temple precincts, thereby fulfilling the commandment to "rejoice in the presence of God" (Deut. 16:11). With the destruction of the Temple, Shabbat became the model for festival observance. We "rejoice" in the festival in much the same way that we "remember," "honor," and "delight" in Shabbat: through preparation; including guests at the table; lighting candles; the recitation of *Kiddush* and *Havdalah*; having a festive meal that features *challah* and that begins with *Hamotzi* and ends with *Birkat Hamazon*; singing *zemirot*. The festival *Kiddush* (*Gates of Prayer*, 723–24), like its Sabbath counterpart, consists of two blessings: *borei peri hagafen*, the blessing over wine; and the *Kiddush* proper, the praise of God who "sanctifies Israel and the festivals." On the first night of the festival, we add the blessing *Shehechiyanu* (" . . . who has given us life, sustained us, and permitted us to reach this season"). In most respects, the details of these observances are the same on festivals and Shabbat.

In addition, the Torah's requirement to "rejoice in your festival" means that formal mourning is suspended for the observance of the holiday. *Shivah*, the seven-day period of mourning that begins with the burial of the deceased, is terminated when the festival intervenes. All other physical manifestations of an individual's mourning are removed before the onset of the holiday. The *chagim* share this feature with the non-pilgrimage festivals of Rosh Hashanah and Yom Kippur. Shabbat, by contrast, which is a day of honor (*kavod*) and delight (*oneg*) but not a time when we are required to "rejoice," does not bring *shivah* to an end.

Weddings are not held on festival days. The reason for this is in part the same as that which explains why we do not hold weddings on Shabbat: the formation of a marriage is the creation of a legal contract and the acceptance of a set of legal obligations, acts which are not in keeping with the nature of the day. There is, however, another reason which pertains specifically to the festivals: since the festival is a time of rejoicing for all Israel, we should not mix our own personal *simchah* with that of the community as a whole.

The joy of the festival is expressed as well in the synagogue liturgy. In the *Kedushat Hayom* benediction of the *Tefillah*, as well as in the *Kiddush* recited over wine, we praise God, who has ordained this festival. During the worship service we say *Hallel* (Pss. 113–18) in praise of God's redemptive acts in the history of the Jewish people. And we insert the passage "Be mindful of Your people" (*ya'aleh veyavo*) into the third blessing of *Birkat Hamazon*.

The Festival Prohibitions. It is a *mitzvah* to abstain from work on the festivals. According to tradition, all activities ordinarily prohibited on

Shabbat are also prohibited on *yom tov* (the festival day: i.e., the first and seventh days of Pesach; Shavuot; the first day of Sukkot; and Shemini Atzeret/Simchat Torah. The rules concerning work on Rosh Hashanah are the same as those of the festivals). There are, however, some important exceptions. One may perform labor in order to prepare food to be consumed on the festival day. It is also permitted to transfer a flame from an existing fire (although kindling a flame is forbidden, as on Shabbat) as well as to carry objects in the public thoroughfare. These exceptions do not apply to Yom Kippur, on which the traditional prohibitions against work are in every respect as stringent as those of Shabbat.

Reform Judaism teaches that the festivals, like Shabbat, are set aside for sanctification. Individuals should refrain from those activities which do not contribute to the spirit of holiness. Children and university students should not attend classes on *yom tov* but should instead participate in worship services. In the event that a school schedules classes or ceremonies on a festival, the Jewish community should take a firm stand, insisting either that the ceremony be held on a different day or that alternative arrangements be made for Jewish students.

Chol Hamo'ed (The Intermediate Days of the Festival). The five intermediate days of Pesach and the six days between Sukkot and Shemini Atzeret are called *chol hamo'ed*, literally "the non-sacred days of the festival." They are "non-sacred" in that, unlike *yom tov*, the first and last days of the festival, it is permitted to do most kinds of work on *chol hamo'ed*. Yet these days are still part of the festival. Since many of the festival's observances (*matzah* and the abstention from eating leaven on Pesach; the *sukkah* and the *lulav* on Sukkot) are maintained on *chol hamo'ed*, each day can be an opportunity for rejoicing and for preserving the festive atmosphere.

Weddings may be held on *chol hamo'ed*. On mourning during the festival period, see the discussion in Chapter 4.

The Second Festival Day (Yom Tov Sheni Shel Galuyot)

On the fifteenth day of the [first] month is God's Feast of Unleavened Bread . . . On the first day you shall celebrate a sacred occasion: you shall not work at your occupations . . . The seventh day shall be a sacred occasion: you shall not work at your occupations. (Lev. 23:6–8)

According to the Torah, the "sacred occasion" (*mikra kodesh*), the festival day or *yom tov*, occurs at a fixed time on the Jewish liturgical calendar and lasts for one day. Rabbinic tradition prescribes that Jews living in the Diaspora (outside the land of Israel) observe a second day of *yom tov* for the following holidays: the first and seventh day of Pesach; Shavuot; Rosh Hashanah; the first day of Sukkot; and Shemini Atzeret. This means that Pesach becomes an eight-day festival; Sukkot and Shemini Atzeret/Simchat Torah lasts for nine days; and Shavuot and Rosh Hashanah are each observed for two days.

The extra day was added due to difficulties in communication between Jerusalem, where the Sanhedrin (the Great Court) determined the Jewish calendar, and the Jewish Diaspora. In ancient times, the new moon (Rosh Chodesh) was declared by the judges of the Sanhedrin on the basis of testimony brought to them by eyewitnesses in the land of Israel. The court would then proclaim the new month and send word of the proclamation by means of a series of torches that were lighted on hilltops. When observers on the next hilltop saw the lighted torch waved to and fro, they would light their own torches to signal the observers stationed on the hilltop beyond them and so on. This chain stretched all the way to Babylonia, so that the large Jewish community there would learn quickly that the new month had begun. They could then begin to number the days to the festivals: Pesach and Sukkot occur on the fifteenth day of their respective months; Shavuot occurs fifty days after the beginning of Pesach, and so forth.

The difficulty with this method of communication lay in the fact that a Jewish calendar month can consist of either twenty-nine or thirty days, so that Rosh Chodesh can occur on either the thirtieth or thirty-first day of the preceding month. The Samaritans (*kutim*), a neighboring people whose relations with the Jews were strained, were able to sabotage the system by lighting torches on hilltops on the thirtieth night of the month, even if Rosh Chodesh had not yet been declared. The Diaspora Jews would draw the mistaken conclusion that the new month had begun; they would count the required number of days and begin the festival one day early. To counteract this threat, the Sanhedrin determined to send messengers to spread word that the new month had begun. This system was not as efficient as the old one. The messengers could not reach the entire Diaspora within two weeks; the outlying communities therefore could not receive official word as to the proper date on which to begin counting toward the festival. Because of this doubt, communities which lay beyond a two-week's journey from Jerusalem began to observe *yom tov* for two days, that is, fifteen days after both the thirtieth and the thirty-first day of the preceding month, the two days on which Rosh Chodesh might have been declared in Jerusalem. Eventually, this custom was adopted by all Jews living outside the land of Israel.

The two-day observance of Rosh Hashanah was an exceptional case, since the New Year falls on the first day of the "seventh month" (Tishri). One year, the Talmud tells us, the witnesses to the new moon did not arrive in Jerusalem until nearly sundown the next day, leading to confusion in the Temple as to which day, the thirtieth or thirty-first of Elul, was Rosh Chodesh and Rosh Hashanah. To forestall this problem, it was decreed that Rosh Hashanah should always be observed for two days, even within the land of Israel. This is the practice observed in Israel today, where Rosh Hashanah is observed for two days, while every other *yom tov* is a one-day observance.

The two-day observance of *yom tov*, in other words, originated out of doubt (*safek*) as to which day was in fact the biblically-ordained festival day. Yet this doubt has long since disappeared. Even in ancient times, as noted in our discussion of the calendar, the formulae for determining the months and years were widely known. The Talmud therefore asks: now that we know how to set the calendar by means of mathematical calculation, no longer relying upon eyewitness testimony and messengers to inform the Diaspora, why do we not return to the original, biblical standard of observing *yom tov* for one day only? The answer, recorded in the form of a decree (*takkanah*) issued by the rabbinic authorities in the land of Israel, was that the Diaspora must retain its ancestral custom, lest one day a hostile government forbid the Jews from studying the Torah and hence from learning the computations which set the calendar. This decree was adopted by all Diaspora communities that observed the rabbinic tradition.

From early in its history, the Reform movement has criticized the practice of *yom tov sheni* on several grounds. First, since Jews in fact have determined their calendar for centuries through mathematical calculations—since we know very well just when Rosh Chodesh is going to occur—the second day is clearly no longer necessary as a response to calendrical doubt. Second, the Talmud's rationale for retaining *yom tov sheni* has lost its persuasive force. The formulae for determining the calendar are now open to all, to Jews and non-Jews alike; they are no longer the sort of religious knowledge that a hostile government would proscribe as "Torah." Third, Reform Judaism rejects the notion that we are bound to observe the decrees of past authorities even when the reasons which prompted them to issue these decrees no longer exist. Finally, the economic hardships involved in observing a second festival day convinced Reform leaders that the interests of Jewish religious life would be better served by eliminating *yom tov sheni* than by maintaining it. Reform Jews have therefore returned to the standard, as prescribed by the Torah, that each *yom tov* be observed for one day. The one exception to this is Rosh Hashanah, which many Reform congregations in North America have lately begun to observe for two days.

The "Special Sabbaths"

Jewish tradition speaks of five "special Sabbaths" which occur during the six-week period prior to Pesach.

1. *Shabbat Shekalim* occurs on the Shabbat preceding Rosh Chodesh Adar (in a leap year, Rosh Chodesh Adar II) or on Rosh Chodesh itself when that day coincides with Shabbat. In Temple times, according to tradition, all Jews were required to contribute one-half shekel annually toward the upkeep of the sanctuary and the purchase of animals to be offered for public sacrifice. Since the Temple's financial year began in Nisan, this contribution was collected during the month of Adar. On Shabbat Shekalim we remember that practice, and we consider our own obligations toward the maintenance of our synagogues and other Jewish institutions. We read from the Torah, in addition to the weekly portion, the passage Exodus 30:11–16, which describes the collection of the half-shekel from the Israelites in the desert. The *Haftarah* is II Kings, 12:5–16 (traditionally, 12:1–17), which describes contributions made toward the Temple in the days of King Jehoash.

2. *Shabbat Zakhor.* On the Shabbat preceding Purim, the additional Torah reading is Deuteronomy 25:17–19, which contains the commandment to "remember" (*zakhor*) the unprovoked attack by Amalek upon our people in the wilderness (Exod. 17:8–16) and to "blot out the memory of Amalek from under heaven." This theme continues in the traditional *Haftarah*, I Samuel 15:2–34, which de-

scribes a war between the Israelites and the Amalekites during the days of King Saul. The king of the Amalekites was named Agag, which is significant because Haman, the villain of the Purim story, is called an "Agagite" (Esther 3:1). Haman is therefore considered a descendant of Amalek, a nation which in our national memory has become identified with anti-Semitism and causeless hatred of the Jews. Thus, the Amalek passage is read on the Shabbat before Purim. Today, Shabbat Zakhor is an opportunity to reflect upon the persecutions we have suffered through our history and upon the ways we might best respond to them. Due to the violent nature of the Samuel passage, Reform practice substitutes a selection from the Book of Esther (7:1–10; 8:15–17; or 9:20–28), which preserves the connection between Amalek and Haman.

3. *Shabbat Parah* occurs after Purim, on the Sabbath immediately preceding Shabbat Hachodesh (see below). Besides the weekly portion, we read Numbers 19:1–9 (traditionally, 19:1–22), which speaks of the ceremony of the red heifer, an essential element in ritual purification. In ancient times, all Jews were required to bring the Passover sacrifice to the Temple, yet they were not permitted to enter that holy place in a state of ritual defilement. The need to purify themselves was an integral part of the preparations for the festival; hence, the laws concerning ritual purification are read at this time of the year, when we are readying ourselves for our own observance of the upcoming holiday. The *Haftarah*, Ezekiel 36:22–36 (traditionally, 36:16–38), continues the theme of the day by speaking of moral and spiritual purification, an apt complement to the ritual setting of the Torah reading.

4. *Shabbat Hachodesh* occurs on the Sabbath immediately preceding Rosh Chodesh Nisan or on Rosh Chodesh Nisan when it occurs on Shabbat. The special Torah reading for the day is Exodus 12:1–20, in which God instructs Moses and Aaron in the laws of the very first Passover in Egypt. Tradition tells us that God spoke these words on the first day of Nisan. The *Haftarah*, Ezekiel 45:16–25 (traditionally, the reading continues to 46:18), speaks of the festival sacrifices in the Temple. This Shabbat, marking the beginning of the month in which Israel was redeemed from Egypt, helps to focus our attention upon the approaching holiday and its theme of liberation.

5. *Shabbat Hagadol* (the "Great Sabbath") is the Shabbat which precedes Pesach. It is called "great" because of the great miracle which, according to legend, was performed for our ancestors in Egypt on that day. When the time had come for Israel to be redeemed from slavery, God commanded the people to take lambs into their homes on the tenth day of the month. They were to keep the lamb until the fourteenth of the month, when they were to sacrifice it as the Passover offering (Exod. 12:3ff.). The miracle lay in the fact that the Egyptians, who worshiped the lamb as a god, saw the Israelites prepare to slaughter that sacred animal and were powerless to stop them. According to tradition, the tenth of Nisan that year fell on Shabbat; it therefore became customary to declare the Shabbat preceding Pesach as Shabbat Hagadol in remembrance of that miracle. There is no special Torah reading on this day. The *Haftarah* is Malachi 3:4–24, which concludes with the prediction of the coming of Elijah to herald God's "great" day. Since Elijah is traditionally associated with the coming of the Messiah, this passage is timely at Pesach, with its focus upon the liberation of Israel from bondage.

Pesach

Seven days you shall eat unleavened bread; on the very first day you shall remove leaven from your houses . . . You shall observe the Feast of Unleavened Bread, for on this very day I brought your ranks out of the land of Egypt . . . In the first month, from the fourteenth day of the month at evening, you shall eat unleavened bread until the twenty-first day of the month at evening. No leaven shall be found in your houses for seven days. (Exod. 12:15–19)

You shall not eat anything leavened with [the paschal sacrifice]; for seven days thereafter you shall eat unleavened bread, bread of distress—for you departed from the land of Egypt hurriedly—so that you may remember the day of your departure from the land of Egypt as long as you live. (Deut. 16:3)

For six days you shall eat unleavened bread. (Deut. 16:8)

They shall eat [the Passover sacrifice] with unleavened bread and bitter herbs. (Num. 9:11)

You shall explain to your child on that day: "It is because of what God did for me when I went free from Egypt." (Exod. 13:8)

The prayer book calls Pesach (or Passover) *zeman cheruteinu*, the season of our liberation. It commemorates the Exodus from Egypt, a central and defining event in the religious history of the Jewish people. We recall this pivotal experience frequently in our worship. The festival begins at sundown, at the conclusion of the fourteenth day of the month of Nisan, and lasts for seven days.

Like Shavuot and Sukkot, Pesach is a *chag*, a pilgrimage festival, celebrated through the *mitzvot* of *simchah*, rejoicing, and *shevitah*, abstention from work. In addition, its observance is characterized by *mitzvot* unique to Pesach itself: *matzah* (the eating of unleavened bread); *maror* (the eating of bitter herbs); *chametz* (abstention from eating leaven); *bi'ur chametz* (the removal of leaven from the home); and *haggadah* (participation in the Seder meal and telling the story of the Exodus).

Matzah. It is a *mitzvah* to eat *matzah* on the evening of the fifteenth day of Nisan, at the Seder, in remembrance of the haste in which our ancestors left Egypt (Exod. 12:39), of our humble beginnings and compassion for the poor and oppressed (Deut. 16:3), and of the paschal sacrifice that our people offered to God in Egypt and thereafter (Exod. 12:8; Num. 9:11). Tradition does not require one to eat *matzah* during the remainder of the festival, although some authorities hold that it is a special *mitzvah* to do so.

The word *matzah* means "unleavened bread." This implies, first of all, that *matzah* (pl., *matzot*) is *bread*, a foodstuff baked from one of the "five grains": wheat, barley, rye, oats, or spelt. And it is *unleavened*, which means that the *matzah* dough must be placed in the oven quickly, before it undergoes the process of fermentation (*chimutz*). All "Passover *matzot*," those packed in boxes labeled "kosher for Passover" (*kasher lepesach*) meet this definition, as do such by-products as *matzah* meal. Among Passover *matzot*, however, are two varieties which deserve special mention.

1. *Matzah meshumeret* ("*shemurah matzah*"). Exodus 12:17, according to the traditional understanding, bids us to "guard" or "watch" the *matzot*, that is, to make sure that the dough does not ferment and become *chametz*. Most Passover *matzot* are "watched" from the time of kneading: as indicated above, once the dough is mixed with water, care is taken to insure that the mixture is placed in the oven before it has a chance to ferment and to leaven. Some authorities,

however, assert that the required "watching" must take place earlier, from the time when the grain is harvested. Such *matzah*, baked from grain that was carefully stored from the moment of harvest to prevent it from coming into contact with water, is called *matzah meshumeret* or "*shemurah matzah*" ("watched" or "guarded *matzah*"). Some observant Jews have fully adopted this stringency and do not eat any *matzah* during the entire Pesach festival that is not *meshumeret*. Others will be sure to eat *matzah meshumeret* at the Seder, in fulfillment of the actual commandment to eat unleavened bread. For our purposes, it is sufficient to note that this practice is a custom, a voluntarily-adopted standard, and not a ritual requirement. Regular Passover *matzot* are fully acceptable for use at the Seder and throughout the festival.

2. *Matzah ashirah* ("enriched" or "egg *matzah*"). *Matzah* is ordinarily baked from dough consisting of a mixture of flour and water. *Matzah ashirah* is baked from flour mixed with liquids other than water, usually fruit juice or eggs (hence the common term "egg *matzah*"). The Talmud declares that such mixtures do not ferment, and Sefardic Jews accordingly eat *matzah ashirah* during Pesach. Traditional Ashkenazic practice, however, forbids *matzah ashirah* during Pesach for all but the old, the infirm, or the very young, out of fear that fermentation does take place when flour is mixed with fruit juice or eggs. Even if one eats *matzah ashirah* during the festival, one cannot use it to fulfill the *mitzvah* of eating *matzah* at the Seder. The Seder *matzah* must be the plain variety, baked from a flour-and-water dough.

Maror. It is a *mitzvah* to eat *maror*, or bitter herbs, on the fifteenth day of the month of Nisan, at the Seder, in remembrance of the bitterness of our enslavement in Egypt (Exod. 1:14). Various vegetables qualify as *maror*. Although many people choose romaine lettuce as the preferred species of "bitter herb," Ashkenazic tradition often favors horseradish. By "horseradish" we mean the *root* of the plant itself, that is, freshly-grated horseradish, rather than the bottled variety, which contains other ingredients.

Chametz and "Kosher for Passover." It is a *mitzvah* to abstain from eating leaven, or *chametz*, during the entire seven days of Pesach. According to tradition, the prohibition against eating *chametz* begins about an hour before midday on Erev Pesach (14 Nisan), that is, some six or more hours before one eats *matzah* at the Seder.

Among Reform Jews, abstaining from *chametz* may take many forms, from not eating such obviously leavened foods as bread and cake to the more stringent avoidance of all *chametz* and *chametz* mixtures.

Chametz refers not only to leavened bread but to any product made from the five species of grain—wheat, barley, rye, oats, and spelt. These grains are called *chametz* because their flour undergoes the process of leavening (*chimutz*) when mixed with water. Traditional practice forbids the eating of products made of the leavened grains themselves (*chametz be'ayin*) as well as any mixture containing them (*ta'arovet chametz*) during Pesach. These grains may be consumed during Pesach only when baked in the form of *matzah* or *matzah* by-product, under careful supervision which insures that the dough does not have a chance to leaven before it is placed in the oven.

Rice and Legumes. Other vegetables which resemble the "five grains," notably rice and legumes (*kitniyot*) such as peas and beans, are not *chametz*. Thus, according to the Talmud and the leading codes, it is permitted to eat these foods on Pesach. Ashkenazic Jews, however, have long observed the practice of abstaining from rice and legumes, as well as grains such as corn, during the festival. This custom has various explanations. For example, these foodstuffs are said to be prohibited because the rice and legumes sold in the marketplace inevitably contained small amounts of grain. Other authorities write that cooked dishes made with the permitted substances closely resemble those containing *chametz*, thereby leading to the possibility that the people may permit themselves to eat *chametz* mixtures as well. Still others worried that, despite the Talmud's assertions, rice and legumes do indeed ferment when soaked in water. Whatever its origins, the custom never spread into Sefardic and other Jewish communities. Moreover, not all Ashkenazim were convinced by these explanations; we find Ashkenazic halakhic scholars as late as the eighteenth century expressing skepticism as to the correctness of this customary prohibition.

From its beginnings, the Reform movement has relaxed this custom and permitted the consumption of rice and legumes during Pesach. Some liberal Jews may wish to abstain from these foods out of personal piety, as an affirmation of familial tradition, or in solidarity with general

Ashkenazic practice. There is, however, no religious requirement that they do so.

Bi'ur Chametz. It is a *mitzvah* to remove leaven (*chametz*; foods made from wheat, barley, rye, oats, and spelt) from one's possession prior to the beginning of Pesach. This *mitzvah* is separate and distinct from the prohibition against eating *chametz*.

This requirement is based upon Exodus 12:15. According to most authorities, that verse demands only that we eliminate *chametz* from our legal possession or ownership. This can be accomplished through the process of nullification (*bitul*), a declaration to the effect that one's *chametz* is ownerless or does not exist. That is to say, we fulfill the *mitzvah* when we mentally "remove" ourselves from all legal attachment to our *chametz*. As an extra precaution, the ancient Rabbis added the requirement of *bi'ur chametz*, the destruction or physical removal of the leaven in our possession. Unless we eliminate our *chametz*, they reasoned, we might inadvertently eat some of it during the festival. Moreover, the process of "nullifying *chametz*" is successful only if one completely and sincerely renounces all claim to it, with no mental reservations whatsoever. Since this is not an easy thing to do, the Rabbis decreed the physical removal of leaven.

Jewish tradition combines both these procedures. On the evening of 14 Nisan, the night before the Seder, after the house has been cleaned for Pesach, it is customary to conduct a symbolic search for *chametz* (*bedikat chametz*). Prior to the search, the following blessing is recited:

> *Barukh atah Adonai Eloheinu melekh ha'olam asher kideshanu bemitzvotav vetzivanu al bi'ur chametz.*

> Blessed are You, Adonai our God, Sovereign of the universe, who hallows us through the *mitzvot* and commands us to burn *chametz*.

Following the search, one recites a formula of *bitul*: "All *chametz* in my possession which I have neither seen nor destroyed, I declare to be annulled and like the dust of the earth." This formula is said again the next morning, after one has burned or otherwise destroyed the *chametz* found during the previous night's search. Through its recitation, the *chametz* that is not physically eliminated from one's property is "removed" in accordance with the terms of Exodus 12:15.

The requirement of *bi'ur* presents its own difficulties. It is, after all, economically unfeasible to destroy large amounts of leaven prior to

Pesach. Rabbinic law therefore developed another means of "removing" *chametz*: one may sell the leaven to a non-Jew prior to noon on the day before Pesach. The transfer of the *chametz* is conducted as an actual sale. The Gentile buyer is in all respects its true legal owner, even though both parties assume that the buyer will not take physical possession of the *chametz* during Pesach and both know that the seller will buy it back immediately upon the conclusion of the festival. In this way, it is officially "removed" from one's ownership, thereby fulfilling the terms of Exodus 12:15.

The problem with this device, of course, is that it is a legal fiction. Even though it is sold, the *chametz* remains exactly where it is: stored in the Jew's home, shop, or other property. The sale of leaven has effectively repealed the old rabbinic decree of *bi'ur*, the physical "removal" of *chametz*. Jewish ritual practice has therefore come full circle, back to the original "Toraitic" standard: we remove *chametz* by eliminating it from our *legal* possession while it remains in our *physical* possession.

Adhering to this logic, Reform Judaism holds that one may properly remove *chametz* by adhering to the "Toraitic" standard. No "sale" is necessary. One who does not destroy or physically eliminate *chametz* may store it away or cover it from view. This is tantamount to nullification and accords with the traditional understanding of Exodus 12:15.

The Seder Table

It is a *mitzvah* to participate in the Seder and to recite the Haggadah, the narrative of the Exodus from Egypt. The Seder is a ritual meal at which we tell the story of the Exodus and eat the special foods of Pesach.

Preparations. In front of the leader of the Seder or in front of each participant, a special plate is set. On it (or next to it) are the following items:

Three matzot. Two of these represent the two loaves (*lechem mishneh*) which appear at every Shabbat or festival meal. The third *matzah*, which will be broken in two, is particular to the Pesach ritual. With its first half we perform the actual *mitzvah* of eating *matzah* on the Seder night, which must be performed over a *perusah*, a piece, rather than an entire *matzah*. The second half is the *afikoman*, which is consumed at the end of the meal.

Maror. Romaine lettuce or horseradish root, symbolic of the bitterness of Egyptian slavery.

Charoset, a mixture of apples, wine, and spices, representing the mortar with which our ancestors made bricks during their bondage in Egypt.

Parsley or any green herbs, symbolic of springtime.

Two cooked dishes (tavshilin), symbolic of the Pesach and *chagigah* (festival) sacrifices that were brought to the ancient Temple and consumed at the Seder. Most Ashkenazic Jews use a roasted shankbone (*zero'a*) to symbolize the Pesach offering and a boiled or roasted egg (*beitzah*) to represent the *chagigah*.

Wine, for it is a *mitzvah* to drink four cups of wine during the Seder. A traditional explanation is that each cup corresponds to one of God's four promises of redemption for Israel in Exodus 6:6–7. Some follow the custom of adding a fifth cup. Today, this cup is popularly (if inaccurately) associated with the "cup of Elijah the prophet," set upon the Seder table as a symbol of our hope in the ultimate redemption of Israel and humanity. The Haggadah of the Reform movement, while retaining the "cup of Elijah," restores the optional fifth cup as "an additional cup set aside for the future."

The Seder

The Torah sets forth the commandments to be fulfilled on the first night of the festival: to partake of the Passover sacrifice, to eat the *matzah* and the *maror*, and to recount the tale of the Exodus. The Seder as we know it, however, is a product of the early Rabbis, an elaborate ceremonial meal which they modeled upon the banquet or "symposium" feast of the surrounding Hellenistic society. The symposium, which was often devoted to philosophical conversation, resembled our Seder in a number of ways. The meal consisted, for example, of several distinct courses, each accompanied by wine. The main course was preceded by an "appetizer," usually vegetables and greens dipped into condiment. Those present would eat while reclining on individual couches. Participation in such a meal was emblematic of the status of *ben chorin*, a free person, a citizen of the state. The Rabbis, of course, translated those customs into symbols of Jewish significance. In turn, subsequent generations added to the content of the Seder. Indeed, every Jewish community has brought something of its own to this ritual. If the essence of this *mitzvah* is the personal experience of liberation—"In every generation one must view oneself as having come forth out of Egypt"— then it is no wonder that Jews everywhere and at all times have told the stories of their own lives in the language of the biblical narrative of redemption and of its rabbinic commentary. *A Passover Haggadah: The New Union Haggadah*, the current Seder ritual of the North American Reform movement, is our own contribution to this age-old process of Jewish self-narration.

The Seder ritual consists of the following steps, found on the indicated pages of *A Passover Haggadah*:

1. *Kadesh*, "Sanctification of the Day" (pp. 21–25), is recited over the first cup of wine. The blessing over wine, *borei peri hagafen*, is followed by *Kedushat Hayom*, the festival *Kiddush*. If the Seder takes place on Friday night, the appropriate phrases are inserted for Shabbat. If it occurs on Saturday night, the blessings *borei me'orei ha'esh* ("Creator of the lights of the fire") and *Havdalah* follow the *Kiddush*. We recite the blessing *Shehechiyanu* ("who has kept us in life") following *Kiddush* (or *Havdalah*), immediately before drinking the wine.

It is traditional to drink the wine while reclining on our left side. This reenacts the ancient Hellenistic practice, mentioned above, for "free people" to eat their festive meals in this position. Such has not been the custom for many centuries; still, the practice is retained symbolically, so that one should recline to the left side while drinking the four cups of wine and eating the *matzah*, the foods that represent our liberation from bondage. Reform practice dispenses with reclining. Since we no longer follow this ancient custom at our festive meals during the year, it no longer expresses the status of freedom. It is therefore not necessary for us to adopt it on the night of Pesach.

It is also traditional practice to wash one's hands at this point of the Seder, in the ritual manner known as *netilat yadayim*, in which one pours water from a cup or pitcher onto one hand and then onto the other. This ceremony is performed twice during the traditional Seder: immediately prior to *karpas*, the eating of the green vegetable; and immediately before *motzi-matzah*, the eating of the bread. The practice of *netilat yadayim* is a remnant of the laws governing ritual purity and impurity in the ancient Temple. Our Haggadah does not include these handwashings, since Reform Judaism tends in general to omit observances that evoke the Temple and the priesthood and express hope for their restoration.

2. *Karpas* (pp. 25–26). Each person takes the parsley or other green vegetable, dips it in salt water, vinegar, or other condiment, recites the blessing *borei peri ha'adamah* ("who has created the fruit of the earth") and eats it.

3. *Yachatz* (p. 26). The leader breaks the middle *matzah*. One half will serve for the actual *mitzvah* of eating *matzah* during the meal, and the second half will be the *afikoman*.

At this point of the Seder (p. 28), *A Passover Haggadah* offers the option to continue with the eating of *matzah* and *maror* or to defer them until page 60. The first option reflects the ancient practice, when Jews who assembled at the Temple for the Passover sacrifice would first eat the meal and then proceed to tell the story of the Exodus. The second is the familiar, traditional practice, in which the *matzah* and *maror* are eaten immediately prior to the festive meal.

4. *Maggid* (pp. 26–60), the narration of the Exodus event, is the major portion of the Seder ritual. Tradition requires that the story be told in response to a child's questions concerning the unusual rituals of the evening, hence, the "Four Questions" (p. 29), which give the child an opportunity to "ask" why the customs surrounding the meal on this night differ from those of other nights. Indeed, many other rituals associated with the Seder are explained as pedagogical devices designed to elicit the curiosity of the children. The "answer" to the questions begins with "We were slaves to Pharaoh in Egypt . . . " (Deut. 6:21; p. 34).

Tradition offers some guidelines as to how the story is to be told. For example, we begin with *degradation*, our origin as slaves to Pharaoh and to idolatry, and we end with *praise* of God, who set us free and who gave us Torah. In addition, the core of the story is a *midrash* (homiletical expansion) upon Deuteronomy 26:5–8. Most important is the requirement that the story be related in a language that its listeners understand. The Passover narrative, that is, is no purely ritual act but a means of internalizing the experience of slavery and redemption in those who hear it. To a significant extent, the Haggadah accomplishes this goal by reminding us of the story's continuing relevance. "For more than one enemy has risen against us. In every generation, in every age, some rise up to plot our annihilation. But a Divine Power sustains and delivers us" (p. 45). The Haggadah, moreover, stresses in several places that today we are not truly free, that we await the final redemption, the ultimate fulfillment of the promise of the Exodus. The story of Pesach, in other words, is *our* story, the account of our own as-yet uncompleted lives and not merely a tale of ancient times. Our text, *A Passover Haggadah*, offers supplementary readings that treat the great themes of the Passover narrative in the context of the historical experience of our own generations.

Following the narration of the Exodus event, we explain to ourselves the significance of three items of the Seder plate: *pesach* (the shankbone), *matzah*, and *maror* (pp. 53–56). Their significance lies in their role in the Passover story: we utilize them today at our Seder as reminders of both what happened to us in Egypt and of how our ancestors celebrated this festival at the Temple in days of old. We then recite the mishnaic passage "In every generation . . . ," by which we make clear that the story of slavery and redemption is not merely something that happened centuries ago; it is *our* story as well. In this spirit, having *personally* experienced liberation from bondage, we joyously recite the first two psalms of the *Hallel* (pp. 59–60) in celebration of God's redemptive power in our people's history. The *Maggid* concludes with the recitation of *Birkat Ge'ulah*, the "blessing of redemption," over the second cup of wine. We recite the blessing *borei peri hagafen* and drink the wine.

5. *Motzi-Matzah* (p. 28). If we did not eat the *matzah* prior to the recitation of *Maggid*, we do so at this point. The leader takes the three *matzot* in hand, and we recite two benedictions: *Hamotzi*, the blessing we say before eating bread, and the following *berakhah* concerning the special *mitzvah* of this evening:

> *Barukh atah Adonai Eloheinu melekh ha'olam asher kideshanu bemitzvotav vetzivanu 'al akhilat matzah.*

> Blessed are You, Adonai our God, Sovereign of the universe, who hallows our lives through commandments, who has commanded us regarding the eating of *matzah*.

The uppermost *matzah* and the middle, broken *matzah* are then broken and distributed among the group, who eat them.

6. *Maror* (p. 28). We take some of the *maror*, dip it into the *charoset*, and recite the benediction:

> Barukh atah Adonai Eloheinu melekh ha'olam asher kideshanu bemitzvotav vetzivanu 'al akhilat maror.

> Blessed are You, Adonai our God, Sovereign of the universe, who hallows our lives through commandments, who has commanded us regarding the eating of *maror*.

We eat the *maror*.

7. *Korekh* (pp. 28–29). In the days of the Temple, the sage Hillel fulfilled the *mitzvot* of Passover night by eating all three ritual foods—the Pesach sacrifice, the *matzah*, and the *maror*—together. In remembrance of his custom and in solidarity with all generations of the Jewish past, we combine *matzah* and *maror* (the latter dipped in *charoset*) and eat them together at this point in the Seder.

8. *Shulchan Orekh* (p. 61). The meal is served.

9. *Tzafun* (p. 61). The *afikoman* is eaten. The second half of the middle *matzah* was "hidden" (*tzafun*) at *Yachatz*, above. The custom has developed in some homes for the children to search out the "hidden" piece of *matzah*. The *afikoman* is the last food to be eaten during the Seder.

10. *Barekh* (pp. 61–68). We say *Birkat Hamazon*, the grace recited after eating bread. The blessing concludes with the recitation of *borei peri hagafen* and the drinking of the third cup of wine.

We open the door "for Elijah" (pp. 68–71).

11. *Hallel* (pp. 71–75). The recitation of *Hallel*, begun at the end of *Maggid*, is concluded. Our Haggadah provides a selection from Psalms 115–18. At this point in the traditional Seder the fourth cup of wine is consumed. Our Haggadah reserves the final cup for *Nirtzah*, the conclusion of the Seder. Some of the familiar Seder songs, such as *Chad Gadya* ("An Only Kid") and *Echad Mi-Yode'a* ("Who Knows One?"), are placed here, rather than after *Nirtzah*, as in the traditional Haggadah.

12. *Nirtzah* (pp. 91–93), the conclusion of the Seder. We pray that God will find our service acceptable and speed our ultimate redemption ("Next year in Jerusalem!"). We recite *borei peri hagafen* and drink the final cup of wine.

Passover Services

Synagogue services for Pesach follow the festival liturgy (*Gates of Prayer*, pp. 455–572). The festival days of Pesach are the first day and the seventh day; the intermediate days are *chol hamo'ed*. *Yizkor* (the memorial service) is recited by many congregations on the seventh day. A portion of the *Hallel* is recited on each day of Pesach. The Torah portion for the first day of Pesach is Exodus 12:37–42 and 13:3–10, and the *Haftarah* is Isaiah 43:1–15. The seventh day reading is Exodus 14:30–15:21 (which includes the Song at the Sea), and the *Haftarah* is II Samuel 22:1–51. When one of the days of *chol hamo'ed* is Shabbat, the Torah portion is Exodus 33:12–34:26, and the *Haftarah* is Ezekiel 37:1–14. Each day of *chol hamo'ed* has its own Torah reading (for a list, see the Notes to this section). The Song of Songs is read on the Shabbat during Pesach (or on the last day of the festival, should that day be Shabbat).

Reform congregations observe each *yom tov* for one day only. When the "eighth day" of Pesach (or the "second day" of Shavuot) falls on Shabbat, Reform congregations (and all congregations in Israel) will resume reading the cycle of weekly *sidrot* (Torah portions). Other Diaspora congregations will read Deuteronomy 14:22–16:17, the traditional portion for that day, along with its *Haftarah*, Isaiah 10:32–12:6. This means that for some weeks, and perhaps months, the Reform lectionary will be "one step ahead" of the Torah readings in other Diaspora synagogues, until such time as those congregations can "catch up" by reading two relatively short Torah portions on the same Shabbat. In order to preserve uniformity in the reading of the Torah throughout our community, it has been suggested that Reform congregations spread the reading of the weekly *sidra* over two Sabbaths (the "eighth day" of Pesach/"second day" of Shavuot and the following Shabbat), so that by the time of that second Shabbat all Diaspora congregations will be reading from the same portion. Alternately, a Reform congregation might repeat the festival reading from the previous day, or it may join other Diaspora congregations in reading from Deuteronomy 14:22–16:17, resuming the weekly cycle on the following Shabbat.

The seventh day of Pesach is a *yom tov*, a festival day. The festival liturgy is recited. In addition, Reform congregations hold *Yizkor* (memorial services) on this day. Unlike Shemini Atzeret, however, it is not considered a festival in its own right but rather a continuation of the Pesach holiday. For this reason, although we recite *Kiddush* at synagogue and at the festive meal on the evening of the seventh day, we do not say the blessing *Shehechiyanu* as we do at the *Kiddush* which comes at the beginning of a festival. Neither is the full *Hallel* recited on the last day of Pesach, as it is in traditional congregations on all other festival days; rather, one recites the abbreviated *Hallel* on both *chol hamo'ed* and on the concluding festival days.

The Omer

The period between Pesach and Shavuot is called the "Counting of the Omer" (*sefirat ha'omer*), after the ancient rite of the bringing of the first sheaf (*omer*) of the barley harvest to the priest (Lev. 23:9–14). This ceremony began "on the day after the *shabbat*" (23:11), which rabbinic tradition understands to mean the day after the festival (*yom tov*), that is, the second day of Pesach. Starting from that day, the Torah also instructs that "you shall count off seven weeks. They must be complete: you must count until the day after the seventh week—fifty days" (23:15–16). The festival of Shavuot is observed on the fiftieth day.

Reform Judaism has generally regarded this "counting" as a regulation of the calendar: the community is to count seven weeks from Pesach to the conclusion of the spring harvest, so that the harvest may be concluded by the Shavuot festival. There is no need, in other words, to count the days in a ritual manner. Jewish tradition, on the other hand, holds that the counting is a separate *mitzvah*, a concrete observance in its own right, a memorial of the days when the harvest ritual was observed in the Temple. This *mitzvah* can be seen as a means of linking Pesach, the season of our liberation, to its ultimate fulfillment in Shavuot, the season of the giving of the Torah. There is no "freedom," in other words, without Torah, without a system of meaning to be found in Jewish life and existence. The counting, which lasts for forty-nine days, takes place at night, commencing with the second night of Pesach. Those who "count the Omer" recite the following benediction:

Barukh atah Adonai Eloheinu melekh ha'olam asher kideshanu bemitzvotav vetzivanu 'al sefirat ha'omer.

Blessed are You, Adonai our God, Sovereign of the universe, who hallows us through the *mitzvot* and commands us regarding the counting of the Omer.

One then says: "This is the (first, second, etc.) day of the Omer." From the seventh day, one counts the weeks as well, for example, "this is the tenth day of the Omer, a total of one week and three days."

The weeks between Pesach and Shavuot are customarily a period of some solemnity. Tradition recounts that thousands of Rabbi Akiva's students died of a plague during these weeks, a plague brought on "because they did not treat each other with respect." In commemoration of that sad event, the community engages in a number of mourning practices: weddings are not scheduled, haircuts are not taken, and celebrations of music and dance are not held during the Omer. The great exception to this rule is 18 Iyar, or "Lag Ba'omer," the thirty-third day of the period, a day on which the plague is said to have stopped. Lag Ba'omer is a break in the period of mourning; those activities otherwise proscribed during the Omer may take place on that day. The fifth of Iyar, Yom Ha'atzma'ut (Israel Independence Day), is also recognized by many traditionally-observant Jews as a joyful interruption of the Omer's solemnity, although those Orthodox Jews who for ideological reasons do not celebrate Yom Ha'atzma'ut will continue to observe the Omer's restrictions on that day. The Reform movement has largely abrogated these customs, which have no basis in either the Bible or the Talmud. One custom we have retained, however, is the study of one of the chapters of the mishnaic tractate *Avot*, the "Ethics of the Fathers" *(Pirkei Avot),* on each of the Sabbaths between Pesach and Shavuot.

Shavuot

You shall count off seven weeks . . . Then you shall observe the Feast of Weeks to Adonai your God. (Deut. 16:9–10)

On the third new moon after the Israelites had gone forth from the land of Egypt, on that very day, they entered the wilderness of Sinai. (Exod. 19:1)

> The Torah was given to Israel on the sixth day of the third month. (*B. Shabbat* 86b)

The Torah itself never connects the festival of Shavuot with God's revelation to Israel at Sinai. The holiday is simply called "Weeks" (*shavuot*), because it occurs at the end of the seven-week period of "counting" which commences with Pesach. It bears other biblical names as well—*katzir*, "harvest," and *bikkurim*, "first fruits"—which testify that, in ancient days, this day was associated exclusively with the end of the spring harvest season. Rabbinic tradition, however, noting the close proximity between the date of this festival and the date given for the Israelites' arrival at Sinai in Exodus 19:1, holds Shavuot to be the anniversary of the revelation; hence, in the prayer book, the holiday is referred to as *zeman matan torateinu*, the season of the giving of the Torah. Our observance of this festival today blends these two aspects: we give thanks to God for the bounty of nature as we rededicate ourselves to living with God in a covenantal relationship.

Religious Services. It is a *mitzvah* to observe Shavuot seven weeks after Pesach, on the sixth of Sivan. The services follow the festival liturgy (*Gates of Prayer*, pp. 455ff.). The *Hallel* is recited, and the Torah reading includes the Ten Commandments. *Yizkor* (the memorial service) is recited by many congregations. It is customary to read the Book of Ruth on Shavuot. Many reasons are given for this practice. One holds that Ruth, as the archetype of all who "choose" or convert to Judaism, accepted the Torah in the way that our ancestors did at Sinai, which we commemorate at this festival. We are all, that is to say, "Jews-by-choice," and we *as a people* made our choice on Shavuot.

It is a *mitzvah* to reaffirm the covenant and our acceptance of the Torah on Shavuot. One way to do so is through the custom of *tikkun leyl shavuot*, a vigil of Torah study carried on during the night of Shavuot, sometimes lasting until dawn.

The ceremony of Confirmation is often held on or near Shavuot. Just as our people accepted the Torah on Shavuot, so do our confirmands reaffirm their commitment to the covenant.

Special Observances. It is customary to decorate the home and the synagogue with greens and fresh flowers on Shavuot. This reminds us of the spring harvest and of the ancient ritual of the bringing of the first fruits (*bikkurim*) to the Temple. It is also customary to eat dairy dishes on Shavuot, because (among other explanations) Jewish tradition compares the words of Torah to milk and honey.

Sukkot, Shemini Atzeret, and Simchat Torah

On the fifteenth day of the seventh month, when you have gathered in the yield of your land, you shall observe the festival of Adonai seven days: a complete rest on the first day, and a complete rest on the eighth day. On the first day you shall take the product of *hadar* trees, branches of palm trees, boughs of leafy trees, and willows of the brook, and you shall rejoice before Adonai your God seven days . . . You shall live in booths seven days . . . in order that future generations may know that I made the Israelite people live in booths when I brought them out of the land of Egypt . . . (Lev. 23:39–43)

Like Pesach and Shavuot, the season of Sukkot and Shemini Atzeret combines elements of the biblical harvest festival with the commemoration of formative events in our people's history. It is, on the one hand, the most singularly joyous of the pilgrimage festivals. The tradition speaks of it simply as *zeman simchateinu*, "the season of our rejoicing." Indeed, when the rabbinic texts refer to *hechag*, "*the* festival," without any other qualification, they generally mean Sukkot, the most festive time of the year, "a welcome change of religious pace from the solemn days of prayer and introspection of Rosh Hashanah and Yom Kippur." As the "festival of ingathering" (Exod. 23:16), the conclusion of the harvest time, it is an appropriate occasion for both happiness and thanksgiving. Yet along with the joy we express for our portion of nature's bounty comes the realization that the material blessings of life are fragile and transitory at best. By "dwelling in the *sukkah*," a temporary structure which offers imperfect shelter from the winds and rains of autumn, we call to mind the precariousness of life itself and the knowledge that we realize true joy only when we dedicate our lives to values that are eternal.

The Observance. It is a *mitzvah* to observe the festival of Sukkot. The holiday begins on the fifteenth day of the month of Tishri and lasts for seven days. The eighth day, 22 Tishri, is Shemini Atzeret, a separate festival in its own right, the concluding day of the Sukkot season. In Reform congregations, which generally observe one day of *yom tov* rather than two, the actual festival days are the first day of Sukkot and

Shemini Atzeret. The second through the seventh day are *chol hamo'ed*, the intermediate days of the festival. Simchat Torah, the festival of "rejoicing in the Torah," is observed on Shemini Atzeret.

The Sukkah. It is a *mitzvah* for every Jew to participate in the building and the decoration of a *sukkah*, whether at one's home, at the home of friends, or at a synagogue or other community institution. It is particularly meritorious to make a symbolic start to this work of building immediately after the conclusion of Yom Kippur and the breaking of the fast.

As our tradition defines it, the *sukkah* is a temporary structure that is fit for human habitation. Thus, its height may not exceed twenty cubits, or about ten meters, since to build it that high would require walls sturdy enough to support a permanent structure. Nor may its height be lower than ten handbreadths, or about fifty centimeters, for such a structure would be considered unfit for even temporary habitation. The area of the *sukkah*, that is, the area underneath its "roof," must be sufficient to allow an individual to eat a meal within it. The essence of the *sukkah* rests in the *sekhakh*, the material which serves as its roof or covering. The *sekhakh* must consist of detached vegetation, such as cut branches, plants, and narrow strips of wood, and there must be enough of it so that the amount of shadow it casts exceeds the amount of sunlight that enters the *sukkah*. The walls of the *sukkah* (there must be at least three), by contrast, may be constructed out of any material, so long as they are sturdy enough to withstand a normal wind. The walls, if they are anchored in the roof of the *sukkah*, must extend to within three handbreadths of the ground. The *sukkah* must have a roof; should the walls come together in the manner of a conical hut, the structure is not a valid *sukkah*. A structure which does not meet these requirements—a tent, for example—is not a *sukkah*. Nor does an indoor *"sukkah,"* such as decorations placed on the *bimah* of a synagogue, serve as an acceptable substitute.

A "permanent" *sukkah* is valid, provided that the structure was built with the intention that it serve as a *sukkah*. If the structure serves some other purpose during the year, some new *sekhakh* must be added in order to demonstrate that it now fulfills the *mitzvah* of *sukkah*.

It is a *mitzvah* to celebrate in the *sukkah*. The Torah requires that we "dwell" in the *sukkah* for seven days. We fulfill this *mitzvah* primarily by eating meals in the *sukkah*, especially on the first night of the festival.

Whenever we eat or recite *Kiddush* in the *sukkah*, we say a special benediction following the blessing over the food:

Barukh atah Adonai Eloheinu melekh ha'olam asher kideshanu bemitzvotav vetzivanu leishev basukkah.

Blessed are You, Adonai our God, Sovereign of the universe, who hallows us through the *mitzvot* and commands us to dwell in the *sukkah*.

It is a special *mitzvah* to welcome guests (*hakhnasat orechim*) to the *sukkah*. The liturgy, in fact, includes a special ceremony to welcome to the *sukkah* symbolic "guests," the biblical patriarchs and matriarchs (*ushpizin*) who are said to visit us on successive days of the festival. This ceremony enhances our appreciation of the holiness of the day and of our responsibility to extend ourselves to all in hospitality.

Lulav and Etrog. It is a *mitzvah* to take up the *lulav* and *etrog* every day during the Sukkot festival. The *etrog* is the fruit of the citron; the *lulav* is the combination of a palm branch (the "*lulav*" proper), two branches of willow (*aravah*), and three branches of myrtle (*hadas*). Together, these "four species" (*arba'ah minim*) are seen as the fulfillment of Leviticus 23:40 ("On the first day you shall take the product of *hadar* trees, branches of palm trees, boughs of leafy trees, and willows of the brook"). The *lulav*-bundle is taken in the right hand, with the leaves facing upward, in the direction of their natural growth. The *etrog* is taken in the left hand, with its tip (*pitam*) facing downward. Holding the *lulav* and *etrog* so that they touch each other, we recite the benediction:

Barukh atah Adonai Eloheinu melekh ha'olam asher kideshanu bemitzvotav vetzivanu 'al netilat lulav.

Blessed are You, Adonai our God, Sovereign of the universe, who hallows us through the *mitzvot* and commands us to take up the *lulav*.

On the first day of Sukkot, we add the blessing *Shehechiyanu*. We then turn the *etrog* so that its tip faces upward, in the direction of its natural growth, and we wave the *lulav* and *etrog* in the six directions (the points of the compass, up and down), symbolically acknowledging the sovereignty of God over nature.

In traditional synagogues, congregants march with their *lulavim* and *etrogim* in a procession (*hakafah*, a "circuit") around the sanctuary on each of the days of Sukkot, except for Shabbat. This is done to commemorate the similar procession around the altar in the ancient Temple. A Torah scroll is removed from the ark and rests upon the reading desk, so that the *bimah* will symbolically resemble the altar. Liturgical poems called *hoshanot* are recited, beseeching God to "save" (*hosha*) and help us prosper. On the seventh day of Sukkot, known as Hoshana Rabbah, all the Torah scrolls are removed and seven complete *hakafot* are made around the sanctuary.

It is desirable to acquire one's own *lulav* and *etrog*. By selecting a beautiful *lulav* and *etrog*, one enhances the performance of this *mitzvah*.

Religious Services. The services on the first day of Sukkot follow the festival liturgy (*Gates of Prayer*, pp. 455ff.). The ceremony of "taking" the *lulav* and *etrog*, performed every day during Sukkot, may be done at any time during daylight hours. It customarily follows the *Tefillah*, since the *lulav* is waved during *Hallel*, recited upon the conclusion of the *Tefillah*. The Torah reading for the first day of Sukkot is Leviticus 23:33–44, and the *Haftarah* is Zechariah 14:7–9, 16–21. The Torah portion for Shabbat *chol hamo'ed* is Exodus 33:12–34:26, and the *Haftarah* is Ezekiel 38:18–39:7. The Torah is read on each day of the festival; for a list of the readings in *chol hamo'ed*, see the Notes to this section. The Book of Kohelet (Ecclesiastes) is read on the Shabbat during Sukkot. The book's theme, the "vanity" of all our strivings, reminds us, as does the *sukkah*, of the transitory nature of life.

Shemini Atzeret. The Torah (Lev. 23:36) describes the eighth (*shemini*) day of the Sukkot festival as *mikra kodesh*, a "sacred occasion," and *atzeret*, a "gathering." What is the purpose of this "gathering," other than that of concluding the festival season? The Rabbis liken it to the example of a king who beseeches his subjects who have come to celebrate with him: "Stay with me yet one more day, for it is difficult for me to part from you." According to Jewish tradition, the festival of Sukkot, when we rejoice in the natural bounty of God's world, is a celebration on behalf of all humankind. On Shemini Atzeret, we turn inward to renew the intimate bond between God and the Jewish people. The connection between Sukkot and Shemini Atzeret thus affords us the opportunity to reflect upon our understanding of the One who is both the Creator of all the World and the God of Israel whom we have encountered in our own history.

Although it comes at the very end of the Sukkot celebration and is called, like Sukkot, *zeman simchateinu*, "the season of our rejoicing," Shemini Atzeret is *not* Sukkot but a holiday in its own right. We do not celebrate in the *sukkah*, nor do we take up the *lulav* and *etrog*. Rather, we recite the festival liturgy (*Gates of Prayer*, pp. 455ff.) as we do on every *yom tov*. In addition, some Reform congregations say *Yizkor*.

Simchat Torah. It is a *mitzvah* to participate in the Torah procession honoring the completion and the beginning of the cycle of Torah readings on Simchat Torah, which is observed in Reform congregations on the day of Shemini Atzeret. This celebration originated during early medieval times, based upon the fact that the final portion of the Torah, *Vezot Haberakhah*, was read on the second day of Shemini Atzeret. Our practice is to read from two Torah scrolls. From the first, we read Deuteronomy 34:1–12; from the second, Genesis 1:1–2:3. On the morning of Atzeret/Simchat Torah, the *Haftarah* is Joshua 1:1–18.

The Torah service on this evening and day is especially festive (*Gates of Prayer*, pp. 538–43). We remove all the Torah scrolls from the ark and conduct seven *hakafot* (circuits) around the sanctuary. The *hakafot* are accompanied by singing and dancing, symbolizing our joy that the study of Torah never ceases among us. In many synagogues, every member of the congregation is called to the Torah. The children, too, are called to the Torah in one, collective *aliyah*.

In some Reform congregations, it is customary to hold Consecration, a special ceremony for children entering religious school, on the night of Simchat Torah. Others celebrate this event on the Shabbat during Sukkot.

Rosh Hashanah

> In the seventh month, on the first day of the month, you shall observe complete rest, a holy day commemorated with loud blasts. You shall not work at your occupations. (Lev. 23:24–25)

The holiday we call Rosh Hashanah, observed in the ancient Temple as a day of *teru'ah*, or blasts of the *shofar*, was not celebrated as a "new year" festival in biblical times. The fact that it occurs on the first day of the seventh month (Tishri), rather than the first month (Nisan), indicates that more than one system of calendation may have been in existence during that time. Later Jewish tradition eventually came to recognize the first day of Tishri, the seventh biblical month, as the beginning of the new calendar year. Moreover, Rosh Hashanah took on an important spiritual dimension that complemented its chronological function. It became known as *Yom Hadin*, the Day of Judgment, on which "all mortals pass for inspection before God." Today, Rosh Hashanah is a solemn time, the first of the "Ten Days of Repentance" that culminate in Yom Kippur, the Day of Atonement. Yet it is also a *yom tov*, a day to celebrate before God. This celebration, if more muted than our joy on the pilgrimage festivals, finds its expression in the knowledge that "the gates of repentance are always open." The color white, with which many congregations adorn their ark and Torah scrolls at this time of the year, testifies to our optimism that the hard work of repentance will bear ample spiritual fruit: "Be your sins like crimson, they can turn white as snow" (Isa. 1:18). In these words lie our conviction that we can triumph over weakness and sin, and our faith that we will, as the age-old blessing puts it, be inscribed for the coming year in the Book of Life.

The Month of Elul. It is a *mitzvah* to prepare for the *Yamim Nora'im*, the Days of Awe, during the preceding month of Elul. Some communities recite *selichot*, special penitential prayers, every day (except for Shabbat) from Rosh Chodesh Elul to Yom Kippur. Our practice, adapted from Ashkenazic custom, is to recite *selichot* late at night, usually on the Saturday night that precedes Rosh Hashanah. Some congregations follow the custom of sounding the *shofar* at the end of each weekday morning service during Elul (except for the day of *erev Rosh Hashanah*, the day that precedes the New Year) as a reminder of the approaching season of atonement.

It is customary in some communities to visit the graves of relatives during Elul and during the Days of Awe. Similarly, it is customary to increase the giving of *tzedakah* during this time, since this act, along with repentance and prayer, is an integral part of the process of reconciliation between ourselves and God.

Religious Observance. It is a *mitzvah* to observe Rosh Hashanah on the first of Tishri. The day is known for the grand style of its synagogue liturgy, including the *shofar* ritual. The service is marked by special music, featuring a motif (*nusach*) unique to the High Holiday season.

While synagogues are encouraged to utilize this motif, they should keep in mind that congregational participation is a central goal of Reform Jewish worship. Music, whether "traditional" or not, that is unfamiliar to the congregation should be introduced gradually, so as not to diminish the worshipers' active participation in the service.

The liturgy follows the general structure of festival worship. There are, however, a number of changes peculiar to Rosh Hashanah and the High Holidays. Special inserts in the *Tefillah* emphasize the themes of God's sovereignty and judgment, along with our hope for God's forgiveness. *Hallel* is not recited following the morning *Tefillah,* for even though Rosh Hashanah is a *yom tov,* it is an occasion for spiritual reflection and self-searching, an inappropriate setting for songs of joy. The penitential prayer *Avinu Malkeinu* follows each recitation of the *Tefillah.* The most obvious liturgical change is the *shofar* service (described below). The Torah reading for Rosh Hashanah is Genesis 22:1–19, the *Akeidah,* or "binding of Isaac." An alternate Torah reading is Genesis 1:1–2:3, the story of creation, and some Reform congregations which observe a second day of Rosh Hashanah will read this "alternate" portion on that day. The *Haftarah* is from I Samuel, with alternates from Nehemiah 8, Isaiah 55, or Jeremiah 31.

The Shofar. It is a *mitzvah* to hear the sound of the *shofar* on Rosh Hashanah. The *shofar* is generally the horn of a ram, symbolic of the ram that substituted for the sacrifice of Isaac (Gen. 22:13). The *shofar* should be curved or bent, to symbolize our humility as we confront our sins and stand before God in judgment.

Traditionally, the *shofar* is sounded at least twice on Rosh Hashanah morning: once following the reading of the Torah and *Haftarah* during the *Shacharit* service and then again during the *chazan's* repetition of the *Musaf* prayer (*Tefillah*). Since Reform liturgy does not contain a *Musaf* service, we sound the *shofar* immediately following the *Haftarah* (*Gates of Repentance,* pp. 138–51). Yet in doing so, we borrow heavily from the traditional *Musaf* liturgy, for it is there that the *machzor* (the High Holiday prayer book) develops the three great themes of Rosh Hashanah: *Malkhuyot,* God's sovereignty over the world; *Zikhronot,* God's remembrance of the covenant that binds God to Israel through all time; and *Shofarot,* God's revelation of Torah to us and our age-old hope for the redemption of Israel and all the world. As in the traditional *machzor,* each of these themes makes up a liturgical unit, composed of an introduction, verses from each section of the Bible pertaining to the theme, and a paragraph that ends with a closing benediction (*chatimah*). Following each *chatimah*, the *shofar* is sounded.

The person who sounds the *shofar* (the *toke'a* or *ba'al teki'ah*) recites the benediction:

> *Barukh atah Adonai Eloheinu melekh ha'olam asher kideshanu bemitzvotav vetzivanu lishmo'a kol shofar.*

> Blessed are You, Adonai our God, Sovereign of the universe, who hallows us through the *mitzvot* and commands us to hear the sound of the *shofar*.

This is followed by the blessing *Shehechiyanu*.

The ancient Rabbis deduced from the Torah that we are obligated to hear nine sounds from the *shofar* on Rosh Hashanah: that is, a series of the three notes *teki'ah—teru'ah—teki'ah* sounded three times. But while the Sages agreed that the note *teki'ah* consists of one simple blast, they were not sure of the definition of *teru'ah*. Is it the note that *we* today call *teru'ah*, nine staccato blasts? Is it the note that we call *shevarim*, three short blasts? Or is it both *shevarim* and *terua'ah*? To make sure that the observance was performed properly, it was ordained that we should hear three sets of *shofar* sounds: *teki'ah—shevarim/teru'ah—teki'ah*, three times; *teki'ah—shevarim—teki'ah*, three times, and *teki'ah—teru'ah—teki'ah*, three times. Our practice, to hear three sets consisting of one of each of these combinations, follows the contemporary Ashkenazic custom for the *shofar* ritual during the *Musaf* service.

Shofar on Shabbat. We sound the *shofar* even when Rosh Hashanah falls on Shabbat. Traditional *halakhah* prohibits this, not because sounding the *shofar* is considered a form of "work" but because one might be tempted to carry it through the public thoroughfare to an expert to learn the skill of *shofar*-blowing. Since such carrying *is* prohibited on Shabbat, the Rabbis decreed that the *shofar* not be sounded on that day. Their decree did not, of course, nullify the *mitzvah* of *shofar* in their communities, for the people would in any case be able to hear the *shofar* on Sunday, the second day of the New Year festival. In those Reform communities where it is customary to observe Rosh Hashanah for one day only, to adhere to the rabbinic decree would render it impossible for us to fulfill this biblical *mitzvah* and deprive us of the *shofar* ceremony for that year. We therefore sound the *shofar* on Shabbat.

The Second Day of Rosh Hashanah. Most North American Reform congregations, following the calendar set forth in the Torah (Lev. 23:24; Num. 29:1), observe Rosh Hashanah for one day, on the first of Tishri. Yet this holiday differs from all the other festivals in that it is observed for two days even in the land of Israel. A growing number of Reform congregations have adopted this practice and observe a second day of Rosh Hashanah.

The Mitzvot of the Day. Rosh Hashanah is called a *yom tov*, a festival day. As such, we observe it at home as we do the other festivals, with the lighting of candles, *Kiddush*, a festive meal over *challah*, and *Havdalah* at its conclusion. It is customary, prior to the blessing *Hamotzi* which begins the meal, to dip a piece of apple into honey. We recite the following:

> *Yehi ratzon milfanekha Adonai Eloheinu velohei avoteinu shetechadesh aleinu shanah tovah umetukah.*

> May it be Your will, our God and God of our people, to renew for us a good and sweet year.

We then say the appropriate blessing (*borei peri ha'etz*), eat the apple, and proceed to *Hamotzi*.

As on other festivals, it is *mitzvah* to refrain from work on Rosh Hashanah. Children and students should not attend school on that day.

The Days of Awe

> For transgressions against God, the Day of Atonement atones; but for transgressions of one human being against another, the Day of Atonement does not atone until they have made peace with each other. (*M. Yoma* 8:9)

The days between Rosh Hashanah and Yom Kippur are called *Hayamim Hanora'im*, the "Days of Awe." Their "awe" lies in each person's consciousness during this penitential season of the nearness of God. While the community as a whole may repent of its sins and make atonement at any time of the year, as individuals it is especially appropriate to do so at this season, for we are to "seek God when God can be found" (Isa. 55:6).

The Observance. It is a *mitzvah* to reflect upon our behavior during the ten-day period beginning with Rosh Hashanah and concluding with Yom Kippur. This reflection involves several elements:

Repentance (*teshuvah*, literally, "return"). What is repentance? "It is when the sinner abandons an evil deed, removes the very thought of it from the mind, and resolves with sincerity never to repeat that action." True repentance has occurred when one who has the opportunity to repeat a sinful act refuses to do so and when that refusal stems "not from fear or from weakness, but from the fact of repentance itself."

Reconciliation. It is not enough that one repents privately. We must seek reconciliation, especially during these ten days, with those whom we have wronged during the past year.

Forgiveness. It is a *mitzvah* to forgive those who have wronged us and have asked for our forgiveness.

Shabbat Shuvah. The Sabbath between Rosh Hashanah and Yom Kippur is called Shabbat Shuvah, taking its name from the first word of its *Haftarah, shuvah yisrael,* "Return, O Israel" (Hos. 14:2). The liturgy on this Shabbat, as well as the weekday liturgy during the Days of Awe, includes special passages in the *Tefillah* expressing the theme of the season. This Shabbat is an important introspective prelude to Yom Kippur, and one should make a special effort to attend services on that day.

Yom Kippur

For on this day atonement shall be made for you to cleanse you of all your sins; you shall be clean before God. It shall be a sabbath of complete rest for you, and you shall practice self-denial; it is a law for all time. (Lev. 16:30–31)

Mark, the tenth day of the seventh month is the Day of Atonement. . . . Do no work whatever . . . on the ninth day of the month at evening, from evening to evening, you shall observe this your sabbath. (Lev. 23:27–32)

Rabbi Akiva said: Rejoice, O Israel! Before whom are you purified? Indeed, who is it that purifies you? It is none other than God, as it is said (Ezek. 36:25): "I will sprinkle clean water upon you, and you shall be clean." (*Mishnah Yoma* 8:9)

The Torah portrays Yom Kippur primarily as a cultic festival, a day centered almost exclusively upon the Temple. It was on this day that the *kohen gadol*, the high priest, performed the complicated rituals and sacrifices which purified the Temple of the defilement that had attached to it as a result of the sins of the Israelite people, which had caused God's presence to depart from their midst. Yet there was another aspect to the day: *atonement*, the cleansing of the people themselves. The people, to be sure, did not take an active part in these atonement rituals. Their role was to serve as an attentive and expectant audience outside the Temple precincts, awaiting the hoped-for successful outcome of the high priest's service. Their role, according to the Torah, was to abstain from work and to practice "self-denial." Our tradition has defined "self-denial" as *inuyim* ("afflictions"): fasting and refraining from certain other activities that satisfy our physical needs.

With the Temple's destruction, this second aspect of Yom Kippur came to predominate. The "atonement" we now perform is turned inward; it is an act of self-purification, the purging of our own lives from the stain of our misdeeds. We continue to fast, understanding this self-denial as a cleansing of soul, an act of self-discipline and a sign that on this day we rise above our most basic biological necessities in order to focus our attention upon matters of the spirit. The Temple is remembered in the content and structure of the synagogue liturgy. Our prayers traditionally last all day long, as did the service of the high priest. We recall his service in poetic form, and the recitation of *Ne'ilah* at the conclusion of Yom Kippur hearkens back to the time when the "closing of the gates" was a feature of the Temple's everyday ritual. Finally, the drama of the ancient sacrifice has become an internal drama, which we experience as a grand spiritual and emotional sweep which takes us from the haunting melody of *Kol Nidrei* at *Ma'ariv*, through the recitation of the prayers, *selichot* (poems of supplication and penitence) and *viduyim* (confessions of sin), culminating in *Ne'ilah*, when we stand one last time before God in the fading moments of this, the year's holiest day.

Although the prevailing mood of the day is a somber one, Yom Kippur is also an occasion for joy. Repentance and reconciliation with God and our fellow human beings, a process we begin formally on Rosh

Hashanah and pursue with urgency during the Days of Awe, reaches a climax on this day. And our tradition recognizes this as a *successful* climax. The end of the day should leave us feeling physically exhausted and morally exhilarated, for we know that God will receive our sincere and prayerful repentance with love. "Rejoice, O Israel!" sang Rabbi Akiva in the house of study long ago, for you may be certain that on this day you *shall* be made pure.

The Observance. It is a *mitzvah* to observe Yom Kippur on the tenth day of the month of Tishri, to repent of our sins and moral shortcomings on that day, and to seek reconciliation with our families and with those we may have offended prior to its onset. It is especially appropriate to perform acts of charity, *tzedakah*, in the days leading to Yom Kippur as a visible sign of one's spiritual determination to lead a life of goodness during the coming year.

Erev Yom Kippur. The ninth of Tishri, Erev Yom Kippur, is regarded by tradition as a semi-holiday. It is a *mitzvah* to eat a large meal on this day, not merely in preparation for the next day's fast but as an expression of joy and confidence "that Yom Kippur will bring us goodness and blessing and that God will pardon our sins and grant us a good new year."

The late-afternoon meal on Erev Yom Kippur is called *se'udah mafseket* (the concluding meal before the fast). There are no special rituals connected with this meal. We do not recite *Kiddush*, for it is not yet Yom Kippur, and this meal must be completed *before* the onset of the holy day. Since the meal has something of the air of a festive occasion, it is appropriate to have bread, to say *Hamotzi*, and to conclude with *Birkat Hamazon*.

Yom Kippur Lights. It is a *mitzvah* to light and to recite the appropriate blessing over the Yom Kippur lights after the meal and before leaving for the synagogue:

> *Barukh atah Adonai Eloheinu melekh ha'olam asher kideshanu bemitzvotav vetzivanu lehadlik ner shel (shabbat ve-) yom hakipurim.*

> Blessed are You, Adonai our God, Sovereign of the universe, who hallows us through the *mitzvot* and commands us to kindle the lights of (Shabbat and) Yom Kippur.

The kindling of the light serves as the formal beginning of Yom Kippur. Therefore, unlike the Shabbat and festival light, it is kindled *after* the meal, since it is forbidden to eat once Yom Kippur has begun.

Fasting. It is a *mitzvah* to fast, to abstain from both food and drink, throughout Yom Kippur. The Torah commands us to practice "self-denial" (literally, "you shall afflict yourselves") on this day, and the tradition identifies this affliction (*inu'i* or *inu'i nefesh*) with fasting. The fast begins with the kindling of the Yom Kippur lights and concludes at the end of Yom Kippur, with the sounding of the *shofar* at *Ne'ilah*. Children below the age of Bar/Bat Mitzvah should be taught to fast beginning with a few hours' fast and increasing it each year until, when they are thirteen, they can fast the entire day. Pregnant women and those who are ill should follow the advice of a physician on fasting.

Religious Services. The heart of the Yom Kippur experience is congregational worship. It is a *mitzvah* to attend all the services on Yom Kippur, beginning with *Ma'ariv* in the evening and ending with *Ne'ilah* and the sounding of the *shofar* the next day. Memorial services (*Yizkor*) are held on Yom Kippur (*Gates of Repentance*, pp. 477–94). *Havdalah* is recited at the end of Yom Kippur (*Gates of Repentance*, pp. 526–28). A joyous "break-the-fast" meal is served following Yom Kippur. A congregation should not schedule this meal until nightfall, when Yom Kippur is actually over.

Refraining from Work. It is a *mitzvah* to refrain from work on Yom Kippur. The same rules that govern work on Shabbat apply as well to Yom Kippur.

Beginning the Sukkah. It is customary to make a symbolic start in building the *sukkah* immediately after the break-the-fast, to symbolize that our repentance is genuine and that we turn at once to the performance of a *mitzvah*.

Purim

The study of Torah is interrupted for the reading of the Megillah. If this is so, then the reading of the Megillah certainly supersedes all other *mitzvot*. (Maimonides, *Yad, Megillah* 1:1)

It may seem odd that Purim, a seemingly "minor" holiday frequently regarded as a "children's festival," is ascribed such importance by the tradition. When we consider the matter more carefully, however, we perceive the wisdom behind this talmudic statement cited by Maimonides. The *Megillah*, the biblical scroll of Esther, recounts the courageous acts of Esther and Mordecai through which the Jews triumphed over enemies bent upon their destruction, maintaining their self-respect and religious integrity, and refusing to bow before any authority but God. This theme of Jewish survival as a tiny minority in the midst of a sea of often-hostile nations is a central element in the story of the Jewish people. It is *our* story, an indelible feature of our consciousness as a community and as individuals. Therefore, when the time comes on Purim to read that story, there is no more important duty to fulfill. All of us gather to hear it, for "a numerous people is the glory of the King" (Prov. 14:28). The large crowd and the carnival atmosphere of this day are expressions of our joy at the fact of our survival and our belief that the struggle against bigotry and persecution can be won again as it was in ancient times.

The Observance. It is a *mitzvah* to observe Purim on the fourteenth of the month of Adar (or, in leap years, the fourteenth of the second Adar). That was the day, according to the biblical account, when the Jews in unwalled towns of the Persian empire "rested" from their victorious struggle over their enemies "and made it a day of feasting and merrymaking." Jews who lived in walled cities, such as the capital of Shushan, "rested on the fifteenth" (Esther 9:16–19). For this reason, Jews today who live "in cities which were walled in the days of Joshua"—Jerusalem, for example—celebrate Purim on 15 Adar (or second Adar), the day commonly referred to as "Shushan Purim."

The Reading of the Megillah. It is a *mitzvah* to read *Megillat Esther*, the biblical book of Esther, on Purim. Traditionally, the *Megillah* is read at both evening and morning services. It is especially important to fulfill this *mitzvah* as part of a congregation.

The reading of the *Megillah* is preceded by three blessings:

> *Barukh atah Adonai Eloheinu melekh ha'olam asher kideshanu bemitzvotav vetzivanu al mikra Megillah.*

Blessed are You, Adonai our God, Sovereign of the universe, who hallows us through the *mitzvot* and commands us concerning the reading of the *Megillah*.

Barukh atah Adonai Eloheinu melekh ha'olam she'asah nissim la'avoteinu bayamim hahem bazman hazeh.

Blessed are You, Adonai our God, Sovereign of the universe, who performed wondrous deeds for our ancestors in days of old, at this season.

The third benediction is *Shehechiyanu*.

Following the *Megillah* reading, we recite the blessing *harav et riveinu* ("who pleads our cause"). (For the liturgy of the *Megillah* reading, see *The Five Scrolls*, pp. 86–87.)

A number of customs are associated with the reading. The reader unrolls the scroll and folds it so that it looks like a letter (*igeret*), since the text refers to itself as a "letter of Purim" (Esther 9:29). Since Haman, the enemy of the Jews, is regarded by tradition as a descendant of Amalek, a nation known for its implacable and unreasoning hostility toward us, we make noise at every mention of the name Haman, in boisterous fulfillment of the commandment to "blot out the name of Amalek" (Deut. 25:19).

The Other Mitzvot of the Day. Like other holidays, Purim is marked in our prayer service. We recite the passage *'al hanissim* (*Gates of Prayer*, p. 46) during the *Tefillah* and in *Birkat Hamazon* as a remembrance of God's deliverance. We do not, however, recite the *Hallel* during *Shacharit*, the morning service, because this deliverance, unlike our rescue from Egyptian bondage, was not complete: even after the downfall of Haman we remained under the domination of the Persian king. The Torah reading, appropriately, is Exodus 17:8–16, which recounts the war waged by Amalek, the reputed ancestors of Haman, against our people in the Sinai wilderness.

We read in the book of Esther (9:22) that the days of Purim are a time for "feasting and merrymaking" and for "sending gifts to one another and presents to the poor." From this verse the tradition derives the other aspects of the celebration of this holiday:

"Feasting and Merrymaking." The atmosphere of Purim is one of nearly unrestrained merrymaking. "It is a *mitzvah* to hold a festive

meal on Purim." Traditionally, this meal is held following *Minchah* (the afternoon service) on the day of Purim.

"Sending Gifts." Purim is the season of *mishloach manot* (popularly, *"shelach manos"*), the sending of gifts to friends. These gifts are ready-to-eat foods. The word *manot*, "portions," is plural; thus, we are to send at least "two portions [that is, two different kinds of ready-to-eat food or drink] to one person."

"Presents to the Poor." It is a *mitzvah* to send gifts to the poor on Purim. It is better to emphasize *tzedakah* on Purim than to spend large amounts of money on our feasting and on gifts to our friends, "for there is no greater joy than to cause the poor to rejoice."

Chanukah

The eight days of Chanukah begin on the twenty-fifth day of Kislev. We do not speak eulogies on these days; neither do we fast. For when the Greeks entered the Temple, they polluted all of its oils, and when the Hasmoneans defeated them, they searched and found only one small cruse of oil, hidden away under the seal of the high priest. It contained but enough pure oil to light (the *menorah*) for one day. Yet a miracle occurred: the *menorah* was kindled from this oil for eight days. From then on, these days were set aside as a festive occasion for the rendering of praise [*Hallel*] and thanksgiving. (*B. Shabbat* 21b)

While historians debate the causes and outcomes of the war in which the followers of Judah Maccabee defeated the Syrian Greek armies of Antiochus Epiphanes (second century B.C.E.), there is no denying that Chanukah, the holiday which celebrates that victory, evokes in our minds stirring images of Jewish valor against overwhelming odds. The refusal to submit to the religious demands of an idolatrous empire, the struggle against total assimilation into Hellenistic culture and the loss of a unique Jewish identity, the fight for Jewish political autonomy and self-determination—all of these themes are rooted in our observance of this holiday. Chanukah, which means "dedication," is the festival at which Jews the world over re-dedicate themselves to the task of standing against those forces which would efface our Judaism, of keeping alive the flame of Jewish religion, culture, and nationhood so that it may be passed on to yet another generation.

Literally, of course, the "dedication" of which Chanukah speaks is the re-dedication of the Temple, its purification from the defilement caused by the Greeks during their occupation of that holy place. This leads the Rabbis to remind us of yet another central theme of this holiday. According to legend, the *Shekhinah*, God's divine presence, dwelled on earth from the beginning of time. When the first human generations sinned, corrupting the world, the *Shekhinah* departed from earth and ascended into Heaven. It was only the actions of righteous generations that brought the *Shekhinah* back to us, a work culminating in the dedication of the *mishkan* (tabernacle), God's "dwelling place" in the desert, a "home" for the *Shekhinah*. The *mishkan* served as a model of the Temple in later times. Although the Temple for which the Maccabees struggled has long since been destroyed, the ceremony of the *mishkan*'s dedication, which is the Torah reading for the days of Chanukah, reminds us of the need in our own day to build lives and communities that are worthy of serving as dwelling places for the presence of God.

The Observance. It is a *mitzvah* to observe Chanukah for eight days, beginning with the twenty-fifth day of Kislev. The actual "*mitzvah*" of Chanukah, as tradition understands it, consists of kindling the Chanukah lights in one's home. Prior to lighting the *menorah*, we recite the following blessings:

Barukh atah Adonai Eloheinu melekh ha'olam asher kideshanu bemitzvotav vetzivanu lehadlik ner shel chanukah.

Blessed are You, Adonai our God, Sovereign of the universe, who hallows us through the *mitzvot* and commands us to kindle the light of Chanukah.

Barukh atah Adonai Eloheinu melekh ha'olam she'asah nissim la'avoteinu bayamim hahem bazman hazeh.

Blessed are You, Adonai our God, Sovereign of the universe, who performed wondrous deeds for our ancestors in days of old, at this season.

On the first night, we add the benediction *Shehechiyanu.*

One candle is lit for each night. The candle for the first night is placed on the right side of the eight-branched *menorah* (*chanukiyah*). On each subsequent night, an additional candle is placed to the immediate left of the previous night's candle, so that the kindling begins with the newest light. Since these lights are holy, it is forbidden to make practical use of them; therefore, we use a special "servant" (*shamash*) candle to light the others. It is an Ashkenazic custom that each member of the household, including children, kindles his or her own Chanukah lamp.

Since it is traditionally forbidden to light a fire on Shabbat, on Friday evening the Chanukah lights are kindled *before* the Shabbat lights and on Saturday night they are kindled *after* the *Havdalah* ceremony.

"To Proclaim the Miracle." We should proclaim in public the miraculous events that transpired in the days of the Maccabees. A number of features of Chanukah observance are connected with this requirement. We kindle the lights at sundown, because that is the time when passers-by coming home from work are most likely to see them. When possible, we place the *menorah* where it can be visible from the outside. And we do not fulfill the *mitzvah* of Chanukah by lighting an electric *menorah* because we use electricity for illumination during the entire year; thus, an electric *menorah* is not sufficiently special to call attention to the miracle.

Synagogue Services. During Chanukah, the passage *'al hanissim* is recited as part of the *Tefillah* (*Gates of Prayer*, p. 45) and in *Birkat Hamazon*. *Hallel* is recited during *Shacharit* at the conclusion of the *Tefillah*. The Torah reading for each day is taken from Numbers 6:22–8:4, which recounts the dedication of the *mishkan* by the Israelites in the Sinai wilderness. On Shabbat, we read the weekly portion, and we may follow the traditional practice of adding the daily Chanukah reading from a second scroll. If Rosh Chodesh Tevet, which occurs on the sixth or seventh day of Chanukah, coincides with Shabbat, we might read from three Torah scrolls: the weekly portion from the first; the portion for Rosh Chodesh from the second; and the portion for Chanukah from the third. The *Haftarah* readings for Shabbat during Chanukah are Zechariah 4:1–7 (traditionally, 2:14–4:7) and (if Chanukah includes two Shabbatot) I Kings 7:40–50 (or 8:54–66).

Tisha Be'Av and Yom Hashoah

Take us back, O God, to Yourself, and let us come back; renew our days as of old! (Lam. 5:21)

The observance of Tisha Be'Av, the ninth day of the month of Av, poses some special problems for Reform Jews. The day is one of fasting and mourning, for the destruction of both the First and the Second Temple in Jerusalem is said to have taken place on that day. While other tragic events in Jewish history may have coincided with the ninth of Av, it is the Temple's destruction (*churban habayit*) which dominates the day's ritual and liturgy. Reform theology has not generally looked upon the loss of the Temple and the expulsion of the people of Israel from its land as a catastrophe to be lamented by liberal Jews. In the words of the Pittsburgh Platform: "We consider ourselves no longer a nation, but a religious community, and, therefore, expect neither a return to Palestine, nor a sacrificial worship under the sons of Aaron." Some Reform prayer books ignore Tisha Be'Av altogether; others have gone so far as to transform the day into one of joy as well as sadness, for on the day when the Temple was laid waste and the Jewish people was scattered over the face of the earth, Israel accepted the religious mission to disseminate the knowledge of God to all mankind. Since some reformers regarded this as the essence of Israel's eternal religious mission, they saw the destruction of the Temple and the sacrificial cult as a progressive and positive moment in our history as a people.

This point of view was never a unanimous one. Other Reform thinkers emphasized that, however much we feel at home in our Western lands and however little we feel the need to pray for a restoration of sacrificial worship, the tragedies and sufferings of Jewish history cannot be erased by the experience of but a few years of Enlightenment and Emancipation. The ninth of Av is a moment of great power in the Jewish calendar, the time when we give voice to our sadness as a people for the calamities which have befallen us. The Holocaust is a reminder that deliverance has not yet come to us, that unspeakable horror can be visited upon us even in our "progressive" age. It is no surprise, then, that generations which live in the shadow of such events, whatever their attitude toward Temple and sacrifice, will continue to observe this day as a mark of solidarity and identification with the fate and destiny of the Jews in all lands and in all times. In the American Reform movement, this observance is expressed by the appearance of a synagogue liturgy for Tisha Be'Av and Yom Hashoah (Holocaust Memorial Day) in *Gates of Prayer*, pp. 573–89.

Tisha Be'Av. It is part of the traditional observance of Tisha Be'Av to fast from sundown to sundown. In this way, the fast of the ninth of Av is more stringent than any other of the Jewish year save Yom Kippur. Following *Ma'ariv*, the evening service, the synagogue lights are dimmed, the congregants sit on the floor or on low benches, and the biblical book of Lamentations and other *kinot* (dirges) are chanted. A liturgy for the reading of Lamentations is found in *The Five Scrolls*, pp. 253–66. At *Shacharit*, the morning service, *tallit* and *tefillin* are not worn, in fulfillment of the midrashic interpretation of Lamentations 2:17 and 2:1. The Torah reading in the Reform ritual is Deuteronomy 4:25–41; in the traditional ritual, it is Deuteronomy 4:25–40. The *Haftarah* is II Samuel 1:17–27 (traditionally, Jer. 8:13–9:23). *Kinot* are recited again. At *Minchah*, the afternoon service, the *tallit* and *tefillin* are worn, symbolizing our hope in redemption even at the moment of our greatest sorrow, for it was at *Minchah* time that the fire which burned down the Temple was kindled. The Torah is read (Exod. 32:11–14; 34:1–10), and the *Haftarah* is Isaiah 55:6–56:8.

It is customary not to hold weddings on Tisha Be'Av, since the day is not a proper time for the expression of joy. Even if we do not observe this fast, we avoid conducting weddings on Tisha Be'Av out of historical consciousness and respect for *Kelal Yisrael*, the Jewish people.

Yom Hashoah. It is a *mitzvah* to remember the six million Jews murdered during the Nazi Holocaust on Yom Hashoah, Holocaust Memorial Day. The twenty-seventh day of Nisan was set aside by the Israeli Knesset for this purpose. The day is observed in Reform communities in a variety of ways befitting a day of national mourning. Congregations may hold special services for Yom Hashoah (*Gates of Prayer*, 573–89), study issues relating to the Holocaust, and discuss ways of preventing other catastrophes. *Tzedakah* may be given to projects that preserve the memory of the victims of the Holocaust. Weddings should not be held on this day.

Yom Ha'atzma'ut

For Zion's sake I will not keep silence; for Jerusalem's sake I will speak out, until her right shines forth like the sunrise, her deliverance like a blazing torch. (Isa. 62:1)

Yom Ha'atzma'ut, Israel Independence Day, occurs on the fifth of Iyar. It is a *mitzvah* for every Jew to celebrate on that day the establishment of the State of Israel and to proclaim the indelible importance of Israel in Jewish life. As a religious festival, not merely a national one, Yom Ha'atzma'ut should be marked by public worship; a liturgy for Israel Independence Day is found in *Gates of Prayer*, pp. 590–611. This liturgy includes the *Hallel* and the reading of the Torah.

Orthodox Jews, including those who are pro-Zionist, find these innovations controversial. It is not a settled matter for them whether Yom Ha'atzma'ut may be observed as a kind of *yom tov* with religious rites. The halakhic debates over the issue are complex, but they all seem to revolve around one central question: Do we perceive the hand of God in the establishment of the modern Jewish state? Do we regard the events leading to 5 Iyar 5708 (1948) as a miraculous sign of God's redemptive power in the history of our people, in the same way that we have understood the events commemorated by the festivals of Purim and Chanukah? If the answer is "yes"—and for Reform Jews the answer is certainly "yes"—then it is proper to establish a religious festival, complete with liturgy and rites, as a response to the establishment of the State of Israel.

4

The Life Cycle

Birth and Childhood

And God said: let us make the human being in our image, after our likeness. (Gen. 1:26)

Rabbi Simlai was asked: why does God speak in the plural, "let *us* make mankind"? He responded: God addresses the male and the female themselves. God says: you, Adam, were created from the dust of the earth, and you, Eve, from Adam's body. From now on, *we* shall create the human being, in *our* image and *our* likeness. Man and woman, together with God, shall create human life. (*Y. Berakhot* 9:1, 12d)

Our biblical ancestors looked upon children as one of God's choicest blessings and the inability to bear children as a sorrow for which one prayed for relief. We, too, affirm that it is a *mitzvah* for men and women, recognizing the sanctity of their marriage partnership, to bring children into the world. And it is a special *mitzvah* for us as Jews to bear children, in fulfillment of the age-old ideal of Jewish life and marriage and as an act of faith in God and in our future a people. Reform Judaism encourages couples to consider family size within the context of Jewish history, especially in light of tragic recent events which have decimated our numbers and of the challenge of the Jewish future. When we Jews have children, we affirm our commitment to our heritage, and we say "*no*" to all the forces that would conspire to put an end to our people.

Jewish Status and "Patrilineal Descent"

I make this covenant, with its sanctions, not with you alone, but both with those who are standing here with us this day before Adonai our God and with those who are not here with us this day. (Deut. 29:13–14)

> How do we know that all future generations of the Jewish people, both those born of Jews and those who convert to Judaism, were present at Mount Sinai? Because the Torah says "... and with those who are not here with us this day." (B. Shevu'ot 39a)

Who, precisely, is a Jew? What do we mean when we speak of the Jewish *community*? The answer that Reform Judaism offers is, in many important ways, the same answer given by all other Jews. In other, no less important respects, it differs. At the intersection of these similarities and differences lie the roots of one of the most persistent and challenging controversies facing world Jewry today.

History. Reform Judaism accepts in broad outlines the traditional definition of Jewish status: to be a "Jew" one must be a member of the Jewish people, a status obtained either through birth or conversion. Jewish identity, that is to say, is not determined purely by the individual, exclusively as a matter of personal belief or a feeling of attachment. One does not become a Jew merely by declaring "I am a Jew" or "I accept the Jewish religion." One must either be born a Jew or become a Jew through a process recognized and administered by the community. In this sense, "Jewishness" is roughly analogous to citizenship in a political commonwealth. To be a citizen, one must either be a "natural-born" citizen or one must complete the formal process of naturalization, a process defined and governed by the laws of that commonwealth. Conversion, our form of "naturalization," will be treated in Chapter 5. The present discussion concerns the acquisition of Jewish status through birth.

According to *halakhah*, Jewish status is determined on the basis of matrilineality; that is, the child of a Jewish mother is a Jew, even when the child's father is a Gentile. On the other hand, the offspring of a Gentile mother is a Gentile, even if the father is a Jew. By *halakhah*, of course, we mean traditional Jewish law as worked out in the rabbinic literary sources. Prior to the rabbinic period, we find little trace of the principle of matrilineal descent among the Jews. The Bible in fact seems to recognize a purely patrilineal standard, according to which the child of an Israelite father follows the father's status, regardless of the identity of the mother. Something of the patrilineal principle remains in the later *halakhah*, which holds that the child of two people who are permitted to marry each other inherits the status of the father rather than that of the mother. Thus, the child of a priest (*Kohen*) and a female

Levite or Israelite is a *Kohen* (or *Kohenet*), a member of the priestly clan. But when the mother is a Gentile, the child is a Gentile; to become a Jew, that child must undergo conversion.

It is not clear why the rabbinic tradition abandoned the biblical principle of patrilineal descent in favor of the standard which follows the mother's line. The Rabbis, we presume, had their reasons. What is clear is that those reasons, whatever they may have been, do not necessarily speak to the situation of Reform Jewry in our time. Our community must struggle with the tension between the tradition, which exerts much influence upon us, and the modern world, which since the time of the Emancipation in the late-eighteenth and early-nineteenth centuries has profoundly affected our conceptions of Jewish identity. And unlike the ancient Rabbis, our community, especially in the United States, confronts the phenomenon of mixed marriages in ever-increasing numbers. We sense a pressing need to formalize the status of the children of these marriages, many of whom are active members of our communities.

The Central Conference of American Rabbis (CCAR) has grappled for decades with the issue of the Jewish status of children of mixed marriages. In 1947, the Conference adopted a resolution declaring that in the case of children of Gentile mothers and Jewish fathers, "the declaration of the parents to raise them as Jews shall be deemed sufficient for conversion." This decision was in keeping with the traditional definition of Jewishness: the child of a Gentile mother is a Gentile and requires conversion. True, this "conversion" could be accomplished simply by the parents' declaration, but this was in keeping with the long-standing policy of the Conference to do away with the requirement for special "initiatory rites"—such as circumcision or immersion in the *mikveh*—for conversion to Judaism (see Chapter 5). By 1961, however, an important change had occurred in the discussion of status. The CCAR *Rabbi's Manual* published that year declared:

> Reform Judaism accepts such a child [i.e., born of a Jewish father and a non-Jewish mother] as Jewish *without a formal conversion* [italics added] if he attends a Jewish school and follows a course of studies leading to Confirmation. Such procedure is regarded as sufficient evidence that the parents and the child himself intend that he shall live as a Jew.

The 1961 formulation may simply have described the situation that existed *de facto* in Reform congregations, where these children were accepted as Jews if raised as Jews. Still, its appearance in an official rabbinic document was an important religious event, for it introduced *de jure* a radical new element into the determination of Jewish status. Previously, rabbinic tradition had defined a "Jew" as a person either born of a Jewish mother or a convert to Judaism. Now, the North American Reform rabbinate was suggesting a third means of proving one's Jewishness: the determination to lead a Jewish life. The child of a Jewish father and a Gentile mother, regarded by *halakhah* as a non-Jew, no longer needed to "convert" to Judaism. Rather, the child was accepted as Jewish without need of a formal conversion upon the presentation of "sufficient evidence" that he or she identifies as a Jew and intends to live as such.

By 1983, the CCAR was ready to take one further step. If the child of a Gentile mother in a mixed marriage could become Jewish by virtue of the parents' intent to raise him or her as a Jew, then it no longer seemed reasonable to treat the child of a Jewish mother and Gentile father any differently. The problem of mixed marriage was now "an unprecedented situation." In most cases of mixed marriage, regardless of which parent is Jewish,

> the non-Jewish extended family is a functioning part of the child's world, and may be decisive in shaping the life of the child. It can no longer be presumed *a priori*, therefore, that the child of a Jewish mother will be Jewish any more than the child of a non-Jewish mother will not be.

Thus, the 1983 Resolution on Patrilineal Descent applies the same requirements to the children of all mixed marriages:

> The Central Conference of American Rabbis declares that the child of one Jewish parent is under the presumption of Jewish descent. This presumption of the Jewish status of the offspring of any mixed marriage is to be established through appropriate and timely public and formal acts of identification with the Jewish faith and people . . .
>
> Depending on circumstances, *mitzvot* leading toward a positive and exclusive Jewish identity will include entry into the covenant, acquisition of a Hebrew name, Torah study, Bar/Bat Mitzvah, and *Kabbalat Torah* (Confirmation). For those beyond childhood claiming Jewish identity, other public acts or declarations may be added or substituted after consultation with their rabbi.

Analysis. What, in detail, is the position of North American Reform Judaism, as enunciated by the CCAR, on Jewish status? The following observations have been culled from the text of the 1983 resolution, the history behind that text, and its subsequent interpretation in the responsa literature and other CCAR publications.

> 1. *The resolution is advisory rather than halakhic in the traditional sense.* "It does not establish a new definition of Jewish identity, for its preamble states expressly that it means to be operative only for Reform Jews in North America, not for all Jews everywhere."

This statement, taken from the CCAR's *Rabbi's Manual*, hints at the enormous controversy which attended and still attends the Conference's doctrine of "patrilineal descent." Although the 1983 resolution was arguably a logical outgrowth of a CCAR policy that had been developing over decades, its adoption brought much greater attention to this policy than it had ever before received. For the first time in at least two millennia, the rabbinic leadership of a significant segment of world Jewry had publicly and formally resolved to alter the accepted halakhic definition of Jewish status. And although the majority of those rabbis assembled at the 1983 convention of the CCAR believed that the situation of Jewish life in our time warranted this change, they were well aware that they were legislating only for the North American Jewish community. Orthodox and Conservative Jews did not then nor do they now accept the doctrine of "patrilineal descent" as legitimate. Liberal and progressive Jewish communities outside of North America, too, reject the doctrine. This means that, unless and until this difference of opinion is successfully resolved, many individuals recognized as Jews by North American Reform congregations will *not* be accepted as Jews by communities in this continent and elsewhere that do not adhere to "patrilineal descent."

There are those who predict that the conflicting definitions of Jewishness will lead to demographic disaster, to an unbridgeable rift among Jews who can no longer determine with any certainty just who is a member of the people of Israel. Others discount these predictions as overstated, noting that the controversy over "who is a Jew?" has been around for a long time and it has yet to produce such a dire outcome. But whatever the consequences of the 1983 resolution, Reform rabbis and congregations have a moral obligation to inform their members that the controversy continues and that our movement's definition of Jewishness is by no means universally accepted.

2. *Jewish descent may be from either parent.* The term "patrilineal descent" is in fact a misnomer. The Reform movement presumes the child of *one* Jewish parent, either mother or father, as Jewish. In fact, the 1983 resolution is in one significant respect more stringent than the traditional definition of Jewish status. The child of a Jewish mother and a Gentile father, whom the *halakhah* regards as clearly Jewish, enjoys but a *presumption* of Jewish status which must be "established" by "appropriate and timely public and formal acts of identification."

3. *Biology remains a crucial factor.* The 1983 resolution places great importance upon a child's performance of acts that indicate a personal commitment to Judaism. Yet biological descent remains a crucial factor in the determination of Jewish identity. The child of *two* Jewish parents remains, as before, definitely Jewish, inheriting his or her Jewishness from the parents. The child of *one* Jewish parent inherits a *presumption* of Jewishness from that parent, a presumption that may be established by subsequent Jewish behavior. The child of *two Gentile* parents is, as before, definitely a non-Jew. To become a Jew, he or she must undergo a formal conversion to Judaism.

It may seem incongruous that a person born of two Jewish parents is "automatically" Jewish even if he or she performs no mitzvot or does not behave in any way as a Jew, while one who identifies as a Jew and leads in all respects an exemplary Jewish life is considered a Gentile merely because his or her parents were not Jewish. Yet this is a fact of Jewish life. We call ourselves the *people* of Israel, and when we do so we give voice to the historical conception of Israel as an historical, national, ethnocultural entity. We are not a "church," a purely *confessional* enterprise: the fact that one "believes" in Judaism or "feels" that he or she is a Jew is not a sufficient indicator of Jewish status. This does not mean that belief and action are irrelevant. A Jew can reject Judaism, to the point that he or she is regarded as an apostate deserving of exclusion from the community. Yet this does not contradict the "peoplehood" definition of Jewishness. Even an apostate remains technically a Jew, and his or her return to the community is not viewed formally as a "conversion."

The Reform position on the Jewish status of children of mixed marriages must be considered, therefore, as a continuation of as well as a departure from Jewish history and experience. The 1983 resolution modifies but does not repeal the influence of biology upon Jewish status. Biology, it is true, is no longer an "automatic" determinant of Jewishness, even for the child of a Jewish mother; Jewish status in a case of mixed parentage is *tentative*, awaiting confirmation. But the child of one Jewish parent, by virtue of that biological fact, enjoys a presumption of Jewishness that is not available to the child of two Gentile parents. And when the child of one Jewish parent acts in such a way as to establish that presumption, this action is seen, not as a conversion, but as the confirmation of a status derived, albeit tentatively, from biology.

4. *Both descent and behavior are crucial in determining Jewish status under the resolution.* The Jewish status of a child of a mixed marriage cannot be determined "automatically" either by biology or by behavior. Both elements, descent from one Jewish parent *and* the performance of *mitzvot* that lead to a "positive and exclusive Jewish identity," must be present, and they must be present during childhood. Reform responsa hold that adults who were born to one Jewish parent but who, as children, never performed "appropriate and timely public and formal acts of identification with the Jewish faith and people" require conversion in order to establish their Jewish identity.

5. *The resolution applies only to children raised exclusively as Jews.* Judaism makes exclusive demands upon the individual. One cannot successfully be both a practicing Jew and a communicant of another religion. Adult Jews who adopt another religion, even though they do not formally renounce their Judaism, are considered apostates. It follows that children of one Jewish parent who are raised simultaneously in more than one religious tradition do not qualify for Jewish status under the doctrine of "patrilineal descent," even if they perform "appropriate and timely public and formal acts of identification with the Jewish faith and people." Rather, we regard them as Gentiles until such time as their parents decide to raise them exclusively as Jews. If the parents never make this decision, the children will require conversion in order to establish their Jewish status. The "appropriate and timely public and formal acts of identification" of which the 1983 resolution speaks do not automatically confer Jewish status. They serve rather to establish the *presumption* of Jewish status, as evidence that Judaism is, in the words of the resolution, the

child's "positive and exclusive" religious identity. A child raised simultaneously in Judaism and another religious tradition does not develop a "positive and exclusive" Jewish identity; therefore, the presumption of Jewish status is disproved, and the resolution does not apply to that child. He or she will require conversion prior to observing Bar or Bat Mitzvah in the synagogue.

The 1983 resolution also does not apply to the child of a mixed marriage raised in a home where two religions are actively practiced on an equal basis, even though the parents declare their intent to raise this child as a Jew and not simultaneously in two religious traditions. While the child may perform "appropriate and timely" Jewish acts, such as attending religious school, these acts must be "meaningful" evidence of Jewish identification. In an environment where the home is both a Jewish *and*, say, a Christian one, where Christian symbols and observances are at least as prominent as their Jewish counterparts, it is highly doubtful that the child will develop a "positive and exclusive" Jewish identity. A child born and raised in such a home will require conversion to Judaism prior to observing Bar or Bat Mitzvah in the synagogue.

Adoption

Whoever raises an orphan in his house is regarded by the Torah as the child's physical parent. (*B. Sanhedrin* 19b)

The one who raises a child is called "parent," not the one who begets the child. (*Exodus Rabbah* 46:6)

Adoption, the institution through which an individual or individuals become the legally-recognized parents of a child that is not their biological offspring, is not mentioned in classical Jewish sources. Those sources do refer to a situation of legal guardianship, in which the guardian (*apotropos*) assumes the legal responsibility for raising the child, but the guardian is not referred to as a "parent." Still, Jewish practice has developed over time in response to the reality that families *are* created and expanded through adoption. Rabbinic thinking has centered upon two distinct yet related questions raised by the adoptive relationship: What is the status of the adoptive parents toward the child? And how is the Jewish status of the adopted child to be determined?

Adoptive Parents and Their Children. The adoptive parents are in every respect *the* parents of that child. Though many authorities hold that the commandment to "honor your father and your mother" (Exod. 20:12; Deut. 5:16) refers exclusively to one's biological parents and that no such obligation exists toward adoptive parents, others assert that the duty to honor our parents stems from the love and guidance they have bestowed upon us during the years of our childhood and growth. "Parenthood," in other words, is established not by biological fact but by the real bond between parent and child, a bond that exists in adoptive families. This view accords with our own understanding of the essence of parenthood and our recognition of adoptive families as families in every way. For this reason, it is our practice that a child must say *Kaddish* and observe all mourning rites for an adoptive parent, for he or she is the child's *real* parent.

The Jewish Status of Adopted Children. Adopted children whose biological parents were Jewish are themselves Jews by virtue of birth. An adopted child born to Gentile parents requires conversion. When the child is adopted at a young age, he or she like any other Jewish child receives a Hebrew name in a synagogue ceremony and is called *ben/bat* ("son/daughter of") the Jewish adoptive parents. Alternately, some special readings might accompany the child's circumcision or naming ceremony.

There are no religious prohibitions against the adoption of a child based upon the child's race or ethnicity. The racial descent of a child has absolutely no significance in Jewish law.

Adoption Agencies. Adoption agencies affiliated with and sponsored by the Jewish community should establish and maintain effective Jewish priorities in the placement of children. This means that, whenever feasible, children should be placed with families in which both parents are Jews, by birth or conversion. Within this category, preference should be given to families with a clear and discernible commitment to Judaism.

Circumcision (Berit Milah)

As for you, you and your offspring to come throughout the ages shall keep My covenant . . . every male among you shall be circumcised. You shall circumcise the flesh of your foreskin, and that shall be the sign of the covenant between Me and you. And throughout the generations,

every male among you shall be circumcised at the age of eight days.
(Gen. 17:9–12)

On the eighth day the flesh of his foreskin shall be circumcised. (Lev.
12:3)

In Jewish tradition, the *mitzvah* of circumcision is "the first commandment given to our father Abraham, the very seal of God upon our flesh."
The circumcision (*milah*) of male children is the eternal sign of the
covenant (*berit*) between God and the descendants of Abraham; hence
berit milah, "the covenant of circumcision." The ritual removal of the
foreskin (*orlah*) has assumed an extraordinary religious significance for
Jews. As the forging of the most physical kind of bond between Israel
and its God, it is indelible testimony of our identity as a community
set apart and distinguished, "bound through the generations to serve
God and to tell of God's praise."

Within Reform Judaism, by contrast, attitudes toward circumcision
have been much more ambivalent. Reform Jews have often criticized
the ritual on both intellectual as well as aesthetic grounds. The more
radical among them called for its abolition as an outdated, even barbaric
ritual. Most, though they continued to circumcise their sons, down-
played the religious significance of the act, even to the point of eliminating the religious ceremony. Recent decades, however, have witnessed
a rebirth of interest among Reform Jews in *berit milah* as a ritual of
Jewish identification. In 1963, it could be said that "the ancient practice
of circumcising a male child . . . is strictly observed" within the Reform
movement; by 1979 it had become "a *mitzvah* to circumcise a male child
on the eighth day." The strongest evidence of this rebirth is the establishment of the Berit Milah Board of Reform Judaism, which trains and
certifies physicians and other licensed practitioners to serve as *mohalim*
or *mohalot* (specialists in the performance of circumcision) for the Reform community. Reform Judaism has thus come full circle, from a
hesitant, arm's-length stance toward *berit milah* to one of full ritual
affirmation and participation.

The Ceremony of Berit Milah. The *berit milah* service may be held at
home, but it is entirely appropriate to perform it in the synagogue as a
means of stressing the communal religious aspect of the occasion. The
traditional ceremony begins with a processional, in which the baby is
carried into the room on a pillow by a man (*kvatter*) and a woman

(*kvatterin*). The congregation greets the infant with the words "*barukh haba*," "blessed be he that comes." The child is placed upon a chair designated as *hakisei shel Eliyahu*, the throne of the prophet Elijah, who is said to be present at the circumcision ceremony. He is then placed upon the lap of the *sandak* or *sandakit* (see below) or upon a sturdy table where the *sandak/it* holds him during the circumcision. Immediately before performing the circumcision, the *mohel/et* recites the following blessing:

> *Barukh atah Adonai Eloheinu melekh ha'olam asher kideshanu bemitzvotav vetzivanu 'al hamilah.*

> Blessed are You, Adonai our God, Sovereign of the universe, who hallows us through the *mitzvot* and commands us concerning circumcision.

Following the circumcision, the parents recite the blessing:

> *Barukh atah Adonai Eloheinu melekh ha'olam asher kideshanu bemitzvotav vetzivanu lehakhniso beverito shel Avraham avinu.*

> Blessed are You, Adonai our God, Sovereign of the universe, who hallows us through the *mitzvot* and commands us to enter our son into the covenant of Abraham.

The congregation responds: "Just as he has entered the covenant, may he likewise embark upon a life blessed with Torah, marriage, and good deeds."

In the traditional ceremony, when the circumcision has been completed the blessing *asher kidash* (". . . who sanctified the beloved one from the womb . . . Blessed is Adonai, who establishes the covenant") is recited over a cup of wine and the child's Hebrew name is bestowed. The person reciting the blessing drinks from the cup; the infant, too, shares a few drops from the cup by sucking from a cloth soaked in wine. In Reform practice, we recite the *Shehechiyanu* blessing (". . . who has kept us in life, sustained us . . .") at the *milah* ceremony.

It is preferable that the *berit milah* take place in the presence of a *minyan* (ten Jewish adults), in order to emphasize the festive and public nature of the event. Nonetheless, if we cannot gather a *minyan*, we perform the circumcision in the presence of fewer than ten.

The Procedure. Ritual circumcision consists of three separate acts: *milah*, the cutting of the foreskin; *peri'ah*, the tearing or cutting of the mucous membrane covering the glans; and *metzitzah*, "suction" to remove the blood from the wound.

Most physicians today perform circumcision by using surgical clamps which protect the glans and achieve hemostasis, the reduction of blood flow, during and following the procedure. The clamps combine *milah* and *peri'ah* into one process. There is no objection to the use of clamps rather than the *izmeil*, the traditional *mohel*'s knife, to perform *milah* and *peri'ah*.

Metzitzah was traditionally performed by oral suction. While some Orthodox *mohelim* continue this practice, it was discarded by many Jewish communities during the nineteenth and twentieth centuries. Since *metzitzah* is not a ritual requirement but was originally instituted for medical purposes, the use of surgical swabs to wipe away the blood meets these purposes and is a sufficient replacement for the old method.

There is no valid objection to the use of anesthetics as part of the circumcision procedure, particularly if the boy is older than an infant.

The Mohel/et. The person who performs the circumcision should be one whose life meets the highest standards of Jewish belief and practice as we understand them. A certified *mohel/et*, who combines professional skill with a profound commitment to Judaism, is the best choice. When the services of a *mohel/et* cannot be arranged, the circumcision may be performed by a qualified physician or medical professional, preferably a religious Jew who appreciates the nature of *berit milah* as a religious ceremony rather than merely a medical procedure. Failing that, another qualified Jewish practitioner may circumcise. If no such person is available, a Gentile may perform the medical procedure, but the religious service should be conducted by the family, the rabbi, or another suitable Jewish representative.

Other Participants. The *kvatter* (male) and *kvatterin* (female) are honored with the task of bringing the child into the room where the *milah* will take place. A non-Jew may serve as *kvatter/in*. The *sandak* (or *sandek*) holds the child during the procedure. The *sandak*'s role is an exalted one, and the parents should seek out an especially righteous person who is worthy of the honor. In some communities, the rabbi served as the permanent *sandak* for all circumcisions; in others, the honor was bestowed upon a grandparent or even upon the child's father. Although it is customary to translate the word *sandak* as "godfather," this individual has no legal responsibility toward the child beyond the circumcision ceremony.

When Is the Ceremony Held? The *berit milah* takes place on the eighth day of the child's life, even should that day fall on a Shabbat, a festival, or Yom Kippur. Exceptions to this rule include babies born at twilight on Friday or Saturday and babies born by cesarean section. Circumcision may be postponed only for valid medical reasons. If postponed, it does not take place on a Shabbat, festival, or Yom Kippur.

The circumcision should not take place prior to the eighth day. If for any reason the circumcision was performed prematurely, it is still considered valid; there is no need to perform the ceremony of *hatafat dam berit* (the taking of a drop of blood) to render the procedure ritually acceptable. Yet as a matter of religious practice, Reform Judaism insists that circumcision be performed on the eighth day, for by observing this ritual requirement we affirm that *berit milah* is a sacred religious rite and not merely a medical procedure.

The *berit milah* customarily takes place during daylight hours, from sunrise on. It should not be performed at night.

Special Circumstances

1. A *mohel/et* should perform the circumcision of the son of an unmarried couple, since the child requires circumcision whether his parents are married or not. The community may, based upon its sense of propriety, require that the *milah* be held privately, without the usual public ceremony.

2. We circumcise the son of a mixed-married couple on the basis of the CCAR Resolution on Patrilineal Descent. If the parents are unmarried, we would want some assurance that the child will be raised as a Jew before granting their request. The child of a non-Jewish mother is, under traditional *halakhah*, a non-Jew, and the circumcision would be considered part of the child's conversion ritual. The North American Reform movement accepts the child of a Jewish father and a non-Jewish mother as potentially Jewish; a Reform *mohel/et* will perform the circumcision, and the synagogue will welcome the child as a member of the community. In such a case, however, we have a moral obligation to inform the parents that not all

streams of Judaism accept their child as Jewish without a formal conversion.

3. When a mixed-married couple wishes to have their son both circumcised and baptized, we should refuse to perform the *berit milah* ceremony. His parents' determination to raise him as both a Jew *and* as a Christian indicates that they are not ready to fulfill the *mitzvah* of bringing him into the covenant community and of rearing him exclusively in the Jewish faith and tradition. There is no such thing as a "half-Jew"; one is either a Jew or one is not. It is important that we discourage parents at the outset from raising their children simultaneously in two religious traditions.

4. Similarly, we should refuse to perform *berit milah* for "Messianic Jews," whom we regard as Christians (see Chapter 2). These individuals have by their own choice separated themselves from the covenant community. To perform the circumcision would be to lend our endorsement to that choice as a legitimate Jewish decision.

5. When parents refuse to circumcise their son, the child should not be named at a synagogue service. Since we affirm circumcision as an essential sign of the covenant, we should do everything in our power to encourage it. To hold a naming ceremony would create the false impression that such a ceremony is an adequate substitute for *berit milah*.

6. Circumcision does not create Jewish identity. A boy who is born Jewish is a Jew, even if his parents do not have him circumcised during infancy. While we would encourage him to become circumcised upon reaching religious majority, we treat him as fully Jewish with respect to Bar Mitzvah and other community rites.

7. When Jewish parents request a surgical circumcision but do not want a *berit milah* ceremony, a *mohel/et* should refuse to do the procedure. Again, circumcision is for us a religious act; to treat it as mere surgery is to deny its Judaic significance.

Naming and Covenant Ceremonies

Jewish tradition does not know of a service for female infants comparable to *berit milah*. A girl received her Hebrew name as part of a simple synagogue ritual. Her father would be called to the Torah, usually on the Shabbat following her birth, and a blessing (*"mi sheberakh"*) would be recited announcing her name. In Sefardic communities, the naming would take place within a celebration called *zeved habat* held either in the synagogue or at home. Yet for all its festivity, this ceremony does not replicate the religious significance of *berit milah*, the moment that a boy is "entered into the covenant." Reform Judaism holds that a woman participates actively in the covenant (*berit*) between God and Israel just as a man does. In 1975, therefore, the Central Conference of American Rabbis resolved that congregations ought to introduce "life-cycle ceremonies for females equivalent to those now offered for males."

These ceremonies are quite new on the Jewish scene, and no uniform liturgy yet exists. An example of a covenant service for girls (*hakhnasat bat laberit*), to be held either at home or at the synagogue, is included in the *Rabbi's Manual*, pp. 16–24.

It is a *mitzvah* to give a Jewish child a Hebrew or Jewish name, and it is a Reform custom to name the child in the synagogue even when the child has already been named at the *berit milah* or covenant ceremony. One's Hebrew name is traditionally linked to that of one's father: for example, "Reuven *ben* (son of) Ya'akov." Reform practice mentions the names of both parents: "Reuven *ben* Ya'akov *ve*-Leah." In Ashkenazic practice, the custom is to name a child after a relative who has died, while Sefardim tend to name their children after living relatives. Reform practice allows either option. Jews-by-choice may name their children after a Gentile parent, since Jewish tradition recognizes that the proselyte continues to owe honor and respect to his or her parents.

Redemption of the First-born Son (Pidyon Haben)

In Jewish tradition, the first-born son is to be "redeemed" from God. This originates in the belief that God "acquired" the Israelite first-born by sparing them from *makkat bekhorot*, the last plague before the Exodus from Egypt, the destruction of the first-born Egyptian sons (Exod. 12:29). Like all other persons or things sanctified to God's service, the first-born could alter that status only upon the payment of a fee to the Temple; the Torah sets this fee at five shekels, payable upon the child's thirtieth day of life (Num. 18:16). The requirement applies to a son who is first-born to his father ("the first-fruits of his strength," Deut.

21:17) and mother ("he that breaches the womb," Exod. 13:2). A child born by cesarean section does not "breach" the womb and hence is exempt from the requirement of redemption, as is the child whose father or mother is a priest (*Kohen*) or a Levite.

Since Reform Judaism no longer recognizes a hereditary priesthood and does not believe that the first-born son ought to occupy a status that is different from other sons and daughters, this ceremony is incongruous for Reform Jews.

Bar/Bat Mitzvah

At thirteen years of age, one begins to fulfill the *mitzvot*. (*M. Avot* 5:21)

A Jewish child traditionally reaches majority at the age of thirteen (for a boy) or twelve (for a girl). At that point, he or she becomes a full-fledged member of the community and takes on the obligations of an adult Jew. The term *bar mitzvah* or *bat mitzvah* means simply "one who is obligated to perform *mitzvot*." No special ritual is needed to mark this change in status from childhood to adulthood. It occurs automatically, just as one automatically "becomes an adult" under civil law at age eighteen or twenty-one. During the Middle Ages, however, the custom arose to mark the occasion of a boy's coming into adulthood by calling him to the Torah and by arranging a festive meal (*se'udat mitzvah*). From these beginnings emerged the familiar custom of the Bar/Bat Mitzvah as a rite of passage for Jewish youth.

The Reform movement in North America has struggled over the Bar/Bat Mitzvah. At one time, this ceremony was on the verge of extinction in Reform congregations. Most of them preferred to replace Bar/Bat Mitzvah with Confirmation, which they considered a more enlightened and appropriate ceremony for modern Jews. Yet the enduring popularity of Bar/Bat Mitzvah prevailed, and today, in our communities, Bar/Bat Mitzvah is "virtually universally observed by Reform Jews." It is considered "a *mitzvah* to be called to the reading of the Torah" at the time when one reaches the age of religious majority. The overwhelming majority of the Reform rabbinate recognizes the value of the observance of Bar/Bat Mitzvah as a means of encouraging the intensified study of Hebrew and Jewish liturgy, of strengthening Jewish identity and participation in synagogue life, and of inculcating Jewish values and responsibility.

Age. No gender distinction is made in the age at which the ceremony occurs. Both boys and girls become Bar/Bar Mitzvah at the age of thirteen.

Nature. The ceremony of Bar/Bat Mitzvah is both a religious occasion and a time for celebration. Often, however, the festivities become so lavish that they detract from the religious dimensions of Bar/Bat Mitzvah. Rabbis and congregations are urged to establish the appropriate standards to insure that the emphasis is placed upon the true significance of this moment in the young person's Jewish life.

The observance of Bar/Bat Mitzvah is an indication that the young person has met certain identifiable standards in his or her Judaic and Hebraic education. Among these standards are commitment to performing *mitzvot* and to continuing with formal Jewish study at least through (but hopefully not ending with) Confirmation. The rabbi of the congregation should be consulted as the final authority in matters related to standards for Bar/Bat Mitzvah.

Time. Since it involves calling a young person to the Torah, a Bar/Bat Mitzvah "ceremony" may theoretically be held at any service when the Torah is regularly read, such as Shabbat, festivals, Rosh Chodesh, and Mondays and Thursdays at *Shacharit.* It is clearly not permitted to schedule a Bar/Bat Mitzvah on a day when the Torah is not read. It is also inappropriate to celebrate a Bar/Bat Mitzvah on a fast day or on the High Holidays, even though the Torah is read then, since a family ought not to celebrate a moment of personal joy on a day observed by all Israel as a time of somber reflection. Similarly, we should not celebrate Bar/Bat Mitzvah on a festival day: the joy of that day is of a special communal and religious nature, and "we do not confuse one joy with another."

A Bar/Bat Mitzvah "service" is *not* a private ceremony. Reform practice strongly prefers that Bar/Bat Mitzvah be observed at a regularly-scheduled Shabbat service of the congregation. The essence of Bar/Bat Mitzvah, after all, is that the child is now ready to assume a full and active role in the religious life of the community. Such a role involves attendance at the congregation's religious services. The congregation should therefore be present to mark the occasion. Since the Bar/Bat Mitzvah "ceremony" is a *public* worship service, any events which our congregations customarily mark at public worship services, such as baby-namings and blessings of couples about to be married, may therefore take place at the Bar/Bat Mitzvah service and are not regarded as "intrusions" upon a family celebration. Congregations should see to it that the "regular" service attenders who are not specially invited to the Bar/Bat Mitzvah celebration do not feel excluded from a service that belongs to them as well.

The so-called *Havdalah* Bar/Bat Mitzvah ("so-called" because the Torah is in fact read at the *Minchah* or afternoon service for Shabbat and not at *Havdalah* on Saturday night) presents a special challenge to our conception of Bar/Bat Mitzvah as a communal religious event. On the one hand, since we do read from the Torah on Shabbat afternoon, it would be permissible to schedule a Bar/Bat Mitzvah for a late afternoon *Minchah*, to be followed by *Havdalah* when Shabbat ends. In most of our congregations, however, there is no regularly-scheduled Shabbat *Minchah* service, and the "*Havdalah* Bar/Bat Mitzvah" takes on the aspect of a private celebration for invited guests. True, it is often convenient for the family to schedule the Bar/Bat Mitzvah ceremony for late Shabbat afternoon, as a means of combining the worship service with the evening festivities and to allow those who work on Shabbat to attend. Yet convenience is the wrong reason to schedule the ceremony at that time. Bar/Bat Mitzvah is emphatically a *public* event, reflecting a young person's commitment to the community and readiness to lead the congregation in worship. There may exist some exceptional circumstances in which the Bar/Bat Mitzvah might best be scheduled at Shabbat *Minchah*. Outside of those circumstances, though, the ceremony should take place in the context of a regularly-scheduled congregational worship service.

Special Situations

1. *Divorce.* In the Bar/Bat Mitzvah "ceremony," the role of the young person is primary. While it is customary and encouraged for both parents to take part in the service, neither enjoys an inherent "right" to participate. In cases of divorce where family relationships have become especially strained or embittered, participation should be adjusted in order to spare embarrassment to the young person becoming Bar/Bat Mitzvah.

2. *Non-Jewish Relatives.* Non-Jewish parents and relatives of the Bar/Bat Mitzvah may take part in the service in accordance with the

guidelines concerning the participation of non-Jews in synagogue ritual discussed in Chapter 1.

3. *Special Needs Youngsters.* The Bar/Bat Mitzvah "ceremony" is not an achievement test that measures "excellence" according to how well the young person performs. It is an occasion for marking a transformation from childhood to religious adulthood. All Jewish children make this transformation at age thirteen. Therefore, physically and mentally disabled children who cannot reach the standards of Hebraic or educational achievement that we expect of others should be encouraged to accomplish the most they can. Just as they are expected to receive the best Jewish education that the community can provide, so too do we want to include them in the events of the Jewish life cycle to the fullest possible extent. Blessings can be memorized; Torah portions can be shortened; deaf children can speak to the congregation with the aid of an interpreter. In severe cases, substitutes may be found for the reading from the Torah in order to allow the young person to mark this significant occasion in his or her life as a Jew.

4. A Jewish boy who for some reason has not been circumcised may be called to the Torah. Like all other Jewish children, he becomes Bar Mitzvah at the appropriate age, and while he now bears the responsibility of having the circumcision performed, he is permitted to mark his entry into adulthood in the synagogue.

5. *Adult Bar/Bat Mitzvah.* In one sense, the "Adult Bar/Bat Mitzvah" is a contradiction in terms. By virtue of age, every adult Jew *is* a Bar/Bat Mitzvah, a full member of the Jewish religious community. Still, many adults today wish to study toward an "Adult Bar/Bat Mitzvah," either because they never marked this occasion formally as children or in order to reenact that special moment upon a significant anniversary. This is to be encouraged, especially since it enables an adult learner to become more familiar with Hebrew, Jewish liturgy, and religious values.

Confirmation

The ceremony of Confirmation was adopted by Reform Jews in Germany in the early nineteenth century. Held at the end of a prescribed course of study, its purpose was to "confirm" the young person in his or her acceptance of the major doctrines of Jewish faith. Although the ceremony, openly borrowed from Christian liturgical practice, aroused opposition even among liberal-leaning Jews, it became widely accepted within Reform Judaism, particularly with the decline of the observance of the Bar Mitzvah. Even today, when Bar/Bat Mitzvah has become a central element in the life-cycle observance of the Reform community, "it is a *mitzvah* to be confirmed in the Jewish religion as a member of the Jewish people." Reform Jews see Confirmation as a useful supplement to Bar/Bat Mitzvah, which continues to center upon the attainment of *ritual* proficiency: reading from the Torah and leading the service. Confirmation, by contrast, stresses a general knowledge of Judaism, which is as necessary as Hebraic and liturgical skills to the full education of the Jewish person. Because it takes place at a later age than Bar/Bat Mitzvah, Confirmation allows the young adult to express a more mature understanding and acceptance of his or her responsibilities as a Jew. The ceremony makes concrete our commitment to the need for continued Jewish study beyond the age of thirteen. And, perhaps most importantly of all, it enables the young Jewish adult to reenact as an individual the dramatic moment at Sinai when the Israelite people said "yes" to the Torah.

Marriage

It is not good for man to be alone; I shall make for him a fitting helper. (Gen. 2:18)

Jewish teaching holds that marriage is the natural state of humankind. Our tradition identifies marriage with "the good," the essential happiness to which human beings aspire. When we read in the story of Creation that it is not "good" for the human being to dwell alone, the Rabbis comment, "One who has no wife lives without *goodness*." Even though one already has children and has thereby fulfilled the *mitzvah* to "be fruitful and multiply," one must still strive to marry, for "it is not *good* for man to be alone." To live alone in splendid isolation would have encouraged in God's creature the delusion that he, too, is a god. Against this, our tradition teaches that it is only *God* who lives alone. Human beings, finite and limited as they are, require "fitting helpers" to achieve their fullest potential, the "goodness" of which Torah speaks.

Does this mean that those who do not marry cannot realize happiness and good things in their lives? Hardly. Each human being is a unique person, and no general rule or principle, however exalted, can possibly address the specific reality of each and every member of our incredibly varied species. Many human beings are quite happy alone, leading lives of fulfillment and contentment. We do not condemn them for their decision to live as singles. We say, rather, that above and beyond the choice made by any one person there exists an ideal for humankind which Judaism proclaims and to which it directs our prayerful attention. That ideal is marriage, the proper framework for family life. If the single life is the right decision for particular individuals, it is the wrong decision for humanity as a whole. On the contrary, says Torah: we belong together, husbands and wives clinging to each other as one flesh (Gen. 2:24). It was not good for the first man to dwell alone, and it is not good for *us*—the collective, human "us"—to dwell alone.

Judaism's powerful emphasis upon the value of marriage is reflected in the fact that it calls marriage *kiddushin*, from the word *kadosh*, "sacred"or "holy." Marriage, in other words, is a sacred union, according to the essential meaning of that Hebrew term. The *sacred* belongs to God; it is separate, set apart from profane, everyday experience. Marriage, too, belongs to God, and it is the only social arrangement of human life that our tradition describes in this way. Like all else that is holy, marriage is an exclusive and inviolate thing, a reality in which the Divine Presence is manifest. Indeed, the prophets and mystics of Israel in all ages have seen this bond between wife and husband as a metaphor and model for the eternal bond which links Israel to its God.

Jewish Marriage

The Mitzvah. It is a *mitzvah* for a Jew to marry and to live together with his or her spouse in a manner worthy of the traditional designation *kiddushin*—set apart for each other in a sanctified relationship. It is also a *mitzvah* for husband and wife to take pleasure in sexual union. The tradition frowns upon sexual relations between two unmarried persons and encourages couples to come together in Jewish marriage. A premarital or non-marital sexual relationship, however "permanent," is not *kiddushin*, and we do not treat it as a marriage.

History. The act of marriage was construed by the Rabbis as a kind of acquisition (*kinyan*), based upon the language of the verse, "a man takes a bride" (Deut. 24:1), "taking" being a synonym in legal language for acquisition. The "acquired" wife, though not chattel to her husband, was part of his legal domain (*reshut*) and forbidden to marry another man until such time as she "acquired herself," leaving her husband's legal domain by means of his death or divorce. The husband, by contrast, was not "acquired," not part of his wife's legal domain, and he was permitted, under biblical law, to marry more than one wife. Yet the Rabbis of the Mishnah and Talmud almost never used the term *kinyan* to refer to marriage. They preferred the word *kiddushin*, translated above as "a sacred union," a term of their own invention which conveys something of the ritual nature of the marital relationship. Just as a sanctified person or object is reserved exclusively to God or to the Temple, so is the wife "sanctified" to her husband and forbidden, by the laws of adultery, to any other man.

Kiddushin is in fact the second of three distinct stages of the Jewish marriage process. The first of these is *shidukhin*, "engagement," a promise to marry at some future date. If the promise is broken, it cannot be enforced "in kind"; neither side can demand that the other honor the agreement against his or her will, since marriage is valid only with the consent of both parties. Yet though the couple remain unmarried, the agreement may require that the side which broke the engagement pay compensation to the aggrieved party. *Kiddushin* (sometimes called *erusin*) itself is an act of legal "betrothal" or espousal, in which a man and a woman forge a marital union that can be broken only through death or divorce. The couple do not live together as husband and wife, however, until the time of *nisu'in*, "nuptials," which takes place under a canopy (*chupah*) symbolizing the bridal chamber or marital home. Originally, much time (up to a year) could elapse between *kiddushin* and *nisu'in*, but during the medieval period it became customary to hold the two ceremonies at one and the same time and place. This, of course, is our custom today.

Consequences. Jewish marriage brings about a host of significant legal consequences for the bride and groom. Marriage establishes an exclusive conjugal relationship between husband and wife and thus creates, from the time of *kiddushin*, the legal possibility of adultery, which in traditional Jewish law means sexual relations between a man and the wife of another man. It also broadens the definition of incest (*arayot*), the forbidden sexual unions listed in Leviticus 18 and expanded by rabbinic law, to include a number of relatives by marriage. Marriage—here, specifically, the act of *nisu'in*—also creates monetary obligations and corresponding rights for both husband and wife. The husband, for example, is obligated under traditional *halakhah* to provide for his wife's food, clothing, shelter, and medical care, among other needs. In return, the husband enjoys the use of his wife's income during the marriage, and he inherits her estate upon her death.

The Contribution of Reform Judaism. In traditional Jewish practice, the husband is the dominant figure in the marital relationship. The man is the active party in the creation and the dissolution of marriage: it is he who "takes" a wife and he who issues the document of divorce. It is he who controls the family in general and its wealth in particular. The wife in marriage was often subject to severe legal and financial disabilities. Even those passages in traditional literature which register noble sentiments concerning marriage are unquestionably male-centered. Jewish marriage, in other words, may have been a "sacred union," but its traditional structure strikes us with its inequity.

The *halakhah*, we should note, was sensitive to this situation and sought in various ways to redress the imbalance between husband and wife. The Rabbis instituted the document known as the *ketubah,* which specified the wife's financial claims on her husband in the event their marriage came to an end so that "it would not be easy for him to divorce her." They permitted husband and wife to stipulate that the wife would maintain control over her own income and property, enabling her to maintain financial independence from and equality with her husband. Rabbinic law has for a full millennium prohibited a husband from divorcing a wife without her consent, and it does allow the wife to sue for divorce, that is, to ask the authorities to pressure her husband into divorcing her. These remedies demonstrate that the Rabbis were aware of the injustice done to Jewish wives under the law, and they strove mightily to rectify the system's most egregious defects. Yet their efforts, while significant, failed to solve the most obvious problem: the structure of Jewish marriage is decisively weighted in favor of the husband. As long as this fact remained unaltered, the basic inequity could not be righted.

Reform Judaism has taken the insight of the tradition, namely that equity and justice must be done, and proclaimed it as principle. In the

Reform Jewish view, *kiddushin* continues to establish a bond of exclusivity between a man and a woman, but this bond is understood as *mutual* in character and in force. Husband and wife are consecrated *to each other* unconditionally; they are set apart for each other and only for each other. Each spouse passes into the other's domain (*reshut*). A betrayal of marital fidelity by either partner is equally abhorrent. Each enjoys an equal claim to financial authority and responsibility within the marriage. Thus, while we retain the vocabulary and the symbolism of traditional Jewish marriage, we demand that these be interpreted and applied equally, to both husband and wife, so as to remove any suggestion of the dominance of one partner over the other.

Mixed Marriage

> You shall be for Me a kingdom of priests, a holy nation. (Exod. 19:6)

History. The concept of holiness (*kedushah*), from which the tradition coins the name for Jewish marriage (*kiddushin*), carries the meaning of "separate" or "distinct." Each spouse is consecrated to the other, set apart for each other in a sanctified relationship. Like the Temple, the Shabbat, or the festival, the Jewish marriage is made "holy" by means of rules that enforce its distinctiveness, its separateness from all other conjugal relationships, no matter how similar. And the most obvious example of this in Jewish tradition is the prohibition against mixed marriage, the marriage between a Jew and a non-Jew. Jewish marriage is distinct from all other kinds of marriage because it takes place only between two Jews.

Judaism resists mixed marriage because, in denying the distinctiveness of Jewish marriage, it weakens the fabric of family relationship and the survival potential of the Jewish community. It is therefore a *mitzvah* for a Jew to marry a Jew so that the sacred heritage of Judaism can be transmitted from generation to generation.

The Jewish opposition to mixed marriage, like most things Jewish, traces its roots to biblical times, when much emphasis was placed upon marrying within the Israelite fold. Even though some noted figures took foreign wives—Moses, Samson, and Solomon come readily to mind—the phenomenon of exogamy, "out-group" marriage, was cited by biblical authors as the chief cause of sin and idolatry among the people. Loyalty to their covenant with God may have led the patriarchs and matriarchs to avoid "out-group" marriage for their children, and it certainly explains the Torah's prohibition against marriage with the seven Canaanite nations (Deut. 7:1). The prophet Malachi (2:11) denounced mixed marriage as a violation of Israel's sacred relationship with God, and Ezra and Nehemiah decreed that Jewish men separate from their non-Jewish wives upon their return from exile in Babylonia. Here, too, the offense was described as the people's failure to remain religiously distinct from the surrounding population.

The rabbinic literature continues this trend, making one major inno-vation: the *halakhah* declares that there is no legal validity to the mar-riage between a Jew and a non-Jew (*ein kiddushin tofsin*). This concept, of course, was hard to reconcile with the life stories of those biblical personalities who did marry foreign wives: how could such great heroes have violated what the Rabbis believed to be a clear standard of Torah law? Yet this difficulty could be resolved, because rabbinic law made provision for religious conversion, an institution unknown in biblical times. Thus, said the Rabbis, conversions must have preceded those biblical instances of mixed marriage. The rule that mixed marriage was legally invalid became a permanent fixture of Jewish law, and no excep-tion was made to it for marriage with Christians or Muslims. Opposi-tion to mixed marriage remained firm in the face of notable violations of the prohibition.

With the modern period, the question of mixed marriage became an actual one for significant numbers of Jews. With emancipation and citizenship, Jews entered the societies of the West as putatively equal citizens, and most governments guaranteed their citizens the right to marry under civil law regardless of religious differences between the couple. The stigma against out-group marriage was no longer such a strong deterrent, particularly when the "out-group" consisted of one's fellow citizens, members of precisely that culture into which Jews wished to integrate. Consequently, the rabbis of western and central Europe and in America had to accommodate themselves to a very dif-ferent social reality of mixed marriage than that which faced their fore-bears. Liberal rabbis tended to accept the validity of mixed marriage on civil grounds; since the law of the state permitted these unions, Jews should look upon them as marriages and not (as did the halakhic liter-ature) as cases of lewdness and sexual license. However, while mixed marriages were *sanctioned* as a matter of legal fact, they were not *sanc-tified* as a Jewish practice. Resolutions to permit rabbinic officiation at mixed marriages were defeated at the Reform rabbinical conferences in

Brunswick (1844) and Breslau (1846). In America, mixed marriage was clearly viewed as a threat to the historical continuation of the Jewish people and was accordingly opposed by the great majority of classical Reform rabbis. The Central Conference of American Rabbis (CCAR) declared in 1909 that "mixed marriages are contrary to the tradition of the Jewish religion and should, therefore, be discouraged by the American Rabbinate." It reaffirmed this view in 1947.

The Current Position. This stance was once again endorsed by the CCAR in a resolution adopted in 1973 which declared the Conference's express "opposition to participation by its members in any ceremony which solemnizes a mixed marriage." The vote that year was the outcome of a long, sustained, and sometimes bitter controversy. The proportion of American Jews who married Gentile partners had been on the rise for some decades, and a number of Reform rabbis had responded to this demographic trend by officiating at mixed-marriage ceremonies. They argued that refusal to officiate would drive mixed couples away from the synagogue and discourage them from raising their children as Jews. Much of the Reform Jewish laity agreed, and many congregations began to demand that their rabbis officiate at mixed marriages under certain circumstances. Against this pressure stood those who opposed rabbinic officiation on traditional grounds as well as pragmatic ones: by sanctioning mixed marriage, the CCAR would split off the Reform movement from the rest of the Jewish community and would discourage the Gentile partner from converting to Judaism by removing a major impetus for that decision. The 1973 vote was a victory for the opponents of rabbinic officiation, although the resolution did note that, given the number of Reform rabbis who did officiate at mixed marriages, the members of the Conference "continue to hold divergent interpretations of Jewish tradition."

The controversy continues to this day and shows no sign of abating. As noted, many Reform rabbis in the United States do officiate under some circumstances at weddings between a Jew and a non-Jew, and they justify their position with the claim that a "positive response" to religiously-mixed couples is necessary to insure that their families do not become lost to Judaism. Many other American Reform rabbis, as well as virtually all Reform rabbis in Canada, Israel, Great Britain, Europe, and elsewhere, do not officiate, and their position coheres with the stance that the CCAR has taken in all its statements on the subject. Reform responsa literature, too, opposes rabbinic officiation at mixed marriages, making the following points in support of that opposition:

1. The rabbi, as the officiant at a wedding (*mesader kiddushin*), serves as the agent for Judaism. And Jewish tradition uniformly denies the *Jewish* validity of a mixed marriage. The rabbi does not "marry" the couple, even if the law of the state grants that power to the rabbi. The couple marry each other, and they can do so only "according to the religious traditions of Moses and Israel," that is, as Jews. The rabbi's role at a wedding is to attest that the marriage which is formed at that ceremony meets all the criteria of Jewish validity. A mixed marriage does not meet these criteria.

2. It is the rabbi's task as a Jewish leader and teacher to strengthen Judaism. Rabbinic officiation at mixed marriage is a declaration that the couple's home will be a "Jewish" one, yet this is patently not the case when one spouse has refused to accept Judaism. Although the mixed couple may agree to raise their children as Jews, experience and common sense tell us that it is easier to fulfill this resolve in a family where both parents are Jews. The Gentile partner is *not* a Jew and is in no way bound by *Jewish* history and heritage to pass on a tradition to which he or she feels no personal attachment.

3. We are not indifferent to the marriage decisions of our people. Rabbinic officiation at mixed marriage is a clear signal that it does not matter to the rabbi whether a Jew chooses a Jewish or non-Jewish spouse. We do not wish to send that signal to our children.

4. Religious issues may not be important to the couple contemplating marriage, but they are and must be of paramount concern to the rabbi. The rabbi's sole function at a wedding ceremony is to make sure that the religious values of Judaism occupy a central place in the formation of the couple's union. It is thus appropriate at this time for the couple to make the decision whether they intend to establish a Jewish home.

5. By refusing to officiate at a mixed marriage, the rabbi does not "reject" the couple. The rabbi, in fact, reaches out to the couple by encouraging them to make a sincere and concrete *Jewish* choice. This is accomplished by the non-Jewish partner's decision to convert to

Judaism. We make that offer freely, and we encourage the Gentile partner to accept it. If he or she does not wish at this time to choose Judaism, that is a free choice which should be respected. But, we stress, it is the choice of the Gentile partner to refuse conversion. The rabbi does *not* "reject" the couple, and it is inaccurate, unjust, and simply wrong to place that construction upon the rabbi's decision not to officiate.

6. Whether it is indeed true that by refusing to officiate at mixed marriages rabbis turn away many couples from Judaism (and we know of no solid non-anecdotal evidence to support this claim), it can as easily be said that when we officiate we discourage the Gentile partner from conversion. Many of those who convert to Judaism do so as a result of their decision to marry Jews, and their presence *as Jews* is a source of great strength to our community. By officiating at mixed marriages we may give the mistaken impression that we are indifferent to whether the Gentile partner will or will not choose Judaism. By refusing to officiate until the Gentile partner is ready to make that choice, we emphasize that that decision is a matter of paramount importance to us.

One particular issue surrounding mixed marriage involves the "dual-religion" wedding ceremony. Some couples and families, wishing to "be fair to both sides," will ask that a non-Jewish clergyperson officiate at the wedding along with a rabbi or that there be two separate wedding ceremonies reflecting the two religious traditions. Reform Judaism rejects these suggestions on the basis of its opposition to religious syncretism. The CCAR publicly repudiates the practice of rabbinic co-officiation at weddings with non-Jewish clergy.

At a Jewish wedding—that is, at a wedding of two Jews—it is also improper for a non-Jewish clergyperson or spiritual leader of another faith to officiate on an equal basis with a rabbi. The main officiant (*mesader kiddushin*) must be a person who is competent to attest to the validity of the marriage under Jewish law and tradition, and it is customary that this person be a rabbi. The non-Jewish clergyperson may participate by delivering a homily or a reading, but he or she may not take part in the major part of the liturgy of the wedding service, *kiddushin* and *nisu'in,* to avoid any implication that he or she is performing a Jewish rite.

The Response to Mixed Marriage. We should take no actions of a ritual nature which would imply religious approval of mixed marriage. In congregations where it is customary to offer a blessing during the synagogue service on behalf of couples who are soon to be wed, this blessing should not be offered in the case of a mixed marriage, since to do so would lead to the mistaken inference that we as a Jewish community grant religious sanction to a Jew's decision to marry a non-Jew. Once the marriage has occurred, however, the proper response is one of loving outreach. A decision to enter into a mixed marriage does not, in our eyes, separate this couple from our sphere of care and concern. The Jewish spouse remains a Jew, the couple's children are potentially Jewish, and it is definitely our Jewish obligation to bring the entire family into the midst of the Jewish community. The Jewish partner and the children are welcomed into the congregation as full-fledged members, and we do whatever we can to make the non-Jewish partner feel at home among us. Our goals are to assist fully in educating the children of mixed marriage as Jews; to provide an opportunity for the conversion of the non-Jewish spouse; and to encourage active involvement in the Jewish community and the synagogue.

Some might say that to reach out to a mixed-married couple after refusing to officiate at their wedding is an act of hypocrisy or, at the very least, a serious inconsistency. We reject these charges. We are motivated on this issue, after all, by two important principles: our concern for the integrity of Jewish religious standards and our responsibility for the continuation of Jewish life and identity. Religious Jews must affirm both these values, and there is no contradiction in their doing so. On the contrary: it is only when we insist upon the integrity of the most pivotal Jewish religious standards that we preserve and protect a Jewish heritage that will inspire the loyalty of our children and future generations.

From Engagement to Marriage

Consultation with the Rabbi. It is strongly recommended that the couple consult with the rabbi prior to the scheduling of their wedding. While the content of the premarital consultations will vary with rabbi and couple, these meetings can be an invaluable tool in strengthening the couple's awareness of the meaning of marriage, home, and family in Jewish tradition.

Civil Requirements. The requirements of civil law, such as the marriage license and the blood test, must be satisfied before the Jewish wedding takes place. Reform rabbis do not officiate at weddings unless these marriages are also recognized and permitted by the civil authorities.

Reform Judaism accepts the validity of civil marriage (a marriage solemnized before civil legal authorities). Nonetheless, the couple is urged to undergo a Jewish wedding in addition to their civil ceremony, so as to consecrate their marriage as a religious act. Special care must be taken in the case of Jews who were married in countries where it is or was illegal or dangerous to arrange a Jewish wedding. While we would certainly encourage and assent to their request for a Jewish ceremony, we recognize that their intention has always been to live together in Jewish marriage; we therefore do not tell them that their marriage is "invalid" and that a Jewish ceremony is required.

Testing for Disease. It is a *mitzvah* to be tested for genetic disease prior to marriage. When the tests show a significant likelihood that the couple would transmit the disease to their children, they should seek out the best medical advice and consult with their rabbi.

There is no religious requirement that couples preparing for marriage be tested for other dangerous diseases such as AIDS. It is certainly true that either member of the couple is obligated under Jewish tradition to inform the other if he or she is afflicted with a dangerous disease, and this obligation might reasonably carry a demand that those who belong to population groups that bear a significant risk of contracting a disease submit to testing. The incidence of diseases such as Tay-Sachs among segments of the Jewish community has led the Reform movement to view testing for such genetic diseases as a *mitzvah*. We do not believe that the incidence of other diseases warrants at this juncture a requirement that *all* Jews be tested prior to marriage. Rabbis should emphasize during their pre-marital counseling that testing is highly advisable and perhaps morally essential if either member of the couple has engaged in behavior which would place him or her at significant risk of contracting a dangerous disease.

Blessing in the Synagogue. In many congregations, the bride and groom are called for an *aliyah* to the Torah on the Shabbat prior to their wedding. This is traditionally referred to as an *aufruf* ("calling up"), although in non-liberal synagogues this honor is bestowed upon the groom alone. In other congregations, the rabbi may offer a prayer for God's blessing of the forthcoming marriage.

The Wedding Ceremony

Place. The wedding ceremony should be carried out in an atmosphere of *kedushah*, of sanctity. The most appropriate setting for a wedding is therefore either the synagogue or the home, each of which is regarded by tradition as a *mikdash me'at,* "a sanctuary in miniature." Jewish tradition, however, does not require that a wedding be performed in a specific place. Many couples prefer the Ashkenazic custom of holding weddings outdoors, "under the open sky." For reasons of convenience, weddings are often performed in the place where the reception is to be held. If this is the case, care should be taken to make sure that the surroundings do not offend our religious sensibilities.

The Processional. The formal ceremony of bringing the bride and groom to the *chupah* is usually conducted according to local custom. Those who escort the couple are called *shoshbinim* and *shoshbinot,* "attendants," who traditionally arranged the wedding and prepared the bride and the groom for the ceremony. Since Reform Judaism adheres to the principle of equality between men and women, it is strongly suggested that the bride's father not appear to "give her away."

The Service. Wedding liturgies are found in the *Rabbi's Manual,* pp. 50–84. The following is a description of the major elements of the traditional Jewish wedding service.

The wedding ceremony, as mentioned above, is a combination of two distinct legal acts: *kiddushin* (also called *erusin*), "betrothal," and *nisu'in,* "nuptials." *Kiddushin,* the actual forging of the marriage bond between husband and wife, is effected by an act of *kinyan,* "acquisition." According to *halakhah,* the *kinyan* can be carried out in one of three ways: through the transmission of an object of monetary value (*kesef*); through the transmission of a document declaring the intent to marry (*shetar*); and through an act of sexual intercourse performed with intent to marry (*bi'ah*). This third method was prohibited early on by the Rabbis, and today the universal custom is to perform *kiddushin* with the use of an object of monetary value, usually a ring. Since the monetary value of this object must be known to bride and groom, tradition prefers a plain ring with no jewelry or ornamentation, whose worth is easier to estimate. In our day this concern has disappeared; Reform practice accepts the use of any ring for the wedding. Other objects of value may be used in place of a ring. Immediately before the exchange of the ring, the officiant recites the betrothal benediction (*Birkat Erusin; Rabbi's Manual*, pp. 52–53) over a cup of wine; the blessing *borei peri hagafen* precedes *Birkat Erusin*. If wine cannot be obtained or if for health reasons the couple cannot drink wine, another beverage may be substituted and the appropriate blessing recited. The betrothal benediction praises God for sanctifying Israel through marriage, an institution which involves very strict rules concerning sexual relations and conjugal fidelity.

Traditionally, the groom gives the ring to the bride in the presence of two legally-acceptable witnesses and recites the formula *"Harei at mekudeshet li betaba'at zo kedat Moshe ve-Yisrael"* ("Behold, you are consecrated [betrothed] to me by this ring according to the heritage of Moses and Israel"), or some similar phrase that expresses his intent to marry. The bride's acceptance of the ring is her declaration of consent to the marriage. In Reform Judaism, where the conception of *kiddushin* is an egalitarian one, it is customary for the bride as well to give a ring to the groom and to recite the equivalent formula (*"Harei atah mekudash li"*) to him. Tradition permits the use of a borrowed wedding ring.

The reading of the *ketubah* sometimes follows the ceremony of *kiddushin/erusin*. This corresponds to the historical reality in talmudic and medieval times, when betrothal and marriage were often observed as two separate ceremonies. Since the *ketubah* takes effect only with *nisu'in*, or the "nuptials," it is considered appropriate to read the document prior to that part of the service.

The ceremony of *nisu'in*, "nuptials," involves the recitation of the *Sheva Berakhot*, the seven wedding benedictions (*Rabbi's Manual*, pp. 55–57). In fact, the "wedding benedictions" are six in number, but since these blessings are recited over a second cup of wine, they begin with *borei peri hagafen*. Their content links the marital union to the great themes of Jewish faith and destiny: the creation of the world and of humankind; the hoped-for restoration of Zion and Jerusalem; the prayer for joy and happiness in marriage. After the benedictions are recited, a glass is placed on the floor and traditionally the groom steps on it and breaks it. This custom is frequently explained as a reminder to the couple of the potential for sadness in life; it is therefore a touch of sobering realism in the midst of great joy.

In traditional practice, the couple spend a few minutes alone together in a private room following the wedding ceremony. In addition to affording them a brief respite during an exciting and stressful day, this custom helps fulfill a requirement under the *halakhah*: according to some opinions, the word *chupah* refers to the private meeting (*yichud*) between bride and groom which declares symbolically that they are now married. Another view holds that "*chupah*" refers to a *tallit* that is held over the couple during the *Sheva Berakhot*; from there derives the custom of using a *tallit*, held aloft on four poles or by four people, as a wedding canopy. Some communities, on the other hand, make use of richly decorated, permanent *chupot* for weddings.

A wedding is a public event, the celebration of the establishment of a new household in Israel. Therefore, a *minyan* is traditionally required. If no *minyan* is present, the wedding is still valid. And as a wedding is also a legal ceremony, one which alters the status of two individuals under Jewish law, it is customary that a rabbi act as officiant.

Dignity and Sanctity. The Jewish wedding is a joyous celebration. It is a *mitzvah* to accompany the couple to the *chupah* and to rejoice with them. Yet the wedding is also an occasion of sanctity (*kedushah*). This value should be kept in mind in the planning of the ceremony and its surrounding events.

1. *Music.* It is a long-standing custom to celebrate a marriage with music. A great deal of Jewish music is available and should be selected in consultation with the rabbi, the cantor, or the congregation's music director. Other kinds of music are permissible, although selections drawn from the liturgical traditions of other religions are to be avoided.

2. *Expense.* The sense of *kedushah* should encourage the couple and their families to place appropriate restraints upon the lavishness of the wedding celebration. It is a *mitzvah* to give a gift to *tzedakah* in honor of one's marriage or the marriage of one's children.

3. *Decorum.* Flash photographs should not be taken during the ceremony. It is permissible to record the wedding on videotape, but those who hold the cameras should do so unobtrusively and take care to observe the sense of propriety prevalent in the community.

Times When Weddings Should Not Take Place. Jewish tradition has identified certain days on which it is inappropriate to hold a wedding. We do not schedule weddings on Shabbat and *yom tov*, since one does not enter into binding legal transactions on those days and because they are set aside for delight (*oneg*) or joy (*simchah*) of a communal nature rather than for personal celebrations. On the other hand, most Reform rabbis will officiate at weddings on *chol hamo'ed*. Most Reform rabbis will abstain from officiating on days of national mourning such as Tisha Be'Av and Yom Hashoah. Traditional practice prohibits weddings during the Omer period between Pesach and Shavuot as well as during the three weeks between the fast of 17 Tamuz and Tisha Be'Av (*bein hameitzarim*). While Reform rabbis generally permit weddings during those times, personal observance along with family and communal considerations may warrant a degree of consideration for the traditional custom. Although some Jews do not hold weddings on the days of repentance between Rosh Hashanah and Yom Kippur, weddings are in fact permitted during that time.

The Ketubah. A document, signed and witnessed, attesting that a marriage has taken place will be prepared prior to the wedding and given to the couple. This document may be called a *ketubah*, after the name of the Jewish marriage "contract." The traditional *ketubah* is in fact a promissory note issued by the husband to his wife which specifies both the financial obligations he assumes toward her during the marriage and those owed to her by him or by his estate should the marriage end due to his death or to divorce. The document declares the amount of the husband's basic indebtedness to his wife (*ikar ketubah*) as well as any additional amount (*tosefet ketubah*) which he may decide to promise. In practice both these sums are determined by the communal custom. The *ketubah* will also specify the *neduneya*, or dowry, the property brought into the marriage by the wife and for which the husband accepts financial responsibility. The purpose of the *ketubah* in rabbinic law is to provide economic insurance to the wife and to make it more difficult for the husband to divorce her. The document must be ready to transmit to the wife prior to the wedding (*nisu'in*), because the debt to which it testifies is contracted from that time. Thus, "it is forbidden to marry without first writing the *ketubah*." Under rabbinic law, should the husband fail to write the *ketubah,* the *beit din* will nonetheless act as though one were written, allowing the wife to collect the standard amounts at the end or dissolution of the marriage.

All this holds in legal theory. Today, in practice, the *ketubah* has become a purely symbolic certificate. The financial details concerning the end of the marriage are determined by civil law in most of our communities. While the *ketubah* fell into disuse for many years in North American Reform Judaism, it has lately returned to widespread use. Numerous texts are in circulation, and others are being created all the time. Most of them, written in Hebrew and English rather than the customary Aramaic, speak of the spiritual commitments of marriage in place of or in addition to the financial obligations. One constant feature of Reform *ketubot*, however, is that they speak of the mutual obligations of both partners and not simply those of the husband toward the wife.

Marriage and Family Finances. Jewish law is sensitive to financial obstacles to marriage and has taken steps to overcome them. Jewish communities have often provided assistance to couples whose economic circumstances made it difficult for them to marry. This assistance, called *hakhnasat kallah*, is one of the most sublime forms of *tzedakah*. Our communities today are called upon to act in the spirit of this Jewish value and to render aid to those couples in need of financial help. In addition, Jewish law permits a couple to arrange its finances prior to marriage in such a way as to protect the assets of either spouse.

Divorce

If a man divorces his first wife, even the altar sheds tears. (*B. Gittin* 90b)

Divorce in Traditional Jewish Law. The procedure of divorce, as prescribed by the *halakhah*, is derived formally through *midrash*, a series of interpretations of a single biblical verse: "A man takes a wife and possesses her. She fails to please him because he finds something obnoxious about her, and he writes her a bill of divorcement, hands it to her, and sends her away from his house" (Deut. 24:1). Based upon this passage, the Rabbis declare that a divorce is effected when the husband executes a written document called a *get peturin* or, simply, a *get* and transmits it to his wife in the presence of two witnesses. Once the *get* reaches the wife's legal possession she is divorced, free to remarry. The document must be written specifically to dissolve this marriage, and its text can leave no doubt that the husband desires a complete and final separation from his wife. The writing, transmission, and receipt of the *get* may be performed by agents appointed by the husband and the wife, so that the couple need not be in each other's presence at any time during the divorce proceedings.

The Jewish law of divorce grants a clear legal advantage to the husband over the wife. The Rabbis of talmudic times read Deuteronomy 24:1 strictly: it is the husband who enjoys the exclusive power to initiate divorce. The divorce is valid only when the husband gives his consent to it; the wife, the recipient or "passive" party, may be divorced even against her will. To be sure, the rabbinic tradition has introduced important remedies into the law to provide a measure of equity for the wife. The famous *takkanah* (enactment) of Rabbeinu Gershom b. Yehudah (Germany, tenth century) prohibits a husband from using his Toraitic power to divorce his wife against her will. It also forbids him to marry another woman before divorcing his present wife; this rule, intended to prevent the wife from being stranded while the husband partakes of a new marriage, put a formal end to the biblically-sanctioned (if rarely observed) practice of polygamy among Ashkenazic Jews. The wife is entitled under talmudic law to sue for divorce, and should it find in her favor, the rabbinic court will instruct her husband to accede to her demand. Under certain circumstances the court may even coerce the husband, by physical means if necessary, to do so. Yet the basic inequity has never been erased, for the husband must still give his consent before a divorce can be issued. Judicial coercion may not be sufficient to persuade him to release his wife, and today, in any case, this power is denied to all rabbinic courts outside of Israel. The husband can therefore effectively prevent his wife from remarrying until such time as he deigns to free her. The wife, meanwhile, enjoys no such power over her husband. Should she refuse a justifiable request to accede to a divorce, the *takkanah* of Rabbeinu Gershom may be waived and the husband permitted to marry a second wife.

Reform Judaism and Jewish Divorce. The Reform movement in the United States accepts civil divorce as completely dissolving the marriage and permitting the remarriage of the divorced persons. No *get* or any substitute form of religious divorce is required. Virtually all Reform communities outside of the United States continue to insist upon Jewish religious divorce as a prerequisite for remarriage.

From its beginnings, the Reform movement objected strongly to the inequities of traditional Jewish divorce and to the cumbersome divorce procedures of the rabbinic courts. Some early reformers urged that the process of divorce be modified to meet these criticisms, although little came of their suggestions. In 1843, Rabbi Samuel Holdheim advanced a more radical proposal to do away with religious divorce altogether. He based his argument on essentially legal (halakhic) grounds. Divorce in Jewish tradition, Holdheim contended, is an act of civil or monetary (as opposed to ritual) law. Today, we conduct our monetary affairs according to the civil laws of the states in which we enjoy full citizenship. And since these states make provision for civil divorce, it follows that religious divorce has become entirely superfluous. Once a competent court has dissolved the marriage under civil law, the marriage has ceased to exist under Jewish law as well. Holdheim's suggestion, though never accepted by the German Reform movement, was adopted in the United States at the Philadelphia rabbinical conference in 1869. "The dissolution of marriage," it was declared, "is, on Mosaic and rabbinical grounds, a civil act only which never received religious consecration. It is to be recognized, therefore, as an act emanating altogether from the judicial authorities of the state. The so-called ritual Get is in all cases declared null and void."

In addition to the legal argument, the authors of the resolution drew a sharp theological distinction between marriage, which was to remain under rabbinic supervision, and the dissolution of marriage. The difference, wrote Rabbi David Einhorn in a paper submitted to the Philadelphia conference, is that marriage is an act of sanctification which establishes a religious institution; divorce, by contrast, is the negation and the destruction of that sanctity. Religion presides at the formation of marriage, for when two persons unite in the formation of a sacred union it is the proper function of religion to offer its blessing. But religion has no positive role to play when the marital union comes apart, for how can one "sanctify" that which is destructive of holiness? In Einhorn's words: "If the holy bonds are severed, religion can only tolerate the act in sorrow and silence . . . it cannot invest the act [of divorce] with its consecration."

While the 1869 resolution remains the official policy of the Reform movement in the United States, a growing number of Reform Jews have urged that the movement reconsider its abandonment of religious divorce. The official policy, they note, can be criticized on several grounds. The first is a serious flaw in the legal reasoning which justifies the acceptance of civil divorce. The designation of Jewish divorce as an act of "civil" law is not entirely accurate, for divorce in Jewish legal thinking pertains to ritual as well as to monetary matters. Moreover, Einhorn's distinction between the religious significance of marriage and divorce is less than fully persuasive. If the formation of a sacred union is a "religious" matter, then why should its dissolution be any less a subject of religious concern? Divorce, to be sure, is not commonly regarded as a blessing, something to be sanctified. Then again, neither is death, yet Judaism does not ignore death; rather, it fashions a response to the trauma of loss and bereavement drawn from the vast resources of our ritual and liturgical tradition. Divorce arguably belongs in the same category. The sentiment that Judaism can merely "tolerate" or greet with "silence" a decision for divorce is not as widely shared as it was in Einhorn's day. On the contrary: a policy of "silence" toward a most fateful experience in the lives of couples and their children might well be interpreted as an abdication of religious responsibility.

Such criticisms have led to some very tentative steps toward the recovery of this major rubric of Jewish tradition. The current edition of the *Rabbi's Manual* includes a new liturgy for a "ritual of release" (*seder pereidah*). The ritual, declares the *Manual*, is not a *get*. It does, however, serve as "a form of religious divorce" which, because of its egalitarian nature, is free of a major objection that Reform Jews raise against the traditional divorce procedure. The ceremony, which is entirely optional, permits the couple a measure of religious closure to a union which they likewise formed as part of a religious service. It reassures them that they remain in every way members of the Jewish community, and it reminds them of their continuing obligations to their fellow Jews and (if applicable) to their children.

The inclusion of a divorce ritual in the *Rabbi's Manual* is a significant break with the tradition of Reform practice in the United States, an open recognition that the policy of "silence" has outlived its usefulness.

Reform Judaism, Divorce, and the Jewish World. If Reform Judaism is reconsidering the importance of religious divorce, it does so under the influence of "new intra-religious relationships" (*Rabbi's Manual*, p. 246). Although we think of ourselves as an autonomous community which governs its own affairs, we are also part and parcel of a larger, world-wide Jewish reality in which the subject of divorce lies at the center of a bitter controversy. Traditional *halakhah* defines the offspring of an incestuous or an adulterous union as a *mamzer*, an "illegitimate" child who upon reaching adulthood is forbidden to marry almost all other Jews. Since traditional law does not accept the validity of civil divorce, a Jewish woman who remarries without benefit of religious divorce is still considered legally married to her previous husband. Any child she has by her second husband is the offspring of an "adulterous" union and is therefore labeled a *mamzer*. A considerable number of Reform Jews are the offspring of marriages solemnized following their mothers' civil divorce from previous husbands. These individuals, should they someday wish to marry observant Jews, will find their marriages forbidden. This problem becomes especially acute in Israel, where the *halakhah* as interpreted and applied by the Orthodox rabbinate is, by act of the Knesset, the law of marriage and divorce for *all* Jews, Orthodox or not.

Reform Judaism has abandoned the concept of *mamzerut* (illegitimacy), since it is morally repugnant to place such a crushing disability upon a child whose only "crime" was to be born to his or her parents. The *halakhah*, too, recognizes the injustice of this situation and seeks to remedy it as much as possible. Rabbinic authorities will explore every possible legal pretext in order to declare that a person thought to be a *mamzer* is in fact legitimate and permitted to marry most Jews. One such pretext is to find some legal ground to invalidate the marriage between the mother of the *mamzer* and her first husband; this renders her "second" marriage valid and its offspring legitimate. This approach is taken by some halakhists in Israel to purify entire communities, such as the Karaites and the Ethiopian Jews, from the taint of *mamzerut*. The marriages which have taken place in those communities are found to be *invalid* under the *halakhah*, usually on the grounds that the weddings were not witnessed by "observant" Jews (i.e., those observant of rabbinic law). Since their marriages were never "valid," it follows that "adultery" was never committed and that the offspring of these unions are all legitimate. The same approach is often taken toward Reform Jews. Many Orthodox authorities hold that Reform Jewish weddings are not valid under the *halakhah*; if so, then the wife does not require a *get* before remarriage, and her children from that remarriage are not *mamzerim*. While this may be an effective solution for the problem of *mamzerut*, it is both ironic and offensive that, in order to declare many Reform Jews legitimate, Orthodox rabbis must first declare Reform Jewish marriage—and, by extension, Reform Judaism itself—illegitimate.

Although the laws of *mamzerut* are of no importance in day-to-day Reform Jewish practice, it is vital that Reform Jews understand the ramifications of these laws against the backdrop of what one Orthodox writer calls "the divorce factor." If Jews to our religious right adopt the perception that the entire Reform community, by virtue of its rejection of religious divorce, exists under a suspicion of *mamzerut*, they will refuse to marry Jews born into Reform households. This refusal will lead to an accelerated religious polarization among the Jews, threatening and perhaps destroying forever the notion, central to our ancient faith and self-definition, that Israel is *one* people.

This prospect will not disturb those Orthodox and Reform Jews who are convinced that the great split has already occurred. At any rate, they argue correctly, there seems to be little we can do to prevent it. Even if Reform Judaism in the United States were to adopt a system of religious divorce, our divorces, precisely because they would be administered on an egalitarian basis under the supervision of Reform rabbis, would not be accepted as halakhicly valid by the Orthodox community. The only other recourse would be for Reform Jews to agree to submit their religious divorces to the jurisdiction of Orthodox rabbis, and this, obviously, we are most unlikely to do. Until some other and better solution can be located, then, Reform Jews ought to be kept informed of the situation so that they may participate actively in a discussion that will likely determine the very future of Jewish unity. Reform rabbis should take care to explain the realities of "the divorce factor" to their people, who must be made aware of the Orthodox position, particularly if they are considering the possibility of moving to Israel and having children.

The Agunah. Under the traditional Jewish law of divorce, as noted above, the court does not dissolve a marriage by decreeing divorce. Nor can a wife divorce her husband. It is the husband who either writes the *get* or commissions it to be written by a scribe (*sofer*). In a case of marital conflict, a wife may ask for a divorce and the *beit din*, should it find in her favor, may instruct the husband to issue a *get*. But if a divorce cannot be obtained from him, then the marriage remains legally valid even though the couple no longer live together. The wife is bound to the husband in a marriage that exists in theory but which for all practical purposes has ended. A wife in this situation is called an *agunah*, from the Hebrew word for "anchor." Like a ship chained to the dock, she cannot move; under the *halakhah*, she is forbidden to remarry unless her husband either dies or divorces her.

A woman becomes an *agunah* in either of two circumstances. In the first, her husband has disappeared and has remained missing for a long time. We might be convinced that he is dead, but under *halakhah* that conviction, in the absence of proof of death, is insufficient to dissolve the marriage. In the second, the husband simply refuses to issue a *get* to his wife, even though their marital life has effectively ended. In modern times, the couple may already have been divorced in the civil courts, yet the wife is denied remarriage under the *halakhah* unless and until the husband grants her a Jewish divorce. The potential for extortion is obvious, as the husband is in a position to exact crushing financial demands upon his wife or to force her agreement on matters of child custody and the like as the price for his issuing the *get*.

The case of the *agunah* is the clearest example of the inequity of a divorce law which grants to the husband the exclusive power to dissolve the marriage. Acknowledging this injustice, rabbinic authorities through the centuries have sought to provide relief to the wife who languishes, perhaps for years, in a state of marital limbo. In one respect their efforts have succeeded: the *halakhah* has largely solved the problem of the "missing" husband. The Sages of the Mishnah and the Talmud introduced important leniencies into the Toraitic standards of evidence required to prove the husband's death. These leniencies have since been honed into a complex system of rules and procedures which enable the halakhist in a particular case to craft the proper legal device that will permit the wife to remarry. The second scenario, the case of the recalcitrant husband who simply refuses to divorce his wife, is a much more difficult one. As we have seen, the rabbinic court may require the husband to issue a divorce and may pressure or even coerce him to do so. Today in Israel, the Attorney General is empowered by civil law to imprison a husband who refuses to issue a *get* as a means of inducing him to abide by the decree of the *beit din*. Yet these measures are of limited effect, particularly in countries where the rabbinic courts enjoy no such power of coercion. A husband who withstands the pressures can render his wife an *agunah* until his demands are satisfied, if ever.

Various halakhic solutions have been proposed during the last century which would have the effect of dissolving the marriage without the necessity of securing the husband's immediate consent to a divorce. Yet despite the powerful legal arguments that have been marshaled on behalf of these proposals, they have all been rejected by the leading Orthodox rabbinical authorities. Current efforts to address the dilemma of the *agunah* in the Orthodox world center upon the execution of a pre-nuptial agreement, enforceable under civil law, by which the husband obligates himself in the event of a breakdown of the marriage to pay for his wife's food and maintenance (which at any event he owes to her under the *halakhah*) until such time as he issues a *get*. At present, however, this agreement is not demanded or even accepted as valid by all Orthodox rabbis.

Reform Judaism has eliminated the problem of the *agunah*, of course, either through its acceptance of civil divorce in the United States or its creation of an egalitarian divorce procedure in other countries. Yet we do encounter this issue when Jews from the Orthodox community approach us for remarriage. What is our religious and moral duty in the case of a couple whose Orthodox marriage has come to an end in the civil courts but has yet to be dissolved by a Jewish divorce?

Reform responsa distinguish in this matter between the wife and the husband, yet the organizing principle in both cases is justice. If a Jewish woman married under Orthodox auspices and divorced in the civil courts asks us for remarriage, we should agree to perform the ceremony, even though her husband has refused to issue her a *get*. Her husband's conduct, which renders her an *agunah* under Orthodox practice, is morally inexcusable, and to turn her away would aid and abet his action, whether taken out of spite or out of hope for gain. Let us, however, consider the reverse situation: a man who was divorced in the civil courts but who refuses to issue a *get* to his wife comes to us and asks us for remarriage. In this case, we say "no." Although we accept the validity of civil divorce, the primary issue is again one of simple justice. This man seeks to exploit us, using our services to secure remarriage for himself while denying that option to his wife. It is true, of course, that the wife could also be remarried in a Reform ceremony, but she wishes to remain Orthodox. Such is her Jewish *choice*, and as a movement committed to religious pluralism we are required to respect her right to choose. Rather than demand that she become a Reform Jew, our task is to do what we can to free her from the bonds which, ironically, the rabbinate of her own community has proven incapable of severing. By denying her a *get*, moreover, her husband violates the implicit promise he made to her at the time of their wedding to respect her and to treat her justly in accordance with Jewish law. We will not act as agents for his immorality. On the contrary: our refusal to grant his request for remarriage may help pressure him to live up to his ethical obligations as a Jew and as a human being.

The Ethics of Divorce. Divorce has never ceased to be a matter of *religious* concern to Reform Judaism. Although we rely upon the action of the civil courts to dissolve marriage, we do so on the grounds that those courts act as our representatives in the matter. When we consider questions and problems relating to divorce, therefore, we continue to draw guidance from the sacred texts of our tradition. Those texts teach us, for example, that it is unethical for a person to divorce a physically incapacitated spouse in order to shelter assets that would otherwise be used to pay the spouse's medical bills. They also teach us that marriage in our view is a legal as well as a spiritual institution. Thus, the personal and financial obligations of marriage continue until the marriage comes to a legal end, even when the couple have separated.

The Jewish Home and Family

Unless God builds a house, its builders labor in vain on it. (Ps. 127:1)

We speak of the Jewish home, like the synagogue, as a *mikdash me'at*, a "sanctuary in miniature." If the synagogue and the house of study provide gathering places for communal worship and learning, the home is where we live the major part of our lives as individuals and as families. And since the Torah's teachings extend to each and every moment of our lives, our homes, no less than our synagogues, must therefore be holy places. We know that unless our homes are dedicated to Jewish life, no synagogue, school, or other outside institution will succeed in transmitting that way of life to the generations which follow us. It is our responsibility to insure that those who work for the preservation and enrichment of Judaism do not "labor in vain," and that responsibility begins at home.

Religious Identity. A Jewish home is one whose religious identity is an exclusively Jewish one. We categorically reject any tendencies toward religious syncretism, the blending of Judaism with other faiths or toward the mixing of two religious traditions together within the context of one household. We recognize the particular difficulties created by mixed marriage, and we know that in such a home the non-Jewish spouse, as an equal partner, may well feel entitled to his or her own religious expression. The fact remains, however, that we cannot grant *Jewish* legitimacy to decisions which run counter to the most essential standards of Jewishness as we understand them. Therefore, the child of a mixed marriage raised in more than one religious tradition cannot be considered a Jewish child. Judaism is an exclusive religious identity. We cannot and do not accept the contention that a person can be successfully Jewish *and* an adherent of another religion. When a child's parents declare their intention to have their child baptized as well as circumcised or named in a Jewish covenant ceremony, we should refuse to perform the Jewish ritual, since that ritual would give the false impression that the child will be raised in the covenant of Israel. Nor can we prepare a child for Bar/Bat Mitzvah when we know that he or she is at the same time studying toward a parallel life-cycle ceremony in another faith. The Union of American Hebrew Congregations has resolved that enrollment in Reform Jewish religious and day schools be open to Jewish children who are *not* also receiving formal instruction in another religion.

These decisions may seem controversial, given the emphasis the Reform movement places upon outreach and the need to present a warm and welcoming attitude toward the mixed-married families in our midst. Many such families are sincerely attempting to work out the question of their religious commitment, and they are not yet ready to declare an exclusive identification with one faith. To place that demand upon them before they are ready, it is argued, may drive them away from us. To this, we would offer three responses, based respectively upon theology, psychology, and common sense. In terms of theology, it is inconsistent for a person or a family to identify simultaneously as an adherent of Judaism and Christianity (or any other religion). To admit these people to our schools and to perform Jewish life-cycle rites for them is to grant our institutional endorsement to their dual identification, and this, as a self-respecting Jewish religious body, we cannot do. In terms of psychology, a decision to raise children in two religious faiths places upon them the burden of ultimately choosing one identification over the other. This is unfair and confusing to the child, and our synagogues must not help contribute to that confusion. It is the parents' responsibility to choose a consistent and coherent religious identity for their children, just as it is their responsibility to provide them with solid foundations for their moral, ethical, and personal lives. And in terms of common sense, we should remind ourselves that we do not "drive people away" from Judaism by proclaiming Judaism. We exist, not as a membership organization, but as a community of Jews committed to teaching Torah. We welcome all Jews into our midst and we want to keep them there, but we cannot afford to do so at the cost of denying the very reason and purpose of our existence. If some Jews decide not to associate with us because they do not share a commitment to even the most basic standards of Jewishness as we understand them, we certainly respect their decision and we regret it. But it is *their* decision, and not our insensitivity, that impels them to leave. Our doors remain open, and we look forward to their return.

Mezuzah: Dedication of the Home

It is a *mitzvah* to affix a *mezuzah* to the doorpost of a Jewish home. The *mezuzah* is the traditional fulfillment of the commandment in Deuteronomy 6:9: "You shall write [these words] upon the doorposts [*mezuzot*] of your house and upon your gates." Two passages from the Torah (Deut. 6:4–9 and 11:13–21), both of which mention the commandment of *mezuzah*, are inscribed by hand upon a parchment which is rolled and inserted into a cylinder or casing and affixed to the upper third of the right doorpost (as one enters the house) in a diagonal position, the top part facing inward. The diagonal setting is a compromise worked out in the tradition between the views of those authorities who require the *mezuzah* to be placed vertically on the doorpost and those who hold that it should rest horizontally. This *mitzvah*, therefore, can be said to embody within itself the virtues of compromise and accommodation, which are all-important as we seek to preserve *shalom bayit*, peace within the household.

There are no special requirements concerning the cylinder or casing, which may be constructed and decorated in many ways. The parchment, however, must be rolled so that the text faces inward, not outward. Those who observe the traditional practice place a *mezuzah* on the doorpost of each room in the house, with the exception of the bathroom.

The responsibility for affixing the *mezuzah* rests upon the one who dwells in a home (not necessarily the owner), who must do so within thirty days after he or she has moved into the home. A home which is to be occupied for less than thirty days is not considered a permanent dwelling, and a *mezuzah* is not required. All this applies to the Diaspora; one who occupies a home in the land of Israel must affix the *mezuzah* immediately, as this fulfills the *mitzvah* of settling in the land. Prior to affixing the *mezuzah*, one recites the following blessing:

> *Barukh atah Adonai Eloheinu melekh ha'olam asher kideshanu bemitzvotav vetzivanu likbo'a mezuzah.*

> Blessed is Adonai our God, Sovereign of the universe, who hallows us with the *mitzvot* and commands us to affix the *mezuzah*.

It is customary to invite friends to a ceremony of *chanukat habayit*, dedication of the home, at which the *mezuzah(ot)* will be affixed to the doorpost. A liturgy for this ceremony can be found in *On the Doorposts of Your House*, pp. 138–41.

Torah Study and Jewish Education

We are taught that *talmud torah keneged kulam*, "the study of Torah equals all the other *mitzvot* in importance." This is true, of course, because it is by studying Torah that we learn the other *mitzvot*. Yet Torah study represents more to the religious Jew than a practical guide to the duties of religious life. It is in many ways the *essence* of that life. The study of Torah is an act of Jewish prayer, for it is a cornerstone of traditional Jewish doctrine that God is to be found within the pages of our sacred texts. To study those texts is to take one's place in an eternal conversation between God and Israel as to the nature of the good and holy life. In the Jewish understanding of things, there is simply no better task to pursue. To put it another way: since the Torah is conceived as the very blueprint with which God created the universe, to study that blueprint is to learn the secrets of creation itself. We study, that is, because we are Jews in search of God, and it was for this purpose that we were placed on this earth.

Children. Children should be enrolled in Jewish study, whether in day school or in the synagogue's school, as soon as they are eligible. Many congregations mark the beginning of religious study with a service of Consecration held on or around the festival of Shemini Atzeret/Simchat Torah. This ceremony serves to impress the child and the rest of the congregation with the importance of embarking upon formal Jewish learning. The ceremonies of Bar/Bat Mitzvah and Confirmation are important milestones along the road of the child's Jewish education, but they do not mark the end of that road. The *mitzvah* of Torah study lasts a lifetime.

Adults. The *mitzvah* of *talmud torah* is incumbent upon a Jew throughout life. Adults should study Torah, whether or not they received a formal Jewish education during childhood. They should study together with their children at home. It is particularly worthwhile for parents to attend Jewish study classes at the synagogue during the time their children are in religious school, for in so doing they demonstrate to their children by their own example the importance of Torah study. Adults who have not celebrated Bar/Bat Mitzvah or Confirmation but who are involved in continuing Jewish education should consult their rabbi as to the possibility of observing these joyous events in later life.

Hebrew. It is a *mitzvah* to learn and teach the Hebrew language. Hebrew connects us to Jews and to Jewish communities in all ages and locales. It is the language of Torah, of the State of Israel, and of Jewish religious and cultural creativity throughout history. The renaissance of Hebrew prayer in the Reform synagogue is but the most obvious expression of the movement's commitment to the Hebrew language as a medium of Jewish expression.

Between Parents and Children

It is the responsibility of parents to teach Torah to their children. The synagogue and the school are indispensable means to this end, and the community bears the obligation of providing for these institutions and for the training of teachers and other educational specialists. But the child's essential religious and moral development occurs at home, based upon values established and exemplified by his or her parents. It is therefore incumbent upon parents to insure that theirs will be a truly and unmistakably Jewish household. Home rituals, such as blessings recited over the meal and Shabbat and holiday observance, are the core of Jewish life and ought to be experienced as such in the Jewish home. It is a *mitzvah* to set aside time for daily prayer. When there are no services at the synagogue or if one cannot attend the synagogue, the home is a perfectly appropriate place for the prayer service. A Jewish home should have a Jewish library, and time should be set aside for regular Torah study.

The Torah enjoins that each person "honor your father and your mother" (Exod. 20:12) and that "you shall each revere your mother and your father" (Lev. 19:3). According to the tradition, "honor" refers to the parent's physical needs: the adult child is obliged to feed, clothe, and provide for housing and sustenance for parents who cannot do these things for themselves. "Reverence" involves matters of respect: the child does not appropriate the parent's customary place, does not publicly contradict the parent's words, and does not refer to the parent by his or her first name. These duties are to be taken most seriously, note the Rabbis, because we owe the same obligations of "honor" and "reverence" toward God (Prov. 3:9 and Deut. 6:13).

These non-financial duties do not cease when the children grow into adulthood, but their observance at that point becomes problematic. To what extent may a parent expect deference from an adult child, especially when this deference may interfere with the child's marriage and family life? The child is not expected to heed the parent's instruction to violate another religious obligation. Tradition teaches that should the parent protest the child's desire to move to the land of Israel, to go to another city to learn Torah, to marry the person whom the young person wishes to marry, or to make peace with one of the parent's enemies, the child may ignore these objections. In general, the parent is warned against placing excessive demands upon the child. In an intergenerational conflict within the family, one's primary responsibility is toward spouse and children. When husband or wife objects to what he or she considers undue interference from the spouse's parents, the spouse must heed that objection over any sense of obligation owed to the parents. The trend of Jewish thought has been to stress the child's duties toward the parents but to limit the circumference of these duties so that the child would not be subjugated to every whim and desire of the older generation.

One of the obligations owed to a parent is that of financial support. It is therefore appropriate for communities to compel children to contribute toward the care of their aged parents. Jewish tradition disputes whether a child may compel an aged or ailing parent to enter a nursing home over the parent's objections. On the one hand, the very nature of the *mitzvah* to honor one's father and mother emphasizes the child's *personal* responsibility to provide the needed care, and the love we are expected to show to those who brought us into the world, raised us, and taught us would seem to require no less. Yet there are times, say the authorities, when a child is physically or emotionally incapable of providing the proper care and supervision for the parent, and in those situations the child is permitted to hire others to provide that care. This is certainly the case today, when complex and specialized treatment regimens far beyond the ability of the family are prescribed for the aged and infirm. The best that can be said, perhaps, is that in every case of this nature the children should carefully examine their own motives. If they are certain that their intended course of action is not undertaken out of selfish desires but rather truly for the good of the parent, then that action adheres to the standards of honor and reverence.

Kashrut and Reform Judaism

Many Reform Jews observe certain traditional dietary disciplines as part of their attempt to establish a Jewish home and life style. Each Jewish family should study *kashrut* and consider whether it may enhance the sanctity of their home.

The above statement taken from *Gates of Mitzvah* represents a revolution in the religious thought of North American Reform Judaism. Through most of its history the Reform movement has been closely identified with the rejection of *kashrut*, the traditional Jewish dietary laws. In 1885, the framers of the Pittsburgh Platform stated this position in no uncertain terms:

> We hold that all such Mosaic and Rabbinical laws as regulate diet, priestly purity, and dress originated in ages and under the influence of ideas altogether foreign to our present mental and spiritual state. They fail to impress the modern Jew with a spirit of priestly holiness; their observance in our days is apt rather to obstruct than to further modern spiritual elevation.

Although both the Columbus Platform of 1937 and the Centenary Perspective of 1976 take a more positive stance toward ceremonial observance than does their predecessor, neither mentions the dietary laws at all, let alone favorably. None of this meant that Reform Jews were somehow forbidden to "keep kosher" or that no Reform Jews ever chose to do so. It implied, however, that in the eyes of Reform Judaism the observance of the dietary laws was at best irrelevant to a proper conception of liberal Jewish religious life. Reform Jewish leaders and thinkers were, when not openly hostile, at least supremely indifferent to the entire issue. This indifference is reflected in the fact that out of nearly 1100 published Reform responsa we find only one *teshuvah* which deals with a substantive matter of *kashrut* and that Rabbi Solomon B. Freehof's comprehensive *Reform Jewish Practice* does not refer to the subject at all. At no time prior to 1979 did any official Reform rabbinic document suggest that Reform Jews ought to think positively about the observance of *kashrut* or consider adopting it into their religious lives.

Gates of Mitzvah effectively reverses this trend. The book marks the first time that an "official" American Reform movement publication has looked favorably upon *kashrut* as a religious option. With the publication of *Gates of Mitzvah*, it is no longer the movement's official position that the dietary laws offer no spiritual meaning to today's Reform Jew. This means that while some Reform Jews will continue to find nothing of value in the observance of *kashrut*, those who do are encouraged to adopt it as a *mitzvah* which enhances the sanctity of the home.

What accounts for this change to a more positive attitude? It stems, first and foremost, from an acknowledgment of historical and religious fact: *kashrut* has been a basic element of Judaism for too long for Reform Jews—as Jews—to ignore. Put differently, we have come to recognize that Reform practice does not exist in isolation from historical Jewish religious experience, nor does it trace its roots exclusively to the European Enlightenment of the late-eighteenth century. If Reform Judaism has done away with certain aspects of traditional observance, it does not declare its independence from tradition itself. Reform religious expression takes shape rather within the broader context of historical *Jewish* religious life, and the centrality of *kashrut* to Jewish religious life can hardly be overstated. Since biblical times, the Jews have recognized a very real religious dimension to the preparation and consumption of food; the Jewish response to God's call has always included a dietary regimen. Through the discipline of *kashrut*, Jews have traditionally imposed sanctity upon the most elemental human necessity, transforming the physical act of eating into a symbolic sacrifice to God. As Jews, we are part of that tradition, that historical continuity, and this implies that the traditional Jewish sense of the holy is not foreign to us. It no longer makes sense to declare, by dint of "reason" or "enlightenment," that the dietary laws *cannot* be a source of spiritual fulfillment to the Reform Jew. On the contrary: it is more reasonable for a movement which sees itself as an authentic expression of Jewish religiosity to urge its members to think about *kashrut* as an authentic mode of Jewish observance and to consider the value of bringing its practice into their homes and lives.

There are any number of compelling "reasons" that might motivate a Reform Jew to adopt *kashrut*. Some of these are: 1) identification with the contemporary and historical Jewish religious experience; 2) the authority of the religious tradition itself, both biblical and rabbinic; 3) a desire to have a home in which any Jew might feel free to eat; 4) a desire to place limits upon one's diet as an expression of ethical responsibility toward nature.

For Reform Jews, the decision to choose *kashrut* as a mode of religious life is not an "all or nothing" option. The dietary laws involve several major rubrics: the abstention from "forbidden species" of meat, such as pork and shellfish and products made from those species; the separation of meat and dairy products; the consumption of kosher meat, that is, meat slaughtered and prepared according to ritual requirements. Reform Jews may decide to observe all of these practices, some of them, or even none of them. They may decide to observe them at all times or only when dining at home. Some Reform Jews believe that a vegetarian diet, based upon a refusal to slaughter animals for food, sanctifies their lives by showing reverence for nature.

Again, the choice is up to the individual or the household. Because *kashrut* can mean different things to different Reform Jews, and because no consensus has yet emerged within the movement as to the "best" decision a Reform Jew can make about it, the level of dietary observance is largely a matter of personal rather than communal decision. This state of affairs may or may not change in the future. One thing, though, can be said with certainty: the question of *kashrut* is no longer irrelevant to the discussion of Reform Jewish religious life.

Death and Mourning

> The Torah commands us to mourn when our relatives die.
> (Maimonides, *Yad, Avel* 1:1)

The above statement is a controversial one. The Bible contains no explicit statement that "thou shalt mourn," the literature of Talmud and Midrash never derives such an obligation from a biblical verse, and not all subsequent rabbis agree with Maimonides' claim that he has found one. Yet even if the Torah does not "command" us to mourn, it has much of importance to say to the mourner in times of tragedy. It teaches that God stands by us in our trial: "Though I walk through the valley of the shadow of death, I will fear no evil, for You are with me" (Ps. 23:4). It reminds us of the transience of grief, that life and hope will conquer despair: "Weeping may linger in the evening, but joy comes in the morning" (Ps. 30:6). And it instructs us therefore to be steadfast in our faith even when death should shake us to the core: "Adonai gives, and Adonai takes away; praised be the name of Adonai" (Job 1:21). From these sentiments, as well as from the descriptions of mourning practices which we do find in biblical literature, the Rabbis constructed a religious institution of great richness and complexity.

The importance of our mourning practices lies most obviously in the fact that they respond to our deepest spiritual and emotional needs as human beings. All of us experience loss and grief in our lives, and almost all of us, even those who are not religiously observant, tend to look toward the tradition for comfort, for its affirmation of hope against despair, and for its assurance that, even at the darkest times, life itself retains its sanctity. Mourning, too, is a predominant *public* concern of the Jewish people. Jewish communities invest considerable human and economic resources into the establishment and maintenance of burial societies, funeral homes, and cemeteries. All of this activity on the intellectual, individual, and social level testifies to the great care with which Judaism, as a way of life, has developed the means of expression whereby mourners can confront the reality of death and "channel emotions into a productive expression of grief." The goal of these practices is as exalted as it is simple: "To offer consolation in the face of death by reaffirming life, moving mourners slowly back to the normal routine of life." To achieve this aim, to heal the shattered, grief-stricken heart, is arguably the most important task that a religious tradition can possibly accept upon itself. Thus, even if his position cannot be proven on textual grounds, Maimonides may still be judged correct on the level of substance: the Torah could not have failed to instruct us in the need and the way to confront our grief. We must conclude that somehow in the deep resources of its teachings, the Torah *does* command us to mourn.

The Approach of Death

Visiting the Sick. It is a *mitzvah* to visit and to care for the sick (*bikkur cholim*). For details, see Chapter 6.

Confession. It is a *mitzvah* for the critically ill person to recite a special prayer, traditionally known as the Confession (*Vidui*), in contemplation of death. It is also a *mitzvah* for an individual (not necessarily a rabbi) to help the dying person to say this prayer or to recite it on his or her behalf. Texts of this prayer may be found in *On the Doorposts of Your House,* pp. 160–61, and the *Rabbi's Manual,* pp. 106–9.

Traditional literature requires that while we should encourage the dying to confess, we must not inform them of the gravity of their medical condition, "lest they weep and their heart break" and so hasten their death. Some Reform responsa concur with this position or slightly modify it, counseling that we tell patients of their critical or terminal condition when they repeatedly and explicitly request to know the truth. The most recent responsa take the view that, in general, it is to the patient's advantage to be informed of all aspects of his or her medical situation. In this way, the person may feel a sense of control over his or her destiny, which in turn can be a powerful boost to the morale and an aid in healing.

Ethical Wills. It is a *mitzvah* to prepare an ethical will for the moral edification of the family. Examples of such wills are found in *Gates of Mitzvah,* pp. 139–43.

From Death to Funeral

Keri'ah and *Tzidduk Hadin.* It is a *mitzvah* for those present at the patient's bedside to recite the following *berakhah* upon his or her death:

> *Barukh atah Adonai Eloheinu melekh ha'olam dayan ha'emet.*

> Blessed is Adonai our God, Sovereign of the universe, the Righteous Judge.

This blessing is called *Tzidduk Hadin,* "the justification of the decree," a statement of faith by which we affirm the ultimate goodness of God and God's world even in the face of grievous loss. The burial service is also called *Tzidduk Hadin,* since the proclamation of God's righteousness is a major theme of its liturgy (see *Rabbi's Manual,* pp. 152–53).

The mourner traditionally rends his or her garment upon witnessing or hearing of the death of a relative. The "mourner" is anyone who is obligated under *halakhah* to practice the rituals of mourning (*avelut*): that is, the parent, child, sibling, or spouse of the deceased. The rending of the garment, called *keri'ah*, is traditionally performed in a standing position. For most relatives, a tear in the length of one handbreadth is made in the right front side of the outermost garment of the upper body. For a parent, a tear is made in all one's garments over the left side, that is, until one's heart is bared. In Reform practice, the rite of *keri'ah* is left to the discretion of the mourners. Some do not perform it at all; others pin a torn black ribbon to the spot of the outer garment which is traditionally rent; others observe the traditional ritual in its entirety. It is customary for many Reform Jews to perform *keri'ah* immediately before the funeral service.

Aninut. The period between death and burial is called *aninut*, and the relative of the deceased is called *onen* or *onenet*. The *onen/et*'s sole preoccupation is to bury his or her dead; therefore, he or she is exempt from all positive religious obligations that might occur during that time. On Shabbat, when we do not bury the dead, the *onen/et* observes the normal obligations of a religious Jew.

The period of mourning begins with the burial of the deceased. Following the funeral, visitors are encouraged to pay their respects at the home of the mourners. Although it is a *mitzvah* to console the bereaved and to help them in any way we can, the hours or days before burial are not the proper time to make condolence calls. The custom of pre-funeral visitation in the chapel is contrary to Jewish tradition and is to be discouraged.

Funeral Preparations. Tradition forbids us from making specific funeral arrangements before a person's death. Nonetheless, more general preparations, such as the purchase of burial plots, should be done before the time of need.

Occasionally, a person will instruct relatives not to mourn for him or her. Are the relatives bound to honor that request? The answer depends upon whether we believe that these rites exist for the honor of the dead (*kevod hamet*) or for the honor of the living (*kevod hachayim*). Tradition regards some aspects of mourning—for example, the funeral eulogy—as serving the honor of the dead; therefore, the deceased may forego the honor, and we heed the instruction "do not eulogize me." The practices of *shivah* and *sheloshim* (the seven- and thirty-day periods of mourning) are more difficult to determine, since one can argue that these are performed either for the honor of the dead or for the living. The most prevalent attitude is that the concrete expression of grief upon the death of a loved one is a religious duty as well as a psychological necessity. In any event, when the deceased leaves instructions which seem to run counter to Jewish tradition, the mourners should consult the rabbi.

Preparation of the Body; Autopsy; Donation of Organs. Following its careful cleansing and washing, the body is wrapped in inexpensive white linen shrouds (*tachrichim*). This is true even for the leaders of the community, in order to avoid bringing shame upon those who cannot afford an opulent funeral. Reform Jews may observe these customs. In all cases, the body should be released to a reputable Jewish funeral director or *chevra kadisha*, a Jewish communal burial society, with instructions that it be prepared for burial. It is praiseworthy for Reform Jews to participate in the work of the *chevra kadisha*, whose function it is to wash, guard, and dress the body for burial. The contemporary funeral director represents in many ways the professionalization of the traditional *chevra kadisha*. While there is no prohibition against using the services of a non-Jewish funeral director, particularly when a comparable Jewish institution is not available, it is preferable to engage a Jewish mortician in fulfillment of the *mitzvah* of burial. We also encourage the formation of communal burial societies which encourage lower-cost funerals and distribute their profits to *tzedakah*.

Reform Judaism permits autopsies so long as they are clearly performed for the purpose of increasing medical knowledge. Jewish tradition tends to frown on autopsy because it is said to violate several ritual prohibitions: *nivul hamet*, desecration of a corpse; *hana'ah mehamet*, deriving benefit from the dead; and the unnecessary delay of burial. These objections may be waived in criminal investigations, when an autopsy is essential in the service of justice as a means of establishing the cause of death. Similarly, autopsy is permitted in cases of *pikuach nefesh*, when the information to be gleaned through the procedure may help save another's life. Yet most Orthodox authorities sanction autopsy only when the patient to be saved is "in our presence," that is, when there is a person here and now who can benefit from the results gained from the procedure. The possibility that someone, someday might be saved thereby is not, in their view, sufficient cause to override the prohibition. For this reason, most halakhists forbid routine autopsy even for the purpose of medical education. The Reform view is that the study of medicine is most certainly an instance of *pikuach nefesh*. If autopsy is an essential feature of medical education, it makes little sense to declare that we approve of the saving of life but not of the means by which medical professionals are trained to accomplish that goal. Moreover, in our day of rapid transportation and instantaneous communication, once-important considerations of time and place are now irrelevant. The entire world is "in our presence," and we can be sure that there are patients who can benefit from the knowledge to be gained through autopsy. It is therefore unreasonable to place geographical or chronological boundaries upon the right of medical professionals to take action to preserve human life.

Our position presumes that the remains will be treated with the respect due to the human body (*kevod hamet*). The burial of the parts of the body should be arranged as soon as possible following the procedure.

For similar considerations, Reform Judaism approves the donation of the organs of one's body for the purpose of transplantation, either to save a life or to heal a deficiency. An individual may also donate his or her entire body to science, provided that the institution which is to receive the body is known to treat the body with respect and that, when the study is completed, the remains are buried or cremated.

Closing the Coffin. Jewish tradition is opposed to the practice of public viewing of the deceased in an open coffin. The family may, if they wish, view the body privately, but the coffin must be closed before the funeral service begins.

Embalming. Jewish tradition frowns upon embalming, both as a foreign custom and as an unnecessary delay in the body's decomposition. Death, as the end of one's physical existence on this earth, means that one "returns unto the dust." The traditional beliefs concerning immortality relate to the soul, spirit, or mind; no purpose is served in preserving the physical human body through chemical means. When a funeral must be delayed or when the body must be shipped elsewhere for burial, legal requirements may make embalming a necessity. When this happens, care should be taken to avoid any disrespectful treatment of the body (*nivul hamet*). The body's organs and blood, when removed for legally-required embalming, should be preserved for burial.

The Funeral Service and Burial

Burial; Cremation; Entombment. It is a *mitzvah* to bury the dead with all proper respect. Jewish tradition defines this *mitzvah* as the burial of the body in the earth. While Jewish dead were once interred in caves or mausoleums, burial in the ground has for centuries been the normative practice, regarded as the most direct means for "returning the body to the earth." Objections to mausoleum interment might be met by surrounding the coffin in its casing with earth. Burial at sea is contrary to Jewish tradition and should be avoided except in cases of dire emergency.

Some Reform Jews have adopted the practice of cremation. While this method of handling the dead is certainly contrary to Jewish tradition, there is no clear-cut prohibition of cremation in the halakhic literature. Cremation can be justified religiously in that it rapidly achieves the decomposition of the body. Ecological arguments, too, can be offered for it. It has been opposed, on the other hand, as a denial of faith in bodily resurrection; as an unnecessary imitation of Gentile practice; and as a reminder of the fate of our people in the crematoria of the Holocaust. The Reform rabbinate seeks to discourage cremation, when possible, in favor of the more traditionally Jewish practice. When a family has decided upon cremation, however, Reform rabbis do not refuse to officiate at the service.

Responsibility for Burial. The *mitzvah* to bury the dead is incumbent first of all upon the heirs of the deceased. A spouse buries the deceased spouse. In the event that no heirs are available to provide for burial, that responsibility falls upon the community as a whole. If the family can afford to pay the funeral expenses, the community is entitled to levy a charge for those services. In the event of poverty, the community provides the funeral.

Timely Burial. Jewish tradition strongly emphasizes the need for speedy burial, regarding the delay of burial (*halanat hamet*) as an act of disrespect to the dead. Delay is permitted in order to make adequate preparations for the funeral and to allow the mourners to gather.

Days When Burial Does Not Take Place. Funerals do not take place on Shabbat, Rosh Hashanah, Yom Kippur, or *yom tov* (the major days of the festivals), since on these days Jews traditionally abstain from the kinds of labor required as part of the burial process. Some leniencies apply to Rosh Hashanah and *yom tov,* but we observe the widespread custom not to bury the dead on those days. While *halakhah* permits Jews to perform the labor of burial on the second day of the festival, the sensitivities of some relatives may argue against holding the funeral on that day; the rabbi should be consulted. Funerals may take place on all other days.

Arrangements. Simplicity and dignity govern the funeral arrangements. The dead are dressed in plain linen shrouds rather than in expensive garments that testify to the deceased's wealth and social position. It is preferable to use a simple wooden coffin, both because of its lack of ostentation and because wood does not excessively retard the decomposition of the body. Coffins made of other materials are acceptable, but again, simplicity of design and construction is the rule. Flowers are not utilized as decorations at many Jewish funerals. While Reform practice does not forbid flowers, the same rules of simplicity and dignity govern their use. Families are encouraged to request that gifts to *tzedakah* be made in lieu of flowers.

The Funeral Service. A liturgy for the funeral is found in the *Rabbi's Manual,* pp. 111–62. The service, like the blessing recited before the rending of the garment, is referred to as *Tzidduk Hadin,* the acceptance of the divine decree: even now, in our grief, when we cannot perceive the justice of God, we declare our faith that, in spite of everything, justice shall triumph and our consolation will come. It is a *mitzvah* to attend a funeral service (*halvayat hamet*). Even the study of Torah is postponed in order to assist in the burial of the dead. Traditionally, this is understood as the service of burial itself. If the mourners schedule a private interment, the *mitzvah* can be fulfilled by attending a service at a chapel or a funeral home.

Funeral services are sometimes held entirely at graveside. Frequently, however, a service will be held at a funeral home or at some other location prior to the procession to the cemetery. Some communities permit funeral services to be held in the synagogue and allow the coffin to be present there during the service. Some observe the custom of halting the funeral procession at the synagogue so that an appropriate prayer such as *El Malei Rachamim* might be said.

It is a *mitzvah* to speak well of the dead. The eulogy (*hesped*) is a central feature of the funeral service. "What is a proper *hesped*? One lifts the voice to describe the deceased so as to break the heart, to inspire tears, to speak his praise," provided that the speaker does not exaggerate that praise beyond reason. Reform Judaism permits eulogies to be recited on any day.

Most Reform communities do not observe the custom of *ma'amadot*, halting the cortege seven times during the recitation of *Tzidduk Hadin*. The seven halts are said to correspond to the seven times that the word *hevel* ("vanity" or "emptiness") occurs at the beginning of the book of Ecclesiastes.

The funeral service consists of three major liturgical elements: *Tzidduk Hadin*, the prayer *El Malei Rachamim*, and the *Burial Kaddish*. Customs vary as to the order of these elements. In some communities, they are all recited prior to the burial; in others, burial precedes the liturgy. Tradition prescribes that the mourners remain at the graveside for the lowering of the coffin and the refilling of the grave. Some follow the custom of helping to fill the grave. If the family chooses not to remain at the cemetery for the completion of the burial, a representative should remain behind until the grave has been completely filled.

The mourners of the deceased recite *Kaddish* at the graveside. Reform Judaism encourages but does not require a *minyan* for the recitation of *Kaddish*. When the mourners leave the graveside, it is customary to have them pass through two rows of those attending, who recite to them the traditional words of consolation:

> *HaMakom yinachem etchem betokh she'ar avelei tziyon virushalayim.*

> May God grant you comfort among all those who mourn for Zion and Jerusalem.

Some individuals will observe, upon leaving the cemetery, the customs of plucking up some grass and earth, casting these behind them, and reciting the verses Psalms 72:16 and 103:14, which contrast the eternity of the spirit with the mortality of life on earth. Some will wash their hands and recite the verse Isaiah 25:8 ("May God swallow up death forever").

Special Situations

Burial of Non-Jews. Reform Judaism permits the burial of the non-Jewish family members of Jews in Jewish cemeteries. The interment is accompanied by a liturgy of our own devising; under no circumstances should a non-Jewish religious burial service be used, nor should any non-Jewish religious symbolism be displayed during the funeral or on the tombstone. This permit is restricted to the family members of Jews. Other non-Jews, including a prospective convert who had not yet completed the process of becoming a Jew, are not buried in Jewish cemeteries. The funeral service for a non-Jew is not held in the synagogue.

Burial of Jews in Non-Jewish Cemeteries. Since the establishment of particularly Jewish cemeteries is a long-standing custom in our tradition, we strongly encourage that Jews bury their dead in Jewish cemeteries. If a community cannot afford its own cemetery, the Jewish graves may be located in a separate section of the general cemetery, spaced or hedged from the other graves. An exception is burial in a national military cemetery when that cemetery is considered the property of all citizens and is in no sense associated with another religion.

When the burial takes place in a non-Jewish cemetery, a rabbi will officiate, provided that the funeral service is Jewish.

Burial of Apostates. We bury the apostate Jew in a Jewish cemetery, since every Jew, including those who have separated themselves from the community, deserves a proper burial. However, many of the honors normally bestowed upon the memory of the dead, such as the eulogy, are withheld from the apostate. We are obliged to care for the relatives of the apostate, since the comfort of mourners is a duty we owe to the living rather than to the dead.

A special stringency exists in the case of Messianic Jews, since their theology, which gives the unacceptable impression that Christianity is an acceptable form of Judaism, is particularly offensive and dangerous to the Jewish community. We treat Messianic Jews as Christians and not as apostates, so long as they do not return to Judaism; we do not bury them in our cemeteries.

Burial of Suicides. We bury suicides in a Jewish cemetery. The ancient prohibition against doing so is based upon the conception of suicide as the conscious and willful taking of one's life. Over time, however, Jewish tradition has come to view suicide as the result of mental and emotional desperation and, virtually by definition, an irrational, non-willful act. Jewish law puts an extraordinarily strict construction upon the definition of "suicide"; therefore, even if all evidence points to suicide and even if that evidence satisfies the investigative authorities as to the cause of death, our custom is to bury these individuals, to engage in mourning rituals for them, and to eulogize them appropriately.

Burial of the "Wicked." It is a *mitzvah* to conduct a regular funeral service for all Jews, regardless of the style of their lives. All should be treated with respect and buried in the Jewish cemetery in the midst of their families. While tradition suggests that the "wicked" should not be buried next to the righteous, this law pertains to the days of the ancient Sanhedrin, the high court which had the power to apply these judgments to individuals. Today, the *mitzvah* of burial and respect takes precedence.

Rites of Fraternal Orders. Non-Jewish religious liturgy should not be used at Jewish funerals. We do not regard the ceremonial rites of most fraternal orders as "religious" practices. We therefore permit them, provided that such rites be placed at the end of the service so that they do not detract from the primacy of the Jewish mood or message.

The Cemetery

Reverence. In a technical sense, the tradition does not recognize the existence of a distinct entity known as a "Jewish cemetery" as the proper place for Jewish burial. The requirement is merely that an individual be buried *betokh shelo*, in property that he or she owns, and this need not be located within a plot of ground specially fenced-off for this purpose. As such, a "Jewish cemetery" is simply a cluster of Jewish graves; it is not a special area, let alone a "sacred" one, defined by rules that distinguish it from all other space.

The historical custom of the Jewish people, however, has taken a different direction. In practice, the cemetery *is* a special place, and we relate to it as such. The *halakhah* does not require that Jewish communities acquire ground to establish cemeteries, as it *does* require them to establish synagogues, but Jews have tended from the very beginnings of their settlement in a particular town or region to make the purchase of land for a cemetery one of their first communal acts. And although the classical sources do not speak of a formal service of dedication for a cemetery, it has become customary in recent centuries to arrange such a service. The entire cemetery, both the graves and the land which is set aside for future burials, is treated with the utmost respect, with the reverence normally accorded the synagogue. While it is permitted to pray in the cemetery, it is inappropriate to hold public worship services there on a regular basis or to bring a Torah scroll onto the grounds.

Reverence implies the prohibition against deriving material benefit (*hana'ah*) from the grave or from anything connected with the burial. From this prohibition, some learn that it is likewise forbidden to walk across graves, since that, too, is a "benefit" to be avoided. In general, though, walking across a grave is permitted so long as this is a temporary, chance crossing and is not done in an attitude of disrespect.

Ownership. Jewish communities historically have made great efforts to own outright the land on which they bury their dead. Again, this is not an absolute requirement of Jewish law, which prescribes simply that the deceased own the grave in which he or she is buried. Yet the custom to own the cemetery itself has prevailed, and tradition today frowns upon the sale of any unused part of cemetery land. Nonetheless, a Jewish community may bury its dead in a Jewish section of a general cemetery. The Jewish section should be separated from the general section by a wall, a fence, or an evergreen hedge that will indicate the separation all through the year.

A community that acquires and maintains a cemetery has the right to govern its use. So long as proper provisions are made for the burial of the poor and indigent, a community may restrict the use of its cemetery to members of the synagogue or to those who affiliate with the community by a specified means.

Although it is the property of its sponsoring organization, there is no objection to naming a cemetery after an individual. This should, however, be done in full cognizance of the feelings and sensitivities of the community.

The Grave. The graves in the cemetery may be aligned in any direction, although it is customary that the graves in any one section all face in a uniform direction.

It is generally forbidden to bury two persons in a single grave. Each must have his or her own resting place. The exception is the burial of a small child "who slept with its parent in life" along with the parent. It is also forbidden, generally, to bury one coffin on top of another, even when space in the cemetery is at a premium. If, however, at least six handbreadths of earth separate the two coffins, it is permitted to bury one on top of the other.

Cremains may be buried in a Jewish cemetery. Indeed, cemetery burial is the most proper means of disposing of the ashes. The ashes of each individual should be buried separately, in a manner similar to bodies, and not intermingled with those of others.

Disinterment. Jewish tradition frowns upon disinterment as a dishonor to the dead. Exceptions to this rule include disinterment for reburial in a family plot, in a Jewish cemetery, or in the land of Israel. Similarly, if the deceased had given instructions prior to death that he or she be reburied in another grave, those instructions are honored. If there is concern that floods, vandalism, or some other calamity will desecrate the graves, the dead may be reinterred in a safer burial place. If disinterment is indicated in order to collect legal evidence, particularly in a capital case, the exhumation is permitted. If a body is removed from a grave, that grave may be used for the burial of another.

No special ritual is required when the body is reinterred. However, some suggest that the relatives observe the rites of mourning until sundown that day.

Mourning

Jewish tradition prescribes several periods of mourning (*avelut*), differing in intensity and in level of obligation. In the Reform view, the observances of the mourning period exist as a means of helping us to confront our grief, to work through it, and ultimately to return to the "land of the living" with a renewed spirit and determination to lead lives of goodness. The customs of *avelut*, in other words, come to benefit the mourners and not to subject them to excessive, empty discipline. Thus, while we encourage mourners to adopt the traditional practices of *avelut* in solidarity with Jews around the world and throughout countless generations, we counsel them to do so in ways that will actually be helpful in bringing comfort to them in their distress.

We have already seen that the period between death and burial is referred to as *aninut*. The period of mourning as such begins with the closing of the grave and the return from the cemetery.

Shivah, "seven," refers to the seven days following the funeral. The first day of *shivah* is the day of the funeral itself, lasting from the burial until sundown. *Shivah* concludes after *Shacharit* (morning) services on the seventh day. Mourning begins with the meal of consolation (*se'udat havra'ah*) supplied to and prepared for the mourners by friends upon their return from the cemetery. The meal, and the entire *shivah* period, should not be an occasion for lavish feasting and the serving of refreshments to all who visit the home, but rather a time for family and close friends to come together to lend their strength to the bereaved.

A memorial candle is kindled in the home upon the return from the cemetery and is kept burning throughout *shivah*. During *shivah*, mourners are encouraged to remain at home, except for Shabbat and holidays, when the mourner attends services at synagogue. The first three days of *shivah* are considered the most intense period of mourning. During that time, tradition forbids mourners to work even if they are poor. For the rest of *shivah*, the mourner may work privately at home if economic necessity forces this. Three days are the minimum period of mourning in Reform Judaism, and in some communities they have taken the place of *shivah* as a whole. This, however, is not the desirable norm: Reform Jews ought to observe all seven days of *shivah*.

Traditionally, mourners during *shivah* wear the garment or ribbon which was torn in the ritual of *keri'ah* and sit on low stools or on the floor of the house. They observe several traditional *inuyim*, or personal "afflictions": they do not wear leather shoes, bathe or anoint themselves except for hygienic reasons, engage in sexual intercourse, or inquire about the welfare of another. These prohibitions have been officially disregarded in Reform practice since the Breslau rabbinical conference of 1846. The wishes of the family, however, are paramount, and the mourners are encouraged to express their sadness through the traditional prohibitions should they find it meaningful to do so.

During *shivah*, worship services should be conducted at the house of mourning, that is, the home of the deceased or, if this is not possible, at the home of a designated family member. These are the regular daily worship services, which afford the mourners an opportunity to recite *Kaddish* as well. While a *minyan* is not an absolute requirement for reciting *Kaddish* in Reform Jewish practice, it is certainly encouraged, and efforts should be made to secure a *minyan* for the home service. While the service need not be led by a rabbi, it is considered proper for a learned person to deliver a *devar torah* or message of consolation from sacred literature.

Sheloshim, "thirty," is the thirty-day period following the funeral. *Shivah* is the first seven days of *sheloshim.* During the next twenty-three days, the ritual restrictions of mourning are less severe. One may return to work, for example, but one should avoid joyful social gatherings and entertainments. Mourners should not hold their wedding during *sheloshim* unless plans had been firmly made and delay would cause an undue hardship. In any event, the wedding should not take place during *shivah.* Mourners may attend the wedding of their children, along with the wedding meal, but they should avoid participating in the entertainments. A child who has lost a parent may observe Bar/Bat Mitzvah during *shivah* or *sheloshim,* although the accompanying festivities should be either canceled or appropriately subdued.

Shabbat, Yom Tov, and Mourning. Shabbat is one of the seven days of *shivah* and does not cancel it. On the Sabbath, mourners do not observe the outward, public signs of *avelut* (*devarim shebefarhesya*). They wear their normal Shabbat clothes; they do not wear the torn garment or ribbon. They attend synagogue, where it is traditional for the congregation to offer them comfort immediately following the singing of *Lekha Dodi* on Friday night. It is customary not to call the mourner to the Torah or to lead services in the synagogue during *shivah* (although the mourner may lead services in the home). On the other hand, the private and inward practices of mourning (*devarim shebetzina*) are observed at home on Shabbat.

A *yom tov* (Pesach, Shavuot, Sukkot, Rosh Hashanah, Yom Kippur) cancels *shivah.* For example, if the burial takes place on the afternoon before the onset of the *yom tov*, mourning is observed for one hour and the holiday cancels the observance of *shivah. Chol hamo'ed* (the intermediate days of the festival) are counted as part of *sheloshim,* even though one does not traditionally observe the outward signs of mourning on those days. Thus, if the burial took place on the day before Pesach, *shivah* ends with the beginning of the festival. The seven days of Pesach count as part of the remaining twenty-three days of *sheloshim,* leaving a total of sixteen days out of *sheloshim* to be observed at the conclusion of the festival. If a *yom tov* occurs after *shivah* has ended, it cancels the remainder of *sheloshim*. Thus, if burial takes place on the day before Rosh Hashanah, Rosh Hashanah cancels *shivah* and Yom Kippur will cancel the rest of *sheloshim*.

These calculations embody a powerful religious message: the mourner does not cease to be a Jew, a member of the covenant community, even during his or her sadness. Jews are traditionally obliged to rejoice on the festival, and that obligation is incumbent as well upon the mourner. However, the cancellation of the period of *avelut* may exact a heavy emotional toll upon the survivors, who are denied the opportunity to express their grief along the lines specified by Jewish tradition. For example, when burial occurs the day before Yom Kippur, the Day of Atonement cancels *shivah* and Sukkot cancels *sheloshim*. The mourners will therefore have observed *shivah* for less than one day and *sheloshim* for less than four days. In order to allow for a proper period of mourning, Reform Judaism permits the mourners to adopt the private and inward observances of *shivah* at the conclusion of the festival should they so wish. Similarly, when the burial occurs during *chol hamo'ed*, although *shivah* does not traditionally start until the conclusion of the festival, we may encourage that it be held during the intermediate days.

The Twelve Months. During the twelve-month period following the death of a parent, one recites *Kaddish* and traditionally avoids festive meals and entertainments.

Kaddish. It is a *mitzvah* for mourners to recite the *Kaddish* in memory of the dead at home services during *shivah* and in synagogue thereafter. If there are no daily services in the vicinity, mourners may recite *Kaddish* at home or privately. For a parent, one says *Kaddish* for a full year; for other relatives, one recites *Kaddish* until the end of *sheloshim*. The *mitzvah* is incumbent upon the mourners themselves and is not fulfilled by engaging someone else to recite *Kaddish* in one's place.

Structure and Practice. Kaddish began not as a memorial prayer for the dead—its text, indeed, makes no mention of the subject—but as a declaration of God's praise and of hope in the coming of the messianic kingdom. In its original, shorter form it was recited at the conclusion of sermons of *aggadah* (homiletical lessons on the Torah). Since the preachers delivered these sermons in Aramaic, the vernacular of their audience, the *Kaddish* itself was recited in that language, and the fact that we continue to say *Kaddish* in Aramaic testifies to the liturgical and ritual power of this prayer. Later, we find congregations reciting *Kaddish* at the conclusion of the Torah reading and following the study of rabbinic literature, at the end of the *Tefillah*, and as a kind of punctuation between the different sections or rubrics of the service. The theme of consolation (*nechemta*) may have encouraged the use of *Kaddish* as a memorial prayer, the *Mourner's* (or *"Orphan's"*) *Kaddish* (*Kaddish Yatom*), a custom that developed later than these other usages.

In traditional prayer books, the *Kaddish* appears in various forms depending upon its liturgical function. All forms include the paragraphs beginning with *yitgadal* ("May God's great name be exalted") and *yitbarakh* ("May the name of the Holy One be praised"), which surround the congregational response *yehei shemei rabbah . . .* ("May the great name of God be praised").

1. The *"Full Kaddish"* (*Kaddish Shalem*), which adds the passages *titkabal tzelotehon* ("May the prayers of all Israel be accepted . . ."), *yehei shelama rabbah* ("May abundant peace . . ."), and *oseh shalom bimeromav* (in Hebrew: "May the One who makes peace in the Heavens . . ."), is recited at the conclusion of the *Tefillah*.

2. The *"Half Kaddish"* (*Chatzi Kaddish*) or *"Reader's Kaddish"* omits all but the first three passages and is said prior to *Keri'at Shema* (the recitation of Shema; that is, immediately before *Barekhu*), as an introduction to the *Musaf* prayer, at the conclusion of the Torah reading, and at other times.

3. The *"Rabbis' Kaddish"* (*Kaddish Derabbanan*) substitutes the passage *al yisrael ve'al rabbnan* ("May abundant peace be upon Israel and its Torah scholars . . .") for *titkabal* and is recited after the study of a passage of Talmud or other rabbinic literature.

4. The *"Great Kaddish"* (or *"Burial Kaddish"*), whose first paragraph includes an expansion on messianic themes, is traditionally recited at funerals or at the conclusion of the study of an entire tractate of the Talmud.

5. The *Mourner's Kaddish* (*Kaddish Yatom*) omits the passage *titkabal*. It is said by the mourners in attendance at the service, who also customarily recite the *Kaddish Derabbanan* at the appropriate times.

In a traditional service, *Kaddish* is therefore recited many times. The *Mourner's Kaddish* in particular is repeated often (after *Aleinu*, the Psalm of the Day, and various other readings), due to its popularity and enduring appeal. Reform Judaism has greatly reduced the number of times that *Kaddish* is recited. Indeed, the *Union Prayer Book* preserves only one *Kaddish* per service: the *Mourner's Kaddish*. This reflected the reality that despite its complex history and varied usage the *Kaddish* is best known as a memorial prayer. More than that: while the text of the traditional *Kaddish Yatom* focuses exclusively upon consolation and hope and does not mention death at all, the *Union Prayer Book*'s version includes a paragraph which beseeches God's blessings upon the departed. This paragraph was frequently omitted in Reform synagogues, where congregants preferred to recite the more traditional text, and it does not appear in *Gates of Prayer* and *Gates of Repentance*. The latter prayer books, too, restore the *Chatzi Kaddish* as an introduction to *Barekhu* and the recitation of *Shema*.

Reform congregations stand as a whole for *Kaddish*, and many tend to recite it in unison, in view of the fact that, after the Holocaust, there are many Jews who have no one but ourselves to say *Kaddish* for them.

Special Circumstances

1. *The Stillborn and the Infant.* Jewish law does not require mourning for a stillborn or miscarried fetus (*nefel*), since the fetus is not considered a viable human person. A *nefel* is any infant which dies within thirty days of birth, provided it is certain that the pregnancy had not yet reached its full term. If, however, the fetus had gestated for nine months, the parents are required to mourn even if it dies immediately upon birth. This detail of observance is considered a leniency in that it spares the family the disciplines involved in *shivah* and *sheloshim*. On the other hand, many families might wish to practice the rites of mourning, in full or in part, as a means of dealing with a grief that can be as painful as that experienced over the loss of any loved one. The tradition, we should note, *permits* one to observe mourning even for persons toward whom one is not *obliged* to

mourn. We would encourage families in this situation to consult with their rabbi.

2. *Gentile Relatives.* "The proselyte is like a newborn child." The Jew-by-choice, according to this powerful talmudic statement, is a brand-new person whose life is indelibly transformed from what it was before. One traditional implication of this idea is that *halakhah* does not recognize any legal bonds between the proselyte and his or her Gentile relatives. Many authorities therefore hold that the convert is not required, and indeed may be forbidden to say *Kaddish* for or to mourn those relatives. Yet Jewish law also declares that proselytes are duty-bound to show honor and respect to their parents, for conversion to Judaism does not relieve one of an elemental moral responsibility recognized by all faiths and cultures. Since honoring one's parents includes the *mitzvah* of mourning and memory, Reform Judaism permits and encourages the Jew-by-choice to recite *Kaddish* and to observe the rites of mourning for his or her non-Jewish parents and relatives.

3. *Adopted Children.* Relatives by adoption are required to recite *Kaddish* and to observe the rites of mourning for each other.

4. *Criminals; Abusive Relationships.* A child is required to honor his or her parents. This includes the obligation to say *Kaddish* for the parent even if the latter was a criminal or acted in an abusive way toward the child. The rites of burial and mourning are seen by tradition as a means of effecting the deceased's atonement for sin; thus, although one may act in such a way as to forfeit the honor owed by one's children, the children ought to mourn and say *Kaddish*. In this way, they can confront the bitterness of the relationship and hopefully come to feel at peace with the parent's memory. Since this issue is a matter of dispute within the tradition, however, the child of a criminal or an abusive parent is encouraged to consult with a rabbi.

5. *Delayed Funeral.* When burial is delayed beyond a reasonable period (for example, if the person died while in another country and the body cannot be returned home quickly), the observances of *shivah* begin once the body has been placed in an appropriate coffin. When the deceased is to be transported to another place for burial,

mourners not accompanying the body begin *shivah* once they have turned away from the funeral procession back to their homes.

If a person has disappeared and is presumed dead, *shivah* begins from the moment that the family has given up hope of recovering the body.

6. *Delayed News of a Death.* If one hears of the death of a relative within thirty days of burial, the news is called *shemu'ah kerovah*, "timely news"; *keri'ah* takes place and *shivah* begins upon receipt of the report. If one receives the report more than thirty days after the burial (*shemu'ah rechokah*, "delayed news"), one is traditionally obligated to observe mourning for but a short time on the day the news is received.

Yahrzeit and Yizkor

It is a *mitzvah* to observe *yahrzeit*, the anniversary of the day of death, by reciting *Kaddish* and attending synagogue services. As its Yiddish name implies, *yahrzeit* originated as an Ashkenazic observance in the Middle Ages, although similar customs are observed by Sefardic Jews, some of whom refer to the anniversary of a death as *nachalah*. It is customary to light a memorial candle on the *yahrzeit*. If candles are unavailable, an electric light may be used. On Shabbat or *yom tov*, the kindling should take place prior to the kindling of the Shabbat or festival lights.

In Reform practice, the names of the dead are often recited in the synagogue on the Shabbat nearest the *yahrzeit*. While some Reform Jews observe *yahrzeit* on the anniversary of the secular date of death, it is preferable to observe the Hebrew date. If the death occurred in the month of Adar, the *yahrzeit* is observed in Adar I during a leap year. If the death occurred during Adar II in a leap year, the *yahrzeit* is observed in Adar II in all subsequent leap years.

Yizkor, or the memorial service, is recited by the congregation on Yom Kippur, the last day of Pesach, Shavuot, and on Shemini Atzeret/Simchat Torah. Congregations which observe two days of a festival will hold *Yizkor* on the second day of Shavuot and on the first day of Shemini Atzeret/Simchat Torah. It is a *mitzvah* to attend these services and to recite *Kaddish* for one's deceased relatives. We do not encourage the custom of keeping children whose parents are alive away from *Yizkor* services. Young people should be taught the Jewish way of remembering the dead.

The Tombstone. It is a *mitzvah* to erect a marker or a tombstone (*matzevah*) in memory of the dead. In most communities, the mourners wait for a year before placing a monument at the grave, on the principle that no memorial is necessary during the first year when the death is so recent. Local custom, however, often encourages that the marker be placed within the year.

The monument should be a simple one, containing the Hebrew as well as the English name of the deceased. Various materials may be used to construct it, and various kinds of inscriptions may be permitted; in each case, local custom and standards of decorum are decisive. It may be set either at the head or the foot of the grave, although cemeteries will usually insist upon uniform placement of all markers. A marker may be erected in the absence of a body, in the event the body of the deceased cannot be found or when tombstones must be moved from ravaged cemeteries.

Jewish law and tradition require no special ritual for the setting or unveiling of a tombstone. Since, however, it has become customary to do so, special liturgies are provided in the *Rabbi's Manual*, pp. 165–79, and *On the Doorposts of Your House*, pp. 181–91. Once the marker is set, it becomes part of the grave and is therefore forbidden for other use.

Visiting the Cemetery. It is customary to visit the graves of loved ones before the High Holidays, though not on days of rest and joy such as Shabbat and *yom tov*. Many congregations hold memorial services at the cemetery during these visits. Liturgies are included in the *Rabbi's Manual*, pp. 180–89.

Although certain days such as *yahrzeit* are regarded as appropriate for visiting the cemetery, there is no prohibition against visiting prior to the anniversary of death or during *sheloshim*.

5

Conversion

The Jew-by-Choice

But Ruth replied, "Do not urge me to leave you, to turn back and not follow you. For wherever you go, I will go; wherever you lodge, I will lodge; your people shall be my people, and your God my God. Where you die, I will die, and there I will be buried." (Ruth 1:16–17)

In Jewish tradition, Ruth is the model of the *ger tzedek*, the "true proselyte." Pledging to follow her mother-in-law Naomi back to Judah rather than remain with her own Moabite family, Ruth does more than change her address. In the view of the Rabbis, she adopts a new faith, a new nationality, a new identity. Seeking to build their true home among the Jewish community, she and all those who choose Judaism are "like a newborn child," born this time within the covenant, claiming their share of the heritage of Israel. And because he or she is a brand new human being, it is customary to call the Jew-by-choice "the son/daughter of Abraham and Sarah," the progenitors of the Jewish people, for as the midrash teaches, they created *new lives* by bringing others into the covenant that God had established.

That one born a Gentile can choose to become a full member of the Jewish people is, in some ways, a radical notion. The Bible itself does not know of the institution of "conversion," whereby an individual freely adopts the religion of Israel and becomes a full-fledged member of the community. The Hebrew word for "convert," *ger* (fem. *giyoret*), is the word the Bible uses for the "resident alien," the "stranger" who sojourns in a land not his own. Under biblical law, the *ger* does take part to some extent in the religious life of the community, and when he does, the same law applies to him as to the Israelite. The Torah demands as well that we guarantee the *ger* justice and economic protection. Yet these very requirements testify to the *ger*'s essential inequality in the society. He requires our care and concern precisely because he is a powerless "stranger" who, like the widow and the orphan, is especially vulnerable to economic and social oppression. And in one important respect, the *ger*'s status is inferior to that of the widow and the orphan; since he has no Israelite family, he enjoys no share in the land, the ultimate source of prosperity and social standing. The Torah does command us to love the stranger, because we were "strangers in the land of Egypt"; yet with all that, the *ger* remains a stranger in our midst just as *we* were aliens in a foreign land.

By rabbinic times, however, the word *ger* had come to mean a "proselyte," one who has adopted the religion of Israel. The Talmud speaks of the *ger tzedek*, the "true proselyte," a "naturalized citizen" of the Jewish commonwealth. This citizenship requires that the proselyte undergo a formal ceremony whose rituals evoke the experience of our ancestors who received the Torah at Sinai. This teaches, the Rabbis tell us, that the *ger* has the same portion and stake in the God of Israel and the Torah of Israel as do "natural-born" Israelites, for just as all generations of Israelites are said to have been present at the giving of the Torah, the Rabbis teach that all those who would one day convert to Judaism were also there. The *gerim* are now full members of the covenant community, in possession of the Torah and subject to all its *mitzvot*.

In theory, then, the *ger* or *giyoret* is truly one of us, no longer a "stranger" but a Jew who shares our history and our destiny in all respects. In practice, however, the matter is not so simple. Traditional *halakhah* maintains some significant legal distinctions between *gerim* and Jews by birth. Moreover, the attitude of the community toward the Jew-by-choice has never been unequivocally positive and accepting. On the contrary: the literary sources, beginning with those of the ancient Rabbis, express a good deal of ambivalence. We read, for example, that the *ger* is especially dear in God's sight, for God has explicitly commanded us not to oppress him, and that when one converts to Judaism he receives a reward as though he had studied Torah all his days. The *ger* may recite the words "our God and the God of our ancestors" which appear in the liturgy, for though he did not descend from the tribes of Israel, he is the child of Abraham himself, the "ancestor of many nations." But we also hear that "*gerim* delay the coming of the Messiah" and that "misfortune upon misfortune overtakes those who accept proselytes" into the community. These passages in turn spawned a literature of interpretation, itself divided between positive and negative opinions. The adoption of either a positive or a negative attitude toward converts and conversion throughout Jewish history was no doubt heavily influenced by the environment in which the community found itself as well as the way in which its members perceived themselves as Jews. Even today, to those Jews who see themselves predominantly as an ethnic community and who experience the outside world as essentially unfriendly or hostile to our people, the tradition offers many citations which discourage conversion as a serious threat to Jewish life. Some communities have recently gone so far as to prohibit conversion entirely. The opposite, however, is also true: those who approach the general culture with a positive attitude can find support in the tradition for the open acceptance of proselytes and for defining conversion in general as something to be welcomed and encouraged.

The Reform movement has enthusiastically chosen this positive approach, as the many outreach programs sponsored by our synagogues and other institutions attest. Some of our leaders have even urged the movement to seek proselytes actively. These proposals are often based upon the notion that, some two millennia ago, the Jews engaged in aggressive missionizing among the Gentiles. While the existence of such missionary activity is open to debate and while Jewish legal thought does not speak of a positive duty to seek proselytes, the idea is not entirely foreign to the tradition. Abraham and Sarah, after all, converted some of their neighbors to their new faith as they set off on their journey to the land that God had promised to show them. And the Talmud records the view that "the Holy One exiled Israel among the nations only in order that proselytes might be added to them." It is as though the ancient sources are telling us that the Torah is too important to keep to ourselves. Particularly in these times, when Jewish identity and self-definition has come under the extraordinary challenges posed by assimilation and intermarriage, the Reform movement regards conversion as an affirmation of Judaism in the face of all those influences which conspire to render it irrelevant to our world.

It is therefore a *mitzvah* for us to welcome Jews-by-choice into our communities and to make no distinctions between them and ourselves. It is a *mitzvah* for Jews-by-choice to consider themselves totally Jewish and to be, in practice as well as in theory, fully empowered and participating members of the Jewish people. Our goal, as individuals as well as institutions, must be the removal of any vestiges of discrimination which hinder the complete acceptance of the *ger* or *giyoret*. Reform Judaism is committed to equality for the Jew-by-choice, and our moral standing as a movement may well be judged largely in terms of how well we fulfill that commitment.

The Ger Toshav (*The "Almost" Proselyte*)

Rabbinic tradition speaks of another kind of proselyte: the *ger toshav*, a term which usually denotes a Gentile who has adopted a number of Jewish practices without fully converting to Judaism. The term may be the rabbinic equivalent for what other sources call "God-fearers," individuals who were attracted to Jewish ethics, theology, and custom and who attached themselves to the synagogue. The *halakhah* defines the *ger toshav* as a Gentile who declares the intention to observe the seven "Noachide Laws," the *mitzvot* that according to rabbinic tradition are incumbent upon all human beings (the "children of Noah"). This declaration is made formally, in the presence of a *beit din*, a rabbinic court.

By the talmudic period, the term *ger toshav* had long since ceased to designate a concrete reality (if it ever did). Jewish law today does not recognize a status of "semi-proselyte"; one either becomes a Jew-by-choice, or one remains a Gentile. To the extent that this term is used at all in Jewish law, it designates those Gentiles, in particular Muslims and Christians, who are monotheists and do not worship idols.

Some proposals have been raised in Reform circles to designate the non-Jewish spouse or other relative of the synagogue member as a *"ger toshav."* The contention is that we would thereby reflect the reality within our congregations, where non-Jewish relatives are not outsiders but play an active social role and feel very much "at home." Reform responsa do not accept this suggestion, for two reasons. First, the term is largely meaningless. Since *"ger toshav"* can apply today to *any* person who adheres to a monotheistic religious faith, whether or not that person is related to a Jew, it conveys no special status for non-Jewish relatives that most other non-Jews do not already possess. Second, to create a special status called *"ger toshav"* might imply that this individual is a "virtual Jew" who enjoys the right and the obligation to participate with Jews on an equal basis in religious services and in the leadership of the congregation. Yet these rights and obligations flow from full membership in the Jewish community; they are restricted to Jews, who are bound with God in a covenantal relationship. While we welcome the non-Jewish relative into the fellowship of the congregation, he or she can properly gain full participation in the community by becoming a Jew. We invite—indeed, we actively encourage—him or her to take this step. In the meantime, until they are ready to make this choice, we would not establish a special status for non-Jewish family members which might serve as a disincentive for them, ultimately, to choose conversion.

Requirements for Conversion

Course of Study. Conversion is the product of a reasoned, informed, and sincere decision by a non-Jew to accept the obligations of Judaism. Thus, a basic knowledge of Jewish life and expression is essential to the conversion process. Most rabbis require that the prospective Jew-by-choice complete a course of study covering Jewish beliefs, practices, and liturgy. They will also require regular attendance at synagogue services and participation in religious observances and communal events, so that the candidate can experience Jewish life at first hand before making a final decision for conversion. The content of the course of study and the length of the period of preparation are determined by the rabbi and may vary depending upon the circumstances of the individual case.

Sincerity. Ideally, the candidate should come to Judaism out of a sincere affirmation of Jewish faith, a desire to live fully as a Jew, and a willing acceptance of Jewish destiny. As the Talmud puts it, "when a person seeks to convert to Judaism, we say to him, 'Do you not know that the Jews today are oppressed and persecuted, that they live in a lowly state, and that terrible suffering is their lot?' If he replies, 'I know all of this, and I pray that I might be worthy to share their fate,' he is accepted without delay." To become a Jew means to accept the Torah and its commandments with no reservations whatsoever. The proselyte should not choose Judaism out of such "ulterior" motives as economic gain, social or political advancement, or the desire to marry a Jew.

Yet it is no simple thing to measure the sincerity of another person's stated intent. A decision to convert to Judaism might be motivated by a combination of factors, some of which we find "sincere" and others not. And over time, a person who chooses Judaism for the "wrong" motivations can come to desire it for the "right" ones. A person, for example, who converts in order to marry a Jew may eventually learn to love Judaism and to identify fully as a member of the Jewish people. The Talmud itself presents examples of such individuals. For that matter, it is difficult to imagine a more "sincere" purpose for choosing Judaism than the desire to join one's spouse in creating a cohesive Jewish home and family. Given the complexity of human behavior and the near impossibility of sorting out "sincere" from insincere motivations, Jewish law leaves the decision to the discretion of the rabbi, who must determine whether the candidate for conversion chooses Judaism for reasons the community would find acceptable. And in the context of our culture and our time, we do not believe that those who wish to convert to Judaism "for the sake of marriage" should be rejected as "insincere."

The Convert's Beliefs. A candidate's sincerity is judged by his or her demonstrated desire to practice Judaism in accordance with our beliefs and interpretations. We insist that the convert declare his or her free choice to enter the covenant between God and Israel, renounce all other faiths and religions, pledge loyalty to the Jewish people, and promise to live a Jewish life and to raise his or her children as Jews. As Reform Jews, we define our range of acceptable "beliefs and interpretations" as liberally as we can; as we avoid dogmatism within our community, we do not impose strict standards of "correct" doctrine upon those who wish to enter it. For example, since Jews subscribe to many widely varying conceptions of God, we do not disqualify a prospective convert for his or her version of these conceptions, even if they tend toward agnosticism. On the other hand, we are a religious community, and we therefore share in common certain ideas as to what that designation means. We do not accept an avowed atheist as a convert, for the acknowledgment of the existence of God and of God's covenant with Israel is essential to our understanding of Judaism as a religion. Although there are born Jews who might be described as atheists, it is vital to remember that conversion is a *religious* decision rather than simply a social or ethnic one. A convert, that is, chooses *Judaism* as well as the Jewish people. One who wishes to join our community but who rejects the most central elements of Jewish religion as we interpret it is not ready for conversion. Similarly, a Christian who wishes to become a Jew but cannot abandon all belief in the divinity of Jesus is not accepted for conversion.

When Family Members Do Not Join in the Decision to Convert. Reform responsa are divided as to whether we should accept a proselyte whose spouse and family do not share his or her desire to become a Jew. Some argue that, as we urge against mixed marriage, we ought not to create a new mixed marriage by converting one spouse to Judaism. Moreover, Judaism as we understand it is not simply a matter of personal choice but part of a pattern of family and communal life. It would be virtually impossible for this proselyte to live in accordance with the ideals of Jewish life. He or she should rather remain a "Jew at heart" and a friend of the Jewish people without formally entering the community until such time as his or her family are prepared to do likewise. On the other hand, one can argue that conversion is very much a *personal* decision and that we should welcome into our midst any individual who has demonstrated sincere attachment to Judaism and to the people of Israel.

The way in which the candidate pursues the study and preparation for conversion is perhaps the best evidence of his or her sincere intentions. One obvious indicator might be this: if the candidate is the parent of young children, does he or she intend to raise them as Jews? If the answer to this question is "no," then that indicates the individual's lack of readiness to accept the title of "Israel."

The Conversion Rituals

Jewish law prescribes several initiatory rites for conversion. A male proselyte is circumcised, and both male and female proselytes immerse in a *mikveh* (a ritual pool) or other suitable body of water. If the male was already circumcised before his conversion, a drop of blood is taken from the spot that was once covered by his foreskin. Immediately prior to their immersion all proselytes are ceremonially informed of their obligations under the Torah. Upon emerging from the water, the candidate is a Jew in all respects. Like the born Jew, the proselyte's Jewish identity is a permanent one. Should the Jew-by-choice subsequently abandon Judaism for another religion, tradition regards him or her (as it regards a born Jew who adopts another faith) not as a Gentile but as an apostate Jew.

The ancient Rabbis understood these rituals as a reenactment of the process by which, in their recounting, our ancestors prepared themselves to receive Torah at Sinai. "Just as your ancestors entered the covenant through circumcision (*milah*), immersion (*tevilah*), and a sacrificial offering, so too does the proselyte enter the covenant through circumcision, immersion, and a sacrificial offering." With the destruction of the Temple and the end of the sacrificial cult, the Rabbis did not wish to deny the sincerely committed individual the opportunity to choose Judaism. They therefore ruled that in the same way that Israel worships God today without rendering sacrifices, so the *ger* may enter the community without bringing such an offering.

These rites are practiced everywhere by Orthodox and Conservative Jews and by Reform Jewish communities outside the United States. Reform Jews in the United States, however, have generally followed the resolution adopted by the Central Conference of American Rabbis in 1893 which declares that the initiatory rites of circumcision and immersion are no longer required for conversion. The proselyte need only declare orally and in writing before an "officiating rabbi, assisted by no less than two associates" that he or she accepts the Jewish faith and intends to live in accordance with its *mitzvot*. The resolution was supported by a lengthy report, which made three general arguments. First, the Torah itself never establishes initiatory rites as a condition for the admission of proselytes to the community. Second, the ancient Rabbis themselves authored no such requirement, so that the practice of circumcision and immersion for converts is a matter of neither Toraitic nor rabbinic law but rather of custom. And third, even some Jewish legal authorities in the Middle Ages hold that the initiatory rites are not indispensable. The report, combined with the tendency of late-nineteenth century Reform to emphasize the rational and ethical aspects of Judaism over its ritual elements, convinced the assembled rabbis and their successors to do away with the demand that Jews-by-choice be circumcised and/or immersed in a *mikveh*.

Each of these three points is, to say the least, quite controversial. Subsequent Reform responsa have criticized them in detail and have concluded that, as a matter of rabbinic argument, the report which accompanies the 1893 resolution fails to prove its case. Nonetheless, the resolution itself has never been rescinded, and it still embodies the official position of the CCAR on the subject of conversion rituals: neither circumcision nor immersion is required for the acceptance of proselytes. The rabbi thus has the option to accept for conversion individuals who sincerely wish to become Jewish but who are terrified of the prospect of circumcision.

Yet to say that these rites are not "required" is not to say that they are "forbidden," nor is it to say that they are irrelevant to Reform Jewish concern. A great deal has changed in the century that has passed since the CCAR resolution. In part, this change is of a piece with the transformation of Reform Jewish attitudes toward ritual and ceremony in general. If our predecessors looked askance at much of the Jewish ritual tradition, our own outlook is a great deal more affirmative, and we have restored much that they excised. With respect to conversion, we no longer necessarily emphasize, as did our forebears, the intellectual and "spiritual" elements of the process to the exclusion of the ritual ones. Many Reform Jews recognize today "that there are social, psychological, and religious values associated with the traditional initiatory rites." Among these values is the understanding that conversion is not simply a choice of a new belief-system but a decision to join a historical community which defines itself in ethnic and national as well as religious terms. To "become a Jew" means to become a member of that community as a whole, of the Jewish *people*, and not merely that segment of it called "Reform." If so, then the proselyte ought to enter the community by means of the procedures recognized as valid by all Jews, not only Reform Jews. A difficulty for this argument, of course, is that conversions conducted under Reform auspices are *not* accepted as valid by all Jews. Orthodox rabbinical authorities declare that our conversions are of no force whatsoever, even when they are accompanied by circumcision and immersion. If such is the case, one might well ask, what do we accomplish by following the traditional halakhic procedures?

This is a powerful critique, and many Reform Jews find it compelling. There are no easy answers to it. One obvious response, however, is to suggest that we Reform Jews do not adopt any traditional practice, including the rites of conversion, in order to convince other Jews of our religious legitimacy. We adopt it because it makes sense to *us*. We are Jews; the tradition is as much "ours" as "theirs." We, no less than they, find meaning in the forms and standards through which our people have for many centuries expressed their understanding of God, the world, and themselves. Reform Jews who favor the traditional conversion rites do so out of a particular understanding of Jewish history and religious experience, an understanding which persuades them that there ought to be *one* procedure for entry into the *one* people of Israel. They thus declare their abiding faith in the unity of our people, despite (and perhaps because of) Orthodox opposition, despite everything which divides us and sets Jew against Jew.

For these reasons, while many Reform rabbis continue to adhere to the 1893 resolution of the CCAR, many others will encourage or require the traditional rites for conversion. So long as the resolution remains on the books, these rites are not mandatory for all Jews-by-choice, yet they remain serious and relevant options for conversion under Reform auspices. Indeed, recent responsa argue that they should serve as the norm, to be dispensed with only in unusual circumstances. To the extent that these rites possess meaning for the community and for the Jew-by-choice, they should be encouraged.

Circumcision of Male Proselytes. When circumcision is part of the rite of conversion, the *mohel* recites the following benediction before the procedure:

> *Barukh atah Adonai Eloheinu melekh ha'olam asher kideshanu bemitzvotav vetzivanu lamul et hagerim.*

> Blessed are You, Adonai our God, Sovereign of the universe, who hallows us through the *mitzvot* and commands us to circumcise proselytes.

Following the circumcision, the *mohel* recites this blessing:

> *Barukh atah Adonai Eloheinu melekh ha'olam asher kideshanu bemitzvotav vetzivanu lamul et hagerim ulehatif mehem dam berit, she'ilmalei dam berit lo nitkayemu shamayim va'aretz, shene'emar: im lo veriti yomam velayla chukot shamayim va'aretz lo samti. Barukh atah Adonai, koret haberit.*

> Blessed are You . . . who commands us to circumcise proselytes, taking from them the blood of the covenant, for were it not for the blood of the covenant even heaven and earth could not survive, as it is said [Jer. 33:25]: "were it not for My covenant day and night, then I have not established the laws of heaven and earth." Blessed are You, Adonai our God, who has established the covenant.

When a circumcised male chooses Judaism, traditional practice requires that a drop of blood be taken from the spot where his foreskin was originally located. This symbolic *milah* allows the proselyte to reenact the circumcision by which our ancestors are said to have entered the covenant of Sinai. No benediction is recited over this ritual, however, since there is a dispute in the law as to whether the taking of a drop of blood (*hatafat dam berit*) is in fact required, and we do not pronounce a blessing containing God's name when it is uncertain that the act over which we say it is obligatory. Many Reform rabbis who do require circumcision for conversion follow those authorities who accept the existing circumcision as sufficient and will not insist upon *hatafat dam berit*. Others, however, will observe the traditional rite.

Mikveh and Immersion. To be ritually valid, the immersion must take place in at least forty *se'ah* (191 gallons) of water from a natural source (*mayim chayim*). This includes natural bodies of water fed by springs, such as rivers, streams, oceans and lakes, as well as rainwater and melted ice or snow. It excludes water drawn by human agency from a well or other reservoir (*mayim she'uvim*). If forty *se'ah* of water from a natural source has been collected in a pool, however, the remainder of that pool may be filled with drawn water. The prevalent custom is for the immersion to take place in a *mikveh*, a ritual pool built permanently into the ground which contains at least forty *se'ah* of natural water, usually rainwater conveyed from rooftops to the *mikveh* itself. The pipes which convey the water to the *mikveh* must be constructed in such a way that they are not subject to ritual impurity. If a *mikveh* is unavailable, a swimming pool built into the ground may be used for immersion.

The convert removes all clothing and immerses fully in the *mikveh*, so that the water covers his or her entire body. Upon emerging from the water, he or she recites:

Barukh atah Adonai Eloheinu melekh ha'olam asher kideshanu bemitzvotav vetzivanu 'al hatevilah.

Blessed are You, Adonai our God, Sovereign of the universe, who hallows us through the *mitzvot* and commands us concerning ritual immersion.

The Jew-by-Choice and the Community

When a *ger* resides with you in your land, you shall not wrong him. The *ger* who resides with you shall be to you as one of your citizens; you shall love him as yourself, for you were *gerim* in the land of Egypt. (Lev. 19:33–34)

The Torah commands us to love the proselyte, to treat him or her in every way as though he or she is—and always has been—one of us. This means, among other things, that we take care to avoid giving the impression to the Jew-by-choice that he or she remains an outsider. We do not remind proselytes of their foreign origin, for we, too, were once foreigners in a land not our own; we know the experience of insult and exclusion, and we must not commit these offenses against those who come to dwell among us.

The Jewish Name. "A proselyte is like a newborn child." Along with its powerful spiritual component, this talmudic statement carries some important legal consequences as well. In strict halakhic terms, the Jew-by-choice severs all familial ties with his or her non-Jewish relatives. The most obvious expression of this, as noted at the beginning of this chapter, is the custom of naming the convert "*ben/bat Avraham avinu ve-Sarah imeinu*," "the son/daughter of our ancestors Abraham and Sarah." Although this custom does not have the status of "law" in the classic literary sources, it is long attested in Jewish practice. It testifies to our belief that the Jew-by-choice is in fact "one of us," the direct descendant of the first patriarch and matriarch of our people, who distinguished themselves by bringing others into the new community of faith.

As this is not an absolute requirement, the practice may be waived in certain circumstances. An adopted child, when converted to Judaism, is named after his or her adoptive Jewish parents. Similarly, a child who converts along with his or her parent(s) may be named "son/daughter of" the parent(s), rather than of Abraham and Sarah.

Non-Jewish Relatives. Although in principle the Jew-by-choice is a "newborn child," he or she in fact remains a member of an extended family of non-Jewish relatives. In recognition of this fact, Jewish tradition teaches that the proselyte is required to render honor to his or her Gentile parents. Their relationship must be acknowledged (even if, as a matter of legal theory, it no longer exists) because a Jew must act in accordance with the highest ethical standards, and among these is the duty to show respect to those who raised us in the world. For this reason, the proselyte observes mourning and recites *Kaddish* for his or her Gentile relatives.

The Convert's Privacy. If we are not supposed to remind *gerim* of their past, why do we refer to them publicly (for example, when calling them to the Torah) as *"ben/bat Avraham ve-Sarah"*? Why, too, do we maintain records of their conversions in our files? Does this not embarrass them, violating our commitment to treat them as "one of us" without any distinction? The answer is that conversion, like any other life-cycle event, is a matter of public record. Indeed, in that a conversion requires the presence of a Jewish court (*beit din*), its public nature is even more pronounced than that of most of our rituals, which are not generally classified as judicial acts. We might add that the fact that a person has chosen Judaism should be the occasion of pride and not of embarrassment; there is absolutely no reason to be ashamed that one is "the son/daughter of Abraham and Sarah." However, because we oppose gossip and recognize a right to privacy for all persons, we must act so as to safeguard the *ger* or *giyoret* from becoming the subject of unnecessary public discussion.

Special Circumstances

Conversion in Cases of Doubtful Jewish Status. A person qualifies for Jewish status in either one of two ways: through birth or through the formal process of conversion. Reform Jews define "birth" to include the terms of the CCAR's 1983 Resolution on Patrilineal Descent: a person may claim Jewish status if he or she is the child of one Jewish parent and if he or she has met the other requirements of the Resolution. On the other hand, a person descended from Jewish grandparents or more distant ancestors but whose parents were Gentiles does not have a valid claim to Jewish status. Such a person must undergo conversion in order to be accepted as a Jew.

At times, doubt arises as to the status of an individual who is already a member of the Jewish community. In such cases, the fact that he or she has lived as a Jew in our midst may allow us to presume his or her Jewishness in the absence of clear evidence to the contrary. If, however, we know that he or she was born a Gentile and has never converted to Judaism, a formal conversion is necessary in order to confer Jewish status. The rabbi may, of course, shorten or waive the required period of study if the individual already possesses knowledge sufficient for conversion.

Incomplete Conversion. In extraordinary circumstances, a rabbi may declare that a person has become a Jew even though he or she did not complete all the requirements of the conversion process. This is based upon the CCAR's resolution of 1893 which determined that the formal initiatory rites (circumcision and immersion) are no longer necessary for valid conversion. Since many rabbis do, however, require these rites for conversion, the application of this rule will vary from community to community.

Conversion of Children. Although conversion to Judaism is usually restricted to adults, the *halakhah* does provide for the conversion of children. In communities which follow the traditional halakhic definition of Jewish status, this doctrine allows for the conversion of the child of a Jewish father and a non-Jewish mother. It also serves to permit the conversion of an entire family, children along with their parents.

The idea that children may convert to Judaism is a curious one. Conversion, after all, is understood as an informed and rational choice to accept Judaism and its obligations. How can a minor, who under *halakhah* as well as in other systems of law is considered incapable of expressing legal consent, be said to "choose" Judaism and its duties? The tradition answers that either the parent or the rabbinical court (*beit din*) substitute their consent for that of the child. They are permitted to do this because we hold that to become a Jew is a benefit rather than a disadvantage. We "may confer a benefit upon another person even without that person's informed consent" because we presume that he or she would not object to possessing the benefit; similarly, we may presume that the child would not object to receiving Jewish status. This presumption, however, is a limited one: the child may renounce his or her Jewishness upon reaching the age of Jewish majority. From that point on, once the young person is seen "acting as a Jew," his or her Jewish status is considered permanent. In practical terms, the ceremony of Bar/Bat Mitzvah ratifies the conversion that took place during childhood.

Teenagers are a special case. Since they are no longer "children" under Jewish law, they are theoretically capable of choosing Judaism. On the other hand, our contemporary culture does not recognize them as adults, a fact which raises the specter of complications under civil law should we accept them for conversion without the consent of their parents or guardians. We must be concerned, too, with the familial, social, and psychological factors which may have led to a teenager's decision to convert. Teenagers may, therefore, be admitted to courses of study and be allowed to participate in the congregational activities at the discretion of the rabbi. Formal conversion, however, should not occur until they have reached the age of adulthood as recognized by the general community.

On conversion of adopted children, see the discussion on adoption in Chapter 4.

6

Medical Ethics

The performance of medicine is a *mitzvah*. One who does so diligently is worthy of praise; but one who delays in securing medical treatment is like a shedder of blood. (Nachmanides, *Torat Ha'adam*)

Healing and the Jewish Tradition

The practice of medicine is a *mitzvah*, a fundamental religious obligation incumbent upon the Jewish people.

While this statement might strike us as obvious and unexceptional, the attitude it conveys is far from unanimous in Jewish tradition. The Torah never explicitly commands us to practice medicine, and some biblical passages are highly critical of physicians and those who resort to them. This negative attitude stems, in large part, from the fact that for much of its history medical "science" was not far removed from the arts of black magic, which the Bible condemns in no uncertain terms. Yet there are weighty theological objections to medicine as well, and these have to do with the Bible's conception of God as Creator of the universe and therefore the Source of both sickness and health. If God is the cause of all that happens to us, it stands to reason that illness is a sign of divine displeasure, a punishment for our misdeeds. And if such is the case, the proper response to illness is not medicine but prayer and repentance. Do we not read that "I am Adonai, your healer" (Exod. 15:26)? Does this verse not teach us that all healing belongs to God? If so, then to employ the services of a physician in search of a natural cure for disease betrays a lack of faith in the mercy of Heaven. Thus, the biblical author criticizes King Asa of Judah because "in his illness he sought not God but rather physicians" (II Chron. 16:12). The Talmud contains statements in a similar vein. According to one legend, King Hezekiah wins praise for hiding away a medical book as a means of encouraging the people to turn to God, and not to physicians, for healing. Elsewhere, the Talmud suggests that human beings committed a serious error when they began to practice medicine; "they should instead have learned to seek God's mercy." Perhaps this is what the Mishnah has in mind when it declares in no uncertain terms that "the best physician is deserving of hell."

This point of view finds a powerful expression in the commentary of Rabbi Moshe ben Nachman (thirteenth-century Spain), known as Nachmanides or Ramban, to Leviticus 26:11. God, Ramban tells us, offers us an existence entirely distinct from that which is the lot of all other peoples, whose lives are governed by the normal workings of nature. Israel, by contrast, is to receive blessings and suffer curses as a direct result of its success or failure in keeping God's covenant. Nowhere is this distinction more evident than in the area of medicine and health. For God's people, disease will occur not because of natural causes but because we have transgressed against the Torah. Illness comes upon us as a punishment for our wickedness; its cure is effected when we repent of our evil and take up the *mitzvot* once more. Such a community has no need of physicians; "what place do doctors have in the house of those who perform God's will?" Unfortunately, Ramban continues, our ancestors did not have sufficient faith to sustain this state of affairs. When they became ill they consulted physicians, preferring natural medicine to the spiritual regimen prescribed by the Torah. For this reason, "because medicine became a habit with them," God annulled Israel's exemption from the laws of nature. From then on, we have had no recourse but to consult the doctor when we become sick, for "the door that does not open to *mitzvot* must open to the physician." Since we have determined to resort to physicians, the Torah grudgingly permits them to practice their art. Yet were we to return and walk fully in God's ways, we should have nothing to do with them.

Nonetheless, despite these objections, the bulk of Jewish thought assumes a positive and affirming attitude toward the practice of medicine. This is demonstrated most clearly by the many rabbinic scholars, including Nachmanides, who were physicians and who wrote medical literature. It is expressed, too, by the tradition's spirited defense of medical practice against the theological criticisms described above. Yes, God is our Healer. But since the Torah does not require us to depend upon miracles, all those passages which seem to condemn the practice of medicine must be interpreted otherwise. King Asa's sin, we are told, was not that he consulted physicians but that he placed his reliance entirely upon them, forgetting that the physician is God's agent in the treatment of disease and that the patient must pray for healing *as well as* go see the physician. If King Hezekiah put away a medical text, says Maimonides, the book must have contained forbidden or dangerous lore which the unlearned might misuse; the king could not have been so foolish as to oppose the practice of medicine itself. If the Mishnah states that "the best physician is deserving of hell," this refers either to one who injures or kills his patients as a result of his arrogant refusal to consult with other doctors or to one who refuses to treat those who cannot afford to pay. As for Nachmanides' essay on Leviticus 26:11, some authorities reject his theory outright, while others note simply that today we are forbidden to ignore medicine and the rest of the laws of the natural world. Therefore, the Talmud instructs that "one who is in pain should go to the physician" and forbids a scholar from living in a town where no doctor is available.

The Torah, it is true, does not explicitly command us to practice medicine. On the other hand, it does instruct that one who causes a bodily injury to another must see to it that the injured person receives medical treatment (Exod. 21:19). From this verse, rabbinic tradition derives that a physician is permitted to practice medicine in the first place. This permission is essentially a "license" which allows the physician to engage in his craft without fear that he thereby frustrates the will of God. Jewish law, however, understands the *permission* to practice medicine as a *mitzvah*, a requirement to do so. Some authorities derive this requirement from the general rule concerning the preservation of life, or *pikuach nefesh*. This rule itself is based upon Leviticus 18:5: "These are the *mitzvot* which one shall do and live by them," to which the Rabbis add: "and not *die* by them." By this, they meant two things: that the performance of virtually any other *mitzvah* may be set aside if it is found to endanger life; and that the Torah itself sees the preservation of life as its highest goal, so that we are commanded to take all reasonable action, including the practice of medicine, necessary to protect our lives. Others see medicine as an aspect of the duty to rescue those in danger: "Do not stand idly by the blood of your neighbor" (Lev. 19:16). Whatever its textual source, the status of medicine as *mitzvah* is unquestioned in Jewish religious thought; "whoever delays its performance is guilty of shedding blood."

The definition of medicine as a *mitzvah* implies a set of moral duties on the part of the patient, the physician, and the community at large.

The Patient. Judaism exhorts us to "choose life" (Deut. 30:19), and medical science is a significant, concrete expression of the human determination to realize this goal. It is the responsibility of every person to seek medical care in time of illness. To refuse lifesaving medical treatment is to commit suicide, to choose death over life. The obligation to treat one's illness takes precedence over other religious duties, with but the rarest of exceptions; to fulfill another religious obligation (say, the observance of Shabbat or Yom Kippur) at the expense of receiving vital medical treatment is the act of a "pious fool." Even the person who is gravely ill and near death is obliged to seek medical care, since the dying person is still alive and continues to bear the duty to preserve the life that remains.

Does this mean that the individual has no choice in the matter? Is a person never permitted to refuse treatment? Must one who is ill seek out any and every drug, surgery, or other available procedure, even when these offer no hope of cure, in order to postpone death, however briefly? The answer to these questions is "no." As we shall see, the determination of one's moral and religious responsibility in the face of disease depends greatly upon how we define the purposes of "medicine" in the particular case. To put it another way, we are obliged to consult physicians, as long as what they offer us is actual *medicine*: therapeutic and efficacious treatment of our ailment. If what they offer is not medicine, if their remedies are of no therapeutic benefit to us, then we are under no moral obligation to accept them. This rule, of course, does not spare us the necessity of making some difficult and complicated judgments. It does, however, suggest the manner in which Jewish tradition would have us think through the issues that illness forces us to confront.

The Physician. If medicine is a *mitzvah*, then those who are expert in its practice bear certain responsibilities toward their patients and the wider community which sharply distinguish them from other workers. Physicians do, to be sure, work for a living, and we shall see that Jewish tradition demands that we provide for their financial security. As performers of a most cherished *mitzvah*, however, medical professionals must be constantly aware of the moral duties which place clear and significant limits upon their personal and economic freedom.

The Community. Many of the discussions in the field of medical ethics take place on the level of the personal: what is the proper course to take with respect to *this* patient in this particular set of circumstances? Yet beyond the confines of the immediate situation stand the community, the society at large which provides the resources needed to provide medical care for the individual patient. Jewish tradition recognizes that the ultimate responsibility for the performance of the *mitzvah* of medicine rests neither with the patient nor the physician but with the community as a whole. This fact does not reduce the obligations already shouldered by individuals; it does, however, refute the notion that medical treatment is entirely a private matter to be determined by market forces and agreements between individuals. We would say, rather, that the provision of adequate health care to all is emphatically a public responsibility.

Bikkur Cholim: *Visiting and Caring for the Sick*

It is a *mitzvah*—not merely a kindness—to visit the sick. *Bikkur cholim* includes the responsibility to care for the sick person's physical, economic, and personal needs, to relieve his or her isolation, and to pray for his or her recovery. This "visiting," in other words, is seen as critical to the health of the patient, although it should be carried out so as not to tire or burden him or her.

Between Physicians and Patients

The Physician: Status, Training, and Compensation. The practice of medicine, as we have seen, is the fulfillment of the *mitzvah* to save life. Yet though this *mitzvah* is incumbent upon all of us, only those who are well-trained and licensed by the proper authorities may serve as physicians. Once a person possesses this training, however, he or she is morally required to offer medical services to those who seek them, just as the *dayan* (rabbinical judge or rabbi) who has sufficient knowledge of Torah is obligated to provide religious instruction to the community.

The comparison that tradition draws between the status of the physician and that of the rabbinical judge or rabbi applies as well to the issue of financial compensation. Like the rabbi, the physician performs a *mitzvah*, a religious obligation. A *mitzvah* is something we do because it is *right*, because we are supposed to do it, not because we are paid to do it. Hence, there is a difficulty in justifying on religious grounds the payment of fees to the physician for doing that which, after all, he or she *must* do in any case. The texts resolve this difficulty by pointing out that, precisely because the *mitzvah* to save life is an obligation that is shared by all of us, it is unreasonable to require a particular portion of the community (i.e., the physicians) to perform it at their own expense. Moreover, if physicians received no financial compensation, few if any individuals would wish or be able to devote themselves to the practice of medicine and to the rigorous study and preparation that practice demands. The solution, as in the case of the rabbi, is to forbid doctors from accepting payment in return for their medical expertise but to permit them to be paid for their expenses and for the value of their time. The sources do not specify the proper level of this compensation, although some contemporary authorities suggest it should be set at a rate competitive with that offered to other similarly educated professionals.

The Physician's Right to Strike; Medical Treatment for the Indigent. If doctors are entitled to compensation, are they similarly entitled to withhold their services when they feel that the level of compensation is inadequate? In some countries, physicians do strike from time to time against the state-sponsored health care systems. In other countries, where the provision of medical care is a private matter, physicians will sometimes refuse to treat patients who lack sufficient funds or health insurance. Does Jewish thought permit them to take such action?

We might reply that since the practice of medicine is a *mitzvah* a physician is not permitted to refuse treatment to a patient for financial reasons. A religious obligation does not cease to be a religious obligation on account of its expense. And since the duty to save life outweighs virtually all other religious obligations, we might conclude that the physician must provide life-sustaining treatment for all who seek it, regardless of their ability to pay. Yet the question is not so simple. The physician is a human being, possessed of a certain inalienable dignity, which includes that which we might call economic freedom. The free person cannot be made a slave to the financial demands of others. Jewish law entitles the worker to quit his or her job even after beginning it, and workers are allowed to organize and adopt trade policies which determine the prices they charge to the public. In addition, a strong argument can be made that the ultimate responsibility for the performance of the *mitzvah* of medicine rests upon the community or society as a whole, and not upon the physicians in particular. If so, then it is the duty of the community to provide funding for medical care, and it is unfair to demand that the physicians provide it in the absence of adequate compensation.

Reform responsa literature recognizes both these arguments as cogent, a fact which requires that a careful balance be drawn. This balance entails the following considerations:

1. Every member of the community enjoys the right to adequate medical care. Medicine is a *mitzvah*, and this particular *mitzvah* is paramount in importance. To deny access to life-sustaining medical care on the basis of inability to pay is repugnant to Jewish moral teaching. While societies may debate the best, the most equitable, and the most efficient means of delivering health care to all, *that* it must be delivered cannot be doubted.

2. Physicians are entitled to organize on behalf of their economic interests and to press for adequate compensation. They are not in principle required to shoulder a disproportionate share of the responsibility to care for the indigent. But this does not permit them to withhold their services from the public, particularly from those who cannot afford to pay for those services at the level that the physicians deem adequate. A physician is ethically bound to provide medical care to those who seek it, either personally or by making arrangements for the patient to see another doctor. In the event of an unavoidable conflict, the lives and health of the poor take precedence over the economic requirements of the physicians.

Medical Confidentiality. Conversations between physicians and patients, like those between an individual and a clergyperson, counselor, or lawyer, are commonly protected by expectations of confidentiality. Under any but the most extraordinary circumstances, physicians are morally bound to honor those expectations. This is true, first of all, as a simple matter of trust: the physician makes an explicit or implicit promise of confidentiality, and the patient is entitled to expect the physician to honor that promise. Second, confidentiality is an essential element of good medical care. Successful treatment demands that the patient provide the physician with a full account of all necessary medical information, and many persons might hesitate to speak freely if they fear that their words will be shared with others. It can thus be argued that doctors could not perform the *mitzvah* of medicine in the best manner possible unless they are prepared to guarantee that their patients' communications will be held in the strictest confidence.

Under what "extraordinary circumstances" may a physician reveal confidential information concerning a patient to a third party? There is no question that the physician is obligated to do so in a case of danger to human life. The preservation of life, after all, is the supreme *mitzvah*. All of us, including the physician, are forbidden "to stand idly by the blood" of our fellow human beings (Lev. 19:16). Thus, when a physician knows that a patient afflicted with a life-threatening disease is engaged in conduct that might spread that disease or endanger other people in some way, the physician is required to inform the proper authorities of the patient's condition. This obligation may well extend to other circumstances in which life and limb are not at issue. Consider, for example, the case of a person engaged to be married who suffers from cancer or some other serious (though non-communicable) disease. Consider as well the case of a person who, unbeknownst to a prospective spouse, is physically incapable of conceiving a child. In both these instances, the person's prospective spouse would likely suffer significant (though not life-threatening) harm were he or she not to know the medical facts in advance. The person afflicted with the disease or condition is morally required to reveal that fact to the intended spouse. And many authorities teach that the person's physician, too, is obligated to reveal this information. To remain silent, they suggest, is to violate both the commandment to "not stand idly by the blood" of one's neighbor and the prohibition against placing a "stumbling-block before the blind" (Lev. 19:14), that is, withholding vital information from one who is innocently "blind" to the truth.

Even when the physician has sworn an oath to maintain strict confidentiality, most opinions hold that there still exists an overriding moral duty to release information in these circumstances. The theory, stated in traditional language, is that the people of Israel have already "sworn" an oath (at Sinai) to observe the *mitzvot*. Thus, any subsequent oath that would bind us to violate a *mitzvah* is nullified by our existing obligation.

Reform responsa stress, however, that each case must be judged very carefully and on its own merits before the physician or other counselor decides to reveal confidential information to a third party. One must particularly weigh all plausible outcomes of the decision; it just may be that more harm will accrue from revealing the information than from guarding its secrecy. In addition, the relevant civil law of the jurisdiction should be taken into account. The physician is in any case required to observe that law, and Jewish tradition, under the principle of *dina demalkhuta dina*, "the law of the state is binding," would recognize the validity of the details and restrictions of civil law even though their specific content may differ from the Judaic principles we have discussed.

The Patient's "Right to Know." May a physician or a hospital withhold vital medical information from a patient? Traditional Jewish law answers "yes." The majority view in the *halakhah* is that a person whose condition is grave should not be informed of that fact. The physician's primary task, after all, is the *mitzvah* of medicine, the saving of life. Most traditional authorities believe that to communicate "bad news" to patients frustrates that task by causing the patients to despair, to lose hope in the possibility of recovery, and ultimately to hasten their deaths. Similarly, the *halakhah* cautions against transmitting such information to the patient's relatives, lest they communicate their sorrow to the patient. To the argument that one has a "right to know" of one's own medical condition, the tradition would respond that the patient's overriding concern, like that of the physician, should be the preservation of life rather than some abstract conception of rights and liberty.

Until several decades ago, this opinion predominated in the medical profession as well. The prevailing tendency among doctors was to conceal from patients diagnoses of terminal illnesses, particularly cancer, for as long as possible. Reform responsa, too, adhered to this position. As one rabbi noted, strict veracity is not the only value we seek to uphold. Tradition tells us that even God "bends" the truth from time to time for the sake of such lofty goals as peace and domestic tranquillity, when full disclosure would lead to unnecessary strife and bitterness. The doctor is likewise entitled to refrain from communicating information which, in his or her professional judgment, would be harmful to the patient's spirits and will to live.

This situation has changed radically in recent years, with the advent of the doctrine of patient autonomy. It is widely accepted today that patients have a right to know all relevant information concerning their health and medical condition. The notion that "the physician knows best" is rejected as excessively paternalistic and an insult to the patient's essential dignity as a human being. Medical thought, too, has taken a sharp turn on this issue. Physicians, who are aware today as never before of the crucial importance of the spiritual dimension of healing, have come to see that it is generally to the advantage of the patient to be well-informed of his or her condition. A feeling of control over one's fate, a sense that one can make knowledgeable decisions concerning one's medical treatment, can be a powerful boost to morale and an antidote to depression. By contrast, when physicians keep secrets, their patients will sense a loss of control which may well exacerbate their feelings of despair.

Newer Reform responsa, as well as some which emanate from within the Orthodox community, reflect this contemporary thinking. The point is not that the old rulings were "wrong" but rather that they were based upon presumptions concerning the welfare of the patient which no longer reflect our understanding. There may, of course, be individual cases where good judgment would counsel the physician to withhold some information from the patient. Yet as a general principle, the strategy of concealment is no longer tenable on either ethical or medical grounds. In all but the most exceptional cases, a patient ought to be made aware of any and all information concerning his or her medical condition.

Medical Malpractice; The Physician's Liability for Damages. Jewish law grants the physician a wide immunity from monetary liability for damages caused by errors of professional judgment. So long as the physician is properly trained, licensed to practice, and performs the medical function in a conscientious manner, he or she cannot be sued in court for damages. This immunity, to be sure, is not absolute. Physicians who cause damages through clear negligence (defined as conduct which a reasonable person—or in this case, a trained professional—should know will likely lead to harm) are indeed required to compensate the patients. By this standard, however, physicians are not liable for damages resulting from factors other than obvious negligence. For example, a doctor prescribes a particular drug or therapy because he or she, exercising careful and proper professional judgment, believes that such is the proper treatment for the patient's condition. The treatment may unexpectedly prove to be ineffective or harmful to the patient. Yet so long as "careful and proper" judgment was used, the physician is exempt from liability.

The sources offer two explanations for this exemption. First, our tradition defines medicine as a *mitzvah*, a religious duty and a commanded act. Doctors should not be held liable for unintentional damages resulting from an act that, after all, the Torah requires them to perform. The second explanation holds that doctors are protected against many damage claims on the basis of an ancient rabbinic ordinance adopted *mipnei tikkun ha'olam*, "for the betterment of the world." To insure that individuals would be willing to practice medicine and fulfill the *mitzvah* of saving life, the Sages of old granted immunity to physicians from many of the claims for compensation that might arise as a result of their work. These two theories share a deep concern for the negative social consequences that would occur should doctors be held liable for unintentional damages. Under such circumstances, few persons would wish to enter the medical profession and subject themselves to such grave financial risk.

Yet these theories, which support a lenient stance regarding the physician's liability, could be used to argue just as persuasively for the opposite point of view. Precisely because the practice of medicine is a *mitzvah* and involves *tikkun ha'olam*, we might conclude that physicians and medical institutions must adhere to a moral standard that exceeds the legal minimum. We would say, from the point of view of Jewish law, that doctors should at all times perform their duties with an awareness that they are acting according to the higher aspirations of the tradition, seeking the betterment of the world and the welfare of all. We would posit that medical professionals are forbidden to take any actions that run counter to these "higher aspirations" and are thus held to a higher standard of conduct than the mere avoidance of negligence.

A Reform responsum shows how these considerations influence moral thinking. In the case under discussion, twenty-two patients at a hospital, all of them children, accidentally received transfusions from blood contaminated with the AIDS virus. The patients and their families sued for damages. These suits failed, due primarily to the finding by the civil courts that the hospital met the "standards of the time" in its blood-testing procedures and was not guilty of negligence. The question was raised: does Jewish law also exempt the hospital from liability?

The responsum acknowledges that, in the absence of actual negligence, the Jewish legal tradition might well, like the civil law, rule in the hospital's favor. Yet the responsum ultimately rejects this argument, applying instead the more stringent standard of the "higher aspirations" of Jewish law. Judged according to this criterion, the hospital's conduct was morally insensitive, perhaps even repugnant, because it tends to convey to the community the impression that the hospital is unconcerned over the horrifying human tragedy that resulted from its error. By refusing to compensate the victims of that error, the hospital seriously weakened the public's trust and confidence in the medical establishment and in its ability to perform faithfully the *mitzvah* of *pikuach nefesh*, the saving of life. The destructive social consequences of the hospital's actions make it imperative that we reject its appeal to the "standards of the time." The institution should rather have set for itself a higher and more exalted measure of judgment. Compensation should therefore have been offered to these patients.

We have, therefore, two possible approaches to the subject of medical malpractice, both of them based upon the same principles. The definition of medicine as a *mitzvah* practiced for the sake of making the world a better place can support an exemption of physicians from many kinds of financial liability. Conversely, it can serve as an argument that doctors adhere to a higher standard of conduct than that which the letter of the law requires from them. These approaches may appear contradictory, but they are both, in fact, true. Each represents a conception of religious and moral value that we regard as essential to our idea of the ethically good life. On the one hand, we surely do not demand that all persons at all times live up to the highest possible moral standards. This would be an unreasonable expectation of flesh-and-blood human beings. Since physicians are human beings too, the tradition requires that the rules concerning medical malpractice and liability for damages be drafted accordingly. Yet on the other hand, the physician in many respects is not an ordinary human being, and a hospital is no ordinary place of business. They are our agents for the fulfillment of the paramount *mitzvah*, the saving of life. Their effectiveness in doing so depends in large part upon their ability to retain our trust, confidence, and respect. It is accordingly not unreasonable to ask that medical professionals adhere as closely as possible in their practice to our tradition's higher aspirations rather than to its legal minimum.

We accept, in other words, the lenient *and* the stringent points of view, because both reflect our understanding of the purposes of the *mitzvah* of medicine. There exists no formula by which we can determine in some abstract way whether to rule leniently or stringently in any actual case. Each instance must be examined on its own merits, against the backdrop of everything we know about reality and everything we believe about right and wrong. At times, our conception of the nature of medical practice will lead us to "go easy" on physicians, holding that they ought to be exempt from liability; on other occasions, that same conception will convince us that the physicians should have adhered to a higher standard of conduct, and we will hold them accountable for their failure to do so. We do not know before we confront the individual case just which conclusion will emerge from it. Nor are we absolutely sure, when we have reached that conclusion, that our answer is "right" while other possible and plausible responses are "wrong." Precision, as we know, is the province of mathematics and (perhaps) the physical sciences; it seldom accompanies the process of moral or religious reasoning, especially on "hard" questions that admit of more than one plausible solution. Our goal is not precision but rather *confidence*: the conviction that, so long as we have considered each case carefully and prayerfully, the conclusions we have reached are the best ones we could have reached, the products of the most persuasive readings of our tradition as we honestly understand it. When we attain that conviction, then we know we have done our moral and religious duty, even if we concede that others might well have arrived at answers different from our own.

The Frontiers of Medical Science

Reform Judaism looks upon the advancement of science and human knowledge as a positive thing. Our movement has accepted modernity and embraced it with enthusiasm. We do not shrink from the challenges that modernity poses to the old ways of living and thinking; we seize these instead as opportunities for intellectual and spiritual growth as human beings and as Jews. One of our guiding principles of medical ethics must therefore be the affirmation of the fruits of scientific research and technological progress. The discoveries and breakthroughs of modern medicine have eliminated diseases, lengthened our life span, and offered hope to untold millions of human beings who otherwise would have been forced to accept their suffering as the decree of fate. If the physician is God's agent in the act of healing, then the medical wonders that have sprung forth from modern laboratories are without question concrete evidence of God's healing power at work in our midst.

With all that, however, our faith in modernity is not naive. Not all the options it offers us are good ones, and not all of its gifts are to be accepted without question. We are aware of the problems as well as the promise of the "brave new world" that has emerged during the last two centuries. We have witnessed the application of nuclear energy both for good and for incalculable evil; the profound and often disastrous effects of technology and industry upon our land, air, and water; and the harnessing of science, sophisticated communications, and mass transportation by Nazi Germany for the express goal of exterminating an entire people. We cannot and do not regard the progress of science as an unmixed blessing. We wonder, instead, whether it portends fearful consequences for humankind, a species whose state of moral development may not be sufficient to guarantee that it will use its physical powers with wisdom and restraint.

Because we both affirm modern science and view its effects with wariness, our approach to the new and advanced medical technologies must combine caution with enthusiastic acceptance. The goal is to think carefully and thoroughly about the implications, both positive and negative, of all the discoveries that occupy what we call the frontiers of science. If our conclusions are tentative, this simply means that the process of our thinking and analysis is not yet complete, if it ever will be. For this reason, the "answers" drawn from Reform responsa literature on these matters constitute, in a way quite similar to science itself, a work-in-progress.

Scientific Technologies and Human Reproduction

Artificial Insemination. One of the earliest scientific innovations in the area of human reproduction was artificial insemination, whereby a woman is impregnated through the insertion of semen into her womb by means other than normal sexual intercourse. The procedure was first used successfully in 1866. The earliest rabbinic discussions of the subject also date from about that time, although most of the leading articles and responsa appeared during the middle of the twentieth century.

Traditional authorities generally approve of that form of artificial insemination known as AIH, that is, when the semen donor is the husband of the woman to be impregnated. In cases of impotence or of low sperm count, this technique may be the only means by which the husband can father children and thus fulfill his obligation to "be fruitful and multiply." Some halakhists disagree, claiming that, according to *halakhah*, legal paternity is established only when the child is conceived in the normal manner; a child conceived by artificial insemination is not in fact the legal offspring of the semen donor, and its birth does not enable him to fulfill the *mitzvah* of procreation. Another issue is the traditional prohibition against "emitting seed for no purpose" (*hotza'at zera levatalah*): if, as is often stated in the sources, marital intercourse is the only occasion during which it is proper for a man to bring forth semen, then artificial insemination may violate this rule. The majority opinion, however, holds rather sensibly that so long as the intention is to conceive a child, no matter how "artificial" the method, the emission of semen cannot be said to have no legitimate purpose. Still, in view of these concerns, some authorities will permit AIH only as a last resort, when it is obvious that a couple can conceive a child by no other means.

Orthodox opinion is virtually unanimous in prohibiting AID, artificial insemination when the semen donor is a man other than the woman's husband. In this case, since the child would not be the husband's offspring, its birth would not help him fulfill his *mitzvah* to bring children into the world. Some scholars, moreover, hold that the insertion of "foreign" seed into the womb of a married woman is tantamount to adultery. Those who do not accept that idea—adultery, after all, involves an act of forbidden intercourse, which is certainly not the case here—nonetheless worry that the child might one day marry a blood relative of his or her biological father. Traditional authorities, too, exhibit a profound revulsion to the suggestion that a woman accept into her womb the semen of a man other than her husband. This revulsion is not, strictly speaking, a legal argument, based upon source citation, precedent, and textual analysis. It is rather a moral argument, derived from a deep conviction that for a woman to consent to AID is to transgress the most fundamental standards of sexual modesty and propriety to which all Jews should adhere. Thus do Orthodox authorities, with but one notable exception, condemn AID as a *to'evah* ("abomination") and a *ma'aseh ki'ur* ("an act of ugliness").

Reform responsa, on the other hand, are much more accepting of both forms of artificial insemination. This is true for several reasons:

1. Although we are aware of the moral seriousness of this technological intervention into human procreation, we dissent vigorously from the attitude displayed by many Orthodox rabbinic scholars. It is a good thing, indeed a *mitzvah* to enable Jewish couples to bear children, particularly in a period of our history when the Jewish population has declined and the Jewish birthrate has dwindled. The new reproductive technologies give us a wonderful opportunity to help bring Jewish children into the world. These procedures, therefore, are not to be viewed as threats to morality but as gifts of God through the medium of human intelligence. True, this technology can be abused. Yet *all* technologies, from the most simple to the most complex, can be manipulated for the wrong purposes. The mere possibility of their abuse must not deter us from considering the immense good that they can do. In any event, to refer to modern reproductive technologies as "abominations" is to perpetrate a tragic injustice upon childless couples and to distort the message of a tradition which commands us to choose life.

2. The various halakhic concerns raised by traditional responsa, such as the possibility that the child might grow up to marry a blood relative, are too statistically far-fetched to take seriously.

3. In their analysis of artificial insemination, traditional authorities pay little if any attention to the wishes and desires of the women involved. Much consideration is given, for example, to the issue of legal paternity, because the rabbis are more likely to permit the procedure if the child conceived in this manner helps the semen donor to fulfill his obligation "to be fruitful and multiply." Yet this *mitzvah*, according to Jewish tradition, is incumbent upon males only, and not upon women. As a matter of strict religious law, a woman is not commanded to have children; her desire to do so, while understandable on emotional grounds, is therefore of little halakhic relevance. For this reason, virtually every Orthodox halakhic authority forbids AID, which enables a woman—but not her husband—to bring a child into the world. Reform Judaism, by contrast, views all religious obligations through the lens of gender equality. A Jewish woman, no less than a Jewish man, fulfills a *mitzvah* by having chil-

dren. We are therefore much more likely to look favorably upon the use of a donor's semen, even though the child is not the biological offspring of a woman's husband.

In Vitro Fertilization. This technique is utilized when a woman's fallopian tubes are blocked or damaged, preventing the sperm from reaching the ovum. An ovum is removed surgically, placed in a container, and fertilized with freshly-drawn semen. The fertilized embryo is then implanted into the womb, where it continues its development.

In vitro fertilization (IVF) raises some of the same religious concerns discussed above in connection with artificial insemination. One of these is the question of legal parenthood: does *halakhah* regard the child conceived by this procedure as the legal offspring of the biological parents, the donors of the semen and the ovum? Some traditional authorities view the embryo as in all respects the child of the biological parents, while others declare that the bonds of legal parenthood do not exist between the donors of the genetic material and an embryo conceived outside the womb. As is the case with artificial insemination, those Orthodox scholars who believe that the child is not the legal offspring of the semen donor are less likely to permit the use of the procedure. In addition, some halakhic writings condemn IVF as a morally repugnant act which carries frightening implications for the future of the family and of society at large.

Reform responsa, again, take a more affirmative view of this technological advance in human reproduction. We consider IVF a medical procedure, a legitimate measure undertaken in response to the disease of infertility. Since it does not entail unacceptable physical risks to the woman involved, there is no reason to advise against it. We hold that parenthood is determined according to genetic criteria: regardless of the physical environment of the conception, the child is the offspring of the man and the woman who donated the semen and the egg. And, again, the couple's desire to have children is a matter of paramount concern to us. Even were we to accept the view that the child conceived through IVF is not their legal offspring, we would not deny them the hope that this procedure holds out to them. Thus, while we share the concern that science and technology, if left to operate without careful moral scrutiny and supervision, can create serious problems that we would wish to avoid, we cannot condemn in vitro fertilization as "morally repugnant." On the contrary: it is potentially a great blessing for childless couples, a blessing for which we should be deeply grateful.

One particular difficulty raised by IVF is that the procedure usually involves the fertilization of many eggs at one time in order to insure the successful conception and implantation of at least one embryo. What is to be done with the embryos which are not implanted in the womb? Does their disposal constitute the unwarranted destruction of potential human life? The issue of the legal and moral status of the human fetus is considered below in our discussion of abortion. It should be noted here, however, that although the wanton destruction of human embryos deserves condemnation on moral grounds, the disposal of embryos in this case cannot be termed "wanton" or immoral. The embryos were created as a necessary part of the procedure of IVF; so long as that procedure itself is judged to be moral and good, a legitimate medical therapy, then the destruction of the remaining embryos is justified as the necessary, if unintended, consequence of a morally permissible act. The embryos may be discarded, provided that this act be done with the dignity due to them as potential human life. They may be utilized in medical research, again provided that they are handled with dignity. Should an embryo be offered to another couple, that couple are regarded as the adoptive parents of the child upon birth; the woman and the man who donated the egg and the semen are the child's biological parents.

Surrogacy. The term "surrogate mother" describes an arrangement in which a woman other than the partner of the biological father gestates the fetus. There are, broadly speaking, two kinds of surrogacy. In the first, the woman who conceived the embryo is unable or unwilling to gestate it and the embryo is transferred to the womb of another woman who carries it to term. The second kind of surrogacy involves a woman who both conceives and gestates the embryo. Here, typically, the wife of the biological father is unable to conceive a child. The couple enters into a contractual arrangement with a woman who, in return for a fee, is artificially inseminated with the sperm of the biological father, carries the child to term, and relinquishes it to him and to his wife.

The objections to surrogacy are weighty. Apart from the issue of legal parenthood (since the child in the second example would have to be adopted by the father's wife before she could be regarded as the legal mother), there are real concerns as to the moral propriety of bringing a third party into the act of childbirth in this manner. A surrogacy contract can be seen as degrading both to the contracting couple, who negotiate what may seem to be the purchase of a child, and to the "surrogate mother," whose service as a reproductive "vessel" might be considered an affront to her inherent human dignity. Such an agreement may weaken the marriage of the contracting couple and, if she is married, of the "surrogate mother" as well. In addition, the woman who bears the child may well face serious emotional trauma following its birth and surrender. Finally, surrogacy raises the very real possibility for economic exploitation. We ought to feel discomfort at the prospect of well-to-do couples offering large sums of money to poor women to act as "childbearers-for-hire." On the other hand, surrogacy can be viewed as a great *mitzvah* which a fertile or healthy woman can perform for a childless couple. Women may enter freely and willingly into these arrangements; who are we to say that they thereby "degrade" themselves? The relationship between the couple and the surrogate need not be an exclusively legal and financial one, nor does it necessarily threaten the stability of marriages when those involved make a mature and careful decision concerning the contract.

Jewish tradition would seem to offer precedents for surrogacy of the second kind, in which the surrogate is the biological mother of the child. In the Bible, Sarah, Rachel, and Leah offer their maidservants to their husbands, and the children thus conceived are regarded as the legal offspring of the biological father and his wife. The analogy breaks down, however, in that the maidservants became the concubines of Abraham and Jacob; they enjoyed a legal status that was common enough in ancient Near Eastern society but which has long since disappeared. Today's surrogate mother is not the concubine of the biological father, and we would not wish to invoke that legal institution to describe a relationship with a woman who, unlike the concubine, is a free person possessing full legal control over her destiny.

For this reason, the Reform responsum on this issue addresses surrogacy as a new and unprecedented phenomenon. If we are to seek analogies, we would compare surrogacy to artificial insemination and in vitro fertilization, a *medical* technique rather than (or as much as) a social and legal arrangement. We place it, like those other techniques, in the category of healing, a remedy for childlessness. And since it is undertaken in the service of *mitzvah*, we give it our hesitant approval as we await "further clarification of medical and civil legal issues." We caution in the strongest terms that the parties involved must not enter into a surrogacy agreement without much careful thought and counseling concerning its attendant medical, legal, and psychological risks.

Sex Preselection. By various techniques, scientists are able to increase the probability that a couple who wish to conceive either a male or a female child will be able to fulfill their desire. Yet is it religiously or morally proper for parents to preselect the gender of their child? Traditional Judaism would seem to answer this question in the affirmative. Talmudic literature contains passages conveying the folk wisdom of the period on this subject. As befits a patriarchal society, people seem to have been interested in learning how they might bear sons rather than daughters. The "technology" of the Rabbis—a couple might attain a male child by placing their bed in a particular direction, by abstaining from intercourse immediately prior to the wife's menstrual period, and so forth—strikes us today as superstition rather than good science. Nonetheless, these statements indicate that the Rabbis did not condemn as immoral the attempt by prospective parents to insure that their children would be of a preferred gender.

The existing Reform responsum on this subject concurs with this traditional attitude, provided that the techniques employed by scientists are as "moral, simple, and safe" as those discussed in the rabbinic texts. On such grounds, however, one can raise several objections to these techniques. If the ancient Rabbis approved of sex preselection, this may stem from the fact that their methodologies were inefficient—that is, they frequently did *not* work—and accordingly did little to alter the gender makeup of their communities. Today, as the methodologies employed for sex preselection become increasingly efficient, we may confront some rather serious problems of gender imbalance and the social instability which would result precisely because the technologies *do* work. Then, too, our Reform Jewish commitment to gender equality suggests that we should look skeptically upon the favoring of one gender over another in any way: what kind of message do we send by preselecting the sex of our children to conform to our desires? Such considerations teach us that we should think long and carefully before availing ourselves of the technologies of sex preselection.

Genetic Engineering. Science is now capable of altering the genetic structure of living organisms, thereby introducing planned improvements into the biological makeup of plants, animals, and human beings. There are some good arguments in favor of doing this. The world can benefit from the creation of new and disease-resistant strains of food crops and animals. Scientists might develop particular versions of mice and other animals that are especially suitable for laboratory research. We could protect the environment through the rapid manufacture of synthetic versions of natural resources. Genetic engineering in human beings offers us hope that we might correct hereditary defects and strengthen the mental abilities, physical prowess, and positive character traits of men and women.

On the other hand, powerful objections can be raised against genetic engineering. Some of these have to do with the effects of such procedures. Even if we discount as extreme and fantastic the possibility of a "brave new world," of attempts to create a race of super-beings that would dominate all others, we still are not certain that the "improvements" we introduce into genetic structure are in fact beneficial. The creation of new species of plants and animals can affect the world's ecosystem in ways that we cannot predict in advance. The same knowledge which permits the alteration of species in beneficial ways, moreover, can also be put to the service of immense evil. A world which shivers in the shadow of existing thermonuclear, chemical, and biological weapons systems is understandably frightened at the prospect of genetic warfare. Such dangers are real enough to give pause to even the most optimistic proponent of these new technologies. A second set of arguments goes to the nature, rather than the effects, of genetic engineering. As moral beings, we question whether we have the right to manipulate the various plant and animal species for our own benefit. As religious people, we justifiably ask whether it is proper for us to assert such dominance over the very structure of a natural world which we did not create. Who are we to play God? When we alter the genetic characteristics of the forms of life, are we not treading upon ground that ought to be reserved to the exclusive control of the Creator of all life?

At first glance, it would seem that Jewish tradition condemns efforts to manipulate the biological structure of plants and animals. The Torah declares (Lev. 19:19):

> You shall observe my laws. You shall not let your cattle mate with a different kind[*kilayim*]; you shall not sow your field with two kinds of seed [*kilayim*]; you shall not put on cloth from a mixture of two kinds of material [*kilayim sha'atnez*].

It is possible to interpret these words as a prohibition against altering species in any way. The Talmud indeed suggests that the "laws" of which the verse speaks are the "laws of nature," that is, the divinely-ordained boundaries which define the species. The divisions between the species must never change. One who alters them suggests thereby that God's creation was imperfect and insufficient, thus betraying a lack of faith and trust in the wisdom of the Creator.

In fact, however, rabbinic authorities who have discussed this subject tend to understand this law rather strictly: the Torah forbids the specific act of the *mating* of two separate species, but it does not speak to the issues of genetic engineering. The story of Jacob's selective breeding of Laban's sheep in Genesis 30 tells us that some form of genetic science or eugenics was known and practiced in ancient times. Indeed, we have always been willing to "improve upon nature," and we have not necessarily regarded attempts to do so as denials of the goodness of God's creation. In the biblical account of creation, God bids human beings to "subdue" the earth (Gen. 1:28), and this has been understood as the granting of permission for humankind to exert control over all of nature. Yes, this control can be and, sadly, has been abused; our record of cruelty to animals and environmental pollution testifies amply to this. But the possibility that one might abuse a right or a privilege does not imply that the right or privilege does not exist; nor does it necessarily mean that humankind can never be trusted with that power.

How do we resolve this dilemma between our reluctance to tamper with the natural order and our conviction that we ought to pursue knowledge wherever it leads, particularly when we can accomplish much good in doing so? In the end, the *mitzvah* of medicine is the single most influential factor in our thinking. We are obliged, religiously and morally, to seek remedies for disease, and genetic engineering today offers a most promising source for many such remedies. It is certainly true that we must proceed with the utmost caution in the field of genetic technology. Our own recent history, in which we have suffered the horrific medical and eugenic experiments of the Nazis, renders us all the more sensitive to the potential misuse of power by scientists and those who pretend to be scientists. Still, precisely because *pikuach nefesh*, the duty to save life, is an overriding concern in Jewish moral teaching, and precisely because we regard science as a primary means of fulfilling the *mitzvah* of healing, we may be ready to accept genetic changes made for medical purposes.

Birth Control

According to Jewish tradition, it is a *mitzvah*, a religious duty, to have children. Yet tradition recognizes that there are times when a couple might justifiably not be prepared to have children or to increase the size of their family, and it acknowledges that sexual intercourse within marriage carries a value of its own even when it does not and cannot lead to procreation. For these reasons, Jewish law permits the use of birth control methods, including some artificial contraceptives, under these circumstances.

Reform Judaism respects the right of parents to determine how many children they shall have, although we emphasize that bringing Jewish children into the world remains a special *mitzvah* and encourage couples to consider the matter of family size carefully and with due regard to the problem of Jewish survival. We discourage such permanent methods of birth control as sterilization and vasectomy.

Abortion

Reform responsa support the decision of a woman to terminate her pregnancy in a wide but not unlimited range of circumstances. This is not merely an expression of political ideology but a carefully considered interpretation of Jewish law. Yet in *halakhah* as in politics, abortion is a deeply controversial question.

All opinions agree that Jewish law permits—indeed, requires—an abortion when the procedure is necessary to save a woman's life. This rule is based upon a statement in the Mishnah which declares that the fetus is destroyed in cases of dangerous childbirth, because "her [the mother's] life precedes [or 'takes precedence over'] its life." The text cautions, however, that once the major part of the fetus has emerged from the womb "it may not be harmed, for the life of one human person [*nefesh*] does not supersede that of another." The disagreement begins when we inquire as to the precise interpretation of the Mishnah's language. A number of commentators hold that the Mishnah permits this abortion because the fetus, though possessing a separate life, is not a "legal person" [*nefesh*] and does not enjoy the full range of protections which accompany that status. So long as it remains a fetus—that is, so long as it remains *in utero*—it may be sacrificed to save the mother, since as a *nefesh* her life takes precedence over its life. Once it emerges from the womb it may not be harmed, since from that moment the infant is a full legal person whose life cannot be subordinated to that of another. Other authorities, meanwhile, explain that the abortion is permitted because the fetus is compared to the "pursuer" or "aggressor" (*rodef*), who according to Jewish law may be killed if necessary in order to protect his or her potential victim. Once the fetus has emerged from the womb it may not be harmed, because at that point it is impossible to determine biologically just which person, the child or the mother, is the "pursuer" and which is the "victim."

This disagreement over interpretation leads in turn to widely differing legal conclusions. Authorities who hold that the Mishnah permits abortion because the fetus is not yet a *nefesh* may extend this permission to circumstances of less than mortal danger to the mother. They will sanction abortion for purposes of the mother's "healing" (*refu'ah*), even when her life is not in jeopardy, because the vital interests of the mother, as a full legal person, "take precedence" over the life of the fetus. Thus, abortions are warranted when the continuation of the pregnancy threatens grave physical or psychological consequences which would seriously impair the woman's functioning, even though her life is not in jeopardy. Those who believe that the Mishnah requires the abortion because the fetus is an "aggressor" tend to permit the procedure only in such circumstances where it can be convincingly argued that it is necessary to save the mother from mortal danger.

While the latter, more stringent position is favored by most contemporary Orthodox authorities, Reform responsa side with the more lenient view. We reject the comparison of the fetus to an "aggressor" as forced, unpersuasive, and contradicted by the texts themselves. We believe that the Mishnah's case is better explained by the theory that the fetus is not yet a *nefesh* and may therefore be sacrificed on her behalf. We accept as well the implication of this theory that the mother's "healing" is a sufficient warrant for abortion, even in cases where her life is not threatened by childbirth.

Just what, however, do we mean by "healing"? For better or worse, there exists no ironclad set of criteria which can answer this demand in the abstract. The decision for or against abortion cannot be made by applying a series of hard and fast rules. The determination rather must be made and measured against the circumstances of each particular case. It is a matter of *judgment*, in which a woman who contemplates abortion, hopefully in consultation with her physician and her rabbi, carefully and prayerfully considers all the relevant factors and issues in order to reach that decision which makes the best moral sense to her. Yet the Reform responsa tradition does contain some general lines of approach which, though they do not provide a sure answer to any particular case, might help direct and challenge our thinking on this issue as a whole.

1. We do not encourage abortion, nor favor it for trivial reasons, nor sanction it "on demand." The termination of a pregnancy, even though it is not the killing of a person, is nonetheless the destruction of a human life, a *potential* person. It is a step which must not be taken lightly; the mere desire to have an abortion is not, in and of itself, sufficient reason for it. An abortion must rather be justified, demanded by reasons and arguments that we as liberal Jews find acceptable and compelling.

2. Abortion is maternally indicated: the termination of a pregnancy is justified when the failure to do so would likely result in "great pain," of a physical or psychological nature, to the mother. Again, while it is difficult to define "great pain" with precision, the standard implies that an abortion is warranted only for "healing," for reasons that are serious and profound. These may include cases of pregnancy brought on by rape or incest and instances where the fetus is afflicted with severe birth defects. When the birth of the child would lead to severe emotional trauma for the mother, an abortion may be performed. On the other hand, abortion is not justified as a means of birth control, for economic or social reasons, or for any other consideration that does not involve severe physical and emotional harm to the mother.

3. It is easier, from the standpoint of Jewish law, to justify an abortion during the first forty days of pregnancy. However, if an abortion can be justified on moral grounds, the procedure may be performed up until the moment of birth.

Abortion is therefore both a *morally serious* and a *morally justifiable* procedure. It is morally serious in that it should not be undertaken without good and sufficient cause. Not *all* abortions are morally proper, and it is the task of religious and moral thought and argument to distinguish those cases in which abortion is warranted from those cases in which it is not. Abortion is morally justifiable in that, in a range of instances, "good and sufficient cause" can be found. What counts as "good and sufficient" is a matter of judgment and open to dispute; not all reasonable persons will necessarily agree with a woman's decision that an abortion is the best and morally proper course of action. It is a judgment, nonetheless, which can and must be made. For this reason, Reform Judaism assumes a "pro-choice" stance on the political controversy over abortion. We do not claim that a decision for abortion is always "right." We insist, rather, that the determination of the rightness of an abortion can be made only by the woman herself, in the context of her own life and religious commitment. The government, police, courts, lawyers, and politicians should not deny to women the right to choose for themselves a morally justifiable course of action.

An aborted or miscarried fetus may serve as a subject of medical research and as a source of organs for transplant, in the same way that a human corpse may be used for these purposes. Since the fetus is not a *nefesh*, a full legal person, the needs of the living and the duty to save life (*pikuach nefesh*) permit us to make use of it for these purposes, provided that the remains be treated with dignity.

Extreme Illness and the Approach of Death

Refusing Medical Treatment. Jewish tradition teaches that the preservation of life is the supreme and overriding *mitzvah* or religious obligation. Since medicine is the primary means by which we fulfill this obligation on a daily basis, it follows that we have a duty to seek out and to accept medical treatment during time of illness. "Medical treatment," in this sense, would include such preventive measures as immunizations, periodic "routine" examinations, and proper nutrition. Preventive medicine, that is, those actions which according to the consensus of medical opinion contribute to the avoidance of disease and the preservation of health, is also medicine, and it is surely encompassed by our conception of the *mitzvah* of healing. For example, vaccinations against disease are considered "proven remedies" by competent medical opinion, and it is therefore our obligation to utilize them. A synagogue is well within its rights to demand, as do many school districts, that children be immunized against disease prior to being admitted to the congregational school. But does the obligation to seek out medical treatment mean that a patient never has a choice in the matter, that he or she must always follow the physician's orders and may never decline any form of medical treatment?

While the logic of Jewish tradition, which commands us to "choose life" and which sees medicine as a *mitzvah*, might suggest that the patient indeed has no right to refuse treatment, this conclusion is only partially correct. In some situations the patient is well within his or her rights to say "no" to the doctor's prescription. It is important to understand the theory behind this statement, since knowledge of that theory and its underlying principles can help us to determine whether any particular case is one in which it is permissible to refuse treatment.

The obligation to practice medicine and to avail ourselves of medical treatment is a subset of the more general duty to save life. Fundamental to that duty is the element of *ability*: one is required to take action to save the life of another only in a situation where one is capable of doing so, that is, when the action taken has a reasonable chance of success. One is not obligated to take useless actions which do not contribute to the rescue of another from danger, for such actions are not defined as "the saving of a human life." The same can be said in the particular example of medicine: the obligation to heal applies only when one "is able to save the endangered person" by medical means. The point of medical practice, after all, is to *heal*, to take measures which in the considered judgment of the profession are *therapeutic*, which contribute to the successful treatment of disease. To do otherwise, to administer harsh drugs and invasive surgeries which do not have therapeutic value, is the very opposite of "medicine"; it is *chavalah*, the causing of unnecessary physical harm to the human body.

With this distinction in mind, rabbinic scholars suggest that while a person does have a moral duty to accept medical care—indeed, the refusal of treatment is a violation of the *mitzvah* to preserve life and may be tantamount to suicide—this duty applies only to those medical procedures which are tested and proven and which offer a reasonable prospect of successful treatment. If, however, a particular remedy is experimental in nature or if its effect on the disease is at best uncertain, then the patient is not obligated to accept it. Under such circumstances, the treatment is no longer classified as "lifesaving" and is thus no longer a moral obligation, a *mitzvah*. While the physician and the patient may choose to resort to that remedy, they are under no religious requirement to do so.

This understanding of the nature of medicine allows us to make some judgments concerning treatment with a good deal of moral confidence. For example, under the heading "therapeutic" and "successful treatment" we would include all medical procedures, such as immunization, antibiotics, and routine surgery that physicians expect will lead to the prevention or the cure of the disease in question. Other therapies, though they do not produce a "cure," also fall under this heading because they are able to control the disease as well as can be expected and allow the patient a reasonable degree of function. These treatments, such as insulin for diabetes and dialysis for chronic renal disease, may not offer a cure, but they do offer *life*; they are included therefore in the *mitzvah* to preserve life itself. When, however, a patient has entered the final stage of terminal disease, medical procedures which can at best prolong this stage but can neither reverse nor halt the decline are not required. A cancer patient, for example, would accept radiation and/or chemotherapy so long as these offer, according to informed medical opinion, a reasonable chance of reversing or controlling the malignancy. Once this prospect has disappeared and the therapies can serve only to prolong the patient's suffering by delaying his or her inevitable death from the disease, they are no longer considered *medicine*; the patient may refuse them.

The standard which we employ here is by no means free of difficulty. Terms such as "therapeutic," "successful treatment," and "reasonable degree of function" are inherently ambiguous. For this reason, a number of Orthodox rabbinical authorities rule that we are obliged to maintain the struggle to prolong life until its very last instant. Since we can never be absolutely certain that a patient has no hope for recovery, and since every moment of life is sacred, possessing inestimable value in the sight of God, these authorities argue that we have a moral obligation to maintain medical treatment until death has overpowered our attempts to save the patient's life. We respectfully but firmly disagree. Although decisions concerning medical treatment, like all moral decisions, are never completely free of uncertainty, we believe it is quite possible to distinguish between treatments which offer a reasonable hope for success and those which do not. We believe that we can tell the difference between treatments which serve a credibly therapeutic function and those which can do nothing but prolong the agony of the dying patient. We believe, in other words, that we practice *medicine* in order to heal, rather than to delay to no discernible purpose a patient's suffering and impending death. There comes a point when all the technologies which comprise the physician's arsenal can no longer achieve the purpose for which they are intended. When that point has arrived in the life of any person, the application of these therapies and techniques can no longer be defined as *medicine*, as healing, as *pikuach nefesh*.

True, it is no easy task to determine just when that point has arrived. We will frequently disagree among ourselves as to just what counts as "successful treatment." We believe, however, that we have no recourse but to face this uncertainty directly and to make our decisions by way of careful reasoning and intensive argument. Moral decision-making, we must remember, is not determined by precise mathematical formulae. It is a judgment, a choice between two or more plausible alternatives. We do not make this choice arbitrarily; we do not think that all the alternatives are equally good or equally bad. We decide as carefully and as thoroughly as we can, weighing the information at our disposal and the circumstances of the case against the teachings of Jewish tradition as we understand them. What emerges from this process, from the moral discussion or argument we conduct within our communities and within ourselves, is a decision that we can never be sure is absolutely "correct." It is, however, the best we can do. It is all we are expected to do. And it is most assuredly what we *must* do if we are to fulfill what is expected of us as religious Jews and moral beings.

"Dangerous" Treatments and the Treatment of Severe Pain. The purpose and justification of medical practice is the *mitzvah* of saving life. It is something of a problem, therefore, when physicians prescribe therapies which involve serious risks to the patient. Major surgery and powerful drugs bring with them the probability of harmful side-effects, some of which may actually shorten the patient's life, an outcome that seemingly contradicts the very point of medicine. Yet Jewish tradition has always understood that medicine involves unavoidable risks that are justifiable so long as the intent behind them is a medically legitimate one: the battle against disease. Simply put, it is permissible to undergo "dangerous" treatment for a disease that, in the absence of the treatment, will lead to certain death. Traditional authorities differ, to be sure, as to the degree of risk that one is allowed to accept in the name of healing. Some hold that the survival rate for the therapy in question must be at least fifty percent, while others believe that even a slight chance of survival justifies the use of a risky procedure, so long as death

is certain without it. The Reform position is that the determination of an acceptable level of risk should be left in the hands of the patient or, if the patient is incapable of expressing consent, the patient's family. On the other hand, as our discussion in the preceding section indicates, the patient is not morally obligated to accept an unproven or experimental remedy for disease.

It is permissible to administer powerful doses of medication and potentially dangerous surgery in order to relieve a patient's suffering and pain. This applies even if the therapy might shorten this person's life, so long as the intent behind it is to alleviate pain and *not* to hasten the patient's death. The relief of pain is a proper medical objective, and the treatment of suffering falls under the heading of legitimate *refu'ah*, healing.

The Treatment of the Terminally Ill. While the precise definition of the concepts "disease" and "illness" has long been a subject of medical, philosophical, and sociological debate, we proceed on the basis of the following presumptions, commonly held in our community. By "terminal illness" we do not mean a chronic illness or a disease which, though incurable, is subject to medical control. The term rather denotes a disease (that is, a condition which the preponderance of contemporary medical opinion identifies as such) which cannot be defeated or controlled and which will lead inevitably to the patient's death. This is an important distinction to bear in mind. We do not call an illness "terminal" simply because it is incurable and will likely result in death for the patient at some date in the distant future. An illness is "terminal" when death is reasonably imminent, when the patient has on account of the disease lost much of his or her ability to function normally and is clearly and unquestionably in the process of "dying" as we generally understand that term.

Discontinuation of Treatment. The right to refuse treatments that are medically ineffective, discussed above, implies the right to discontinue treatments which may have been useful previously but which have now lost their medical benefit: that is, they no longer serve a legitimate medical function. Jewish tradition teaches that, while we are forbidden to hasten a patient's death, we are permitted to remove all factors which delay that death unnecessarily, which prolong the process of dying without offering a hope for recovery or stabilization. We hold that when a medical procedure, whether drug, surgery, or machine, has lost its therapeutic effectiveness, and its continued use may constitute at best a delay of the patient's reasonably imminent death, the procedure may be discontinued.

Heroic Measures. A terminally-ill person (or his or her family, in the absence of that person's ability to consent) may refuse drastic treatments such as cardiopulmonary resuscitation (CPR) and mechanical ventilation when he or she enters a medical crisis. In addition, devices such as ventilators or heart-lung machines which sustain a patient's vital signs may be disconnected when it is clear that the medical condition is irreversible and that death would occur imminently without these machines. We bear no moral obligation to fight incessantly to postpone death as long as possible, to preserve every last instant of human life. We do not understand as "medicine" the brief delay of a patient's otherwise imminent death. While measures must be taken for the comfort of the patient and for the relief of pain, there is no medical nor moral justification for compelling a person at the end-stage of a disease to accept a treatment which at best, can buy a bit of extra time but which cannot reverse the course of the disease that will soon lead to his or her death.

Reform Judaism accepts the standard of "brain death" as a sufficient criterion of death (see pp. 256–57). Therefore, when a patient's brain activity has irreversibly ceased, the machines that maintain his or her cardiac and respiratory functions should be discontinued.

Artificial Nutrition and Hydration. A terminal patient can be kept alive by means of food and water supplied through tubes inserted into the veins, nose, or stomach. May these tubes be disconnected, thereby allowing the patient to die? The answer depends upon whether we define artificial feeding as a form of medical treatment, for as we have seen, medical treatment may be refused or discontinued when it loses its therapeutic effectiveness, when it no longer serves a function that we would reasonably describe as "healing." There are, indeed, reasons why we would consider artificial feeding to be a medical procedure. The tubes, like "medicine" in general, are introduced as a response to disease, and it is difficult to distinguish them from such other indisputably "medical" devices as the ventilator: both keep the terminal patient alive, and the withdrawal of either will result in death from the disease that warranted its introduction in the first place. On the other hand, a real and desirable distinction can be made between artificial nutrition and other forms of treatment. Unlike the ventilator and other sophisticated machinery, food and water are universal human needs: all human beings, and not only the sick, require nutrition and hydration in order to live, and we generally hold our duty to feed those who are dependent upon us to be a separate moral obligation of its own. In addition, the fact that we receive these substances through a machine does not necessarily transform them into "medicine," since food and water in any case reach us at the end of a long chain of production, transportation, and distribution technologies.

Rabbinic opinion, like that of ethicists, is sharply divided on this subject. Reform responsa have generally permitted the removal of feeding tubes, although the most recent discussion of the issue sounds a more cautionary note, taking quite seriously the distinction between nutrition and medicine. This division suggests the very real moral difficulty involved in the removal of artificial feeding and hydration. The discontinuation of these measures should never become a routine procedure. It is preferable that artificial feeding be maintained so that, when death does come, it will come for reasons other than deprivation of food and water.

Treatment for Accompanying Illnesses. Frequently, a dying person is afflicted with a disease that is not directly related to his or her terminal illness and which can be successfully treated. Is it permissible for the patient to refuse treatment for the accompanying illness or disease? For example, a person suffering from Alzheimer's disease has previously requested that, once the disease has entered its final stage, all life-prolonging medical care be withheld from her. This request specifically includes "antibiotics," even though antibiotics offer the prospect of successful treatment for infections not related to the disease which will ultimately cause her death. It is nonetheless permissible for her or her legal guardians to refuse the antibiotics. We would define medicine as the treatment of a human being, the whole person, rather than a collection of various syndromes. When a patient is "terminal" and when death is reasonably imminent (again, a measurement which cannot be determined with precision but which calls for careful judgment and analysis), "successful treatments" for accompanying diseases no longer serve a reasonable therapeutic function *for that person* and constitute a needless hindrance to the patient's death. They may be refused or discontinued.

Euthanasia and Assisted Suicide. Jewish tradition prohibits suicide, by which we mean the willful, premeditated taking of one's own life. Similarly, it prohibits euthanasia or "mercy killing" as a response to terminal illness, to disability, to depression, or to whatever leads a person to conclude that life is "no longer worth living." On the contrary, since life is a gift from God, to whom we owe the ultimate responsibility for its use, it is to be cherished and safeguarded until its very last moments. "A dying person," we are taught, "is like a living person in all respects." Thus, one who takes any action to hasten the death of the dying person is guilty of bloodshed, no less than one who kills a healthy individual, and this is true even if the killing is done out of the "best" of motives.

There are cases, to be sure, when other values override the preservation of life. A Jew is obligated, the sources tell us, to suffer death rather than to violate the commandments against idolatry, adultery and incest, and murder. To accept martyrdom in such instances is to uphold the commandment of *kiddush hashem*, the sanctification of God's name through one's decision to die. Moreover, the tradition looks with great sympathy upon individuals who take their lives under the duress of physical and emotional agony. According to the *halakhah*, such persons are not "suicides," for they do not act out of rational premeditation but are driven to do so by powerful forces out of their control. This understanding attitude, however, does not mean that Judaism "permits" suicide as a response to illness, pain, or despair, any more than we would "permit" a person to commit a crime so long as he or she is legally insane. And it certainly remains forbidden to accede to a dying person's request for euthanasia.

Reform responsa literature affirms this traditional teaching, for several reasons.

1. We affirm Judaism's declaration of the inestimable value of human life. The existence of life within us, a life stamped with the very image of God, is what makes us human, and it calls forth from us a sense of reverence and humility. To take it upon ourselves to kill a human being, even out of "good intentions," is the opposite of reverence: it is the ultimate arrogance, by which we proclaim that we

are masters over the very thing—life itself—which our faith teaches must be protected against our power to destroy.

2. All of us wish to avoid pain and suffering, and none of us wishes to see a loved one in agony. But suffering does not, in and of itself, justify the killing of a human being. It is, rather, part of the human condition. We remain human even when we suffer, and the ethical choices that face us at that time are essentially the same as those that face us at all times: to determine what we, human beings in covenant with God, shall do with the strength that remains to us. Our faith bids us to make this determination by choosing *life*. When we make that choice, to *live* even in the face of debilitating illness, we proclaim that we refuse to give in to the counsel of despair. This, rather than euthanized death, is the response that Torah would have us make to suffering.

3. Decisions for assisted suicide are often based upon judgments concerning the "quality of life." Yet such judgments are inescapably subjective, since they are determined by each person's individually arrived-at conclusion that "my life is no longer worth living." Once we grant that any person has the right to act on such a conclusion, we have little or no principled reason to deny any other person that right to do so. We would have no reason to deny euthanasia to the chronically ill, the severely disabled, the depressed, the aged, and the infirm, none of whom necessarily suffers from what we might define as a "terminal illness" but all of whom might well decide that death is better than life. Such a situation, rife with the potential for tragic abuse, is incompatible with Jewish teaching as we understand it.

Jewish tradition does *not* demand that we struggle against illness with all our might until the bitter end. Our duty is to practice medicine, to heal, to save life; and once it becomes clear that our technologies no longer serve what we would define as a reasonably therapeutic purpose, we are permitted to withdraw those treatments, even if in doing so we allow the patient to die sooner than she or he otherwise would have died. Indeed, since tradition suggests that it is forbidden to delay unnecessarily the inevitable and imminent death of a terminal patient, it is arguably our *obligation* to discontinue these therapies. But our obligation to heal the sick and to care for them does not include the right to kill them, even out of compassion. For when we define "compassion" so as to include the right to kill another person, we have transgressed the most basic and elemental moral standards of the Judaism we profess.

Cryonics. This term, along with its alternative "cryobiology," refers to the practice of freezing bodily organs or even an entire body in order to suspend life functions for a period of time. The ultimate goal (though it is not yet a practical possibility) would be to freeze the body of a dying person in order to revive it at a later, perhaps a much later date, when a cure for the person's illness will have been found. Assuming that such a technology were feasible, would it be permissible in the view of Jewish teaching?

There are some arguments we could cite in favor of cryonics. To allow an individual to conquer disease in this fashion might well be defined as a legitimate end of the *mitzvah* of medicine, whose goal after all is to heal the sick. In addition, this technology offers the prospect of a wider range of control over our lives and destinies. Yet the economic costs of large-scale investment in cryonics would likely divert our resources from other and arguably more important medical and social objectives. Moreover, the social costs involved in preserving the lives of a significant number of individuals must also be considered. What would be the effect upon a future society of their emergence from suspended animation? What physical and psychological effects would long-term freezing have upon these in-dividuals themselves? Is the attraction of cryonics a legitimate ex-pression of the biblically-sanctioned longing for "length of days," or is it an example of humankind's hubris and arrogance, the drive for physical immortality above all things? Since much of our thinking about morality flows from the premise that human life is finite, the possibility that we may conquer our finitude might well shake the foundations of many of our most important ethical commitments.

Reform responsa, noting that cryonics remains a theoretical "science" only, link the freezing of the human body with the preceding discussion concerning our treatment of the terminally ill. Just as it is forbidden to delay the death of a terminal patient when no legitimate medical pur-pose can be served thereby, it would be permitted to freeze a human being *only* if there were a tested remedy available for his or her disease and if this remedy involved freezing. The freezing of a body on the mere hope that someday a remedy may be found is not legitimate medicine and should therefore be considered as an unwarranted delaying of death and as contrary to the spirit of the Jewish legal tradition.

Organ Donation and Transplant

It is permissible to transplant organs from a corpse into the body of a living person for legitimate medical reasons. Transplantation does not violate the traditional prohibition against deriving benefit from a corpse, nor do we consider it an act of contempt for the corpse. On the contrary: the use of organs *post mortem* as a means of fulfilling the *mitzvah* of healing is an act of respect for the dead, for it allows them to be a source of life even when their own lives have come to an end. For this reason, it is also permissible to establish repositories or "banks" for the storage of human organs for future transplant.

It is permissible and praiseworthy for a healthy individual to donate part of his or her own body (a kidney, bone marrow, etc.) to be transplanted into the body of a sick person. The most obvious Jewish religious objection against doing so is the prohibition against committing suicide, which also forbids one from placing one's own life in unnecessary danger even in order to rescue another. This principle would seem to deny to any individual the right to endanger his or her life by undergoing surgery, which always involves an element of risk, to remove an organ for donation. There is, however, a long debate in the literature over the scope of this prohibition. While some authorities interpret it quite strictly, declaring that one may never expose oneself even to a limited degree of risk for the purpose of saving a life, others conclude that we are permitted and even obligated to subject ourselves to a measured degree of danger when doing so will rescue another person from mortal danger. We hold this latter position to be the superior and compelling interpretation of Jewish moral teaching; thus, it is a *mitzvah* to volunteer an organ such as a kidney for transplant. We should keep in mind, too, that the surgery necessary to remove the organ has become a routine procedure which, while not precisely "risk-free," poses but a relatively small degree of danger to the donor.

On the other hand, the permission to place oneself in potential danger in order to save another does *not* apply when the motive for assuming that risk is economically driven and morally suspect. This is particularly true when we consider the practice of the sale of human organs for transplant. "Merchants" will offer large sums of money to entice individuals to sell kidneys or other organs. This is a reprehensible practice, and the doctrines of economic freedom or personal autonomy cannot be cited in defense of it. Given that the seller in this situation is most likely a person living in dire economic circumstances, his or her agreement to sell a bodily organ hardly constitutes a rational acceptance of a limited degree of risk. Nor do we accept the contention that such a sale is an act of righteousness or *gemilut chassadim* in that it helps save another's life. The trafficking in human organs is much more about money and profit than it is about medicine. It is an affront to our sense of justice, posing an enormous opportunity for the economic oppression of the poor, particularly those living in poverty-stricken countries. It should be banned by our society and denounced by the medical profession.

The procedures of heart and liver transplant pose a special difficulty. In order to be useful for transplant, these organs must be removed from the body of the donor while they are still functioning. This is done when the donor has entered the state of "brain death" and has accordingly been pronounced dead, even though his or her heartbeat and respiration are maintained artificially. The definition of death in Jewish law, however, has been traditionally understood to consist of three criteria: absence of bodily movement; cessation of heartbeat; and cessation of respiration. By this standard, a patient connected to a respirator or a heart-lung machine is still alive, even in the absence of brain activity, because he or she continues to breathe and the heart continues to function. To remove a beating heart is therefore to kill the donor, and for this reason the heart transplant operation would be absolutely forbidden under Jewish law.

Recently, however, some rabbinical authorities have come to accept "brain death" as a sufficient criterion of death according to *halakhah*. In their view, the primary sign of death as enunciated by the Jewish legal tradition is the total and irreversible cessation of independent respiration. The absence of heartbeat is not in itself an essential criterion of death; rather, it has long served as evidence that respiration has indeed ceased irrevocably. In our own time, we need no longer look to the heart for that evidence. The cessation of independent respiratory activity can be determined through a series of careful and thorough clinical tests which establish that the entire brain, including the brain stem, which controls respiration, has ceased to function. Medical consensus now holds that the absence of brain function is the equivalent of the traditional cardiorespiratory indicators of death. Jewish law can concur with this consensus, since brain death means that the patient has lost any and all possibility of recovering independent vitality, including breathing. Thus, a person who is "brain dead" *is* dead, and his or her organs may be removed and transplanted into the body of a recipient.

Reform Judaism accepts the cessation of brain activity as a sufficient legal and moral criterion for death. Our sources understand the absence of breathing and heartbeat as signs and indicators of death, not as death itself. Since the determination of brain death signals that the body has irreversibly lost its ability to maintain these vital functions on an independent basis, the brain death standard satisfies the demands of both Jewish tradition and simple moral sense. When clinical tests establish beyond medical doubt that brain activity has irreversibly ceased and that circulation and respiration are maintained solely through mechanical means, the patient is dead and the body's organs may be removed for transplant.

Medical Experimentation on Human Subjects

A person may volunteer to serve as a subject in a controlled and careful scientific experiment whose goal is to test and discover medical knowledge. As we noted in our discussion of organ donation, it is a *mitzvah* to rescue those in danger, and we hold the view that one is permitted to assume a limited degree of risk in order to save those who confront a clear and present threat to their lives. By these standards, one is surely permitted to take part in an experiment that may reveal lifesaving information. In some cases, where the potential for saving lives is real and relatively immediate, participation in such experiments could well assume the status of a moral duty.

There are, however, limits to this right and duty. The phrase "controlled and careful scientific experiment" implies that the procedure must be meticulously and rigorously supervised. Moreover, the procedure might be unacceptable because it involves intolerable side-effects, such as agonizing pain, which it is the obligation of medicine to relieve. These limits apply even to those suffering from terminal disease, for it is the first task of medical science to treat *this* patient, the one before us, rather than to use him or her as a subject in the hope that others might someday benefit. As is often the case, we must draw here a balance between two moral obligations, that which we owe to others and that which we owe to ourselves, and like all such balances, this one is difficult to determine in advance of each particular case. Still, the conscientious consideration of these principles can help us when we confront the opportunity to take part in clinical trials to distinguish between acceptable and unacceptable risks.

May experimental medical procedures be tested upon a patient without his or her consent? Consider the development of new methods of cardiopulmonary resuscitation (CPR). There exists a great need to test new emergency therapies, procedures which will afford us the opportunity to save many lives that will be lost if we are restricted to current methods. These therapies must be tested in actual practice, in emergency situations where it is impossible or impractical to obtain the consent of the patient or of a suitable legal surrogate. The tests would, of course, be supervised by experts who would instruct the emergency workers to switch to the standard methods of CPR in the event that the experimental procedures fail to work. Yet it is unavoidable that, in a small percentage of cases, the critical condition of the patients might actually worsen prior to the cessation of these tests.

Experimental lifesaving technology may *in certain cases* be tested without the consent of the patient. The *mitzvah* of medicine requires that we continue to develop new and more effective means of saving life. It is an ethical duty for all of us to participate in the fulfillment of this *mitzvah*, which some of us can do by serving as subjects in carefully controlled experiments. Thus, our consent to participate in emergency testing can be presumed. This presumption, however, is limited by the condition that the life of *this* patient, a life in clear and present danger, takes priority. The overriding ethical responsibility is to save the life before us, and this life may not be sacrificed on behalf of lives that might potentially be saved as a result of the experiment. Thus, the physicians must be reasonably certain that the experimental therapy is neither significantly more dangerous or less efficacious than the standard therapies. If there is reason to suspect that *this* individual will fare worse under the experimental method, he or she must be given the standard treatment. The experiment must be immediately discontinued once it becomes evident that the new therapy is not achieving the desired result for *this* patient.

Cosmetic Surgery

Jewish law prohibits us from causing physical injury (*chavalah*) to ourselves without sufficient justification. The debate over cosmetic surgery within the tradition accordingly centers upon the precise definitions we give to this prohibition. Some assert that, so long as a particular cosmetic procedure is not unusually risky and is being contemplated for honorable reasons, the surgery does not violate the guidelines set forth by our sources and sages. Others, however, argue that cosmetic surgery, like all other medical treatment, is permitted only for *refu'ah*, for healing, for legitimate *medical* purposes. The desire to improve one's physical appearance is, in and of itself, not such a "legitimate medical purpose." Indeed, it may be viewed as an act of arrogance, a desecration of the human form, and an example of misplaced values: with all the important work that we need to do in the field of medicine and healing, is the enhancement of physical beauty truly a proper end to which we ought to apply our knowledge and resources?

Reform responsa view the latter position as the better interpretation of Jewish teaching. Our reverence for the sanctity of the human body prohibits us from the capricious manipulation of its form, and surgery intended merely to improve one's physical appearance should be discouraged. There are, of course, exceptions to this general rule. We believe that reconstructive surgery, the restoration of one's appearance to an approximation of its former state, is a proper medical objective and not merely cosmetic. Surgery to correct what are generally regarded as physical deformities is also permissible. Moreover, for some persons "mere" cosmetic surgery may serve a useful medical purpose in enhancing a sense of psychological and emotional well-being. This is a determination which must be made in each individual case, although we think the argument is too frequently raised and too easily exaggerated. As we understand it, Judaism admonishes us to place less emphasis than we are prone to do on material values and to concentrate upon the development of deeper and more lasting measurements of self-worth and satisfaction. We ought to resist undertaking surgery intended solely for the improvement of physical appearance.

By "surgery," we do not refer to such comparatively non-invasive procedures as the piercing of the ear. In such a case, since the community has long accepted these for cosmetic purposes, we would have no objections, provided that the procedure poses no significant health risk.

On the other hand, tattooing and more extreme forms of body piercing, when not undertaken as part of a regimen of medicine or reconstructive surgery, are most difficult to reconcile with Jewish tradition, which commands us to strive for holiness and to treat our bodies with reverence and respect. They are to be regarded as *chavalah,* as pointless manipulation of the human form, rather than adornment.

Priorities in Medical Treatment

How should we allocate our medical resources or facilities when these are too limited to serve all those in need of them? This question may be applied to individual patients or to the larger community or society. In the case of individuals, the problem might involve two or more persons in need of an organ transplant when only one organ is available: how shall we determine which person receives it? On a communal level, what principles should guide our decisions concerning the funding of medical objectives?

Jewish tradition offers several different avenues by which we might approach answers to these questions.

1. *Equality of Persons.* Each human person, created in the divine image, is equally precious in God's sight; accordingly, "we do not dispose of one person in order to save another." This principle of equality is expressed quite powerfully in the talmudic question: "Who is to say that your blood is redder than that of another person? Perhaps his blood is redder than yours." Thus do the Rabbis affirm the principle that the life of every person is of equal importance and that we are not permitted on moral grounds to allow the life of one human being to take precedence over that of another. It would follow from this principle we may not base lifesaving medical decisions upon considerations of the comparative worth of persons. All are equal; if choices are necessary, these should be made by arbitrary means, such as a lottery, or a first-come, first-served procedure. In this way, "fate" spares us the awful task of deciding "who shall live and who shall die."

2. *Social Value.* On the other hand, some passages in our sources indicate that we *do* set priorities in the performance of moral duties based upon the "worth" of persons or upon their position in society.

A *mishnah* declares that when the lives of a man and a woman are simultaneously in danger, we are to save the man first. The man takes precedence over the woman as well with respect to our obligation to return a lost object. A woman precedes a man in being provided with clothing and being redeemed from captivity. If both persons are men, then we adopt a scale of priorities which follows the traditional structure of genealogical status: the *Kohen* precedes the *Levi*, followed by the Israelite, and so forth. The Talmud explains these priorities in terms of each person's correspondence to the religious ideals of biblical and rabbinic Judaism. Thus, the man takes precedence over the woman because he has more *mitzvot* (religious obligations) to perform; the *Kohen* comes first because of his high cultic standing. And given that the highest of all Jewish religious values in the eyes of the Rabbis is the study of Torah, it is no surprise that the text teaches that "a *mamzer* (a child born of an adulterous or incestuous union) who is a Torah scholar takes precedence over a high priest who is an ignoramus."

Some rabbinic authorities think that this list of priorities offers us practical guidance concerning the allocation of limited medical resources. Reform Judaism, of course, rejects this system, based as it is upon gender and priestly distinctions, as morally irrelevant and offensive. Yet its existence raises some interesting and difficult questions for us. It is possible to infer from these texts that, if we are able to identify the highest values of our own culture and society, we would likewise be justified in awarding precedence to those "better citizens" whose lives embody these values to the greater degree and whose survival would contribute in a more positive way to the welfare of the community. Large-scale allocation decisions might be made in a similar way. Since medical resources are ultimately public property, it can be argued that they should be used in such a way as to maximize the benefit to society as a whole.

3. *Medical Grounds.* The third basis upon which to make these decisions is that of medical need and efficacy: which patient, of the two or more before us, is in greater immediate need of treatment? Which patient is most likely to survive the procedure, to recover from this illness or injury? Those patients who stand a better chance of recovery enjoy a higher priority in receiving our medical resources when

these are not enough to provide for all. This criterion does not rest upon our judgment of the relative worth of persons. It stems rather from our understanding of the *mitzvah* of medicine, which we have seen is an aspect of our moral duty to save life. From this definition, it follows that we ought to practice medicine in such a way that we most effectively save life. Those whom we can save or "cure" take precedence over those we cannot, for to apply our energies and resources to the treatment of those who cannot benefit from them serves a lesser medical purpose, if it indeed serves any medical purpose at all. Similarly, we might infer that as a community we ought to invest our medical resources in such a way that more people, rather than fewer, may benefit from them, since to heal the largest possible number of people is arguably the better way of practicing this *mitzvah*.

The Reform responsa tradition regards this principle as the proper criterion to use. We think that the responsibility to practice medicine requires that we make an active determination as to the best way of practicing it. And we also think that the commitment to the equality of all persons before God is a more coherent reflection of Jewish teaching as a whole than is the idea that we can determine which persons are "better citizens" and more worthy of being saved. The best standard to use in selecting patients for treatment is one which does not demand that we draw invidious distinctions based upon personality, lifestyle, or other similar considerations. Rather, when we must decide which individuals receive our life-sustaining resources, we should strive to do so in accordance with our responsibility to save life—to practice medicine—in the most effective way we can.

Smoking, Alcohol, and Drugs

Smoking. At one time, smoking was generally considered a harmless, even worthwhile pleasure. Many thought that tobacco was a healthful substance, an aid to blood circulation, to digestion, and the like. A number of rabbis shared this opinion, writing in praise of tobacco's benefits to human health. Some even wondered whether a blessing ought to be recited upon smoking, since the pleasure derived from it resembled that of eating, drinking, or the smelling of fragrances. Today, scientific evidence concerning the dangers of smoking is accepted worldwide, and there is no longer any reasonable doubt that tobacco causes disease and death. Reflecting this change, rabbinic opinion now condemns smoking as a threat to human life and health. As Judaism forbids us to endanger our lives needlessly and to treat our bodies with reckless disrespect, so it forbids us to smoke. Those who smoke are under a strict moral obligation to do all in their power to stop smoking. It is wrong as well to encourage smokers in their habit by buying tobacco for them or by offering them a light. Synagogues and other Jewish institutions should prohibit smoking on their premises.

Alcohol and Drugs. Judaism does not condemn the use, in moderation, of alcoholic beverages. On the contrary: the Bible speaks in praise of wine as a substance that "gladdens the human heart" (Ps. 104:15). Wine has always played a visibly central role in Jewish religious culture. This is evident in the fact that the tradition ordains special blessings to be recited prior to and following its consumption, just as it does for bread. The use of wine is required in such ritual practices as *Kiddush*, the "four cups" at the Passover Seder, and the celebration of weddings and *berit milah*. Other intoxicants can serve in place of wine under certain conditions in some (but not all) of these settings.

At the same time, however, we must treat alcoholic beverages with the utmost caution, since they can be a source of pain as well as joy. Wine may serve as an important element in our ritual, but it is by no means indispensable; one who for medical reasons is unable to drink wine or liquor is allowed to substitute non-intoxicants for ritual purposes, including the Passover Seder. We are told to beware of "wine when it is red," for its color and smoothness hide the reality that "in the end, it bites like a snake" and distorts the workings of the human mind (Prov. 23:31–32). A tradition which values clear thinking and responsible conduct cannot but view drunkenness as an evil. The *shikur*, the drunkard, may be the butt of many jokes, but he is in an essential way held separate from the community: he or she may not perform religious, legal, or political functions and is even forbidden to pray until sober. The clear implication of these sources is that should we decide to use alcohol we must strictly control our consumption of it. Once again, we are reminded that Judaism holds us responsible for failure to treat our health with care and respect. This point is driven home with special urgency given our awareness of the destructive nature of alcoholism, a disease of which our ancestors were but dimly aware. The costs of alcoholism, measured by the personal and social wreckage it leaves in its wake, require that we confront this disease openly and directly, doing whatever we can as a community for those who come to us in their struggle for recovery.

One of the most effective programs of recovery from alcoholism is the "twelve-step" method pioneered by Alcoholics Anonymous and utilized as well in the struggle against other addictions. This approach has saved countless lives and therefore must be considered a blessing. It is also the case, however, that meetings of "twelve-step" organizations often involve Christian religious practices such as the recitation of the "Lord's Prayer." This raises a serious difficulty for Jews, for the integrity of our own religious identity demands that we refrain from adopting ritual and liturgical practices that have become associated with other faiths. A Jewish member of a "twelve-step" group might either stand in respectful silence during the prayer or recite an appropriate substitute such as Psalm 23. We are especially grateful to those in our community who work to incorporate the insights of the "twelve-step" method into a Jewish communal and spiritual setting.

The same admonition applies to other addictive and mind-altering substances. The tradition, as we have seen, permits the use of drugs as long as we do so in service of a legitimate medical purpose. We may administer even the most powerful chemicals, provided that: the goal is to combat disease or to control pain; that the chemicals are prescribed by physicians following protocols established and accepted by the medical profession and by the law; and that the drugs are taken under the careful supervision of qualified medical personnel. Outside of those strict limitations, the taking of drugs is forbidden because they are injurious to physical and mental health. Judaism does not countenance the use of drugs for recreation, nor does it recognize any religious value gained from the "expansion of consciousness" by chemical means. These substances should be avoided, and we should do our utmost to see to it that those addicted to them are given the assistance they need to break that dependency.

AIDS; Tay-Sachs Testing

AIDS. As of this writing, there is still no known cure or immunization for AIDS (Acquired Immune Deficiency Syndrome). Those who suffer from AIDS and those who are infected with the human immunodeficiency virus (HIV) that causes it must be treated with the love and the compassion that our tradition teaches us to bestow upon all those who are ill. The *mitzvah* of *bikkur cholim* (visiting the sick) is especially relevant here, inasmuch as society as a whole has all too frequently responded with rejection and blame to those who bear this disease. Those who suffer from AIDS or carry its virus should be protected against all forms of invidious legal discrimination. We renounce any suggestion that AIDS is a sign of God's punishment visited upon a particular class of sinners. It is rather a disease, and like all other fatal diseases it calls upon us to do all we can to care for those whom it affects and to work toward its eradication. We call upon the governments of the world to support research efforts directed at discovering a cure for AIDS and more effective means of halting its spread.

The Community and the AIDS Carrier. Since AIDS is a fatal disease, one who carries its virus must refrain from behavior which would transmit the disease to others. Sexual intercourse should either be avoided entirely or performed with stringent protection. A person infected with AIDS or HIV must reveal that fact to his or her spouse or sexual partner. Failure to reveal this information means that one poses a mortal threat to the partner, and no one is permitted to endanger the life of another. Rabbis, physicians, or other counselors who know that a person suffers from any dangerous communicable disease are morally obligated to reveal this information to that person's spouse or potential spouse. A medical practitioner who has contracted HIV must inform his or her patients of that fact.

Should the Jewish community institute compulsory testing for HIV as a requirement for marriage? Reform responsa have answered this question in the negative. Apart from the severe difficulties in enforcing any such requirement, we must consider the imperfect nature of the tests for the virus and the fact that compulsory testing is at some basic level an invasion of privacy and an insult to the human dignity of the individual. These concerns would certainly give way in the face of *pikuach nefesh*, our duty to protect life, but there is at the present time no evidence that AIDS has spread into the general population to an extent that it would warrant a general requirement. This judgment could change, of course, if AIDS were to become a widespread phenomenon in the general population. On the other hand, those individuals belonging to "at-risk" groups, segments of the population in which AIDS occurs with significant frequency, or those who have engaged in behavior associated with a high risk of contracting AIDS, are strongly advised to have themselves tested for the virus.

We can condone, though reluctantly, the distribution of free needles to drug addicts as a means of preventing the spread of AIDS through contaminated needles. This position is based upon a simple calculation: while drug addiction is certainly dangerous to the user and to those around him or her, it does not necessarily lead to death, and one can, though with much pain and difficulty, recover from it. AIDS, on the other hand, is always fatal. *Pikuach nefesh*, the saving of life, therefore must take precedence. We might also say that, since the addicts will likely continue to inject drugs whether or not we distribute sterile needles, our decision to do so does not in fact cause them to become addicted or encourage them in their habit. Yet our choice of the lesser of two evils ought not conceal the fact that it *is* nonetheless an evil, and the best response is certainly one that does not force us to choose between them at all. We should work to make drug treatment available to all who need it, so that they may escape the curse of drug addiction as well as that of AIDS.

Tay-Sachs Testing. Tay-Sachs disease is a hereditary disorder caused by the transmission of a defective gene from parents to their offspring. The incidence of this disease is concentrated primarily among Jews of Ashkenazic (Central and East European) origin. Both parents must be "carriers" of the gene in order to transmit the disease to their child, in which case there is a one-in-four chance that the child will be afflicted. The disease is always fatal: the child, born with serious retardation, will die at a very young age.

Genetic testing can reveal if a person possesses the Tay-Sachs gene, and many synagogues and Jewish community institutions sponsor screening programs to allow individuals and couples contemplating marriage or pregnancy to determine whether they are carriers. Some Orthodox rabbis have objected to these tests on the grounds that some Jewish couples, upon discovery that they are carriers, might refrain from marrying or having children, thus preventing them from fulfilling the *mitzvah* of procreation. Although we by all means encourage marriage and childbirth, we do not share these objections. The number of persons who might decide against marriage or childbirth on account of genetic testing is quite small, certainly not large enough to dissuade us from supporting a program that can save a couple and a family from great tragedy. If we have the means by which to discover this information, so vital to the emotional and psychological well-being of a couple, then we must use them; failure to do so cannot be morally justified.

Transsexual Surgery

A transsexual is a person who, though born with the anatomical signs of a male or a female, identifies deeply with the opposite gender. Transsexual surgery, the "sex-change operation," along with other treatments, seeks to correct this situation by removing the existing genital organs and constructing, as far as possible, new genitalia which correspond to the individual's "true" gender. Such treatments are permissible to the extent to which we can define this surgery as legitimate medicine. Reform Judaism accepts the considered judgment of science with respect to this issue, as it does on most other questions of medical ethics. Thus, a sex-change operation can be permitted so long as it is undertaken for "valid, serious reasons" with the aid of "the best available medical tests," such as chromosome analysis, which determine whether this individual is *in fact* more properly identified with the opposite gender. On the other hand, if the persons requesting the surgery are "physically normal" but "for some psychological reason, want to be changed into the other sex," then nothing in Jewish law or tradition would approve their request. In the absence of clear medical necessity, the desire to undergo transsexual surgery is a clear sign of emotional imbalance, and one would not be justified in subjecting him- or herself to the physical dangers involved with the operation. The change of sex, moreover, would result in physical sterilization, a most unfortunate outcome in the eyes of a tradition which places such a high value upon the bringing of children into the world. For this person, the proper course of treatment would be psychological, not surgical.

A transsexual may marry, provided that the surgery was undertaken for the "valid, serious reasons" indicated in the preceding paragraph.

We hold that the gender of a person who has undergone this procedure has in fact been altered, so that one who, as a result of a sex-change operation, is "now" a female may marry a male, and vice versa. It is true that the surgery renders the individual sterile; however, a couple who are incapable of having children can nonetheless contract a valid Jewish marriage.

7

Between Jews and Non-Jews

You shall not copy the practices of the land of Egypt where you dwelt, or of the land of Canaan to which I am taking you; nor shall you follow their laws. (Lev. 18:3)

In the days to come, the mount of Adonai's house shall stand firm above the mountains and tower above the hills; and all the nations shall gaze on it with joy. And the many peoples shall go and shall say: "Come, let us go up to the Mount of Adonai, to the house of the God of Jacob; that we may be instructed in God's ways and walk in God's paths." For instruction shall come forth out of Zion, Adonai's word from Jerusalem. Thus will God judge among the nations and arbitrate for the many peoples. They shall beat their swords into plowshares and their spears into pruning hooks: nation shall not take up sword against nation; they shall never again know war. (Isa. 2:2–4; Mic. 4:1–3)

"No advanced cultural or religious tradition has ever existed in a vacuum." Religion, like any other human institution, develops through a process of sustained contact and communication with its environment. The religion we call Judaism is a product of many influences whose roots lie in surrounding non-Jewish civilizations. Scholars have produced a great deal of research documenting these influences upon the law, the literature, the ritual observances, and the religious thought of the Jewish people in all ages. Judaism has thus never sealed itself off from its surroundings. As the Jewish people have experienced history, so have they changed with it, and have done so by borrowing freely from the cultures of the lands in which they lived. Jews have displayed a positive attitude toward the intellectual achievements of other peoples, a readiness to read their books, to absorb their wisdom, and to use what they have learned thereby to build their own religious civilization. It is therefore impossible to comprehend Judaism without studying the "Gentile" factors which have shaped its beliefs, practices, and institutions.

Yet at the same time, no great system of religious life is but a copy or clone of any other. Each is unique, shaped by forces internal as well as external. Judaism, too, differs essentially from all the religions and cultures in whose midst it has developed, for the simple reason that we Jews have aspired to a separate and distinct religious existence of our own.

We have maintained this distinctiveness primarily in two ways. First, although we have borrowed much from others, we have never done so uncritically. Our borrowing has been much more an act of translation than of stenography. If we have *adopted* stories, laws, rituals, and ideas from our neighbors, we have also *adapted* them to our own purposes, restructuring and reinterpreting them into expressions of a particularly Israelite or Jewish reality. Secondly, we have seen fit to place concrete limits upon what we borrow. Indeed, Jewish tradition teaches that it is a *mitzvah* to say "no" to at least some aspects of Gentile culture. The verse Leviticus 18:3, cited at the beginning of this section, warns the people to reject the practices and the laws of Egypt, the land which they have left, and of Canaan, the land in which they shall settle. The Rabbis understood this prohibition to apply to the customs of all Gentile nations, and Maimonides states its rationale succinctly: "So that Israel might remain distinct from the nations in their manner of dress and behavior, just as it is distinct from them in theology and belief."

This does not mean, of course, that we are forbidden to learn *anything* from our neighbors. Specifically, tradition teaches, the verse prohibits us from adopting the "statutes" (*chukkot*) of other peoples, those religious laws and cultural customs whose adoption would suggest a desire to imitate the Gentiles and to deny our Jewish distinctiveness. By contrast, "Gentile" practices which serve legitimate purposes are permitted. But what do we mean by a "legitimate purpose"? Where do we draw the line between the "good" practices which we may borrow from our neighbors and the "bad" ones we may not? Jewish tradition never developed a litmus-paper test to answer these questions. Rabbis had to consider each issue on a case-by-case basis, making their determination against the backdrop of the social environments in which the community lived. At times, their response was more liberal and accepting, reflecting an optimism that the Jewish community could maintain its distinctiveness even when it opened itself to contact with Gentile culture. At other times, the attitude has been more restrictive. The exact placement of the boundaries, in other words, has always been a matter of dispute. The common denominator in all these disputes, however, has been the understanding among the Jews at all times, in "liberal" as well as in "restrictive" periods, that boundaries must be drawn, that some limits must be set upon the degree of Gentile influence which we are prepared to admit into our religious life. We might therefore describe the Jewish relationship with non-Jewish society as one of creative tension, in which our openness to Gentile culture pulls against a pronounced resistance to that culture.

We find the same creative tension at work in the history of Reform Judaism. A dominant theme in the development of our movement has been our declared openness to the ways of the wider world. Reform Jewish thought, in the spirit of the prophetic passage cited at the beginning of this section, holds that the Jewish people are part *of* the world and are not to set themselves apart *from* it. Accordingly, many Reform Jews have chosen to emphasize the "universalistic" elements of our tradition, particularly those ethical precepts which we hold in common with other traditions, over those primarily ritual aspects of our heritage that seemed "parochial" and which served to set us apart from others. In the realm of religious observance, we have openly and gladly introduced innovations modeled after the standards of taste, decorum, and spiritual uplift that we have drawn from the surrounding culture. In recent years, though, we have become more skeptical about the sufficiency of liberalism and universalism as a Jewish religious program. The reasons for this are no doubt tied to the events of contemporary Jewish history, which have both contradicted our earlier faith in the inevitability of human progress and persuaded us that ethnic pluralism and religious particularism are good things and worth preserving. We are also motivated by a heightened concern over assimilation, which we perceive as a clear and present danger to Jewish survival and which therefore must be resisted. We are convinced today that meaning and holiness can be found in the observance of a religious life style that is its own special path to God, which cannot be reduced to ethics or to any other universal human experience. We wish, in short, to be *Jewish*, a term we define in relation to the history of our *particular* people, which has always sought to maintain a distinct religious and cultural existence of its own. And we know that the desire to preserve our Jewish distinctiveness may demand that we, too, say "no" at times to those outside influences whose acceptance would tend to blur the boundaries that set us apart from other peoples and communities.

We Reform Jews, like all other Jews, therefore seek to draw a proper balance between our positive affirmation of the surrounding culture and the need, at times, to distance ourselves from it. To do so means that we, like they, must exercise careful judgment in order to determine just how to go about the task of living fully in the world while insuring our continued distinctiveness as a people.

The Religion of the Non-Jew

Pagans; Christians and Muslims. Jewish doctrine regards the practice of idolatry as one of the most heinous of sins. The idolater, defined by our tradition as one who worships created things—the sun, moon, stars, statues made of wood or stone—is seen as one whose life is devoid of any spiritual value or moral standards. Hence, our texts contain a great deal of restrictive legislation separating us from idol worshipers and their culture. We are not only forbidden to engage in "alien worship" (*avodah zarah*), but we are also to make no use of and derive no benefit from any object devoted to idolatrous cults. Jews must maintain a strict social segregation from idolatrous peoples, lest "they turn your children away from Me to worship other gods" (Deut. 7:4). Moreover, since our tradition teaches that *all* peoples—all the "children of Noah"—are forbidden to practice idolatry, we are not to take any action that would encourage a Gentile to practice it. For this reason, Jews are to refrain from doing business with Gentiles during the days immediately preceding an idolatrous festival, lest the non-Jew donate the proceeds to his cult or give thanks to his idol for the profit he received from the transaction.

Over time, many of these severe prohibitions were removed or relaxed. While the restrictive laws may have fit the situation in the land of Israel during the era when the Jews constituted a majority of the population, in the Diaspora our people were a minority, dependent upon the surrounding Gentile community for their livelihood. They could not observe the limitations upon commerce prescribed in the Bible and Talmud without severe economic hardship. They also feared that a standoffish attitude toward their neighbors would provoke them to hostility and violence. In addition to these pragmatic concerns, the Jews were aware that the Gentiles among whom they lived differed substantially from those described in the classical sources. With all the theological disagreements that separated Judaism from Islam and Christianity, the rabbis could see that the latter were monotheistic faiths which preach the necessity for moral conduct and that the term *avodah zarah* (idolatry) therefore did not fit them. Ultimately, the medieval rabbinic authorities ruled that neither Christians nor Muslims could be considered idolaters. This decision meant that Jews were permitted to associate fully with Gentiles in most economic contexts.

None of the laws that restrict normal economic and social contact with idolaters applies in any way to Christians or Muslims. We respect Christianity and Islam as venerable monotheistic religious traditions whose communicants find in them great resources of spiritual strength and moral guidance. And to the extent that Judaism shares some important religious and ethical doctrines with Christianity and Islam, we look with favor upon cooperative endeavors between the adherents of these three faiths directed toward the attainment of our common goals and aspirations, particularly in the realm of social justice.

Yet even though we find much of value in Christianity and Islam, the religion we call Judaism is incompatible with either of them. Our tradition, like those of our neighbors, is marked by its own particular teachings, beliefs, and practices. Our commitment to the proposition that the Jewish people (*Am Yisrael*) constitutes a unique and distinctive religious community is a fundamental belief. A non-Jew, therefore, no matter how exalted his or her religion, is not a member of this community. He or she is welcome, of course, to join us through the process of conversion, but conversion is the *only* way that the non-Jew can become a member of the people of Israel. And central to conversion is the requirement that the proselyte accept the Torah, renounce any and all attachment to other religions, and declare exclusive loyalty to Judaism. The non-Jew is certainly welcome to worship in our synagogues and to take advantage of many of the programs offered by our congregations. But until such time as he or she decides to become a Jew, the non-Jew is not entitled to formal membership in our communities and may not exercise leadership responsibilities in them. In addition, the non-Jew does not lead us in worship, and he or she should not perform on our behalf those ritual acts by which we express our identity as the community of Israel.

Fraternal Orders; Meditation Groups. A number of organizations express themselves through forms of ritual behavior that resemble those of religious groups and traditions. In assessing our relationship to these organizations, therefore, it is necessary to ask whether we look upon them as religions or as something else.

The Reform movement does not regard fraternal orders such as the Masons as religions. We do not object, therefore, if members of the order wish to perform their rites at the funeral of a Jewish member, so long as these are kept separate from the Jewish service and so long as the rabbi makes it clear that the Jewish service is of primary importance.

Groups organized for the purpose of meditation and spirituality are not *necessarily* to be considered as "religions." Some of them do not differ greatly from the various approaches to group psychology, and there is no objection to participation in them. Others, however, involve beliefs and theologies which may be in conflict with Judaism, and some are full-blown cults, centered upon idolatrous devotion to a charismatic leader. Jews clearly should not take part in any of the activities sponsored by these latter groups.

Interfaith Services

Joint Services. Joint religious services, in which Jews participate together with members of other faiths, are a common occurrence, especially as a means of commemorating national holidays and marking moments of significance, whether joyous or sorrowful, in the life of the wider community. Unlike regular synagogue worship, the interfaith service is not a specifically Jewish event. It is a ritual and liturgical exercise, held in a synagogue, church, or elsewhere, in which all participate in worship on an equal basis. We affirm the value of such services, keeping in mind the following considerations.

Interfaith services should not take place too frequently, since they tend to emphasize the common teachings and concerns of our faiths and thus perhaps to blur the very real distinctions between them. Should interfaith services become a regular occurrence, we would give the erroneous impression to others and to ourselves that there are in fact no significant differences in the beliefs and customs of our communities.

The service should be conducted in an attitude of complete respect for the differences between each religious tradition. The participants should not be required to read or recite anything contrary to their religious conscience. Moreover, the liturgy and ritual of the ceremony should be "non-denominational" and not sectarian in nature, one in which all the participants can share. Participants should avoid the use of particular theological language which evokes the religious sensibilities of some, but not all, of those in attendance.

Not all Jews wish to take part in interfaith services. We should not let their refusal dictate our own policy in this regard; at the same time, we ought to be mindful of *Kelal Yisrael*, the totality of the Jewish community. We should therefore try to avoid giving needless offense to other Jews by the manner of our interfaith activities.

The "Civil Religion." Social scientists use the term "civil religion" to describe the *sancta* of a secular community, that is, the quasi-religious behavior with which it expresses its sense of self. For example, a nation's flag, national anthem, public holidays, and symbols may evoke within its citizens a mood of devotion somewhat akin to religion. The rituals of patriotism (reciting the pledge of allegiance, standing in silence for the anthem or the passing of the flag) may be performed in a spirit that resembles religious behavior and ceremony. As Jews, we do not recognize the "civil religion," whatever its ritual trappings, as a "religion" in a real sense. Since the "civil religion" therefore does not compete with our own, Jews may express loyalty to their country without abandoning Judaism. Indeed, we have always expressed our concern for the welfare of the state and the general community as part of our worship. Those of us who are citizens of democratic countries are active members of our national communities, and we care passionately about their welfare and good order. In our eyes, to declare loyalty to our country is to give voice to our commitment to *tikkun olam*, to the betterment of the world, because it is within the arena of secular political and social life that we are often called upon to apply the teachings of our prophets.

This affirmation, however, has its limits. Just as it is inappropriate to give the impression that there are no differences between Judaism and other faiths, so too it is inappropriate to act in such a way as to identify Judaism with the civil religion or the cult of nationhood. If "civil religion" is not, technically speaking, to be defined as idolatry, overzealous patriotism surely serves as its functional equivalent. The sanctification of the nation-state and its leaders has been associated with some of the most horrendous acts of barbarism and cruelty of our time. We emphatically do *not* equate "God" with "Country," and we are properly suspicious of rhetoric and ceremony which draw that comparison.

It is certainly not forbidden to take part in patriotic or other communal ceremonies; we do so proudly. Nor is it forbidden to display such national symbols as flags in our synagogues, since these testify to the love and concern that our congregants feel for their country. On the other hand, nothing in our tradition *requires* that the flag be displayed. What is essential is that we think carefully and critically about our behavior as Jewish citizens of our state. Should our thinking lead us to conclude that the display of flags, the singing of anthems, or any other ritual of the "civil religion" is inappropriate in the sacred space of the synagogue, then we may choose to dispense with such rituals. The congregation's patriotism is in no way lessened thereby, for the true test of our love of country lies not in the display of its symbols but in our concern for its well-being and in the work we do to further the cause of justice, compassion, and peace for all its people.

Participation in Non-Jewish Religious Services

We may take part in non-Jewish religious services, so long as our participation is not an act of worship and is restricted to matters that are not religiously offensive to us. A Jew may, for example, read a passage from the Hebrew Scriptures (but *not* from the New Testament) at a Christian service as a gesture of friendship to emphasize the common bonds which link our faiths. Similarly, a Jew may serve as an attendant in a wedding ceremony at a Christian church, since attendance is generally not construed as worship. The attendant should, however, avoid kneeling, bowing, or other specifically devotional acts. In general, "there is no way in the law of permitting any Jewish participation in a trinitarian worship or celebration." Thus, a Jewish child who attends a Christian school should not take part in the school's worship services.

A Jew (for example, a Jewish hospital chaplain) should not perform a Christian sacrament such as baptism, even if requested by Christians to do so. The power of a sacrament, even according to the teachings of those denominations which allow non-Christians to perform them, lies in its essence as a visible sign of the salvific power of Christ and of the religious significance of his birth, death, and resurrection. A Jew cannot believe in these doctrines; hence, a Jew cannot serve as the agent of the Church in bestowing religious salvation upon its adherents. A Jewish hospital chaplain should help facilitate the sacrament and arrange for its performance by a non-Jew. It is, however, inappropriate for that chaplain to conduct the rite or to take part in its liturgy.

The above discussion refers specifically to Christianity and Islam, which are monotheistic faiths. Polytheistic religions, such as Hinduism or the Native American religions, pose a special problem. Although these traditions contain noble philosophical and ethical teachings, it is inappropriate for us to take part in any way in polytheistic rituals. This position, of course, might be reviewed if it becomes clear to us that the adherents of these religions have renounced the polytheistic elements of their traditions. Until such time, however, we may watch their ceremonies and do everything to maintain friendly relationships with members of these communities, but we must refrain from participation. (On our relationship to groups such as "Jews for Jesus" or "Messianic Jews," see Chapter 2.)

Non-Jewish Religious Practices

As noted at the beginning of this section, the exact meaning of the commandment contained in Leviticus 18:3—"you shall not copy the practices"—has been the subject of much argument in Jewish tradition. Given the ambiguity built into the interpretation of this *mitzvah*, it may seem inappropriate that Reform Jews take part in this debate. How, after all, can we declare our unwillingness to "imitate Gentile practice" when other Jews have long criticized many of our ritual innovations, such as prayer in the vernacular and the use of instrumental music in worship, on precisely those grounds? To this, we respond first of all that many of the so-called "Gentile" influences we have adopted are perfectly compatible with Jewish law. Secondly, while Jews have for centuries disputed just *which* practices it is forbidden to "imitate," they have always been convinced of the necessity to preserve a distinctive core of religious behavior that is unmistakably *Jewish*. As we Reform Jews share in this conviction, we assume the responsibility of adding our voices and perspective to this age-old "argument for the sake of Heaven." What follows, then, is a discussion of some of the conclusions that we have reached concerning the boundaries that we draw between our own religious practice and that of our neighbors.

Non-Jewish Liturgy and Music. We Jews have always borrowed from the literary styles of other peoples to create our own liturgy. Much of the beautiful Hebrew poetry that fills the traditional prayer book, for example, was written by Jewish authors who followed the standards that defined poetic excellence in the vernacular (that is, the non-Jewish) literatures of their place and time. We therefore do not insist that our prayer-texts conform to some model of "Jewish" stylistic integrity, since styles of Jewish writing have always been dependent upon and adapted from surrounding cultures. We do draw the line, however, at matters of content, excluding from our worship those literary creations which are identified with Gentile *religious* practice and which are commonly recognized as such. This is the case even when the particulars of a text do not, in the abstract, offend our religious sensibilities. A case in point is the Paternoster, the "Lord's Prayer," whose wording is not explicitly christological and is, on that narrow ground, theologically unobjectionable to us. Its text indeed parallels a number of ancient Jewish prayers. Yet we look past the wording of this prayer to what it *means*, to how it functions in its social and historical context. As a familiar element of Christian worship and devotion, the Paternoster is a particularly Christian practice and emblematic of Christian devotion; it is therefore unacceptable in any Jewish setting. The same is true in the case of music. Jews have long adapted the musical styles of their neighbors, including particular songs and melodies composed by non-Jews. There is no problem with this, so long as we do not borrow their specifically liturgical music. Again, not all Gentile hymns contain lyrics that we find objectionable, but their firm association with non-Jewish worship makes them inappropriate for us. Should individuals or families request that Christian hymns be performed at religious events, we should refuse their request, while reminding them that the tradition of Jewish music, like that of Jewish religious practice in general, is a wonderfully rich storehouse of creativity which most surely contains resources that are fitting for any occasion.

Non-Jewish Religious Celebrations. The most common "non-Jewish religious celebration" at issue in the North American context is the holiday of Christmas. This is one of the predominant celebrations in our society, and much of its tenor is secular (gift-giving, Santa Claus, etc.) rather than overtly christological. For this reason, it is sometimes claimed that Christmas, like Thanksgiving, is part of our "civil religion" and that Jews would therefore be permitted to celebrate Christmas, as we celebrate other secular festivals, so long as this did not involve an explicit act of worship. We reject this claim. Christmas, like Easter, is one of the basic observances of the Christian liturgical calendar; it *is* a religious holiday, regardless of what some people say about it. We should therefore refrain from any act of open celebration, such as participating in "holiday luminary displays." We reject as well the suggestion of joint "Christmas-Chanukah" celebrations. Chanukah is not "the Jewish Christmas." Christmas and Chanukah are rather two different holidays, each with its own distinctive message; they must not be confused with each other. Indeed, as Chanukah commemorates our ancestors' refusal to bow to the influence of a Gentile religious culture, it is doubly inappropriate to assert a likeness between these festivals. Moreover, given the pressures exerted upon us and our young people by conversionary movements such as "Jews for Jesus," we must be wary of any practice that might smack of religious syncretism, the tendency to blur the necessary and important distinctions between our faiths.

On the other hand, there is no reason why we cannot wish "season's greetings" to our neighbors or to exchange gifts with them at this time of the year, since we do these things out of a spirit of friendship and not as a religious observance. Much depends upon the social setting. For example, a Jew need not object to holiday decorations in a place of business, although in countries which guarantee the separation of state and religion such decorations may be inappropriate in public schools and government institutions. We are stricter, however, when Jewish children are involved, so that they not be given the impression that Christmas is a holiday that they ought to celebrate.

It has become customary in many communities for Jews to substitute for Christian workers so that the latter may spend the day with their families. This is a praiseworthy deed, but we should remember that "praiseworthy deeds" do not necessarily take precedence over our own religious life. Thus, in years when Christmas or Christmas Eve falls on Shabbat, our volunteering should be confined to hospitals and to institutions of public safety, since our tradition teaches that the protection of life does supersede the restrictions against performing labor on Shabbat. It would *not* be proper, however, to substitute for salespeople, postal clerks, and other workers not directly involved in lifesaving activities.

Other Practices. A number of questions relating to Jewish use of non-Jewish religious practices are discussed elsewhere in this volume, particularly with respect to funeral and mourning observances; see Chapter 4.

1. *Incense.* A Jewish congregation may use incense as part of their worship service, provided that they do not do this in conscious imitation of the worship customs of particular Gentile groups.

2. *All-Night Vigils.* Numerous groups in our society make use of the all-night vigil as a means of demonstrating in support of social causes. Although the all-night vigil is familiar from Christian devotional practice and is undoubtedly borrowed from that context, Jewish tradition also knows of it. The recitation of *selichot*, penitential prayers, traditionally begins late at night and continues until dawn; some communities encourage those members who are able to remain awake for prayer and study during the night of Yom Kippur; and the *tikkun leyl shavuot*, the practice of remaining awake to study Torah through the night of the festival of Shavuot, is a well-known feature of that holiday's observance. It is permissible to participate in such an observance for a secular cause, although it is praiseworthy to add the Jewish element of study to our participation.

3. *The Synagogue.* On non-Jewish participation in synagogue ritual, see Chapter 1. On non-Jews as members and officers of congregations, and on questions of synagogue construction and architecture, see Chapter 2.

Carillon Music. We note above that it is permissible to borrow non-Jewish musical compositions, styles, and motifs for our worship, so long as we exclude music that is specifically liturgical and is generally recognized as such. This proviso holds true as well for such architectural features as carillon bells. Since the ringing of bells is firmly associated with Christian churches, synagogues should not adopt this custom for themselves.

Flowers. Floral decorations are a common feature in our synagogue sanctuaries and social areas. These displays may include any type of flower, including varieties that enjoy a strong symbolic attachment to Christianity or other religions. We might, for the sake of appearances, wish to impose some limitations; for example, we may wish to avoid the use of the lily at the season of Easter. This is not, however, a firm requirement.

Concerts. It is permissible, under certain conditions, to hold non-Jewish events such as concerts in the synagogue. Does this permission extend to performances which include such compositions as requiems, masses, and the like? After all, many of the great compositions of our Western musical heritage originated as liturgical pieces in church practice. The answer requires that we determine just how we experience these selections when we hear them in concert. If we imagine that we are listening to a liturgical exercise, then clearly it is unwise to allow their performance in a synagogue. Since it is more likely, however, that we regard them as "great music" rather than as explicitly liturgical pieces, they may be performed in the synagogue.

8

Reform Judaism and the Jewish Community

All Jews are responsible for one another. (*B. Shevuot* 39a)

The above saying is familiar to us from its frequent use in sermons and communal *tzedakah* campaigns. Its sentiment, the notion that somehow each Jew is accountable for the safety and the well-being of every other, is a clarion call to Jewish unity. That sentiment, however, is based upon a translation of a talmudic text, and while the English is a passably accurate rendition of that text—*kol Yisrael arevim zeh bazeh*—it nonetheless misses an essential element of it. The Hebrew word *arevim*, generally translated as "responsible," is in fact the plural for *arev*, which means "guarantor," one who insures that another person will fulfill a particular legal obligation. One who co-signs a borrower's note is an *arev*, from whom the lender is entitled to seek repayment should the borrower fail to make good on the debt. Our talmudic passage applies this legal concept of accountability to a religious context. To say that "all Jews are *arevim* for each other" is to say that every Jew is a guarantor for every other Jew's performance of the commandments and that God, who gave us the Torah on condition that we observe its precepts, is entitled to hold each of us "responsible" should another Jew fail to fulfill his or her religious duties.

Understood in this way, the passage sounds less morally stirring than it does in its customary translation. It also conveys an idea that we might well find troubling. The suggestion that it is the business of every Jew to insure that other Jews perform the *mitzvot* offends our most deeply-held beliefs in the right to privacy and the autonomy of the individual.

Our religious lives, we tend to think, are our own business, and most of us would resent other Jews snooping into what we regard as our own private realm. Even were we not so offended, to raise the possibility of this kind of intervention implies that we all agree upon exactly what a *mitzvah* is, that is to say, the specific nature and content of our duties under the covenant. It must be so, for only when we know what our obligations are can we hold ourselves and each other "responsible" for our failure to meet them. Such agreement, however, is often lacking in Reform Judaism, where we often bristle at any attempt by others, whether they be rabbis or laypersons, individuals or organized bodies, to restrict our freedom by defining Judaism for us, telling us what we as Jews must do. Perhaps we ought to be glad, then, that translation is *not* an exact science. For while the looser translation of this passage— "all Jews are responsible for one another"—is a conception of Jewish unity that we certainly affirm, the more literal translation says more than most of us may be willing to say.

Yet there may be some good reasons why we should not be so quick to discard the literal translation. For all the difficulties it causes, it still imparts a truth that Reform Jews do accept. That "truth" is the conviction that the Jews—all of us, whatever our theological direction—are participants in a common religious enterprise. Our tradition teaches that "we all stood at Sinai" and heard the voice of God, to which we responded, "All that God has said we will faithfully do [*na'aseh venishma*]." It is indeed the case that we Jews disagree among ourselves, and radically so, over the precise content of that divine message, over the correct interpretation of what God expects of us. But all religious Jews, Reform and otherwise, join together in the understanding that we are responding to God's invitation. All of us define that invitation and response as a covenant, an eternal bond between God and the *entire* Jewish people. We all declare, in other words, that the point of our Jewish existence is religious: the Jewish people exist by virtue of a promise we made to "faithfully do" according to the terms of the covenant. And we made that promise as a collective body, the people of Israel.

We acknowledge, therefore, that all Jews share a common religious destiny and that, to fulfill this destiny, we need each other. We do not comprehend ourselves merely as individuals, each seeking his or her personal spiritual pathway through life. On the contrary: we are *Israel*, a collective reality that is greater than the sum of its parts. And this self-image implies that each of us is *responsible*, not only for our own religious lives, but for the quality of Jewish religious life as a whole. This responsibility, as we see it, does not require that we interfere in the religious choices made by our fellow Jews, to compel them to "do the right thing." We liberals find religious coercion to be morally repugnant. Just as we denounce it when exerted against us, so we renounce any desire to employ it against others. But *responsibility* does require that we hold ourselves accountable for the quality of Jewish religious life, our own and that of the wider community. It requires that every Jew is obliged to work to improve that quality, to help create the conditions under which each member of the family of Israel can do his or her part toward the fulfillment of our common religious purpose.

It is in this sense that we can read our saying according to its literal translation. "All Jews hold themselves responsible for the religious lives of all other Jews," for it is only within this community called Israel that we can work out our Jewish religious existence. And it is in this sense that we can best understand the tradition of Reform Jewish thought concerning our relationship to the entire Jewish community.

Israel and Zionism

The fifth day of the month of Iyar is Israel Independence Day, which is recognized as "a permanent annual festival in the religious calendar of Reform Judaism."

The above sentence indicates just how far the Reform movement has traveled in its attitude toward Zionism and Jewish nationalism. In its early days, Reform Judaism was distinguished by its belief that the Jewish people was a purely religious and not a national community, a community whose "homeland" was the entire world. The first reformers believed in a rational and enlightened Judaism, a key element of which was a devotion to the tenets of universalism. As they saw it, there was no room in such a faith for a conception of Jewish nationalism, the idea that Israel remains a people like other peoples and that it retains any hope for a national existence. The Jew's national attachments were rather to the country in which he or she enjoyed the rights of citizenship. The Pittsburgh Platform proclaimed that, as a "religious community" and not a "nation," we do not look forward to "the restoration of any laws concerning the Jewish state." Indeed, at the end of the nineteenth century and into the beginning of the twentieth century, Reform Judaism in the United States was, at least in its official, institutional expression, an essentially anti-Zionist movement. Resolutions of the Union of American Hebrew Congregations and the Central Conference of American Rabbis criticized and even condemned the Zionist enterprise. "America is our Zion," the movement's representatives announced; "We totally disapprove of any attempt for the establishment of a Jewish state." In 1917, the government of Great Britain issued the Balfour Declaration, which recognized the right of Jewish self-determination in Palestine, a moment enshrined as a glorious one in Zionist history. For its part, however, the Central Conference of American Rabbis took the opportunity to express its opposition once again to the Zionist movement. While its members resolved that "we naturally favor the facilitation of immigration to Palestine" for persecuted Jews, nonetheless "we do not subscribe to the phrase in the declaration which says, 'Palestine is to be a national home-land for the Jewish people.'"

Yet even during its "classical" phase, Reform Judaism contained within its ranks a significant Zionist camp. Some leading Reform rabbis and thinkers were active in the Zionist movement as early as the nineteenth century. If their influence did not then carry the institutions of Reform Judaism along with them, their views over time began to predominate. Part of the explanation for this change lies in demography. The Jews of Eastern European ancestry who began to join American Reform congregations during the early twentieth century held a much more positive attitude toward the concepts of Jewish ethnicity and nationalism than did Reform Jews of German background. As Reform rabbis began to speak more openly of the unbreakable bond between "the faith of Israel" and "the people of Israel," the portrait of Judaism as a belief system devoid of all national attachments lost much of its appeal. By 1937, the Columbus Platform could affirm "the obligation of all Jewry to aid in [Palestine's] upbuilding as a Jewish homeland." The horror of the Holocaust and the creation of the State of Israel in 1948 also did much to soften the ideological anti-Zionism of the movement. Reform acceptance of Zionism and its participation in the work of Jewish national renewal has remained on an upward trajectory in recent decades, so much so that the 1976 San Francisco Platform could endorse *aliyah*, emigration to Israel, as a legitimate religious option for Reform Jews. In 1977, the Association of Reform Zionists of America was founded, heralding a new, more activist phase of Reform Jewish involvement in Zionist activity and Israeli life.

In 1997, in commemoration of the centenary of the first World Zionist Congress, the Central Conference of American Rabbis adopted "Reform Judaism and Zionism: A Centenary Platform." The document represents a formal and explicit rejection of the anti-Zionist ideology of the early decades of Reform Judaism. It sets forth a view of how North American Reform Jews today ought to understand the role of *Eretz Yisrael* (the land of Israel) and *Medinat Yisrael* (the State of Israel) in the life of *Am Yisrael* (the Jewish people). Its principles may be summarized as follows:

1. The Jewish people, throughout its two-thousand-year dispersion, never abandoned its hope for national rebirth. That rebirth, the establishment of the State of Israel, is an historic triumph for us. We understand this triumph in moral as well as political terms, for *Yisrael* is not a nation like all others. The renewal of Jewish nationhood in *Eretz Yisrael* is a necessary condition for the redemption for which our tradition yearns. Yet political statehood does not automatically signal that redemption. Our dreams will not be fulfilled until the Jewish people, whether in Israel or the Diaspora, experiences a spiritual rebirth, living up to the high ideals of its religious tradition.

2. The lack of a national state is synonymous in our world with political powerlessness, the effects of which were most tragically illustrated by the fate of our people during the Holocaust. We welcome the reassertion of state power that is crystallized in the government of Israel. We also hope that this power will be used not merely for military and political ends but to construct and to safeguard a society that guarantees human and civil rights for all its citizens.

3. The State of Israel is the spiritual and cultural focal point of the Jewish world. At the same time, founding of the state does not imply the negation or the end of the Diaspora. Indeed, Israel and Diaspora Jewry are mutually dependent, accountable for one another, and partners in shaping the quality and the future of Jewish life.

4. As a result of this mutual bond, we Reform Jews owe a number of obligations toward Israel. These include: to pledge our financial and political assistance; to learn Hebrew; to travel to Israel and to study

there; to encourage *aliyah* (immigration to Israel); and to teach Israelis about the values of Liberal Judaism.

5. Israel likewise has obligations to the Diaspora. Given the prevalence of conflicting religious views among the Jewish people, the State of Israel best serves *Am Yisrael* by maintaining a pluralistic society in which no one interpretation of Judaism takes precedence over another.

Based upon these principles, we might say that Reform Judaism holds love for *Yisrael*, the people and the state, to be a *mitzvah*, a religious duty. This love involves concern for the material welfare of our fellow Jews and of the State of Israel. Similarly, it demands that we engage ourselves constructively toward the betterment of Jewish religious life and to the furtherance of liberal Jewish ideals in Israel as well as in the Diaspora.

Israel: Conflicts and Priorities

Traditional Judaism is a religion consisting of many concrete religious acts and duties. It is not surprising, therefore, that from time to time two of these duties or *mitzvot* will come into inevitable conflict. Both of them make legitimate demands upon us that we feel obliged to fulfill, but we cannot perform both *mitzvot* simultaneously. We have to choose between them, and this requires some system for setting priorities, some method by which we can determine which *mitzvah* takes precedence over the other. In response to this dilemma, rabbinic tradition has developed a number of rules or rules-of-thumb which help one make the necessary choices in situations of this kind. The value of these rules for us lies not solely in the answers they yield but in the direction they give to our thinking. The rules teach us a set of Judaic criteria by which we might analyze the options before us; they show us how one might "think Jewishly" through a problem on the way to finding a solution.

Occasionally, we may face conflicts between our love for the State of Israel and other important religious obligations. Here, too, we are called upon to set priorities, to determine which *mitzvah* takes precedence over the other. And here, too, it is perhaps more important to us that we "think Jewishly" about this dilemma, so that whatever our answer might be we shall be able to defend it in *Jewish* terms as the best possible

Jewish choice that we could make. Two Reform responsa offer examples of how we might accomplish this task.

In the first responsum, Rabbi Solomon B. Freehof discusses the case of a couple who saved for years in order to visit Israel for a month. They have now decided to divert this money toward paying their children's college expenses. The question: have they the right to do so? Is it not a supreme religious duty to visit *Eretz Yisrael*?

Freehof begins his discussion by asking whether Jewish tradition considers it a *mitzvah*—that is, an "obligation," as opposed to a "good deed"—to settle in the land of Israel. Surprisingly enough, this is a question of great controversy in the halakhic literature. Some authorities hold the possession and settlement of *Eretz Yisrael* to be among the highest religious duties of the Jewish people and the individual Jew. Others, however, hold that the commandment to settle the land applied in the days of Joshua and King David. Others say the commandment was suspended when the Jews were exiled from the land. Some believe that the *mitzvah* will be reinstated only with the coming of the Messiah. Moreover, notes Rabbi Freehof, nowhere in the literature is a brief visit to the land of Israel described as a *mitzvah*. Thus, there exists no Jewish religious reason to hold the parents to their original intention to use this money for a trip to Israel. This is especially the case when the alternative objective, to pay for their children's education, is valued so highly in Jewish tradition. One might therefore surmise that the parents are obliged to use the funds for education, but such is not the case. This is a question of the children's secular, rather than religious education, and secular study "is of no concern in Jewish religious law." Therefore, "the parents can do as they wish"; neither alternative is preferable *on Jewish grounds* to the other.

One can argue with the particular points made on either side of this equation. One might say that, if there is a controversy as to whether the settlement of *Eretz Yisrael* is truly a *mitzvah*, the Jewish people has "voted with its feet" in favor of that interpretation of the tradition which answers the question in the affirmative. On the other hand, it is not necessarily the case that Jewish tradition is indifferent to the value of a secular education. A powerful strain within the tradition holds that the study of the world *is* the study of Torah, since through learning about God's creation we gain a deeper understanding and appreciation of God's glory. Rabbi Freehof's central point, however, is that no matter how we answer the question or whatever weight we accord to the

considerations on either side, we ought to "think Jewishly" toward solutions to problems such as these. His responsum provides an example
of this kind of thinking.

In the second case, a Jew discovers that the company for which he
works has contracted to develop technology systems with military applications for Arab countries which do not have peace treaties with
Israel. He is torn between loyalty to his company and devotion to the
Jewish people and the Jewish state. He would like to inform the Israeli
consulate about his company's activities, but as his company would
surely discharge him if it discovered that he has leaked information, he
is also concerned about his livelihood and that of his family.

The responsum acknowledges that devotion to the State of Israel is a
high religious value for us. At the same time, it is possible that by
revealing company secrets this person would violate the laws of his own
country. This calls into question another important religious value: the
principle *dina demalkhuta dina*, "the law of the state is the law," binding
upon its Jewish as well as its other inhabitants. One of the major justifications offered in traditional sources for this principle is that the residents of the state willingly accept the validity of its laws. This is
certainly the case in a democratic state: since all citizens participate in
the making of the laws, they stipulate in advance their acceptance of
them. The individual in question is bound to obey the laws against
espionage, because these are laws of his own making and because they
pertain to the legitimate legislative power of the state. He therefore is
prohibited *under Jewish law* from violating his nation's statutes by in-
forming the Israeli government. In the event that civil law does not
forbid the sharing of this information he may choose to do so, but since
he thereby places his job in jeopardy he will have to draw a balance
between his concern for Israel and his financial obligations toward his
family. While this decision has to be made according to the circumstances of the specific case, the responsum notes that he may find guidance in the Jewish teaching that, when allocating funds for *tzedakah*,
our obligations to our own family members and those closest to us take
precedence over all others. Moreover, he should weigh the risks to both
sides. Should he keep silent, the risks to Israel are uncertain at best, but
should he speak out, the risks to his family are concrete and immediate;
immediate danger, in Jewish law, takes precedence over potential danger. For these reasons, this individual is under no religious obligation

to inform the government of Israel of his company's activities, even if by doing so he violates no law of the state.

Here, too, the answer provided by the responsum can be criticized. Granted that the *mitzvah* of love for Israel does not necessarily override any other legitimate religious goal or duty, one might still object that our attachment to the Jewish state requires that we act in a spirit of nobility and self-sacrifice, that we reach for a higher standard than the responsum demands. Yet the fundamental consideration, again, is the question of how we think about the moral dilemmas that confront us. Whatever the solutions we determine, we ought to arrive at them by Jewish means, by balancing the alternatives against the values of Jewish tradition as we, Jews with a modern and liberal outlook, understand them.

Reform Judaism and Other Jewish Groups

Reform Jews are part of the larger Jewish community. This, however, does not diminish our distinctiveness. While we are connected to other Jews by bonds of history, peoplehood, and affection, the significant religious differences between segments of the Jewish people divide us into sectarian camps. There is quite obviously a tension between these forces, between our desire for Jewish unity and the fact of Jewish diversity, between our wish to act in concert with all other Jews and our determination to remain true to the liberal values that make us who and what we are. We respond best to this tension by acknowledging both sides of the dilemma. We reach our hands across the religious and ideological divides to all our Jewish brothers and sisters; we are their people and they are ours, and we seek to work together with them toward the realization of our common Jewish aspirations. Yet because we remain committed to a religious course whose rightness we fervently proclaim, we will not compromise our basic principles for the sake of an imagined and ephemeral Jewish unity.

What we demand for ourselves we must be ready to safeguard for others. We believe, therefore, that each segment of the Jewish community ought to enjoy the freedom to pursue its own path to religious fulfillment *within* the structure of *Kelal Yisrael*, as an integral element of the Jewish people. The concept that best summarizes this stance is that of Jewish religious pluralism, the notion that the Jewish people can and ought to have both unity and diversity, that Jews who hold widely differing theological, ideological, and halakhic perspectives can nonetheless accept that those who disagree with them are also Jews, members in good standing of a united Jewish community.

While easy to advocate, pluralism is a great deal more difficult to achieve. For one thing, not all Jews believe in it. Jewish religious pluralism makes perfect sense to Reform Jews, because as religious liberals we affirm the possibility of multiple roads to God and varying interpretations of Judaism. This affirmation is not shared by many Orthodox Jews, who are *not* religious liberals, who believe that there is but one correct way for a Jew to walk, and who look upon other approaches to Judaism as violations of Torah and denials of religious truth. It is vital to remember, therefore, that in calling for Jewish religious pluralism we do not ask that any Jewish group forsake its identity and core values. We do not demand that for the sake of Jewish unity Orthodox Jews become liberals any more than we would consent to becoming Orthodox. We neither seek nor expect their approval of our understanding of Judaism. What we do ask of them is simply that they recognize that all Jews, regardless of those things which drive them apart, are united by a common destiny and that they must work together toward its fulfillment. We ask them to acknowledge that we Reform Jews are not going to abandon our commitment to our own religious path; that we are as sincere in devotion to our path as they are to theirs; and that we therefore deserve to be treated in a spirit of seriousness and mutual respect. These acknowledgments are the very stuff of Jewish religious pluralism, without which there can be no such thing as Jewish unity. We do not believe that this is too much to ask of other Jews. And we cannot and will not accept anything less.

Another problem is that pluralism is not and cannot be unlimited. To say that there is more than one right way to be Jewish does not mean that *any* way, *any* interpretation of Jewish religion is equally valid or acceptable to us. From time to time, we liberals too must draw the necessary lines to distinguish who we are from who we are not, the beliefs we affirm from those we reject. It is difficult for Reform Jews to set limits, for this requires that we establish standards which exclude certain ideas from our midst, and to liberal ears this sort of thing smacks of censorship. It reminds us, in point of fact, of the very intolerance we sometimes encounter at the hands of other Jews. Yet set limits we must, for unless a religious community can define itself, determining what it does and does not believe, it is not a religious community at all. A religious community can exist only when its members share basic commitments by which they distinguish good from evil, right from wrong, true from false, commitments which enable them to conduct a coherent moral conversation or religious argument. As liberals, we understand that limits must be set, standards insisted upon, and shared commitments identified. When we draw lines, however, we seek to do so as broadly as possible, to be as inclusive as we can. We exclude only those doctrines that contradict the most fundamental premises of Reform Judaism, ideas that we cannot accept and yet remain the kind of Jews we believe and proclaim ourselves to be.

Religious Pluralism in Israel. The State of Israel is the single most concrete expression of the unity of the Jewish people. All Jews have a stake in its existence, survival, and prosperity. The State of Israel itself recognizes its connection to the entire Jewish people in the form of the Law of Return, which guarantees the right of *aliyah*, immigration and citizenship, to all Jews. Israel's Proclamation of Independence (*Megilat Ha'atzma'ut*), issued on 5 Iyar 5708 (May 14, 1948) states that full freedom of religion and conscience is to be guaranteed to all citizens of the state. The Reform movement has called repeatedly upon the government of Israel to reject any attempt to amend the Law of Return and deny Jewish status to individuals who convert to Judaism under Reform auspices. We urge as well that Israel extend full religious freedom to all Israeli Jews by ending the religious monopoly currently exercised by the Orthodox rabbinate. If Israel is truly the "Jewish state," it must cease to discriminate against Jews on the basis of their religious beliefs. It must stand for Jewish religious pluralism.

Reform Support of Orthodox Institutions. Many Reform Jews provide financial support and *tzedakah* to Orthodox institutions and causes. This support can be a positive contribution toward Jewish unity. However, we should take care to distinguish between Orthodox institutions that are friendly toward us from those which are not. In particular, we should not support those institutions which are hostile to religious pluralism and are unwilling to accept us and our movement.

Cooperation with Orthodox Institutions. Jewish religious pluralism often calls upon us to join together in common action with our fellow Jews, not only on matters over which we all agree, but also in areas where sharp disputes exist.

A case of marriage and divorce illustrates this point. An Orthodox man refuses to issue his wife a *get,* a Jewish divorce, even though their marriage has been ended by civil divorce. The Orthodox rabbi, seeking to pressure this man to issue a *get,* has asked the city's Reform and Conservative congregations to deny him membership and to refuse to perform his wedding should he seek to marry a second time. This presents us with a difficult choice. On the one hand, the Orthodox rabbi seeks to do justice for a woman who, still regarded as married under traditional Jewish law, cannot remarry and rebuild her life until she receives a *get* from her (former) husband. On the other hand, since Reform Judaism accepts the validity of the wife's civil divorce, to accede to the Orthodox rabbi's request is to cooperate in an essentially Orthodox institution which we have abandoned for good reasons of our own. This woman, from our perspective, is not trapped in an existing religious marriage; she could easily remarry were she to come to us for that service. It is also arguably unfair to exert "pressure" on her former husband, who in obtaining a civil divorce has done all that we would legally require of him. Our cooperation, moreover, simply allows the Orthodox world to pretend that it is doing something to remedy a moral evil—the inequity of divorce laws which allow a husband to make his wife an *agunah*—rather than finding a true solution for it.

A Reform responsum rules in favor of assisting the Orthodox rabbi, justifying its decision on grounds of pluralism. If Reform Judaism took the position that there is but one right version of Jewish truth (that is, the Reform version), it would then be quite proper to insist that all Jews accept our own standards of practice. But this is not our position. We believe instead in pluralism, the acceptance of the fact that other Jews practice their Judaism differently than we do. Though we may disagree with their interpretations, we do not insist that all Jews become Reform Jews. The woman in question is an Orthodox Jew, and pluralism forbids that we impose upon her our own version of Judaism. It rather demands of us that we respect her religious beliefs and do what we can to enable her to remarry within the Jewish religious context that she has chosen for herself. Our duty to aid Jews in need, particularly those suffering from oppression and injustice, is the overriding consideration in this case.

In another case, an individual petitions a Reform congregation, the only synagogue in its small community, for the right to hold an Orthodox service in its building on a regular basis. Again, as liberals we accept the doctrine of Jewish religious pluralism, and this argues for an affirmative response to the request. Yet pluralism is not the only doctrine in question here. There is also such a thing as "Reform Jewish integrity," our readiness to stand up for our fundamental affirmations as a religious community. An Orthodox worship group would deny equal religious access to women, whom it would not count in the *minyan*, and to Jews-by-choice who convert under our auspices, whom Orthodox Jews probably will not recognize as valid proselytes. We clearly do not accept these Orthodox teachings, which strike at our very legitimacy as a Jewish religious movement, yet to allow this group to meet regularly under our roof might imply otherwise. A Reform responsum declares that the group may assemble in our building. Again, we seek to extend a helping hand to those whom we regard as our brothers and sisters, and we do not demand that they follow our version of Jewish practice. We do insist, however, that legal or symbolic measures be taken to make clear to all that this Orthodox *minyan* is a separate community and not a sub-group of our own congregation, so that we not give the impression that Reform Judaism endorses every aspect of this group's theology. Basing itself upon talmudic precedent, the responsum concludes that two groups that conflict over Jewish practice may coexist within the same community so long as each retains its separate and distinct identity.

Hebrew Christians, Messianic Jews, and Jews for Jesus. A member of these groups, like any apostate, may be a "Jew" in the narrow, "biological" sense: one who is born a Jew remains part of the entity called "Israel," the people who according to our tradition stood at Sinai and responded affirmatively to the voice of God. Yet a Jew can indeed forsake the covenant, the binding relationship between God and Israel that defines what we mean by Judaism. A Jew who adopts Christianity has abandoned the covenant of Israel. Whatever his or her motives in doing so, and we may presume these to be quite sincere and heartfelt, this person has made a religious choice that is fundamentally contradictory to and incompatible with any understanding of Jewish religion that our community can recognize and accept. To admit this person into our religious community is to say that Judaism, as we know and practice it, can accommodate a belief in Jesus of Nazareth as son of God, Messiah, prophet, authoritative religious teacher, and the exclusive path to "salvation." We do not and cannot accommodate such a belief. Our definition of Jewish religious pluralism cannot be extended so as to encompass a doctrine that we do not identify in any way as "Jewish."

Humanistic Jews. Some Jewish congregations organize themselves under the banner of "Humanistic Judaism," a Jewish "religious" movement that is neutral or indifferent with respect to God. Unlike other liberal Jews (and unlike, for that matter, many Orthodox Jews) who acknowledge that many different conceptions of God exist and can be accommodated within Jewish belief, Humanistic Judaism simply removes God according to *any* conception from its official religious program. Its liturgy and ritual therefore omit all references to God, including such texts and prayers as the *Shema*, the *Tefillah*, the *Kaddish*, and the *Aleinu*. A humanistic Jewish congregation does not qualify for membership into the Union of American Hebrew Congregations, the congregational body of North American Reform Judaism.

Reform Judaism does not impose a theological test upon individuals wishing to join our congregations. We recognize that Reform Jews as individuals subscribe to a wide spectrum of theologies, of beliefs about God, and that some Reform Jews can be accurately described as atheists or agnostics. The question here, however, is the admission to the institutional Reform movement of a congregation that is formally dedicated to a full and sophisticated theology that denies either the existence of God or the relevance of God to the life and religion of Jews. For the movement to admit this congregation to membership would be to declare that atheism and agnosticism are acceptable versions of Reform Jewish thought and theology, recognized by an official Reform Jewish body as equally legitimate to all other versions. Such a declaration, given the centrality of God to the historical religious quest known as Reform Judaism, would contradict what we know and believe our religion to be. Individual Reform Jews must and will make their own decisions, but as a movement that teaches a coherent and substantial religious message, "we ground our lives, personally and communally, on God's reality." The congregation's system of beliefs lies therefore outside the realm of historical Reform Judaism. While it is certainly free to pursue the truth as it sees it, it must do so outside the institutional Reform movement.

9

Judaism and Society

Reform Judaism teaches that it is a *mitzvah* for the Jew to work for the betterment of society. We do not believe that the Torah's instruction concerning social justice applies only within the context of the Jewish community. We think rather that the commandment to "do that which is right and good in the sight of God" (Deut. 6:18) requires us to act as a holy people in every aspect of our daily lives, in our contact with all our fellow human beings, in our social and economic pursuits no less than in our ritual activities. It is for this reason that Reform Jews have always emphasized the eternal message of the biblical prophets. That message calls us to a life of social action, a never-ending effort directed toward mending the world (*tikkun ha'olam*), of transforming our communities into places of justice and compassion for all.

Our teachings concerning social justice, the message of Torah directed toward our life in the world, are expressed in various ways. Reform Jewish leaders involved in the struggle for social justice have set forth their views and arguments in a number of books. The institutions of our movement, such as the Union of American Hebrew Congregations (UAHC) and the Central Conference of American Rabbis (CCAR) regularly speak out on the issues of the day in the form of resolutions adopted at their conventions. A third source for these teachings is our responsa literature. Unlike many of our resolutions, these responsa are not statements of ideology and of political commitment. Responsa are "judicial" in approach, seeking to ground their conclusions firmly in the texts and sources of the Jewish legal tradition, interpret its teachings from a liberal perspective, and apply them to questions of moral and ethical concern. Since the Reform responsa literature is the primary focus of this book, the following discussion will center mostly, though not exclusively, upon the treatment of social justice issues in that literature.

Tzedakah

> If there be a needy person among you . . . do not harden your heart . . . Rather, you must open your hand and lend him sufficient for whatever he needs. (Deut. 15:7–8)

> It is a positive *mitzvah* to give *tzedakah* in accordance with one's means. And one ought to perform this *mitzvah* more carefully than any other, for a poor person may die as a result of one's failure to give promptly. . . . Do not say "why should I lessen my own fortune by giving my money to this poor person?" Bear in mind, rather, that the wealth we possess is but held in trust, for the purpose that we might use it to perform the will of the One who deposited it with us. (*Tur, Yoreh De'ah* 247)

In Jewish tradition, *tzedakah* is a *mitzvah*: a religious duty. It is more a tax than a voluntary contribution; even the poor person who receives *tzedakah* is obligated to give of his or her substance to *tzedakah*. The word itself is derived from the Hebrew root meaning "justice" and "righteousness," the need to put things in their proper order. It therefore should not be confused with "charity," from the Latin *caritas*, which connotes the "heartfelt" emotions of sympathy and compassion that lead one to give voluntarily to relieve the suffering of the unfortunate. Ideally, of course, *tzedakah* ought not to exclude "charity"; one should *want* to do the right thing rather than perform that duty grudgingly and in a mean spirit. Yet if one must choose between *caritas* and *tzedakah*, our tradition quite prudently gives preference to the latter. To call our act of giving to the poor "*tzedakah*" means that we are obliged to help them even when we would rather not, even when our sympathies are not aroused. We help the poor for the same reason that we fight for justice: it is our moral and religious obligation to do so. *Tzedakah*, we might say, comes to fulfill God's requirements rather than our own desire to feel good about ourselves.

Tzedakah, conceived as justice, means that the needs of the recipient lie at the heart of our concern. "You must open your hand and lend him sufficient for whatever he needs," says Deuteronomy 15:8. The Rabbis interpret this to mean that we must provide the poor with *whatever* they lack, whatever they require in order to maintain themselves at what the community considers a decent standard of living. This might involve gifts of cash or the provision of the tools by which the poor can learn to support themselves; the important thing is that we give primary consideration to the poor, and not to our own wishes, in determining our *tzedakah*. This includes the emotional as well as the material needs of the poor. For example, the Deuteronomy verse says that we must "lend" the poor that which they lack. How can this be, when we know that the poor most frequently cannot repay what they receive, that *tzedakah* usually involves an outright gift? The Rabbis teach that the word "lend" comes to tell us that when a poor person is too proud or ashamed to accept our gift, we call the *tzedakah* a "loan"—a "loan" we never intend to collect—in order to spare the person's feelings.

Priorities in Tzedakah. It is, of course, a monumental undertaking to eradicate poverty or other social ills. Our communal as well as personal resources are limited, and this means that we have to make difficult choices concerning the proper allocation of our *tzedakah* funds. Does Jewish tradition advise us as to the priorities that should determine these choices? In some respects it does, but the messages it offers us are decidedly mixed. Jewish law, for example, establishes a preference for local giving, teaching that we are obligated to care for those closest to us before we address the needs of others. "A member of one's family takes precedence over everyone else . . . The poor of one's household take precedence over the poor of one's city. And the poor of one's own city take precedence over the poor of other cities." This principle allows us to draw some practical ethical conclusions. For instance, we generally look upon the provision of nursing care for the elderly in our community as a public, communal responsibility, as well we might: the costs of establishing and maintaining facilities and the expense involved in supporting their residents are far beyond the financial ability of most individual families. Yet the community that accepts this responsibility is justified in demanding that the children or other close relatives of nursing home patients take seriously the rule that "a member of one's family takes precedence." The children or relatives have a moral obligation to provide a level of financial support that is appropriate to their means, and the community is entitled to exert both moral and social pressure upon them to bring about this end.

The strong local impulse which drives the Jewish law of *tzedakah* must be balanced, however, against other trends that direct our attention outward, toward assisting those who are not our immediate relatives and who dwell farther away. Thus, one who contributes to a communal *tzedakah* campaign must abide by the allocations decisions of those who administer that campaign; one cannot insist that one's contribution be directed toward his or her own relatives or favorite local cause. The sources, too, offer a powerful practical argument to be made against exclusively local giving: local needs will usually overwhelm our resources before they can be directed to worthy causes beyond our immediate vicinity. If we never contribute *tzedakah* elsewhere until we have completely discharged our responsibilities to our own families, then those poor persons who do not have prosperous relatives or who dwell in poor communities will never receive any assistance. We do not allow this to happen. Were we to refuse to give to "foreign" causes before we have entirely solved our local problems, we never would contribute toward the relief of world hunger; we never would take part in the struggle against disease and poverty on other continents; and we would never have been able to make the Zionist dream a reality and build the Jewish state. Rather, along with the principle that favors local giving, we must conclude that there are important objectives outside of our immediate communities, in Israel and in the Diaspora, which must be met and which make legitimate claims upon our attention. We may owe a special duty to care for those closest to us, but this does not exempt us from the duty to contribute toward the meeting of needs elsewhere.

In a similar way, the traditional obligation to give *tzedakah* was an entirely Jewish obligation: we owed no such responsibility toward those outside the community of Israel. This notion may strike us as parochial, but it does have a point: we Jews must see first to our own communal requirements and interests, since no one else will support them if we do not. For this reason, it is still quite proper to say that Jews have a special responsibility to contribute to Jewish causes. Yet this "special responsibility" does not exhaust our *tzedakah* obligations. The ancient Rabbis already instructed their people to provide *tzedakah* to non-Jews who were in need, "in the interests of preserving peaceful relations" (*mipnei darkhei shalom*). And if such a principle could be taught when the Jews were under Roman domination, when we did not enjoy equal rights with all other residents of the country, how much more does its ethical demand apply to us. In our own communities, in which we possess full citizenship, we owe a corresponding responsibility to address the needs and problems of our societies alongside our fellow-citizens. We contribute to non-Jewish causes, therefore, not just out of self-interest, to "preserve peaceful relations," but because we recognize that it is the right thing to do.

Ultimately, all decisions concerning the allocation of *tzedakah* involve the drawing of a balance between competing obligations: local or non-local, Jewish or non-Jewish. Traditional sources speak of these obligations, but they do not answer for us the question of how best to resolve such competition, let alone how to distribute our *tzedakah* funds in detail. Perhaps that is the true message of the tradition on our subject: that while we can imagine such a thing as an order of priorities in giving, we must not take those priorities so literally that they blind us to the legitimate needs of those who rank lower on the scale. In the end, we owe a moral duty to *all* who need our help. The decisions as to how best to distribute our available *tzedakah* resources must be made by each Jew and each Jewish community, according to their best judgment.

Gifts to Organizations Inimical to Reform Judaism. We Jews have a special responsibility to provide for Jewish causes and to join with the rest of our people in the fulfillment of common Jewish objectives. This responsibility does not, however, extend to supporting organizations that deny the religious legitimacy of Reform Judaism and work against our political rights in Israel and elsewhere. We refuse to provide financial assistance to these groups. This is more than simply a matter of self-interest and self-preservation; indeed, the tradition itself suggests that we are obliged to withhold *tzedakah* from those whose behavior is antithetical to the cause of Jewish unity.

Halakhah declares that "one who intentionally violates a *mitzvah* and who has not repented does not deserve sustenance from us." The explanation given for this seemingly harsh statement is that our obligation to provide for our fellow Jews lies precisely in the fact that they are our *fellow* Jews, whom the Torah calls our "brothers," our kinfolk, members of our community. This relationship is a powerful one, but it is not indestructible. There comes a point at which, by means of behavior that destroys this attachment to community, a Jew can separate him- or herself from us and ceases in any effective sense to be our "brother." At that point, our duty to support that person likewise ceases. This text, we believe, speaks to the contemporary situation in which some Jews and Jewish groups have in essence declared war upon us. Their militant and extremist antagonism to Reform Judaism, which threatens the cause of Jewish unity to which we are committed, is a transgression against the Jewish people. By means of their actions, they have separated themselves from the rest of the community of Israel. They do not wish to be our "brothers," our family. If so, that is their choice, but we should certainly not support that choice by offering them our financial assistance.

Reform Jews *should*, however, participate in united, communal *tzedakah* campaigns, even though some of the money raised will go to Orthodox institutions that are not entirely friendly toward us. Our objection to supporting such institution lies in their opposition to Jewish unity; the very fact that communal campaigns are "united" counteracts that opposition through its assertion that we are all "brothers and sisters" who reach out to the rest of our people, including those with whom we disagree over religious and political questions. Such campaigns deserve our active support.

Support for Reform Jewish Organizations. Our tradition speaks unequivocally of the need for Jews to establish and to support synagogues. It does not speak as directly of a requirement to support national and international Jewish organizations, yet some sources teach us that this, too, is an obligation. In ancient times, all Jews were required to contribute one-half shekel to the maintenance of the Temple in Jerusalem. In the Middle Ages, Jewish communities developed sophisticated structures of local and regional government which were empowered to collect taxes to meet the community's financial obligations toward the Gentile authorities and to fund the operation of Jewish communal institutions. These governmental bodies also possessed the authority to enact ordinances (*takkanot hakahal*) to regulate a wide range of communal relationships and public behavior. The rabbis found support for these structures in talmudic law, ruling that individual Jews were bound to act according to the decisions—which included the assessment of taxes—adopted by the legitimate representative bodies which governed their communities. In our own time, bodies such as the Union of American Hebrew Congregations (UAHC), the organized movement of North American Reform synagogues, reflect this heritage of Jewish communal organization. These bodies work on our behalf, represent us on the regional and national levels, and provide religious and educational services which local congregations would find difficult or im-

possible to provide on their own. Reform synagogues are therefore morally obliged to support the national organization at the level set by its
duly elected representatives. Reform rabbis, as interpreters of our tradition, are morally obliged to support the dues-collection and fundraising efforts of the UAHC.

Synagogue Fundraising. A number of ethical issues surround the various
means by which synagogues raise and allocate funds to support themselves and their programs. These are discussed in detail in Chapter 2.

Tzedakah on Shabbat and Festivals. Frequently, Jewish communities
find that Shabbat and the festivals are the most convenient time to
conduct matters relating to *tzedakah*. It is on those occasions that relatively large numbers of Jews can assemble for meetings and projects.
Beyond considerations of convenience, moreover, one might say that it
is particularly appropriate to fulfill this *mitzvah* on the holy days, so
that we might worship God through prayer, the study of Torah, *and*
the performance of good deeds. It is true that the actions taken in the
name of these good deeds—the collection of money, participation in
community clean-up campaigns, building and repairing the homes of
the poor—may violate the prohibitions against work (*melakhah*) and
related activities on these days. Reform Jews, however, set these prohibitions aside in cases when we believe that the sanctity of the day will
be encouraged and nurtured thereby. Given the centrality of social justice to our conception of Reform Judaism, it could be argued that the
cause of sanctity is best served when we utilize the time afforded us by
Shabbat and the festivals to do the work of *tzedakah*.
   Yet this argument reflects but one element of our attitude to
religious observance. We may reserve the right to depart from
traditional observances of Shabbat and the festivals, but to the extent
that these observances define the nature of those days as categories
of Jewish religious experience, we are not free to ignore them
altogether. Shabbat and festivals, no less than *tzedakah* and social
justice, are also *mitzvot*; the so-called "ritual" aspects of Jewish life
are no less *Jewish* to us than are its so-called "ethical" components.
When Shabbat and social action collide, we know of no formula by
which to declare that it is necessarily Shabbat which must give way.
Indeed, given our movement's recent emphasis upon the strengthening
of Shabbat observance among our people, we have reason to decide

for Shabbat over the *tzedakah* project, so that we do not allow the "good deeds" of *tzedakah* to obliterate the holiness of that day. Shabbat and festivals are not simply twenty-four-hour periods that we may fill as we like with productive and useful activities; they are *holy* days, periods of time that exist for their own inherent purposes and make their own legitimate demands upon us. Unless the cause is a dire emergency that cannot wait until after the conclusion of Shabbat or the festival, we do not take part in projects which involve activities that transgress upon the religious sanctity of that day.

Jewish law permits communities to conduct meetings on Shabbat and festivals for the purpose of raising and determining the distribution of *tzedakah*, provided that no monetary transaction takes place until the conclusion of the day. This explains the custom of some congregations to conduct auction-style sales of *aliyot* and other synagogue honors during Shabbat and festival services, and also for the scheduling of appeals for the congregation and communal *tzedakah* agencies at such special services as Yom Kippur night (*Kol Nidrei*). Reform responsa take a dim view of the former custom. The sale of synagogue honors is an affront to the sense of the sanctity of the holy day, and this tends in our eyes to outweigh the monetary benefits we might accrue from the auction. As for the latter practice, we have argued that communities should take great care that meetings for *tzedakah* do not involve activities that would constitute a flagrant violation of the mood of Shabbat or the holiday. In addition, these meetings should impinge as little as possible upon the service itself. The "*Kol Nidrei* Appeal," for example, might take place prior to the beginning of the service, before *Kol Nidrei* itself, at a time when Yom Kippur has not yet begun.

Business Ethics

The wages of a laborer shall not remain with you until morning . . . You shall not falsify measures of length, weight, or capacity. You shall have an honest balance and honest weights. (Lev. 19:13, 35–36)

When you sell property to your neighbor, or buy any from your neighbor, you shall not wrong one another. (Lev. 25:14)

You shall appoint magistrates and officials for your tribes . . . and they shall govern the people with due justice. (Deut. 16:18)

The Jewish passion for social justice is perhaps best expressed in the complex of traditional teachings that touch upon our conduct in the marketplace. The relationships between buyer and seller and between worker and employer are subjects of Judaism's extraordinary moral concern. Even the existence of a legal system, which the Rabbis derive from the instruction in Deuteronomy 16:18 to appoint "magistrates and officials," is bound tightly to the conception of an honest and ethical economic environment. In the words of Maimonides, the "officials" of whom that verse speaks are the marshals of the court "who accompany the magistrates as they inspect the markets and the places of commerce, to see to it that the prices and the units of measurement are just." The judges and other authorities, that is to say, do not merely sit and wait for litigants to approach them with matters that require adjudication. The officers of the court must be pro-active, seeking out and rectifying instances of commercial wrongdoing before these turn into actual court cases. Since there is no justice in a community whose marketplace is corrupt, those whose task it is to guarantee justice for all must also serve as supervisors over business activity, to insure that it is conducted according to the letter and spirit of Torah.

This implies that Jewish tradition favors a regulated marketplace, and in many respects this implication is correct. We should not thereby conclude, however, that the tradition favors a particular kind of economic system over all others. Nor does the tradition's positive view of market regulation mean that Judaism is unmindful of the facts of economic life, of such "iron laws" as the fluctuation of prices according to supply and demand, and of the requirement of healthy competition for the maintenance of prosperity. Every aspect of the *halakhah* concerning business activity demonstrates that the Rabbis understood economics and that they did not wish to stifle the market by placing unreasonable demands upon the merchant. To say that Judaism favors a regulated marketplace is to say instead that the Rabbis do not glorify business for its own sake. Business, like every other human endeavor, is an arena in which we work out our duty and aspiration to live lives of holiness. Like every other activity, business is to be evaluated not by its own terms but by the criteria of justice and fairness: we determine it to be "good" and acceptable to the extent that it can meet those criteria. Like every other human activity, therefore, business must be directed by moral principles. In this sense, Jewish tradition does not regard "business ethics" as an external and artificial interference with the "natural" workings of the market. The opposite, in fact, is the case: it is justice itself, the demand for righteous and ethical conduct in our business dealings, which comes first and is the true measure of the worth of our economic lives.

Economic Dignity; Fair Wages and Prices. God proclaims: "The people of Israel are My servants" (Lev. 25:55). To this the Rabbis add: "and they are not the servants of servants." Liberal Jews read this teaching as a declaration of the fundamental economic dignity of every human being. One who seeks to serve God must do so as a free person, not as a slave to the economic demands of others. Thus, the worker may quit the job after beginning it, "even though half the day has gone by"; one cannot be compelled to work against one's will. And central to that freedom is the idea that workers ought not to be compelled to work for wages and under conditions that deny their dignity as free people.

One of the ways in which workers have sought to safeguard their economic freedom is through organization. The Talmud already mentions the power of "the dwellers of the city" to band together to enact regulations aimed at setting wages, prices, and working conditions. Later *halakhah* defines craft or trade associations, in this regard, as a "city": these groups may adopt their own regulations, and they may levy fines against those members who violate the group's enactments. Recent authorities have extended this concept to labor unions. But while workers unquestionably may set the terms of their employment and to withhold their services from their employers, it is not so clear that Jewish law recognizes their right to strike and to use all the methods of economic coercion that such a job action entails. Strikes often carry severe economic consequences in their wake, not only for the workers and employers in the affected industry but also for the wider community. Most halakhists, relying upon the relevant talmudic passage, require that labor conflicts be brought before "a prominent person" (*adam chashuv*), a court or some other suitable agency for compulsory arbitration; both employer and workers would be bound by the arbitrator's decision. This method serves, ideally, as a compromise that would balance the conflicting interests of workers, employers, and the public. In the absence of a mechanism for compulsory arbitration, however, workers are entitled to resort to strikes when they are convinced that their employer "has violated the terms of employment that are generally accepted in the community." These violations may include unsafe or unsanitary working conditions as well as wages that fall below a satisfactory level.

The words "satisfactory level" do not imply an ideal level of income for each worker. Wages and salaries, like prices for goods and services, are set by the market, that is by supply and demand. But while Judaism recognizes the market's existence, it does not sanctify the market or assert that it is controlled by some benign "invisible hand" which, if only left undisturbed, will guide the economic affairs of the world to the general good. Rather, the course of the market can be influenced in one way or another, in the interests of this or that group, and the power to organize is accordingly a legitimate means by which labor can attempt to do this. So long as their demands are reasonable—that is, so long as they do not tend to distort the workings of the economy so as to cause unacceptable hardship to their employers or to the public at large—workers may engage in job actions to support them.

Some contemporary halakhic opinion regards inflation as a sufficient justification for strikes on the part of workers. Inflation of the currency causes a decline in the real value of wages and is thus, in fact, an annulment of the contract between the workers and the employer who promised to compensate them at a certain level for their services. It might be argued, of course, that by winning higher wages these workers will simply be contributing to the very inflation that eats into the value of their salaries and that the better course of action would be to ask for no wage increase (or even to accept a cut in pay) in order to help society bring inflation under control. This sort of sacrifice may make a certain amount of economic sense, but so long as *anyone* in the economy is benefiting from the inflationary conditions it is not incumbent on workers to abandon their right to maintain their standard of living.

The market may set the price for goods and services, but the market can be distorted. Beyond the normal and accepted fluctuations of supply and demand which cause prices to rise and fall, it is possible that a particular item or service may unknowingly be purchased or sold at a level excessively above or below its general market price. The tradition refers to this price distortion as *ona'ah*, literally, "oppression," a form of robbery, prohibited by Leviticus 25:14. The sources fix this level at one-sixth the true market value of the item or service. When the transaction is concluded at a price that differs from the competitive price by more than one-sixth—say, an item that usually markets for sixty dollars is purchased mistakenly for seventy-five dollars or for forty-five dollars—the injured party can nullify the sale. The "injured party" can be the seller as well as the buyer, for both sides are entitled to a fair price.

If the difference lies within that one-sixth range—the sixty-dollar item sells for sixty-five or fifty-five—the sale stands, since we presume that both sides will waive an error of less than one-sixth. When the error is exactly one-sixth—the sixty-dollar item sells for seventy or for fifty— the sale is valid, but the injured party may demand a refund of the price differential within a reasonable period of time.

The rule of *ona'ah* applies only when either side pays the price mistakenly or unknowingly. If, however, the seller discloses his or her true cost and says, "I sell it to you at such-and-such over that cost," should the buyer accept the seller's offer the sale is valid no matter what the price. Moreover, the "fair price" is difficult to determine for many of the goods and services that are bought and sold in the marketplace, particularly in an affluent society. In the absence of a system of communal price controls or guidelines—and such systems are known in Jewish history and permitted under Jewish law—it may be impossible to establish just what that "fair price" is. Yet the very fact that Jewish tradition offers us a principle called *ona'ah* affords us a tool with which to critique the market on moral grounds. There exists, that is to say, a standard of price fairness according to which we judge all transactions. And even if this standard exists only as an ideal, it *is* an ideal. It demands that all business activity be conducted so as to protect either side of a transaction, particularly when the actions of buyers or sellers lead to economic hardship.

Deception. It is forbidden to deceive the other party in a business transaction, to create a false impression which leads that party to make a decision that he or she might otherwise have avoided. This deception is called *geneivat da'at*, which literally means "theft of the mind." The concept is often used in Jewish discussions of advertising practices, particularly with respect to the ways that products are deceptively disguised so as to encourage unwary buyers to purchase them. A Reform responsum applies it to a different setting. It has become a widespread practice among elderly persons in the United States, prior to being placed in a nursing home, to transfer their assets to their children. This device permits them to shield their property from those institutions, to claim poverty and thus have the government or the Jewish community finance their nursing care. To the extent that civil law permits this subterfuge, it is nonetheless deception, *geneivat da'at*, and should be discouraged.

Competition. Economic competition is a complex issue in Jewish law. The ancient sources dispute the propriety of competition as a business tactic: "Rabbi Yehudah says a storekeeper should not distribute parched grain and nuts to children, for this gets them into the habit of coming into his store. Nor should he cut his price excessively. The Sages, however, permit both practices, saying that such a storekeeper is worthy of praise." The ruling of the Sages, which is the accepted position of the *halakhah,* is explained on the grounds that the aggressive storekeeper does nothing wrong by using advertising methods that the other merchants can also utilize; moreover, by lowering his own price he forces his competitors to lower theirs, thereby benefiting the consumer market. Another passage teaches that the residents of a neighborhood are entitled to adopt rules forbidding the location of particular businesses in their midst. Yet once such a business has been established, they may not prevent another from locating there by claiming that the new entry harms the existing merchant. From this, we might conclude that Jewish law grants priority to the general welfare, concern for the market and for customers as a whole, over that of individual merchants.

At the same time, halakhic authorities have allowed communities to restrict competition when there is a well-grounded fear that the entry of new businesses into a small market will cause economic ruin or the disappearance of a needed service. Again, the overriding concern is the welfare of the community as a whole rather than the prosperity of this or that commercial venture. The rise of the professional rabbinate affords an example of such restraint of competition. To engage the services of a rabbi, it was necessary to provide for his sustenance; accordingly, many medieval Jewish communities adopted rules that guaranteed the local rabbi a monopoly over such rabbinic services as weddings and court functions. Another case in point is that of copyright, specifically the copyrighting of sacred Jewish books, which arose soon after the development of printing. To undertake the publication of a major text such as the Talmud or Maimonides' *Mishneh Torah* involved significant expenses, which the publishers sought to recoup by securing exclusive rights to the printing of that text for a period of time. Rabbinic authorities approved of this institution, which amounted to a ban against competition, in order to insure the availability of the books. These examples show once again that the rabbis did not sanctify the free market; while it remained the economic ideal, they were willing to intervene for the sake of the public good. Determining when the needs of the community dictate that restrictions be placed upon competition is, of course, a difficult judgment to make; but the community, our tradition teaches, is indeed empowered to make that judgment.

In some cases, our definition of "the general welfare" takes on particularly Jewish overtones. One Reform responsum deals with the case of a Jewish funeral director in a city who suddenly finds himself facing competition from a Gentile funeral home in a nearby city which charges considerably less for its services. On the matter of price, there is little to dispute: our tradition, as we have seen, does not object to competition which results in the lowering of prices to all. On the other hand, the issue here is the burial of the dead, which is a *mitzvah*, a religious duty for Jews. It is in the interests of the community to maintain a Jewish funeral home, even if the community must subsidize its operation. Thus, while there is no grounds in Jewish law for preventing the opening of a new funeral home, it is an obligation for Jews to support the existing Jewish establishment.

Personal Ethics

Do not go about as a talebearer among your people. (Lev. 19:16)

Keep far from speaking lies. (Exod. 23:7)

Gossip and Privacy. Jewish sacred texts do not tend to speak of legal or human "rights." Rather, our sources express themselves in a language of "commandments" and "obligations" (*mitzvot*). This does not mean that Judaism necessarily ignores the value of what we today designate as "rights" but simply that our tradition frames these values as duties we owe to our fellow human beings rather than as entitlements we expect from them. For example, the *halakhah* nowhere declares explicitly that human beings have the "right" to own property. On the other hand, from the fact that the Torah forbids us to steal from our neighbors and requires us to compensate them for damage we cause to their possessions we may deduce that Jewish law for all practical purposes acknowledges this "right": my property belongs to me, and I am entitled to initiate court proceedings to rectify wrongful trespass against it. Similarly, while there is a great deal of discussion in our society about the "right" to medical care, no such discussion can be found in our Jewish sources. They *do* say, however, that the practice of medicine is a *mitzvah* which falls under the category of our moral duty to save life. If this is a religious obligation we owe to all, then we can infer that there is no justification for society's denial of medical treatment to any citizen due to his or her inability to pay for it. The declaration that this is our duty equals a "right" to medical care, although our sources do not use that precise language to communicate the idea. In every case, therefore, if we wish to know whether Jewish tradition includes a particular "right," we must inquire as to the corresponding duties and obligations it imposes upon us as part of our response to the voice of Sinai. If these obligations forbid me from interfering with your freedom to possess a certain thing or to engage in a specific activity, then we can conclude that you (and I) enjoy a "right" to that thing or activity.

This is the case when we consider the idea that we call the "right to privacy." Jewish law, again, does not express this concept explicitly. Yet it does forbid us from taking actions which tend to invade the private lives of others. For example, the Bible forbids a creditor from entering the home of a debtor to collect a pledge (Deut. 24:10–11). A home owner, too, may take action to protect his or her household from the prying eyes of neighbors. And then there is the prohibition against gossip, *rekhilut*, which the sources compare to the activity of a peddler, *rokhel*: "One should not act like a peddler, carrying the words of one person to another." On its least severe level, the prohibition covers any sort of talking about another individual, even if what we say is true and causes no damage to that person's reputation. A greater degree of harm is caused when we engage in *lashon hara*, when we actually slander the reputation of another person, even if our statements are factually correct. The worst offense of all is committed when we use falsehood to destroy the good name of another person. The Rabbis have long condemned the practice of gossip and slander in no uncertain terms, to the point that the impurity of slander is compared to that of leprosy and that the sin of *lashon hara* is said to be equivalent to the sins of idolatry, sexual immorality, and murder combined. Engaging in *lashon hara* is also held to violate other commandments, such as the negative "Do not hate your brother in your heart" (Lev. 19:17) and the positive "You shall love your neighbor as yourself" (Lev. 19:18). We should note, as well, the widespread custom to conclude the recitation of the *Tefillah*, the central prayer of our liturgy, with the brief text which begins: "My God, preserve my tongue from evil and my lips from speaking deceitfully," restating in the first person the sentiments of Psalm 34:14. The powerful tone of these rabbinic statements leaves no doubt that one's name, the reputation by which one is known throughout the community, is to be treated with reverence. It must be safeguarded against trespass by others, just as one's home deserves protection from unwanted physical or visual intrusion. And since Jewish tradition demands that we accord each other the same protections of dignity that flow from a "right to privacy," it therefore makes sense to speak of a Judaic conception of that right.

The existence of a "right" to privacy implies that any intervention into our individual lives by outside factors, including communal and governmental agencies, must be viewed with caution. The burden of proof, we would say, is shouldered by those who would pry into our homes, our affairs, our lives. It is up to them to establish that this intrusion is necessary and justified; it is not up to us to prove that we deserve protection against them. One example of this sort of determination concerns the question of compulsory testing for AIDS (acquired immune deficiency syndrome), a disease generally transmitted through sexual intercourse. The spread of AIDS during the 1980s and 1990s convinced some observers of the need for a system of compulsory testing for HIV (human immunodeficiency virus, which causes AIDS) as a prerequisite for marriage. A Reform responsum advised against such a step for a number of reasons. Chief among these was its judgment that no danger was present in this situation (that is, in the general population, as opposed to particular "at-risk groups") that was so significant as to warrant the intrusion into personal privacy that is the inevitable consequence of compulsory testing. Another case involved a question of employment. A young rabbi, seeking to serve a congregation, has learned that he tests positive for Huntington's disease, a genetic illness which begins to cause neurological dysfunction during one's forties or fifties and which leads to certain death. He wonders whether he should reveal this information to the pulpit committee of the congregation before it decides whether to engage him as the synagogue's rabbi. The responsum ruled that the individual's "right" to protection against gossip and slander takes precedence over the congregation's "right" to know about its rabbi's private life. So long as the rabbi, in his informed and sincere judgment, is convinced that his genetic condition will not adversely affect the performance of his duties during the projected contract period, he is not obligated to share this medical information with the congregation.

These cases demonstrate that the individual enjoys, on Judaic grounds, a "right" to privacy. They also indicate that this right may be set aside under conditions judged serious enough to warrant that step. Privacy, in other words, may be a "right," but like other rights it is not absolute, because it must coexist along with the "rights" of others. Still, that the burden of proof rests with those who would disregard rather than safeguard individual privacy shows that our tradition views this "right," and the basic human dignity it comes to protect, with the utmost seriousness.

Is Gossip Ever Permitted? May we engage in gossip about a third party for the sake of some higher purpose than gossip itself? For example, when a husband and wife engage in gossip, can we say that the openness of their communication, their ability to talk about *everything* with each other, contributes to the intimacy of their relationship and to the preservation of domestic peace *(shalom bayit),* which is itself a *mitzvah?* To this question, a Reform responsum answers in the negative. Gossip may be frequent and common among us, but it remains a prohibition nonetheless, and no relationship with another person, however close, suffices to justify the commission of an act that we hold to be wrong. An act such as this is called a *mitzvah haba'ah beaveirah,* a *mitzvah* accomplished by means of sin, and as such not that much of a *mitzvah* at all. We can never expect to eradicate gossip from our world, and we certainly cannot hope to eliminate it from conversations we carry on with those who are closest to us. Yet this fact does not mean that we are somehow required to sanctify gossip as a good thing. There are better and more positive ways of achieving marital harmony than engaging in gossip and slander, and our better selves would counsel us to seek out those paths.

Confidentiality. Under ordinary circumstances, information held in confidence about another person may not be revealed. However, in serious cases confidence must be disregarded. For example, one who has information that another person's life or health is in danger must communicate that information even though it was received in confidence. We learn this from the *mitzvah* in Leviticus 19:16, "do not stand idly by the blood of your neighbor," which rabbinic tradition interprets as imposing upon us a positive obligation to save the life of one who is threatened. And this obligation, *pikuach nefesh,* takes precedence over virtually every other duty, including that of safeguarding an individual's privacy.

How does this affect information obtained through a professional relationship, such as that between physician and patient or attorney and client? The legal status of this information, of course, is determined by the law of the state. In the eyes of Jewish tradition, on the other hand, a professional counselor is just as obligated to reveal lifesaving information as is everyone else; the counselor, no less than the rest of us, is bound by the *mitzvot* and must fulfill the duty of which we read in Leviticus 19:16. We do not infer from this that the counselor may reveal any and all information confided by the client, but rather that the counselor must make a careful judgment as to whether this particular information, if revealed, could save another person from death or harm. Thus, when a physician knows that a patient who is about to be married is inflicted with a dangerous, communicable disease, the physician must reveal that information to the patient's prospective spouse. The patient in this case is considered a *rodef*, a "pursuer" who poses a clear and present mortal danger to a victim, and we are permitted to take drastic action if necessary to stop the pursuer from doing harm. Even when there is no physical danger to the prospective spouse, one might argue that the information should be revealed for the good of the subsequent marital union. The physician or counselor, however, must weigh the advantages of revealing the information against the harm that would be caused thereby, particularly to the patient or client.

The Disabled and the Community

> Said Rav Yosef: were someone to prove to me that blind persons are obligated to observe the *mitzvot*, I would hold a feast for all the rabbis! (*B. Bava Kama* 87a)

Rav Yosef was an outstanding scholar in talmudic Babylonia. He was also blind. And this fact lends unique significance to his remark, cited above. Rav Yosef's statement is not that of a detached observer, but the voice of one who is deeply and personally involved in the discussion into which he has intervened. It is the voice of a disabled person, a member of a class of individuals all too often excluded from our community, its life and activities, demanding to be heard before his fate, and that of those who share his disability, has been sealed. It is a voice too seldom heard, in our tradition and in our world, but a voice which, when we but pay it attention, transforms the way we perceive the disabled as fellow creatures of God.

The matter under discussion in this passage is the question whether the blind, as a class of persons, are to be considered exempt from the duty to perform the *mitzvot* of the Torah. One might think that a blind person would indeed wish to be exempt from the regimen of religious duties incumbent upon the rest of the community. But Rav Yosef wishes to be a Jew in the fullest sense of that term, a member of a community linked to its God through the bond of Torah. In such a community, the performance of *mitzvot* is the way that one expresses one's attachment and acts out one's destiny. In such a community, which sees the ritual *mitzvot* as the key to its daily, sacred relationship with God, to be exempted from the obligation to perform these *mitzvot* is to be excluded from the mainstream of Jewish religious experience. And Rav Yosef most certainly wants no part of that.

The *halakhah*, it turns out, answers Rav Yosef in the affirmative: the blind *are* included within the obligation to perform *mitzvot*. Yet it does not extend his plea for inclusion to Jews with other disabilities, whose physical and mental conditions have historically separated them from the rest of the community. The most obvious of these are the deaf-mute (*cheresh*) and the mentally disabled (*shoteh*), who are exempt from all the *mitzvot* because like a minor child (*katan*) they lack the ability to form legal intent and to take responsibility for their actions. The physically disabled are excluded from *mitzvot* whose formal definition requires actions that they are not able to perform. For example, one who has no arms, or the severely-injured person who cannot move his arms, is exempt from the *mitzvah* of *lulav*, since he cannot "take" the *lulav* and *etrog* with his hand as the law requires. The Rabbis do not substitute some other means of fulfilling this *mitzvah*, even in spirit, so as to offer a degree of religious satisfaction to these people. And this leads to the impression that the Rabbis saw "disability" purely as a subject for formal classification, a way of determining whether or not one was obligated to perform the *mitzvot*, but not as a problem to be overcome. That is, it would seem they were more concerned for the technicalities of the law than for the spirit and the feelings of those who were excluded for these reasons from the community of *mitzvot*. Indeed, the Rabbis seem more interested in hiding away the disabled, in separating them from the rest of the community, so that our normal patterns of religious life might not be disturbed by the ridicule, pity, or lurid contempt that the sight of the disabled might stir in the rest of us. Thus, we read that a priest (*Kohen*) who is physically "blemished" may not recite the priestly benediction for the congregation (see Num. 6:22–27), "lest the people gaze at him."

Fortunately, our texts do not demand such an interpretation. The Rabbis did on occasion reach out to the disabled, drawing them into the mainstream community as far as this was possible. For example, while deaf-mutes, who could not be counted upon to form intent and take responsibility for their actions, were not technically permitted to marry, the Rabbis established a procedure by which they would be able nonetheless to marry and to build a family life. Traditional authorities, moreover, were perfectly capable of recognizing that scientific advancements could render old definitions irrelevant. The development of schools and languages for the deaf, which enabled them to communicate intelligibly among themselves and with others, permitted halakhists to conclude that the deaf-mute does possess the ability to form legal intent and should therefore be held responsible for performing all the *mitzvot*. And regarding the *shoteh*, rabbis came to distinguish between the mentally retarded and the truly incompetent. Accordingly, say one noted authority, the retarded person who can achieve even the level of understanding of a six-year-old should be welcomed into the worship of the congregation. Taken together, these instances comprise what we might call an "inclusionary insight," a degree of awareness on the part of traditional authorities that those with disabilities ought not simply to be defined out of the religious community but rather brought into it. To put it another way, the cry of Rav Yosef may yet be heard by those who take our tradition seriously.

Reform responsa develop this inclusionary insight into a consistent and guiding theme. We should not define disabled persons into categories based upon what they cannot do but rather see them in terms of what they can accomplish as members of our communities. They should be encouraged to participate to the fullest extent possible in our religious and social life. This determination, to mean anything, must be more than a platitude. It demands from us real investment of resources, time, and understanding. We must recognize our moral (as it is increasingly our legal) obligation to make our physical facilities accessible to those with disabilities. Similarly, our synagogues must redouble their efforts to provide the disabled with the tools they require for inclusion:

large-print and Braille prayer books; hearing aids; sign-language interpreters; new computer technologies. Our schools must recognize their responsibility to provide the education needed to help the disabled participate fully in Jewish life, and this recognition carries in its wake the need to hire specialists and to acquire the appropriate materials. We know that these demands are complex and expensive, but they are no less vital for that. If synagogues, schools, and other communal agencies must move slowly and gradually toward the full integration of disabled persons, they should not allow a policy of "all deliberate speed" to divert their attention from the ultimate goal: the maximum inclusion of disabled persons in Jewish life.

Human Sexuality

> Therefore a man shall leave his father and his mother and cleave to his wife, and they shall become one flesh. (Gen. 2:24)

Non-Marital Sexual Relations. The Jewish tradition's teachings concerning human sexuality can be understood as a series of footnotes to Genesis 2:24. That verse establishes marriage as the proper framework for human sexual relationship. To the extent that sexual relations take place within a marital union, tradition sees them in a positive light. But what of non-marital sexual relations? Is it ever proper for two unmarried, consenting adults to engage in sexual intercourse?

The answer to this question, perhaps surprisingly, is not so simple. Our sources, at least in theory, contain two broad approaches on the subject. The first is that of Maimonides, who learns from his reading of biblical and rabbinic literature that one who has intercourse without benefit of marriage (*kiddushin*) violates the prohibition against harlotry (*kedeishah*; Deut. 23:18). The second position is taken by such luminaries as Nachmanides, who declares that "harlotry" refers only to casual, non-marital sex. By contrast, the Torah allows a man to form a stable sexual relationship with a woman other than his wife; this woman is called a concubine (*pilegesh*), and the Bible recounts that our ancestors did take concubines alongside their wives. Maimonides, for his part, writes that only the king of Israel is permitted to take a concubine. The terms of this dispute are rooted in our biblical past, but its outcome might have significant implications for our practices today. If Nachmanides is correct, if concubinage is not prohibited by the Torah, then we could adopt that institution, adjust it to the egalitarian temperament of our time, and declare that Judaism permits the establishment of long-term, non-marital sexual relationships between consenting adults.

This conclusion, however, is more than a bit problematic. For one thing, even those who, like Nachmanides, believe that the Torah does not technically forbid concubinage caution that the institution should be forbidden today on moral grounds. This has become the predominant view among most authorities: the moral and social evils that would result from such unions demand that we not allow them. Our task, they would say, is to promote marriage and not alternatives to it.

This has been the approach of Reform responsa as well. We do not ignore the fact that much sexual activity goes on outside of wedlock and that it has become a common practice for unmarried couples to live together conjugally, either preparatory to or as a substitute for marriage itself. The question we face as a religious community is not whether to acknowledge this reality but whether we should sanctify it. Shall we teach, in the name of Torah, that these relationships offer a legitimate religious alternative to marriage? Shall we teach that, so long as these relationships are stable and monogamous, affording the couple the opportunity to experience sexual and emotional intimacy, they partake of the Jewish ideal and therefore attain a measure of sanctity (*kedushah*)? Reform responsa answer this question with an unequivocal "no." According to Jewish thought, the "sanctity" of a marital relationship lies precisely in the legal and moral restrictions which surround it: the prohibition of extramarital relations and adultery, and the requirement of a divorce to release the parties to form new relationships. These restrictions are part and parcel of what marriage, as the ideal state of sexual union, is supposed to be: a private process of separation and elevation, characterized by a serious and long-term commitment which, though not unbreakable, cannot be ended merely on the whim of the parties involved. Non-marital sexual unions, because they do not recognize such restrictions, therefore frustrate the very Jewish ideal of which they claim to partake. As Reform responsa see it, there is no such thing as a "measure" of *kedushah*. A couple are either prepared to marry, to enter into the sacred commitment of *kiddushin*, or they are not prepared to do so. We realize that many will not be thus prepared to take upon themselves the commitments required by the Judaic ideal. But that ideal remains the goal which we hold out to all; it is what we advocate as the proper framework for human sexual fulfillment and family life.

None of this implies that we condemn those who live together without benefit of marriage as "sinners"; we do not believe this, and it offends us that others do. Nor does it mean that we are indifferent to those who choose this path for themselves. On the contrary: these individuals, like all of us, live their lives under the Torah's demand for ethical and moral conduct. The absence of *kedushah* does not entail a vacuum of morality: these relationships, while not marriage, should nevertheless be constructed along the very lines that our tradition sets for all human relationships. They can be ethical and moral to the extent that they are free from manipulation, deceit, and foreseeable harm. These persons should therefore accord each other the fullest amount of human respect, honesty, and consideration. We should remember, however, that Judaism asks far more of us than ethical behavior alone. It asks us to distinguish our sexual conduct in the most exalted manner possible. This means that marriage should be the goal of our sexuality. And it would therefore be inconsistent for us to teach that other, acceptable goals exist.

Homosexuality. Reform Jewish attitudes on the issue of homosexuality have undergone a deep transformation in recent years. This transformation reflects a similar movement within Western culture as a whole, and it conflicts radically with much of what our tradition has to say on the subject. We do not regret this conflict, for to the extent that our understanding of the nature of human sexual orientation surpasses that of our ancestors, we perceive a moral obligation to part company with their judgments, strictures, and rules. At the same time, however, Reform Jews are not all of one mind as to what, precisely, this change of attitude demands of us in religious terms. As such, our stance as a religious movement on the array of questions surrounding human sexual orientation is currently in a state of flux. Someday soon, a broad consensus may emerge; and then again, it may not. The immediate prospect is therefore one of dispute and disagreement, debate and argument within our camp. The immediate task, whatever the outcome of the debate, is to see that it is conducted in an atmosphere of mutual respect and tolerance for opposing points of view.

Homosexuals in Society. The Reform movement has committed itself unequivocally in support of full legal and social equality for homosexuals in our communities. This means that gays and lesbians should be protected from all forms of discrimination by government, business, and other agencies in terms of employment, housing, and every other aspect of economic life. Homosexuals must be guaranteed the freedom to make decisions regarding their personal lives free from outside political interference. Gay and lesbian couples should be afforded the rights and benefits, both legal and economic, of civil marriage. We in the Reform movement, too, call for equal opportunity for homosexuals within our own professional ranks. We reject, in particular, any suggestion that a candidate's homosexuality be used as a bar to deny automatically his or her entry into the rabbinate.

On Homosexual Marriage; Should Rabbis Officiate? The statements in the above paragraph reflect a broad consensus within the Reform movement. This consensus breaks down, however, when we ask whether the union of a gay or lesbian couple is to be regarded as a marriage or as the equivalent of marriage and whether a rabbi ought to officiate at a wedding ceremony for a homosexual couple. The dispute over this question involves widely divergent points of view on the nature of human sexual orientation, the definition of Jewish marriage, and our relationship to the Jewish tradition's understanding of marriage and the family.

These sharp disagreements are explored in a lengthy Reform responsum in which a majority of the Responsa Committee holds that rabbis should *not* officiate at these ceremonies. A minority of the Committee, meanwhile, argued that rabbis should officiate. Given the intensity and sensitivity of this issue and the passions that surround it, the Committee decided to incorporate both sides of the dispute within its responsum. The result is an attempt to present each side's arguments as completely, as honestly, and as powerfully as possible, in the framework of a single, unified literary structure. The hope is that the movement as a whole might see the responsum as an example of how this vociferous ideological debate might be conducted in Jewish terms, honestly and forthrightly, yet in an atmosphere of mutual respect and commitment to continued dialogue toward the achievement of common ground.

Both sides of the debate proceed from an analysis of Jewish traditional teaching concerning homosexual relations. The Torah explicitly prohibits male homosexual intercourse, calling it an "abhorrence" (*to'evah*), an act which, along with such other abhorrences as adultery and incest, defiles the land. A people called to holiness must keep far from such practices. Female homosexual activity is not mentioned by the Torah, but the rabbinic tradition condemns it nonetheless. To the extent that the sources offer a rationale for these prohibitions, it lies in the concern that homosexual relations will lead to a breakdown in the institution of marriage, the bearing of children, and the boundaries of "normal sexuality." Homosexual relations, in this view, are an *indulgence*, a choice of carnal pleasure that is destructive of the order of nature and of the most basic unit of social life.

How do we understand these teachings? What do they call upon us to do? We might respond that the biblical and rabbinic tradition concerning homosexual relations no longer makes a persuasive claim to our allegiance. This is because that tradition does not speak to the condition of human sexual orientation as we understand it today. The Torah and the rabbinic sources punish individuals who *choose* of their own free will to engage in homosexual acts. They do not address, because they could not conceive of it, the phenomenon called *homosexuality* which, like heterosexuality, is not a choice or a preference; it is not something that one decides to do or not to do. It is simply the way one is. The sources also do not know, again because the reality of ancient times did not permit their authors to see this, of the possibility that gays and lesbians might establish stable, monogamous, and loving relationships with their partners. We know of such relationships; the "possibility" has become a concrete reality before our eyes. This is undoubtedly the reason why many in our society no longer respond with "abhorrence" to homosexual people and couples. Knowing them as flesh-and-blood human beings who live and work alongside the rest of us has helped to personalize for us that which we once stigmatized as a deviation from the sexual norm.

For reasons such as these, it no longer makes sense to many of us to deny to homosexual people the access to the blessings and spiritual satisfactions of marriage. As liberals, we are heirs to a tradition of thought which holds that a human being's most personal decisions are properly left to private discretion with a minimum of interference from the state or the community. As liberal *Jews*, our religious outlook permits us to set aside those aspects of our ancestral tradition which no longer reflect our consciousness of reality and morality. Given that we no longer respond to homosexuality as an "abhorrence," and given that Judaism holds *marriage* to be the best and most proper framework within which a couple may express their personal and sexual intimacy, many of us feel that the time has come to offer gay and lesbian Jews the opportunity to sanctify their unions in precisely the way that heterosexual couples have sanctified theirs.

There is, however, another way of perceiving the situation and of responding to the question of rabbinic officiation while affirming our religious and moral responsibility toward gay and lesbian members of our communities. It begins with an appreciation of the indispensable role of tradition in shaping the ways in which we Jews respond *as* Jews to the world around us. When we engage in Jewish ritual activity, we do so not simply because we find it "meaningful" or because it offers us spiritual and emotional comfort, although we certainly hope that our rituals achieve these ends. Rather, our rituals and ceremonies reflect our sense of ourselves as Israel, as a community that expresses its religious identity in ways that are *particular* to its own experience and consciousness. To illustrate: most religious traditions contain something called a "wedding ceremony," a collection of rites that accompany a couple through a major moment of transformation in their lives. This is because marriage, the formation of the family unit, is a universal human experience, and a religion will surely find the means to respond to that experience in terms of its own concepts, values, and ways of understanding the world. As Jews, we have our own wedding ceremony, and while in a very general sense it "does" what other wedding ceremonies "do," it is at the same time radically unlike any of them. The Jewish wedding is a set of ritual responses, drawn from our historical experience as a religious community, that translates a universal social institution into a *particularly* Jewish one. To put it differently, Judaism does not offer "marriage"; it offers *Jewish* marriage, an inescapably particular kind of marriage, a ceremony in which Jewish couples reaffirm their participation in Jewish community and Jewish destiny as they prepare to create their households and families. While other forms of marriage exist and other ways of understanding the human tendency to couple and to build lives together are available, the only way that we as a religious community can respond to the reality of marriage is through the web of symbols, ideas, and commitments that constitute the Jewish wedding.

This means that when we ask the question "should rabbis officiate at wedding ceremonies for same-sex couples?" we are asking first and foremost whether rabbis, as teachers of a religious tradition that empowers them to speak in its name, can plausibly interpret that tradition so as to define these ceremonies as a form of *Jewish* marriage. For many of us, the answer to this question is "no." Jewish tradition knows of one kind of Jewish marriage, and that is *kiddushin*. And whatever *kiddushin* means to us, it cannot be interpreted, no matter how cleverly and creatively we read our texts, to sanctify as "marriage" a sexual union between individuals of the same gender. It is true, of course, that we Reform Jews have always felt free to reject those features of our religious tradition that strike us as morally objectionable. We could, therefore, do the same in this case. Yet not all of us perceive a moral imperative to redefine the nature of Jewish marriage. Yes, we view homosexuality differently today than ever before. But while this "enlightened" view demands many things of us—that we vigorously oppose all social and economic discrimination against homosexuals; that we reach out to gays and lesbians, previously consigned to the margins of Jewish community life, and bring them into its center—it does not require that we establish a system of Jewish marriage for persons of the same gender. We agree that our understanding of homosexuality as an orientation rather than as a choice removes it from the category of "sin." It bears emphasis, however, that the fact that a pattern of behavior is in some way "involuntary" does not in and of itself mean that we must sanctify it. Indeed, we do not know what causes human sexual orientation, or, for that matter, even what a "sexual orientation" *is*. In the absence of firm knowledge, many of us are hesitant to draw the kinds of conclusions which we would require in order to justify so radical a departure from age-old Jewish tradition and universally-accepted standards of Jewish religious practice.

For these reasons, a majority of the Responsa Committee answered the question of same-sex wedding ceremonies in the negative, while the minority answered in the affirmative.

Some suggest that these difficulties might be resolved were we to use terms other than *kiddushin* or "marriage" to describe gay or lesbian unions. Perhaps it would be better to speak of "commitment ceremonies" whose liturgy and rituals make it obvious that we are not dealing with "marriage" as traditionally conceived but rather witnessing the creation of a very different sort of bond, defined by a unique set of rules and expectations. On the other hand, it can be said that the "commitment ceremony" is surely intended as the substitute for the wedding and that it seeks to establish the functional equivalent of marriage. Many rabbis hold that Jewish tradition empowers them to "officiate" only at ceremonies of *Jewish* marriage. And the only form of *Jewish* marriage that exists is *kiddushin*. Thus, for the same reason that many Reform rabbis do not "officiate" at ceremonies of mixed marriage, they would not wish to "officiate" at a ceremony of commitment which establishes a form of marriage other than *kiddushin*.

The divisions within Reform Judaism on this question are therefore principled, deep, and irreconcilable. This does not, however, mean that the two sides cannot or should not search for common ground. That common ground exists in the acknowledgment, shared by both sides, that it is a *mitzvah* to welcome gays and lesbians into our communities and to accompany them, as we accompany all of our people, along the path of Jewish life. This *mitzvah* requires that we recognize homosexual unions as *households*, the nuclear social and family units which compose our communities and whose strength and stability are primary Jewish religious concern. Whether or not we accord these unions the status of "marriage," we know that we are dealing with a Jewish home, the classic environment of the Jewish experience. As such, all the rituals and ceremonies that pertain to the Jewish home, to the celebration of a family's joys and the observance of its sorrows are as appropriate with respect to the homosexual household as with any other. To accept homosexual couples as full households—an acceptance we do *not* offer to unmarried heterosexual couples—is to invite them to express their partnership according to the full range of possibilities afforded by the Jewish ritual tradition.

It is in the nature of "common ground" that neither side will find it fully satisfactory. Many will see the "majority position," which rejects the call to officiate at homosexual wedding ceremonies but concurs that these unions can constitute Jewish households and families in every respect, as an unpalatable compromise. Yet this position represents, just as does the "minority position," the best effort by a group of rabbis to grapple with forces and ideas that seem to pull us as Jews in opposite directions. It is not always a simple thing for liberal Jews to identify the single "right" answer to a Jewish religious question, if such a single answer exists. All we can do is the best we can do. Through continued study, discussion, and argument—passionate but respectful—we can yet hope to arrive as a community at the kind of consensus agreement that has eluded us thus far on this issue.

The Environment

What makes environmentalism a *Jewish* issue? We are of course deeply interested in the quality of our air, the purity of our water, and the preservation of the earth, but our concern for these things is no different than that expressed by non-Jews. Is there a specifically Jewish value at stake in the public discussions over environmental policy, a principle that should spur us as Jewish individuals or as a Jewish community to action?

The most obvious candidate is the Jewish legal principle of *bal tashchit*, the commandment "not to destroy." We first encounter this *mitzvah* in the biblical interdiction against the destruction of fruit-bearing trees during a military siege against an enemy city (Deut. 20:19–20). The Rabbis expand it into a much wider prohibition. It is now forbidden to destroy wantonly *any* fruit-bearing tree, during war *or* peacetime. It is forbidden as well to destroy wantonly any objects of value—clothing, implements, buildings, water sources, and food—under the heading of *bal tashchit*. "Wanton destruction" is defined as destruction which serves no useful or acceptable purpose. Thus, it is permitted to cut down a fruit-bearing tree if it is found to be damaging other trees, or causing damage to another person's property, or even if its wood is valuable. If, on the other hand, the destruction serves no other purpose than to destroy (*derekh hashchatah*), or if it is carried out in a fit of anger, the act is said to violate the *mitzvah*.

At first glance, *bal tashchit* would seem to offer little support to environmental activism. Even the most inveterate polluters, individuals or corporations who dump prodigious amounts of toxic waste into the air and water or who slash and burn their way through the rain forests, will claim that they do so for a legitimate purpose, in pursuit of legitimate economic ends, rather than for the sake of sheer destruction. Indeed, one could argue that this principle, far from demanding the protection of the natural environment, in fact authorizes us to take any and all actions, no matter how physically destructive, so long as they can be justified in the name of economic gain. Yet Jewish tradition explains the commandment to the opposite effect. Its purpose is to train our minds and hearts to love that which is good and to despise that which is evil; we are therefore obliged to resist all our human tendencies toward destructive behavior.

> This is the way of the truly pious and the ethical, those who love peace, who rejoice when good things happen to others and who strive to bring

them close to Torah. They will not destroy even the smallest mustard seed, they anguish over the sight of waste, and they strive with all their power to save whatever they can from wanton destruction. It is not so with the wicked, who delight in the destruction of the world . . .

This *mitzvah* does not demand that we deify the natural world; we are, after all, permitted to make use of the environment as a treasure-house of resources, materials to be used in our own interest. But it does forbid us to deify economics, a god that would have us perceive the air, water, and land as mere capital, as means to the acquisition of our selfish purposes. It calls upon us to *honor* the world, urging us in our contact with our environment to act at all times as though we are "pious" and "ethical." The principle of *bal tashchit* does not prevent us from building homes, from planting crops, from cutting down forests, and from mining the earth. But it does serve as a constant reminder that the world around us is not our possession, to do with as we wish. On the contrary: the world belongs to an Owner who sets the rules as to its proper use.

The task of *Jewish* environmentalists, therefore, is to define just what we mean by "wanton" destruction. Does this term include only those acts of vandalism as make absolutely no economic sense to anyone? Or is it a wider concept that can reasonably apply to acts of environmental exploitation which, though serving as a source of pleasure or gain for the few, are potentially devastating to the long-term health and happiness of the many? If we choose the first definition, then the *mitzvah* of *bal tashchit* has very little to say to us as we ponder the great issues of ecological policy. But if its second definition is more plausible—and Reform Judaism is persuaded that it is—then the *mitzvah* serves as a real basis for an environmentalism that is truly *Jewish* in its source. This does not free us of the difficult task of balancing environmental protection against the legitimate economic needs of the community. But it does give us a platform upon which we, as Jews, might respond to the challenges that threaten our environment.

War

Nuclear War. Questions relating to the conduct of a nation's foreign and defense policy are usually left to political judgment. Jewish tradition, as noted above, can speak only in broad generalities on these issues, and as such can be interpreted as supporting either side of a particularly complex issue. Nuclear war is one such issue. On the one hand, nuclear war raises no special moral problem that is not already posed by war itself. That is, nuclear war differs from other wars not in its propensity to cause death and destruction—all wars do that—but simply in the extent of its effects. And since war itself can be justified as a necessary means of national self-defense in a violent world, the same might be said of nuclear war. According to this line of thinking, a nation is permitted to develop the weapons, strategies, and tactics needed to defend itself from nuclear intimidation. On the other hand, Jewish thought has always understood war as a *limited* phenomenon, an activity which, however violent, must be conducted within accepted ethical boundaries. These have to do, first of all, with the Torah's legislation concerning the treatment of the inhabitants of a beleaguered city and distinctions between combatants and non-combatants. Nuclear war, unlike even the most destructive sorts of conventional warfare, renders the observance of these limitations impossible. Indeed, to the extent that a thermonuclear conflict would result in the "mutually-assured destruction" of both sides, the "aggressor" as well as the "victim," it is doubtful that this sort of combat qualifies under the traditional permit of self-defense. These observations do not mean that we should advocate unilateral nuclear disarmament, but they do suggest that we should not delude ourselves into thinking that the existence of nuclear arsenals poses no new or special problem in human history. They constitute a most disturbing fact: that military technology has overpowered the ethical concepts with which we have always sought to define and thereby limit the conduct of war. The control and ultimate elimination of these weapons of mass destruction are matters of the highest import for us all.

On the Redemption of Captives. One of the tactics favored by criminals and terrorists is the kidnapping of innocent persons to be held for ransom. The government of Israel, among others, has amassed much bitter experience in dealing with hostage-takers. And Jewish tradition speaks quite directly to this issue.

Rabbinic literature refers to the *mitzvah* of the redemption of captives (*pidyon shevuyim*) as a high obligation, greater even than *tzedakah*. Yet the obligation does have its limits. We are not to redeem captives "for an amount that exceeds their monetary value" on account of "the welfare of society" (*mipnei tikkun ha'olam*). Assuming that we have some way of determining this "monetary value" in contemporary terms, what is the "welfare" that the Rabbis had in mind? The texts offer two possibilities. First, we are concerned that the payment of exorbitant ransoms might bankrupt the community; second, the knowledge that Jews will pay dearly to rescue their captives might tempt other would-be kidnappers to seize more Jewish hostages. If we adopt this second explanation, we would place strict limits on the amount that even wealthy individuals might pay to redeem their relatives, since high ransoms might lead to further kidnapping and endanger the safety of other Jews in the future. Halakhic authorities have generally accepted this view with respect to communities and governments. That is to say, while individuals are free to pay whatever they wish for the safe return of their loved ones, the first responsibility of a government is to the safety of all its citizens and not only the hostages.

The government of Israel has wrestled with this very problem in its dealings with hostage-takers. Does its legitimate concern for the safety of hostages justify the payment of an unreasonable price for their return, a price that will no doubt encourage other terrorists to utilize this weapon? One contemporary halakhist argues that the clear and present danger to the hostages outweighs the potential danger to future captives and therefore justifies the payment of any demand that the kidnappers set. We disagree, especially with the contention that the other citizens of the country are only "potentially" at risk. This is particularly the case with Israel, whose citizens live under the constant threat of terrorist action. Rather, the policy with regard to hostages must be set in each case in accordance with the best available judgment of the political and security situation. While in some cases the government will give in to the demands of the terrorists, in other cases it will resist those demands. While this policy, arrived at after consultations with military and diplomatic experts, cannot guarantee that mistakes will never be made, it is the surest means by which a government can best discharge its ethical responsibilities to its people against the backdrop of a harsh political reality.

Suggestions for Further Reading

"Reform Jewish religious practice" is a vast and wonderfully complex field, much too large and deep and interesting to be contained within the covers of one book. That is true, at any rate, of *this* one book. While I have tried to make its description of the roots, theory, and details of our practice informative and comprehensive, I have had to treat some matters in an all too cursory fashion and have had to omit others altogether. For this reason, I hope that reading this book encourages you to want to learn more about any of the subjects included therein. Of all the works that I have consulted and relied upon in the preparation of this volume (and these are listed in full in the Bibliography), the following are those which I have found particularly useful and would readily recommend to those readers interested in further study.

Rabbinic Literature. To understand Reform Jewish practice, we must understand its roots in the rabbinic legal tradition. The best way to do that is to study the halakhic literature that the Rabbis produced. The Mishnah and the Babylonian Talmud, the basic sources of rabbinic thought on matters of religious practice, exist in English translation, but as is the case with the original texts, a good commentary is an indispensable requirement if we wish to comprehend them. Over the centuries, many commentaries have been written on the Mishnah, opening that compendium of Oral Torah to experts and beginners alike. For today's reader, the most comprehensive and accessible Mishnah commentary is that of Pinchas Kehati, whose work, *Mishnayot Mevo'arot,* provides a wealth of context and detail. Those who can handle Hebrew will find Kehati's Hebrew original quite lucid and readable. It is also available in English translation as *The Mishnah*. Chanokh Albeck's *Shishah Sidrei Mishnah* is the classic "modern" Mishnah commentary, valuable especially for its extensive endnotes; alas, it is not translated into English. Talmudic commentary is a different story: the efforts of Rashi and other scholars notwithstanding, the Talmud has remained a most difficult work to those lacking extensive training and preparation. Yet recent years have witnessed remarkable accomplishments in this field. First and foremost of these is the commentary of R. Adin Steinsaltz, which expertly guides the student step-by-step through the Talmud's complex arguments and which supplies much useful supplementary material. The "Schottenstein" edition of the Talmud, edited by Hersh Goldwurm and Gedaliah Zlotowitz, offers another comprehensive running commentary to the text, along with the best brief summary of traditional talmudic scholarship available in any language. In a similar way, numerous handbooks and introductions to the study of the Talmud are now available to assist beginning and intermediate students in talmudic terminology, language, and method. The best of these include the "reference guide" volume of the Steinsaltz series, Edward Boraz's *Understanding the Talmud*, and Yitzchak Frank's *The Practical Talmud Dictionary*. Finally, Judith Abrams' three-volume series of remarkable introductions truly open the gates of the Talmud to the beginning student.

Jewish Law and Religious Observance. Jews have studied the Talmud with unceasing intensity for fifteen hundred years. This study has produced a massive literature in its own right, the commentaries, codes, and responsa that make up the corpus of Jewish law, and it is from this literature that the Jewish people have derived the substance and constructed the patterns of their religious observance. The single best summary of the form and substance of this literature is Menachem Elon's four-volume *Jewish Law*. Though his descriptions and conclusions are at times outdated and subject to dispute, his book remains beyond question the standard introduction to the field. As to the nature of Jewish law—that is, how the *halakhah* works and has functioned throughout Jewish history—Louis Jacobs' *A Tree of Life* and Moshe Zemer's *Evolving Halakhah* offer comprehensive and penetrating analyses from a liberal perspective and thus are interesting to compare with such Orthodox works as Bleich's *Contemporary Halakhic Problems*.

Other good sources for liberal Jewish halakhic thought are the collections edited by Walter Jacob and Moshe Zemer, published by the Freehof Institute of Progressive Halakhah.

There are many good general surveys of traditional Jewish religious observance. The best of these is Isaac Klein's *A Guide to Jewish Religious Practice*. Klein offers a comprehensive overview of traditional Jewish ritual life (prayer; Shabbat and festival observance; *kashrut*; mourning practice; marriage, divorce, and family law), incorporating the relevant teachings and rulings of the Conservative movement up to 1979. The book boasts a wealth of information expressed in a concise style unsurpassed for its clarity. The reviewer's cliche "this book belongs in every good Jewish library" must have been specifically coined, I think, for Klein's *Guide*. If, on the other hand, you're looking for *the* comprehensive reference work, you can hardly do better than Shelomo Ganzfried's *Code of Jewish Law*, Hyman Goldin's translation of Ganzfried's *Kitzur Shulchan Arukh*. Despite its name, this work is not precisely an abbreviated version of the great code of Karo and Isserles but rather a popular and widely-studied summary of those details of Jewish law that pertain to ritual observance. Those who can handle the Hebrew will appreciate that the text of the *Kitzur* appears opposite the translation. A more recent version of Ganzfried's work is Avrohom Davis' translation, *The Metsudah Kitzur Shulchan Arukh*. A less-detailed but still quite useful introduction is Hayim Halevy Donin's *To Be a Jew*. For those who can read Hebrew, Eisenstein's *Otzar Dinim Uminhagim* is a fine one-volume summary of the "laws and customs" of Jewish religious life.

Reform Jewish Observance. The most recent comprehensive statements on the religious observance of the Reform movement are the books of the "Gates" series: *Gates of Mitzvah*, edited by Simeon J. Maslin; *Gates of the Seasons*, edited by Peter S. Knobel; and *Gates of Shabbat*, by Mark Dov Shapiro. Solomon B. Freehof's two-volume *Reform Jewish Practice and Its Rabbinic Background* is to date the most ambitious attempt to summarize the distinctive observances of Reform Judaism along with "the traditional rabbinic laws from which they are derived" (p. 15). Though clearly outdated (the "combined edition" of 1963 is a reprint of the 1944 original), Freehof's work remains a valuable treasury of source material and a wonderful example of traditional rabbinic thought at work during the "classical" phase of American Reform Judaism. It is, in many respects, the model for the present volume. For a source of information that is simultaneously rich and concise, see W. Gunther Plaut's Historical and Halakhic Notes to the CCAR *Rabbi's Manual*, edited by David Polish. Michael A. Meyer's *Response to Modernity*, the definitive history of the Reform movement in Judaism, treats a number of issues of religious observance.

The Reform responsa comprise by far the largest body of Reform Jewish writing on questions of ritual and ethical practice and hence the major source of data for this book. They are valuable not only for the answers they reach but rather—and probably more so—as a model of liberal Jewish halakhic thinking and argument. As of this writing, the responsa are collected in twelve published volumes: eight by Solomon B. Freehof, three by Walter Jacob, and one by W. Gunther Plaut and Mark Washofsky. The latest responsa—that is, those written since 1996 and not yet printed in bound volumes—are published on a regular basis in the *CCAR Journal* and available online at the CCAR's webpage (*www.ccarnet.org*).

Liturgy and Worship. The serious Reform Jew wishes to understand how Reform worship is related to and diverges from that of other Jews. A good *siddur* (traditional Jewish prayer book for daily, Shabbat, and festivals) and *machzor* (the traditional prayer book containing the liturgy for the High Holidays or the special poetic additions for the three "pilgrimage" festivals) are therefore essential texts. There are many editions. My own recommendations focus on prayer books that accompany the liturgy with good commentaries. The best of these, I think, is still that of the late British Chief Rabbi J.H. Hertz, *The Authorised Daily Prayer Book*. The *Art Scroll Siddur*, edited by Rabbi Nosson Scherman, is quite popular with Orthodox congregations in the English-speaking world, as are the *machzorim* that Scherman has edited for Rosh Hashanah, Yom Kippur, and the festivals. The commentaries to the Art Scroll prayer books may not satisfy Reform tastes, but they supply much detail concerning the rules (*halakhah*) of traditional worship.

For an academic or "scientific" history and description of Jewish prayer, the standard treatment is Ismar Elbogen's *Jewish Liturgy*. Although Elbogen published his first edition in 1913, the English and Hebrew translations of his German original are updated by the notes of such scholars as Joseph Heinemann, Jakob Petuchowski, and Chaim Schirmann. Stefan C. Reif's magisterial *Judaism and Hebrew Prayer* takes a sweeping historical approach and covers the latest scholarly trends and controversies. Reuven Hammer's *Entering Jewish Prayer* and *Entering the High Holy Days* are also quite useful. On the music of synagogue worship, see A.Z. Idelsohn, *Jewish Music in Its Historical Development*.

The current standard prayer books of the North American Reform movement are *Gates of Prayer* (daily, Shabbat, and festivals) and *Gates of Repentance* (High Holy Days), edited by Chaim Stern. Each of these is accompanied by a volume of Lawrence A. Hoffman's comprehensive commentary, *Gates of Understanding*, containing essays and notes that provide the historical, cultural, and halakhic background so vital to a proper appreciation of Reform liturgy. Jakob Petuchowski's *Prayerbook Reform in Europe* is a thematic history of the development of Reform liturgy; his second chapter is a fine brief introduction to the major outlines of the Jewish prayer service. On the creation of a distinctly American tradition in Reform liturgy, see Eric Friedland's *Were Our Mouths Filled With Song*.

The Congregation. Jewish congregations in North America are voluntary associations, and their style of administration and finance is patterned largely after that of similar associations in the surrounding society. This fact distinguishes them sharply from the structure of the *kahal*, the traditional Jewish community, which enjoyed a great deal of legal autonomy and whose political power extended over every Jewish individual and institution in its locale. On the other hand, while the tradition of Judaic political thought and public law no longer controls the actions of the Jewish community, it continues to serve as an important source of guidance. Reform responsa dealing with communal matters, for example, draw heavily upon this tradition and cite it liberally. Several works provide an exceptionally good introduction to this field. Louis Finkelstein's *Jewish Self-Government in the Middle Ages* is the classic text, containing a treasury of communal *takkanot* (ordinances) that speak to a wide range of issues. On the legal theory that justifies the existence of a "community" as a political entity, along with its right to exert power over individuals and institutions, see Menachem Elon, *Jewish Law*, 678–779.

Law does not operate in a vacuum. The law that defines a community's life and institutions is born and takes its shape in response to the conditions of the social, economic, and cultural environment in which the community exists. Conversely, the law does not passively accept the dictates of the world; rather, the ways in which a community reads and understands its law will do much to affect the ways in which it perceives the conditions of society and the demands of the time. For penetrating analyses of the reciprocal relationship between Jewish life and Jewish law through history, one can hardly do better than to study the incomparable researches of Jacob Katz. On Jewish society in the late Middle Ages, see his *Tradition and Crisis* and *Exclusiveness and Tolerance.*

On the synagogue as a concrete institution, the volumes by Joseph Gutmann—*The Jewish Sanctuary* and *The Synagogue: Studies in Origins, Archaeology, and Architecture*—are particularly helpful. The development of the rabbinate as an institution is summarized with great clarity in Simon Schwarzfuchs, *A Concise History of the Rabbinate.* For American developments, see David J. Zucker's *American Rabbis* and the articles by Jeffrey S. Gurock, Abraham J. Karp, and David Polish in *America Jewish Archives*, 1983. The volume *Rabbinic Authority*, edited by Elliot L. Stevens, contains some valuable discussions by Reform rabbis on issues surrounding the role of the rabbi in the context of contemporary liberal Judaism. On the cantorate, Abraham Joshua Heschel's wonderful essay "The Vocation of the Cantor" is a classic. Leo Landman's *The Cantor: An Historic Perspective* is a book-length treatment. Those who read Hebrew will profit from Mordekhai Hakohen's concise description of the cantor's role in his *Mikdash Me'at*, 145–52.

Sabbath and Holiday Observance. The general works cited above, in the section "Jewish Law and Religious Observance," contain good discussions on Shabbat and festivals. What follows is a listing of books and articles devoted to specific topics.

Yehoshua Noivirt's *Shemirath Shabbath: A Guide to the Practical Observance of the Sabbath* is the most comprehensive collection of the details of Shabbat observance from the perspective of contemporary Orthodoxy. The home liturgy for Shabbat, including *Kiddush*, the blessing of the children, and *zemirot* (table songs), can be found in most prayer books. Abraham E. Millgram's *Sabbath: The Day of Delight* is a wonderful anthology. For representative liberal approaches, see Mark Dov Shapiro's *Gates of Shabbat*, Chaim Stern's *On the Doorposts of Your House*, and Ron Wolfson's *The Shabbat Seder.*

The Jewish calendar is a complex phenomenon, difficult for those who are mathematically challenged (such as the author of this book) to fathom. The articles listed in the Bibliography by Bernard J. Bamberger ("The Festival Calendar"), Alexander Guttmann ("The Jewish Calendar"), and E.J. Wiesenberg ("Calendar") contribute greatly toward a better understanding.

There are many books dealing with the festivals, their themes, symbolism, and observances. For sheer halakhic detail from an Orthodox (and *yeshivah*-world) perspective, the single best work is S.Y. Zevin's *The Festivals in Halakhah*.

Passover is exceptionally rich (or complicated; take your pick) in matters of ritual observance. For the traditionally observant there are, first of all, issues of *kashrut*, the special rules concerning abstention from *chametz* during the festival, disposal of *chametz* in one's possession, and the preparation of the kitchen for the holiday. The single most detailed collection of the laws of Pesach *kashrut*—from an Orthodox perspective—including an up-to-date listing of "kosher for Passover" products, is the yearly pamphlet compiled by Avrohom Blumenkrantz. Jeffrey M. Cohen's *1,001 Questions and Answers on Pesach* does not deal in such specific detail but is quite informative. The Passover Haggadah exists in thousands of printed editions. Many of them accompany the liturgy of the service with commentaries, each according to its own spirit and outlook, that add much to the experience of the Seder evening. *A Passover Haggadah: The New Union Haggadah,* edited by Herbert Bronstein, is the standard text-plus-commentary for the North American Reform movement, offering a great deal of material to enrich the service. The Conservative movement's *Passover Haggadah: The Feast of Freedom,* edited by Rachel Anne Rabinowicz, is also quite good. Two representative and useful contemporary Orthodox publications are Nosson Scherman's *The Haggadah Treasury* and Shlomo Riskin's *The Passover Haggadah.*

The Life Cycle. Again, many of the general works cited in the section "Jewish Law and Religious Observance" cover the subjects included under this heading.

The question of Jewish status—"who is a Jew?"—receives a thorough treatment in S.Z. Abramov's *Perpetual Dilemma,* 270–320. Though dated, the book covers all the main issues and problems. Reuven Bulka's *The Coming Cataclysm* and Irving Greenberg's *Will There Be One Jewish*

People by the Year 2000? are useful perspectives from Orthodox rabbis. On the concept of "patrilineal descent," see the CCAR's *Rabbi's Manual*, edited by David Polish, at page 227. On the development of the "traditional" definition of Jewishness, see Shaye J.D. Cohen, "The Origins of the Matrilineal Principle in Rabbinic Law."

Michael Gold's *And Hannah Wept* discusses, among other issues, the questions surrounding the adoption of children in Jewish law and custom. On circumcision, the articles in Lewis M. Barth's *Berit Milah in the Reform Context* are a wealth of historical, theological, medical, and halakhic information. For an "insider" account by a *mohel*, including a brief summary of the laws of ritual circumcision, see Henry C. Romberg's *Bris Milah*. For a serious discussion of the meaning of Bar/Bat Mitzvah from a liberal Jewish perspective, see Jeffrey K. Salkin's wonderful *Putting God on the Guest List*.

Maurice Lamm's *The Jewish Way in Love and Marriage* is a good general treatment of marriage laws and customs. Reuven Bulka's *The RCA Lifecycle Madrikh*, 69–87, contains the forms and the rules for the traditional *ketubah* and *tena'im*, as well as for a pre-nuptial agreement intended to encourage a husband to issue a Jewish divorce to his wife when instructed to do so by a rabbinical court. The traditional law and procedure of divorce are presented with great clarity by Isaac Klein, *A Guide to Jewish Religious Practice*, 465–508. Shlomo Riskin's *Women and Jewish Divorce* offers a good treatment of the *agunah* problem and a suggestion for (hopefully) solving it. Hebrew readers will want to consult Benzion Schereschewsky's *Dinei Mishpachah*, the standard summary of the law of marriage and divorce for Jews in the state of Israel.

Of the many guides to the laws and customs of mourning and burial, the following deserve special mention: Chaim B. Goldberg's massive *Mourning in Halakhah: The Laws and Customs of the Year of Mourning*; Maurice Lamm's *The Jewish Way in Death and Mourning*; and Aaron Felder's *Yesodei Smochos*. Those who read Hebrew will find much detail and source material in Greenwald's *Kol Bo 'al Avelut*.

Kashrut. For an impressively clear summary of this complex subject, my choice is I. Grunfeld's two-volume *The Jewish Dietary Laws*. Binyomin Forst, *The Laws of Kashrus*, is quite possibly the most detailed one-volume treatment. James M. Lebeau's *The Jewish Dietary Laws: Sanctify Life* offers a Conservative Jewish perspective.

Conversion. Conversion to Judaism as we know it is largely a phenomenon of rabbinic law; see, in general, Bernard J. Bamberger, *Proselytism in the Talmudic Period.* The Bible, of course, speaks of the *ger,* the "stranger" in the midst of the community; as to whether this person was equivalent to the "proselyte" of rabbinic times, see Jacob Milgrom, "Religious Conversion and the Revolt Model for the Formation of Israel." Maurice Lamm's *Becoming a Jew* is a comprehensive look at conversion in Jewish law and life from an Orthodox point of view. For a liberal view, see the volume *Conversion to Judaism in Jewish Law,* edited by Walter Jacob and Moshe Zemer and published by the Freehof Institute of Progressive Halakhah. For good discussions of the dynamics of conversion, the process by which an individual becomes a Jew and by which the community accepts that individual into its midst, see the following three books: Lydia Kukoff, *Choosing Judaism*; Anita Diamant, *Choosing a Jewish Life: A Handbook for People Converting to Judaism and for Their Family and Friends*; and Stephen Einstein and Lydia Kukoff, *Introduction to Judaism: Instructor's Guide and Curriculum.*

Medical Ethics. Most book-length surveys of the *halakhah* of healing are written from the Orthodox perspective. Some good examples are Fred Rosner's *Modern Medicine and Jewish Ethics*; *Jewish Bioethics,* edited by Fred Rosner and J. David Bleich; and Immanuel Jakobovits' *Jewish Medical Ethics.* *Jewish Medical Law* by Avraham Steinberg is a concise handbook. Hebrew readers will want to consult the medical-halakhic journal *Assia,* whose articles reflect a wide range of Orthodox opinion and not exclusively the most stringent viewpoints. *Nishmat Avraham,* edited by A.S. Avraham and arranged according to the order of the *Shulchan Arukh,* is a most helpful compilation of the opinions of the leading halakhic and contemporary Orthodox authorities on medical issues. Yet non-Orthodox scholars have by no means abandoned the field to their colleagues on the right. Elliot N. Dorff's *Matters of Life and Death: A Jewish Approach to Modern Medical Ethics* is an outstanding and richly documented survey. David Feldman's *Health and Medicine in the Jewish Tradition,* a much shorter and more lightly-footnoted work, is quite useful as a brief summary. For the opinions of Reform rabbis, see the volumes *Death and Euthanasia in Jewish Law* and *The Fetus and Fertility in Jewish Law,* edited by Walter Jacob and Moshe Zemer and published by the Freehof Institute of Progressive

Halakhah. Reform responsa are another invaluable source for Reform Jewish thinking on medical issues; see above, under "Reform Jewish Observance."

Between Jews and Non-Jews. For a look at how rabbinic Judaism perceives the Gentile and his place in the Judaic religious system, see David Novak's *The Image of the Non-Jew in Judaism.* Jacob Katz, in his *Exclusiveness and Tolerance*, surveys the changing disposition and attitudes of Jews toward their Gentile neighbors during medieval and modern times. The tenth chapter of that book devotes special attention to the thought of R. Menachem Hameiri, who helped blaze new paths toward a deeper understanding of Christianity and Islam among halakhic scholars. See as well Gerald J. Blidstein, "Menahem Meiri's Attitude Toward Gentiles." A number of the essays in Laurence J. Silberstein and Robert L. Cohn's *The Other in Jewish Thought and History* are quite informative. Hebrew readers may consult the article on the Gentile in the *Encyclopedia Talmudit*, edited by Meir Berlin and S.Y. Zevin, 5:286–366, for a comprehensive summary of the laws concerning the status of the non-Jew in traditional *halakhah.*

Reform Judaism and the Jewish Community. The story of the Reform movement's developing attitude toward Zionism is told in David Polish, *Renew Our Days: The Zionist Issue in Reform Judaism.* The essays and responsa in *Israel and the Diaspora in Jewish Law*, edited by Walter Jacob and Moshe Zemer, consider various aspects of the complex relationship between Jews living inside and outside the land of Israel from the perspective of liberal halakhic thought. For Orthodox perspectives on the possibilities of and limitations upon Jewish unity, see Jonathan Sacks, *One People?*; J. David Bleich, *Contemporary Halakhic Problems*, 3:84–96; and Jacob Schacter, ed., *Jewish Tradition and the Non-Traditional Jew.*

Judaism and Society. The social conscience of the North American Reform movement is expressed in such works as Albert Vorspan's *Reform Judaism and Social Action* and the volume *Jewish Dimensions of Social Justice: Tough Moral Choices of Our Time* by Albert Vorspan and David Saperstein. The application of Jewish values and *halakhah* to economic life is discussed in detail in Meir Tamari's *With All Your Possessions: Jewish Ethics and Economic Life*, and Aaron Levine's *Econom-*

ics and Jewish Law. Haim Cohn's *Human Rights in Jewish Law* is a definitive statement of its subject matter. For introductions to traditional Jewish thought concerning political theory and the nature of government, see the works of Martin J. Sicker, *The Judaic State* and *What Judaism Says About Politics*, as well as Mark Washofsky, "Halakhah and Political Theory." On the attitude of the traditional sources toward the disabled, see Judith Z. Abrams, *Judaism and Disability: Portrayals in Ancient Texts from the Tanach to the Bavli*. Those interested in the ecological teachings of Jewish tradition should consult *The Jewish Sourcebook on the Environment and Ecology*, edited by Ronald H. Isaacs. For the Jewish law and ethics of warfare, see Reuven Kimelman's *The Ethics of National Power: Government and War from the Sources of Judaism*. *Responsa in War Time*, published by the National Jewish Welfare Board, is a collection of rabbinic writing concerning issues faced by Jewish soldiers during World War II. What is most interesting about the collection is that the committee issuing the responsa was composed of Orthodox, Conservative, and Reform rabbis. One wonders sadly whether such cooperation among the branches of Judaism can occur only during an international emergency. Finally, Hebrew readers may consult Shelomo Goren's *Meshiv Milchamah* for a detailed survey of the *halakhah* as it applies to a Jewish army and to the conduct of war.

Notes

The following abbreviations are used in the Notes:

B.	*Babylonian Talmud*
Bach	*Bayit Chadash*
M.	*Mishnah*
Resp.	*Responsa*
Shakh	*Siftei Kohen*
T.	*Tosefta*
Taz	*Turei Zahav*
Tur	*Arba'ah Turim*
Y.	*Talmud Yerushalmi*
Yad	*Mishneh Torah*

Introduction

xiii **Rabbinic Judaism and Jewish Law:** The single best source of information on the literature of Jewish law is the appropriately entitled *Jewish Law: History, Sources, Principles,* the four-volume translation of Menachem Elon's monumental *Hamishpat Ha'ivri.*

xiii **"the Rabbis" or "the Sages" . . . :** The history and literature of the rabbinic period are the subject of a great deal of scholarly research. The scholars, as one might expect, are deeply divided over just about every issue of significance, a fact which makes the study of the period such a fascinating endeavor. H. L. Strack and G. Stemberger, *Introduction to the Talmud and Midrash,* is the standard reference work regarding the origin, nature, and editing of the major rabbinic literary genres. For overviews of the period (and a glimpse of the scholarly controversies concerning it), see Jacob Neusner, *The Oral Torah;* Ephraim E. Urbach, *The Halakhah: Its Sources and Development;* David Halivni, *Midrash, Mishnah, and Gemara;* and Shmuel Safrai, ed., *The Literature of the Sages.* David Kraemer's *The Mind of the Talmud* provides a good treatment of the Babylonian Talmud's dialectical style and conception of truth. Barry Holtz, ed., *Back to the Sources*, is a very good collection of essays on the classic Jewish texts, among them the rabbinic texts described here.

xv **Rabbi was quite selective . . . :** The tannaitic texts which Rabbi omitted from his Mishnah are called *baraita* (pl. *baraitot*), an Aramaic word that means "external material." Yet though Rabbi excluded them from his work, the Rabbis saw them as vital tools in their quest to learn and to understand the Oral Torah. Many of the *baraitot* are therefore preserved in the Talmud and in other collections of rabbinic literature.

xv **dispute (*machloket*) . . . :** See *M. Avot* 5:17 on the distinction between "good" and "bad" halakhic controversies.

xvii **scholars known as *geonim* . . . :** See Robert Brody, *The Geonim of Babylonia and the Shaping of Medieval Jewish Culture*, for a comprehensive introduction to the *geonim* and their literature.

xvii ***commentaries:*** The *geonim* did not produce a running commentary to the entire Talmud. Academic scholars differ as to why this was so. Avraham Grossman, *Chakhmei Tzarfat Harishonim*, 429–36 cites political reasons, while Brody, *Geonim*, 163–64, suggests pedagogical ones. Yet there does exist a sort of geonic commentary on the entire Talmud, in the form of Binyamin Menashe Levin's *Otzar Hageonim* (1928–1943), which collates the geonic material known to that time according to the order of the text of the Bavli. The most renowned single commentary (*peirush*) to the Talmud is that of Rashi (R. Shelomo b. Yitzchak), who lived in northern France and the Rhineland during the eleventh century. Rashi's work, a comprehensive step-by-step guide through the Bavli's linguistic and logical complexities, quickly caught on in the world of Jewish scholarship and became the standard commentary to the Talmud. Its exalted status is evident in the fact that to this day it is printed along with all standard editions of the Talmud, located on the inside margin of the page, which is considered a place of honor.

xvii **derive new ideas from them:** This is the role of the literature called *chidushim*, "novellae." The commentaries called *tosafot*, an edited version of which are printed on the standard Talmud page opposite that of Rashi, are a famous example of such *chidushim*. They penetrate to a deeper level of textual analysis, locating problems in the text, contradictions between passages, and difficulties in the positions of previous commentators such as Rashi; by resolving these problems, the author of the *chidushim* creates new understandings of the text and of the *halakhah* which flows from it. Those new understandings, in turn, will serve as grist for the intellectual mill of subsequent commentators who study, critique, and build upon them.

xvii ***codes* . . . :** On the codes in general, see Menachem Elon, *Jewish Law*, 1138–452, as well as Isadore Twersky, *Introduction to the Code of Maimonides*. Among the most famous codes are the *Mishneh Torah of* R. Moses Maimonides (Rambam; twelfth-century North Africa) and the sixteenth-century *Shulchan Arukh* of R. Yosef Karo and R. Moshe Isserles. This latter work is accepted by today's Orthodox Jews as the most "authoritative" halakhic code. Yet this should not obscure the fact that during the succeeding four centuries rabbis have written numerous commentaries on the *Shulchan Arukh*, some of which are customarily included in the standard printed editions of that text. The task of these commentaries is to link the rulings of Karo and Isserles directly to their talmudic sources and to defend, qualify, or modify those rulings in response to criticisms from other scholars. To "study the *Shulchan Arukh*," in other words, means to study the work *and* its commentaries, which provide the indispensable background to the text and which locate its words within the ongoing debates that forge the *halakhah*.

xvii ***responsa* . . . :** Aside from Elon, *Jewish Law*, 1453–528, the outstanding survey is still Solomon B. Freehof, *The Responsa Literature*. Recent scholarship has shown a growing interest in the study of responsa as a literary genre, rather than simply as a repository of historical and cultural data. See Peter Haas, *Responsa: Literary History of a Rabbinic Genre*, as well as Mark Washofsky, "Responsa and Rhetoric" in John C. Reeves and John Kampen, eds., *Pursuing the Text: Studies in Honor of Ben Zion Wacholder*.

xix ***Reform Judaism and the Halakhah*:** For considerations of theory and practice, see the introductions to the following volumes: Solomon B. Freehof, *Reform Responsa* and *Reform Jewish Practice and Its Rabbinic Background*, 2 vols.; Walter Jacob, ed., *American Reform Responsa* and *Contemporary American Reform Responsa*; W. Gunther Plaut and Mark Washofsky, eds., *Teshuvot for the Nineties*; Simeon J. Maslin, ed., *Gates of Mitzvah: A Guide to the Jewish Life Cycle*; Peter S. Knobel, ed., *Gates of the Seasons: A Guide to the Jewish Year*; Mark Dov Shapiro, *Gates of Shabbat: A Guide for Observing Shabbat*. See also the articles in Walter Jacob, ed., *Liberal Judaism and Halakhah*, as well as the essays by W. Gunther Plaut and Jakob J. Petuchowski in Bernard Martin, *Contemporary Reform Jewish Thought*. For an Israeli perspective see Moshe Zemer, *Evolving Halakhah,* the translation of his *Halakhah Shefuyah*. Also useful are the volumes published by the Freehof Institute for Progressive Halakhah and edited by Walter Jacob and Moshe Zemer (*Dynamic Jewish Law*; *Rabbinic-Lay Relations in Jewish Law*; *Conversion to Judaism in Jewish Law*; and *The Fetus and Fertility in Jewish Law*).

xix **In the formative period of Reform Judaism . . . :** See Alexander Guttmann, *The Struggle Over Reform in Rabbinic Literature*.

xx **"describe present-day Reform Jewish practices . . . ":** Freehof, *Reform Jewish Practice,* 2:15.

xxi **sketchy or even non-existent biblical references . . . :** For example, the Bible tells us to "remember" the Sabbath and to call it a "delight," but it is the Talmud which tells us that we fulfill these *mitzvot* through *Kiddush* and the festive meal; see p. 76. Our Seder, whose description we find in the rabbinic sources, differs significantly from the Bible's description of the Passover meal (Exod. 12). The Torah tells us to "take" four species of plants and to dwell in "booths" during the Sukkot festival (Lev. 23:40–42), but it is the Talmud and the *halakhah* which define precisely what these are. The Torah tells us to sound the *shofar* on Rosh Hashanah (Num. 29:1), but it is the Rabbis who tell us *how* this is to be done. In all of these cases, the Shabbat and holiday observances that we know and that color and characterize Reform Jewish religious life are the products of *rabbinic* thought and are discussed and developed in the *halakhic* literature.

xxiv **the opinion, held by some of the greatest teachers of Jewish law . . . :** Among these is Maimonides, who writes in the introduction to his great code, the *Mishneh Torah,* that no rabbi or court is bound to interpret the sacred texts in a particular way merely because a preceding authority ruled thus. Rather, "one follows the interpretation that one considers correct."

xxiv **the "correct" halakhic ruling is not determined by the weight of precedent . . . :** For a powerful summary of this point, see Elon, *Jewish Law,* 983–85.

Chapter 1: The Worship Service

1 **Jewish prayer . . . is first of all a *mitzvah* . . . :** See *Yad, Tefillah*, ch. 1, where Maimonides, based on the sources cited at the beginning of this chapter, describes prayer as a Toraitic commandment.

1 **Jewish prayer . . . was to be a direct and immediate expression of what we feel:** Talmudic tradition defines the essence of prayer as heartfelt supplication (*rachamei*); B. *Berakhot* 20b and B. *Sotah* 33a. See also *M. Avot* 2:13. At first, writes Maimonides, this prayer had no fixed text; its content was largely up to each individual. It was only later that, in response to a decline in language ability among the returnees from the Babylonian exile (see Neh.13:24), that the Sages ordained a fixed text. Against this, Nachmanides (Ramban) argues that prayer was never a commandment of the Torah. Human beings began to pray, not because the Torah or any other source of authoritative instruction commanded them to do so, but because prayer reflects the natural urge of people to pour out their hearts to God. Prayer was thus never a ritual obligation until the Sages of old established it as a fixed practice. See Ramban's *hasagah* (critical note) to Maimonides' *Sefer Hamitzvot*, positive commandment no. 5. Significantly, both these accounts are united in their description of the origin of Jewish prayer as the heartfelt expression of the worshiper's soul. For a "scientific history" of Jewish prayer, an account of the liturgy which reflects the findings of modern academic research, see Ismar Elbogen, *Jewish Liturgy: A Comprehensive History*; Joseph Heinemann, *Prayer in the Talmud*; Ruth Langer, "The Impact of Custom, History, and Mysticism on the Shaping of Jewish Liturgical Law" (Phd diss., HUC-JIR, 1994); Jakob J. Petuchowski, *Prayerbook Reform in Europe*; and Stefan Reif, *Judaism and Hebrew Prayer*.

2 ***keva* and *kavanah* . . . :** Petuchowski, *Prayerbook Reform*, 22–30.

2 ***tachanunim*:** Elbogen, *Jewish Liturgy*, 66–70. Ironically, the "supplications" in time became a set rubric of the service with a fixed text.

2 ***piyyutim*:** see Ezra Fleischer, *Shirat Hakodesh Ha'ivrit Bimei Habeinayim* and Jakob J. Petuchowski, *Theology and Poetry*.

2 **removing the *piyyutim* . . . :** Petuchowski, *Prayerbook Reform*, 30.

2 **that served only to lengthen the service . . . :** See *Shulchan Arukh, Orach Chayim* 1:4: "it is better to recite a few supplicatory prayers with devotion *(kavanah)* than to recite many without devotion."

2 **"when prayer becomes a fixed thing . . .":** Ascribed to R. Eliezer, at *M. Berakhot* 5:4. What precisely is this "fixed thing"? The Talmud (*B. Berakhot* 29b) suggests several interpretations. Some hold that he refers to one who regards prayer solely as a burden or duty to be discharged rather than as a source of spiritual renewal. Others say that a "fixed prayer" is one whose wording is always the same and does not include anything new or innovative. There is a wide difference between these views. According to the first, a prayer with a fixed text can be "a true supplication" so long as the worshiper recites it with the proper devotion. According to the second, every prayer text must be "new," differing in some way from all previous versions.

3 **The Reform *siddur* . . . :** See Lawrence A. Hoffman, ed., *Gates of Understanding*, vols. 1 and 2.

3 **a fairly set liturgical structure:** Chaim Stern and A. Stanley Dreyfus provide a detailed commentary to *Gates of Prayer* in Hoffman, *Gates of Understanding*, 1:177ff. Much of the material in this section is taken from their work. See also Jacob, *Contemporary American Reform Responsa*, no. 133.

3   **Introductory Prayers and Readings:** See *M. Berakhot* 5:1; *Shulchan Arukh, Orach Chayim* 93:1.

4   ***Barekhu:*** A ritual invitation to a group to recite a benediction, known already in late antiquity; see *M. Berakhot* 7:3 and *Sifre Deuteronomy*, no. 306.

4   ***Shema:*** Recited twice daily, evening and morning (Deut. 6:7: "when you lie down and when you rise up"; *M. Berakhot* 1:3; Rambam, *Yad, Keri'at Shema* 1:1).

4   **In the Reform rite . . . :** The traditional *Shema* is made up of three paragraphs: Deut. 6:4–9; Deut. 11:13–21; and Num. 15:37–41. Reform practice omits the second paragraph because it deals with the theme of retribution and the third because it mentions the commandment to wear ritual fringes (*tzitzit*) on our garments; "they are regarded as questionable or unessential within the present liturgical context" (Hoffman, *Gates of Understanding*, 2:186; Petuchowski, *Prayerbook Reform*, 82). *Gates of Prayer*, ed. Chaim Stern, retains the last two verses of the third paragraph, which, because they mention the doing of "all of My commandments," contains the essence of that paragraph; *Yad, Keri'at Shema* 1:2.

4   ***Barukh shem kavod:*** Originally part of the Yom Kippur Temple ritual; see *M. Yoma* 3:8. Since it does not belong to the text of Deuteronomy 6, it is traditionally recited in an undertone. Another explanation is that when he ascended to receive the Torah, Moses heard the angels utter this praise to God and brought it down to Israel. Since it in fact belongs to the heavenly choir, we do not advertise our possession of it by reciting it aloud. The one exception is, again, on Yom Kippur, "when we are as pure as the ministering angels" and thus have a right to it; *Deuteronomy Rabbah* 2:36.

4   **The *Shema* is preceded . . . :** *M. Berakhot* 1:4. Reform practice, following the practice of most congregations in the land of Israel (*Eretz Yisrael*), omits the third blessing after the evening *Shema*, *Barukh Adonai le'olam*, which is not part of the original *Keri'at Shema*. See Elbogen, *Jewish Liturgy*, 87–88.

4   **to stand during the recitation of the *Shema*:** Traditional *halakhah* follows the opinion of the school of Hillel, *M. Berakhot* 1:3, that one reads the *Shema* in whatever posture that one had previously assumed. Since the preceding two benedictions after *Barekhu* are read while seated, one remains seated for the *Shema*. Some authorities even forbid one already seated to rise for the *Shema* (*Shulchan Arukh, Orach Chayim* 63:2; *Mishnah Berurah*, no. 5), since this would give the impression that one is following the rejected practice of the school of Shamai, who hold that we stand for the morning *Shema*. On the other hand, the *halakhah* does demand that one recite the *Shema* from a position of respect; thus, one is prohibited from reciting it while lying on one's back or face. One who is walking must come to a halt to recite the first verse of the *Shema* (*B. Berakhot* 13b; *Y. Berakhot* 2:1; *Yad, Keri'at Shema* 2:2–3). Even when sitting, one must do so "as though standing in awe and reverence (before God)" (*Kesef Mishneh, Keri'at Shema* 2:2). We may therefore conclude that tradition rejects the literal interpretation of the Hillelite view: what is important is not so much that one remain seated as that one assume a posture that expresses the individual's devotion when uttering the *Shema*. By prescribing that we stand during the recitation of the *Shema*, Reform practice in fact adheres to the spirit of the tradition by favoring that form of posture most closely associated with reverence and *kavanah*. *Gates of Prayer* has the congregation remain standing from *Barekhu* through *Shema* and *Barukh shem kavod*. This instruction corresponds to the letter as well as the spirit of traditional practice in that the worshiper does not change posture to read the *Shema*.

4 On the history of the *Kaddish* see Elbogen, *Jewish Liturgy*, 80–84, and Hoffman, *Gates of Understanding*, 2:47–50. The *Kaddish* exists in several forms:

1) *Kaddish Shalem* (the *"Full" Kaddish*), which traditionally concludes the *Tefillah*. It consists of six paragraphs, the fourth of which asks that God accept Israel's prayer.

2) *Kaddish Derabbanan*, recited by mourners following the study of rabbinic literature. The fourth paragraph of *Kaddish Shalem* is replaced by a prayer for the welfare of teachers and students of Torah.

3) *Kaddish Yatom*, the *Mourner's Kaddish*: It omits the fourth paragraph of *Kaddish Shalem*.

4) *Kaddish Le'itchadata*, the *"Burial Kaddish,"* recited at the funeral and, probably due to its emphasis upon resurrection and the messianic hope, at the conclusion of the study of a tractate of the Talmud.

5) *Chatzi Kaddish*. Reform practice retains *Kaddish Yatom* and *Chatzi Kaddish*. On Shabbat evening, *Gates of Prayer* does not recite *Chatzi Kaddish* between *Shema* and *Tefillah* but does use it, as does the traditional *siddur*, to mark the transition from *Kabbalat Shabbat* to the evening service proper.

4 **the evening *Tefillah*, which is theoretically a non-obligatory prayer:** The evening prayer was originally regarded as a voluntary rather than obligatory practice. In traditional congregations, it is thus recited silently and not repeated, to distinguish it from the obligatory prayers. This distinction, however, no longer makes sense, since for nearly fifteen hundred years its inclusion in the *Ma'ariv* prayer service has by common custom been accepted as obligatory; B. *Berakhot* 27b; *Yad, Tefillah* 1:6.

· 4 ***The Tefillah*:** See Elbogen, *Jewish Liturgy*, 24ff. Current scholarship suggests, *contra* Elbogen and others, that the *Tefillah* originated as one complete unit rather than in stages and that this prayer was ordained by a rabbinic institution (the Sages of Yavneh, ca. 90 C.E.) rather than compiled from the prayers of a number of different worship communities; see Ezra Fleischer, "Lekadmoniyut Tefillot Hachova Be-Yisrael," *Tarbiz* 59 (1990): 397–441.

5 **For weekdays, *Gates of Prayer* offers . . . :** See *Gates of Prayer*, 37–47. The traditional *Tefillah* is made up of nineteen *berakhot*, each a text treating a specific theme: 1) *avot*, God of Israel's history; 2) *gevurot*, God's power manifest in nature and through resurrection; 3) *kedushat hashem*, our sanctification of God's name; 4) *da'at*, knowledge; 5) *teshuvah*, repentance; 6) *selichah*, forgiveness; 7) *ge'ulah*, Israel's redemption; 8) *refu'ah*, healing; 9) *birkat hashanim*, economic sustenance; 10) *kibbutz galuyot*, the ingathering of our exile; 11) *mishpat*, justice, restoration of the Sanhedrin; 12) *birkat haminim*, condemnation of the wicked and of Israel's enemies; 13) *'al hatzadikim*, blessing for the righteous; 14) *binyan yerushalayim*, the rebuilding of Jerusalem; 15) *mashiach ben David*, the coming of the Messiah; 16) *shome'a tefillah*, for God to hear our prayer; 17) *avodah*, the acceptance of our worship, rebuilding of the Temple; 18) *hoda'ah*, thanksgiving; 19) *birkat kohanim*, priestly benediction, peace. In order to bring these texts into line with Reform Jewish thought, *Gates of Prayer* reworks a number of them and omits benediction no. 12 altogether.

5 **The evening *Tefillah* is recited aloud . . . :** The other *tefillot* are traditionally recited silently and then repeated by the prayer leader (*sheliach tzibur*), thus allowing all worshipers, including those unable to pray on their own, to fulfill their obligations by responding *amen* to the leader's benedictions.

5   *Aleinu*...: See Hoffman, *Gates of Understanding*, 1:250–51. *Gates of Prayer* offers the "traditional" version of this prayer (615–16) as well as alternates.

5   **Introductory Prayers and Readings:** See Elbogen, *Jewish Liturgy*, 72–80. "When one awakes, one recites 'the soul that You have given me...' (*Gates of Prayer*, 53) ... when one opens one's eyes, one says 'Blessed is the Eternal our God, who opens the eyes of the blind,' (*Gates of Prayer*, 286)," etc.; *B. Berakhot* 60b; *B. Menachot* 43b; *Tosefta Berakhot* 7:18; *Yad, Tefillah* 7:3–12. In addition, it was customary for some to study Torah early in the morning before reciting the *Shema*. This became a means by which all persons might fulfill the *mitzvah* of daily Torah study. Hence, *berakhot* are recited, and passages of the Bible and rabbinic literature are recited. See *B. Berakhot* 11b; *Yad, Tefillah* 3:10–11; *Shulchan Arukh, Orach Chayim* 47; *Gates of Prayer*, 52–53, 284–85.

5   ***Pesukei Dezimra:*** Based upon the recitation of Psalms 145–50 (traditionally lengthened on Shabbat and festivals). See *Yad, Tefillah* 7:12: not part of the "core" synagogue liturgy, these rubrics were not originally recited in the synagogue but by individuals, at the proper moment upon rising in the morning or in preparation for the recitation of the *Shema* and the *Tefillah*.

5   **The Recitation of the Shema**...: *M. Berakhot* 1:4.

5   **The *Tefillah*:** The text of the final benediction, *birkat kohanim*, in the evening service (*Shalom Rav*...) differs from that in the morning service (*Sim Shalom*...).

5   **Kedushah, the "Sanctification,":** See Elbogen, *Jewish Liturgy*, 54–62. Its opening phrase declares its purpose: we, the community of Israel assembled in prayer, sanctify God's name on earth just as the angelic choir sanctifies it in heaven, as we read in Isaiah 6:3. The terms "community" and "choir" are significant in that the *Kedushah* is recited by Israel as a public, a corporate body. We sanctify God as one, a unity once symbolized by the Temple in Jerusalem and now expressed by the synagogue community. Thus, one who prays in the absence of a *minyan* traditionally does not recite *Kedushah*.

5   **Deuteronomy 6:4:** The *"Shema Yisrael,"* which in the traditional prayer book appears in the *Kedushah* of the *Musaf* service for Shabbat and festivals. Since Reform practice omits that service, the verse is inserted into the *Kedushah* for *Shacharit* on those days.

5   *Hallel:* See the discussion in Chapter 3.

5   **The Reading of the Torah:** See Elbogen, *Jewish Liturgy*, 129ff. A list of Torah readings is found at Hoffman, *Gates of Understanding*, 1:271–84, and see Chapter 3 of this volume. The *Haftarah* is traditionally taken from the prophetic books of the Bible. Reform practice may substitute a selection from the Writings when the prophetic reading for that day is deemed inappropriate on thematic grounds. The readings listed in this book are from Hoffman, *Gates of Understanding*. Other texts may list alternative *Haftarah* portions.

5   **Concluding Prayers:** Traditionally, the *Musaf* prayer follows the Torah reading on Shabbat, festivals, and Rosh Chodesh. Just as the other scheduled *Tefillot* correspond to elements of the priestly ritual in the ancient Temple, this prayer represents the additional (*Musaf*) sacrifice offered on those days (see Num. 28 and 29). The theme of sacrifice dominates the text of the *Musaf* prayers; indeed, tradition sees *Musaf* as the fulfillment of Hosea 14:3, "instead of bulls, we will pay the offering of our lips" (*Tosafot, Berakhot* 26a, s.v. *iba'ya*). For that reason, Reform practice omits this *Tefillah*. See A.Z. Idelsohn, *Jewish Liturgy and Its Development*, 277–78.

6   *Ashrei*: "R. Avina said: whoever recites Psalm 145 three times daily is assured of a place in the World-to-Come" (*B. Berakhot* 4b). Hence, the traditional *siddur* has *Ashrei* twice during the *Shacharit* service and once during *Minchah*. Its recitation also fulfills the principle that one ought to recite the *Tefillah* after having read words of Torah (or Scripture); see *Y. Berakhot* 1:1 (2a) and *Tosafot, Berakhot* 2a, s.v. *me'amatai*.

6   **Readings for Shabbat and festivals:** For Shabbat, these include selections from the *kedushah desidra*; see Elbogen, *Jewish Liturgy*, 70–71.

6   **essentially the same as for *Shacharit*:** The afternoon *Tefillah* contains the *Kedushah* but, in many versions of the Ashkenazic rite, it recites *Shalom Rav* rather than *Sim Shalom* as the text of the final benediction. *Gates of Prayer* accords with those variants of *minhag Ashkenaz*, such as Frankfurt am Main and the R. Eliyahu, the Gaon of Vilna, which adopt *Sim Shalom* for Shabbat *Minchah*. In the traditional *siddur*, the Torah reading precedes the *Tefillah*.

6   **Reform Jews by and large did not cover their heads . . . :** For the developing Reform attitudes toward *kippah, tallit,* and *tefillin* see Michael Meyer, *Response to Modernity: A History of the Reform Movement in Judaism*, 251–52, 273, and 374 and Hoffman, *Gates of Understanding*, 2:56–62.

6   **In 1963 . . . :** Freehof, *Reform Jewish Practice*, 1:43.

7   **the Pittsburgh Platform . . . :** For a full text see Meyer, *Response to Modernity*, 387–388.

8   **By the middle of the twentieth century . . . :** On the Columbus Platform see Meyer, *Response to Modernity*, 317–20 and 388–91.

8   **Centenary Perspective of 1976:** See Meyer, *Response to Modernity*, 391–94.

9   **"we willingly move also . . . ":** Jacob, *American Reform Responsa*, no. 2.

10 *Kippah*: The Lauterbach responsum is Jacob, *American Reform Responsa*, no. 5 (and following him, see idem, no. 1 and Freehof, *Reform Jewish Practice*, 1:43–46). Among his sources are Tractate *Soferim* 14:15; *Leviticus Rabbah* 27:6; and *Chiluf Minhagim Bein Benei Bavel Livenei Eretz Yisrael*, no. 42. The Sefardic custom is recorded in *Yad, Tefillah* 5:5 (and not 4:5, as printed in the responsum) and *Sefer Hamanhig*, ed. Yitzchak Rafael, 1:84. The "later authorities in central and eastern Europe" include R. Shelomo Luria, *Resp. Maharshal*, no. 72, and R. Ya'akov Reischer, *Resp. Shevut Ya'akov* 3:5. The quotation "there is no prohibition whatever...but as a matter of propriety..." is from R. Eliyahu, the Gaon of Vilna, *Bi'ur Hagra, Shulchan Arukh, Orach Chayim* 8:2.

11 **One may quibble over Lauterbach's interpretation . . . :** For example, Lauterbach's "propriety" and "good manners" do not catch the essence of the Gaon of Vilna's term *musar*, which connotes "correct religious conduct": it is correct to keep the head covered, says the Gaon, even if it is not a Toraitic requirement, for "those who seek to be holy stand before God at all times." This wording lends a much more serious tone to the practice than does the suggestion that it is a matter of "propriety" alone. Luria stops far short of declaring that Jews have a right to ignore the custom and to pray bareheaded. Reischer clearly does not favor the removal of headcovering during prayer. Rather, since there is no absolute requirement to cover the head, he permits Jews to doff their hats when a high-ranking Gentile government official visits the synagogue and when the failure to show respect in this fashion might kindle his anger against the community. Reischer also encourages the worshipers to explain the Jewish custom to the official; hopefully, he will permit them to keep their heads covered.

Finally, it is possible that the *Chiluf Minhagim* passage does not refer to headcovering at all; see B. M. Levin's edition of that work, 85–86.

11 **"the custom of our ancestors is Torah . . . "**: *Machzor Vitry*, 226, and many other places in medieval Ashkenazic literature. On the dominant force of *minhag* in Jewish practice generally, see Elon, *Jewish Law*, 880ff.; on its dominant role in the early history of Ashkenazic practice see Yisrael Ta-Shema, *Minhag Ashkenaz Hakadmon*; and on the seriousness with which Jews relate to it, see Hoffman, *Gates of Understanding*, 2:56–62.

12 **partakes deeply of the realm of symbolism . . . :** Hoffman, *Gates of Understanding*, 2:62.

12 **For those concerned about building . . . :** See Jacob, *Questions and Reform Jewish Answers*, no. 8: "[when we decide to restore once-discarded practices] we should make the changes which express our mood while continuing to recognize the validity of practices of a former generation."

12 **"for those who wear the *tallit*"**: *Gates of Prayer*, 48, 282. On the history of *tallit* in Reform practice see Hoffman, *Gates of Understanding*, 3:56–62.

13 **recited while standing . . . :** *Shulchan Arukh, Orach Chayim* 8:1 and *Mishnah Berurah*, no. 2.

13 **immediately prior to donning the *tallit* . . . :** The rule for *birkat mitzvot*, a benediction over a *mitzvah* such as the wearing of *tzitzit*, is that it is said *over le'asi'atah*, immediately prior to the performance of the act it describes (*B. Pesachim* 7b; *Yad, Berakhot* 1:3 and 11:7; *Shulchan Arukh, Orach Chayim* 25:8). A major exception to this rule is the benediction said over the lighting of the Shabbat candles, which must be kindled prior to the recitation of the *berakhah*. Another exception is the blessing recited by the proselyte at the time of ritual immersion; it is recited *after*, and not before he or she immerses in the *mikveh*.

13 **If the *tallit* is large enough . . . :** There is a dispute among the medieval authorities as to whether one is required literally to wrap oneself in the *tallit*. Some, citing Deut. 22:12 ("you shall make tassels ... with which you cover yourself"), declare that the act of "covering" or wrapping the head is part of the *mitzvah*. For this reason, some Jews will leave the *tallit* in place upon their heads during the entire service. Jewish mystics also suggested that by keeping the head covered with the *tallit* one achieves a more powerful devotion (*kavanah*) and concentration upon prayer. Other authorities, noting that the text in Num. 15:37–41 does not mention "wrapping," hold that this is not required. Accordingly, the benediction, which says *lehitatef* ("to wrap oneself") is interpreted as referring to a higher, "ideal" standard but not one expected of all. The order described in the text is a common procedure by which the individual can *yotzei shetei hade'ot*, take note of both opinions. In this "compromise" method, one leaves the *tallit* in place over the head "for as long as it would take to walk a distance of four cubits," i.e., a brief yet significant measure of time. See *Shulchan Arukh, Orach Chayim* 8:3 and *Mishnah Berurah*, no. 4.

13 **"one is surrounded by *mitzvot*"**: *Shulchan Arukh, Orach Chayim* 8:4.

13 **the daylight hours:** Num. 15:39 says of the fringe that "you shall see it"; rabbinic interpretation holds that this exempts one from the requirement of *tzitzit* at night (*B. Menachot* 43a). In practical terms, this means that one does not recite the benediction over *tzitzit* unless one puts on the *tallit* during daylight. Thus, the service leader who wears the *tallit* at night need not say the *berakhah*. On *Kol Nidrei*, many take care to don it and recite the benediction before sundown; Isserles, *Orach Chayim* 18:1.

13   **the night of Yom Kippur (*Kol Nidrei*):** Isserles, *Orach Chayim* 18:1 and *Mishnah Berurah*, no. 6. On the resemblance of Israel to the angels on Yom Kippur, see *Pirkei deRabbi Eliezer*, ch. 46.

13   **In addition . . . :** Freehof, *Modern Reform Responsa*, no. 7; Jacob, *Contemporary American Reform Responsa*, no. 131; *Magen Avraham, Orach Chayim* 18, no. 2; *Arukh Hashulchan, Orach Chayim* 18, no. 7. Some authorities base this custom on the story in *B. Rosh Hashanah* 17b, which reports that God appeared to Moses "wrapped in a *tallit* like a *sheliach tzibur* [service leader]" when God recited the thirteen attributes of mercy (Exod. 34:6).

13   **Women wear the *tallit* . . . :** Jacob, *American Reform Responsa*, no. 4.

13   **a positive commandment . . . which pertains to a particular time:** M. *Kiddushin* 1:7. There are numerous exceptions to this general rule; see *B. Kiddushin* 34a. According to Ashkenazic tradition, many women voluntarily adopted some of these commandments upon themselves, and they were allowed to recite the blessing (". . . who has commanded us . . .") when they did so; see *Hilkhot Harosh, Kiddushin* 1:49, *Tosafot Eruvin* 96a-b, s.v. *dilma*; Isserles in *Shulchan Arukh, Orach Chayim* 17:2.

13   **a sign of arrogance . . . :** Isserles, *Orach Chayim* 17:2.

13   **"we do not allow . . . ":** *Arukh Hashulchan, Orach Chayim* 17, no. 3.

13   **"for those who wear *tefillin*":** *Gates of Prayer*, 48–49.

13   **After donning the *tallit* . . . :** One puts on the *tallit* first and then puts on the *tefillin*. Two reasons are cited for this: 1) "we seek to rise in the ascending order of holiness," and the *tefillin*, which contain words of Torah, are of a higher degree of sanctity than the *tzitzit*; 2) "the more frequent observance takes precedence over the less frequent one," and the *tallit*, unlike the *tefillin*, is worn every day. See *Arukh Hashulchan, Orach Chayim* 25, no. 1.

13   **your weaker arm . . . :** *B. Menachot* 36b–37a; *Shulchan Arukh, Orach Chayim* 27:1,

14   **slightly above the original hairline:** Deut. 6:8 reads: "let them serve as a symbol between your eyes" (*bein 'einekha*). Rabbinic tradition does not take this literally, drawing a comparison between this verse and the "between your eyes" of Deut. 14:1, which is understood as referring to the hair. *B. Menachot* 37b; *Shulchan Arukh, Orach Chayim* 27:9.

14   **Barukh shem kevod . . . :** *Shulchan Arukh, Orach Chayim* 25:5. There is a dispute among the authorities over the passage in *B. Menachot* 36a. Some (Rashi, s.v. *lo sach*; Rambam, *Yad, Tefillin* 4:4–5) read it as requiring only one *berakhah* for the *tefillin* unless one engages in conversation between putting on the *shel yad* and the *shel rosh*; the Sefardic rite has adopted this custom. Others (*Tosafot*, s.v. *lo sach*) believe that the Talmud requires two blessings in any case, one over each *tefillah*. The Ashkenazim take the latter position, but they are not entirely convinced it is the correct one. They therefore recite *Barukh shem kavod ...*, which is customarily said whenever one has recited a blessing that is unnecessary (*Shulchan Arukh, Orach Chayim* 206:6), just in case the law in fact follows those who require only one benediction.

14   **upon which are written the following sections of the Torah:** the relevant passage in *B. Menachot* 34b is subject to two interpretations. Rashi (*B. Menachot* 34b, s.v. *vehakorei*) and Maimonides (*Yad, Tefillin* 3:5) place the passages in each *tefillah* in the order in which they occur in the Torah: that is, Exod. 13:1–10; Exod. 13:11–16; Deut. 6:4–9; and Deut. 11:13–21. Rabbeinu Tam (R. Ya'akov b. Meir, Rashi's grandson and a leading tosafist) disagrees, holding that the order of the Deuteronomy

passages be reversed (*Tosafot, Menachot* 34b, s.v. *vehakorei*). While most *tefillin* follow the custom of Rashi and Rambam, others are made according to the interpretation of Rabbeinu Tam (hence, people will speak of "Rashi *tefillin*" and "Rabbeinu Tam *tefillin*"). While most people who wear *tefillin* will wear only the "Rashi" variety, the most stringently pious may wear two sets of *tefillin* to insure that they have followed whichever interpretation is correct. Some will wear both sets simultaneously while others will wear the "Rashi *tefillin*" for the first part of the morning service, remove them after the *Tefillah*, and replace them with the "Rabbeinu Tam *tefillin*." See *Shulchan Arukh, Orach Chayim* 34:1–3.

14   **Taken together, they call to mind . . . :** See *Sefer Hachinukh,* mitzvot 421 and 422.

14   **Tefillin are not worn at night . . . :** *B. Menachot* 36a-b, on Exod. 13:10; *Shulchan Arukh, Orach Chayim* 30:2.

14   **on Shabbat and festivals . . . :** *B. Menachot* 36b; *Shulchan Arukh, Orach Chayim* 31:1, *Mishnah Berurah,* no. 3.

15   **There is a dispute . . . :** *Shulchan Arukh, Orach Chayim* 31:2. The Sefardic practice is given mystical backing by the Zohar to Song of Songs 1:2. Those Ashkenazim who wear *tefillin* during *chol hamo'ed* will either recite the benedictions in a whisper, so as not to publicize the existence of the halakhic dispute, or dispense with them altogether, so as not to recite blessings which, if the Sefardim are right, are unnecessary; Isserles, *Shulchan Arukh, Orach Chayim* 31:2, *Mishnah Berurah,* no. 8.

15   **many Ashkenazim . . . :** Chassidim, however, follow the Sefardic practice in this case (as they do in many others, under the influence of the *siddur* of R. Yitzchak Luria, the "Ari" of Safed) and do not wear *tefillin* on *chol hamo'ed;* see Aharon Wertheim, *Halakhot Vehalikhot Bachasidut,* 79–81. In this, ironically, they are joined by their great opponent R. Eliyahu, the Gaon of Vilna, who deduces from the relevant talmudic passages that *tefillin* should not be worn on *chol hamo'ed; Bi'ur Hagra, Orach Chayim* 31.

15   **From its early days in Europe . . . :** Meyer, *Response to Modernity,* 24–25, 54, 88.

15   **The use of the vernacular . . . was not unprecedented:** The first translations of Scripture, the *Targumim,* date from the Second Temple period, as did the custom to appoint an authorized translator, the *meturgeman,* to render the text of the Torah into Aramaic, the language of the people, during its public recitation. See Neh. 8:7–8 and, in general, Elbogen, *Jewish Liturgy,* 153–56. The present-day Reform custom of translating the Torah text for the congregation is a revival of this practice (*Gates of Understanding,* 1:231). Translations and vernacular commentaries on the prayer book had long been available, and much devotional literature, intended especially for women, circulated among Jews throughout the world. Prominent in this category are the *techinnes* or *techinot,* prayers written for and sometimes by women for use in private devotion or as a substitute *siddur,* to be read by the individual during the synagogue service; see Solomon B. Freehof, "Devotional Literature in the Vernacular," *CCAR Yearbook,* 33 (1923): 375–415; Tracy Guren Klirs, comp., *The Merit of Our Mothers: A Bilingual Anthology of Jewish Women's Prayers*; and Chava Weissler, "*Tkhines* and Women's Prayer," *CCAR Journal,* 39 (4), Fall 1993: 75–88. Some prayers in the *siddur* itself, most notably the *Kaddish,* were originally composed in Aramaic and remained in the liturgy long after that language had ceased to be a Jewish vernacular.

15   **The reformers defended their innovation . . . :** See the arguments of Abraham Geiger, cited in Petuchowski, *Prayerbook Reform,* 100. The halakhic arguments begin with *M. Sotah* 7:1, which lists other liturgical rubrics as well. *B. Sotah* 32b cites the

midrash: "'Hear O Israel' (Deut. 6:4)—that is, in any language one 'hears' (compre-hends)." *B. Sotah* 33a defines prayer as *rachamei*, a supplication, so that "let him pray in the language in which he knows how to direct his heart to God" (Rashi, s.v. *tefillah*); *Shulchan Arukh, Orach Chayim* 62:2 and 101:4. For an extended discussion see Freehof, *Reform Jewish Practice,* 1:36–38.

15   **it is preferable to pray in a language one understands . . . :** *Magen Avraham, Orach Chayim* 101, no. 5, from *Sefer Chassidim,* ed. Wistinetzki-Freimann, no. 9.

16   **for abandoning ancestral *minhag* . . . :** *Arukh Hashulchan, Orach Chayim* 101, no. 9.

16   The prohibition against adopting the "statutes of the nations" (*chukat hagoy*) is de-rived from Lev. 18:3. See *B. Sanhedrin* 52b and *Sifra,* ed. Weiss, 85a.

16   **"practices which reflect legitimate purposes . . . ":** Plaut and Washofsky, *Teshuvot for the Nineties,* no. 5751.3. See also Freehof, *Reform Jewish Practice* 1:20. Sources include Isserles, *Shulchan Arukh, Yore De'ah* 178:1; *Beit Yosef, Yore De'ah* 178; *Resp. Maharik,* no. 88. See the introduction to section 7.

16   **Finally, opponents of reform . . . :** See especially *Resp. Chatam Sofer* 6:86; *Mishnah Berurah* 62, no. 3, and *Bi'ur Halakhah* to 101, no. 4.

17   **Hebrew never totally disappeared . . . :** On the return of Hebrew in synagogue liturgy see Meyer, *Response to Modernity,* 373.

17   **"it is a *mitzvah* to learn . . . ":** Maslin, *Gates of Mitzvah,* 20.

17   **"bilateral symmetry":** Hoffman, *Gates of Understanding,* 1:155–156.

17   **opposition from the rabbinic leaders . . . :** Much of this is included in the pamphlet *Eleh Divrei Haberit,* a collection of rabbinic responsa in opposition to the reforms introduced at the Hamburg Temple in 1818; see Meyer, *Response to Modernity,* 57–61. For the prohibition against playing musical instruments on Shabbat and festivals see *B. Eruvin* 104a, *Yad, Shabbat* 23:4, and *Shulchan Arukh, Orach Chayim* 338:1. The playing of a musical instrument is not considered a form of "work" (*melakhah*); therefore, it is not a violation of the Toraitic prohibitions against work on Shabbat. However, the rabbis prohibit the playing of an instrument as falling into the category of *shevut,* an activity that ought to be prohibited because it transgresses the spirit of the day or as a safeguard against committing more serious prohibitions. One should refrain from playing an instrument, they say, "lest one be tempted to repair it," because repair would involve a number of activities that are indeed defined as *melakhah.* For the prohibition on week-days as a sign of mourning over the Temple's destruction see *M. Sotah* 9:11, *B. Gittin* 7a, *Yad, Ta'aniot* 5:14, and *Shulchan Arukh, Orach Chayim* 560:3.

18   **The reformers rejected . . . :** See *Resp. Nogah Hatzedek,* a collection of rabbinic opinions defending the very same reforms instituted in Hamburg. The argument that instrumental music is permitted "for purposes of *mitzvah*" is that of R. Aharon Chorin at p. 21. His source is Isserles in *Shulchan Arukh, Orach Chayim* 560:3, who in turn relies upon Karo's *Beit Yosef, Orach Chayim* 560 and earlier sources. These authorities would not likely have applied the permit to religious occasions other than weddings, but the reformers argued that the logic behind it permits *us* to do so. See also Freehof, *Current Reform Responsa,* no. 7, and Solomon B. Freehof, *A Treasury of Responsa,* 160. And just as the *mitzvah* of prayer overrides the rabbinic decree con-cerning the mourning for the Temple (if, indeed, we were still to accept the relevance of that decree), it overrides as well the decree forbidding the playing of instruments on Shabbat "lest one be tempted to repair it." On the "imitation of Gentile religious practices," see p. 19 and the introduction to Chapter 7.

18 **"and in the meantime . . . "**: Freehof, *Reform Jewish Practice*, 1:43.

18 **Jewish liturgical music stems from many sources . . .** : See A.Z. Idelsohn, *Jewish Music*. On the influence of modern Israeli music in the American Reform synagogue, see William Sharlin, "Israel's Influence on American Liberal Synagogue Music" in Hoffman, *Gates of Understanding*, 1:122–28.

18 **A piece of music will be regarded as inappropriate . . .** : Freehof, *Current Reform Responsa*, no. 7, where Rabbi Freehof declares that a "sensual, riotous jazz concert" would insult the sanctity of a synagogue building and is inappropriate for liturgical use.

18 **At other times . . .** : Jacob, *Questions and Reform Jewish Answers*, no. 18.

19 **Much Jewish liturgical music . . .** : On the inter-relationships between Jewish and Christian liturgical music see Eric Werner, *The Sacred Bridge*.

19 **a song . . . written by a non-Jewish composer . . .** : Jacob, *Questions and Reform Jewish Answers*, no. 19.

19 **a musical selection firmly identified with another religion . . .** : Jacob, *Contemporary American Reform Responsa*, no. 195, and Plaut and Washofsky, *Teshuvot*, no. 5752.11. The latter responsum suggests that the concept of *chukat hagoy*, the unacceptable imitation of the "statutes of the nations," is a relevant issue for Reform Jews, particularly in a time of widespread religious and cultural assimilation. See Chapter 7.

19 **Judaism places great emphasis . . .** : B. *Berakhot* 7b–8a; *Yad, Tefillah* 8:1; *Shulchan Arukh, Orach Chayim* 90:11.

19 **"matters of sanctification"**: B. *Berakhot* 21b and B. *Megillah* 23b.

19 **They include . . .** : "The reading of the Torah" refers to the public reading from a Torah scroll, not to reading from a printed text (*chumash*). The requirement for a *minyan* is found in M. *Megillah* 4:3; B. *Megillah* 23b; B. *Berakhot* 21b; *Yad, Tefillah* 8:4–6; *Shulchan Arukh, Orach Chayim* 55:1.

20 **the schedule of the statutory prayers . . .** : The traditional prayers of *Shacharit*, *Minchah*, and *Musaf* correspond to the daily and festival sacrificial offerings. *Ma'ariv* or *Arvit* corresponds with the burning of the twilight sacrifice, which took place at night. *Ne'ilah*, the closing service following *Minchah* on Yom Kippur, corresponds to the service which occurred daily at twilight, at the "closing of the gates" of the Temple. See *Yad, Tefillah* 1:5–7, and Elbogen, *Jewish Liturgy*, 127.

20 **The Rabbis derive this requirement . . .** : See B. *Megillah* 23b. The Rabbis match Lev. 22:32 ("I will be sanctified *in the midst of* the people of Israel) to Num. 16:21 ("Remove yourselves *from the midst of* this congregation [*eidah*]): thus, "sanctification" must be done "in the midst of " the people, and this "midst" is defined as a "congregation." They then cite Num. 14:27 ("How long must I bear this evil *congregation* [*eidah*]?"), referring to the spies who returned from the Promised Land. Since only ten of the twelve spies had actually given a negative report about the land, it follows that a "congregation" consists of at least ten people.

20 **since only adult males are enjoined . . .** : It is possible to interpret traditional *halakhah* in such a way as to include women among the category of "commanded" with respect to these ritual *mitzvot* and so to count them in the *minyan*. One method is that proposed by R. Joel Roth (in Simon Greenberg, ed., *The Ordination of Women as Rabbis*, 127ff.), who argues that one who voluntarily commits him/herself to performing a *mitzvah* on a regular basis may attain the status of "commanded." Another builds upon the theory that women are exempt from the positive, time-bound com-

mandments because as wives and mothers they are constantly engaged in the performance of the *mitzvot* of homemaking and child-rearing, and we have a rule that "one who is presently performing a *mitzvah* is exempt from performing another *mitzvah*" (see *Resp. Mishpetei Ouziel*, 1:237–38). On halakhic grounds one could therefore question whether the "role" of women in our communities in this day and age truly qualifies them for this exemption.

21   **An old Palestinian tradition ... :** Tractate *Soferim* 10:6, based upon *midrashic* readings of Judg. 5:2.

21   **Some authorities ruled it permissible ... :** *B. Berakhot* 47b; see R. Tam, *Tosafot, Berakhot* 48a, s.v. *veleit*, and Rav Hai Gaon, cited in *Hilkhot Harosh, Berakhot* 7:20. On counting a woman see *Beit Yosef, Orach Chayim* 55, s.v. *vekhatuv bamordekhai*, in the name of R. Simchah of Vitry.

21   **These ideas were ultimately rejected:** *Tosafot* and *Hilkhot Harosh* in the places cited; *Yad, Tefillah* 8:4; numerous other authorities cited in *Beit Yosef, Orach Chayim* 55; *Shulchan Arukh, Orach Chayim* 55:4. But see Isserles ad loc.: some are lenient in this regard "in an emergency situation."

21   **One idea that did survive ... :** *Y. Megillah* 3:4; *Tosafot, Megillah* 23b, s.v. *ve'ein*; *Shulchan Arukh, Orach Chayim* 55:2–3.

21   **It was also decided ... :** *Yad, Tefillah* 8:4. This rule is apparently drawn from the "rejected" opinion in *Soferim* 10:6; see *Kesef Mishneh* ad loc.

21   **An exceedingly brief responsum ... :** Jacob, *American Reform Responsa*, no. 3. In citing the "old Palestinian custom," the responsum is unclear as to whether it counsels reducing the numerical definition of a *minyan* or doing away with the *minyan* requirement altogether. In this instance, perhaps ironically, the importance of preserving the institution of public worship is cited to justify a permission for that worship in the absence of the traditional "public." This is no doubt a reflection of the growing centrality of the synagogue in American Jewish life and of the felt need to do everything possible to see to it that services take place, with or without a *minyan*.

21   **In 1963, Rabbi Solomon B. Freehof ... :** Freehof, *Recent Reform Responsa*, no. 1. But there are problems with Freehof's reasoning here; see Plaut and Washofsky, *Teshuvot*, no. 5752.17, n. 4.

21   **In 1992, Rabbi Walter Jacob ... :** Jacob, *Questions and Reform Jewish Answers*, no. 4.

22   **In 1993, the Responsa Committee ... :** Plaut and Washofsky, *Teshuvot*, no. 5752.17.

23   **devotion to a religion of reason ... :** See the Pittsburgh Platform (Meyer, *Response to Modernity*, 388), par. 6. See also Meyer, 205ff., for a discussion of the influence of Kant upon the religious thought of Hermann Cohen and Leo Baeck, among other leading Reform thinkers.

23   **"Furthermore ... ":** Jacob, *American Reform Responsa*, no. 6, at 23.

23   **"we consider ourselves no longer a nation ... ":** Pittsburgh Platform (Meyer, *Response to Modernity*, 388), par. 5.

23–24   **its stance toward non-Jewish religious observances and customs:** See Chapter 7.

24   ***ger toshav*** ("resident alien"; see Gen. 23:4) is the Talmud's designation for the Gentile who accepts upon him- or herself the "seven Noachide commandments" (*B. Sanhedrin* 56a–b: the prohibitions against idolatry, cursing God, murder, adultery and incest, robbery, and the eating of flesh torn from a living animal, along with the

commandment to establish courts of justice). This acceptance is made in a formal declaration before a rabbinic court (*beit din*); B. *Avodah Zarah* 64b; *Yad, Melakhim* 8:10–11 and *Isurei Bi'ah* 14:7–8. The *ger toshav* was permitted to dwell in the land of Israel and was included within the sphere of a Jew's ethical duties, but he was not the ritual equivalent of a Jew; for example, one could lend money to him at interest (*M. Bava Metzi'a* 5:6; B. *Bava Metzi'a* 71a), and he was not to take part in sacrificial rituals such as the paschal offering (Exod. 12:45 and *Mekhilta* ad loc.).

Should the non-Jew who associates with the Jewish community by way of marriage be considered a *ger toshav*? Non-Jews who live in our societies, after all, profess religions which observe what our tradition refers to as the seven Noachide commandments (on Judaism's attitude toward the great monotheistic religions, see Chapter 7). To enjoy that status, it is argued, would allow the non-Jewish family member to feel more at home within the congregation. From the standpoint of traditional Jewish law, though, this does not work. Maimonides, for example, rules that the institution of *ger toshav* is in force only when the Jubilee (Lev. 25:8ff.) is practiced (i.e., when the Temple is standing and when all the Jewish people dwell in the land of Israel); see *Yad*, loc. cit. And even if Maimonides is wrong, it should be remembered that the title *ger toshav* does not confer upon the Gentile anything approaching equal religious status in the religious life of the community of Israel. Such equality is reserved for the *ger tzedek*, the "true proselyte," the Jew-by-choice; see Jacob, *Contemporary American Reform Responsa*, no. 162. For more on the *ger toshav*, see Chapter 5.

25   **The line drawn in the responsa . . . :** See Plaut and Washofsky, *Teshuvot*, no. 5754.5, to date the latest Reform responsum on the subject, and Jacob, *American Reform Responsa*, no. 6. Many will wonder whether concepts such as "obligatory prayer" have any relevance within a liberal religious context. It should be pointed out that the word *chovah*, "obligation," describes not only a theological principle but a category of Jewish liturgical experience: prayers classified as *chovah* form the core of the Jewish people's public and communal worship of God. They are thus to be distinguished from prayers called *reshut*, "voluntary," which pertain more to the private and individual religious sphere. That distinction, regardless of our attitude concerning religious obligation, continues to be relevant within Reform Jewish observance.

25   **Leadership of services:** That the Gentile chorister is not a *sheliach tzibur* is a point made by Freehof in *Reform Jewish Practice*, 2:71, and in Jacob, *Contemporary American Reform Responsa*, no. 132. Plaut and Washofsky, *Teshuvot*, no. 5754.5, calls the custom to use non-Jews singers to perform essential rubrics of the liturgy "an anachronism for our time," "an historical error" which "represents a phase of Reform history which can no longer serve as a precedent" for contemporary decision-making.

25   **The Torah Service:** This position (see Plaut and Washofsky, *Teshuvot*, no. 5754.5) differs somewhat from Rabbi Freehof's suggestion that a Gentile may be called to the Torah, "since the Bible is sacred to Jews and Christians alike," provided that he or she recite a specially-composed blessing that is more suitable to a non-Jew (Freehof, *Current Reform Responsa*, no. 23). The difficulty with Freehof's position is that the "Bible" in question, the Hebrew Scriptures, is not the same book to Christians as it is to Jews. A religious Christian regards the Hebrew Scriptures as the so-called "Old Testament," a collection of literature which contains a revelation that was completed or superseded by the coming of Jesus. This, of course, is not what we Jews mean by "Torah." Moreover, being "called to the Torah" serves as a symbol of one's membership in the religious community constituted by devotion to this Torah and its study; this would tend to exclude even the non-Jew who does not identify as a Christian.

Rabbi Freehof reversed his position in a later responsum (*Today's Reform Responsa*, no. 3), where he rules that a Gentile bridegroom should *not* be called to the Torah on the Shabbat prior to his wedding to a Jew.

26 **Benedictions:** On the issue of Shabbat candle-lighting, see Freehof, *New Reform Responsa*, no. 7.

26 *birkhot nehenin*: A complex subject, mainly because *M. Berakhot* 8:8 instructs that one may respond "*amen*" to a benediction recited by a Samaritan. Many medieval halakhists permit the same response to a blessing recited by any Gentile. See Plaut and Washofsky, *Teshuvot*, no. 5754.5 at nn. 15–24, for a lengthy analysis. The conclusion drawn from the sources, however, is that this permit applies to a situation that has already occurred (*bedi'avad*). A *berakhah* is a declaration of God's praise, and the word "*amen*" is an affirmation of the truth of that declaration by the one who hears it. In this sense, it does not matter whether the praise is uttered by a Jew or a Gentile. Indeed, as one authority notes, this very logic would require the same response if the *berakhah* is recited by an apostate Jew; yet none of the halakhic writers would suggest that an apostate Jew *should* be called upon to say a benediction over a meal for the community. Similarly, the Gentile is not allowed in principle (*lekhatchilah*) to recite a benediction on the community's behalf. We take the position that the recitation of a blessing prior to a meal which celebrates a religious event (*se'udat mitzvah*) is precisely the same kind of public leadership role which, in a Jewish religious community devoted to the observance of Jewish religious life, ought to be reserved to Jews.

26 **Conversely, a non-Jew may participate . . . :** Jacob, *American Reform Responsa*, no. 6.

27 **Historians do not take literally . . . :** Elbogen, *Jewish Liturgy*, 129ff., suggests that the liturgical reading of the Torah began with readings for the festivals only, as a means of instructing the people in the laws of each particular festival. From there, the practice grew to include readings for the "special Sabbaths" during the weeks prior to Pesach, and then to readings for every Shabbat. Next came the readings on Mondays and Thursdays, so that residents of outlying villages who traveled to the larger towns for market and for courts which met on those days could hear the Torah. Finally came the readings for Purim, Chanukah, and fast days, a practice which testifies to the by then well-developed conviction that each "special" day must have its own Torah reading.

27 **"Let all who thirst . . . ":** See *B. Bava Kama* 82a.

27 **Following the ancient Babylonian practice . . . :** *B. Megillah* 29b. This differed from the Palestinian "triennial" cycle, which divided the Torah into as many as 155 sections and completed its reading in either three or three and one-half years. See Elbogen, *Jewish Liturgy*, 132–33; Jacob Mann, *The Bible as Read and Preached in the Old Synagogue*; and Joseph Heinemann, "Hamachzor Ha-'telat-shenati' Veluach Hashanah," *Tarbiz* 33 (1964): 362–68. The "triennial cycle" adopted today in many liberal congregations is *not* the same as the ancient Palestinian version. It rather divides each weekly ("Babylonian") *sidra* into three parts; the first third of each *sidra* is read every week the first year; the second third the second year, etc. Thus, while the weekly portions return every year (*Shabbat Bereshit, Shabbat Noach,* etc.), the reading of the Torah is completed in three years. Unlike both the Babylonian and the Palestinian customs, this one does not read the entire Torah consecutively. For a list of the *sidrot*, see Hoffman, *Gates of Understanding*, 1:271ff.

27 **These are read . . . :** Some shorter portions are combined, especially in a non-leap year (when there is no second month of Adar in the Hebrew calendar), to insure that the reading cycle is concluded by Simchat Torah. These are: *Vayakhel-Pekudei;*

Tazri'a-Metzora'; Acharei Mot–Kedoshim; Behar-Bechukotai; Chukat-Balak; Matot-Mas'ei; Nitzavim-Vayelekh. The cycle as it is observed today reads *Bamidbar* on the Shabbat preceding Shavu'ot; *Va'etchanan* on the Shabbat following Tisha Be'Av; *Nitzavim* on the Shabbat preceding Rosh Hashanah; and *Tzav* on the Shabbat preceding Pesach in a non-leap year. See *Yad, Tefillah* 12:2.

27   **Reform congregations customarily read a segment . . . :** The reading was shortened in order to preserve decorum and retain the congregation's attention (Freehof, *Reform Jewish Practice*, 1:31). On the prohibition against talking during the Torah reading see *B. Sotah* 39a; *Yad, Tefillah* 12:9; *Shulchan Arukh, Orach Chayim* 146:2.

27   **The reading at the *Minchah* . . . :** *B. Megillah* 31b; *Shulchan Arukh, Orach Chayim* 135:2.

27   **at the Friday night service:** Freehof, *Modern Reform Responsa*, no. 1. See *Resp. Meshiv Davar*, no. 16: to read the Torah in public at a time other than those which are determined by tradition would require the congregants to pronounce benedictions which are unnecessary (*berakhot levatalah*), a possible violation of Exod. 20:7, "you shall not pronounce the name of God in vain" (*B. Berakhot* 33a). Yet as the author of that responsum notes, it is not clear that it is forbidden to read the Torah in public at other than the traditionally-specified times. And in congregations which do not hold services on Shabbat morning, Friday night is the only time the Torah benedictions are recited on Shabbat. Accordingly, no "unnecessary" blessings are said.

28   **On festivals and Rosh Chodesh . . . :** Hoffman, *Gates of Understanding*, 1:281–84. On the second festival day in Reform Judaism, see Chapter 3. This creates something of a problem when the eighth day of Pesach falls on Shabbat. Since Reform congregations do not regard that day as a festival, they would ordinarily resume the cycle of weekly *sidrot* which had been interrupted by the holiday. Yet this would leave them out of step with other synagogues in the Diaspora, which wait until the following Shabbat to resume the cycle. Since "it is not convenient that for a number of weeks we should be in dislocation as to Torah reading with the rest of American Jewry" (Freehof, *Current Reform Responsa*, no. 10), various suggestions have been made to synchronize the Reform lectionary with that of other synagogues: the reading for the seventh day of Pesach can be repeated the next day (ibid.), or that Shabbat's weekly portion can be spread over two weeks, so that by the second week the non-Reform congregations will have "caught up" (*Gates of Understanding*, 1:271). Alternately, the congregation may read from the traditional selection for the eighth day of Pesach (Deut. 14:22–16:17) when this day coincides with Shabbat.

28   **Reform congregations generally dispense with . . . :** The reading from the second scroll traditionally consists of passages from Numbers 28–29, which recount the sacrifices offered on each day in the ancient Temple. This tradition is not explicitly mentioned in the Talmud, and the early authorities assumed it to be a geonic enactment; see *Tosafot, Megillah* 31b, s.v. *veshe'ar; Hilkhot Harosh, Megillah* 4:10; *Siddur Rav Amram*, ed. Goldschmidt, 174. Reform Judaism, which does not look back upon the sacrifices with nostalgia or toward their restoration, returns to talmudic practice and does away with the reading from the second scroll.

28   ***Aliyot:*** See Elbogen, *Jewish Liturgy*, 138–42, and Jacob, *American Reform Responsa*, no. 38, on the historical development of the procedure of the Torah reading. On the relationship between the *oleh/ah* and the reader, see *Shulchan Arukh, Orach Chayim* 141:2–3.

28 **"in Reform congregations . . . "**: Freehof, *Reform Jewish Practice*, 1:33. See also Elbogen, *Jewish Liturgy* (which originally appeared in 1913), 140. The biblical custom is that of Deut. 31:10–13 and Neh. 8:1–8.

28 **But as one recent responsum has noted:** Plaut and Washofsky, *Teshuvot*, no. 5754.5.

29 **Reform congregations divide the Torah reading . . . :** The traditional number of *olim* is found in *M. Megillah* 4:1–2. The ascending number corresponds to the ascending degree of sanctity of each set of holy days; see *B. Megillah* 22b. On weekdays, it is forbidden to add to the number of *olim*, since this would delay the people from getting to work and thus be considered an unnecessary burden upon the congregation (*tircha detzibura*). On Shabbat, when people do not have to get to work, it is thus permitted to honor more than seven people with *aliyot*. While the law technically allows more people to be called up on festivals as well, standard Ashkenazic practice is to limit the number to five so as to distinguish the greater sanctity of Shabbat (Isserles in *Shulchan Arukh, Orach Chayim* 282:1; R. Nissim Gerondi to Alfasi, *Shabbat*, fol. 12b).

29 **Tradition requires . . . at least ten verses . . . :** *B. Megillah* 21b: the number "ten" corresponds with the Ten Commandments or with the "ten words with which the world was created" (*M. Avot* 5:1).

29 **The *oleh/ah* is traditionally called . . . :** Freehof, *Contemporary Reform Responsa*, no. 6. One who never received a Hebrew name or who has forgotten that name may nonetheless be called to the Torah. On reciting the blessings in Hebrew, see Jacob, *Contemporary American Reform Responsa*, no. 135: "we have felt that customs are binding and should be followed wherever possible."

29 **The procedure for the *berakhot* . . . :** See *Shulchan Arukh, Orach Chayim* 139. Some *olim* will close the Torah scroll prior to reciting the blessing before the reading. This follows the view of Rabbi Meir, *B. Megillah* 32a, who worries that should the scroll remain open, people will erroneously assume that the *oleh* is reading the blessings themselves from the Torah. The *halakhah* is decided according to Rabbi Yehudah, who does not believe that the people will make this error and that therefore the scroll may remain open during the blessing. Nonetheless, many today follow R. Meir's more stringent practice (see *Tosafot, Megillah* 32a, s.v. *golelo*). All seem to agree that the scroll be closed during the concluding blessing to indicate that the reading has been completed.

29 **This order of priority . . . is problematic:** for two reasons. First, due to the absence of genealogical records, the priestly status of all *Kohanim* is regarded officially as a matter of doubt, and a number of halakhic rulings are based upon the existence of this doubt. See Freehof, *Reform Jewish Practice* 1:46–49. Second, the precedence of priest and Levite in ritual matters is not necessarily set in stone. The rule is derived from several biblical verses, most famously Lev. 21:8; see *B. Gittin* 59b and *Shulchan Arukh, Orach Chayim* 135:3–4. While the talmudic Rabbis believed that the *Kohen* could waive his right to be called first to the Torah, they decreed that he should not do so "in order to preserve peace" (*mipnei darkhei shalom*): unless the *Kohen* reads first, unseemly quarrels will break out as congregants vie for the honor. This may have been true in ancient times; the question is whether it is an accurate description of contemporary reality. The experience in Reform synagogues, where *aliyot* are distributed without any accompanying strife and contention, suggests that it is not.

29   **some leading halakhic authorities . . . :** who interpret the passage in *B. Gittin* 59b differently. The priority, in their view, should be set according to level of Torah

knowledge; the Torah scholar should precede the priest (Maimonides, *Commentary to M. Gittin* 5:8; *Resp. Rashba*, 1:119; *Resp. Rivash*, no. 204).

30 **Any Jewish adult may be called to the Torah:** While it is permitted to call children to the Torah (*B. Megillah* 23a; *Shulchan Arukh, Orach Chayim* 482:3), it is customary not to do so until they have reached the age of religious majority (*Mishnah Berurah* 482, no. 12). It is considered improper for children to read from the Torah in a service conducted by or for adults, with the exception of such special occasions as Simchat Torah (Jacob, *American Reform Responsa*, no. 38, no. 1).

30 **congregation may refuse to call an "unworthy" person . . . :** Jacob, *American Reform Responsa*, no. 39.

30 **individuals who refuse to meet their financial obligations . . . :** Jacob, *Contemporary American Reform Responsa,* no. 149. On the right of the congregation to exclude such a person from being called to the Torah, see *Resp. Tashbetz,* 2:261. On the value of including the sinner within the community of Torah readers, see *Sha'arei Efraim* 1:17. See also *Shulchan Arukh, Orach Chayim* 619:1: on Kol Nidrei, the night of Yom Kippur, we declare formally that transgressors—i.e., those formally excommunicated—may take part in communal worship. "A public fast which does not include the entire people, the sinners as well as the righteous, is not a fast," for even as the sweet-smelling incense included the ingredient *chelbenah* (galbanum) which on its own has a foul odor, so too is Israel at its best when all of its members, the bad as well as the good, join together as one (*B. Keritot* 6b).

30 **tefillat nedavah . . . :** See *Yad, Tefillah* 1:9.

31 **tachanunim:** See Elbogen, *Jewish Liturgy,* 66–71. Just as the *Tefillah* became fixed over time, so have the *tachanunim* become a rubric with a regular text printed in prayer books. This does not affect their nature as private prayer, however; there is no halakhic requirement that a worshiper recite the "official" text of the prayers of supplication. The *tachanunim* are traditionally omitted on Shabbat, festivals, and other days when it is considered inappropriate to beseech God for one's personal needs.

31 **The traditional *siddur* will contain . . . :** For a typical American example see Philip Birnbaum, *Hasiddur Hashalem. / Daily Prayer Book,* 103–17.

31 **"take root among our people . . .":** Chaim Stern, ed., *On the Doorposts of Your House,* ix.

31 **the liturgical formula . . . :** The full formula is *Barukh atah Adonai Eloheinu melekh ha'olam,* "Praised are You, O God, Sovereign of the universe," following R. Yochanan in *B. Berakhot* 40b that "any benediction which does not mention both the Name and the sovereignty of God is not a proper benediction." A blessing taking the short form, omitting the words *Eloheinu melekh ha'olam,* is called *semukhah lechaverta,* literally "dependent upon a preceding benediction." Such a form is used for the closing formula (*chatimah*) of a long benediction or as a benediction in a series of *berakhot,* the first of which mentions God's sovereignty and in effect "covers" the rest. *Yad, Berakhot* 1:5; *Shulchan Arukh, Orach Chayim* 214:1. A famous exception to this rule is the first benediction of the *Tefillah,* which leaves out *melekh ha'olam.* This is explained by the fact that the benediction speaks of "the God of Abraham," and since Abraham "proclaimed God king throughout the world" the mention of his name *is* a statement of God's sovereignty; *Tosafot, Berakhot* 40b, s.v. *amar.*

31 **They are classified according to . . . :** *Sefer Abudarham,* beginning of *Hilkhot Berakhot.* That the *berakhot* are of rabbinic origin is an assumption that runs throughout the talmudic literature; see *Yad, Berakhot* 8:12. Yet this did not prevent the Rabbis

from trying to find scriptural support for the practice of reciting blessings. One such explanation: if the Torah requires us to recite a *berakhah* after we have eaten our fill (i.e., *Birkat Hamazon*, Deut. 8:10), then surely it demands it while we are still hungry! Others say that no proof text is necessary; it is simply "forbidden for one to enjoy the goodness of this world without first praising God's Name." See *B. Berakhot* 35a.

32 *Birkat Hamazon* **is not held to be "rabbinic"** . . . : See *B. Berakhot* 48b and parallels. The tradition holds that the requirement to say grace and its liturgical structure are derived from Deut. 8:10; by contrast, the texts of the *berakhot* are attributed to Moses, Joshua, David, and Solomon (*B. Berakhot* 48b). On the other hand, Maimonides may not regard the number of benedictions to be a Toraitic requirement; see *Yad, Berakhot* 1:1 and Rambam's *Sefer Hamitzvot*, positive commandment no. 19, and *Beit Yosef, Orach Chayim* 191. Although some traditions dissent, the generally accepted view holds that only the first three benedictions of *Birkat Hamazon* are part of the Toraitic component. *Hatov vehametiv* is a rabbinic ordinance; hence, the custom to say "*amen*" following the third benediction (*boneh yerushalayim*) as a means of marking the end of the Toraitic segment of the grace (*B. Berakhot* 45b–46a; *Shulchan Arukh, Orach Chayim* 188:1–2).

32 **recited after one has eaten bread** . . . : the quintessential foodstuff over which one customarily makes a proper meal. This follows the view of the Sages in *M. Berakhot* 6:8, as opposed to Rabban Gamliel, who recites *Birkat Hamazon* over any of the "seven species" with which the land of Israel is blessed (Deut. 8:8), as well as to R. Akiva, who holds that *Birkat Hamazon* is said over any foodstuff so long as it makes one's meal. *B. Berakhot* 44a; *Yad, Berakhot* 3:2; *Shulchan Arukh, Orach Chayim* 208:1. On the content of the benedictions of *Birkat Hamazon* see *B. Berakhot* 48b–49a; *Yad, Berakhot* 2:1–7; *Shulchan Arukh, Orach Chayim* 187–89.

33 **When three or more persons eat together** . . . : *M. Berakhot* 7:1ff.; *Yad, Berakhot* 5; *Shulchan Arukh, Orach Chayim* 192ff.

33 **When the company numbers ten or more** . . . : *M. Berakhot* 7:3, following R. Akiva, who makes no distinction between a company of ten and more numerous gatherings.

33 **"abbreviated" forms of the *Birkat Hamazon*:** Jacob, *Questions and Reform Jewish Answers*, no. 79. For the full text and an abbreviated version see Stern, *On the Doorposts of Your House*, 9ff. The earliest "abbreviated" text is the one-line blessing of Benjamin the shepherd in *B. Berakhot* 40b, though the Talmud concludes that this may substitute only for the first benediction (*birkat hazan*) rather than for the entire grace; *Shulchan Arukh, Orach Chayim* 187:1. That workers and others pressed for time may say an abbreviated *Birkat Hamazon* is discussed in *B. Berakhot* 16a; see *Yad, Berakhot* 2:2 and *Shulchan Arukh, Orach Chayim* 191:1.

33 *Berakhah achat me'ein shalosh*: *B. Berakhot* 44a–b; *Yad, Berakhot* 3:3 and 8:1; *Shulchan Arukh, Orach Chayim* 208:1–2. For texts, see Stern, *On the Doorposts of Your House*, 24–26.

34 *hamotzi lechem*: "Bread" is solid dough from any of the five grains (wheat, barley, rye, oats, spelt) baked in an oven. This includes bagels, rolls, and matzah. Sefardim consider matzah to be a cracker and—except on Pesach, when it serves as bread—recite *mezonot* over it, so long as it is eaten as a snack and not as part of a fixed meal. (See *Resp. Yechaveh Da'at*, 3:12, for sources and analysis). Toast and French toast require *hamotzi*.

34 *borei peri hagafen*: "Wine" here means grape wine. Other wines (apple, blackberry, cherry, etc.) take the blessing *shehakol*. Brandy and cognac lose the character of wine

and hence take *shehakol*. Grape wine mixed with other fruit juices (e.g., *sangria*) remains "wine" and takes *borei peri hagafen* (*Shulchan Arukh, Orach Chayim* 202:1).

34   ***borei minei mezonot*:** The proper blessing for cake, pie, pastry, crackers, pretzels, and pizza. This *berakhah*, however, is said only when these foods are eaten as snacks. When eaten as a meal or in an amount equivalent to the amount of bread that one would eat with a meal, these foods take *hamotzi* (and *Birkat Hamazon*); see *Shulchan Arukh, Orach Chayim* 168:6 and *Mishnah Berurah* ad loc. *Mezonot* is also recited over cooked dishes and processed foods made from the "five grains," such as oatmeal and many breakfast cereals. Rice is an exceptional case. Though not one of the "five grains," it is considered sufficiently sustaining as a food to require *mezonot*. Though it is not certain that our "rice" is the correct identification of the Talmud's *orez*, the custom is to say *mezonot* over dishes of cooked rice. See *Shulchan Arukh, Orach Chayim* 208:7 and *Mishnah Berurah* and *Bi'ur Halakhah* ad loc.

34   ***borei peri ha'eitz*:** A "tree" is a tree, bush, or shrub whose stem survives the winter and does not require replanting (*Tur, Orach Chayim* 203, and Isserles, *Orach Chayim* 203:2). Other fruits and vegetables are considered "fruits of the earth." Thus, bananas and strawberries take the blessing *ha'adamah* rather than *ha'eitz*. If one mistakenly says *borei peri ha'adamah* over a fruit of the tree, no other benediction is required, since the tree itself grows from the soil. This does not, however, work in reverse: if one says *borei peri ha'eitz* over a fruit that grows from the soil, one must compensate for the error by reciting the blessing *ha'adamah* (*Berakhot* 40a; *Shulchan Arukh, Orach Chayim* 206:1). To take this blessing (or *ha'adamah*, where appropriate), the fruit or vegetable must exist in its original form. Thus, fruit juice and most fruit soups take *shehakol* (*Tosafot, Berakhot* 38a, s.v. *veha'i; Shulchan Arukh, Orach Chayim* 202:8).

34   ***borei peri ha'adamah*:** When a fruit or vegetable is normally eaten only when it is cooked, it takes *shehakol* when it is eaten raw; if normally eaten raw, it takes *shehakol* when eaten cooked (*B. Berakhot* 37a; *Shulchan Arukh, Orach Chayim* 205:1).

34   ***shehakol nihyeh bidevaro*:** This is the proper benediction for foods which do not grow from the earth (meat, dairy products, eggs, mushrooms, water). It is also said over fruit juices, soups, and sauces, provided that significant chunks of the fruit or vegetable are not visible in the soup or sauce, as well as over foodstuffs made of processed fruits and vegetables. For example, potato chips and corn flakes are generally made of flattened potatoes and corn; they require *ha'adamah*, because the foodstuff continues to exist in its original form. When these are made out of potato or corn flour, however, their original form has been changed, and they take *shehakol* (*Shulchan Arukh, Orach Chayim* 205:4 and *Mishnah Berurah*, nos. 15 and 17). If one recites *shehakol* by mistake over any food, the blessing is valid (*M. Berakhot* 6:2; *Yad, Berakhot* 8:10; *Shulchan Arukh, Orach Chayim* 206:1). When in complete doubt as to the proper blessing over a particular food, one says *shehakol* (*Shulchan Arukh, Orach Chayim* 204:13).

34   **When foods are combined . . . :** As the traditional staple of human sustenance, bread is automatically the more "important" food; *hamotzi* alone is sufficient. Foods containing one of the five grains take *mezonot* unless the grains are an insignificant ingredient in the whole. In other cases, one recites the blessing over that ingredient which one desires more than the other or over the ingredient which exists in the greater quantity than the other. See, in general, *M. Berakhot* 6:7, and *Shulchan Arukh, Orach Chayim* 212.

34   **some of the other *birkhot nehenin* . . . :** For other blessings, both traditional and new, see Stern, *On the Doorposts of Your House*, 27–33.

35   **some of the *birkhot hoda'ah*:** See, in general, *M. Berakhot* 9:1–5.

35   ***shehechiyanu*:** Tradition distinguishes between occasions at which one recites *shehechiyanu* and occasions when *hatov vehametiv* is appropriate. One says *shehechiyanu*: 1) on festivals and holidays that occur at fixed times, over some of the *mitzvot* which accompany them, and at certain life-cycle events (*B. Eruvin* 40b; *Yad, Berakhot* 11:9); 2) when the joy is one's own and is not shared by others. For example, if one purchases a house and implements, one says *shehechiyanu*, but if one's family derive satisfaction from those things one says *hatov vehametiv* (*B. Berakhot* 59b); 3) upon seeing a fruit that has ripened for the first time in a particular season (*B. Eruvin* 40b). At all other joyous times, one says *hatov vehametiv*. For details, see *Shulchan Arukh, Orach Chayim* 222, 223, and 225.

35   ***dayan ha'emet*:** "One must praise God over the bad things that occur just as one praises God for the good things"; *M. Berakhot* 9:5. This means that one should utter the blessing *dayan ha'emet* in sincerity and pureness of heart, in full acceptance of God's sovereignty even at this unhappy moment (*B. Berakhot* 59b; Rashi, s.v. *lekabolinhu besimchah*; Bartenura to *M. Berakhot* 9:5). One recites this benediction at the time of *keri'ah*, the ritual tearing of one's garment upon hearing of or witnessing the death of a close relative.

35   ***hagomel*:** The Talmud (*B. Berakhot* 54b) enumerates four persons who must recite *Birkat Hagomel*: 1) one who returns from a sea voyage; 2) one who completes a journey through the wilderness; 3) one who recovers from an illness; 4) one who has been released from prison. Most authorities rule that this list is not exhaustive; the custom is to recite *Birkat Hagomel* over any experience of personal deliverance from danger (*Resp. Rivash*, no. 336; *Shulchan Arukh, Orach Chayim* 219:9, and *Mishnah Berurah*, no. 31). Should the blessing be recited as a matter of course after an airplane flight? Some say yes, since by its nature air travel is analogous to sea travel (*Resp. Igerot Moshe, Orach Chayim,* 2:59). Others say that the blessing is recited after any journey involving "danger" and that danger is measured by the length of the trip; thus, the blessing is recited after any journey, whether by land or by air, of somewhat more than an hour in duration (*Resp. Yabi'a Omer, Orach Chayim* 2:14).

Chapter 2: The Congregation

36   **"Any community . . .":** This ruling by Rambam has long puzzled his commentators, since it has no explicit source in rabbinic texts. The commentary of R. Yosef Karo, *Kesef Mishneh*, which seeks to provide the sources for Rambam's decisions, passes over this one in silence. *Migdal Oz* calls it Rambam's "introduction" to the laws of the synagogue; i.e., it is a phrase of Rambam's own device and not an actual, talmudically-supported law. What follows is a suggestion as to how he might have derived this requirement from Jewish tradition.

36   **Tradition teaches . . . :** See Chapter 1, "The Minyan."

36   **a *sanctuary* in miniature . . . :** *mikdash me'at*; derived in a *midrash* on Ezek. 11:16, is in *B. Megillah* 29a. But while the Temple was a truly "priestly" institution, the synagogue has always been administered by the community as a whole, by laypersons who have made their own rules, albeit in careful consultation with the sages of the rabbinic tradition. On the long history of Jewish communal self-government see Louis Finkelstein, *Jewish Self-Government in the Middle Ages*; Elon, *Jewish Law*, 678–

779; and Mark Washofsky, *"Halakhah* and Political Theory" in *Modern Judaism* (October, 1989): 289–310.

37   **An adult . . . :** *Suggested Constitution and By-Laws for Congregations,* Art. V, sect. 1. When does one become an "adult"? Jewish tradition generally holds that this occurs at age thirteen, but it tends to set a later age—usually twenty—for some matters that fall under the heading of "public responsibility." See Yitzchak Gilat, *Perakim Behishtalshalut Hahalakhah,* 29–31. In our synagogues, one may not exercise voting rights so long as one is dependent upon one's parents for financial support. He or she remains a member of the "family unit," part of the family's membership in the synagogue; Jacob, *Contemporary American Reform Responsa,* no. 152.

37   **"to promote the enduring and fundamental principles . . . ":** *Suggested Constitution,* Art. II.

37   **According to Rabbi Solomon B. Freehof . . . :** Freehof, *Recent Reform Responsa,* no. 12, at 65. On Gentile membership in a congregation, see *Suggested Constitution,* Art. V, sec. 2; Jacob, *Contemporary American Reform Responsa,* nos. 161 and 162; Jacob, *American Reform Responsa,* no. 10; Freehof, *Reform Responsa for Our Time,* no. 47.

37   **In the case of a mixed-married couple . . . :** A relaxation of the stricter position of Rabbi Kaufman Kohler and Rabbi Jacob Z. Lauterbach (Jacob, *American Reform Responsa,* no. 12).

37   **He or she may not, however, serve as an officer in the congregation . . . :** See *Suggested Constitution,* loc. cit.; Jacob, *Contemporary American Reform Responsa,* nos. 163–164; Freehof, *Reform Responsa for Our Time,* no. 53.

37   **Jews who have converted to another faith . . . :** Plaut and Washofsky, *Teshuvot for the Nineties,* no. 5753.10.

37   **Unmarried Jewish couples . . . :** A Jew is entitled to join a synagogue and does not forfeit that privilege by living with a partner in an unmarried relationship. Children born out of wedlock are not regarded as "bastards" *(mamzerim)* under traditional Jewish law; that designation is applied to the offspring of incestuous and adulterous unions (*M. Yevamot* 4:13; *Yad, Isurei Bi'ah* 15:1). Even a *mamzer,* moreover, is expected to live a Jewish life and is entitled to learn Torah. In Reform Judaism, where the traditional disabilities that attach to this status are disregarded in any case, there is absolutely no reason to discriminate against the children of an unmarried couple.

37   **While the synagogue should refrain . . . :** *Responsa Committee,* no. 5756.10.

38   **A congregation is entitled to withhold membership . . . :** Jacob, *American Reform Responsa,* no. 16.

38   ***cherem* or *nidui* . . . :** *Shulchan Arukh, Yore De'ah* 334.

38   **communal punishments of lesser severity . . . :** This refers to *nezifah,* a kind of public tongue-lashing which exposed an individual to embarrassment but did not carry with it the social isolation of excommunication; *B. Mo'ed Katan* 16a; *Hilkhot Harosh, Mo'ed Katan* 2:7; *Shulchan Arukh, Yore De'ah* 334:14.

38   **As one responsum puts it . . . :** Jacob, *American Reform Responsa,* no. 15.

38   **A synagogue may restrict . . . :** Freehof, *Contemporary Reform Responsa,* nos. 45–46.

38   **The Establishment of a Congregation:** *Resp. Rivash,* no. 253; Isserles, *Choshen Mishpat* 162:7.

38   **Some authorities . . . :** *Magen Avraham, Orach Chayim* 154, no. 23; *Resp. Be'er Yitzchak, Orach Chayim,* no. 24.

39   **On the other hand ... :** *Resp. Radbaz* 3:910 (472); *Resp. Chatam Sofer, Choshen Mishpat* 12, sec. 3; *Arukh Hashulchan, Choshen Mishpat* 162, par. 10.

39   **Reform responsa accordingly uphold ... :** Jacob, *Contemporary American Reform Responsa*, no. 137.

39   **Jewish tradition, however, tends to encourage large numbers ... :** The following are examples from rabbinic literature. One who has not seen the massive synagogue of Alexandria, Egypt, "has not seen the glory of Israel"; *T. Sukkah* 4:3; *B. Sukkah* 51b. It is preferable to recite *Havdalah* in public and the *Megillah* in a crowded setting; *B. Berakhot* 53a; *Shulchan Arukh, Orach Chayim* 690:18 and *Mishnah Berurah* ad loc., no. 61. Even if one can assemble a *minyan* in one's home, it is better to pray at the synagogue; *Magen Avraham, Orach Chayim* 90, no. 15. It is better to pray in a larger synagogue than a smaller one; *Mishnah Berurah, Orach Chayim* 90, no. 28.

39   **Tradition does recognize some exceptions ... :** If a synagogue is so large and crowded that one cannot hear the service or the Torah reading, one ought to pray in a smaller, quieter setting; *Mishnah Berurah,* loc. cit. Chassidic *minhag* generally favors smaller prayer-groups over larger congregations; Wertheim, *Halakhot Vehalikhot Bachasidut,* 68–71. At least one authority rules that a member of a synagogue enjoys a "property" right over his seat and can prevent the congregation from admitting new members if the increased number of worshipers interferes with his "right of way," making it difficult for him to reach his place and uncomfortable for him once he gets there; *Resp. Rivash,* no. 253; Isserles, *Choshen Mishpat* 161:7 (and see *T. Bava Metzi'a* 11:9). Others reject this theory out of hand; *Resp. Mashat Binyamin,* no. 4, and *Arukh Hashulchan, Choshen Mishpat* 161, par. 11.

39   **Reform responsa have held that it is improper ... :** Plaut and Washofsky, *Teshuvot,* no. 5752.12; Jacob, *American Reform Responsa,* no. 9.

40   **"capable men who fear God ... ":** The translation of the Hebrew *anshei chayil,* which has military connotations (compare the modern Hebrew *chayal,* "soldier"), thus conveying the notion of strength, energy, leadership potential, and wisdom; see Nachmanides to Exod. 18:21.

40   **to the point that some have suggested ... :** Rashi on the verse. The word *chayil* also means "wealth" (see Deut. 8:17–18).

40   **Just as the *sheliach tzibur* ... :** See *Shulchan Arukh, Orach Chayim* 53:4–5. For the *gabai tzedakah* see *Yad, Matanot Aniyim* 9:1.

40   **not to give even the appearance of improper conduct ... :** *Yad, Matanot Aniyim* 9:8–9. The *gabai* should be "blameless in the eyes of God and Israel" (*Tur, Yore De'ah* 257; Isserles, ad loc.): i.e., he or she be free of wrongdoing and of the suspicion of wrongdoing. See *M. Shekalim* 2:2; *Exodus Rabbah* 51:2; *Arukh Hashulchan, Yore De'ah* 257, nos. 9–12.

40   **We do not expect perfection ... :** See Plaut and Washofsky, *Teshuvot,* no. 5754.17, concerning a synagogue trustee accused of dishonest business practices.

40   **A person should not be penalized or removed from office on grounds of mere suspicion ... :** *Shakh, Yore De'ah* 257, no. 4, though one accused of wrongdoing must answer to the charges; *Arukh Hashulchan, Yore De'ah* 257, no. 13. On the efficacy of repentance to restore a person to communal office, see Freehof, *Today's Reform Responsa,* no. 51, *Magen Avraham, Orach Chayim* 53, no. 8, and *Mishnah Berurah,* no. 22.

41   **It is up to the congregation . . . :** See Freehof, *Today's Reform Responsa*, no. 51: by electing the individual to office the congregation indicates its acceptance of his or her *teshuvah*.

41   **a payment of one-half shekel . . . :** Considered even in biblical times as a regular, annual assessment on the people: II Kings 12:5ff.; II Chron. 24:4ff.; Neh. 10: 33–34; and Josephus, *Antiquities*, 9.8.2 and 18.9.1. The mishnaic tractate *Shekalim* describes how this tax was collected, and the present-day observance of Shabbat Shekalim commemorates that collection. Halakhic tradition understood the annual half-shekel payment to be a Toraitic commandment: *She'iltot*, ch. 64; *Halakhot Gedolot*, ed. Warsaw, p. 6; Rambam, *Sefer Hamitzvot*, positive commandment no. 171 and *Yad, Shekalim* 1:1; and see Ramban and Ibn Ezra to Exod. 30:12.

41   **The community . . . was also empowered to levy taxes:** *T. Bava Metzi'a* 11:12 (printed version); *Yad, Tefillah* 11:1.

41   **Some rule . . . :** R. Meir of Rothenburg (13th century), cited in *Mordekhai, Bava Batra*, ch. 479; *Shulchan Arukh, Orach Chayim* 53:23.

41   **Others maintain . . . :** *Resp. Maharam Padua*, no. 42; Isserles, *Shulchan Arukh, Orach Chayim* 53:23 and *Choshen Mishpat* 163:3, end.

41   **Still others hold . . . :** *Resp. Chatam Sofer, Choshen Mishpat*, no. 167.

41   **"and are thus in accordance with the main spirit of the law" . . . :** Freehof, *Reform Jewish Practice*, 2:32 ("all matters of taxation are decided according to established community custom"; *Resp. Terumat Hadeshen*, no. 344, and Isserles, *Shulchan Arukh, Choshen Mishpat* 163:3).

42   **Assessment of Dues:** See Jacob, *Contemporary American Reform Responsa*, no. 151. The case involved a wife who worked at minimum wage and whose husband, "a man of considerable means," resigned his membership. Since in this case the family's standard of living was set according to the husband's wealth, there was no justification to make an exception for synagogue dues and to measure them against the wife's smaller income.

42   **Collection of Dues:** See *Mordekhai, Bava Batra*, ch. 476: "it is the custom...that a person cannot exempt himself from local taxes by leaving the city after the obligation has taken force."

42   **"the resignation of any member . . . ":** *Suggested Constitution*, Art. IV, sec. 8.

42   **Jewish law traditionally discourages . . . :** *B. Gittin* 88b; *Yad, Sanhedrin* 26:7; *Shulchan Arukh, Choshen Mishpat* 26:1.

42   **In our time . . . :** R. Solomon B. Freehof notes the prevailing custom in even Orthodox communities today to bring monetary disputes before the civil courts (*Reform Responsa*, Introduction, 7–8). The justification for this prohibition, as stated by Rashi to Exod. 21:1, is to refrain from bringing credit to the pagan deities in whose name the non-Jewish court does justice. Since we do not hold the Gentiles among whom we live as pagans (see Chapter 7), this reason to avoid using their courts no longer applies.

42   **Moreover, it has always been permitted . . . :** *B. Bava Kama* 92b; *Yad, Sanhedrin* 26:7; *Shulchan Arukh, Choshen Mishpat* 26:2 and Isserles ad loc.

42   **the spirit of Jewish tradition generally opposes . . . :** Freehof, *Recent Reform Responsa*, no. 44/Jacob, *American Reform Responsa*, no. 17. The quotation ("general feeling in the Jewish community . . . ") is on p. 207 of Freehof's volume. Rabbi Freehof holds that the collection of delinquent building pledges in the civil courts "is contrary both to the

letter and the spirit of Jewish legal tradition." The sources supplied in the foregoing ("it has always been permitted") conflict with his interpretation, though his concern for *chilul hashem* remains valid. However, his statement (p. 208) that a Jewish "Document of Gift" (*shetar matanah*) cannot be collected in a Gentile court is not supported by the source he cites (*Shulchan Arukh, Choshen Mishpat* 68:1).

42   **Gifts and Donations:** see Chapter 4.

43   **Torah study *(talmud torah)* ...:** B. *Shabbat* 127a.

43   **Thus, a synagogue building may be sold ...:** M. *Megillah* 3:1. Similarly, a synagogue may be turned into a *beit midrash*, a school for Torah study, but the *beit midrash* may not be turned into a synagogue (B. *Megillah* 26b; *Yad, Tefillah* 11:14).

43   **On this basis, halakhic authorities have concluded ...:** *Resp. Harosh,* 13:14; *Shulchan Arukh, Orach Chayim* 153:5; see B. *Arakhin* 6b. Donors who contribute to the synagogue and to other worthy endeavors do so with the implicit acceptance of local custom, which recognizes the community's power to redirect the gifts to purposes other than those originally intended; *Resp. Rashba,* 5:249; Isserles, *Shulchan Arukh, Yore De'ah* 259:2.

43   **The making of ... improvements ...:** *Responsa Committee,* no. 5756.3.

43   **A congregation, for example, is permitted to discontinue ...:** Plaut and Washofsky, *Teshuvot,* no. 5753.18.

44   **One of the reasons why persons are permitted ...:** *Resp. Rashba* 1:581.

44   **To summarize ...:** See *Responsa Committee,* no. 5756.3 and Freehof, *Modern Reform Responsa,* no. 24.

44   **Donations from Disreputable Persons:** *Resp. Rashba* 1:581; Isserles, *Shulchan Arukh, Yore De'ah* 249:13.

44   **According to the Talmud, sinners are permitted ...:** B. *Chulin* 5a. See *Yad, Ma'aseh Hakorbanot* 3:4.

44   **Some later authorities ...:** Isserles, *Yore De'ah* 254:3; *Magen Avraham, Orach Chayim* 154, no. 18.

44   **Others reject this analogy ...:** *Resp. Mabit* 1:214; *Shakh, Yore De'ah* 254, no. 5.

45   **On this matter, Reform responsa advise ...:** Freehof, *Current Reform Responsa,* no.14; Jacob, *Contemporary American Reform Responsa,* no. 146. On accepting donations from a sinner, see *Yad, Tefillah* 12:6: "we do not tell a wicked person: 'add to your sin by neglecting a *mitzvah.*'" Our conclusion apparently conflicts with the above ruling of Rashba that one who donates an object to the synagogue is entitled to inscribe his name upon it. On this basis, R. Haim David Halevy has ruled that a congregation may not refuse this right to a donor. If the congregation does not wish to place his or her name upon the donated object, its only recourse is to refuse the donation altogether or to see to it that the object is presented or funded by more than one donor; *Resp. Aseh Lekha Rav* 8:55. Yet a primary justification for Rashba's ruling is that by making this gift the donor wishes to establish his good name in the sight of God and the community. This reasoning would not apply to a criminal or notorious person, who cannot establish a "good name" by means of a monetary gift without first repenting of his or her evil deeds. Rather, we would say that a person has a *general* right to have his or her name associated with a gift, but this general right does not apply in cases where that association would contradict the moral and religious purposes which the synagogue represents.

45   **Fundraising:** On the sale of High Holiday tickets, see Jacob, *Contemporary American Reform Responsa*, no. 150. On the sale of ritual honors, see idem, no. 150 and Jacob, *Questions and Reform Jewish Answers*, nos. 40 and 42. On kickback schemes, see idem, no. 42. Such an arrangement raises the specter of unfair business competition, the subject of considerable halakhic discussion. See *B. Bava Batra* 21b–22a and *Shulchan Arukh, Choshen Mishpat* 156.

45   **Gambling:** See *M. Sanhedrin* 3:3 and *B. Sanhedrin* 24b–25a: the proceeds of gambling are but one step removed from robbery, and the robber is not trusted as a witness. See as well Maimonides' commentary to *M. Sanhedrin* 3:3: "the gambler occupies himself with an activity that offers no benefit to human civilization." This does not, however, disqualify the occasional gambler "who has another occupation"; see *Yad, Edut* 10:4. On Judaism and gambling, see Leo Landman, "Jewish Attitudes Towards Gambling," *Jewish Quarterly Review* 58 (1967): 34–62.

46   **Some prominent halakhic scholars . . . :** *Resp. Zera Emet* 3:144 and *Resp. Panim Me'irot* 3:43. For a different opinion, see *Resp. Chakham Zvi*, no. 123.

46   **It is therefore inaccurate to say . . . :** See Isserles, *Choshen Mishpat* 370:3: "the custom to permit dice-playing is widespread; only the 'professional' dice-player is disqualified as a witness."

46   **Nonetheless, it is just as inaccurate . . . :** See *Resp. Rivash*, no. 432: gambling may be legal, but it is morally reprehensible.

46   **the spirit of the tradition, as we interpret it . . . :** See Jacob, *Contemporary American Reform Responsa*, nos. 166–67, and Freehof, *Current Reform Responsa*, no. 15, along with the following resolutions of the Central Conference of American Rabbis: *CCAR Yearbook* 89 (1979): 97; and idem, 59 (1949): 179.

46   **The congregation sets the level . . . :** On the enforcement of *tzedakah* obligations see *B. Ketubot* 49b (which deals as well with the issue of child support), *B. Bava Batra* 8b; *Yad, Matanot Aniyim* 7:10; *Shulchan Arukh, Yore De'ah* 248:1.

47   **What, precisely, is our responsibility . . . :** See Jacob, *Contemporary American Reform Responsa*, nos. 138 and 152.

48   ***yisrael mumar*** or ***yisrael meshumad:*** On these terms, see Stanley Wagner, "The *Meshumad* and *Mumar* in Talmudic Literature" in M. Katz, ed., *The Jacob Dolnitzky Memorial Volume*. A great deal of confusion exists over these terms, which are often used interchangeably in the texts. Yet neither person, nor even the *min* (a member of a sect deemed heretical by the Rabbis), however reprehensible his conduct or however worthy of banishment from the community, is ever said to lose his basic identification as a Jew.

48   **the convert to Christianity or Islam . . . :** The first century C.E. "Jewish-Christian" sects were an exception to this rule. With their disappearance and the triumph of "Gentile Christianity," however, the two faiths came to regard themselves as separate and religiously distinct entities. The current "Messianic Jewish" groups are a self-conscious effort to erase the boundaries.

48   **ceases to be the "son" of his Jewish father . . . :** See *Otzar Hageonim, Kiddushin*, no. 80: "once he has adopted another religion, he loses the sanctity of Jewish status."

48   **Others suggested that we no longer recognize his marriage as valid . . . :** An opinion cited in *Tur, Even Ha'ezer* 44. It is, however, a minority view, and traditional *halakhah* continues to require a divorce in such a case.

48   **"A Jew, even though he sins, remains a Jew":** *B. Sanhedrin* 44a. The text, a midrashic play on Joshua 7:11, refers in fact to the entire people of Israel: though they transgress God's commandment, they remain Israel, the covenant people. Medieval authorities, beginning with Rashi in the eleventh century, read this text as referring to the individual Jew: even though he abandons the covenant, he remains a member of the covenant community. See *Teshuvot Rashi*, ed. S. Elfenbein, nos. 171, 173, and 175.

49   **This conception did not . . . :** See Jacob Katz, *Halakhah Vekabalah*, 255–69.

49   **The gates of repentance . . . :** Some authorities require that repentant apostates mark their return to Judaism with a formal ceremony; this was *not*, however, regarded as a "conversion"; Isserles, *Shulchan Arukh, Yore De'ah* 268:12, refers to it as *divrei chaverut*, a kind of "membership" ritual. See Jacob, *Contemporary American Reform Responsa*, no. 64, and Plaut and Washofsky, *Teshuvot*, no. 5754.13.

49   **Reform Judaism's attitude toward the non-Jewish world . . . :** See Chapter 7.

49   **And given that contemporary attitudes toward other religions are not nearly so hostile . . . :** See Freehof, *Modern Reform Responsa*, no. 30. For the citations from the Centenary Perspective, see Meyer, *Response to Modernity*, 392.

51   **From the inception of the Reform movement in Europe . . . :** See Meyer, *Response to Modernity*, 90–91, 204, and 289ff.

51   **We would therefore not label atheists or thoroughly secularized Jews as "apostates" . . . :** This does not mean that atheism is considered a valid expression of Judaism. It does mean, however, that Reform Judaism does not regard atheism or "secular humanism" as *religions* to which one converts or commits oneself.

52   **The Jew . . . who converts to another religion remains a Jew in our eyes . . . :** Jacob, *American Reform Responsa*, no. 71; see *B. Yevamot* 47b; *Yad, Isurei Bi'ah* 13:17; *Shulchan Arukh, Yore De'ah* 268:2.

52   **As Rabbi Solomon B. Freehof writes . . . :** Freehof, *Modern Reform Responsa*, no. 30.

52   **The apostate is not accepted as a member of a synagogue . . . :** Plaut and Washofsky, *Teshuvot*, no. 5753.10.

52   **he or she may not ascend the *bimah* . . . :** Plaut and Washofsky, *Teshuvot*, no. 5753.13.

52   **their children may enroll in our religious schools:** Jacob, *Contemporary American Reform Responsa*, no. 66. There is a long tradition in the *halakhah* which absolves the descendants of apostates of any blame for their forebears' renunciation of Judaism. Since they were raised as Gentiles, their continued apostasy is not seen as the result of a conscious choice on their part. Rather than punish them, "we should draw them toward us with words of reconciliation, so that they return to the truth of Torah" (*Yad, Mamrim* 3:3). A stricter opinion is recorded in R. David ibn Zimra's comment to that ruling of Maimonides. Our own position follows Rambam's more lenient (and, we think, more realistic) view.

52   **the apostate may be buried in a Jewish cemetery . . . :** Freehof, *Recent Reform Responsa*, no. 27; R. Shelomo ben Adret, quoted in *Beit Yosef, Tur, Yore De'ah* 334; *Shakh, Yore De'ah* 334, no. 18; *Resp. Chatam Sofer, Yore De'ah* 341.

52   **Hebrew Christians, Messianic Jews, and Jews for Jesus:** Plaut and Washofsky, *Teshuvot*, nos. 5754.1 and 5753.10; Jacob, *Questions and Reform Jewish Answers*, nos. 110 and 242; Jacob, *Contemporary American Reform Responsa*, nos. 66, 67, and 68; Jacob, *American Reform Responsa*, no. 150.

53   **The Returning Apostate:** For a general survey and analysis, see Stanton M. Zamek, "Even Though He Sins He Remains a Jew: The Repentance of the Returning Apostate" (Rabbinic thesis, HUC-JIR, 1996).

53   **Thus, say some authorities . . . :** *Resp. Rashbash*, no. 89; *Beit Yosef, Yore De'ah* 268, end (in *Bedek Habayit*).

53   **Other authorities demand . . . :** *Chidushei Haritva, Yevamot* 47b; *Nimukei Yosef* to Alfasi, *Yevamot*, fol. 16b. Even Rashbash, who does not require immersion or a formal court ceremony, prescribes a special prayer to be recited at the *berit milah* of a previously uncircumcised apostate.

54   **Reform responsa, in general . . . :** Jacob, *Contemporary American Reform Responsa*, no. 64; Plaut and Washofsky, *Teshuvot*, no. 5754.13. .

54   **The Synagogue Building: Consecration:** Freehof, *Contemporary Reform Responsa*, no. 1. The practice of conducting a dedication service for a new synagogue is mentioned in *Resp. Halakhot Ketanot* 2:179. See also *Resp. Chatam Sofer, Orach Chayim*, no. 156. Representative liturgies are found in Y.D. Eisenstein, *Otzar Dinim Uminhagim*, 138, and Hyman Goldin, *Hamadrikh: The Rabbi's Guide*, 63–71.

54   **The building becomes a holy place . . . from the moment it is first *used* as a synagogue:** *Y. Megillah* 3:1 (73d); *Hilkhot Harosh, Megillah* 4:1; *Shulchan Arukh, Orach Chayim* 153:8.

55   **the money raised for synagogue construction . . . :** *B. Bava Batra* 3b; *Shulchan Arukh, Orach Chayim* 153:5 and 13.

55   **Thus, a synagogue building under construction . . . :** Freehof, *Recent Reform Responsa*, no. 45.

55   **Jewish tradition permits the sale . . . :** See, in general, Freehof, *Contemporary Reform Responsa*, no. 1; Freehof, *Reform Jewish Practice*, 2:32–35; *M. Megillah* 3:1 (*B. Megillah* 25b–26a); *Yad, Tefillah* 11:14; *Shulchan Arukh, Orach Chayim* 153:2.

55   **toward an appropriate religious purpose . . . :** Ideally, the money realized from the sale of any item of sanctity must be put toward the purchase of an item of greater sanctity. This follows the rule "that which is holy must be elevated to higher degrees of holiness, not degraded to lower ones" (*ma'alin bakodesh ve'ein moridin; M. Menachot* 11:7). A synagogue may be sold to raise funds for the redemption of captives, to fund Torah education, and to provide for the marriage of orphans in the community; *Resp. Harosh* 13:14; *Shulchan Arukh, Orach Chayim* 153:6.

55   **If the sale enjoys the full legal approval of the community . . . :** *B. Megillah* 26a–b; *Yad, Tefillah* 11:17; *Shulchan Arukh, Orach Chayim* 153:7.

55   **Originally, this sanction applied . . . :** *B. Megillah* 26a; *Tosafot* ad loc., s.v. *keivan; Yad, Tefillah* 11:16; *Shulchan Arukh, Orach Chayim* 153:7.

55   **During the last several centuries . . . :** R. Binyamin Selonik offered two arguments on behalf of the right of the large-city congregants to sell the synagogue: 1) the political structure of Jewish communal government today empowers community leaders to sell the building, even in a large city; 2) if the synagogue was built with the stipulation that its congregants shall enjoy full ownership over it, they can sell the building without the consent of others (*Resp. Mashat Binyamin*, no. 33, and *Mishnah Berurah* 153, no. 32. See also *Resp. Penei Yehoshua*, 1:4). See as well *Magen Avraham, Orach Chayim* 153, no. 12: a synagogue in a large city may be sold if worshipers no longer enter there to pray. On this basis, R. Moshe Feinstein concludes that a synagogue located in a formerly Jewish neighborhood may be sold. Since the Jews no

longer enter it on a regular basis to pray, we can presume that even those Jews from other communities, whom tradition regards as part owners of this large-city synagogue, would consent to its sale (*Resp. Igerot Moshe, Orach Chayim*, 1:50).

56   **The synagogue building may be sold to any interested buyer . . . :** *B. Megillah* 27a; *Shulchan Arukh, Orach Chayim* 153:9.

56   **The building may therefore be sold to a Christian congregation . . . :** Freehof, *Reform Jewish Practice*, 2:35–36. While others would disagree, this position follows the view, taken by some prominent halakhists and accepted by Reform Judaism, that Christianity is not a form of idolatry; see Chapter 7.

56   **the spirit of the tradition would argue . . . :** See Freehof, *Contemporary Reform Responsa*, no. 2, on the sale of a synagogue building to a group espousing an anti-Semitic philosophy. Moreover, the permit to sell a synagogue "for virtually any purpose" is hardly unanimous. Though maintained by the *Shulchan Arukh* and other authorities, there is significant opposition to it in the *halakhah*. See *Mishnah Berurah* to 153:9, in *Bi'ur Halakhah*. The conclusion, therefore, is that while we may sell the synagogue to anyone we wish, we *ought* to take care that the new owners will not use it for notorious purposes (*Mishnah Berurah*, no. 58).

56   **It is true that Jewish law permits a congregation . . . :** R. Eliyahu Mizrachi (16th-century Turkey), cited by *Magen Avraham, Orach Chayim* 154, no. 17: since the building itself was not the object of worship, it is not disqualified as a synagogue. See *Resp. Sho'el Umeshiv* 1, part 3, nos. 73, 74, and 75; *Resp. Melamed Leho'il, Orach Chayim*, no. 20; Jacob, *Contemporary American Reform Responsa*, no. 148. *Mishnah Berurah* to 154:11, in *Bi'ur Halakhah*, prohibits the conversion of a Catholic church, which contains various statuary, into a synagogue. Reform Judaism disagrees with both his technical reasoning and his assumption that Christianity, especially its more iconic sects, is idolatry.

56   **Reform Judaism does not regard Christianity and Islam . . . as forms of idolatry . . . :** See Chapter 7.

56   **"to declare publicly that these two forms of worship . . .":** Freehof, *Contemporary Reform Responsa*, no. 3, p. 22.

56   **Jewish congregations . . . ought to seek their own distinct quarters . . . :** Jacob, *Questions and Reform Jewish Answers*, no. 51; Jacob, *Contemporary American Reform Responsa*, no. 148; Freehof, *Contemporary Reform Responsa*, no. 3.

On renting to a university, see Jacob, *Questions and Reform Jewish Answers*, no. 59. On renting to a church, see Freehof, *Reform Jewish Practice*, 2:44–45, and Freehof, *Contemporary Reform Responsa*, no. 9.

56   **Architecture and Landscaping:** Freehof, *Reform Jewish Practice*, 2:8–12; Jacob, *Questions and Reform Jewish Answers*, no. 55; Jacob, *Contemporary American Reform Responsa*, no. 140.

57   **it was forbidden . . . to plant trees in their courtyards:** Based upon Deut. 16:21, "Do not plant an *asherah*, any kind of tree, near the altar of God." This translation is the traditional understanding (see *Sifrei*, Rashi and Nachmanides on the verse, and *Yad, Avodat Kokhavim* 6:9) which understands *asherah* to be a living tree that served as an object of idol-worship. Current biblical scholarship, however, believes that the *asherah* was a manufactured object, probably a wooden pole (hence the Hebrew *'etz*, which can be rendered as "tree" or "wood"); see *Anchor Bible Dictionary*, 1:485–86, and the translation of Deut. 16:21 in *The Torah*, Jewish Publication Society of Amer-

ica, 1962. Even if one reads *asherah* as "tree," it does not necessarily follow that the prohibition against planting trees in the Temple courtyard applies as well to the synagogue. The first to so apply it is *Resp. Maharam Schick, Orach Chayim*, nos. 78–79. Other authorities, however, do not believe that the prohibition holds outside of the Temple courtyard; see *Resp. Maharsham* 1:127 and 6:17.

On the prohibition of new architectural styles, compare the stringent *Resp. Yehudah Ya'aleh, Orach Chayim*, 1:39, to the more lenient *Resp. Noda Biyehudah, Orach Chayim*, 2:18. On the subject of imitating Gentile religious practice, see the discussion in Chapter 7.

57 **"Richly equipped as the synagogue is . . . ":** Jacob, *American Reform Responsa*, no. 25.

57 **the issue of access . . . for the physically disabled:** Plaut and Washofsky, *Teshuvot*, no. 5752.5.

57 **Jews traditionally face in the direction of Jerusalem . . . :** The precedent for this practice is perhaps Daniel 6:11. See *M. Berakhot* 4:5 and *B. Berakhot* 30a; *Yad, Tefillah* 5:2; *Shulchan Arukh, Orach Chayim* 94:1.

57 **it has therefore become customary to place the ark against the eastern wall . . . :** *Yad, Tefillah* 11:2 and *Hagahot Maimoniot* ad loc.; *Shulchan Arukh, Orach Chayim* 150:5. Since the earth is round, it is true that one could just as easily face west. Still, tradition has established that "our" direction toward Jerusalem and the land of Israel is east (*Tur, Orach Chayim* 94; Isserles, *Shulchan Arukh, Orach Chayim* 94:5).

58 **Reform synagogues should, wherever possible . . . :** Jacob, *American Reform Responsa*, no. 18.

58 **"the Divine Presence is everywhere" . . . :** *B. Bava Batra* 25a.

58 **it is the worshiper's spiritual orientation . . . that counts:** See *M. Berakhot* 4:5 and the discussion in *B. Berakhot* 30a: that Israel "shall pray towards this place" (the Temple; I Kings 8:30) means that they should direct their hearts (if they are unable to direct their bodies) toward the sanctuary.

58 **In a synagogue whose sanctuary faces . . . :** Freehof, *Reform Jewish Practice*, 2:12–16. See *Taz, Orach Chayim* 94, no. 1, and *Resp. Meshiv Davar* 1:10.

58 **the desk or table from which the Torah is read . . . :** See Freehof, *Reform Jewish Practice*, 2:16–20. On locating the *bimah* in the center of the sanctuary, see *Yad, Tefillah* 11:3; *Tur, Orach Chayim* 150; Isserles, *Orach Chayim* 150:5.

58 **aroused much opposition from traditionalists . . . :** See especially *Resp. Chatam Sofer, Orach Chayim*, no. 28, who argues that the placement of the *bimah* in the center of the sanctuary is dictated by talmudic law (*B. Sukkah* 51b, the description of the enormous synagogue of Alexandria) and not, as suggested by R. Yosef Karo (*Kesef Mishneh, Tefillah* 11:3), by practical concerns. See also *Mishnah Berurah, Bi'ur Halakhah, Orach Chayim* 150, s.v. *be'emtza*, and *Arukh Hashulchan Orach Chayim* 150, no. 9, who condemn the attempts to move the ark from the center of the sanctuary as egregious departures from sacred Jewish tradition.

58 **And they could cite weighty halakhic opinion . . . :** R. Yosef Karo, in *Kesef Mishneh, Tefillah* 11:3.

58 **Rabbinic tradition interprets this instruction . . . :** *B. Sanhedrin* 21b, although the verse apparently refers to the great lyric poem *ha'azinu*, which follows immediately. See Rashi to Deut. 31:19.

58   **The purpose of this commandment . . . :** *B. Bava Batra* 14a; *Sefer Hachinukh,* mitzvah 365.

58   **"more precious to us than gold" . . . :** Cf. Ps. 19:11.

58   **One may fulfill this requirement . . . :** *Yad, Sefer Torah* 7:1; *Tur, Yore De'ah* 270.

59   **it is considered as though that individual . . . :** *B. Menachot* 30a.

59   **The *sofer* or scribe who writes . . . :** See Jacob, *Questions and Reform Jewish Answers,* no. 135.

59   **the *sofer* is traditionally a male, although . . . :** Plaut and Washofsky, *Teshuvot,* no. 5755.15 (which suggests in broad outline a curriculum for such a program) and Jacob, *Questions and Reform Jewish Answers,* no. 135. At this writing, a program for the training of Reform *soferim/ot* is being planned.

59   **Scrolls Fit and Unfit for Use:** See *Yad, Sefer Torah* 10:1, for the twenty distinct errors which render the Torah scroll *pasul.*

59   **Indeed, some (though not all) authorities require . . . :** Jacob, *Questions and Reform Jewish Answers,* no. 137. For those who require removal, see *Magen Avraham, Orach Chayim* 154, no. 14 and *Resp. Noda Biyehudah, Orach Chayim,* 1:9. For those who permit the keeping of a *pasul* scroll, see *Sefer Chassidim,* no. 934 (after *B. Berakhot* 8b and elsewhere: the broken tablets of the Ten Commandments were kept in the ark along with the set Moses carved in Exod. 34); and *Resp. Binyan Tziyon* 1:97. See Freehof, *Contemporary Reform Responsa,* no. 24, which permits the keeping of an unfit (*pasul*) Torah scroll in the Ark.

59   **a congregation may find it necessary to conduct the reading . . . :** See Jacob, *Contemporary American Reform Responsa,* no. 69. Tradition prohibits the reading of a *chumash* (a scroll containing less than an entire *sefer torah*) in a public service on the grounds that it insults the honor of the congregation (*B. Gittin* 60a); the congregation presumably forgives this insult when the Torah portion cannot be read in any other way. While no blessing is recited over a reading from a printed *chumash* (Isserles, *Shulchan Arukh, Orach Chayim* 143:2), if the community possesses only a *chumash* the reading itself should be done "so that the practice of Torah reading should not be forgotten" (*Magen Avraham* 143, no. 2).

59   **the customary benedictions should be omitted . . . :** though some authorities permit the public reading from a defective Torah scroll and require a benediction over it (*Mordekhai, Megillah,* ch. 3). Among these is Maimonides, who notes (*Responsa,* ed. Freimann, no. 43) that the blessings are not recited over the scroll itself but over the reading, the words that are pronounced; a blessing is therefore in order whether the scroll is properly written or not. Our suggestion, to omit the benedictions, follows the consensus among most scholars (*Shulchan Arukh, Orach Chayim* 143:3; *Mishnah Berurah* ad loc.) who distinguish between *keri'at hatorah,* the public reading from the Torah, and *talmud torah,* the activity of Torah study. The latter is usually done without a Torah scroll. While blessings are recited over the act of Torah study, they are not exactly the same as those said over the public reading and they may already have been pronounced at the beginning of the service (see *Gates of Prayer,* 52, and 284). The public reading of the Torah, by contrast, is a ritual act that ought to be accomplished with a proper Torah scroll; when such a scroll is not available, it is proper to omit the benedictions to note the difference between Torah *study* and Torah *reading.*

59 **The Honor Due to the Torah Scroll:** *B. Kiddushin* 33b; *Yad, Sefer Torah* 10:9; *Shulchan Arukh, Yore De'ah* 282:2.

60 **One removes the Torah from the ark . . . :** Freehof, *Current Reform Responsa*, no. 9. The prevailing Ashkenazic custom is that the Torah is taken with the right arm and carried on one's right side; (*Maharil, Din Keri'ah ve-Sefer Torah*, no. 2, Isserles, *Orach Chayim* 134:2, and *Arukh Hashulchan, Orach Chayim* 134, no. 4, based upon Deut. 33:2 and Song of Songs 2:6).

60 **It is not necessary to stand during the Torah reading . . . :** *B. Sotah* 39a; *Shulchan Arukh, Orach Chayim* 146:4 and *Taz,* ad loc. Some authorities do urge that congregants stand during the reading: just as our ancestors stood to hear the Torah at Sinai (Exod. 19:17), we too should stand, as though hearing and accepting the Torah for the very first time. Others recommend standing during the recitation of *Barekhu* and *Barukh shem kevod* in the Torah blessings, as these are "matters relating to sanctification"; *Mishnah Berurah* 146, no. 19.

60 **If the Torah scroll is dropped . . . :** See Freehof, *Contemporary Reform Responsa*, no. 25. This custom (of fasting) is not mentioned in the Talmud or any of the great codes and is enforced with varying degrees of strictness.

60 **It is customary to stand while the ark . . . is open:** See *Taz, Yore De'ah* 242, no. 13. When it rests upon the *bimah* or in the ark, the Torah scroll is in a different spatial domain (*reshut*) than are we. We are therefore not in its "presence" and are not, strictly speaking, required to stand. However, the desire to show honor to the Torah has led to the custom of standing while the ark is open.

60 **Some authorities advise against . . . :** Freehof, *Contemporary Reform Responsa*, no. 23.

60 **Others say . . . :** Jacob, *Questions and Reform Jewish Answers*, no. 137.

60 **There is general agreement . . . :** Freehof, *Current Reform Responsa*, no. 19. See *Shulchan Arukh, Orach Chayim* 135:14, which does cite such a prohibition from the *Mordekhai, Rosh Hashanah*, ch. 1, par. 450: the honor of the *sefer torah* requires that we go to *it* rather than have it brought to us. Most later authorities reject this view, for the sensible reason that the sick and the imprisoned are incapable of "going to" the Torah reading; see *Mishnah Berurah* ad loc., no. 46, and his *Bi'ur Halakhah* ad loc.

60 **The scroll should not be moved from the synagogue . . . :** See *Responsa Committee*, no. 5758.9, "Transporting a Torah Scroll to a Private Bat Mitzvah Ceremony."

60 **It is forbidden to burn or destroy sacred texts . . . :** *B. Makkot* 22a (on Deut. 12:4); *Yad, Yesodei Hatorah* 6:1.

60 **This prohibition does *not* apply to impermanent writing . . . :** Freehof, *Current Reform Responsa*, no. 6; *Resp. Igerot Moshe, Yore De'ah* 1:173.

60 **When a Torah scroll has become worn or *pasul* . . . :** *B. Megillah* 26b; *Yad, Sefer Torah* 10:3; *Shulchan Arukh, Orach Chayim* 154:5 and *Yore De'ah* 282:10; Jacob, *Contemporary American Reform Responsa*, nos. 108–9; *Responsa Committee*, no. 5757.4: and Jacob, *American Reform Responsa*, no. 72, which suggests a liturgy for the burial of a damaged *sefer torah.*

60 **A *pasul* Torah scroll may be divided up . . . :** Freehof, *Today's Reform Responsa*, no. 28.

60 **Sale and Ownership of the Torah Scroll:** *B. Megillah* 27a; *Tosafot, Bava Batra* 8b, s.v. *pidyon*; *Shulchan Arukh, Yore De'ah* 270:1. *Arukh Hashulchan, Yore De'ah* 270,

no. 16, includes medical expenses in the list of approved purposes for the sale of a *sefer torah*.

60   **For this reason, it is certainly permitted . . . :** Jacob, *Questions and Reform Jewish Answers*, no. 138; Freehof, *Reform Responsa for Our Time*, no. 52.

61   **It is also permitted to use the Torah scroll as a means of fundraising . . . :** Jacob, *Contemporary American Reform Responsa*, no. 232. This is not considered to be disrespectful to the Torah. See *Birkei Yosef, Yore De'ah* 270, s.v. *ve-eino rasha'i lemokhro*, who quotes a number of opinions permitting the sale of a Torah scroll by auction, and *Resp. Panim Me'irot* 3:43, who permits the raffling of a *sefer torah*.

61   **Individuals will frequently place their own Torah scrolls . . . :** Jacob, *Questions and Reform Jewish Answers*, no. 136; Jacob, *American Reform Responsa*, no. 40. See *Resp. Maharik*, no. 161, end, and *Resp. Maharshal*, no. 15. A "well-established custom" is one that has been recognized and attested by local rabbinic authorities and not merely a case of "so-and-so remembers that. . . ."

61   **Decorations:** See Freehof, *Current Reform Responsa*, no. 3, and Freehof, *Modern Reform Responsa*, no. 4, on the history of these ornaments. While most of them are not mentioned in the Talmud, they eventually came to reflect the holiness of the *sefer torah* itself. See *Yad, Sefer Torah* 10:4, and *Shulchan Arukh, Yore De'ah* 282:16.

61   **Some rule . . . :** *Yad* and *Shulchan Arukh,* loc. cit.

61   **others permit . . . :** *Hilkhot Harosh, Megillah* 4:5.

61   **Graven Images:** See Freehof, *Reform Jewish Practice*, 2: 20ff., Jacob, *American Reform Responsa*, no. 24, Jacob, *Questions and Reform Jewish Answers*, no. 50.

62   **Those who permit the placement . . . :** *Ran* to Alfasi, *Avodah Zarah*, fol. 18b–19b; R. Efraim of Regensburg (12th century), cited in *Mordekhai, Avodah Zarah*, ch. 840; see also *Yad, Avodat Kokhavim* 3:10–11 and *Shulchan Arukh, Yore De'ah* 141:6–7. Another argument is that the prohibition applies only to complete images; thus, even a human likeness may be rendered so long it is not a representation of the entire human form (*Hilkhot Harosh, Avodah Zarah* 3:5; *Shulchan Arukh, Yore De'ah* 141:7, cited as "some say").

62   **While some authorities worry . . . :** *Resp. Radbaz*, no. 1178; *Resp. Avkat Rokhel*, no. 63; *Resp. Mabit*, no. 30.

62   **others write . . . :** *Resp. Chesed Le'avraham, Yore De'ah*, no. 39; R. Avraham Yitzchak Hakohen Kook, *Igerot*, no. 10.

62   ***hiddur mitzvah*:** The concept is based upon the rabbinic understanding of Exod. 15:2: "this is my God, whom I shall glorify": we glorify God by adorning the *mitzvot*, by using a beautiful *lulav*, a beautiful *sukkah*, etc. (*B. Shabbat* 133b; *Mekhilta* to Exod. 15:2), or by performing a *mitzvah* according to a higher standard than is absolutely required (see Rashi, *B. Pesachim* 99b, s.v. *lo yokhal*). The idea is that we expend additional effort and resources in order to raise our level of observance from the minimally acceptable (e.g., "any *shofar* will do") to the aesthetically pleasing ("we *ought* to use a bigger *shofar* that makes a deeper sound"), so as to show that our performance of a *mitzvah* is a joyful privilege and not merely a rote act in fulfillment of an obligation. While understandable, this desire might easily lead to unreasonable and burdensome expenditures; the Rabbis therefore place a limit on this extra effort. Our expenses on behalf of *hiddur mitzvah* should not exceed more than one-third of the original cost of the object (*B. Bava Kama* 9b).

63   **The Ark:** On the distinction between *tashmishei kedushah* ("appurtenances of the sacred"; i.e., implements relating to the Torah scroll) and *tashmishei mitzvah* ("appurtenances of *mitzvah*"; e.g., a bag which holds a *tallit* or *tefillin*), see Freehof, *New Reform Responsa*, no. 5. On the sanctity of the *tik*, see *Yad, Sefer Torah* 10:4. On the distinction between the *tik* and our ark, see *Or Zaru'a* 2, ch. 386, although *Resp. Chatam Sofer* 6:10 argues that our ark possesses a higher sanctity. On the permit to sell an ark see *Resp. Melamed Leho'il, Orach Chayim*, no. 18, and *Resp. Seridei Esh* 2:18. On the conversion of an ark to a bookcase, see Freehof, *New Reform Responsa*, no. 5, and *Taz, Orach Chayim* 154, no. 7.

63   **The Menorah:** Freehof, *Reform Jewish Practice*, 2:24–25. B. *Avodah Zarah* 43a; *Yad, Beit Habechirah* 7:10; *Shulchan Arukh, Yore De'ah* 141:8, *Shakh* ad loc.; *Resp. Chakham Zvi*, no. 60; R. Yitzchak Halevy Herzog, *Responsa, Yore De'ah*, no. 48.

63   **National Flags:** Jacob, *American Reform Responsa*, no. 22, and Plaut and Washofsky, *Teshuvot*, no. 5753.8. The latter explicitly rejects the patriotic rhetoric of an earlier responsum (*American Reform Responsa*, no. 21, from 1954). That the flag is not considered an idol is a point made as well by R. Moshe Feinstein, *Resp. Igerot Moshe, Orach Chayim* 1:46. While Feinstein clearly prefers that the flags *not* be in the synagogue, he does not find their placement to violate religious law. We concur with his analysis, though we vigorously reject his responsum's description of national flags as "nonsense" and his condemnation of Zionism and the Israeli state.

63   **This is not to say that the flag is a religious symbol . . . :** Jacob, *Questions and Reform Jewish Answers*, no. 195. Thus, a worn Israeli flag should be disposed of in a dignified manner but not necessarily in accordance with the rules of disposal for worn sacred objects.

64   **Proper and Improper Use of the Synagogue:** Freehof, *Modern Reform Responsa*, no. 32.

65   **"levity" and "idle chatter" . . . :** B. *Megillah* 28a; *Yad, Tefillah* 11:6; *Shulchan Arukh, Orach Chayim* 151:1. See Freehof, *Current Reform Responsa*, no. 7, where the distinction is drawn between "culture" and "good music" on the one hand and "sensual, riotous jazz" on the other. Jacob, *Questions and Reform Jewish Answers*, no. 52, rules against the performance of a cabaret singing group in the sanctuary.

65   **it is appropriate to take steps . . . :** Freehof, *Modern Reform Responsa*, no. 32; Jacob, *American Reform Responsa*, no. 20.

65   **Weddings may be conducted in the sanctuary . . . :** Maslin, *Gates of Mitzvah*, 32; Freehof, *Reform Jewish Practice*, 1:85–86; *Reform Responsa*, no. 46, at 198.

65   **although not before the open ark . . . :** Freehof, *New Reform Responsa*, no. 42. It is the custom to open the ark at certain particular points in the public liturgy; the wedding is a private service. Also, since it is the custom to remain standing while the ark is opened, this practice would present an inconvenience for those in attendance.

65   **We do not share this concern . . . :** Alongside the frivolity argument, some Orthodox authorities, especially the leading nineteenth-century Hungarian opponents of the Reform movement, forbid weddings in the synagogue on the grounds that the custom was instituted to imitate Gentile religious practice (*Resp. Chatam Sofer* 1:98 and *Resp. Maharam Schick, Even Ha'ezer*, no. 87). On the other hand, synagogue weddings were never forbidden in Germany (*Sefer Maharil, Hilkhot Chatunah; Resp. Yad Halevi*, 2:61) or in most Sefardic communities (*Resp. Ta'alumot Lev*, 3:57 and *Resp. Yabi'a Omer* 3:10). R. Moshe Feinstein rules that there is today no prohibition against weddings in the synagogue (*Resp. Igerot Moshe, Even Ha'ezer* 1:93).

65   **New Year's Eve:** Freehof, *Today's Reform Responsa*, no.11, and Plaut and Washofsky, *Teshuvot*, no. 5753.15.

66   **Gambling:** Jacob, *American Reform Responsa*, no. 168.

66   **Smoking:** Freehof, *Current Reform Responsa*, no. 13.

66   **The Rabbi:** On the history of the rabbinate, see Simon Schwarzfuchs, *A Concise History of the Rabbinate*. On the halakhic debate over the professional rabbinate and rabbinical compensation see Jacob, *American Reform Responsa*, no. 165, and Richard Rheins, "The Development of the Professional Rabbinate as Evidenced in the Halakhic Sources" (Rabbinic thesis, HUC-JIR, 1989). Much of the opposition stems from the midrashic interpretation of Deut. 4:5: just as Moses—the original "rabbi"—taught Torah to Israel without remuneration, so too should we all (*B. Berakhot* 29a). The solution to this problem was the theory of *sekhar batalah*: the rabbi is compensated not for the teaching of Torah (which he does for free) but for the loss of time that, were he not serving as rabbi, he could have devoted to gainful employment. *Halakhah* uses the same theory to permit compensation of physicians for performing the *mitzvah* of healing (*Shulchan Arukh, Yore De'ah* 336:2). For opposing viewpoints on rabbinic compensation, see Rambam's commentary to *M. Avot* 4:5 ("Do not make of the Torah a spade with which to dig"), and *Resp. Tashbetz*, nos. 142–148.

67   **CCAR's *Code of Ethics for Rabbis*:** See *CCAR Yearbook* 103 (1993): 179–87. The reader should consult that document for further details concerning the issues discussed in the text.

67   **Ordination:** Plaut and Washofsky, *Teshuvot*, 5753.4. The ancient ceremony of ordination is patterned after Moses' ordination of Joshua (Num. 27:18). On *semikhah* and the status of the *musmakh* (one who has received ordination), see *B. Sanhedrin* 5a and 13b; *B. Gittin* 88b (on Exod. 21:1); *B. Sanhedrin* 56b (on Exod. 22:7–8); *B. Bava Kama* 84a–b; and *Yad, Sanhedrin* 4:1–11. Today, "we are all *hedyotot* [i.e., non-ordained scholars]; we do not exercise the power of Toraitic jurisdiction"; *Tur, Choshen Mishpat* 1. Thus, a rabbi's rulings are null and void in the absence of community acceptance (*Tur, Choshen Mishpat* 3). On contemporary ordination see *Resp. Rivash*, no. 271; Isserles, *Yore De'ah* 242:14; *Arukh Hashulchan, Choshen Mishpat* 1:14; and Breuer, "Hasemikhah Ha'ashkenazit," *Zion* 33 (1968): 15–46.

68   **Reform Judaism discourages the practice of "private ordination"** . . . : Plaut and Washofsky, *Teshuvot*, no. 5753.4.

68   **persons who have received rabbinic certification** . . . : *Responsa Committee*, no. 5759.3.

69   **Duties and Prerogatives:** On funerals without the participation of a rabbi, see Jacob, *Contemporary American Reform Responsa*, no. 90. It is true, of course, that Jewish tradition does know of priests. The biblical priests (*kohanim*) played a central and exclusive cultic role in the Temple. Moreover, the *kohanim* today retain some of their priestly prerogatives (*matanot kehunah*) in traditional Judaism: the *Kohen* is called first to the Torah, recites the priestly benediction at festivals, is an essential participant in the ceremony of *pidyon haben*, etc. Still, in almost all aspects of contemporary Jewish ritual life, including the prayer service and most life-cycle events, the priest plays no formal role. The rabbi need not be a *Kohen*, nor does the rabbi serve as a substitute for a *Kohen* in any act where the tradition requires a priest's participation.

69   **could insure a proper degree of competent supervision** . . . : The need for expert supervision over weddings is usually based upon the statement in *B. Kiddushin* 6a:

"one who does not understand thoroughly the laws of marriage and divorce should have nothing to do with these matters."

69   **it has become customary . . . for weddings to be performed by the rabbi:** One of the earliest evidences of this is a responsum of Maimonides (12th century) indicating that the local rabbinical authority was present at all weddings (*Resp. Rambam*, ed. Freimann, no. 156). See Jacob, *American Reform Responsa*, no. 130.

69   **"the performing of marriages is . . . the exclusive function of the rabbi":** Jacob, *American Reform Responsa*, no. 130, p. 401; idem, no. 131.

70   **Rabbinic Jurisdiction:** *Code of Ethics for Rabbis*, 180–83; Jacob,*Contemporary American Reform Responsa*, no. 1.

70   **the rabbi's relationships with the other rabbis and religious professionals of the congregation . . . :** For example, the senior rabbi must accord an assistant or associate rabbi the same freedom of the pulpit and opportunities for professional growth and development that the senior enjoys. The assistant or associate must consult with the rabbi concerning life-cycle ceremonies and other duties. For details, see *Code of Ethics*.

71   **Rabbinic Fees and Salaries:** *American Reform Responsa*, no. 165; *Code of Ethics*, 183–84.

71   **The Cantor:** See Elbogen, *Jewish Liturgy*, 370–71, and Jacob, *Questions and Reform Jewish Answers*, no. 1. On the qualifications for the *sheliach tzibur*, see B. *Ta'anit* 16a–b; *Shulchan Arukh, Orach Chayim* 53:4–5, especially Isserles ad loc. In the talmudic passage, the verse Jer. 12:8—"she (Israel) has uttered her voice against Me; therefore, I have rejected her"—is interpreted as directed against those who allow unfit persons to serve as *sheliach tzibur*.

Chapter 3: Sabbath and Holiday Observance

73   **"island of holy time in a sea of secular activity":** Peter S. Knobel, ed., *Gates of the Seasons: A Guide to the Jewish Year*, 17.

73   **four separate *mitzvot* . . . :** See *Yad*, Shabbat 29:1 and 30:1ff.

74   **a "foretaste of the World-to-Come":** B. *Berakhot* 57b. See also M. *Tamid* 7:4: "On Shabbat, the Levites in the Temple used to recite 'A psalm, a song for the Sabbath day' (Ps. 92:1): a psalm and song for the World-to-Come, a world that is entirely Shabbat and rest forever more."

74   **"the art of living . . . ":** Mark Dov Shapiro, ed., *Gates of Shabbat: A Guide for Observing Shabbat*, 1.

74   **Reform thought on the subject of Sabbath observance . . . :** See W. Gunther Plaut, *A Shabbat Manual*, 2–4.

74   **These books have emerged . . . :** For the quotations in the text, see Plaut, *A Shabbat Manual*, 1–8 ; Knobel, *Gates of the Seasons*, 17; and Shapiro, *Gates of Shabbat*, 91–95.

74   **It is a *mitzvah* to prepare for Shabbat . . . :** Knobel, *Gates of the Seasons*, 24; Shapiro, *Gates of Shabbat*, 97. Some sources classify this *mitzvah* under the heading of *zakhor*, to obligation to "remember" the Shabbat: one should remember the Shabbat all week, organizing one's life and the life of one's household around the coming of the holy day (*Mekhilta* to Exod. 20:8). Thus, if a good thing should come one's way during

the week, one should save it for the Sabbath. *B. Beitzah* 15b–16a. Others see it as an aspect of *kavod*, the duty to "honor" the Sabbath;" *Yad, Shabbat* 30:5–6.

75 **for the giving of tzedakah . . . :** Knobel, *Gates of the Seasons*, 25. See *B. Bava Batra* 8b, *Yad, Matanot Aniyim* 9:1 and 6, and *Shulchan Arukh, Yore De'ah* 256:1: *tzedakah* was traditionally collected and distributed every Friday, to enable the poor to prepare for Shabbat.

75 **Kindling the Shabbat Lights (Hadlakat Hanerot):** Knobel, *Gates of the Seasons*, 25.

75 **The Rabbis ordained this practice . . . :** *B. Shabbat* 25b; Rashi, s.v. *chovah*; *Tosafot*, s.v. *hadlakat*, *Yad, Shabbat* 5:1 and 30:5; and *Shulchan Arukh, Orach Chayim* 263:2. The practice of kindling the Shabbat lamp, while not mentioned in the Bible, is assumed by the Mishnah (see *M. Shabbat* 2:1ff.). The Talmud links the practice to a biblical prooftext: Lam. 3:17, "my life was bereft of peace." This, say the Rabbis, refers to the Shabbat lamp, since one who lives in darkness knows no peace (*B. Shabbat* 25b, and Rashi, s.v. *hadlakat ner beshabbat*).

75 **For this reason, the Shabbat candles should be large enough . . . :** *Shulchan Arukh, Orach Chayim* 263:9; *Magen Avraham*, no. 16; *Kitzur Shulchan Arukh* 75:2; Freehof, *Contemporary Reform Responsa*, no. 10.

75 **It also marks the formal beginning of Shabbat . . . :** Some put the formal beginning of Shabbat at a later point, at the recitation of the evening prayer prior to nightfall. See *Shulchan Arukh, Orach Chayim* 263:10 and Isserles ad loc.

75 **the special responsibility of women . . . :** *M. Shabbat* 2:6; *Shulchan Arukh, Orach Chayim* 263:2.

75 **since they tended to be at home preparing the meal . . . :** *Yad, Shabbat* 5:3.

75 **men are also required . . . :** *Shulchan Arukh, Orach Chayim* 263:2; Freehof, *Reform Responsa*, no. 1.

75 **When does Shabbat begin?:** See *Shulchan Arukh, Orach Chayim* 261:1–3 and *Mishnah Berurah* ad loc. There is general agreement that "night" (*laila*) is the last stage in a progression that begins at "sunset" (*sheki'ah* or *sheki'at hachamah*) and lasts through "twilight" (*bein hashemashot*). Prior to sunset is definitely "daytime" and following twilight is definitely "night." The candles must therefore be lit *before* twilight. But how long, exactly, does twilight last? According to Maimonides (*Yad, Shabbat* 5:4) and others, "twilight" is a period of approximately a quarter of an hour between sunset and nightfall. Another position, attributed to Rabbenu Tam (*Tosafot, Shabbat* 35a, s.v. *trei*), reckons the duration of "twilight" at about one hour. According to this latter position, Shabbat begins earlier and ends later than it does in the eyes of the more lenient position of Maimonides. The customary practice is to follow Maimonides with respect to the beginning of Shabbat and "to add from the weekday to the holy day" (*lehosif mechol 'al hakodesh*) by lighting the candles at eighteen minutes before sunset. Concerning the end of Shabbat, the customary practice follows Rabbenu Tam: i.e., Shabbat concludes about one hour (instead of fifteen minutes) following sunset on Saturday.

75 **The widespread custom, however, is to kindle two lamps . . . :** *Shulchan Arukh, Orach Chayim* 263:1, from *Sefer Kol Bo*, ch. 31.

76 **Most blessings are recited immediately before the performance . . . :** *Shulchan Arukh, Orach Chayim* 25:8. Covering the flame while reciting the benediction is mentioned in Isserles, *Orach Chayim* 263:5 and *Mishnah Berurah*, nos. 26–27.

76 **Blessing the Children:** Knobel, *Gates of the Seasons*, 27, offers a liturgy for this blessing; Maslin, *Gates of Mitzvah*, 41–42. The blessing follows Gen. 48:20, and see Rashi ad loc. Many add verses from the Priestly Benediction (Num. 6:24–26). For the traditional liturgy see S. Baer, *Seder Avodat Yisrael*, 195.

76 **Kiddush:** Knobel, *Gates of the Seasons*, 26. See *B. Pesachim* 106a on Exod. 20:8: "*Remember* the Sabbath day": i.e., "remember" it (call it to mind) over wine. Some authorities, notably Maimonides (*Yad, Shabbat* 29:1, 6) and *Tosafot* (*Pesachim* 106a, s.v. *zokhreihu*), hold that we fulfill the Toraitic requirement of *Kiddush* simply by "saying something," such as the benediction *Kedushat Hayom* ("Blessed are You, Adonai, who sanctifies the Sabbath") during the Shabbat evening *Tefillah.* They view the use of wine as a rabbinic ordinance, based upon metaphorical allusions in Hosea 14:8 and Song of Songs 1:4, undertaken perhaps as a means of enhancing the solemn festivity of the Shabbat meal. Rashi, on the other hand, (*B. Berakhot* 20b, s.v. *Kiddush Hayom*) seems to regard wine as an integral feature of the Torah's *mitzvah* of *Kiddush.* His position is supported by most recent halakhists; see *Arukh Hashulchan, Orach Chayim* 271, par. 3 and *Mishnah Berurah* 271, no. 2, and *Bi'ur Halakhah* ad loc. The latter makes the point that the fulfillment of *mitzvot* must be considered within the social context of one's religious life: an individual surely intends to carry out the requirement of *Kiddush* at home, over the Shabbat meal, rather than during the *Tefillah.*

76 **It therefore consists of two blessings . . . :** The benediction over wine precedes the *Kiddush* benediction; see *B. Berakhot* 51b, following the school of Hillel; *Yad, Shabbat* 29:7, and *Shulchan Arukh, Orach Chayim* 271:10.

76 **While the *Kiddush* should ideally be recited in Hebrew . . . :** Shapiro, *Gates of Shabbat*, 26. Should one not be able to recite the full Hebrew text, one may say the benediction *borei peri hagafen* in Hebrew and the *Kiddush* benediction in the vernacular, hopefully learning the Hebrew for that *berakhah* over time.

76 **it is customary to recite the verses of Genesis 1:31 through 2:3 . . . :** *Yad, Shabbat* 29:7; *Shulchan Arukh, Orach Chayim* 271:10. The requirement to recite these verses, which are part of the traditional text of the *Tefillah* for Friday night, is mentioned in *B. Shabbat* 119b: "Scripture regards the one who says these verses in the Shabbat evening prayer as God's partner in the work of Creation." It is recited over the home *Kiddush* so that the entire household, including those who did not attend synagogue or pray at home (traditionally, the Shabbat evening service *precedes* the meal), may hear the passage and fulfill this requirement.

77 **The proper place . . . :** *B. Pesachim* 101a; *Yad, Shabbat* 29:8; *Shulchan Arukh, Orach Chayim* 273:1. The reason: "if you call the Sabbath a 'delight' [*oneg*]" (Isa. 58:13), and true delight is found at the place where we take our Shabbat meal. See *Beit Yosef, Orach Chayim* 273.

77 **many traditional authorities require that we recite it while seated . . . :** Isserles, *Shulchan Arukh, Orach Chayim* 271:10, from *Sefer Kol Bo; Mishnah Berurah* ad loc., no. 46. Maimonides, *Yad, Sukkah* 6:12, apparently agrees; see Rabad and *Magid Mishneh* ad loc. The kabbalists, on the other hand, held that *Kiddush* be said while standing, for the Sabbath is like a bride, and the wedding benedictions are recited while *standing* under the *chupah.* See *Arukh Hashulchan, Orach Chayim* 271, par. 24.

77 **The *Kiddush* recited in synagogue is not a substitute . . . :** Knobel, *Gates of the Seasons*, 27.

77 **Since wine is traditionally associated with joy . . . :** Shapiro, *Gates of Shabbat*, 25. Cf. Ps. 104:15: "wine, which gladdens the human heart."

77   **the Rabbis decreed . . . :** *B. Pesachim* 106a.

77   **The term "wine" refers to grape wine . . . :** *"Kiddush* is recited only over wine acceptable for the libations upon the Temple altar" (*B. Bava Batra* 97a; *Yad, Shabbat* 29:14). Tradition does not take these words to be exclusive, since they would forbid the use of other beverages for *Kiddush*; see the Notes below concerning the *Kiddush* on Shabbat morning.

77   **unfermented grape juice . . . :** *B. Bava Batra* 97b; *Yad, Shabbat* 29:17; *Shulchan Arukh, Orach Chayim* 272:2.

77   **In some communities . . . :** based upon Prov. 23:31, interpreted to mean that red wine is of higher quality than white wine. See *B. Bava Batra* 97b and Rashbam ad loc., s.v. *ki yitadam.* An opinion in *Y. Shekalim* 3:2 suggests that it is preferable to recite *Kiddush* over red wine, and one authority (Ramban, *Chidushim, Bava Batra* 97b) actually forbids white wine for that purpose. Most, however, permit white wine for *Kiddush,* especially when it is of higher quality than the available red wine (*Tur, Orach Chayim* 472; *Shulchan Arukh, Orach Chayim* 272:4 and *Mishnah Berurah,* no. 10).

77   **If no wine is available . . . :** See Plaut and Washofsky, *Teshuvot,* no. 5755.16, and Jacob, *American Reform Responsa,* no. 47. While alternatives are permitted, the tradition prefers that *Kiddush* be recited over wine whenever possible; see *Mishnah Berurah* 272, no. 32.

77   ***Kiddush* may be recited over the bread . . . :** *B. Pesachim* 106b; *Yad, Shabbat* 29:9; *Shulchan Arukh, Orach Chayim* 272:9.

77   **a Kiddush to begin the noon meal . . . :** Knobel, *Gates of the Seasons,* 46–48. *B. Pesachim* 106a; *Shulchan Arukh, Orach Chayim* 289:1–2.

77   **Frequently, beverages other than wine are used . . . :** *Kiddush* may be recited over a "fine beverage" (*chamar medinah*) other than water which serves in place of wine as the drink of choice in a particular locale. This practice became widespread in eastern Europe, where the available wines were expensive and inferior in quality to other intoxicants. It is generally not followed for Friday night, however, since some authorities oppose the use of any beverages other than wine for *Kiddush.* Moreover, since the evening *Kiddush* must in any case be recited at the meal, tradition prefers the use of bread rather than *chamar medinah* on Friday night when wine is not available. (*Hilkhot Harosh, Pesachim* 10:17; *Shulchan Arukh, Orach Chayim* 272:9 and 289:2; *Arukh Hashulchan, Orach Chayim* 272, pars. 11ff.)

77   **called euphemistically *Kiddusha Rabbah* . . . :** A euphemism, that is, because this *Kiddush* is quite short. Unlike the *Kiddush* on Friday night, which comes to fulfill the Toraitic commandment to "remember the Sabbath day" (Exod. 20:8), the daytime *Kiddush* is but a rabbinic (that is, a lesser) ordinance; *Mishnah Berurah* 289, no. 3.

77   ***Hamotzi:*** Knobel, *Gates of the Seasons,* 28–29.

77   ***challah:*** The Torah requires that a portion of the dough be separated and offered to God; see Num. 15:17–21. Ironically, the word *challah* describes this separated portion, which we are *not* supposed to eat; eventually, however, it came to be applied to the loaves themselves.

77   **preferably unbroken and unsliced . . . :** *B. Berakhot* 39b; *Yad, Berakhot* 7:4; *Shulchan Arukh, Orach Chayim* 274:1. The requirement of whole loaves is *mitzvah min hamuvchar,* "the best way" to perform the ritual, not an absolute requirement. Still, one should strive to bring two uncut loaves to the Shabbat table (Freehof,

Modern Reform Responsa, no. 16). It is perfectly permissible to use a small loaf or even a roll for either of the two *challot.*

77   **double portion of manna . . . :** Exod. 16:22; *B. Shabbat* 117b; *Yad, Shabbat* 30:9; *Shulchan Arukh, Orach Chayim* 274:1.

77   **and covered with a cloth . . . :** Since we are permitted to say *Kiddush* over bread and since bread, the major symbol of the meal, would logically take precedence over wine, we cover the bread as a way of "removing" it from sight. This allows us to use the wine for *Kiddush* and to spare the bread the "embarrassment" of being relegated to second place (*Tur, Orach Chayim* 471).

77   **a ritual washing of the hands . . .** Shapiro, *Gates of Shabbat*, 28–29. Traditionally, the ritual hand-washing is required whenever one eats bread. *Yad, Berakhot* 6:1; *Shulchan Arukh, Orach Chayim* 158:1. The requirement of a vessel is also derived from Temple practice (*B. Chulin* 107a; *Shulchan Arukh, Orach Chayim* 159:1 and *Mishnah Berurah*, no. 1).

78   **salt is often sprinkled . . . :** after Lev. 2:13. See Knobel, *Gates of the Seasons*, 29.

78   **The Shabbat Table:** Knobel, Gates *of the Seasons*, 29; Shapiro, *Gates of Shabbat*, 31.

78   **Even our conversation should be different . . . :** See *B. Shabbat* 113a–b on Isaiah 58:13.

78   **"idle talk" . . . :** *Yad, Shabbat* 24:4 and *Shulchan Arukh, Orach Chayim* 306:1.

78   **It is a mitzvah to conclude the Shabbat meal with the Grace . . . :** Knobel, *Gates of the Seasons*, 29. For the special paragraph for Shabbat, "Eternal God, strengthen our resolve" (*retzei vehachalitzeinu*), see Stern, *On the Doorposts of Your House*, 13.

78   **The Shabbat midday meal . . . :** Shapiro, *Gates of Shabbat*, 46–48. It is called the "morning feast" (*se'udat Shacharit*) in the sources. In former times the Shabbat worship service was conducted much earlier in the day than is our custom; hence, "lunch" would have been served before noon.

78   **a brief *Kiddush* . . . :** *B. Pesachim* 106a. For the liturgy, see Shapiro, *Gates of Shabbat*, 47 and Stern, *Gates of Prayer*, 720.

78   **se'udah shelishit . . . :** *B. Shabbat* 118a. In ancient times, the average person was seldom able to enjoy three fixed meals per day. For this reason, the eating of a third meal fulfills the *mitzvah* of *oneg shabbat*, delighting in the Sabbath (*Yad, Shabbat* 30:9). The meal is traditionally served following the afternoon prayer (*Minchah*) and prior to the conclusion of Shabbat. It can consist of a light snack, should one not be hungry following the noontime meal, provided it includes bread so that *Hamotzi* and *Birkat Hamazon* can be recited.

79   ***Havdalah:*** Knobel, *Gates of the Seasons*, 31; Maimonides regards *Havdalah* as a requirement of Toraitic law, as is *Kiddush*: "One is required to *remember* Shabbat (Exod. 20:8) both when it enters and when it departs" (*Yad, Shabbat* 29:1). Others regard it as a rabbinic ordinance; see *Magid Mishneh* ad loc.

79   **four berakhot . . . :** *B. Berakhot* 52b; *Yad, Shabbat* 29:24; *Shulchan Arukh, Orach Chayim* 296:1.

79   **The blessing over wine . . . :** On "substitute beverages," see the discussion of *chamar medinah* in the Notes above concerning the *Kiddush* at the Shabbat noon meal. Bread cannot be used in place of wine at *Havdalah* as it is with *Kiddush*, since unlike the latter, *Havdalah* is not said in conjunction with a meal at which bread is the principal ritual element; *Shulchan Arukh, Orach Chayim* 296:2 and *Mishnah Berurah*, no. 7.

79   **The blessing over spices . . . :** See Hoffman, *Gates of Understanding*, 1:253.

79   **"additional soul" . . .** *B. Beitzah* 16a. See *Tosafot Beitzah* 33b, s.v. *ki haveinan*: a festival, unlike Shabbat, brings us no "additional soul"; hence, when we recite *Havdalah* at the conclusion of a festival, we do not say a blessing over spices.

79   **The blessing over fire . . . :** One does not recite a blessing over the fire unless one is near enough to it to make use of its light. The practice of cupping the hands and examining the light upon one's fingernails is a means of fulfilling this requirement (*M. Berakhot* 8:6; *B. Berakhot* 53b; *Shulchan Arukh, Orach Chayim* 298:3–4).

80   **God created fire . . . :** *B. Berakhot* 54a; *Pirkei deR. Eliezer*, ch. 20. Adam and Eve were driven from the Garden of Eden at twilight on the sixth day of creation. During the following day, they enjoyed the celestial light of Shabbat, but as the sun set they grew fearful of the gathering darkness, which they were now experiencing for the very first time. God showed them how to create fire, whose light made them feel safe and assured them that God would be with them and their children even in their exile from the Garden.

80   **A candle with multiple wicks . . . :** *B. Pesachim* 103a. If one does not have a special *Havdalah* candle, one may light a candle of any kind, so long as it is a light other than the one which provides illumination for the room. Electric lights, according to some halakhists, are permitted for *Havdalah* (*She'arim Metzuyanim Bahalakhah*, ch. 96, no. 6; *Resp. Tzitz Eliezer* 1:20, par. 13).

80   **"lights" of various colors . . . :** *B. Berakhot* 52b; Rashi, s.v. *harbeh me'orot*.

80   **the *Havdalah* benediction . . . :** In some rites, those present then take a bit of the wine on their fingertips and place it upon their eyelids, as a sign of their love for this *mitzvah* (*Tur, Orach Chayim* 299).

80   **the candle is extinguished in the remaining wine . . . :** to show that this light was kindled only for the *mitzvah* of *Havdalah* and not for any other purpose (*Levush, Orach Chayim* 296:1).

80   **Israel's longing for messianic redemption:** This is especially evident in the hymn *Eliyahu Hanavi*, "Elijah the Prophet," who is said in the tradition to be the harbinger of the Messiah.

80   **a foretaste of the World-to-Come . . . :** *B. Berakhot* 57b.

80   **"never-ending Shabbat" . . . :** *M. Tamid* 7:4.

80   **"the world will be perfected under [God's] unchallenged will":** From the *Aleinu*; *Gates of Prayer*, 616.

80   **Lighting of the Candles (*Hadlakat Hanerot*):** Since the lighting of the candles in the synagogue is a Reform innovation in Jewish practice, no traditional rules apply. Congregants may wish to stand as a sign of respect for the ritual and as a way of demonstrating that its importance is equal to that of the synagogue *Kiddush*, for which we do stand (Freehof, *New Reform Responsa*, no. 6).

81   **In some congregations, the lights are kindled prior to the onset of Shabbat . . . :** Freehof, *Reform Responsa for Our Time*, no. 1; Hoffman, *Gates of Understanding*, 1:201.

81   ***Kabbalat Shabbat*:** Hoffman, *Gates of Understanding*, 1:201–3; Elbogen, *Jewish Liturgy*, 92. The service was created by the kabbalistic scholars of Safed near the end of the sixteenth century as an expansion upon the practice of some ancient sages to greet the Shabbat Queen or Bride at the limits of the city (*B. Bava Kama* 32a–b).

81   **the order of *Kabbalat Shabbat* in the traditional *siddur* . . . :** six psalms (95–99 and 29), corresponding to the six days of creation, followed by *Lekha Dodi*, and Psalms 92 and 93, which evoke the Sabbath. See Daniel Sperber, *Minhagei Yisrael*, 1:67ff..

81   ***Chatzi Kaddish; Keri'at Shema:*** Hoffman, *Gates of Understanding*, 1:203–4.

81   **The *Tefillah*:** The berakhah, *Kedushat Hayom* ends "*mekadesh hashabbat*" ("who sanctifies the Sabbath"). In the traditional *siddur*, this blessing treats the three-fold nature of God's relationship to the world and to humankind: the evening *Tefillah*, *Ma'ariv*, speaks of God as creator of the universe; the morning *Tefillah*, *Shacharit*, acknowledges God's revelation, God's function as teacher of Torah to the people Israel; and the afternoon *Tefillah*, *Minchah*, declares our faith in God's redemption. These themes are most clearly evident in *Gates of Prayer*'s Shabbat Evening Service I (136), Shabbat Morning Service I (309); and in the Afternoon Service (565).

81   ***me'ein sheva* . . . :** Originally instituted for the benefit of latecomers to the service who missed the *Tefillah*; Hoffman, *Gates of Understanding*, 1:205. It may also have been introduced into the service as a replacement for the *Tefillah*, which in traditional congregations the prayer leader (*sheliach tzibur*) does not repeat at the evening service; Elbogen, *Jewish Liturgy*, 94.

81   ***Keri'at Hatorah:*** *Gates of Prayer*, 417ff. Traditionally, the Torah is read at morning services, with the exception of the festival of Simchat Torah, when it is read at night as well. There are two obvious halakhic objections to reading the Torah on Friday night. First, if the Torah will be read on Shabbat morning, the reading on Friday night involves the saying of an unnecessary benediction (*berakhah levatalah*). Second, the Friday night reading is frowned upon as an innovation in ritual practice with no clear source in the Talmud and the legal authorities (see *Resp. Meshiv Davar*, no. 16). These objections do not apply to the Reform context, particularly for those small congregations that do not hold Shabbat morning services. Moreover, since we are not opposed to the introduction of new practices merely because they are innovations, there is nothing "unnecessary" about the benedictions we say (Freehof, *Modern Reform Responsa*, no. 1).

81   **Concluding Prayers:** *Gates of Prayer*, 615ff.

81   **the congregation recites *Kiddush* . . . :** B. *Pesachim* 101a; *Shulchan Arukh, Orach Chayim* 269.

81   **The reason for retaining the congregational *Kiddush* . . . :** *Sefer Kol Bo*, ch. 58.

82   **On *Menuchah* . . . :** The two themes are expressed in the two versions of the Ten Commandments (Exod. 20:11 and Deut. 5:15). See the comments of Rashi and Nachmanides to the Deuteronomy passage.

82   **a prohibition which the Torah mentions . . . :** Exod. 20:10; 31:14; 31:15; 35:2; Lev. 23:3; Deut. 5:14.

82   **The Torah never defines the concept of "work" . . . :** Although the Bible does give examples of prohibited activity (Exod. 35:3; 34:21; Num. 15:32–35; Jer. 17:21–22; Neh. 13:15–17). Exodus 34:21, which mentions "plowing" and "harvesting," may actually suggest a general definition which restricts the prohibition to agricultural labor. The other biblical sources, however, understand the prohibition as applying to other types of labor as well.

82   **thirty-nine general categories . . . :** M. *Shabbat* 7:2.

82   **though at times they concede . . . :** M. *Chagigah* 1:8.

82   **From this fact, declares one *midrash* . . . :** *Mekhilta* to Exod. 35:1, B. *Shabbat* 49b, and Rashi to Exod. 35:2.

83   **Over the centuries . . . :** This expansion has been accomplished largely by way of analogy. Electricity, for example, resembles fire; therefore, just as it is forbidden to kindle or extinguish a fire, it is likewise forbidden to turn an electric appliance on or off. On the other hand, the traditional conception is that the Torah prohibits these labors only in the manner in which they are normally performed. When done in an unusual manner (*kele'achar yad*) or through indirect causation (*gerama*; a common example is the use of an automatic timer to turn lights on or off), an action otherwise prohibited on Shabbat may in fact be permitted or tolerated. For a detailed discussion of all the rules pertaining to work on Shabbat, see Yehoshua Noivirt, *Shemirath Shabbath: A Guide to the Practical Observance of the Sabbath.*

83   **In addition, the Rabbis enacted numerous rules of their own . . . :** The term for these is *shevut*, a decree intended to keep one far from transgressing the actual prohibition against work or from violating the special nature of the day. See *Yad, Shabbat* 21:1 and *Magid Mishneh* ad loc.

83   **"fences around the Torah":** See *M. Avot* 1:1.

83   **a massive and complex subject . . . :** The laws concerning the prohibition of work on Shabbat occupy 115 chapters of the *Shulchan Arukh.*

83   **Reform Attitudes:** See Knobel, *Gates of the Seasons,* 49–59.

83   **"In creating a contemporary approach . . . ":** ibid., 57

84   **Personal Activities:** Shapiro, *Gates of Shabbat,* 49–56.

85   **Jewish tradition allows a community to hold a business meeting . . . :** Isaiah 58:13, "if you refrain from … pursuing your affairs on My holy day," is understood to prohibit us from pursuing our own business on Shabbat; the pursuit of "Heaven's business" (*tzedakah*, the public welfare), by contrast, is permitted. B. *Shabbat* 150a; *Yad, Shabbat* 24:5; *Shulchan Arukh, Orach Chayim* 306:6. See, in general, Freehof, *Contemporary Reform Responsa,* no. 12.

85   **"we have sought in every way to enhance Shabbat . . . ":** Jacob, *Questions and Reform Jewish Answers,* no. 60.

85   **it is inappropriate in the absence of an emergency situation . . . :** Plaut and Washofsky, *Teshuvot,* no. 5751.5; see also Freehof, *Reform Responsa,* no. 8.

85   **Congregational fundraising projects . . . :** *Responsa Committee,* 5756.4; Jacob, *Contemporary American Reform Responsa,* no. 177.

85   ***tzedakah* projects . . . :** *Response Committee,* no. 5757.7; Jacob, *Contemporary American Reform Responsa,* no. 176, and Plaut and Washofsky, *Teshuvot,* no. 5753.22. See also idem, no. 5755.12: "the fact that Shabbat 'conflicts' with another mitzvah or worthy cause does not mean that it is Shabbat which must give way. Indeed, the reverse is often the case." An exception is the saving of life (*pikuach nefesh*), which does supersede the Shabbat restrictions. Thus, concerning the "Christmas *mitzvah*" projects in which Jews substitute for Christian workers on December 24 or 25: when these days coincide with Shabbat, we substitute only for workers engaged in lifesaving activity (hospitals; institutions of public safety); Jacob, *American Reform Responsa,* no. 52.

85   **the synagogue gift shop . . . :** Freehof, *Reform Responsa,* no. 9. Rabbi Freehof argues that the gift shop is an agency that functions for the religious benefit of the commu-

nity; thus, like meetings to discuss *tzedakah* and other *mitzvot*, it is an example of "Heaven's business" that may legitimately be pursued on Shabbat. His suggestion is based upon what he calls "our present vague relationship with the Sabbath laws." Given the powerful emphasis which the Reform movement has in recent years placed upon the observance of Shabbat and its spirit, our "relationship" today may well be less vague. If so, it is appropriate to ask whether this leniency ought to be maintained.

85 **Synagogue Employees:** *Halakhah* permits the Gentile to do work for the Jew on the Sabbath if the transaction is defined as a contract (*kablanut*), in which the employer says "do such-and-such labors for me" and leaves it to the contractor to decide when to do them. The contractor may "decide" to do the work on Shabbat; technically, the Jewish employer does not make this a requirement of the job. The work should not be done openly or "in public," thereby calling attention to the fact that Gentiles are working for Jews on the Sabbath. By contrast, it is forbidden to hire a non-Jew explicitly to work on Shabbat, and it is also forbidden to pay a laborer who is compensated by the day or by the hour for labor performed on Shabbat. Synagogues tend to define their employees as "contractors" for this purpose. See *Shulchan Arukh, Orach Chayim* 244. Like all legal fictions, this one pays homage to an essential value of the law (i.e., that we do not require our employees to work on Shabbat) while seeking a means to loosen its restrictions. In Reform thought, which looks askance at legal fictions generally, the essential issue is one of communal sensibility: we may hire Gentiles to perform labor for us on Shabbat so long as the labor in question does not offend our conception of proper Shabbat observance. See Freehof, *Current Reform Responsa*, no. 53, 225–26.

86 **Weddings:** *B. Beitzah* 36b–37a; *Shulchan Arukh, Orach Chayim* 339:4 and *Even Ha'ezer* 64:5; Jacob, *American Reform Responsa*, no. 136, Freehof, *Recent Reform Responsa*, no. 36; Shapiro, *Gates of Shabbat*, 58. See the discussion on weddings in Chapter 4.

86 **Funerals:** Shapiro, *Gates of Shabbat*, 58; Freehof, *Reform Jewish Practice*, 1:117. See the discussion on funerals in Chapter 4.

86 **Circumcision (Berit Milah):** *B. Shabbat 132a; Yad, Milah 1:9; Shulchan Arukh, Yore De'ah 266:2.*

86 **if an infant's circumcision has been delayed . . . :** Plaut and Washofsky, *Teshuvot*, no. 5755.12.

87 **The Calendar:** Much of the traditional material on the process of calendation can be found in the Mishnah, tractate *Rosh Hashanah*, chs. 1 through 3:1, and its talmudic commentary and expansion. Maimonides reworks these sources in *Yad, Kiddush Hachodesh*, which remains the single best treatise on the laws of the Jewish calendar. For historical background, see Bernard J. Bamberger, "The Festival Calendar" in W. G. Plaut, ed., *The Torah: A Modern Commentary*, 919–23, along with the sources cited there; Alexander Guttmann, "The Jewish Calendar" in Knobel, *Gates of the Seasons*, 7–11; and E.J. Wiesenberg, "Calendar" in *Encyclopaedia Judaica*, 5:43–50.

88 **Reform congregations generally observe Rosh Chodesh for one day . . . :** Hoffman, *Gates of Understanding*, 1:284; Knobel, *Gates of the Seasons*, 139, n. 220. This is consistent with the Reform practice of maintaining each biblical festival day as a one-day observance, rather than celebrating it for two days as do most other Diaspora communities. Yet the reason why festivals are traditionally observed for two days is essentially different from that which explains why Rosh Chodesh sometimes lasts for two days. The second festival day originated because Diaspora communities, far from the Great Court in Jerusalem, were in doubt as to the correct day on which to declare

the holiday. The second day of Rosh Chodesh, by contrast, is not a response to doubt but an integral feature of the calendar system, similar to the addition of a second month of Adar in "leap years." Reform Jews do observe the second Adar because they maintain the basic system of the traditional Jewish calendar. It might therefore be argued that a Reform congregation should observe Rosh Chodesh for two days whenever the traditional calendar so indicates.

88   **unacceptable complications in Jewish ritual life . . . :** See *Yad, Kiddush Hachodesh* 7:1. If Rosh Hashanah (1 Tishri) falls on a Wednesday, Yom Kippur (10 Tishri) will be on a Friday; if Rosh Hashanah occurs on a Friday, then Yom Kippur will fall on a Sunday. In either case, we would have two consecutive days (Yom Kippur and Shabbat) on which it is traditionally prohibited to cook, resulting in serious hardship for the people. If Rosh Hashanah falls on a Sunday, then Hoshana Rabbah (21 Tishri) will occur on Shabbat. A major observance of Hoshana Rabbah is the beating of willow branches upon the altar or the bimah. Lest the people be tempted to carry their willow branches to the synagogue (and thereby violate the traditional prohibition against carrying objects in the public thoroughfare on Shabbat), we make sure that the day does not occur on Shabbat.

89   **The Year:** See *B. Sanhedrin* 11b–12b and *Yad, Kiddush Hachodesh* 4.

89   **The blessing of the new month . . . :** Hoffman, *Gates of Understanding,* 1:236–37. Isserles, *Shulchan Arukh, Orach Chayim* 284:7. Elbogen, *Jewish Liturgy,* 94–95.

89   **"Be mindful of Your people" . . . :** Hoffman, *Gates of Understanding,* 1:192. *B. Shabbat* 24a; *Yad, Tefillah* 2:10; *Shulchan Arukh, Orach Chayim* 222:1. The passage is part of the traditional festival *Tefillah,* indicating that Rosh Chodesh enjoys something of a festive status. It is traditionally included within *avodah,* the seventeenth benediction of the *Tefillah. Gates of Prayer* places it as a separate rubric.

89   **and into the Grace after Meals (Birkat Hamazon):** *B. Shabbat* 24a; *Yad, Berakhot* 2:5; *Shulchan Arukh, Orach Chayim* 224; Stern, *On the Doorposts of Your House,* 13–14.

90   **The Hallel:** Hoffman, *Gates of Understanding,* 1:241–42. According to talmudic tradition, the ancient Rabbis ordained that the full text of this *Hallel* (the word means "praise") be recited on days celebrating God's redemptive power in Jewish history: the eight days of Sukkot and Shemini Atzeret, the eight days of Chanukah, the first day of Pesach, and Shavuot. To these, traditional communities in the Diaspora add the second day of Pesach, Shemini Atzeret (Simchat Torah), and Shavuot. Since Rosh Chodesh is neither a festival (since it is permitted to do work) nor a time of remembrance of God's deliverance, the Rabbis did not decree that *Hallel* be recited that day. The practice to recite it on Rosh Chodesh is a custom (*minhag*) stretching back to Babylonia in talmudic times. Therefore, the *Hallel* is recited in abbreviated form on Rosh Chodesh (Ps. 115:1–11 and 116:1–11 are omitted) as a sign that its recitation on this day is a custom and not a rabbinic decree. See *B. Arakhin* 10b and *B. Ta'anit* 28b; *Yad, Chanukah* 3:5–14; *Shulchan Arukh, Orach Chayim* 222:2.

90   **It is customary to begin the Hallel . . . :** Isserles, *Shulchan Arukh, Orach Chayim* 222:2, reflecting the Ashkenazic practice to recite a blessing over the performance of a *minhag,* an observance based in custom, as well as over a *mitzvah,* an obligation based in Toraitic or rabbinic law (see *Tosafot, Arakhin* 10a–b).

90   **The Torah is read:** *M. Megillah* 4:2; *Yad, Tefillah* 13:4; *Shulchan Arukh, Orach Chayim* 223:1–2. On the difficulties in dividing the first *parashah* of this reading (vv. 1–8), see *B. Megillah* 21b–22a.

90   **In Reform practice . . .** : Hoffman, *Gates of Understanding*, 1:284. This shorter reading corresponds to the custom mentioned in *M. Megillah* 3:6. In traditional congregations, this shorter passage is read from a second scroll when Rosh Chodesh occurs on Shabbat; the weekly portion is read from the first scroll.

90   **It is not forbidden to do work . . .** : There is, however, some evidence that Rosh Chodesh was actually observed as a festival, a day on which work was not performed, during biblical times; see II Kings 4:23 and Amos 8:5. Moreover, Rosh Chodesh resembles the other biblical holy days in that an "additional" sacrifice (*Musaf*) was offered in the Temple on that day (Num. 28:11–15), paralleling the *Musaf* offered on Shabbat and festivals. The custom for women to abstain from work on Rosh Chodesh is mentioned in *Y. Ta'anit* 1:6. The legend concerning the Golden Calf is found in *Pirkei deR. Eliezer*, ch. 44. See *Tur* and *Shulchan Arukh, Orach Chayim* 417.

90   **many Jewish women have chosen to revive the ancient tradition . . .** : Knobel, *Gates of the Seasons*, 101.

91   **Simchah—It is a *mitzvah* to rejoice . . .** : Knobel, *Gates of the Seasons*, 61; Deut. 16:14.

91   **As the Talmud understands it . . .** : *B. Pesachim* 68b and *B. Beitzah* 15b. This insight is based upon the following *midrash*: in one verse, we read that "it is a solemn gathering [*atzeret*] for Adonai your God" (Deut. 16:8); in another, we read that "it shall be a solemn gathering for you" (Num. 29:35). If the festival day is devoted to God, how can it be for *us*? The solution to this dilemma: divide the day, half "for God" (that is, devoted to the study of Torah), and half "for you" (that is, the festive meal).

91   **Originally, this notion of festivity . . .** : See *B. Pesachim* 109a.

91   **We "rejoice" in the festival in much the same way . . .** : Knobel, *Gates of the Seasons*, 61–62.

92   **the recitation of *Kiddush* . . .** : The festivals are also called "sabbaths" (Lev. 23:39 and 23:24, concerning Rosh Hashanah); hence, says Rambam, we learn that there is a Toraitic requirement to recite *Kiddush* on a festival as well as on Shabbat (*Yad, Shabbat* 29:18; and see *Mekhilta, Yitro* 4, ed. Horowitz-Rabin, 229, and *Torah Temimah* to Lev. 23, no. 6). Other authorities hold the festival *Kiddush* to be a rabbinic enactment (*Magid Mishneh* to *Yad* ad loc.; *Magen Avraham, Orach Chayim* 271, no. 2; *Mishnah Berurah, Orach Chayim* 271, no. 2). *Shehechiyanu* is not recited on the seventh day of Pesach, since that day is not considered a festival in its own right; *B. Pesachim* 102b; *Shulchan Arukh, Orach Chayim* 490:7 and *Mishnah Berurah*, nos. 11–13.

92   ***Havdalah . . .*** : The blessing over the spices is traditionally omitted at the conclusion of a festival. That blessing is recited as a consolation for the loss of the "additional soul" with which we are blessed on Shabbat, and "we receive no additional soul on a festival." However, since the festivals are referred to as "sabbaths" (see above paragraph), one might well say this *berakhah* at the *Havdalah* concluding a *yom tov*. In addition, the blessing over fire is also omitted at the conclusion of a festival, since that blessing symbolizes events and laws that relate to Shabbat and *not* to festivals (*Yad, Shabbat* 29:28–29; *Shulchan Arukh, Orach Chayim* 491:1; *Magen Avraham* ad loc.).

92   **formal mourning is suspended . . .** : Knobel, *Gates of the Seasons*, 62–63. For details concerning the suspension of *shivah* by a festival, see the discussion of mourning in Chapter 4.

92   **Weddings are not held . . .** : Ibid., 63, and see the discussion of weddings in Chapter 4.

92   **we should not mix our own personal** *simchah* **. . . :** *B. Mo'ed Katan* 8b–9a; *Yad, Yom Tov* 7:16 and *Ishut* 10:14. Traditionally, this reasoning applies to *chol hamo'ed,* the intermediate days of the festivals of Pesach and Sukkot, as well as to the festival days themselves. In Reform practice, however, weddings may be held on *chol hamo'ed.*

92   **It is a** *mitzvah* **to abstain from work on the festivals:** Knobel, *Gates of the Seasons,* 62.

92   **According to tradition . . . :** On the rules concerning labor on the festivals, see *Yad, Yom Tov* 1:1–4. The distinction between Shabbat and *yom tov* flows from the language of Scripture, which prohibits work (*melakhah*) on Shabbat (Exod. 20:10 and elsewhere) and on Yom Kippur (Lev. 23:28 and Num. 29:7) while prohibiting something called *melekhet avodah,* variously translated as "servile labor" or "normal occupations," on the festival day (Lev. 23:7 and elsewhere). Nachmanides, in his Commentary to Lev. 23:7, defines it as any kind of work that is not directed toward the preparation of food, an act which Exod. 12:16 explicitly allows on a festival day.

93   **Children and university students . . . :** Knobel, *Gates of the Seasons,* 62.

93   **In the event that a school schedules classes or ceremonies on a festival . . . :** Jacob, *Questions and Reform Jewish Answers,* no. 73. Note that this ruling is much more stringent than that offered by R. David Zvi Hoffmann, the head of the Orthodox rabbinical seminary in Berlin during the early years of this century (*Resp. Melamed Leho'il* 1:58). Clearly, the situation in today's America is different; our community's self-confidence and pride in its heritage means that we need not compromise on matters of vital principle.

93   *Chol Hamo'ed***:** Work is traditionally allowed on *chol hamo'ed* only in order to provide for the needs of the festival or for the needs of the community, or in order to avoid significant economic loss, provided that the labor one must do does not involve excessive effort. *M. Mo'ed Katan,* chs. 1–2; *B. Chagigah* 18a; *Yad, Yom Tov* 7:1–2; *Shulchan Arukh, Orach Chayim* 530 and *Mishnah Berurah* ad loc. Some authorities hold that the Torah itself forbids nonessential work on *chol hamo'ed.* Most, however, believe that the Torah does not prohibit excessive labor on the intermediate festival days but that the ancient Rabbis, who sought to insure that these days retain the festive character of the season, instituted the prohibition. See *Tur, Orach Chayim* 530 and *Beit Yosef* ad loc.

93   **each day can be an opportunity for rejoicing . . . :** Knobel, *Gates of the Seasons,* 73, 84.

93   **Weddings may be held on** *chol hamo'ed***:** Freehof, *Reform Jewish Practice,* 1:72–73; Jacob, *Questions and Reform Jewish Answers,* no. 216. This is a Reform innovation. Weddings are traditionally not held on the intermediate days, on the grounds that we do not allow our own joy to interfere with the *simchah* of the festival. Yet this prohibition is not a stringent one. *Halakhah* declares that betrothals (as opposed to the actual wedding) may be solemnized on *chol hamo'ed* and a feast may be held, so long as this does not take place in the bride's home. In addition, a man may remarry a wife he previously divorced and celebrate with a wedding feast. A feast, too, may be held during *chol hamo'ed* to celebrate a wedding held the day before the onset of the festival. These exceptions demonstrate that the prohibition against weddings on *chol hamo'ed* is not as stringent as that against the holding of weddings on *yom tov* itself. See *M. Mo'ed Katan* 1:7; *Yad, Yom Tov* 7:16; *Shulchan Arukh, Orach Chayim* 546:1.

93   **The Second Festival Day:** For a full discussion of the theory behind *yom tov sheni* and the Reform response to it, see *Responsa Committee,* no. 5759.7. For rabbinic sources see *M. Rosh Hashanah* 2:2–4, *B. Beitzah* 4b–5a, and *Y. Eruvin* 3:9. On *yom*

tov sheni as a rabbinic enactment see *Yad, Yom Tov* 1:21–22 and *Kiddush Hachodesh* 5:5. The different origin of the second day of Rosh Hashanah leads to some difficulties in its ritual practice: for example, does one recite the blessing *Shehechiyanu* over *Kiddush* and at the sounding of the *shofar* on the second day? See *Tur, Orach Chayim* 600, and *Shulchan Arukh, Orach Chayim* 600:2 and *Mishnah Berurah* ad loc. On Reform opposition to the two-day *yom tov* see Meyer, *Response to Modernity*, 88, 139, and 259. See also Freehof, *Reform Jewish Practice*, 1:16–19, Alexander Guttmann, *The Struggle Over Reform in Rabbinic Literature*, 9–11, and Plaut, *The Rise of Reform Judaism*, 195–98.

96 **Reform Judaism rejects the notion that we are bound to observe the decrees of past authorities . . . :** This is an old halakhic dispute. The position of Maimonides, *Yad, Mamrim* 2:2, is that a decree issued by a *beit din* and adopted by all Israel remains valid, even if the original justification for that ordinance (e.g., doubt as to the date of Rosh Chodesh; the fear of future persecution) no longer applies. The decree can be overturned only by a court that is "greater" than the one which issued it. Yet since according to traditional Jewish thought no "greater" court will emerge until the restoration of the Sanhedrin in Jerusalem, there is no practical possibility of modifying or annulling the original *takkanah*. This opinion of Maimonides has its critics; see, for example, the note (*hasagah*) of R. Avraham b. David to *Yad, Mamrim* 2:2. For a more complete analysis see *Responsa Committee*, no. 5759.7. We think that this latter view is a better reading of the talmudic sources and that it accords with common sense: if the Rabbis issued a ruling explicitly in response to a particular set of circumstances, then when those circumstances no longer obtain, the rabbinic ruling may be set aside if necessary.

96 **The "Special Sabbaths":** See *M. Megillah* 3:4; *Shulchan Arukh, Orach Chayim* 685:1–7 and *Mishnah Berurah*, n. 1; Hoffman, *Gates of Understanding*, 1:282–83. On the collection of the half-shekel during the month of Adar, see *M. Shekalim* 1:1. Two Torah scrolls are used for the "special Sabbaths." The weekly portion (*parashat hashavu'a*) is read from the first scroll while the special portion for that day is read from the second. When *Shabbat Shekalim* or *Shabbat Hachodesh* occurs on Rosh Chodesh, three scrolls are used: the weekly portion is read from the first; the portion for Shabbat Rosh Chodesh (Num. 28:9–15) is read from the second; and the special portion for that Shabbat is read from the third.

97 **Due to the violent nature of the Samuel passage . . . :** The *Haftarah* is traditionally a reading drawn from the Prophets (*Nevi'im*); see *M. Megillah* 4:2–3. How then can it be drawn from Esther, a book numbered not among the prophetic works but among the *Ketuvim*, or sacred Writings? Reform Judaism would respond that the prophetic spirit—the human apprehension of God's will—may be discerned throughout all of Scripture and not merely in those books labeled as "prophetic."

98 ***Shabbat Hagadol . . . is called "great" because of the great miracle . . . :*** See *B. Shabbat* 87b. The explanation is found first in the literature of the "school of Rashi" in eleventh-century France: *Sefer Ha'orah*, 201; *Sefer Hapardes*, ch. 17; *Siddur Rashi*, ch. 352. See also *Tosafot*, s.v. *ve'oto*; *Shulchan Arukh, Orach Chayim* 430:1. A related explanation holds that this Shabbat is "great" because on this day Israel successfully observed its first *mitzvah* as a people; *Sefer Abudarham, Seder Tefillat Purim*, end, in the name of *Machzor Vitry* (ch. 259). Others suggest that the day is called *gadol* because, on this Shabbat, the congregation remains at synagogue after services to hear the sages expound upon the laws of Pesach; hence, the day seems especially long (*gadol*) (*Shibolei Haleket*, ch. 205).

99   **calls Pesach zeman cheruteinu . . . :** The formula is found in the *Kiddush* for festivals and in the *Kedushat Hayom* benediction in the *Tefillah*; Gates of Prayer, 482, 519, and 721.

99   **We recall this pivotal experience . . . :** The Exodus is a focal point of the *Ge'ulah* ("redemption") benediction which follows the recitation of the *Shema* in the evening and in the morning. It is also mentioned in the *Kiddush*, which describes Shabbat and the festivals as *zekher litzi'at mitzrayim*, "a remembrance of the Exodus from Egypt"; Gates of Prayer, 719, 721.

99   *Matzah:* Knobel, *Gates of the Seasons*, 71.

99   **in remembrance of the haste . . . :** *B. Pesachim* 116b.

99   **of our humble beginnings . . . :** Deut. 16:3 refers to *matzah* as *lechem oni*, which can be translated as "the bread of distress," "the bread of poverty," or simply as "poor bread."

99   **Tradition does not require one to eat *matzah* during the remainder of the festival . . . :** See *B. Pesachim* 120a; *Yad, Chametz Umatzah* 6:1; *Shulchan Arukh, Orach Chayim* 475:7.

99   **although some authorities hold that it is a special *mitzvah* to do so . . . :** Quite possibly because the eating of *matzah* is the one positive religious observance that takes place during the holiday, and it would make little sense religiously to discard it altogether after the Seder. See Ibn Ezra to Exod. 12:15; *Resp. Harosh* 23:3; *Ma'aseh Rav, Hanhagat Hagra*, ch. 181.

99   **"unleavened bread" . . . :** *M. Pesachim* 2:5. Deut. 16:3 speaks both of the prohibition against eating *chametz* and the commandment to eat *matzah*. The Rabbis understand this as a *hekesh*, a comparison made by the Torah itself between these two substances; thus, *matzah* must be made from only those grains which become leaven and which are forbidden to us on Pesach in any form other than *matzah*. *B. Pesachim* 35a; *Yad, Chametz Umatzah* 5:1 and 6:4.

99   *Matzah meshumeret* . . . : See Rashi to the verse. The Jewish Publication Society's translation of the Torah (1962; utilized in Plaut, *Torah Commentary*) reads "you shall observe the [Feast of] Unleavened Bread"; i.e., the word *matzot* is an abbreviation for *chag hamatzot*.

99   **"watched" from the time of kneading . . . :** *Matzot* baked during the rest of the year and which are not labeled "kosher for Passover" are not as carefully "watched" and may therefore be *chametz*, or leaven.

99   **Some authorities, however, assert . . . :** Based upon *B. Pesachim* 40a. Maimonides, *Yad, Chametz Umatzah* 5:9, requires that all grain eaten during the festival meet this standard of "watching." In this, he follows the precedent of Alfasi, *Halakhot, Pesachim*, fol. 12a, and the Babylonian *geonim*. Ashkenzaic authorities did not go so far, preferring a more lenient definition of "watching"; *Hilkhot Harosh, Pesachim* 2:26.

100 **Others will be sure to eat *matzah meshumeret* at the Seder . . . :** i.e., the *matzah* over which the blessings are recited, along with the *afikoman*. See *Shulchan Arukh, Orach Chayim* 253:4.

100 **Regular Passover *matzot* are fully acceptable . . . :** The notion that "watching" must be done from the time of harvesting is based upon a highly contestable reading of *B. Pesachim* 40a; see Sperber, *Minhagei Yisrael*, 1:92–97. A number of authorities hold in any case that the necessary "watching" is from the time of kneading (see

Mishnah Berurah 253, no. 24). *Matzah meshumeret*, in other words, is an unnecessary stringency and, given its high cost, a needlessly expensive one.

100 **Matzah ashirah . . . :** *B. Pesachim* 35b.

100 **Sefardic Jews accordingly eat matzah ashirah . . . :** *Yad, Chametz Umatzah* 5:2; *Shulchan Arukh, Orach Chayim* 462:1.

100 **Traditional Ashkenazic practice, however, forbids . . . :** Isserles, *Orach Chayim* 462:4, based upon such authorities as Rashi, *Pesachim* 36a, s.v. *ein lashin*, and Rabad, *hasagah* to *Yad* ad loc.

100 **The Seder matzah must be the plain variety . . . :** Since the *matzah* we are bidden to eat is referred to as *lechem oni*, or "poor bread" (Deut. 16:3), "enriched" *matzah* does not fulfill that requirement; *B. Pesachim* 36a; *Shulchan Arukh, Orach Chayim* 462:1. Maimonides allows "egg *matzah*" for the Seder (*Yad, Chametz Umatzah* 6:5), apparently because he defines *matzah ashirah* as only that *matzah* whose flour is mixed with wine, oil, or honey (*Magid Mishneh* ad loc.).

100 **Maror:** Knobel, *Gates of the Seasons*, 72.

100 **the bitterness of our enslavement . . . :** *B. Pesachim* 116b.

100 **Various vegetables qualify as maror:** See *M. Pesachim* 2:6; *Yad, Chametz Umatzah* 7:13; and *Shulchan Arukh, Orach Chayim* 473:5. The first of the five species listed there is *chazeret*, or lettuce, which arguably gives it pride of place as the favored kind of *maror*. Moreover, the *midrash* seems to prefer it: "Why do we eat lettuce on Pesach? For just as the lettuce leaf tastes sweet at its beginning (top) but becomes bitter at its end (base), so too was our experience in Egypt, which began with Pharaoh's welcome to Joseph's family and which ended in slavery" (*Y. Pesachim* 2:5).

100 **Ashkenazic tradition often favors horseradish:** The translation of "*tamkha*," the third of the species listed in *M. Pesachim* 2:6; see *Mishnah Berurah* 473, no. 36. Bottled horseradish is packed in water and other ingredients which affect its natural flavor; this renders it something other than *maror* (*Shulchan Arukh, Orach Chayim* 473:5 and *Mishnah Berurah*, no. 38).

100 **Chametz:** Knobel, *Gates of the Seasons*, 68.

101 **According to tradition . . . :** *B. Pesachim* 28b. Deut. 16:3 forbids the eating of *chametz* with the Pesach sacrifice; since that sacrifice was offered after midday on 14 Nisan, the Toraitic prohibition against eating *chametz* commences at that time. The Rabbis subsequently extended the prohibition to one hour (that is, one-twelfth of the daylight time) prior to noon, as a "fence" to keep one from inadvertently transgressing the Toraitic prohibition (*B. Pesachim* 2b; *Yad, Chametz Umatzah* 1:8–10).

101 **Among Reform Jews . . . :** Knobel, *Gates of the Seasons*, 68. See *Responsa Committee*, no. 5756.9.

101 **Chametz refers not only to leavened bread . . . :** *B. Pesachim* 35a.

101 **Rice and Legumes:** Ibid. 35a. For this reason, unleavened bread made from the flour of these foodstuffs cannot be used to fulfill the *mitzvah* to eat *matzah* at the Seder.

101 **according to the Talmud and the leading codes . . . :** *B. Pesachim* 135a and *B. Pesachim* 114b, where Rav Huna permits rice as one of the "two cooked dishes" on the Seder plate; *Yad, Chametz Umatzah* 5:1; *Hilkhot Harosh, Pesachim* 2:12; *Tur* and *Shulchan Arukh, Orach Chayim* 253:1.

101   **Ashkenazic Jews, however, have long observed the practice . . . :** Isserles, *Orach Chayim* 253:1. The practice goes back as far as twelfth- and thirteenth-century France and Provence.

101   **This custom has various explanations . . . :** See *Tur* and *Bach, Orach Chayim* 253, beginning.

101   **we find Ashkenazic scholars . . . :** *Tur* ad loc. R. Ya'akov Emden, *Mor Uketzi'ah* 453, (Germany, 18th century), recounts his own fierce opposition and that of his father, R. Zvi Ashkenazi, to this "mistaken custom" (*minhag ta'ut*). The prohibition was always set aside during years of famine; *Mishnah Berurah* 453, no. 6.

101   **the Reform movement has relaxed this custom . . . :** See Meyer, *Response to Modernity*, 36–37. For an extended discussion of the history of this practice and of options for liberal Jews, see *Responsa Committee*, no. 5756.9.

102   **It is a mitzvah to remove leaven . . . :** Knobel, *Gates of the Seasons*, 67.

102   **According to most authorities . . . :** For a full summary see *Responsa Committee*, no. 5756.9. In *B. Pesachim* 4b, we read that "according to the Torah, nullification alone is sufficient" for removal of *chametz.* See Rashi, s.v. *bevitul be'alma*; Onkelos to Exod. 12:15; *Yad, Chametz Umatzah* 2:2–3; *Tosafot, Pesachim* 4b, s.v. *mide'oraita*; Rabbeinu Nissim to Alfasi, *Pesachim*, fol. 1a; *Chidushei Haramban, Pesachim*, beginning.

102   **On the evening of 14 Nisan . . . :** Unless 14 Nisan commences on a Friday night, since *chametz* is not to be burned on Shabbat. In such a case, the search for *chametz* takes place on 13 Nisan, Thursday night, and the *chametz* is burned on Friday morning.

103   **one may sell the leaven to a non-Jew . . . :** *Tosefta Pesachim* 2:6 (printed editions; 2:12, Lieberman ed.); *Y. Pesachim* 2:2 (28d); *Yad, Chametz Umatzah* 4:6; *Hilkhot Harosh, Pesachim* 2:4; *Shulchan Arukh, Orach Chayim* 248:3.

103   **Adhering to this logic . . . :** *Responsa Committee*, no. 5756.9; Knobel, *Gates of the Seasons*, 67 and 128, n. 144.

103   **The Seder Table:** Knobel, *Gates of the Seasons*, 70–73.

103   **Three *matzot*:** *Shulchan Arukh, Orach Chayim* 473:4 and *Mishnah Berurah*, no. 18; see Rashi, Rashbam, and *Tosafot, B. Pesachim* 116a, top. There are other explanations for the requirement of three *matzot*; see Menachem Kasher, *Haggadah Sheleimah*, 61–62. Some authorities, meanwhile, prescribe only two *matzot*, just as two loaves of bread are present at the table on every other *yom tov* (*Yad, Chametz Umatzah* 8:6; R. Eliyahu, the Gaon of Vilna, *Ma'aseh Rav*, ch. 187). This difference in customs stretches back to geonic times (7th–11th centuries C.E.); see *Otzar Hageonim, Pesachim*, 117–18, and *Berakhot*, 89, no. 249. The Talmud itself never specifies the number of *matzot* to be brought to the table. See Yosef Tabory, *Pesach Dorot*, 269–306.

103   **With its first half . . . :** Matzah is called *lechem oni* (Deut. 16:3), which can be translated as "a poor person's bread." Thus, just as a poor person must be satisfied with less than a whole loaf, so do we fulfill the *mitzvah* of eating *matzah* over a half-loaf (*B. Pesachim* 115b–116a; *Yad, Chametz Umatzah* 8:6).

104   ***Maror***: *A Passover Haggadah,* ed. Herbert Bronstein, 15, following long-standing Ashkenazic custom, specifies horseradish root for *maror.* The present text adds the option of romaine lettuce, which many authorities regard as the "best" kind of *maror*; see the discussion of *maror* in this chapter.

104   *Parsley or any green herbs*: These should be a variety of vegetable other than *maror,* since we shall eat the bitter herb with the appropriate blessing later during the meal; *Mishnah Berurah* to *Orach Chayim* 473, no. 20.

104   *Two cooked dishes (tavshilin)*: M. *Pesachim* 10:3. The Mishnah does not identify these, and the Talmud mentions various customs (*B. Pesachim* 114b). Vegetarians may thus use other foods to substitute for the shankbone. The shankbone reminds us of the outstretched arm (*zero'a*) of God, who delivered us from Egypt, while the egg may symbolize either God's redemptive will or our sense of mourning over the destruction of the Temple (*Mishnah Berurah* to *Orach Chayim* 473, no. 23).

104   *Wine*: M. *Pesachim* 10:1.

104   **A traditional explanation ...** : *Y. Pesachim* 10:1, 37b–c, which gives alternative explanations as well. Our Haggadah matches each of the cups to one of these "promises of redemption." The "original" reason may be that each cup corresponds to a segment of the formal Hellenistic banquet or symposium meal, after which the Seder is modeled.

104   **a fifth cup:** the manuscripts of the Talmud (*B. Pesachim* 118a) cite the opinion of Rabbi Tarfon that a fifth cup is consumed at the Seder, though our printed texts read "fourth" in place of "fifth." The fifth cup is attested in geonic literature and is called optional, as opposed to the required four cups (*Otzar Hageonim, Pesachim*, 126–28, and see *Yad, Chametz Umatzah* 8:10). Medieval sources suggest that the fifth cup corresponds to God's "fifth" and ultimate promise of redemption in Exod. 6:8: "and I will bring them to the land which I swore to give to Abraham, Isaac, and Jacob" (Rabad, *Tamim De'im*, no. 30). Its association with the "cup of Elijah" is a later development. See Knobel, *Gates of the Seasons*, 129, n. 154.

104   **"an additional cup set aside for the future":** *A Passover Haggadah,* 77–79.

104   *The Seder*: See Lawrence A. Hoffman, "Historical Introduction" in Bronstein, *A Passover Haggadah,* 9–12. On the history of the Seder ritual and its relationship to Greco-Roman custom see Ernst Daniel Goldschmidt, *Haggadah shel Pesach* and Barukh M. Bokser, *The Origins of the Seder: The Passover Rite and Early Rabbinic Judaism.*

105   **the following steps ...** : The traditional Haggadah lists fourteen steps. Of these, the CCAR (Bronstein) Haggadah omits the ritual handwashings preceding *karpas* and *motzi-matzah.*

105   *Kadesh*: M. *Pesachim* 10:2; *Yad, Chametz Umatzah* 8:1; *Shulchan Arukh, Orach Chayim* 473:1.

105   **while reclining on our left side:** *B. Pesachim* 99b, *mishnah* (and Rashi, s.v. *afilu ani*); *B. Pesachim* 108a; *Yad, Chametz Umatzah* 7:7–8; *Shulchan Arukh, Orach Chayim* 472:2; Knobel, *Gates of the Seasons*, 73.

105   **while drinking the four cups of wine and eating the *matzah* ...** : But *not* while eating the *maror,* which symbolizes the bitterness of slavery.

105   **Reform practice dispenses ...** : Our Haggadah does not mention reclining, even in its translation of the fourth of the "Four Questions," even though the Hebrew text cites it explicitly (29). In so doing, we follow those medieval authorities who rule that it is not necessary to recline, since free people now eat while seated upright at the table (Raban, *Even Ha'ezer* 74b and *Ra'abyah,* ch. 525). Our contention, like theirs, is that reclining made sense as an expression of freedom only during the time when free men and women (citizens) actually distinguished themselves by feasting in that manner. Today, it is the Seder in its entirety which demonstrates our freedom.

105　*netilat yadayim* . . . : The first hand washing, *urechatz*, takes place immediately prior to *karpas*; the second, *rachatzah*, occurs immediately prior to *motzi-matzah*, the eating of the unleavened bread. In Temple times, some non-priests who wished to adopt for themselves the laws of priestly purity developed the custom of washing their hands in this manner before eating bread and any sort of food that was dipped into a sauce or condiment (the liquids in the sauce were considered a primary agent in the transmission of ritual impurity; see *M. Berakhot* 8). *Netilat yadayim* survives today as a ritual requirement before eating bread; traditionally-observant Jews will perform this ritual throughout the year, reciting the customary blessing for hand washing before they say *Hamotzi*. For this reason, the blessing is recited before the *second* hand washing (*rachatzah*) but not at this point, before *karpas*, since many authorities are of the opinion that hand washing is no longer required before eating foods dipped into condiment. On the other hand, since some authorities *do* think that hand washing is required, the practice is to require the washing here but to dispense with the benediction, lest the hand washing in fact be unnecessary and the blessing superfluous (and to say an unnecessary benediction is a *berakhah levatalah*, a violation of the prohibition against mentioning God's name "in vain" [Exod. 20:7]. See *Shulchan Arukh, Orach Chayim* 158:1, 4; 473:6; and *Mishnah Berurah*, no. 52).

106　**Karpas**: *M. Pesachim* 10:3. The *karpas* reflects the Hellenistic custom of preceding the banquet's "main course" with the eating of vegetables dipped into condiment. The Babylonian Talmud, which is largely unaware of that custom, explains it as one of several pedagogical devices used during the evening to arouse the curiosity of the children so that they will ask, in effect, "why is this night different from all other nights?" *B. Pesachim* 116a; Rashbam, s.v. *chiyuva ledardekei*; *Tur, Orach Chayim* 473. Condiments such as salt water, vinegar, and wine are permitted, so long as one does not use *charoset*, which is reserved as a condiment for the *maror* (*Mishnah Berurah* 473, no. 54). Maimonides, on the other hand, uses *charoset* as the condiment for *karpas* as well as for *maror* (*Yad, Chametz Umatzah* 8:2).

106　**Yachatz**: *Shulchan Arukh, Orach Chayim* 473 and *Mishnah Berurah*, no. 57. We break the middle *matzah*, rather than one of the others, because the three *matzot* follow the order of the evening's ritual. We recite the benediction *Hamotzi* over the first *matzah*. The blessing *'al akhilat matzah* must be said, according to most authorities, over the broken *matzah*; hence, we place it second, between the unbroken pieces. The third *matzah* will be used for *korekh*.

106　**At this point of the Seder** . . . : *A Passover Haggadah*, 28. *M. Pesachim* 10:3. See Goldschmidt, *Haggadah shel Pesach*, 10.

106　**Maggid**: *M. Pesachim* 10:4; *B. Pesachim* 116a; *Yad, Chametz Umatzah* 8:2. Although the Haggadah announces the *maggid* at p. 34, it traditionally begins with *Ha Lachma Anya*, "This is the bread of affliction," on p. 26. That the *haggadah* (the narration or telling) must take the form of an answer to a child's question is suggested by Exod. 12:26, Exod. 13:8, Exod. 13:14, and Deut. 6:20.

106　**the "Four Questions"** . . . : These originate in *M. Pesachim* 10:4, where they are not presented as "questions" at all. Rather, they are the father's instructions to his son, in the event that the son does not possess the intelligence to ask: "How different this night is from all others! On all other nights, etc." Maimonides (*Yad, Chametz Umatzah* 8:2) tells us that "the one who recites the Narration says: How different is this night, etc." The custom for the children to recite this passage, as well as our perception of it as "four questions," is a later development.

106   we begin with **degradation** . . . : *M. Pesachim* 10:4.

106   **our origin as slaves to Pharaoh and to idolatry** . . . : The Talmud (*B. Pesachim* 116a) records a dispute between two authorities over the nature of the "degradation" with which we begin the story. Rav identifies this as "in the beginning our ancestors were idolators," while Shmuel sees the degradation in the fact that "we were slaves to Pharaoh in Egypt." The traditional Haggadah includes both passages; the CCAR Haggadah has them at p. 36 and p. 34 respectively.

106   **Deuteronomy 26:5–8:** *vidu'i habikurim*, the statement recited by the landowner who brings the first fruits of the harvest to the Temple in Jerusalem at the festival of Shavuot.

106   **the story be related in a language** . . . : See Isserles, *Orach Chayim* 473:6.

107   **The Haggadah, moreover, stresses in several places** . . . : See, for example, *Ha Lachma Anya* (p. 26): "Now we are all still bondmen. Next year may we all be free." See as well the "blessing of redemption" (*Birkat Ge'ulah*), recited over the second cup of wine (p. 60): "we look now with hope to the celebration of a future redemption." That redemption, in the traditional Haggadah text, involves the rebuilding of Jerusalem and the restoration of the Temple service, for without the Temple and the sacrifices the Jews remain, at least according to tradition, in a state of exile. A final example: *korekh*, the eating of the *matzah* and the *maror* together in remembrance of Temple times; see the discussion on *korekh* in the Notes, below.

107   **Following the narration** . . . : *M. Pesachim* 10:5. Although the *Haggadah*, 53, instructs the leader to point to the shankbone and to refer to it as "this *pesach*," traditional practice forbids this: since we no longer offer the sacrifice, we cannot point to it as if to say "*this* is the Passover offering." The Hebrew text, in fact, reads "the *pesach* that our ancestors ate when the Temple was standing. . . . " All agree, however, that we *do* point at "this" *matzah* and at "this" *maror*. On *Hallel*, see the section in this chapter on Rosh Chodesh, along with its Notes. Why do we not precede the *Hallel* at the Seder with its customary benediction? For various explanations, see Kasher, *Haggadah Sheleimah*, 139–40. Most likely, the exceptional nature of this *Hallel*, which we do not recite as one unit but divide into two parts, interrupted by dinner and *Birkat Hamazon*, led those who instituted the custom not to require a *berakhah*. The Sefardic custom, to recite *Hallel* along with the introductory *berakhah* at the evening service prior to the Seder, may have originated as an attempt to resolve this problem. A blessing *is* recited at the conclusion of the *Hallel*; see below.

107   **Birkat Ge'ulah** . . . : *M. Pesachim* 10:6.

107   **Motzi-Matzah:** *Shulchan Arukh, Orach Chayim* 475:1. While the *A Passover Haggadah*, 28, instructs us to break the *matzah* prior to the blessings, we follow here the traditional practice and recite *Hamotzi* before breaking the bread. Tonight, *Hamotzi* is said over the top, or unbroken *matzah*.

107   **The leader takes the three matzot** . . . : See *Mishnah Berurah* 473, no. 2, and Kasher, *Haggadah Sheleimah*, 70. In some customs, the leader replaces the two whole *matzot* on the plate and recites '*al akhilat matzah* while holding the broken piece alone.

108   **Maror:** This book follows the traditional practice, in which the *maror* must be eaten by itself and *not* (as indicated in the *A Passover Haggadah*, 28) along with a piece of *matzah*. While *maror* is dipped in *charoset* (*M. Pesachim* 10:3; *B. Pesachim* 115a–b), the *charoset* should be used sparingly, so that it does not blunt the bitter taste of the *maror*. See *Yad, Chametz Umatzah* 8:8 and *Shulchan Arukh, Orach Chayim* 475:1.

108   **Korekh:** B. Pesachim 115a; Yad, Chametz Umatzah 8:6–8. Hillel based his practice upon an interpretation of Num. 9:11, "along with unleavened bread and bitter herbs shall they eat it [the Passover sacrifice]"—that is, he ate all three foods together. Today, in the absence of the sacrifice, halakhic thought holds that we cannot fulfill these *mitzvot* as a "package"; hence, we eat *matzah* and *maror* separately. And since we have already fulfilled those two *mitzvot*, we do not recite a blessing over *korekh*. See *Mishnah Berurah* 475, no. 16.

108   **in solidarity with all generations . . . :** This is our explanation for the practice, which is why we retain it in our Seder even though it evokes a Temple setting and even though we do not hope for a restoration of the sacrifices. Other Jews might see *korekh* as a demonstration of precisely the opposite: our longing for the Messianic future, for the rebuilding of the Temple and for the day when all the *mitzvot*, including those surrounding the sacrificial cult, might be observed again. In this sense, *korekh* shows how the same Jewish ritual practice can serve to unite an entire community even though segments of that community understand the practice in different ways.

108   **Tzafun:** In the Temple, the last food to be tasted was the Passover sacrifice itself. The *matzah* eaten here is a remembrance of that custom. The word *afikoman* (M. Pesachim 10:8) comes from the Greek *epikomios*, or "after-dinner entertainment" familiar at Greco-Roman banquet meals. Such revelry is forbidden at the Seder, which is devoted to the telling of the Exodus story.

108   **Barekh:** M. Pesachim 10:7; Yad, Chametz Umatzah 8:10; Shulchan Arukh, Orach Chayim 479. No wine may be consumed between the drinking of the third and fourth cups, lest one be induced to fall asleep and miss the rest of the Seder.

108   **Hallel:** M. Pesachim 10:7. Hallel concludes with Birkat Hashir, a blessing which follows the liturgical recitation of Psalms. The traditional Haggadah prescribes that this blessing end with a *chatimah* formula ("Barukh Atah . . . "); B. Pesachim 118a; Shulchan Arukh, Orach Chayim 480:1. Our Haggadah maintains a parallelism: as there is no blessing recited *before* the *Hallel*, so there is no *chatimah* recited at its conclusion.

109   **Each day of chol hamo'ed has its own Torah reading . . . :** listed in Hoffman, *Gates of Understanding*, 1:283, as follows: second day of Pesach (= first day of *chol hamo'ed*): Exod. 13:14–16; third day of Pesach (if a weekday): Exod. 23:14–17; fourth day of Pesach: Exod. 34:18–23; fifth day of Pesach (if a weekday): Num. 9:1–5; sixth day of Pesach, Lev. 23:1–8. On Shabbat *chol hamo'ed*, the Torah reading is Exod. 33:12–34:26, and the *Haftarah* is Ezek. 37:1–14. In other congregations, a second scroll is also read on each day of Pesach. On the first day (and the second day, when two days of *yom tov* are observed), the reading from the second scroll is Num. 28:16–25; on the other days of Pesach, the reading is Num. 28:19–25. In congregations which observe two days of *yom tov*, the Torah reading for the second day is Lev. 22:26–23:44; the *Haftarah* is II Kings 23: 1–9 and 21–25.

109   **The Song of Songs . . . :** *Soferim* 14:16; Isserles, *Orach Chayim* 490:9. On the "eighth day" Torah reading in Reform congregations, see Hoffman, *Gates of Understanding*, 1:271 and Freehof, *Current Reform Responsa*, no. 10.

110   **The seventh day of Pesach . . . :** Knobel, *Gates of the Seasons*, 74; *Gates of Prayer*, 546–53. Another explanation for not reciting the full *Hallel* on the seventh day of Pesach, even though it is a *yom tov*, is that on this day we commemorate the drowning of the Egyptians in the sea. Our joy is limited by our sadness at this event, however necessary it was in order to secure our liberation. See B. Sanhedrin 39b.

110 *The Omer:* The ancient rabbinic tradition clashed with that of other Jewish groups, who understood *"shabbat"* as "the Sabbath" and began the count on the first Sunday ("the day after the *shabbat"*) following the beginning of Pesach. According to this latter method, Shavuot would always fall on a Sunday. See *Sifra* to the verse and *B. Menachot* 66a.

110 **Jewish tradition, on the other hand . . . :** R. Nissim Gerondi, Commentary to Alfasi, *Pesachim* fol. 28a; *Yad, Temidin* 7:22.

110 **The counting, which lasts for forty-nine days . . . :** and not fifty days; *Sifra* to Lev. 23:16.

110 **takes place at night . . . :** because of the requirement that seven "complete" weeks be counted: the Hebrew day begins in the evening. *B. Menachot* 66a.

111 **From the seventh day, one counts the weeks as well . . . :** *B. Chagigah* 17b. On the laws of counting the Omer see *Yad, Temidin* 7:22 and *Shulchan Arukh, Orach Chayim* 489:1.

111 **The weeks between Pesach and Shavuot . . . :** *B. Yevamot* 62b. The Talmud does not mention the custom to refrain from rejoicing during this period. That custom is apparently a geonic development; see *Otzar Hageonim, Yevamot,* 141, *Shulchan Arukh, Orach Chayim* 493, and *Magen Avraham,* no. 1.

111 **a day on which the plague is said to have stopped:** The idea that the plague ceased on Lag Ba'omer surfaces in Spain and Provence by the late twelfth–early thirteenth centuries; see *Sefer Hamanhig, Hilkhot Erusin Venisu'in,* ch. 105.

111 **The Reform movement has largely abrogated . . . :** Jacob, *American Reform Responsa,* no. 134 and Knobel, *Gates of the Seasons,* 131–32, n. 167.

111 **the mishnaic tractate *Avot* . . . :** Knobel, *Gates of the Seasons,* 74.

112 **It is a *mitzvah* to observe Shavuot . . . :** Lev. 23:15-16, 21; Knobel, *Gates of the Seasons,* 77.

112 **the Torah reading . . . :** Exod. 19:1–8; 20:1–14 (traditional congregations read all the verses of Exod. 19–20). For those congregations which observe the traditional practice, the reading from the second scroll on both days of *yom tov* is Num. 28:26–31. The *Haftarah* is Isa. 42:1–12, as opposed to the traditional Ezek. 1:1–28 and 3:12. Those congregations observing a second day will read Deut. 15:19–16:17 from the first scroll; if the second day falls on Shabbat, the reading is Deut. 14:22–16:17. The *Haftarah* is Hab. 3:1–19. See Hoffman, *Gates of Understanding,*1:283.

112 *Yizkor . . . :* Knobel, *Gates of the Seasons,* 78.

112 **the Book of Ruth . . . :** *Soferim* 14:18; *Mishnah Berurah,* 490, no. 17; Knobel, *Gates of the Seasons,* 78.

112 **It is a *mitzvah* to reaffirm the covenant . . . :** Knobel, *Gates of the Seasons,* 77 and 133, n. 173. An explanation for the all-night vigil is that, at Sinai, the Israelites fell asleep while awaiting revelation, and God had to awaken them so they could receive the Torah. By staying up all night and studying Torah, we effect a repair (*tikkun*) of this breach; *Magen Avraham, Orach Chayim* 494. See Jacob, *Questions and Reform Jewish Answers,* no. 74.

112 **Confirmation . . . :** Knobel, *Gates of the Seasons,* 77–78; Freehof, *Reform Jewish Practice,* 1:25–26.

112 **greens and fresh flowers . . . :** Knobel, *Gates of the Seasons*, 77. Isserles, *Orach Chayim* 494:3, explains the custom as a reminder of Mount Sinai, which was lush with pasturage for the Israelites' flocks.

112 **first fruits (*bikkurim*) . . . :** The ritual is described in Deut. 26:1ff. and *M. Bikkurim* 3:1ff. On Shavuot as the "festival of the first fruits" see Exod. 23:16 and 34:22; Lev. 23:17; Num. 28:26.

112 **dairy dishes . . . :** Isserles, *Orach Chayim* 494:3.

113 **to milk and honey:** See Song of Songs 4:11 and *Shir Hashirim Rabbah* 1:3. See Knobel, *Gates of the Seasons*, 133, n. 177 and Jacob, *Questions and Reform Jewish Answers*, no. 74. It was once a custom to place trees in the synagogue, as a reminder that the fruit of trees is "judged" on Shavuot (*M. Rosh Hashanah* 1:2). This practice was abrogated, however, by the Gaon of Vilna, on the grounds that Christians use trees to celebrate Christmas. See *Mishnah Berurah, Orach Chayim* 494, no. 10.

113 **Sukkot, Shemini Atzeret, and Simchat Torah:** Knobel, *Gates of the Seasons*, 80.

113 **It is a *mitzvah* to observe . . . Sukkot:** Ibid., 81.

114 **Simchat Torah . . . is observed on Shemini Atzeret:** as is the case in all Israeli congregations. In traditional congregations in the Diaspora, Simchat Torah occurs on the second day of Shemini Atzeret.

114 **The Sukkah:** Knobel, *Gates of the Seasons*, 82. On starting to build the *sukkah* right after Yom Kippur see idem, 54 and 125, n. 127; Isserles, *Orach Chayim* 625 and *Mishnah Berurah*, no. 2. The reason, as stated in *Maharil*, beginning of *Hilkhot Sukkah*: once we have repented and made atonement for our sins, it is fitting that we perform a *mitzvah* as soon as we can.

114 **the *sukkah* is a temporary structure . . . :** See, in general, Plaut and Washofsky, *Teshuvot*, no. 5755.4; *M. Sukkah* 1:1; *B. Sukkah* 2a; *Yad, Sukkah* 4:1; *Orach Chayim* 633:1. R. Zeira, *B. Sukkah* 2a, offers another explanation for the height of a *sukkah*: a *sukkah* requires shade (cf. Isa. 4:6). If the height of the walls exceeds twenty cubits, one dwells in the shade of the walls rather than that of the *sekhakh*.

114 **the area of the *sukkah* . . . :** defined as "seven square handbreadths" (*B. Sukkah* 3a; *Yad, Sukkah* 4:1; *Orach Chayim* 634:1).

114 **the essence of the *sukkah* . . . :** Rashi, *Sukkah* 2a, s.v. *veshechamatah*.

114 **detached vegetation . . . :** *M. Sukkah* 1:1 and 1:4; *Yad, Sukkah* 5:1; *Orach Chayim* 629 and 631. A *sukkah* may not as a rule be built under a tree, since its shade will derive from that tree rather than from the *sekhakh*; see *M. Sukkah* 1:2 and *Yad, Sukkah* 5:12. For special circumstances, see *Orach Chayim* 626:1.

114 **The walls . . . :** *M. Sukkah* 1:1, 5, and 9; *Yad, Sukkah* 4:2, 4, and 16; *Orach Chayim* 630:1ff.

114 **The *sukkah* must have a roof . . . :** See *M. Sukkah* 1:11 and *Sukkah* 19b; *Yad, Sukkah* 4:7; *Orach Chayim* 631:10.

114 **A structure which does not meet these requirements . . . :** Plaut and Washofsky, *Teshuvot*, no. 5755.4; Freehof, *Reform Responsa*, no. 11; Freehof, *Reform Jewish Practice*, 2:27–28. While *bimah* decorations do help to instill the spirit of the holiday, they do not substitute for a valid *sukkah*.

114 **A "permanent" *sukkah* . . . :** Freehof, *Reform Responsa for Our Time*, no. 9; *M. Sukkah* 1:1; *Shulchan Arukh, Orach Chayim* 436:1. When the structure has a permanent roof, this roof must be removed *before* the *sekhakh* is put on; it may then be

placed back over the *sekhakh* to serve as a cover when the *sukkah* is not in use. *Reform Responsa for Our Time*, no. 9; Isserles, *Orach Chayim* 626:3.

114   It is a *mitzvah* to celebrate in the *sukkah*: Knobel, *Gates of the Seasons*, 83.

114   The Torah requires . . . : Lev. 23:42–43. The Rabbis explain: "for seven days one makes the *sukkah* one's permanent dwelling"; See *M. Sukkah* 2:9; *B. Sukkah* 28b–29a; *Yad, Sukkah* 6:5–6; *Shulchan Arukh, Orach Chayim* 639. We "live" in the *sukkah* precisely as we do in our homes the rest of the year. Thus, one is permitted to leave the *sukkah* under conditions such as inclement weather, insects, etc., which would cause one to leave one's permanent home. See *Mishnah Berurah* to *Orach Chayim* 640, no. 13. And see Isserles, *Orach Chayim* 639:2: the cold European autumn climate and the lack of privacy in urban areas render the *sukkah* unfit as a "dwelling" at night; thus, while we continue to eat in the *sukkah*, we are no longer obligated to sleep there.

114   especially on the first night . . . : One is traditionally *required* to eat in the *sukkah* on the first night of the festival, since this observance is compared to the requirement to eat *matzah* on the first night of Pesach; *B. Sukkah* 27a; *Yad, Sukkah* 6:7; *Shulchan Arukh, Orach Chayim* 639:3. On the other nights of the festival, one may avoid this requirement by not eating a full or "fixed" meal over bread. The exception to this is Shabbat, on which we are required to eat a full meal; during Sukkot, this meal is eaten in the *sukkah*.

115   Whenever we eat . . . : Some hold that we say the blessing whenever we enter the *sukkah* to "dwell" there (*Yad, Sukkah* 6:12); the general practice is to say the blessing only when we eat in the *sukkah* (*Magid Mishneh* ad loc.; *Shulchan Arukh, Orach Chayim* 239:8).

115   to welcome guests . . . : Knobel, *Gates of the Seasons*, 84.

115   *Lulav and Etrog*: Ibid., 82–83.

115   every day during the Sukkot festival . . . : In traditional congregations, this *mitzvah* is omitted on Shabbat, as a precaution lest one carry the *lulav* through the public thoroughfare and thereby violate the prohibition against carrying objects on Shabbat (*B. Sukkah* 42b–44a; *Yad, Lulav* 7:18). For the same reason, the *shofar* is not sounded when Rosh Hashanah falls on Shabbat. In Reform practice, both *shofar* and *lulav* are performed on Shabbat.

115   The *lulav*-bundle is taken in the right hand . . . : *B. Sukkah* 37b. The *lulav*, which combines three of the four species, is held with the "stronger" hand (*Shulchan Arukh, Orach Chayim* 651:2–3). The left-handed person, however, may hold the *lulav* in the left hand (Isserles, *Orach Chayim* 651:3).

115   with its tip (*pitam*) facing downward: in order to avoid fulfilling the *mitzvah* to "take" the *lulav* and *etrog* before the blessing is recited.

115   so that they touch each other . . . : *Shulchan Arukh, Orach Chayim* 651:11.

115   we wave the *lulav* and *etrog* . . . : three times in each direction (ibid. 551:9).

115   the sovereignty of God . . . : *B. Sukkah* 37b.

115   In traditional synagogues . . . : See *Shulchan Arukh, Orach Chayim* 660 and 664, including the ritual of the *aravot* (willow branches) on Hoshana Rabbah.

116   one's own *lulav* and *etrog* . . . : Knobel, *Gates of the Seasons*, 83. This flows from the rabbinic interpretation of Lev. 23:40 (the Hebrew word *lakhem* suggests that the species must be "yours"; i.e., owned by you); see *B. Sukkah* 41b. Thus, one cannot fulfill the *mitzvah*, at least on the first day of the festival, by borrowing a *lulav* and

etrog from another. What happens, therefore, when one cannot afford or has failed to purchase a *lulav* and *etrog* of one's own? (Using the synagogue's *lulav* and *etrog* will not suffice, since they are owned in partnership by all the members of the congregation and not in their entirety by the individual who seeks to fulfill the *mitzvah*.) Tradition overcomes this problem through the device of *matanah*, or "gift": one mentally deeds the ownership of the *lulav* to another person so that the latter may perform the *mitzvah* with his/her "own" set. See *Yad, Lulav* 8:10, and *Shulchan Arukh, Orach Chayim* 658:3–5.

116   **one enhances the performance . . . :** The concept is *hiddur mitzvah*, the aesthetic dimension of a ritual act. See Knobel, *Gates of the Seasons*, 162–64, B. *Bava Kama* 9a–b, and *Shulchan Arukh, Orach Chayim* 656.

116   **The services on the first day of Sukkot . . . :** M. *Megillah* 2:5; B. *Sukkah* 43a; *Yad, Lulav* 7:10; *Shulchan Arukh, Orach Chayim* 652:1.

116   **the *lulav* is waved during *Hallel* . . . :** In addition to the waving which follows the benediction '*al netilat lulav.* The *lulav* is waved during the recitation of Psalm 118:1–4, 25 (*hoshi'a na*), and 29, but it is held still during the recitation of God's name.

116   **The Torah is read on each day of the festival:** The readings for *chol hamo'ed* Sukkot, according to Hoffman, *Gates of Understanding*, 1:281–82: second day of Sukkot (= first day of *chol hamo'ed*): Lev. 23:39–44; third day of Sukkot (if a weekday): Exod. 23:14–17; fourth day of Sukkot: Exod. 34:21–24; fifth day of Sukkot (if a weekday): Deut. 16:13–17; sixth day of Sukkot (if a weekday): Deut. 31:9–13; seventh day of Sukkot (Hoshana Rabbah): Deut. 11:10–15. The Torah reading for Shabbat *chol hamo'ed* is Exod. 33:12–34:26; the *Haftarah* is Ezek. 38:18–39:7. In traditional congregations, the Torah reading on each day of *chol hamo'ed* is taken from the appropriate section of Numbers 29. Congregations which observe two days of *yom tov* repeat the reading for the first day on the second, and Num. 29:12–14 is read from a second scroll on both festival days.

116   **Kohelet . . . :** Knobel, *Gates of the Seasons*, 84.

116   **Shemini Atzeret:** Rashi, Lev. 23:36; see B. *Sukkah* 55b.

116   **celebration on behalf of all humankind:** *Bamidbar Rabbah* 21:22. During the days of Sukkot, a total of seventy bulls were sacrificed in the Temple (Num. 29:12–34), corresponding to the proverbial seventy nations of the world. On Shemini Atzeret, one bull is offered (Num. 29:36), corresponding to Israel.

117   **We do not celebrate in the *sukkah* . . . :** *Shulchan Arukh, Orach Chayim* 668:1. Jews who observe two days of *yom tov* will eat in the *sukkah* on Shemini Atzeret, out of the "doubt" over whether this day is actually Shemini Atzeret or the seventh day of Sukkot. Out of this same "doubt," they do not recite the benediction *leishev basukkah*, on the possibility that this day is not Sukkot and there is no *mitzvah* to eat in the *sukkah*. On Simchat Torah, these Jews will not eat in the *sukkah*, since this is definitely *not* the seventh day.

117   **the festival liturgy . . . :** Those who observe two days of *yom tov* remove two Torah scrolls. From the first, they read Deut. 14:22–16:17; from the second, Num. 29:35–30:1. The *Haftarah* is I Kings 8:54–66.

117   **Yizkor:** Knobel, *Gates of the Seasons*, 85.

117   **Simchat Torah:** Ibid., 84–85, and 135, n. 194.

117   **originated during early medieval times . . . :** The Babylonian *geonim* already discuss some of the halakhic problems connected with this festival; *Otzar Hageonim, Beitzah (Yom Tov)*, nos. 62–63 (pp. 28–29).

117   **the final portion of the Torah . . . :** *B. Megillah* 31a; *Yad, Tefillah* 13:12.

117   **Our practice . . . :** In traditional congregations, the reading at night on Simchat Torah is Deut. 33:1–27. In the morning, the remainder of Deuteronomy is read from the first scroll, Gen. 1–2:3 is read from the second scroll, and Num. 29:35–30:1 is read from the third scroll.

117   **seven *hakafot* . . . :** Or fewer, depending upon communal custom; see *Mishnah Berurah* 669, no. 10.

117   **The children, too . . . :** Isserles, *Orach Chayim* 669.

117   **Consecration . . . :** Knobel, *Gates of the Seasons*, 85; Freehof, *Reform Jewish Practice*, 1:26–27.

117   **Rosh Hashanah:** The Torah refers to the springtime month of Aviv (later called by its Babylonian name Nisan; see Exod. 23:15 and Deut. 16:1) as the first month, suggesting that the year begins at the season of Pesach; see Exod. 12:2, Lev. 23:5, and Num. 28:16. On the other hand, the festival of Sukkot takes place at "the end of the year" (Exod. 23:16; see also Exod. 34:22), which would indicate that the new year occurs in the fall. These differing "new years" may reflect different systems of calendation, the former reckoned by the cultic year (that is, for the numbering of the festivals), the latter according to the agricultural year (the harvest season ending in the fall).

118   **Later Jewish tradition . . . :** *M. Rosh Hashanah* 1:1. Note in that Mishnah the persistence of differing calendars for different institutions.

118   ***Yom Hadin* . . . :** *B. Rosh Hashanah* 16b; see *B. Arakhin* 10b.

118   **"all mortals pass for inspection before God":** *M. Rosh Hashanah* 1:2.

118   **"the gates of repentance are always open":** *Deut. Rabbah* 2:12.

118   **The Month of Elul:** Knobel, *Gates of the Seasons*, 39 and accompanying notes. *Pirkei deR. Eliezer*, ch. 46, brings the legend that Moses ascended Mt. Sinai on the first day of Elul, accompanied by the blast of the *shofar* in the Israelite camp.

118   **Some communities recite *selichot* . . . from Rosh Chodesh Elul to Yom Kippur:** the Sefardic custom; *Shulchan Arukh, Orach Chayim* 581:1.

118   **Our practice . . . :** Isserles, ad loc. If Rosh Hashanah falls on a Monday or a Tuesday, *selichot* are recited on the Saturday night of the previous week. The reason is that some Jews observe the custom to fast from sunup to sundown for ten days from *selichot* to Yom Kippur. Since it is forbidden to fast during four of the Ten Days of Repentance (the two days of Rosh Hashanah, Shabbat, and Erev Yom Kippur), we must insure that there be at least four days suitable for fasting between *selichot* and Rosh Hashanah.

118   **sounding the *shofar* . . . :** one series of notes: *teki'ah-shevarim-teru'ah-teki'ah* (*Arukh Hashulchan* 581, no. 1).

118   **visit the graves of relatives:** Knobel, *Gates of the Seasons*, 39–40; *Shulchan Arukh, Orach Chayim* 581:4.

118   **It is a *mitzvah* to observe Rosh Hashanah . . . :** Knobel, *Gates of the Seasons*, 39.

118   **special music . . . :** A.Z. Idelson, *Jewish Music in Its Historical Development*, 110ff.; Jacob, *Questions and Reform Jewish Answers*, no. 65. For a detailed and comprehensive

commentary on the liturgy of the High Holidays, see Hoffman, *Gates of Understanding*, vol. 2.

119   **Special inserts in the *Tefillah* . . . :** Among others: *Zokhreinu*, "remember us unto life," inserted into the first blessing of the *Tefillah* (*Avot Ve'imahot*); the expanded version of the third blessing of the *Tefillah* (*Kedushat Hashem*) on Rosh Hashanah and Yom Kippur; and the special *chatimah* (concluding formula) "*hamelekh hakadosh*" for that blessing during the Days of Awe. Compare *Gates of Repentance*, Chaim Stern, ed., 30–39 to the festival *Tefillah*, *Gates of Prayer*, 481–86. See also the *Tefillah* inserts for "The Ten Days of Repentance," *Gates of Prayer*, 37–47 and 134–41.

119   ***Hallel* is not recited . . . :** *B. Arakhin* 10b and *Rosh Hashanah* 32b; *Yad, Chanukah* 3:6: Rosh Hashanah is a time of "repentance, awe and trembling before God, not a time of effusive joy."

119   ***Avinu Malkeinu* . . . :** Hoffman, *Gates of Understanding*, 2:23–25.

119   **The Torah reading . . . :** Stern, *Gates of Repentance*, 124–36 and 192–206. The traditional Torah readings for the first day of Rosh Hashanah are Gen. 21 and (from a second scroll) Num. 29:1–6; the *Haftarah* is I Sam. 1:1–2:10. On the second day the traditional Torah readings are Gen. 22 and (from the second scroll) Num. 29:1–6; the *Haftarah* is Jer. 31:2–20.

119   **The *Shofar*:** Knobel, *Gates of the Seasons*, 42.

119   **generally the horn of a ram . . . :** *B. Rosh Hashanah* 16a and 26b; *Shulchan Arukh, Orach Chayim* 586:1. Maimonides (*Yad, Shofar* 1:1) accepts *only* the ram's horn, but most authorities permit other animal horns (except for those of cattle and oxen, because those are called in Hebrew *keren* rather than *shofar*) if a ram's horn is not available.

119   **the *shofar* is sounded at least twice . . . :** In communities where it is the custom to hear *me'ah kolot*, "one hundred sounds" of the *shofar* on Rosh Hashanah (see *Tosafot Rosh Hashanah* 33b), the *shofar* is sounded twice more (the placement varies with communal custom) so as to make up an additional forty sounds.

119   **then again during the *chazan's* repetition . . . :** A well-known explanation for this custom is that in ancient days the *shofar* was sounded but once, at *Shacharit*, which was recited at dawn. One year the Romans mistook the early-morning *shofar* blasts as a call to war and massacred many Jews. The Rabbis then decreed that the *shofar* be sounded later in the day, during *Musaf*, to prevent a similar mistake from occurring in the future (*Y. Rosh Hashanah* 4:8, 59c. For another explanation, see *B. Rosh Hashanah* 32b). Once the "old" custom of sounding the *shofar* at *Shacharit* had been reinstated, the later practice was left in place as a remembrance or a precaution. At least one historian suggests that the *shofar* ritual was originally practiced at *Musaf*, rather than *Shacharit*, since it was always associated with the Temple rituals and special sacrifices of the day; see G. Alon, *Jews, Judaism and the Classical World*, 124–32.

119   ***Malkhuyot . . . Zikhronot . . . Shofarot*:** Knobel, *Gates of the Seasons*, 42 and 147–53; Hoffman, *Gates of Understanding*, 2:96–101. The number of verses in each section is traditionally ten (three from Torah, three from Writings, three from Prophets, a final one from Torah). This number is preserved in *Gates of Repentance*'s second service for Rosh Hashanah morning (208–17), although the selection of verses differs from that in the traditional *machzor*.

120   **The person who sounds the *shofar* . . . :** *Gates of Repentance*, 142; *Shulchan Arukh, Orach Chayim* 585:2.

120   **The ancient Rabbis deduced . . . :** *B. Rosh Hashanah* 33b–34a; *Yad, Shofar* 3:1–3; *Shulchan Arukh, Orach Chayim* 590:1–2. *Teru'ah* is described as *yelalah*, or "sobbing," while *shevarim* is called *anachah*, "sighing." Thus we see that, in this discussion of halakhic detail, the Rabbis focused upon the connection between the sound of the *shofar* and the contrite, broken heart.

120   ***Shofar* on Shabbat:** Freehof, *Recent Reform Responsa*, no. 6; Freehof, *Reform Jewish Practice*, 2:53–54. See *B. Rosh Hashanah* 29b; *Shulchan Arukh, Orach Chayim* 588:5. This explanation appears in the Babylonian Talmud, but other sources do not mention the concern that one might carry the *shofar*. See Albeck to *M. Rosh Hashanah* 4:1. The *shofar* was sounded in the Temple on Shabbat, and when the Temple was destroyed Rabban Yochanan ben Zakai decreed that it likewise be sounded on Shabbat "wherever a *beit din* [rabbinic court] is present," presumably to emphasize the equivalence between this rabbinic institution of Torah and the old Sanctuary. Maimonides (*Yad, Shofar* 2:8–9) holds that this *beit din* must consist of judges who possess *semikhah*, the ancient and long-discontinued ordination that was practiced in the land of Israel. Traditional *halakhah* follows his view, and since no one today possesses this *semikhah*, it is prohibited to sound the *shofar* on Shabbat. But R. Yitzchak Alfasi, an eminent eleventh-century halakhist, ruled that the *shofar* is sounded on Shabbat in the presence of *any* established *beit din*; thus, "the *shofar* was sounded before Alfasi's court when Rosh Hashanah fell on Shabbat" (R. Nissim b. Gerondi to Alfasi, *Rosh Hashanah*, fol. 8a, s.v. *venireh*; *Hilkhot Harosh, Rosh Hashanah* 4:1). Our practice, which regards each community as a fully-empowered *beit din*, coheres with that of Alfasi.

121   **The Second Day of Rosh Hashanah:** *B. Beitzah* 4b–5a. See, in general, *Responsa Committee*, no. 5759.7. The calendar was set in ancient times according to eyewitness testimony to the appearance of the new moon. The month of Tishri might begin on either the 30th or 31st day following the beginning of Elul, and the witnesses might not arrive at the Great Court in Jerusalem until late in the day of 30 Elul. The uncertainty over whether that day is to be celebrated as a festival or a weekday led to the rabbinic decree that Rosh Hashanah be observed for two days, even in Jerusalem. There is some evidence that in later times only one day of Rosh Hashanah was observed in the land of Israel, but Diaspora scholars who emigrated there reinstated the second day (*Sefer Hama'or* to Alfasi, *Beitzah*, fol. 3a).

121   **The *Mitzvot* of the Day:** Knobel, *Gates of the Seasons*, 40–43. Some observe the custom of dipping the *challah* into honey following *Hamotzi*.

121   **The Days of Awe:** *B. Rosh Hashanah* 18a; *Yad, Teshuvah* 2:6.

122   **It is a *mitzvah* to reflect . . . :** Knobel, *Gates of the Seasons*, 45–46.

122   **Repentance . . . :** the quotations are from *Yad, Teshuvah* 2:1–2.

122   **Reconciliation . . . :** *M. Yoma* 8:9; *M. Bava Kama* 8:7; *Yad, Teshuvah* 2:9.

122   **Forgiveness . . . :** *M. Bava Kama* 8:7; *Yad, Teshuvah* 2:10.

122   **Shabbat Shuvah:** Knobel, *Gates of the Seasons*, 46. The full *Haftarah* is Hosea 14:2–10; Micah 7:18–20; and Joel 2:15–27; see Plaut, *The Torah: A Modern Commentary*, 1634ff. The Hosea passage is always read, while the particular combination of the verses from Micah and Joel traditionally depends upon whether the Torah portion that day is *Vayelekh* or *Ha'azinu*.

122   **Yom Kippur:** Lev. 16.

123   **We continue to fast . . . :** see Knobel, *Gates of the Seasons*, 53 and 146–147.

123   **The Temple is remembered . . . :** For a full commentary see Hoffman, *Gates of Understanding*, 2:109ff.

123   **We recall his service in poetic form . . . :** On the *Seder Avodah* and its development, see Elbogen, *Jewish Liturgy*, 174, and Hoffman, *Gates of Understanding*, 2:138–44.

123   *Ne'ilah* . . . : See Elbogen, *Jewish Liturgy*, 127. Outside the Temple, *Ne'ilah* was a feature of all fast-day liturgy; later practice retained it for Yom Kippur alone, a fact which heightens the sense of drama at the close of this day.

123   *selichot* . . . : Included in each of the services for Yom Kippur. See Elbogen, *Jewish Liturgy*, 177–84.

123   *viduyim* . . . : Also included at each Yom Kippur service. Each *vidu'i* customarily includes two forms of confession, one short (*ashamnu, bagadnu*, etc.; *Gates of Repentance*, 269), the other longer (*al chet; Gates of Repentance*, 271–72).

124   **It is a *mitzvah* to observe Yom Kippur . . . :** Knobel, *Gates of the Seasons*, 50–51.

124   *tzedakah* . . . : There is an old custom to perform, *kaparot*, an "atonement" ritual, on the day before Yom Kippur. In one form, this ritual involved the slaughter (symbolic sacrifice) of a rooster and the recitation of appropriate biblical verses. The practice was the subject of controversy among halakhic authorities; see *Shulchan Arukh, Orach Chayim* 605 and Isserles ad loc. Some suggested as an alternative to this ritual that coins be placed in a bag and waved in the air; the coins would then be given to the poor (*Chayei Adam*, 144:4). Our suggestion for the giving of *tzedakah* on Erev Yom Kippur is a development on the theme of *kaparot*. In fulfillment of this custom, many congregations conduct food drives to coincide with Yom Kippur.

124   **Erev Yom Kippur:** *B. Yoma* 81b. Lev. 23:32 declares that we begin our self-denial (i.e., fasting) "on the ninth day of the month at evening." This could be interpreted as meaning that the fast begins at sundown on the night *before* Yom Kippur and lasts for two days. Such a requirement is both impractical and a contradiction of the clear biblical evidence that the fast takes place only on the tenth of Tishri (see Num. 29:7). Thus, the Rabbis read Lev. 23:32 as follows: "whoever eats and drinks on the ninth of Tishri is regarded *as though* he or she has fasted for two days." In other words, our joy on this day is part and parcel of the observance of the next day, Yom Kippur, with its mood of somber self-denial.

124   **"that Yom Kippur will bring us goodness . . . ":** *Arukh Hashulchan, Orach Chayim* 604, no. 5.

124   *se'udah mafseket* . . . : *Shulchan Arukh, Orach Chayim* 608.

124   **no special rituals . . . :** It is traditional, however, that one recites the *vidu'i*, the confession of sins, at the *Minchah* service prior to the meal. *B. Yoma* 87b; *Yad, Teshuvah* 2:7; *Shulchan Arukh, Orach Chayim* 607:1.

124   **We do not recite *Kiddush* . . . :** Knobel, *Gates of the Seasons*, 51–52.

124   **must be completed *before* the onset of the holy day . . . :** The principle is that we should "add from the ordinary to the holy"; i.e., we allow the holy day to extend into the afternoon of the preceding day, especially to fulfill the implication of Lev. 23:32 that the fast begins on the ninth of Tishri. Thus, the *se'udah mafseket* must end during daylight so that Yom Kippur may begin with the recitation of Kol Nidrei prior to sundown. Knobel, *Gates of the Seasons*, 51; *B. Yoma* 81b; *Yad, Teshuvah* 1:6; *Shulchan Arukh, Orach Chayim* 608:1.

124   **Yom Kippur lights:** Knobel, *Gates of the Seasons*, 52. This "*mitzvah*" is a custom, mentioned in *M. Pesachim* 4:4, observed by some, but not all, Jews. The Talmud (*B. Pesachim* 53b and Rashi ad loc.) hints at the reason: the light may serve to prevent sexual intercourse, one of the forbidden acts on Yom Kippur (*Yad, Shevitat Asor* 3:10; *Shulchan Arukh, Orach Chayim* 610:1 and *Mishnah Berurah*, no. 1). Later authorities suggest that the light is a sign of the "honor" of the day, much like the Shabbat light (*Arukh Hashulchan, Orach Chayim* 610, no. 3).

125   **Fasting:** Knobel, *Gates of the Seasons*, 53, and 146–47.

125   **the tradition identifies this affliction . . . :** *M. Yoma* 8:1. Other afflictions mentioned there are the abstention from washing, anointing, sexual intercourse, and the wearing of leather shoes.

125   **Children . . . :** *M. Yoma* 8:4; *Yad, Shevitat Asor* 2:10; *Shulchan Arukh, Orach Chayim* 616:2.

125   **Pregnant women and those who are ill . . .** See *M. Yoma* 8:5–6. The laws are found in *Shulchan Arukh, Orach Chayim* 617–18. The category is that of *pikuach nefesh*, the duty to preserve life, traditionally derived from a *midrash* on Lev. 18:5: "These are the *mitzvot* which one shall do and live by them," to which the Rabbis add: "and not *die* by them" (*B. Yoma* 85b). Hence, virtually every ritual requirement is set aside when its performance is judged to be a danger to life. If a physician prescribes that a patient must eat on Yom Kippur, the patient has no right to disobey this instruction. He or she *must* eat, for it is a sin (and definitely *not* a mitzvah) to bring one's life into unnecessary danger.

125   **Religious Services:** Knobel, *Gates of the Seasons*, 53–54.

125   **Memorial services . . . :** See Hoffman, *Gates of Understanding*, 2:146–49. Yizkor is recited in traditional synagogues following the reading of the *Haftarah* at *Shacharit*. Many Reform congregations hold this service in the afternoon, between *Minchah* and *Ne'ilah*.

125   ***Havdalah* . . . :** Traditionally recited at the *Ma'ariv* service, which follows immediately after *Ne'ilah*. Our ritual includes the blessing over the spices. Traditionally, one does not recite this blessing at the end of Yom Kippur, since the spices come to compensate for the loss of the "additional soul" (*neshamah yeteirah*) which we are said to enjoy on the Sabbath day. On Yom Kippur, a day of fasting rather than delight, we do not receive this additional soul. On the other hand, some hold that we *do* say the blessing over spices when Yom Kippur coincides with Shabbat (*Bach, Tur, Orach Chayim* 624; *Shulchan Arukh, Orach Chayim* 624:3, *Mishnah Berurah*, no. 5). Our practice is to say this *berakhah* on whatever day of the week Yom Kippur falls because the day is referred to as a "sabbath" of complete rest (Lev. 23:32); hence, we treat it in this regard as a Shabbat.

125   **"break-the-fast" . . . :** Knobel, *Gates of the Seasons*, 55. The high priest would invite his friends to a festive gathering following the conclusion of his service on Yom Kippur; *M. Yoma* 8:4.

125   **A congregation should not schedule . . . :** Even if services have ended before sundown, the sanctity of Yom Kippur requires that the day itself not be brought to an end before its proper time; Jacob, *Questions and Reform Jewish Answers*, no. 67.

125   **Refraining from Work:** Knobel, *Gates of the Seasons*, 54.

125   **Beginning the Sukkah:** Ibid.

125   **The study of Torah is interrupted . . . :** *B. Megillah* 3a. While this point is the subject of some controversy (see Isserles, *Shulchan Arukh, Orach Chayim* 687:2), many authorities (e.g., *Taz* and *Bi'ur Hagra* to *Shulchan Arukh* ad loc.) hold this position literally: the reading of the *Megillah* on Purim takes precedence over any other *mitzvah* that one might perform at that moment. The only exception is the burial of a *met mitzvah*, a corpse for whom no one else is available to do the work of burial.

126   **This theme of Jewish survival . . . :** See Knobel, *Gates of the Seasons*, 137, n. 210, for another interpretation: the futility of assimilation and the demand that Jews proudly proclaim and live their heritage.

126   **"a numerous people is the glory of the King":** It is a special *mitzvah* to hear the reading of the *Megillah* as part of a large congregation; *Mishnah Berurah* 687, no. 7.

126   **It is a *mitzvah* to observe Purim . . . :** Knobel, *Gates of the Seasons*, 96; *M. Megillah* 1:1; *B. Megillah* 2a–b; *Yad, Megillah* 1:4; *Shulchan Arukh, Orach Chayim* 688:1–3. Smaller communities read the *Megillah* on the previous Monday or Thursday (that is, market days) when Purim fell on another day of the week. This practice was no longer observed in talmudic times (*B. Megillah* 2a) nor is it followed today (*Yad, Megillah* 1:9); Purim is observed everywhere on either the fourteenth or the fifteenth of the month.

126   **The Reading of the *Megillah*:** Knobel, *Gates of the Seasons*, 96. This *mitzvah*, mentioned in *Tosefta Megillah* 2:4 and *B. Arakhin* 2b, is a rabbinic ordinance (see *Yad, Megillah* 1:1), inasmuch as Purim is not mentioned in the Five Books of Moses, the source of "Toraitic" *mitzvot*.

126   **Traditionally the *Megillah* is read . . . :** *B. Megillah* 4a; *Yad, Megillah* 1:3; *Shulchan Arukh, Orach Chayim* 687:1.

126   **as part of a congregation . . . :** See above, "a numerous people is the glory of the King." This is not an absolute requirement; in case of illness or emergency, one may fulfill this *mitzvah* by reading the Book of Esther at home. Still, it is meritorious to "search out a *minyan*," since by reading the *Megillah* we "publicize the miracle" of our redemption (*Shulchan Arukh, Orach Chayim* 690:18, based upon the discussion in *B. Megillah* 5a; *Beit Yosef, Tur, Orach Chayim* 690, end. Some early authorities, in fact, did require a *minyan*). On the benedictions, see *M. Megillah* 4:1; *B. Megillah* 21b; *Shulchan Arukh, Orach Chayim* 692:1.

127   **A number of customs . . . :** *Shulchan Arukh, Orach Chayim* 690:17.

127   **a descendant of Amalek . . . :** "We ought not to sneer at customs such as these, for they were established for a purpose"; *Beit Yosef, Orach Chayim* 690. It is customary to read the names of Haman's ten sons (Esther 9:7–9) in one breath (*Shulchan Arukh, Orach Chayim* 690:15) and for the congregation to chant out loud the "four verses of redemption": Esther 2:5, 8:15, 8:16, and 10:3. The reader then recites the verses.

127   **The Other *Mitzvot* of the Day:** *Shulchan Arukh, Orach Chayim* 693.

127   **We do not . . . recite the *Hallel* . . . :** "How can we recite 'Praise God's name, O you servants of God' (Ps. 113:1, the beginning of *Hallel*) when we are still the servants of Ahasuerus?" *B. Megillah* 14a; *Mishnah Berurah* 693, no. 7.

127   **"Feasting and Merrymaking":** Knobel, *Gates of the Seasons*, 96. See *B. Megillah* 7b, where we find that "one is obligated to become so intoxicated on Purim that one cannot distinguish between 'cursed be Haman' and 'blessed be Mordecai.'" The Talmud cautions us in graphic terms against a too-literal reading of this statement,

and rabbinic tradition has sought to pull back from the more unfortunate applications of this "strange expression" (*Arukh Hashulchan, Orach Chayim* 695, no. 3). See *Mishnah Berurah*, 695, no. 4.

127   **"It is a *mitzvah* to hold a festive meal . . .":** *Tur, Orach Chayim* 695.

128   **following *Minchah* . . . :** Isserles, *Orach Chayim* 695:2.

128   **"Sending Gifts":** B. *Megillah* 7a; *Yad, Megillah* 2:15; *Shulchan Arukh, Orach Chayim* 295:4.

128   **"Presents to the Poor":** B. *Megillah* 7a; *Shulchan Arukh, Orach Chayim* 694.

128   **"for there is no greater joy . . . ":** *Yad, Megillah* 2:17. Rambam continues: "for the one who lifts the spirits of these unfortunates is like the *Shekhinah* (the Divine Presence itself; see Isa. 57:15)."

128   **While historians debate . . . :** For the various theories, see Victor Tcherikover, *Hellenistic Civilization and the Jews*, 175ff.

129   **According to legend . . . :** *Pesikta deRav Kahana, piska* 1.

129   **It is a *mitzvah* to oberve Chanukah . . . :** Knobel, *Gates of the Seasons*, 91.

129   **The actual "*mitzvah*" of Chanukah . . . :** B. *Shabbat* 21b; *Yad, Chanukah* 3:3. Chanukah is properly a home observance; "the kindling of Chanukah lights in the synagogue is no substitute for kindling them at home" (Knobel, *Gates of the Seasons*, 92). Indeed, one who is away fulfills the *mitzvah* when one's spouse or family kindles the lights at home (B. *Shabbat* 23a; *Yad, Chanukah* 4:11; *Shulchan Arukh, Orach Chayim* 677:1). However, one who is not at home at the time of candle-lighting may choose to fulfill this *mitzvah* by lighting the candles at the place where he or she happens to be (Isserles, *Orach Chayim* 677:3; *Mishnah Berurah*, no. 15).

129   **blessings:** B. *Shabbat* 23a; *Yad, Chanukah* 3:4; *Shulchan Arukh, Orach Chayim* 676:1–2.

130   **One candle is lit for each night . . . :** B. *Shabbat* 21b; *Yad, Chanukah* 4:1; *Shulchan Arukh, Orach Chayim* 671:2.

130   **a special "servant" (*shamash*) candle . . . :** *Shulchan Arukh, Orach Chayim* 673:1; Freehof, *Modern Reform Responsa*, no. 19.

130   **each member of the household . . . kindles . . . :** *Yad, Chanukah* 4:2–3; *Shulchan Arukh* and Isserles, *Orach Chayim* 671:2 and 675:3. The "children" here are of school age. See Freehof, *Reform Responsa*, no. 1.

130   **Since it is traditionally forbidden . . . :** Knobel, *Gates of the Seasons*, 92; *Shulchan Arukh, Orach Chayim* 679. The question of Havdalah is complicated. Some authorities hold that we kindle the Chanukah lights *before* Havdalah (*Shulchan Arukh* and Isserles, *Orach Chayim* 681:2). The reason is that we have already said a form of *Havdalah* in the fourth benediction of the Saturday night *Tefillah*; therefore, Shabbat has technically been concluded and it is permissible to light fire. Moreover, they continue, we should seek to postpone the *Havdalah* ceremony (wine, spices, and fire) as long as possible so as to delay the end of Shabbat (*Mishnah Berurah*, no. 2). Other authorities, however, find problems with this procedure and rule that *Havdalah* precedes the kindling of the Chanukah lights (*Taz* to *Orach Chayim* 681:2). We follow this latter position, which we find to be the more logical and consistent of the two: Shabbat starts with the candle-lighting and ends with *Havdalah*, and the Chanukah candles should not "intrude" upon the time marked off by these rituals.

130   **"To Proclaim the Miracle":** *Yad, Chanukah* 3:3; *Tur, Orach Chayim* 671; Knobel, *Gates of the Seasons*, 92.

130   **at sundown . . . :** *B. Shabbat* 21b; *Yad, Chanukah* 4:5; *Shulchan Arukh, Orach Chayim* 672:1.

130   **visible from the outside . . . :** *B. Shabbat* 21b and Rashi, s.v. *mibachutz*; *Yad, Chanukah* 4:7–8; *Shulchan Arukh, Orach Chayim* 671:5–8. However, since the *mitzvah* of Chanukah lies in the *kindling* of the light rather than in its placement, one fulfills the *mitzvah* even when the candles are not visible from the outside; *B. Shabbat* 23a; *Shulchan Arukh, Orach Chayim* 675:1.

130   **an electric *menorah* . . . :** *Resp. Beit Yitzchak, Yore De'ah*, no. 120:5; *Resp. Mishpetei Ouziel* 1:25. See Jacob, *Questions and Reform Jewish Answers*, no. 76: this applies to the observance at home, but for purposes of public display an electric *menorah* is "safer and more aesthetically pleasing."

130   **'al hanissim . . . :** *Shulchan Arukh, Orach Chayim* 682:1.

130   **Hallel is recited . . . :** Ibid., 683.

130   **The Torah reading . . . :** Ibid., 684; Hoffman, *Gates of Understanding*, 1:282.

131   **the destruction of both the First and the Second Temple . . . :** *M. Ta'anit* 4:6.

131   **While other tragic events . . . :** For example, the decree that the Israelites would not be able to enter the Promised Land (Num. 14:26ff.) and the destruction of Beitar are dated by tradition on 9 Av (*M. Ta'anit* 4:6). The expulsion of the Jews from England in 1290 and from Spain in 1492 took place on that day as well. See Knobel, *Gates of the Seasons*, 140, n. 227.

131   **Some Reform prayer books ignore . . . :** Especially the American ones; see Petuchowski, *Prayerbook Reform*, 291–97.

131   **joy as well as sadness . . . :** For example, *Olat Tamid*, the *siddur* of David Einhorn (1809–79), the German-born leader of "radical Reform" in the United States. See Meyer, *Response to Modernity*, 247. See as well Einhorn's sermon, excerpted in Plaut, *Rise of Reform Judaism*, 201–3: "[The commemoration of Tisha Be'Av] has no lesser importance than the revelation of Mount Sinai; for the reform of Judaism recognizes in the destruction of the Temple…a deed in which God Himself reformed the law…. From the grave of animal sacrifice and separate priesthood rose the magnificent phenomenon of a congregation of priests scattered over the entire world….We must not weep over the ruins of Jerusalem, for the Messiah was born in those very ruins! Israel lost a structure of wood and stone so that it might win more souls for God."

132   **Tisha Be'Av:** The fast is observed on the ninth of Av unless that date falls on Shabbat. Since fasting is prohibited on Shabbat (except in the case of the biblically-ordained fast of Yom Kippur), this observance is delayed until Saturday night and Sunday, the tenth of Av.

132   **the fast . . . is more stringent . . . :** See *Shulchan Arukh, Orach Chayim* 550. On the other fast days—10 Tevet, 13 Adar (the fast of Esther), 17 Tamuz, and 3 Tishri (the fast of Gedaliah)—the fast lasts from sunup to sundown only. In addition, on Tisha Be'Av as on Yom Kippur (but not on these other fasts) one is traditionally prohibited from washing, anointing, wearing leather shoes, and engaging in sexual intercourse. See, in general, *Shulchan Arukh, Orach Chayim* 549–59. The Torah and *Haftarah* readings in Reform congregations are noted in Hoffman, *Gates of Understanding*, 1:283. For a descriptive and analytical account of the observance of these fast days see Sandra Cohen, "Mourning the Temple's Destruction: The Laws of Tisha B'av and the Other Public Fasts in the Arba'ah Turim and the Bet Yosef" (Rabbinic thesis, HUC-JIR, 1995).

132 **It is customary not to hold weddings . . . :** *B. Yevamot* 43a; *Yad, Ishut* 10:14 (by implication: it is permitted to *betroth* a wife on this day, since betrothal does not usually involve feasting and rejoicing. It follows that weddings, which are joyful even apart from the feasting, are prohibited); *Shulchan Arukh, Orach Chayim* 551:2 and *Magen Avraham,* no. 9. Although there are indications that at times this prohibition was not strictly observed (*Resp. Mateh Levi,* 2, no. 32), it remains the predominant halakhic view.

132 **Even if we do not observe this fast . . . :** David Polish, ed., *Rabbi's Manual,* 241. See also Knobel, *Gates of the Seasons,* 104, and Jacob, *Questions and Reform Jewish Answers,* no. 217. R. Solomon Freehof (*Recent Reform Responsa,* no. 38) rules that we should avoid large wedding festivities on this day "out of respect for general sentiment," though a small private wedding is permitted. Of course, if we observe Tisha Be'Av as a sign of heartfelt identification with the history of our people and not merely on grounds of "general sentiment," then we would *not* be inclined to hold any weddings, however small, on that day.

132 **Yom Hashoah:** Knobel, *Gates of the Seasons,* 102–3; *CCAR Yearbook* 87 (1987): 87.

133 **Yom Ha'atzma'ut:** Knobel, *Gates of the Seasons,* 102.

133 **a liturgy for Israel Independence Day . . . :** Since many Reform congregations will mark this holiday on Shabbat, the various Shabbat inserts are included in this service. In Israel, however, Yom Ha'atzma'ut is never observed on Shabbat or on Friday. If the fifth of Iyar falls on either day the observance is moved to the preceding Thursday, lest its festivities interfere with preparations for or observance of Shabbat.

133 ***Hallel* and the reading of the Torah . . . :** Hoffman, *Gates of Understanding,* 1:283, suggests the following as possible Torah readings: Deut. 8:1–18; 11:8–21; 26:1–11; or 30:1–16. Possible *Haftarot*: Isaiah 60:1–22; 10:32–12:6; 65:17–25.

133 **The halakhic debates . . . :** detailed in N. Rakover, *Hilkhot Yom Ha'atzma'ut ve-Yom Yerushalayim.* See Y. Shaviv, *Shanah Beshanah, 5756* (Jerusalem: Heikhal Shelomo, 1995): 70: "According to an ordinance of the chief rabbinate of Israel, *Hallel* is recited in the synagogue (some recite the blessings for *Hallel*; others do not), along with prayers for the well-being of the state," but the Torah and *Haftarah* are not read. In addition to the liturgical questions, there is the question of the Omer: Yom Ha'atzma'ut occurs on the twentieth day of that period of semi-mourning. Some Orthodox Jews who observe Yom Ha'atzma'ut will relax the Omer restrictions on that day or in preparation for it. Those who do are more likely to attend community celebrations of Israel Independence Day which involve music and other festivities. Other Orthodox Jews, including most of the *charedim* (ultra-Orthodox), do not observe Yom Ha'atzma'ut as a festival; on the contrary, for them it is a day of mourning. See Mordekhai Hakohen, "Yom Ha'atzma'ut" in Y. Reppel, *Mo'adei Yisrael,* 174–75.

133 **the festivals of Purim and Chanukah . . . :** The Conservative movement's *siddur,* in fact, offers a version of the prayer *'al hanissim* for Yom Ha'atzma'ut which parallels the texts of that prayer for Chanukah and Purim. As on those other festivals, the prayer is inserted into the eighteenth benediction of the *Tefillah.* See Jules Harlow, ed., *Siddur Sim Shalom: A Prayerbook for Shabbat, Festivals, and Weekdays,* 118.

Chapter 4: The Life Cycle

134   **Our biblical ancestors . . . :** See the stories of Abraham and Sarah (Gen. 15–17, 21–22), Rebecca (Gen. 25:19-21), Rachel (Gen. 29:31–30:24), and Hannah (I Samuel 1), as well as the prophetic imagery in Isaiah 54.

134   **it is a *mitzvah* for men and women . . . :** The commandment to "be fruitful and multiply" is found in Gen. 1:28; see *M. Yevamot* 6:6; *Yad, Ishut* 15:1, and *Shulchan Arukh, Even Ha'ezer* 1:1.

134   **And it is a special *mitzvah* . . . :** Jacob, *American Reform Responsa*, no. 132; *Responsa Committee*, no. 5758.3. Despite the great emphasis placed by tradition upon procreation, the marriage of a childless couple is as valid as any other Jewish marriage. While childlessness is a valid ground for divorce and while the community is even empowered to coerce a divorce in such a case (*B. Yevamot* 64a; *Shulchan Arukh, Even Ha'ezer* 154:10), this rule has not been enforced for centuries; *Resp. Rivash*, no. 15; Isserles, *Even Ha'ezer* 1:3; *Responsa Committee*, no. 5758.3; *American Reform Responsa*, no. 132.

134   **Reform Judaism encourages couples . . . :** Maslin, *Gates of Mitzvah*, 11.

134   **Jewish Status and "Patrilineal Descent":** See, in general, *Report of the Committee On Patrilineal Descent*, and Jacob, *Contemporary American Reform Responsa*, no. 38.

135   **According to *halakhah* . . . :** The basic text is *M. Kiddushin* 3:12. See *Shulchan Arukh, Even Ha'ezer* 8:5.

135   **Prior to the rabbinic period . . . :** See Shaye J.D. Cohen, "The Origins of the Matrilineal Principle in Rabbinic Law," *AJS Review* 10 (1985): 19–53. The patrilineal principle is evident in the genealogies of the Israelites, who were numbered "by their families, by their fathers' houses" (Num. 1:2). This implies, as the Talmud notes, that "the line (family) of the father is recognized, and the line (family) of the mother is not"; *B. Yevamot* 54b and *Bava Batra* 109b; *Yad, Nachalot* 1:6.

135   **Something of the patrilineal principle . . . :** *M. Kiddushin* 3:12; *Yad, Ishut* 19:15; *Shulchan Arukh, Even Ha'ezer* 8.

136   **The Rabbis, we presume, had their reasons:** Shaye J.D. Cohen, "Origins of the Matrilineal Principle," suggests some of these: 1) the influence of Roman law, which declares that if one parent is incapable of contracting a valid marriage (*connubium*, similar to the halakhic *kiddushin*) the offspring inherits the mother's status; 2) the rabbinic definition of *kilayim*, "diverse kinds" (cf. Lev. 19:19), in which the offspring of two diverse animal species is judged according to its mother; and 3) the development of the institution of conversion, which allowed Gentile women (and their offspring) to attain Jewish status. From this, it followed that when a Gentile woman does not choose to become a Jew her offspring, too, remains a Gentile.

136   **The Central Conference of American Rabbis (CCAR) has grappled . . . :** The quotations in the following section are taken from the *Report of the Committee on Patrilineal Descent*.

138   ***The resolution is advisory* . . . :** Polish, *Rabbi's Manual*, 227.

138   **There are those who predict . . . :** See Bulka, *The Coming Cataclysm*, and Jakob J. Petuchowski, "Toward Sectarianism," *Moment* 8 (Sept., 1983): 34–36. See also Irving Greenberg, *Will There Be One Jewish People By the Year 2000?*: if current sociological and demographic trends continue, the Jewish people will split apart into two, mutually divided hostile groups who are unable or unwilling to marry each other out of inability to agree on the basic question of Jewish status.

138   **Others discount . . . :** On the history of these predictions in general, see Abramov, *Perpetual Dilemma: Jewish Religion in the Jewish State*, 270–320, and Mark Washofsky, "The Proposal for a National *Beit Din*: Is It Good for the Jews?" in M. Shapiro, ed., *Divisions Between Traditionalism and Liberalism in the American Jewish Community.*

138   **Reform rabbis and congregations have a moral obligation . . . :** Plaut and Washofsky, *Teshuvot for the Nineties*, no. 5752.2, n. 3.

139   *Jewish descent may be from either parent:* See Polish, *Rabbi's Manual*, 227.

140   *Both descent and behavior are crucial in determining Jewish status under the resolution:* See Jacob, *Contemporary American Reform Responsa*, nos. 39, 40, 58, 59.

140   **Reform responsa hold . . . :** Plaut and Washofsky, *Teshuvot*, no. 5754.13; Jacob, *Contemporary American Reform Responsa*, nos. 39, 42 (end), and 59. Even though the 1983 resolution speaks of "other public acts or declarations" to establish Jewish status for those "beyond childhood," the tendency has been to see conversion as the one best "act" for adults whose Jewish status remains questionable.

140   *The resolution applies only to children raised exclusively as Jews:* Plaut and Washofsky, *Teshuvot*, no. 5755.17; Jacob, *Contemporary American Reform Responsa*, no. 61; Jacob, *Questions and Reform Jewish Answers*, no. 109.

141   **a home where two religions are actively practiced . . . :** Plaut and Washofsky, *Teshuvot*, no. 5755.17.

141   **these acts must be "meaningful" evidence . . . :** Polish, *Rabbi's Manual*, 227. The resolution states that "the performance of these *mitzvot* serves to commit those who participate in them, *both parent and child* [italics added], to Jewish life." Jewish life requires an environment in which Judaism is the exclusive religious identification of the *household*, even if one of the parents is not Jewish. The dual-religion household is not one that is committed to *Jewish* life.

142   **The adoptive parents are in every respect *the* parents . . . :** Plaut and Washofsky, *Teshuvot*, no. 5753.12; Jacob, *American Reform Responsa*, no. 62.

142   **Though many authorities hold . . . :** See *Meshekh Chokhmah* to Deut. 5:16; *Resp. Miyam Hahalakhah* 2:18; *Nachalat Tzvi*, 37; *Yalkut Yosef* 6:100.

142   **others assert . . . :** *Sefer Hachinukh*, mitzvah 33; *Sha'arei Ouziel*, 2:184–85; *Resp. Aseh Lekha Rav* 3:39.

142   **say *Kaddish* and observe all mourning rites for an adoptive parent . . . :** Plaut and Washofsky, *Teshuvot*, no. 5753.12; Jacob, *Contemporary American Reform Responsa*, no. 35. The child may choose to observe mourning rites for his or her biological parents, but mourning is an obligation with respect to the adoptive parents, those who raised him or her.

142   **The Jewish Status of Adopted Children:** *Responsa Committee*, no. 5759.1; Jacob, *American Reform Responsa*, no. 63; Jacob, *Contemporary American Reform Responsa*, no. 37; Jacob, *Questions and Reform Jewish Answers*, no. 117. The position enunciated here follows that taken in our responsa literature, which holds that conversion is necessary when a child of Gentile biological parents is adopted by Jews. In the absence of biological descent from Jewish parents a child can become a Jew only through conversion. On naming the adopted child, see *Resp. Igerot Moshe, Yore De'ah* 1:161: since the child has never known any other religion than that taught him or her by the Jewish parents, it is unnecessary to provide a special "conversionary" name (*ben/bat Avraham avinu ve-Sarah imeinu*).

142   **Alternately, some special readings . . . :** Polish, *Rabbi's Manual*, 25–36.

142   **race or ethnicity . . . :** Jacob, *American Reform Responsa*, no. 62.

142   **Adoption Agencies:** Jacob, *Contemporary American Reform Responsa*, no. 36, based upon the priorities traditionally followed in the allocation of *tzedakah* (*Shulchan Arukh, Yore De'ah* 251:3).

142   **Circumcision (Berit Milah):** *Arukh Hashulchan, Yore De'ah* 260, par. 1.

143   **"bound through the generations . . .":** *Tur, Yore De'ah* 260. If Hellenistic authors saw circumcision as a mutilation of the body, the Rabbis declared it the means by which the male form is perfected; *Genesis Rabbah* 11:6. See Lewis M. Barth, ed., *Berit Milah in the Reform Context*, 104–12.

143   **Within Reform Judaism . . . :** See Michael A. Meyer, "*Berit Milah* Within the History of the Reform Movement" in Bartha, *Berit Milah*, 141–51, and Jacob Katz, *Hahalakhah Bameitzar*, 123–49.

143   **"the ancient practice . . .":** Freehof, *Reform Jewish Practice*, 1:113.

143   **"a mitzvah to circumcise . . .":** Maslin, *Gates of Mitzvah*, 14.

143   **The Ceremony of Berit Milah:** Jacob, *Questions and Reform Jewish Answers*, no. 98. For the liturgy, see Polish, *Rabbi's Manual*, 6-15 and the commentary of Richard Levy in Barth, *Berit Milah*, 3–15.

144   **hakisei shel Eliyahu . . . :** See *Pirkei deR. Eliezer*, ch. 29, end. Elijah condemns Israel for having forsaken the "covenant"; i.e., the practice of *berit milah*. In return, God appoints him as the "messenger of the covenant" to be present at every circumcision. Some interpret this as a reward for Elijah's righteous zeal. Others regard it as a punishment: "Since you have cast aspersions upon Israel's faithfulness to Me, you shall attend every circumcision to witness with your own eyes how they fulfill this *mitzvah*"; *Perishah* to *Tur, Yore De'ah* 265, no. 25.

144   **placed upon the lap of the sandak or sandakit . . . :** Likened to an altar, upon which the circumcision is offered as a gift to God (*Sefer Maharil, Hilkhot Milah*, par. 1).

144   **the mohel/et recites . . . :** On the *berakhot*, see B. *Shabbat* 137b; *Yad, Milah* 3:1; *Shulchan Arukh, Yore De'ah* 265:1.

144   **Following the circumcision, the parents recite . . . :** Traditionally, this blessing is recited between the circumcision proper (*milah*) and *peri'ah* (see below); *Tosafot, Shabbat* 137b, s.v. *avi*; *Shulchan Arukh, Yore De'ah* 265:1.

144   **the infant, too, shares a few drops . . . :** The *mohel* also gives the baby a few drops of wine at the recitation of Ezekiel 16:6 during the naming prayer.

144   **In Reform practice . . . :** Also followed by the Sefardim (*Yad, Milah* 3:3; *Shulchan Arukh, Yore De'ah* 265:7), on the grounds that a *berit milah* is a joyous occasion at which the blessing is appropriate. The Ashkenazic custom not to recite it at the ceremony is usually linked to the *absence* of joy: sadness at the infant's discomfort and concern for his life, given that infant mortality is quite high during the first month. To this, one can respond that we recite *Shehechiyanu* over our own happiness at performing the commandment (*Hagahot Maimoniot, Milah* 3:4) and that most infants do in fact survive their first month (*Resp. Rashba* 1:166).

144   **It is preferable . . . :** Jacob, *Questions and Reform Jewish Answers*, no. 97.

144   **Ritual circumcision consists . . . :** M. *Shabbat* 19:6; *Yad, Milah* 2:2; *Shulchan Arukh, Yore De'ah* 264:3.

145   **Most physicians today . . . :** Thomas Goldenberg, "Medical Issues and *Berit Milah*," in Barth, *Berit Milah*, 197–99; Polish, *Rabbi's Manual*, 222. To meet the traditional requirement that at least some blood flow during the circumcision, the *mohel/et* may wish to use a clamp that does not achieve complete hemostasis. Goldenberg recommends the Mogen clamp for this reason. The requirement that blood be drawn during *milah* is likely based upon the rabbinic understanding of Ezekiel 16:6 and upon the association of the blood of the covenant with the blood of the paschal sacrifice in Egypt as acts by which Israel merited redemption from bondage. See Levy, "The Liturgy of *Berit Milah*," in Barth, *Berit Milah*, 12–13.

145   **There is no objection to the use of clamps . . . :** These technologies, both old and new, are intended to facilitate the circumcision and are not regarded as sacred in and of themselves.

145   ***Metzitzah* . . . :** Polish, *Rabbi's Manual*, 222. While *milah* and *peri'ah* are the two essential steps without which the *mitzvah* has not been properly performed (*M. Shabbat* 19:6; *Shulchan Arukh, Yore De'ah* 264:4), *metzitzah* is a hygienic measure (*B. Shabbat* 133b; *Yad, Milah* 2:2); its absence does not invalidate the circumcision. On the controversy surrounding *metzitzah* and its role in anti-Reform polemics in the nineteenth century, see Katz, *Hahalakhah Bameitzar*, 150–83.

145   **anesthetics . . . :** Jacob, *American Reform Responsa*, no. 57; *Resp. Ma'arakhei Lev*, no. 53; *Nachalat Tzvi*, 57.

145   **The *Mohel/et*:** Freehof, *Reform Responsa*, no. 24; Freehof, *Reform Responsa for Our Time*, no. 18; Polish, *Rabbi's Manual*, 221; Maslin, *Gates of Mitzvah*, 15. Some halakhists allow an apostate to circumcise; R. Akiva Eger, *Chidushim, Yore De'ah* 264:1; *Resp. Melamed Leho'il* 2:80. As for Gentiles, the Talmud (*B. Avodah Zarah* 26b–27a) offers two alternative reasons for their disqualification. The first declares that we fear Gentiles may harm the child; the second rejects them because this *mitzvah* is restricted to members of the covenant community. If we follow Rabbi Freehof in accepting the first explanation, we would permit Gentiles to circumcise inasmuch as this fear no longer exists among us. The second explanation, adopted by most commentators, is more difficult to refute. Clearly it is better that the circumcision be performed by one who is part of the community which *milah* symbolizes. On the other hand, Maimonides (*Yad, Milah* 2:1) and Karo (*Shulchan Arukh, Yore De'ah* 264:1) rule that though the procedure ought to be performed by a Jew, the *milah* is *not* considered invalid if performed by a Gentile. While others disagree (see Isserles, *Yore De'ah* ad loc.), we can safely conclude that as a final resort, a Gentile may serve as *mohel/et*.

145   **Other Participants:** Jacob, *Questions and Reform Jewish Answers*, no. 105. On the *sandak*, see *Shulchan Arukh, Yore De'ah* 264:1 and 265:11; Jacob, *Contemporary American Reform Responsa*, no. 30; and *Questions and Reform Jewish Answers*, no. 166.

146   **When Is the Ceremony Held?** Gen. 17:12 and Lev. 12:3; *B. Shabbat* 132a and Rashi, s.v. *uvayom*.

146   **Exceptions to this rule . . . :** Jacob, *Questions and Reform Jewish Answers*, no. 95. *Milah* supersedes Shabbat only when we are certain that Shabbat is the baby's eighth day. Since in both cases it is doubtful whether the birth occurred on Shabbat, it is therefore doubtful whether the baby is in fact eight days old at the next Shabbat. Babies born by induced labor on Shabbat are circumcised the following Shabbat; *Questions and Reform Jewish Answers*, no. 96.

146   **If postponed . . . :** Plaut and Washofsky, *Teshuvot*, no. 5755.12; *Shulchan Arukh, Yore De'ah* 266:2.

146   **The circumcision should not take place prior to the eighth day . . . :** Plaut and
Washofsky, *Teshuvot*, no. 5752.2. Orthodox authorities, following the position of
Shakh, Yore De'ah 262, no. 2, require *hatafat dam berit* to "repair" a circumcision
performed before the eighth day. Our practice concurs with the major earlier authorities (and some important later ones) who hold that *hatafat dam berit* does nothing
to "repair" this mistake and is therefore unnecessary.

146   **Reform Judaism insists . . . :** Polish, *Rabbi's Manual*, 221; Maslin, *Gates of Mitzvah*,
13–14; Jacob, *American Reform Responsa*, nos. 55–56; Freehof, *Reform Responsa*, no.
21. If a *mohel* is not available to perform the circumcision on the eighth day, it is
better to engage the services of another practitioner than to postpone the ceremony;
Jacob, *Questions and Reform Jewish Answers*, no. 100.

146   **during daylight hours . . . :** *M. Megillah* 2:4 and *B. Megillah* 20a. To show our
enthusiasm for the *mitzvah*, we traditionally schedule the *milah* early in the morning,
following *Shacharit* services ("the pious rise early to do the *mitzvot*"; *B. Pesachim* 4a).

146   **It should not be performed at night . . . :** Isserles, *Yore De'ah* 262:1. There is no
"compelling reason" for us to depart from this practice; Jacob, *Questions and Reform
Jewish Answers*, no. 161.

146   **Special Circumstances:**

1. Freehof, *New Reform Responsa*, no. 14.

2. Polish, *Rabbi's Manual*, 227; **If the parents are unmarried . . . :** Jacob, *Questions
and Reform Jewish Answers*, no. 94; **In such a case, however . . . :** Plaut and Washofsky, *Teshuvot*, no. 5752.2, n. 2.

3. Jacob, *Questions and Reform Jewish Answers*, no. 109.

4. Ibid., no. 110. This does not preclude "outreach" to these individuals that will
hopefully encourage them to either convert to Judaism or to make it their exclusive
religious commitment. The concern is rather that by performing *berit milah* we will
give the appearance of affirming or condoning their religious decisions. A Messianic
Jew or a Jew who raises his child as a half-Christian has made a choice that negates
the most basic definition of Jewish identity that we can imagine or accept. He/she
has the "right" to make that choice; we as a community have a corresponding right—
and responsibility—to reject it.

5. Jacob, *American Reform Responsa*, no. 54; Jacob, *Contemporary American Reform
Responsa*, no. 29. Circumcision is for us a religious ceremony; we do not accept
medical and psychological arguments against the practice.

6. Jacob, *American Reform Responsa*, no. 34.

7. Jacob, *Questions and Reform Jewish Answers*, no. 93.

148   *zeved habat* **. . . :** See Herbert C. Dobrinsky, *A Treasury of Sephardic Laws and Customs*, 3–4; 11; 20; 25–26.

148   **In 1975 . . . :** *CCAR Yearbook* 85 (1975): 78.

148   **a Hebrew or Jewish name . . . :** Maslin, *Gates of Mitzvah*, 16–17. See, in depth,
Jacob, *American Reform Responsa*, no. 59.

148   **may name their children after a Gentile parent . . . :** Freehof, *Modern Reform Responsa*, no. 23.

148   *Plidyon Haben*: Yad, *Bikkurim* 11; *Shulchan Arukh, Yore De'ah* 305.

149   **the child whose father or mother is a priest (*Kohen*) or a Levite:** Because the members of the tribe of Levi are dedicated to God's service "in place" of the first-born of the rest of the community; Num. 3:45 and *Shulchan Arukh, Yore De'ah* 305:18.

149   **Since Reform Judaism no longer recognizes . . . :** Maslin, *Gates of Mitzvah,* 18; Polish, *Rabbi's Manual,* 228.

149   **A Jewish child traditionally reaches majority . . . :** *M. Nidah* 5:6; *Yad, Ishut* 2:9-10.

149   **During the Middle Ages . . . :** The custom for the father to say "blessed be the One who has exempted me from legal liability for this one's actions" is mentioned in *Genesis Rabbah* 63:14. See *Maharil, Hilkhot Keri'at Hatorah;* Isserles, *Orach Chayim* 225:2 and *Magen Avraham,* no. 4 (who indicates that the young man led services and was called to the Torah). *Yam shel Shelomo, Bava Kama* 7:37, mentions that the young man delivered a sermon (*derashah*) at the Bar Mitzvah meal. Bat Mitzvah, of course, is a much later innovation. It was introduced in America by Rabbi Mordecai Kaplan for his daughter in the 1920s, although the *Ben Ish Chai* (vol.1, *Re'eh,* par. 17), a nineteenth-century Iraqi work, mentions the custom for a girl to celebrate the day of her majority in a festive way.

149   **The Reform movement in North America . . . :** Aaron Rosenberg, *Divrei Benei Mitzvah,* preamble; Meyer, *Response to Modernity,* 252. See the responsa of R. Kaufman Kohler in Jacob, *American Reform Responsa,* no. 30, and R. Israel Bettan, idem, no. 32, who describe Bar Mitzvah as a outmoded ceremony.

149   **"virtually, universally observed . . . ":** Jacob, *American Reform Responsa,* no. 33, which reverses the earlier responsa.

149   **"a *mitzvah* to be called . . .":** Maslin, *Gates of Mitzvah,* 21.

149   **The overwhelming majority of the Reform rabbinate . . . :** Rosenberg, *Divrei Benei Mitzvah,* par. 1.

150   **Age:** Ibid., par. 2. Bar/Bat Mitzvah is less a *rite de passage* than a "way station in Jewish growth." While girls traditionally reach majority at age twelve, both our commitment to gender equality and the fact that girls and boys study together in school dictate that Bat and Bar Mitzvah be observed at the same age (Polish, *Rabbi's Manual,* 229).

150   **Nature:** Divrei Benei Mitzvah, par. 3; Jacob, *Questions and Reform Jewish Answers,* no. 37. Jewish law empowers communities to enact "sumptuary" regulations which place limits on expenditures for private festivities; see Salo W. Baron, *The Jewish Community: Its History and Structure to the American Revolution,* 2:301–7, and Louis Finkelstein, *Jewish Self-Government in the Middle Ages,* 103, 292, and 374.

150   **the young person has met certain identifiable standards . . . :** Rosenberg, *Divrei Benei Mitzvah,* pars. 4, 5, and 6.

150   **Time:** Ibid., par. 11; Polish, *Rabbi's Manual,* 230.

150   **on a day when the Torah is not read . . . :** Jacob, *Contemporary American Reform Responsa,* no. 156. See Freehof, *Reform Responsa,* no. 4: "To conduct a Torah reading where no Torah reading belongs...merely in order to make the religious service convenient to the social celebration, is to consent to an inversion of values."

150   **"we do not confuse one joy with another":** *B. Mo'ed Katan* 8b.

150   **Reform practice strongly prefers . . . :** Rosenberg, *Divrei Benei Mitzvah,* par. 11.

150   **a *public* worship service . . . :** See Jacob, *Questions and Reform Jewish Answers,* no. 33. Obviously, in the case of special needs where it is legitimately impractical for the

Bar/Bat Mitzvah to come to the synagogue, a worship service may be held at home; idem, no. 36.

151   **The so-called *Havdalah* Bar/Bat Mitzvah . . . :** Rosenberg, *Divrei Benei Mitzvah*, par. 11; *Responsa Committee*, no. 5759.9.

151   **some exceptional circumstances . . . :** For example, in a large congregation where more than one Bar/Bat Mitzvah is scheduled on a Shabbat, the regular Shabbat morning congregation might feel overwhelmed by the overflow of invited guests; Jacob, *American Reform Responsa*, no. 36.

151   **Divorce:** Rosenberg, *Divrei Benei Mitzvah*, par. 9b.

151   **neither enjoys an inherent "right" . . . :** Freehof, *Contemporary Reform Responsa*, no. 5; Jacob, *Questions and Reform Jewish Answers*, no. 32.

152   **Special Needs Youngsters:** Rosenberg, *Divrei Benei Mitzvah*, par. 13. How can we call a severely retarded child a "Bar/Bat Mitzvah" when he or she, due to intellectual limitations, is not held liable for his or her actions under Jewish or civil law? We distinguish between "Bar/Bat Mitzvah" as a legal coming-of-age and the *ceremony* called "Bar/Bat Mitzvah" which centers upon the young person being called to the Torah. Even a minor may take part in the Torah reading, provided he or she knows "to Whom the blessings are addressed" (*B. Megillah* 23a; *Shulchan Arukh, Orach Chayim* 282:3). Thus, there is no formal prohibition against calling this "special needs youngster" to the Torah (Freehof, *Recent Reform Responsa*, no. 3).

152   **who for some reason has not been circumcised . . . :** Freehof, *Current Reform Responsa*, no. 28.

152   **Adult Bar/Bat Mitzvah:** Rosenberg, *Divrei Benei Mitzvah*, par. 14.

152   **Confirmation:** Maslin, *Gates of Mitzvah*, 21–22; Polish, *Rabbi's Manual*, 230–31.

153   **"One who has no wife lives without *goodness*":** *B. Yevamot* 62b.

153   **Even though one already has children . . . :** Ibid., 61b.

153   **it is only *God* who lives alone . . . :** Rashi to Gen. 2:18, from *Pirkei deR. Eliezer*, ch. 12.

154   **Does this mean that those who do not marry . . . :** See Maslin, *Gates of Mitzvah*, 119–21, on "the single person, the single-parent family, and *mitzvot*."

154   **Each human being is a unique person . . . :** *M. Sanhedrin* 4:5.

154   **the prophets and mystics of Israel . . . :** See Maslin, *Gates of Mitzvah*, 28.

154   **It is a *mitzvah* . . . to marry . . . :** Ibid., 29; Rambam, *Sefer Hamitzvot*, positive commandment no. 213; *Sefer Hachinukh*, mitzvah 552.

154   **It is also a *mitzvah* . . . :** Maslin, *Gates of Mitzvah*, 30, and n. 43; see David M. Feldman, *Marital Relations, Birth Control, and Abortion in Jewish Law*, 60–105.

154   **The tradition frowns upon . . . :** Jacob, *American Reform Responsa*, no. 154. The tradition has always placed great emphasis upon sexual chastity and modesty. Maimonides, in fact, holds that all non-marital intercourse is prohibited by Deut. 23:18 (and see Rashi to the verse); *Yad, Ishut* 1:4 and *Moreh Nevukhim* III, ch. 49. He also rules that the concubine (*pilegesh*) of biblical times was permitted only to kings (*Yad, Melakhim* 4:4). Other authorities (Rabad, *Hasagot, Ishut* 1:4; Nachmanides, *Hasagot* to *Sefer Hamitzvot, shoresh* 5) disagreed, yet even they tend to hold that concubinage should not be practiced today, because it would weaken the institution of marriage and because most men would use it as an avenue to immoral

behavior. See, in general, Elyakim Ellinson, *Nisu'in Shelo Kedat Moshe ve-Yisrael*, 40ff. (A concubine, in traditional parlance, is a woman who has neither *kiddushin* nor *ketubah* from a man but enjoys some regular status in his household, less than that of a wife.) The tradition, in other words, has for many centuries sought to annul or remove this institution, and we do not advocate its restoration as a device to sanctify the relationships of couples who do not choose to marry; *Responsa Committee*, no. 5756.10; Jacob, *American Reform Responsa*, no. 133.

155 **History:** *M. Kiddushin* 1:1; *B. Kiddushin* 2a–b; *Yad, Ishut* 1:1–2. See the commentary of Chanokh Albeck, *Shishah Sidrei Mishnah*, 3:308: the terminology of *kinyan* is used only in the first chapter of the mishnaic tractate *Kiddushin*; everywhere else, the act of betrothal is called *kiddushin*.

155 **Just as a sanctified person or object . . . :** *B. Kiddushin* 2b; *Tosafot*, s.v. *de'asar*.

155 **Kiddushin is . . . the second of three distinct stages:** On *shidukhin*, see *B. Kiddushin* 12b; *Yad, Ishut* 3:22; *Shulchan Arukh, Even Ha'ezer* 42:1. On the span of time separating *kiddushin* and *nisu'in*, see *M. Ketubot* 5:2. Already in the geonic period (Babylonia, 7th–11th century C.E.) we find the custom to hold *kiddushin* and *nisu'in* together (*Otzar Hageonim, Ketubot*, no. 82).

155 **Consequences:** Exodus 21:10 speaks of the wife's three "rights" from her husband, which the tradition understands as food, clothing, and sexual relations (*B. Ketubot* 47b). Other financial duties were established by rabbinic law. For a list of marriages forbidden as *arayot*, see Polish, *Rabbi's Manual*, 235–36. On the financial relations between husband and wife, see *Yad, Ishut* 12.

156 **it is he who "takes" a wife . . . :** *B. Kiddushin* 4b: "the text (Deut. 24:1) reads: 'a man takes a wife,' and not 'a woman takes a husband.'"

156 **and he who issues the document of divorce . . . :** Deut. 24:1; *Yad, Gerushin* 1:1ff.

156 **severe legal and financial disabilities . . . :** Maslin, *Gates of Mitzvah*, 31, and n. 44.

156 **"it would not be easy for him to divorce her":** *B. Ketubot* 11a and elsewhere; *Yad, Ishut* 10:7.

156 **They permitted husband and wife to stipulate . . . :** *Halakhah* recognizes the freedom to make such arrangements concerning financial matters; *B. Kiddushin* 19b. See *Yad, Ishut* 12:4, 6; *Shulchan Arukh, Even Ha'ezer* 69.

156 **Rabbinic law has for a full millennium . . . :** On the *takkanah* (enactment) of Rabbeinu Gershom b. Yehudah, see the discussion in this chapter. The *takkanah* was not accepted by Sefardic Jews or the Jewish communities of North Africa and Asia (the *edot hamizrach*). Those communities, however, developed other means of assuring that the husband would not marry a second wife or divorce his wife without her consent. See Friedman, *Ribui Nashim Be-Yisrael*, and Schereschewsky, *Dinei Mishpachah*, 57–67.

156 **allow the wife to sue for divorce . . . :** See *Shulchan Arukh, Even Ha'ezer* 154.

156 **Reform Judaism has taken the insight . . . :** Maslin, *Gates of Mitzvah*, 31; Polish, *Rabbi's Manual*, 238.

157 **Judaism resists mixed marriage . . . :** Maslin, *Gates of Mitzvah*, 36–37.

157 **The Jewish opposition to mixed marriage . . . :** For an extensive historical survey see *CCAR Yearbook* 90 (1980): 86ff. (=Jacob, *American Reform Responsa*, no. 147).

157 **Moses, Samson, and Solomon . . . :** Exod. 2:21; Num. 12:1; Judg. 14:1; I Kings 3:1, 9:16, 11:1.

157   **the chief cause of sin and idolatry . . . :** Judg. 3:6; I Kings 11:2.

157   **the patriarchs and matriarchs . . . :** Gen. 24:3, 27:6, 28:8–9.

158   **Ezra and Nehemiah . . . :** Ezra 9–10.

158   **there is no legal validity . . . :** B. *Kiddushin* 68b; *Yad, Ishut* 4:15; *Shulchan Arukh, Even Ha'ezer* 44:8.

158   **conversions must have preceded . . . :** Thus, Ruth becomes the quintessential convert to Judaism *prior* to her marriage to Boaz (see B. *Yevamot* 47b on the famous passage in Ruth 1:16–18). On the Rabbis' view of the marriages of Samson and Solomon, see *Yad, Isurei Bi'ah* 13:14–16. In the case of Esther, no "marriage" is deemed to have taken place with the Persian king.

158   **Christians or Muslims . . . :** Members of these religions cannot be called "idolaters," yet as non-Jews the rules of mixed marriage apply to them. The prohibition is much more about encouraging marriage among Jews within the community than about prohibiting relationships with "idol worshipers."

158   **With the modern period . . . :** See Meyer, *Response to Modernity*, 134–35, 290.

159   **in 1909 . . . :** *CCAR Yearbook* 19 (1909): 170.

159   **in 1947 . . . :** Ibid., 57 (1947): 161.

159   **The Current Position:** Ibid., 83 (1973): 97; Polish, *Rabbi's Manual*, 242–43; Meyer, *Response to Modernity*, 372.

160   **Reform responsa literature . . . :** Jacob, *American Reform Responsa*, no. 149.

161   **"dual-religion" wedding ceremony:** Ibid., no. 149; *CCAR Yearbook* 92 (1982): 132.

161   **At a Jewish wedding . . . :** Jacob, *American Reform Responsa*, no. 151.

162   **The Response to Mixed Marriage:** Plaut and Washofsky, *Teshuvot*, 5754.10; Jacob, *American Reform Responsa*, no. 147.

162   **The Jewish partner and the children . . . :** Jacob, *American Reform Responsa*, no. 10.

162   **Our goals are . . . :** *CCAR Yearbook* 83 (1973): 97.

162   **Consultation with the Rabbi:** Maslin, *Gates of Mitzvah*, 29.

163   **Civil Requirements:** Ibid., 29–30; Polish, *Rabbi's Manual*, 246. The Jewish legal principle here is *dina demalkhuta dina*, "the law of the government is the law"; B. *Gittin* 10b and parallels. Why does Jewish law, a legal system sufficient unto itself, recognize the validity of the legal acts of a Gentile government? There are various theories. According to one, "those who dwell in the king's land agree to accept him as their master and to be his servants" (*Yad, Gezeilah Ve'aveidah* 5:18; *Shulchan Arukh, Yore De'ah* 369:2). Another theory, much more congenial to our democratic temperament, is that "the normal and ordinary laws of the state are valid because those who dwell there accept those statutes and laws of their own free will" (Rashbam, *Bava Batra* 54b, s.v. *veha'amar shmuel*). Put in a more modern vocabulary, the citizens of the state contract with each other to live by a common set of "ordinary" (i.e., well-known, commonly-enacted) laws. See *Responsa Committee*, no. 5757.1. It must be stressed that the rule *dina demalkhuta dina* applies to civil and monetary matters but not to issues of ritual law such as marriage. The decree of the civil government does not affect the validity of a marriage under Jewish law; thus, a Jewish couple who marry under Jewish religious auspices are considered husband and wife under Jewish tradition even if their marriage is not recognized by the state. We say rather that those who violate the civil legal requirements are rightly punished under civil law, and our acceptance as citizens of that law means that we will refuse

to marry any couple who have not already fulfilled those requirements. See *Resp. Teshuvah Me'ahavah* 1:117; Shmuel Shilo, *Dina Demalkhuta Dina*, 115ff.; Freehof, *Contemporary Reform Responsa*, no. 21.

163 **the validity of civil marriage . . . :** See Plaut, *Rise of Reform Judaism*, 219; *CCAR Yearbook* 57 (1947): 162–64; Polish, *Rabbi's Manual*, 243; Freehof, *New Reform Responsa*, no. 44. Halakhic authorities dispute the validity of civil marriage under Jewish law: that is, when Jews are married under non-Jewish auspices, do they require a Jewish divorce (*get*) in order to remarry? Some hold that civil marriage requires no Jewish divorce, since the couple's decision to wed outside the boundaries of Jewish ritual indicates their intention *not* to be married "according to the laws of Moses and Israel"; (*Resp. Rivash*, no. 6; *Resp. Maharam Schick, Even Ha'ezer* 21; *Resp. Chelkat Ya'akov* 2:184; *Resp. Mishpetei Ouziel Even Ha'ezer* 2:54). Others declare that a Jewish couple's intention to live together as husband and wife establishes the possibility that a valid marriage exists between them; therefore, a *get* is required (*Perushei Ibra* 1:4; *Resp. Tzofnat Paneach* 1–4). Still others urge that a *get* be obtained if possible but will allow the wife to remarry in the event that no Jewish divorce is forthcoming (*Resp. Igerot Moshe, Even Ha'ezer* 73–75. This course is adopted by the rabbinic courts in Israel; see *Piskei Din Rabbani'im* 7:37).

163 **Special care must be taken . . . :** Freehof, *New Reform Responsa*, no. 44.

163 **Testing for Disease:** Maslin, *Gates of Mitzvah*, 30; *CCAR Yearbook* 85 (1975): 79.

163 **There is no religious requirement . . . :** Plaut and Washofsky, *Teshuvot*, 5750.1.

163 **either member of the couple is obligated . . . :** *Resp. Chelkat Ya'akov* 3:136. One afflicted with a dangerous and communicable disease can be termed a *rodef*, a "pursuer" who even unintentionally endangers the life of another. To avert this danger is a requirement of Lev. 19:16, "do not stand idly by the blood of your neighbor"; *M. Sanhedrin* 8:7; *B. Sanhedrin* 73a; *Yad, Rotzeach* 1:14.

163 **population groups that bear a significant risk . . . :** See Shelomo Daichovsky, "Kefiat Bedikah Vetipul," *Assia* 12 (1989): 28–33.

163 **Blessing in the Synagogue:** Maslin, *Gates of Mitzvah*, 30, and 76, n. 42.

164 **Place:** Ibid., 32–33.

164 **The most appropriate setting . . . :** In some communities, rabbis refuse to officiate in any locale other than the synagogue or the home; Polish, *Rabbi's Manual*, 239.

164 **"under the open sky":** Isserles, *Even Ha'ezer* 61:1, as a sign that "your progeny shall be as numerous as the stars of the sky."

164 **do not offend our religious sensibilities:** If the wedding takes place in a Christian home, we should endeavor to remove or conceal any visible religious symbols prior to the ceremony, although the presence of those symbols in no way invalidates the wedding; Jacob, *Contemporary American Reform Responsa*, no. 194.

164 **The Processional:** Polish, *Rabbi's Manual*, 238; Freehof, *Reform Jewish Practice*, 1:86–87.

164 **The Service:** *M. Kiddushin* 1:1; *Yad, Ishut* 1:2; *Shulchan Arukh, Even Ha'ezer* 26:4.

164 **This third method was prohibited . . . :** *B. Kiddushin* 12b.

164 **usually a ring:** Isserles, *Even Ha'ezer* 27:1.

164 **tradition prefers a plain ring . . . :** *Tosafot, Kiddushin* 9a, s.v. *vehilkheta*; *Tur* and *Shulchan Arukh, Even Ha'ezer* 31:2.

165   **Reform practice accepts the use of any ring . . . :** Polish, *Rabbi's Manual*, 238; Freehof, *Reform Jewish Practice*, 1:91–93. No appraisal of the ring is necessary unless a precise value is claimed for it (*Hilkhot Harosh, Kiddushin* 1:8).

165   **Other objects of value . . . :** Jacob, *Questions and Reform Jewish Answers*, no. 220.

165   **Immediately before the exchange of the ring . . . :** B. *Ketubot* 7b; *Yad, Ishut* 3:23; *Shulchan Arukh, Even Ha'ezer* 34:1–2. Some sources indicate that the *berakhah* is recited after the exchange of the ring, perhaps to prevent against the recitation of an unnecessary benediction (*berakhah levatalah*) should the bride refuse to accept the ring (*Hilkhot Harosh, Ketubot* 1:12). The liturgies in the *Rabbi's Manual* vary in their placement of *Birkat Erusin*.

165   **another beverage may be substituted . . . :** Plaut and Washofsky, *Teshuvot*, no. 5755.16; *Shulchan Arukh, Even Ha'ezer* 34:2; *Yad, Ishut* 10:4.

165   **two legally-acceptable witnesses . . . :** B. *Kiddushin* 65a–b and *Sanhedrin* 26a; *Yad, Ishut* 4:6; *Shulchan Arukh, Even Ha'ezer* 42:2. Should the wedding take place in the presence of no witnesses, or one witness, or two invalid witnesses, the marriage is legally invalid.

165   **Traditionally, the groom gives the ring . . . :** B. *Kiddushin* 5b–6a; *Yad, Ishut* 3:1; *Shulchan Arukh, Even Ha'ezer* 27:1–2. The words *kedat Moshe ve-Yisrael* are not required by the Talmud. They were added by later Ashkenazic tradition, apparently as a declaration by the groom that he enters into this marriage on condition that the rabbinic authorities give their consent to it; *Tosafot, Ketubot* 3a, s.v. *ada'ata*.

165   **The bride's acceptance . . . :** A woman is not married against her consent; B. *Kiddushin* 2b; *Yad, Ishut* 4:1; and *Shulchan Arukh, Even Ha'ezer* 42:1.

165   **In Reform Judaism . . . it is customary for the bride as well . . . :** Polish, *Rabbi's Manual*, 238; Maslin, *Gates of Mitzvah*, 32-33. This practice dates back at least to the Augsburg Synod of 1871; see Plaut, *Rise of Reform Judaism*, 217ff.

165   **a borrowed wedding ring:** Freehof, *Recent Reform Responsa*, no. 39; *Shulchan Arukh, Even Ha'ezer* 28:19.

165   **the *Sheva Berakhot* . . . :** B. *Ketubot* 7b–8a; *Yad, Ishut* 10:3; *Shulchan Arukh, Even Ha'ezer* 62:1. The wedding benedictions are also recited, as part of *Birkat Hamazon*, in the home of the bride and groom during the week following the wedding; *Yad, Berakhot* 2:9.

165   **a glass is placed . . . :** See B. *Berakhot* 31a, where the breaking of a glass object serves to interrupt the excessive merriment at a wedding feast. Sefardim tend to recite Psalm 137:5–6—"if I forget you, O Jerusalem . . ."—prior to breaking the glass, explicitly connecting the ritual to the destruction of the Temple; Dobrinsky, *A Treasury of Sephardic Laws and Customs*, 45, and see Isserles, *Orach Chayim* 560:2. See, in depth, J.Z. Lauterbach, "The Ceremony of Breaking a Glass at Weddings" in *Hebrew Union College Annual* 2 (1925): 351–80. While R. Solomon B. Freehof wrote that the custom of breaking a glass "is largely abolished among us" (*Recent Reform Responsa*, no. 80), the practice has returned in contemporary Reform observance.

166   **the private meeting (*yichud*) . . . :** *Shulchan Arukh, Even Ha'ezer* 55:1. Some sources hold that "*chupah*" refers to the moment of *yichud*; others say it is the groom's home itself. See R. Nissim Gerondi, *Commentary to Alfasi, Ketubot*, fol. 1a.

166   **"*chupah*" refers to a *tallit* . . . :** Isserles, *Even Ha'ezer* 55:1; Jacob, *Questions and Reform Jewish Answers*, no. 218. The use of a *tallit* may derive from Ezekiel 16:8, which suggests that in ancient times the legal ceremony of marriage involved the

groom spreading his cloak over the bride; see *B. Kiddushin* 18b and Albeck, *Shishah Sidrei Mishnah*, 3:308.

166   **Some communities . . . :** Jacob, *Contemporary American Reform Responsa*, no. 191. In the event that a wedding is held during *chol hamo'ed Sukkot*, it is perfectly permissible to use a *sukkah* as a *chupah*; idem, no. 181.

166   **a *minyan* is traditionally required . . . :** Ibid., no. 189; *B. Ketubot* 7a–b; *Yad, Ishut* 10:5; *Shulchan Arukh, Even Ha'ezer* 62:4. The requirement is derived by a midrash on Ruth 4:2, where Boaz gathers ten elders in order to arrange his marriage to Ruth.

166   **customary that a rabbi act as officiant . . . :** A wedding is "valid" in the absence of a rabbi; nonetheless, the clear tendency of Jewish tradition is to require appropriate rabbinic supervision at the formation of a marriage.

166   **Dignity and Sanctity:** Maslin, *Gates of Mitzvah*, 34–35.

166   **it is a *mitzvah* to accompany . . . :** *Yad, Avel* 14:1; *Bi'ur Hagra, Even Ha'ezer* 65, no. 1.

166   **Music:** Isserles, *Orach Chayim* 560:3; Maslin, *Gates of Mitzvah*, 34; Jacob, *Contemporary American Reform Responsa*, no. 195; Plaut and Washofsky, *Teshuvot*, no. 5752.11.

166   **Expense:** Maslin, *Gates of Mitzvah*, 35; Jacob, *Questions and Reform Jewish Answers*, no. 221.

166   **a gift to *tzedakah* . . . :** Maslin, Gates *of Mitzvah*, 35.

166   **Decorum:** Ibid., 35; Plaut and Washofsky, *Teshuvot*, no. 5751.14.

167   **Times When Weddings Should Not Take Place:** Maslin, *Gates of Mitzvah*, 31–32.

167   **Shabbat and *yom tov* . . . :** See this book's discussion of each of these special days in Chapter 3.

167   **the days of repentance . . . :** Jacob, *American Reform Responsa*, no. 135. Some prohibit weddings during this period due to its solemnity; *Mateh Efraim* 602:5, and *Kitzur Shulchan Arukh* 130:4. On the other hand, the Days of Awe are not a period of mourning. Weddings are permitted by *Resp. R. Ezriel Hildesheimer, Orach Chayim*, 157b–c; *Resp. Yechaveh Da'at* 1:48; and *Resp. Melamed Leho'il, Even Ha'ezer* 1.

167   **The *Ketubah*:** Maslin, *Gates of Mitzvah*, 34.

167   **The traditional *ketubah* . . . :** *Yad, Ishut* 10:7ff. and 23:12; *Shulchan Arukh, Even Ha'ezer* 66.

167   **"it is forbidden to marry without first writing the *ketubah*":** *B. Ketubot* 7a; *Shulchan Arukh, Even Ha'ezer* 66:1.

167   **should the husband fail . . . :** The amounts specified in the *ketubah* are considered a stipulation imposed by the court which all husbands are presumed to accept prior to marriage (*M. Ketubot* 4:7; *Yad, Ishut* 12:2; *Shulchan Arukh, Even Ha'ezer* 69:1–2). For a detailed treatment of the *ketubah*, see Louis Epstein, *The Jewish Marriage Contract*.

168   **a purely symbolic certificate . . . :** Even in traditional practice, the *ketubah* possesses no concrete financial significance for those Ashkenazic communities which accept the *takkanah* of Rabbeinu Gershom (see the discussion in this chapter), according to which the wife cannot be divorced against her consent. Thus, in the event of divorce, the financial settlement will be determined by negotiations between the parties and not necessarily according to the amounts specified in the *ketubah*. Indeed, most Ashkenazic *ketubot* state standard, purely symbolic amounts.

168   **Reform *ketubot* . . . :** Polish, *Rabbi's Manual*, 237; Maslin, *Gates of Mitzvah*, 34.

168   **Marriage and Family Finances:** Although, for example, one is generally prohibited from selling a *sefer Torah*, a Torah scroll, such a sale is permitted in order to raise the needed resources in order to start a household. *B. Megillah* 27a; *Yad, Sefer Torah* 10:2; *Shulchan Arukh* (and Isserles), *Yore De'ah* 270:1.

168   ***hakhnasat kallah*** . . . : *B. Ketubot* 67b; *Yad, Avel* 14:1; *Shulchan Arukh, Yore De'ah* 249:15.

168   **Jewish law permits a couple to arrange** . . . : See Plaut and Washofsky, *Teshuvot*, no. 5754.9, where two persons afflicted with multiple sclerosis wish to marry. They may stipulate, as a means of making their marriage feasible, that the obligation to provide for a spouse's medical treatment (*M. Ketubot* 4:9; *Yad, Ishut* 12:2) is not incumbent upon either of them.

168   **Divorce:** Maslin, *Gates of Mitzvah*, 35–36.

168   **Divorce in Traditional Jewish Law:** See *Yad, Gerushin* 1 for a list of the Toraitic requirements for valid divorce as well as their midrashic derivations.

169   **the court may even coerce the husband** . . . : *M. Arakhin* 5:6, *M. Gittin* 9:8, *B. Bava Batra* 47b–48a. How may the court coerce a divorce from a husband, who under the law must issue the divorce of his own free will? Maimonides explains that this coercion merely allows the husband's "true" free will to triumph over his evil impulse (*yetzer hara*) which leads him to refuse the order of the court to divorce his wife (*Yad, Gerushin* 2:20).

169   **the *takkanah* of Rabbeinu Gershom may be waived** . . . : through the *heter me'ah rabbanim*, a "permit" granted under the signature of one hundred rabbis; see Benzion Schereschewsky, *Dinei Mishpachah*, 69–71.

169   **Reform Judaism and Jewish Divorce:** Freehof, *Reform Jewish Practice*, 1:99–110; Polish, *Rabbi's Manual*, 244–45; Maslin, *Gates of Mitzvah*, 36. See, in general, Jacob, *American Reform Responsa*, no. 162, and Moses Mielziner, *The Jewish Law of Marriage and Divorce in Ancient and Modern Times*, 130–37.

169   **Virtually all Reform communities outside the United States** . . . : Unlike traditional Jewish divorce, the Reform *get* in most other countries is an egalitarian proceeding. The couple divorce each other; the husband is not the sole "active" party.

170   **the cumbersome divorce procedures** . . . : The process of writing and transmitting a *get* is summarized in 101 paragraphs in *Shulchan Arukh, Even Ha'ezer*, end of 154, and this does not take into account the vast amounts of commentary written in the halakhic literature on every single detail contained within these paragraphs.

171   **divorce in Jewish legal thinking pertains to ritual** . . . : This refers to the division of the *halakhah* into the categories of *mamona* (monetary law) and *isura* (ritual law); on these categories see Elon, *Jewish Law*, 122ff.). Jewish divorce does have much to do with *mamona*, since a divorce nullifies the couple's mutual financial obligations and establishes the wife's right to collect her *ketubah* debt. Yet divorce also falls under the heading of *isura*, because it determined the ritual status of the parties: eligibility for remarriage, questions of adultery and incest, and the legitimacy of children born subsequently to the former wife, all of which are quintessentially ritual matters. See *Responsa Committee*, no. 5756.15. It is true that R. Yechezkel Landau (*Resp. Noda Biyehudah, Even Ha'ezer* 2:114) states that a *get* is a matter of monetary law. Landau makes this point, however, in order to buttress his controversial belief that a *get* must be promulgated by a court of three judges, similar to all other monetary matters (*M.*

Sanhedrin 1:1). He does not say that divorce is *not* also a matter of *isura* or that it has no ramifications for the ritual status of the couple.

171   **"ritual of release"** (*seder pereidah*)**:** Polish, *Rabbi's Manual*, 97–104.

171   **"a form of religious divorce" . . . :** Ibid., 245. As to whether the Reform movement might ever restore a requirement of religious divorce, see the discussion in Jacob, *Questions and Reform Jewish Answers*, no. 233.

172   ***mamzer* . . . :** Deut. 23:3 and Rashi ad loc.; *M. Yevamot* 4:13 and *M. Kiddushin* 3:12; *Yad, Isurei Bi'ah* 15:1; *Shulchan Arukh, Even Ha'ezer* 4:13. The *mamzer*, it must be noted, is not identical to the "bastard" of other legal systems. In Jewish law, a child born "out of wedlock" is not a *mamzer*. A person is illegitimate only if he or she was conceived in an act of incest or adultery.

172   **is forbidden to marry almost all other Jews . . . :** Except for other *mamzerim* and for proselytes; *B. Kiddushin* 72b; *Yad, Isurei Bi'ah* 15:7–8. The offspring of a *mamzer* (male) or *mamzeret* (female) will in almost all cases be considered a *mamzer/et* as well; *M. Yevamot* 8:3; *Yad, Isurei Bi'ah* 15:1.

172   **a Jewish woman who remarries . . . :** Traditional *halakhah* defines "adultery" as an act of sexual intercourse between a married Jewish woman and a Jewish man other than her husband. By contrast, the offspring of a Gentile father and a Jewish mother, even if she is married to a Jewish man, is *not* a *mamzer* (*B. Yevamot* 45b; *Yad, Isurei Bi'ah* 15:3; *Shulchan Arukh, Even Ha'ezer* 4:5).

172   **Reform Judaism has abandoned . . . :** Polish, *Rabbi's Manual*, 224–25.

172   **The *halakhah*, too . . . :** See, in general, Moshe Zemer, "Purifying *Mamzerim*" in *Jewish Law Annual* 10 (1992): 99–114. One who suspects that a *mamzer* has married into a family should not reveal that suspicion publicly; *B. Kiddushin* 71a; Isserles, *Even Ha'ezer* 2:5. In the end of days, God will remove the taint of *mamzerut* from all who bear it; *B.Kiddushin* 71a; *Leviticus Rabbah* 32:7; *Yad, Melakhim* 12:3.

172   **such as the Karaites and the Ethiopian Jews . . . :** the sixteenth-century R. David ibn Zimra permitted Rabbanite Jews to marry Karaites on this basis; *Resp. Radbaz* 1:73 and 4:219. See, in general, the researches by Michael Korinaldi and Menachem Waldman.

172   **Many Orthodox authorities hold that Reform Jewish weddings are not valid under the *halakhah* . . . :** See R. Moshe Feinstein, *Resp. Igerot Moshe, Even Ha'ezer* 1:76–77. The grounds: Reform weddings are not held in the presence of qualified ("observant", i.e., Orthodox) witnesses, and the couple who marry in a Reform ceremony surely do not intend to live as husband and wife "according to the laws of Moses and Israel," i.e., Orthodox *halakhah*. Not all halakhists agree with this position; see the discussion of civil marriage (p. 163). R. Solomon Freehof notes that a Reform Jewish couple clearly intend to live together "according to the laws of Moses and Israel," albeit under a Reform interpretation of those laws. A Reform wedding, therefore, creates a valid halakhic marriage (Freehof, *Recent Reform Responsa*, no. 42; see also Jacob, *Questions and Reform Jewish Answers*, no. 234).

173   **"the divorce factor" . . . :** Reuven Bulka, *The Coming Cataclysm*, 52–57.

173   **Until some other and better solution can be located . . . :** Proposals are occasionally made to establish a national *beit din* (rabbinic court) whose acts would be recognized as legitimate by all streams of Judaism and which might serve to adjudicate matters of personal status such as divorce and conversion. These proposals, while intriguing, have yet to overcome the concerted indifference and/or opposition of

most Orthodox authorities. See Steven E. Foster, "The Community Rabbinic Conversion Board—The Denver Model," *Journal of Reform Judaism* 31 (1984): 25–32 and Mark Washofsky, "The Proposal for a National *Beit Din*: Is It Good for the Jews?"

173 **Reform rabbis should take care to explain . . . :** Polish, *Rabbi's Manual*, 245.

174 **a complex system of rules and procedures . . . :** The literary product of this activity fills 23 folio pages of the *Shulchan Arukh* (*Even Ha'ezer* 17) and six volumes of the *Otzar Haposkim*, the authoritative contemporary restatement of the *halakhah* of marriage and divorce.

174 **Various halakhic solutions have been proposed . . . :** These include: 1) conditional marriage, a stipulation made at the wedding which provides that the marriage be retroactively annulled should the husband refuse a proper request for a divorce; 2) conditional divorce, whereby the husband appoints at the time of the wedding an agent to execute a divorce on his behalf should a competent *beit din* some day require him to do so; 3) annulment of marriage, in which a *beit din* declares the marriage retroactively null and void as a result of the husband's inexcusable conduct. The Conservative movement relies heavily upon the first and third of these measures in order to solve the *agunah* problem within its communities. For a historical summary see Mark Washofsky, "The Recalcitrant Husband: The Problem of Definition" in *Jewish Law Annual* 4 (1981):144–66.

175 **a pre-nuptial agreement . . . :** See Shlomo Riskin, *Women and Jewish Divorce*, for the theory behind such an agreement. The *beit din* of the Orthodox Rabbinical Council of America has approved texts for pre-nuptial and arbitration agreements, included in Reuven Bulka, *The RCA Lifecycle Madrikh*, 72–75. See Bulka's introduction, p. 69: the husband's intransigence in the get process is "behavior which is inexcusable." The Orthodox world, in other words, recognizes the moral tragedy of the *agunah*. It is unfortunate that they have proven unable to go beyond an agreement such as this, which requires the intervention of civil authorities, in order to remedy it. Moreover, other Orthodox groups aside from the "centrist" Rabbinical Council of America do not yet accept even the procedure of the pre-nuptial agreement.

175 **If a Jewish woman married under Orthodox auspices . . . :** Jacob, *Questions and Reform Jewish Answers*, no. 234. We could also frame this decision in traditional halakhic terminology: since talmudic law recognizes a rabbinic power to annul marriages under certain circumstances, our decision to remarry this woman might be regarded as tantamount to an annulment of her existing marriage.

175 **a man who was divorced in the civil courts . . . :** Plaut and Washofsky, *Teshuvot*, no. 5754.6.

175 **the implicit promise he made to her . . . :** The formula by which the husband betroths his wife "according to the laws of Moses and Israel" implies that he subjects his marriage to the moral scrutiny of the rabbis; *Tosafot, Ketubot* 3a, s.v. *ada'ata*. This includes a commitment to "listen to the words of the sages," to heed a rabbinic court decree that he grant his wife a divorce (*B. Bava Batra* 48a). His civil divorce has not freed him from the obligation to live up to these promises.

176 **a matter of *religious* concern to Reform Judaism . . . :** *Responsa Committee*, no. 5756.15 and no. 5758.13.

176 **a physically incapacitated spouse . . . :** *Responsa Committee*, no. 5756.15; Jacob, *Contemporary American Reform Responsa*, no. 86. The husband's duty to pay the wife's medical expenses is declared in *M. Ketubot* 4:9, but that text gives him the right to

divorce her and let her pay for her healing out of her *ketubah*. While the major codes accept this as the *halakhah*, they condemn such a divorce as unethical (*Yad, Ishut* 14:17; *Shulchan Arukh, Even Ha'ezer* 79:3). Other authorities rule that such is *not* the law, that the husband has no power to divorce a wife while she is seriously ill (*Chidushei Harashba, Ketubot* 52b, citing Rabad, who derived the position from *Sifre* to Deut. 21:14). See Plaut and Washofsky, *Teshuvot*, no. 5754.9.

176   **until the marriage comes to a legal end . . . :** *Responsa Committee*, no. 5758.13.

176   **The Jewish Home and Family . . . :** See Rashi to Ps. 127:1, and compare *Leviticus Rabbah* 12:7.

176   **We speak of the Jewish home . . . :** Maslin, *Gates of Mitzvah*, 37, and 83, n. 67.

176   **Religious Identity:** See the discussion on "patrilineal descent" in this chapter, as well as Plaut and Washofsky, *Teshuvot*, no. 5755.17, on the child raised in a home where two religions are practiced on an equal footing.

177   **baptized as well as circumcised . . . :** Jacob, *Questions and Reform Jewish Answers*, no. 109.

177   **Nor can we prepare a child for Bar/Bat Mitzvah . . . :** Jacob, *Contemporary American Reform Responsa*, no. 61; *Responsa Committee*, no. 5758.11.

177   **The Union of American Hebrew Congregations has resolved . . . :** *Reform Judaism* (Spring 1996): 59.

177   **as an adherent of Judaism and Christianity (or any other religion):** On Judaism and Buddhism, see Plaut and Washofsky, *Teshuvot*, no. 5752.3.

178   ***Mezuzah:*** Maslin, *Gates of Mitzvah*, 38.

178   **the traditional fulfillment of the commandment . . . :** *Sefer Hamitzvot*, positive commandment no. 15.

178   **are inscribed by hand . . . :** *B. Menachot* 34a: the words "you shall write them" link the *mezuzah* to the Torah scroll, the *tefillin*, and the *get*, all of which are inscribed by hand. Printed *mezuzah* texts do not meet the requirement; Jacob, *Questions and Reform Jewish Answers*, no. 140 and Freehof, *New Reform Responsa*, no. 3.

178   **inserted into a cylinder . . . :** *Tur, Yore De'ah* 289.

178   **to the upper third . . . :** *B. Menachot* 33a. The Torah compares *tefillin* (Deut. 6:8) to *mezuzah* (Deut. 6:9): just as the *tefillah* (singular for *tefillin*) is bound on the upper arm, so is the *mezuzah* affixed to the upper part of the doorpost. *Shulchan Arukh, Yore De'ah* 289:2.

178   **the right doorpost . . . :** *B. Menachot* 34a; *Yad, Mezuzah* 6:12; *Shulchan Arukh, Even Ha'ezer* 289:2.

178   **in a diagonal position . . . :** Rashi (*B. Menachot* 33a, s.v. *asa'ah kemin nagar* and *pesulah*) holds that the *mezuzah* should be placed vertically along the doorpost. His grandson, Rabbeinu Tam, disagreed, saying that the *mezuzah* should lie horizontally (*Tosafot, Menachot* 33a, s.v. *ha*). While R. Yosef Karo adopts Rashi's view, the *Tur* (*Yore De'ah* 289) notes that many seek to adopt both positions by affixing the *mezuzah* diagonally. R. Moshe Isserles endorses this compromise, which is the common practice today; *Shulchan Arukh, Yore De'ah* 289:6.

178   **the virtues of compromise . . . :** Maslin, *Gates of Mitzvah*, 84, no. 71.

178   **There are no special requirements concerning the cylinder . . . :** Jacob, *Contemporary American Reform Responsa*, no. 71.

178   **the text faces inward . . . :** Freehof, *New Reform Responsa*, no. 12; *B. Menachot* 31b; *Yad, Mezuzah* 5:6; *Shulchan Arukh, Yore De'ah* 288:14.

178   **with the exception of the bathroom . . . :** *B. Yoma* 11b. "The doorposts of your house" excludes those rooms that do not serve as *dirat kavod*, dignified living spaces; *Shulchan Arukh, Yore De'ah* 286:4.

178   **The responsibility for affixing the *mezuzah* . . . :** *B. Menachot* 44a; *Yad, Mezuzah* 5:10; *Shulchan Arukh, Yore De'ah* 286:22. A house trailer, if it is to be one's permanent (more than thirty-day) dwelling, takes a *mezuzah*; Jacob, *Questions and Reform Jewish Answers*, no. 141.

179   **Prior to affixing the *mezuzah* . . . :** Or *mezuzot*: a single blessing suffices if one intends to affix several *mezuzot* throughout the home.

179   **Torah Study and Jewish Education:** On the importance of Torah study, see Maslin, *Gates of Mitzvah*, 73, n. 26, and *Yad, Talmud Torah* 3:1ff.

179   *talmud torah keneged kulam* **. . . :** *B. Shabbat* 127a.

179   **that we learn the other *mitzvot*:** *B. Kiddushin* 40a.

179   **the Torah is conceived as the very blueprint . . . :** *Genesis Rabbah* 1:2.

179   **Children:** Maslin, *Gates of Mitzvah*, 20.

180   **Adults:** Ibid., 22.

180   **Hebrew:** Ibid., 20.

180   **It is the responsibility of parents . . . :** *B. Kiddushin* 29a; *Yad, Talmud Torah* 1:1; *Shulchan Arukh, Yore De'ah* 245:1.

180   **the community bears the obligation . . . :** *B. Bava Batra* 21a; *Yad, Talmud Torah* 2:1; *Shulchan Arukh, Yore De'ah* 245:7.

180   **Home rituals . . . :** See Maslin, *Gates of Mitzvah*, 37–43.

181   **The Torah enjoins . . . :** *B. Kiddushin* 31b–32a; *Yad, Mamrim* 6:2; *Shulchan Arukh, Yore De'ah* 240:2.

181   **we owe the same obligations . . . toward God:** *B. Kiddushin* 30b.

181   **The child is not expected . . . :** See *B. Bava Metzi'a* 32a, *Yad, Mamrim* 6:12, and *Shulchan Arukh, Yore De'ah* 240:15. Lev. 19:3 requires one to revere one's parents *and* "to keep My Sabbaths." The latter is understood as a limitation to the former: if your parents order you to violate any *mitzvah*, you do not heed them.

181   **to move to the land of Israel . . . :** *Resp. Mabit* 1:139.

181   **to learn Torah . . . :** *Shulchan Arukh, Yore De'ah* 240:25.

181   **to marry . . . :** *Resp. Maharik*, no. 167; Isserles, *Yore De'ah* 240:25.

181   **to make peace . . . :** *Tur* and *Shulchan Arukh, Yore De'ah* 240:16.

181   **the parent is warned . . . :** *Yad, Mamrim* 6:8; *Shulchan Arukh, Yore De'ah* 240:19.

181   **When husband or wife objects . . . :** *Yad, Ishut* 13:14.

181   **The trend of Jewish thought . . . :** See Jacob, *American Reform Responsa*, no. 53.

181   **financial support . . . :** Jacob, *Contemporary American Reform Responsa*, no. 26.

181   **Jewish tradition disputes . . . :** Freehof, *New Reform Responsa*, no. 22.

182   **Yet there are times, say the authorities . . . :** See the story of Rav Assi and his mother in *B. Kiddushin* 31b. From there, Maimonides (*Yad, Mamrim* 6:10) deduces that

although a child should strive mightily to care for a parent whose condition has become quite difficult, when this becomes impossible the child is entitled to contract with others who can provide that care. While Rabad (*hasagah* ad loc.) objects to this ruling (see Radbaz ad loc.), such a decision may represent the best possible care for the parent, thus truly fulfilling the *mitzvah* to honor one's parent.

182   **Kashrut and Reform Judaism:** Maslin, *Gates of Mitzvah*, 40. And see the essay in idem, 130–33, upon which much of the discussion in this book is based.

183   **Reform Jewish leaders and thinkers . . . :** See Plaut, *The Growth of Reform Judaism*, 265: the silence on the issue of *kashrut* "is witness to the fact that it no longer was of real concern to the liberal leadership."

183   **only one *teshuvah* . . . :** Jacob, *American Reform Responsa*, no. 51, on the use of Pyrex dishes for both meat and dairy foods. Six other *teshuvot* listed in the indices under *"kashrut"* deal with subjects related to *kashrut* but not with the substance of the dietary laws themselves.

184   **"forbidden species" . . . :** See Deuteronomy 14 and Leviticus 11. The permitted beasts, whether domesticated (*behemot*) or wild (*chayot*), are those which have a cloven hoof *and* which chew the cud. Permitted fish are those with fins and scales. The Torah offers no general characteristics to distinguish between permitted and forbidden fowl; therefore, tradition determines which kinds of birds may be eaten. It is forbidden to consume animal blood (Deut. 12:16, 23–25; for details, see *Yad, Ma'akhalot Asurot* 6), certain animal fats (*chelev*, the internal fats encased in membranes which form a solid layer, as opposed to *shuman*, the fats which are intermingled with the animal's flesh which are permitted) which in ancient times were burned on the Temple altar (Lev. 3:3–4; for details, see *Yad, Ma'akhalot Asurot* 7), and the sciatic nerve (Gen. 32:33; *Yad, Ma'akhalot Asurot* 8).

184   **the separation of meat and dairy products . . . :** Derived from the commandment "you shall not boil a kid in its mother's milk" which occurs three times in the Torah (Exod. 23:19; Exod. 34:26; Deut. 14:21). The literal (*peshat*) sense of this injunction seems to prohibit the ritual act of seething a young goat in its mother's milk, a practice perhaps related to festival observance; see Rashbam and Ibn Ezra to Exod. 23:19 The ancient Rabbis, however, deduced that the three-fold repetition of the command-ment comes to forbid the mixing of all meat and dairy products for any of three purposes: consumption (*akhilah*), cooking (*bishul*), and deriving benefit (*hana'ah*); see B. *Chulin* 113a–116b. On their own authority, the Rabbis extended this prohi-bition to the meat of fowl, prohibiting its mixture with dairy products (B. *Chulin* 113a–b; *Yad, Ma'akhalot Asurot* 9:4). Custom has elaborated upon these principles to the point that separate utensils and dishes are required for dairy and meat meals.

184   **kosher meat . . . :** Permitted species must be slaughtered by the process of *shechitah*, linked by tradition to Deut. 12:21 (B. *Chulin* 28a). An animal that has died on its own or has been improperly slaughtered is called *neveilah* and is prohibited for con-sumption (Deut. 14:21). A properly slaughtered animal which upon examination (*bedikah*) shows physical defects which render it unfit for Jewish ritual consumption is called *tereifah*. Meat fit for consumption must undergo porging (*nikkur*) to remove its forbidden fat (*chelev*) as well as soaking (*hadachah*) and salting (*melichah*) to remove its blood (*dam*).

184   **largely a matter of personal rather than communal decision:** An exception to this statement might be the *kashrut* of kitchens in communal institutions such as syn-

agogues and camps, which some argue should be kosher to permit all Jews to eat there.

184 **The above statement is a controversial one . . . :** The halakhic debate is summarized in *Hilkhot Harosh, Mo'ed Katan* 3:3. While Rambam follows an old geonic tradition that the first day of mourning (*avelut*) is Toraitic, rooted in Lev. 10:19, the sages of northern Europe held that the seven-day mourning period is a rabbinic ordinance. They argue that Lev. 10:19 refers to the status of *aninut*, the period between death and burial, rather than to *avelut* (mourning, which follows burial) per se. See *Sifra* ad loc.

185 **the descriptions of mourning practices . . . :** For example, the biblical mourner will rend his garments; see Gen. 37:29 and 34; Josh. 7:6; and Job 1:20, among many others. Significantly, the Bible explicitly prohibits certain mourning practices as alien or idolatrous (Lev. 19:27–28; Deut. 14:1), and this theme, too, is developed by the later tradition.

185 **the Rabbis constructed . . . :** Even if we accept Rambam's view that the commandment to mourn is found in the Torah itself, the particular means by which that commandment has been fulfilled have been determined by rabbinic thinking and Jewish communal practice. Mourning (*avelut*) therefore is a prime example of the power of "creative ritual" in Judaism, the process by which the Sages and the people develop elaborate structures of religious behavior out of the relatively scant raw materials provided by sacred texts. The subject of death and mourning occupies its own talmudic tractate, the so-called "minor" tractate *Semachot* ("Joys," a euphemism for its true subject matter). In addition, the third chapter of *B. Mo'ed Katan* is a major source for the *halakhah* of mourning. The codified product of this rabbinic thinking fills sixty-three chapters of the *Shulchan Arukh*, and has spawned numerous learned and popular treatises.

185 **"channel emotions into a productive expression . . . ":** Ron H. Isaacs and Kerry M. Olitzky, *A Jewish Mourner's Handbook*, 12.

185 **"To offer consolation . . . ":** Ibid., 14.

186 **Visiting the Sick:** Maslin, *Gates of Mitzvah*, 49.

186 **Confession:** Ibid., 50; *B. Shabbat* 32a; *Shulchan Arukh, Yore De'ah* 338. "Confession," in Jewish tradition, is not a sacrament that is administered by the clergy but an individual's heart-felt admission, rendered directly to God, of his or her failings and weaknesses. See *Yad, Teshuvah*, ch. 2.

186 **Traditional literature requires . . . :** *Semachot* 1:3; *Torat Ha'adam*, ed. Chavel, 46; *Shulchan Arukh, Yore De'ah* 338:1 and *Shakh* ad loc.

186 **Some Reform responsa concur . . . :** Freehof, *Reform Responsa*, no. 28.

186 **or slightly modify it . . . :** Jacob, *Questions and Reform Jewish Answers*, no. 158.

186 **The most recent responsa . . . :** Plaut and Washofsky, *Teshuvot*, no. 5753.2, which notes that some Orthodox writers are also coming to this conclusion. The responsum stresses that this is a *general* statement and that the decision what to tell the patient must be considered carefully on a case-by-case basis. On the patient's "right to know," see Chapter 6.

186 **Ethical Wills:** Maslin, *Gates of Mitzvah*, 51. For an extensive collection of Jewish ethical wills, see Jack Riemer and Nathaniel Stampfer, eds., *Ethical Wills: A Modern Jewish Treasury*.

186 *Keri'ah* **and** *Tzidduk Hadin*: Maslin, *Gates of Mitzvah*, 51.

187 **rends his or her garment . . . :** *Shulchan Arukh, Yore De'ah* 339:3.

187   **The "mourner" is anyone who . . . :** *B. Mo'ed Katan* 20b: one is required to mourn for any relative that a priest (*Kohen*) is obligated to bury (see Lev. 21:2 and *B. Yevamot* 22b); *Shulchan Arukh, Yore De'ah* 374:4. The thought is that if a priest, normally forbidden by the laws of ritual purity from coming into contact with a corpse, is commanded to do so in order to bury these relatives, then surely everyone is commanded to mourn out of respect for those loved ones.

187   ***keri'ah* . . . :** *Shulchan Arukh, Yore De'ah* 340:1ff. A slight cut is made in the garment with a sharp instrument and the tear is completed by hand. For a parent, the entire process is done by hand. Another person may perform the tear upon the mourner's garments; *Pitchei Teshuvah, Yore De'ah* 340, no. 1. When mourning most relatives, one may change into other clothes during *shivah* without having to rend the new garments. For one's parent, the new garments must be torn (*Shulchan Arukh, Yore De'ah* 340:14). For Shabbat, one may change into a new garment without making a tear in it (*Shulchan Arukh, Yore De'ah* 400:1).

187   **In Reform practice . . . :** Maslin, *Gates of Mitzvah*, 54, and 91, no. 99; Polish, *Rabbi's Manual*, 249. The custom of waiting until the funeral to perform *keri'ah* is supported in *Gesher Hachayim*, ch. 4, no. 1.

187   ***Aninut*:** See *M. Sanhedrin* 6:6: while mourning (*avelut*) is a public demonstration of grief, expressed by outward symbols, "*aninut* takes place in the heart alone."

187   **exempt from all positive religious obligations . . . :** such as prayer and the recitation of the *Shema*; *M. Berakhot* 3:1; *Yad, Avel* 4:6; *Shulchan Arukh, Orach Chayim* 71:1. The *onen/et* is not permitted to violate any of the Torah's "thou shalt nots." In addition, the *onen/et* is forbidden to eat meat or to drink wine, except on Shabbat (*B. Mo'ed Katan* 23b), when he or she is obliged to say *Kiddush*.

187   **a *mitzvah* to console the bereaved . . . :** See *M. Pe'ah* 1:1 on *gemilut chasadim*; *Yad, Avel* 14:1.

187   **pre-funeral visitation . . . :** Maslin, *Gates of Mitzvah*, 54.

187   **Funeral Preparations:** Ibid., 52.

187   **Tradition forbids us . . . :** *Semachot* 1:5; *Resp. Rivash*, no. 114; *Shulchan Arukh* and Isserles, *Yore De'ah* 339:1.

187   **Occasionally, a person will instruct relatives not to mourn . . . :** Freehof, *Recent Reform Responsa*, no. 24. See *B. Sanhedrin* 46b–47a; *Yad, Avel* 12:1; *Resp. R. Ya'akov Weil*, no. 4; *Shulchan Arukh, Yore De'ah* 344:10; *Resp. Teshuvah Me'ahavah* 1:174 and 207. Burial itself is a Toraitic commandment, derived from Deut. 21:23. Just as the honor we owe a parent does not authorize us to heed that parent's instruction to violate a *mitzvah*, so the honor we owe the dead does not entitle us to ignore a religious duty at their request.

188   **the mourners should consult the rabbi . . . :** Maslin, *Gates of Mitzvah*, 52.

188   **careful cleansing and washing . . . :** Described in *Kitzur Shulchan Arukh*, ch. 197.

188   **linen shrouds (*tachrichim*) . . . :** See *B. Mo'ed Katan* 27a–b on rabbinic efforts to place limits on funeral expenses; *Yad, Avel* 4:1; *Shulchan Arukh, Yore De'ah* 352:1–2.

188   **It is praiseworthy . . . :** Plaut and Washofsky, *Teshuvot*, no. 5754.8.

188   **a Jewish mortician . . . :** Jacob, *Questions and Reform Jewish Answers*, no. 167. Gentiles are permitted to perform the work of preparation and burial, particularly on the first day of *yom tov* (*Shulchan Arukh, Orach Chayim* 526). However, this is because Jews are not permitted to labor on that day. The main responsibility for the burial

of Jews rests with other Jews, and a community should support its Jewish funeral director(s); Freehof, *New Reform Responsa*, no. 38.

188   **Reform Judaism permits autopsies . . .** : Maslin, *Gates of Mitzvah*, 52–53; Polish, *Rabbi's Manual*, 247. See B. *Bekhorot* 45a, a talmudic report of a permitted autopsy.

188   *nivul hamet . . .* : See B. *Chulin* 11a on Deut. 21:23.

188   *hana'ah mehamet . . .* : B. *Sanhedrin* 47b–48a; *Yad, Avel* 14:21; *Shulchan Arukh, Yore De'ah* 249:1.

188   **unnecessary delay of burial . . .** : It is a *mitzvah* to bury the dead (Deut. 21:23; *Yad, Avel* 12:1), and one does not unnecessarily delay the performance of a *mitzvah*.

189   *pikuach nefesh*: B. *Yoma* 85b on Lev. 18:5; *Yad, Yesodei Hatorah* 5; *Shulchan Arukh, Yore De'ah* 157.

189   **"in our presence" . . .** : *Resp. Noda Biyehudah, Yore De'ah*, 2:210, and *Resp. Chatam Sofer, Yore De'ah*, no. 336. A noted Orthodox authority concedes that "in our presence" does not necessarily mean "in this city"; thus, if we know that there is *surely* a patient who can benefit from this knowledge, the autopsy is permitted; *Chazon Ish, Ohalot* ch. 22, end of par. 32. Another writes that should a patient die from a disease whose cure is unknown, an autopsy may be permitted even when there is no other patient "in our presence" afflicted with the disease; *Resp. Tzitz Eliezer* 4:14.

189   **even for the purpose of medical education:** *Resp. Noda Biyehudah* loc. cit; *Resp. Chatam Sofer* loc. cit; *Resp. Maharam Schick, Yore De'ah* no. 344; *Resp. Yabi'a Omer* 3:23, sec. 26; *Resp. Igerot Moshe, Yore De'ah* 1:151; *Resp. Tzitz Eliezer* 4:14.

189   **The Reform view . . .** : Jacob, *American Reform Responsa*, no. 82; Freehof, *Contemporary Reform Responsa*, no. 49. Among Orthodox scholars, *Resp. Mishpetei Ouziel, Yore De'ah* 28–29, permits autopsy for medical study on grounds of *pikuach nefesh*. And see the statements of *Chazon Ish* and *Tzitz Eliezer*, above: the Reform position, that the increase of medical knowledge overrides our legitimate concern for *nivul hamet*, is the logical interpretation of Jewish law. To the extent that advanced methods of anatomical study may render autopsy unnecessary for medical education, we would agree that the permit for the procedure will have lost much of its rationale. Until then, we support autopsies performed as an integral part of the training of physicians and other medical professionals.

189   **The burial of the parts of the body . . .** : Polish, *Rabbi's Manual*, 247.

189   **donation of the organs . . .** : Maslin, *Gates of Mitzvah*, 52; Freehof, *Contemporary Reform Responsa*, no. 49; Jacob, *American Reform Responsa*, no. 83. Such transplantation does not violate the prohibition against benefitting from the dead, since the transplanted organ now belongs fully to the living person; *Shevet Miyehudah*, 313–14. In addition, the prohibition of *nivul hamet* does not apply "in cases of great need," such as that of a patient who requires a cornea transplant from one who has died; *Resp. Yabi'a Omer, Yore De'ah* 3:23. Some authorities nonetheless prohibit taking organs from the dead on the grounds that the dead are no longer under any obligation to fulfill the *mitzvot*, including that of *pikuach nefesh*, and we are thus forbidden to deny their bodies the respect they deserve (*Resp. Minchat Yitzchak* 5:8; *Resp. Tzitz Eliezer* 13:91). We reason, by contrast, that a person would surely want his body utilized after death in a way which enhances the lives and health of others; *American Reform Responsa*, no. 82. On the donation of organs by a living person, see the discussion in Chapter 6.

189   **An individual may also donate his or her entire body to science . . . :** Maslin, *Gates of Mitzvah*, 53; Freehof, *Contemporary Reform Responsa*, no. 49. Some authorities hold that one may waive the "honor" due to one's corpse for sufficient cause; *Resp. Binyan Tziyon*, no. 170 and *Resp. Tzitz Eliezer* 4:14. Others most strongly disagree; see *Resp. Maharam Schick, Yore De'ah*, no. 347–48 and *Resp. Igerot Moshe, Yore De'ah* 3:140. Should one decide to donate one's body, the ultimate burial of the remains would fulfill the traditional obligation to bury the corpse.

189   **Closing the Coffin:** Maslin, *Gates of Mitzvah*, 54; Polish, *Rabbi's Manual*, 248; Jacob, *Contemporary American Reform Responsa*, no. 91. The open-casket funeral is avoided, traditionally, as an imitation of Gentile religious practice; *Kol Bo 'al Avelut*, 36.

189   **Embalming:** Polish, *Rabbi's Manual*, 248; Freehof, *Reform Jewish Practice,* 1:121.

189   **"returns unto the dust":** The decomposition of the body is seen as having a power to atone for sins which the person committed while alive; *M. Sanhedrin* 5:6.

190   **It is a *mitzvah* to bury the dead . . . :** Maslin, *Gates of Mitzvah*, 54. Deut. 21:23 requires the burial of an executed criminal, and if we are so obligated toward the criminal's corpse, then surely we owe this honor to all others. *B. Sanhedrin* 46b; *Yad, Avel* 12:1; *Shulchan Arukh, Yore De'ah* 362:1.

190   **While Jewish dead were once interred . . . :** Abraham, Sarah, and their descendants were buried in the cave of Machpelah (Gen. 22:16); see also Isa. 22:16; *M. Bava Batra* 6:8; *B. Sanhedrin* 47b on *kever binyan,* the "built grave," and Rashi ad loc. On the subject of mausoleum burial see Freehof, *Reform Responsa*, no. 38 and Freehof, *Reform Jewish Practice*, 1:122ff.

190   **Objections to mausoleum interment . . . :** Plaut and Washofsky, *Teshuvot*, no. 5751.8; *Resp. Igerot Moshe, Yore De'ah* 1:24.

190   **Burial at sea . . . :** Jacob, *Contemporary American Reform Responsa*, no. 104.

190   **Cremation . . . :** See Ibid., no. 51; Freehof, *Reform Jewish Practice*, 1:133ff. The ecological arguments for cremation tend to stress that full-body burial is a waste of land. The traditional arguments against cremation are summarized in *Kol Bo 'al Avelut*, 53ff.

190   **The Reform rabbinate seeks to discourage . . . :** Polish, *Rabbi's Manual*, 248; Jacob, *American Reform Responsa*, no. 100; Maslin, *Gates of Mitzvah*, 56–57.

190   **Responsibility for Burial:** *B. Ketubot* 48a; *Yad, Zekhiah* 11:24; *Shulchan Arukh, Yore De'ah* 348:2.

190   **A spouse . . . :** *B. Ketubot* 47b; *Yad, Ishut* 12:2; *Shulchan Arukh, Even Ha'ezer* 89:1; *Responsa Committee*, 5756.7. When a twice-married person dies, some say that the spouse or the spouse's heirs are responsible for the burial, while others place the duty upon the deceased's own heirs (*Shulchan Arukh, Even Ha'ezer* 89:4). We concur with the former view: the heirs of the spouse pay for the funeral. If the deceased is buried next to a former spouse, then the heirs of that spouse should pay for the gravesite (Freehof, *Today's Reform Responsa*, no. 30).

190   **the community as a whole:** Maslin, *Gates of Mitzvah*, 87, n. 84. The corpse which has no one to attend to its burial is called a *met mitzvah*; whoever encounters the corpse is required to see to its burial. *B. Nazir* 43b; *Yad, Avel* 3:8; *Shulchan Arukh, Yore De'ah* 374.

190   **If the family can afford to pay . . . :** Freehof, *Contemporary Reform Responsa*, nos. 44–45.

190   **Timely Burial:** Polish, *Rabbi's Manual*, 249; Maslin, *Gates of Mitzvah*, 55.

190   **delay of burial *(halanat hamet)* . . . :** M. *Sanhedrin* 6:5; *Yad, Avel* 4:8; *Shulchan Arukh, Yore De'ah* 357:1. The prohibition is drawn from Deut. 21:23, from which the *mitzvah* of burial is derived. The exceptions to the rule of speedy burial are mentioned in these same sources.

191   **Days When Burial Does Not Take Place:** Maslin, *Gates of Mitzvah*, 55; Polish, *Rabbi's Manual*, 249; Freehof, *Reform Jewish Practice*, 1:117–18; Jacob, *Questions and Reform Jewish Answers*, nos. 165–66. The "leniencies" referred to concern the rulings that, if Gentiles perform the forbidden labors, Jews may carry out the actual burial (*B. Beitzah* 6a; *Yad, Yom Tov* 1:23; *Shulchan Arukh, Orach Chayim* 526:1-3).

191   **on all other days:** Jacob, *Questions and Reform Jewish Answers*, nos. 165–66.

191   **Simplicity and dignity . . . :** Our tradition teaches that wealth and riches are ultimately "empty things" that do not reflect life's true purpose (see Ecclesiastes 1); therefore, at death, we take pains not to emphasize them.

191   **a simple wooden coffin . . . :** Maslin, *Gates of Mitzvah*, 55; Jacob, *Questions and Reform Jewish Answers*, no. 175; *Y. Kilayim* 9:4 (32b); *Yad, Avel* 4:4. See *Shulchan Arukh, Yore De'ah* 362:1: it is preferable that the deceased be buried without a coffin, directly in the earth. Should a coffin be used, earth is placed inside to cover the body.

191   **Coffins made of other materials . . . :** Jacob, *Questions and Reform Jewish Answers*, no. 176. The prohibition against the use of metal nails in a wooden coffin has little if any basis in Jewish textual tradition; see Freehof, *Recent Reform Responsa*, no. 32, part C.

191   **Flowers . . . :** Maslin, *Gates of Mitzvah*, 55; Freehof, *Reform Jewish Practice*, 1:135–37.

191   ***Tzidduk Hadin* . . . :** Traditional Ashkenazic practice omits *Tzidduk Hadin* on days when the community does not mourn (Isserles, *Yore De'ah* 401:6; see below, concerning the eulogy). On such days, Psalm 16 is recited in place of *Tzidduk Hadin*. Sefardim do recite *Tzidduk Hadin* on those days (*Shulchan Arukh, Yore De'ah* 401:6).

191   **It is a mitzvah to attend a funeral service . . . :** Maslin, *Gates of Mitzvah*, 56; Polish, *Rabbi's Manual*, 250; *B. Mo'ed Katan* 27b; *Yad, Avel* 14:10; *Shulchan Arukh, Yore De'ah* 343:1.

191   **Even the study of Torah . . . :** *B. Ketubot* 17a.

191   **Funeral services are sometimes held . . . :** Maslin, *Gates of Mitzvah*, 56; Polish, *Rabbi's Manual*, 250.

191   **in the synagogue . . . :** Freehof, *Reform Jewish Practice*, 2:54–58. See *B. Megillah* 28a–b. A "public eulogy" may be held in a synagogue. This is defined as the funeral of a great sage for which a large building is needed to accommodate those in attendance (Rashi, ad loc., s.v. *hesped shel rabim; Yad, Tefillah* 11:7). The *Shulchan Arukh* (*Yore De'ah* 344:19) extends this permit to the wives of scholars. The Sages apparently saw this practice as a special honor for noted leaders of the community.

192   **halting the funeral procession at the synagogue . . . :** Freehof, *Reform Responsa for Our Time*, no. 39.

192   **It is a *mitzvah* to speak well of the dead:** Maslin, *Gates of Mitzvah*, 56; *B. Shabbat* 105b and *B. Berakhot* 6b; *Yad, Avel* 12:1; *Shulchan Arukh, Yore De'ah* 344.

192   **"What is a proper *hesped* ? . . . ":** *Shulchan Arukh, Yore De'ah* 344:1. See *Bach, Tur* 344: some degree of exaggeration is permitted; otherwise, we might *understate* the praise of the deceased.

192   **Reform Judaism permits eulogies to be recited on any day:** Traditionally, eulogies are not recited at funerals held on days when public mourning is forbidden or when *tachanun* is not recited following the *Tefillah*. These days include, among others, Chanukah, Purim, Rosh Chodesh, *chol hamo'ed*, Tu Bishevat, the entire month of Nisan, Lag Ba'omer, and the afternoon before the onset of Shabbat or *yom tov*. See *Shulchan Arukh, Yore De'ah* 401. For us, the *mitzvah* to honor the dead takes precedence over these prohibitions.

192   *ma'amadot* . . . : Polish, *Rabbi's Manual*, 250; B. *Bava Batra* 100b; *Kitzur Shulchan Arukh* 198:12. There are many variations in and explanations for this custom; see Freehof, *Reform Jewish Practice*, 1:129. Isserles mentions that "we halt two or three times" on days when *tachanun* is not said (*Yore De'ah* 358:3); Karo does not mention the custom at all.

192   **Customs vary as to the order** . . . : *Kitzur Shulchan Arukh* 199:9.

192   **Tradition prescribes** . . . : Maslin, *Gates of Mitzvah*, 57.

192   *Kaddish* . . . : Ibid., 57; Polish, *Rabbi's Manual*, 251. Traditionally, this is the *"Burial"* or *"Great Kaddish,"* whose text differs slightly from the more familiar version; Elbogen, *Jewish Liturgy*, 81. Reform practice maintains the *Mourner's Kaddish* for burial.

192   **two rows** . . . : Polish, *Rabbi's Manual*, 251; B. *Megillah* 23b; *Yad, Avel* 13:1–2. On the plucking of grass and the washing of the hands, see *Shulchan Arukh, Yore De'ah* 376:4.

193   **Burial of Non-Jews:** Maslin, *Gates of Mitzvah*, 57; Polish, *Rabbi's Manual*, 250–51; Jacob, *American Reform Responsa*, no. 98. In *American Reform Responsa*, no. 99, R. Solomon B. Freehof develops the theory of the Jewish cemetery which does not forbid the burial of a non-Jew: the cemetery itself is not, according to *halakhah*, a "sacred" place, and the only requirement for burial is that one be interred in one's own ground (*betokh shelo*). Thus, there is no real reason, other than long-standing custom, that a Jewish cemetery (which, by legal standing, is simply an aggregation of Jewish graves) be exclusively Jewish, and the great codes make no such requirement. "Long-standing custom," however, is a powerful force in Jewish religious practice; therefore, individuals and communities have the right to demand that these customs be followed along with the other by-laws of the cemetery (*American Reform Responsa*, no. 99, 1980 addendum). See B.*Gittin* 61a, *Yad, Avel* 14:12, and *Shulchan Arukh, Yore De'ah* 367:1: "we bury the non-Jewish dead together with the Jewish dead for the sake of preserving peace." While Rashi to the Talmud passage notes that this does not mean that the non-Jews are buried in "Jewish graves," it does suggest the possibility that Jews and Gentiles were buried in the same cemetery under certain circumstances (see *Bach* to *Tur, Yore De'ah* 151, end).

193   **a liturgy of our own devising** . . . : Maslin, *Gates of Mitzvah*, 57; Polish, *Rabbi's Manual*, 251.

193   **a prospective convert** . . . : Jacob, *American Reform Responsa*, no. 97. The conversion process may be hastened in the event of a life-threatening illness. Yet the mere intention to become a Jew, however sincerely expressed, does not make one a member of the Jewish people in the absence of a valid conversion.

193   **not held in the synagogue** . . . : Jacob, *Questions and Reform Jewish Answers*, no. 181.

193   **Burial of Jews in Non-Jewish Cemeteries:** Freehof, *Reform Jewish Practice*, 1:122ff.; Freehof, *Reform Responsa*, no. 33.

193   **burial in a national military cemetery** . . . : Freehof, *New Reform Responsa*, no. 25.

193   **a rabbi will officiate . . . :** Polish, *Rabbi's Manual,* 251; Freehof, *Reform Responsa,* no. 33.

193   **Burial of Apostates:** Jacob, *Contemporary American Reform Response,* no. 100; Freehof, *Recent Reform Responsa,* no. 27. The early tradition declares that we do not mourn or even care for the bodies of "those who separate from the community" (*Semachot* 2:10). Having despised Judaism during their lives, they forfeit any claim to its care after their deaths (*Yad, Avel* 1:10). This was *not* understood as a prohibition against burial (*Resp. Rashba* 1:763; Radbaz to *Yad,* loc. cit.), which is after all a *mitzvah,* a religious duty that does not depend upon our feelings toward the dead, but rather an instruction that we withhold from them the normal honors shown to the deceased. We comfort the apostate's mourners: *Shakh, Yore De'ah* 334, no. 18, citing Ramban.

193   **Messianic Jews . . . :** Jacob, *Contemporary American Reform Responsa,* no. 67.

193   **Burial of Suicides:** Polish, *Rabbi's Manual,* 251; Jacob, *American Reform Responsa,* no. 89. The Hebrew term for suicide, *me'abed atzmo leda'at,* suggests a premeditated, rational act. *Semachot* 2:1ff.; *Yad, Avel* 1:11; *Shulchan Arukh, Yore De'ah* 345:1ff., and *Pitchei Teshuvah* ad loc.; *Resp. Chatam Sofer, Yore De'ah* 326; *Resp. Parashat Mordekhai, Yore De'ah* 25; *Resp. Ha'elef Lekha Shelomo, Yore De'ah* 301; *Arukh Hashulchan, Yore De'ah* 345.

194   **to eulogize them appropriately:** Jacob, *American Reform Responsa,* no. 90; *Resp. Kenesset Yechezkel,* no. 37.

194   **Burial of the "Wicked":** Maslin, *Gates of Mitzvah,* 58; *Resp. Chatam Sofer, Yore De'ah,* no. 333.

194   **Rites of Fraternal Orders:** Jacob, *American Reform Responsa,* nos. 91–92.

194   **Reverence:** On the halakhic status of the cemetery see *American Reform Responsa,* no. 99. B. *Megillah* 29a; *Yad, Avel* 14:13; *Shulchan Arukh, Yore De'ah* 368.

195   **The entire cemetery . . . :** Freehof, *Reform Responsa for Our Time,* no. 26; *Hilkhot Harosh, Megillah* 4:9; *Resp. Meir Azaryah of Fano,* no. 56; *Resp. Chatam Sofer, Yore De'ah* 335.

195   **public worship services . . . :** Freehof, *Recent Reform Responsa,* no. 7. See B. *Ta'anit* 16a: Jews have always gone to the cemetery to pray, especially on fast-days, as the intercession of the dead was thought to be effective. The prohibition against bringing a *sefer torah* into a cemetery is found in B. *Berakhot* 18a, based upon Prov. 17:5: we "mock" the inability of the dead to study Torah when we study in their presence. While this reasoning may not appeal to our modern sensibilities, we prohibit the regular use of cemeteries for other religious (let alone secular) purposes out of respect for the dead. Thus (Jacob, *American Reform Responsa,* no. 27), a chapel at a cemetery should be built without an ark, so as to discourage the inclusion of a Torah scroll.

195   **walking across a grave . . . :** Freehof, *Today's Reform Responsa,* no. 20. Isserles, *Yore De'ah* 364:1; *Kol Bo 'al Avelut,* 179.

195   **Ownership:** Freehof, *Reform Responsa for Our Time,* no. 26.

195   **tradition today frowns upon the sale . . . :** Freehof, *Reform Responsa for Our Time,* loc. cit. (p. 134: "it is as if one would sell a room or two in the synagogue for some secular purpose"); *Resp. Melamed Leho'il, Yore De'ah,* no. 125. The cemetery of a defunct congregation must be cared for by other Jews; Freehof, *Modern Reform Responsa,* no. 42. Under very limited circumstances (e.g., the community owns a great deal of cemetery land), it may be permissible to sell some of the land, provided that

the proceeds (as in the case of the sale of a synagogue) are put toward a religious purpose of equal sanctity (Jacob, *Questions and Reform Jewish Answers*, no. 200).

195 **a Jewish section of a general cemetery:** Jacob, *Questions and Reform Jewish Answers*, no. 198; Freehof, *Recent Reform Responsa*, no. 31; *Kol Bo 'al Avelut*, 163. A lease arrangement is permissible, so long as the agreement is carefully worded to guarantee that all decisions concerning burial, ritual, etc. rest exclusively with the Jewish community; *Questions and Reform Jewish Answers*, no. 196.

195 **a community may restrict the use . . . :** Jacob, *Contemporary American Reform Responsa*, no. 101.

195 **naming a cemetery after an individual . . . :** Jacob, *Questions and Reform Jewish Answers*, no. 197.

195 **The Grave:** Freehof, *Current Reform Responsa*, no. 34; Jacob, *American Reform Responsa*, nos. 103–4; *Resp. Chatam Sofer, Yore De'ah*, no. 332.

195 **two persons in a single grave:** Freehof, *Recent Reform Responsa*, no. 29; *Shulchan Arukh, Yore De'ah* 362:3.

196 **one coffin on top of another . . . :** Jacob, *American Reform Responsa*, no. 107; Plaut and Washofsky, *Teshuvot*, no. 5751.8; *Shulchan Arukh, Yore De'ah* 362:4.

196 **Cremains . . . :** Jacob, *Questions and Reform Jewish Answers*, no. 191–92; Freehof, *Modern Reform Responsa*, no. 41; Freehof, *Current Reform Responsa*, no. 37; *Resp. Melamed Leho'il, Yore De'ah*, no. 113.

196 **Disinterment:** *Responsa Committee*, no. 5756.5; Jacob, *Contemporary American Reform Responsa*, no. 111; Freehof, *Today's Reform Responsa*, no. 25; *Y. Mo'ed Katan* 2:4 (81b); *Shulchan Arukh, Yore De'ah* 363:1; *Resp. Chakham Zvi*, no. 50.

196 **vandalism . . . :** Freehof, *Contemporary Reform Responsa*, no. 50; *Resp. Chatam Sofer, Yore De'ah* 353; *Resp. Igerot Moshe, Yore De'ah* 1:246–47.

196 **legal evidence . . . :** Jacob, *Contemporary American Reform Responsa*, no. 110. The arguments are much the same as those which permit autopsy.

196 **that grave may be used for the burial of another . . . :** Freehof, *Reform Responsa*, no. 132. The prohibition of deriving benefit from a grave (*B. Sanhedrin* 47b) applies only to constructed graves and not to those dug in the ground (*Shulchan Arukh, Yore De'ah* 364:1; *Resp. Ketav Sofer, Yore De'ah* 177).

196 **No special ritual . . . :** Jacob, *Contemporary American Reform Responsa*, no. 112.

196 **Mourning:** See Maslin, *Gates of Mitzvah*, 59. The tradition prescribes similar seven-day, thirty-day, and twelve-month periods of rejoicing following one's wedding; see *B. Ketubot* 8a.

197 **Shivah:** Following the principle that "part of a day is equivalent to the entire day" (*miktzat hayom kekhulo*); *B. Mo'ed Katan* 19b and 27a; *Yad, Avel* 1:2; *Shulchan Arukh, Yore De'ah* 375:1.

197 **the meal of consolation (se'udat havra'ah) . . . :** Maslin, *Gates of Mitzvah*, 61; Polish, *Rabbi's Manual*, 252; *B. Mo'ed Katan* 27b; *Shulchan Arukh, Yore De'ah* 378:1. Various foods may be served, but it is customary to include bread, since this is a formal "meal" (*se'udah*) at which the recitation of *Birkat Hamazon* is appropriate, and hard-boiled eggs, a traditional symbol of mourning (*Shulchan Arukh, Yore De'ah* 378:9).

197   **A memorial candle . . . :** A liturgy for the candle-lighting is provided in Stern, *On the Doorposts of Your House*, 176. This is a relatively recent Jewish custom; see Freehof, *Current Reform Responsa*, no. 33.

197   **The first three days . . . :** Freehof, *Reform Jewish Practice*, 1:159; Maslin, *Gates of Mitzvah*, 59. B. *Mo'ed Katan* 27b: "the first three days are for weeping"; *Shulchan Arukh, Yore De'ah* 380:2, 5.

197   **Reform Jews ought to observe all seven days . . . :** Polish, *Rabbi's Manual*, 252.

197   **These prohibitions . . . :** which are detailed in *Shulchan Arukh, Yore De'ah* 380–91. The custom of covering the mirrors in the house of mourning is rooted in folklore and is not insisted upon by Reform Judaism (Freehof, *Reform Responsa*, no. 42, sec. E.). However, as the practice can be defended as a means of rejecting vanity, some may wish to observe it (Polish, *Rabbi's Manual*, 253).

197   **the Breslau rabbinical conference of 1846:** See Plaut, *Rise of Reform Judaism*, 223; Jacob, *American Reform Responsa*, no. 117.

197   **During *shivah*, worship services . . . :** Polish, *Rabbi's Manual*, 253.

197   **at the house of mourning . . . :** See Freehof, *Reform Responsa for Our Time*, no. 27: in the event that the service cannot be held in the deceased's home, it reverts to the home of the effective "head of household." Care must be taken to insure that conflicts over this matter do not destroy the proper atmosphere of mourning.

197   ***minyan* . . . :** Polish, *Rabbi's Manual*, 253.

198   ***devar torah* . . . :** Since Torah study is a source of joy, a mourner is traditionally forbidden to study Torah during *shivah*, with the exception of the "sad" texts of Jeremiah, Job, Lamentations, and the laws of mourning (*B. Mo'ed Katan* 15a; *Yad, Avel* 5:16; *Shulchan Arukh, Yore De'ah* 384). Our position is that the study of Torah is a consolation which we are required to provide to mourners as part of the *mitzvah* of *nichum avelim*. Just as the mourner is permitted to study works of *musar* (ethical discipline) which incline the heart toward repentance (Meiri on *Mo'ed Katan* 21a), he or she is likewise permitted to study Torah when this activity leads to spiritual strength and recovery.

198   ***Sheloshim*:** Maslin, *Gates of Mitzvah*, 59; Polish, *Rabbi's Manual*, 253–54. B. *Mo'ed Katan* 19b (derived from Lev. 10:6 and Num. 6:5); *Yad, Avel* 6:1 (derived from Deut. 21:13). Just as many of the traditional observances of *shivah* have been discontinued in Reform Judaism, so have many of the *sheloshim* regulations. On weddings, see *Yad, Avel* 6:5 and *Shulchan Arukh, Yore De'ah* 392.

198   **Bar/Bat Mitzvah . . . :** Jacob, *Contemporary American Reform Responsa*, no. 159.

198   **Shabbat, *Yom Tov* and Mourning:** M. *Mo'ed Katan* 3:5; *Yad, Avel* 10:1ff.; *Shulchan Arukh, Yore De'ah* 400. Shabbat, because it always falls during *shivah*, does not interrupt mourning; otherwise, there would never be a seven-day period of intense *avelut* (*Tur, Yore De'ah* 400). Another reason: while one is required to rejoice on the festivals, this obligation does not apply to Shabbat.

198   ***yom tov* . . . cancels *shivah* . . . :** B. *Mo'ed Katan* 19a; *Yad, Avel* 10:3ff.; *Shulchan Arukh, Yore De'ah* 399. Shavuot counts as seven days (*Shulchan Arukh, Yore De'ah* 399:8).

199   **Reform Judaism permits . . . :** Maslin, *Gates of Mitzvah*, 60; Polish, *Rabbi's Manual*, 252. See *Shulchan Arukh, Yore De'ah* 399:2: one whose relative dies on a *yom tov* or *chol hamo'ed* observes the private practices of *avelut*, even though *shivah* does not

begin until the conclusion of the festival. It is unreasonable to expect the mourner to pretend that no death has occurred. Thus, tradition forges a compromise between the mourner's public responsibility (to rejoice as a Jew on the festival) and private pain. Our counsel, that the survivor be permitted to take up private mourning following a period of *avelut* shortened by a festival, reflects a similar idea.

199　**The Twelve Months:** Maslin, *Gates of Mitzvah*, 60. Isserles, *Yore De'ah* 376:4, end, recounts the custom of saying this *Kaddish* for eleven months only. According to Jewish folklore, the *Kaddish* helps atone for a parent's sins and to elevate him or her to heaven. By saying it for eleven months, rather than for a full year, we express faith in our parent's righteousness: "Surely he or she was not so wicked as to require a full year of atonement!" (*Be'er Hetev, Orach Chayim* 132, no. 5; *Chayei Adam* 32:18). Reform Judaism does not recognize *Kaddish* as a prayer of intercession for the dead; hence, we recite it for the full year.

199　**It is a *mitzvah* . . . to recite the Kaddish . . . :** Maslin, *Gates of Mitzvah*, 62; 143–45; Jacob, *American Reform Responsa*, no. 118.

199　**Structure and Practice:** On the history of *Kaddish* see Elbogen, *Jewish Liturgy*, 80–84, and Hoffman, *Gates of Understanding*, 2:47–50.

201　**the *Union Prayer Book* preserves only one *Kaddish* . . . :** *Union Prayer Book* 1: 77.

201　**Reform congregations stand as a whole for *Kaddish* . . . :** See Isserles, *Orach Chayim* 56:1: as a prayer rubric "pertaining to sanctification" (*davar shebekedushah*), like *Kedushah* and *Barekhu*, it is appropriate to stand for any *Kaddish*, whether one is a mourner or not. For other customs see *Be'er Hetev*, no. 4, and *Mishnah Berurah*, no. 7.

201　**after the Holocaust . . . :** or out of solidarity with the mourners. Hoffman, *Gates of Understanding*, 2:50; Jacob, *American Reform Responsa*, no. 118 and no. 120, note; Freehof, *Reform Jewish Practice*, 2:114–16. This reflects the traditional practice that, when no mourners are present, *Kaddish* is said for "all the dead of Israel"; Isserles, *Yore De'ah* 376:4 and *Sedei Chemed, Ma'arekhet Avelut*, par. 163.

201　**The Stillborn and the Infant:** *B. Shabbat* 135b and *B. Nidah* 44b; *Yad, Avel* 1:6–7; *Shulchan Arukh, Yore De'ah* 374:8.

201　**The tradition, we should note . . . :** Isserles, *Yore De'ah* 374:6.

202　**to consult with their rabbi:** Maslin, *Gates of Mitzvah*, 58; Polish, *Rabbi's Manual*, 250; Freehof, *Today's Reform Responsa*, no. 48

202　**Gentile Relatives:** *B. Yevamot* 22a.

202　**Many authorities therefore hold . . . :** *Yad, Avel* 2:2, and see *Kesef Mishneh* ad loc; *Shulchan Arukh, Yore De'ah* 374:5.

202　**to show honor and respect to their parents . . . :** *Yad, Mamrim* 5:11, and *Shulchan Arukh, Yore De'ah* 241:9, based in all likelihood upon *B. Yevamot* 22a.

202　**Reform Judaism permits and encourages . . . :** Jacob, *American Reform Responsa*, 123–25; Jacob, *Contemporary American Reform Responsa*, no. 121; *Resp. Zekan Aharon* 2:87.

202　**Adopted Children:** See the discussion on adoption in this chapter.

202　**Criminals; Abusive Relationships:** Jacob, *Contemporary American Reform Responsa*, nos. 122–23.

202　**A child is required . . . :** *B. Yevamot* 22a; *Yad, Mamrim* 6:11.

202   **Since this issue is a matter of dispute . . . :** See *B. Bava Kama* 94b and *Shulchan Arukh, Yore De'ah* 240:18 and Isserles ad loc. According to some, the responsibility to honor a wicked parent holds only if the parent has repented of his or her wrongdoing.

202   **Delayed Funeral:** Jacob, *Contemporary American Reform Responsa*, no. 119; *Shulchan Arukh, Yore De'ah* 375:4.

202   **When the deceased is to be transported . . . :** Jacob, *Contemporary American Reform Responsa*, no. 119; *B. Mo'ed Katan* 22a; *Yad, Avel* 1:5; Isserles, *Yore De'ah* 375:7.

203   **If a person has disappeared . . . :** Freehof, *Recent Reform Responsa*, no. 22; *Semachot* 2:12; *Shulchan Arukh, Yore De'ah* 375:7.

203   **Delayed News of a Death:** Polish, *Rabbi's Manual*, 252. *B. Mo'ed Katan* 20a–b; *Yad, Avel* 7:1; *Shulchan Arukh, Yore De'ah* 402:1. The rule *miktzat hayom kekhulo*, "part of a day is considered the equivalent of a full day," applies.

203   *Yahrzeit* **and** *Yizkor*: Maslin, *Gates of Mitzvah*, 62.

203   **an Ashkenazic observance . . . :** For history, see Jacob, *American Reform Responsa*, no. 127.

203   **similar customs are observed by Sefardic Jews . . . :** Dobrinsky, *A Treasury of Sephardic Laws and Customs*, 75, 86, 94, 107. See *Tur* and *Shulchan Arukh, Orach Chayim* 568:7: Sefardic Jews by the fourteenth century already knew of a custom to fast on the anniversary of the death.

203   **a memorial candle . . . :** Jacob, *American Reform Responsa*, no. 127; *Resp. Maharshal*, no. 46; *Gesher Hachayim* 1:343.

203   **In Reform practice . . . :** Freehof, *Reform Jewish Practice*, 1:181.

203   **it is preferable to observe the Hebrew date . . . :** Jacob, *American Reform Responsa*, no. 127; Jacob, *Questions and Reform Jewish Answers*, no. 209; Maslin, *Gates of Mitzvah*, 62–63. R. Solomon Freehof rules that the secular date may be used for *yahrzeit*; Freehof, *Reform Responsa*, no. 41. However, he justifies his decision in part on the grounds that Jewish families today are out of touch with the Hebrew calendar and would forget the *yahrzeit* should the secular date be forbidden. The later responsa do not make this assumption, and in any event, we might say that we have a special responsibility to teach our congregants a sensitivity toward the Jewish calendar.

203   **the month of Adar . . . :** Polish, *Rabbi's Manual*, 256; Jacob, *Contemporary American Reform Responsa*, no. 127; *Shulchan Arukh* and Isserles, *Orach Chayim* 568:7.

203   *Yizkor,* **or the memorial service . . . :** Polish, *Rabbi's Manual*, 257. For the historical development, see Freehof, *Modern Reform Responsa*, no. 3 and Hoffman, *Gates of Understanding*, 2:146–49.

203   **It is a** *mitzvah* **to attend . . . :** Maslin, *Gates of Mitzvah*, 63.

203   **We do not encourage . . . :** Polish, *Rabbi's Manual*, 257.

204   **The Tombstone:** Maslin, *Gates of Mitzvah*, 63; Gen. 35:20; *M. Shekalim* 2:5.

204   **In most communities . . . :** Polish, *Rabbi's Manual*, 257; Jacob, *American Reform Responsa*, no. 109. See Freehof, *Today's Reform Responsa*, no. 45 for the custom of placing the marker immediately after *shivah*.

204   **The monument should be a simple one . . . :** Maslin, *Gates of Mitzvah*, 64; Polish, *Rabbi's Manual*, 257–58.

204   **local custom and standards of decorum . . . :** Jacob, *Questions and Reform Jewish Answers*, nos. 183–87.

204   **either at the head or the foot of the grave . . . :** Freehof, *Recent Reform Responsa*, no. 30; Jacob, *Questions and Reform Jewish Answers*, no. 182; *Kol Bo 'al Avelut*, 379.

204   **in the absence of a body . . . :** Jacob, *American Reform Responsa*, no. 112; *Resp. Melamed Leho'il* 2:139; *Resp. Mima'amakim* 2:20.

204   **no special ritual . . . :** Maslin, *Gates of Mitzvah*, 64; Polish, *Rabbi's Manual*, 258. A eulogy, however, is customary; *Kol Bo ' al Avelut*, 381.

204   **forbidden for other use:** This is the subject of a dispute; see Isserles, *Yore De'ah* 364:1. However, most opinions forbid the stone for other uses. R. Solomon Freehof forbids the removal of a tombstone when the stone carver claims he was not paid for it; some other form of compensation must be arranged (*Current Reform Responsa*, no. 38).

204   **Visiting the Cemetery:** Maslin, *Gates of Mitzvah*, 64; Isserles, *Orach Chayim* 581:4. Jews traditionally rely upon "the merits of our ancestors" (*zekhut avot*) as an argument that God should forgive our sins (see *Mishnah Berurah* ad loc., no. 27). We might say that the memory of the good deeds of our loved ones, stirred by our visit to their burial place, helps impel us toward repentance (*teshuvah*).

204   **Although certain days . . . :** Freehof, *Reform Responsa for Our Time*, no. 22; *Shulchan Arukh, Orach Chayim* 344:20.

Chapter 5: Conversion

205   **In Jewish tradition . . . :** See *B. Yevamot* 47b. Ruth's speech is treated as a dialogue in which she resists Naomi's attempts to dissuade her from converting to Judaism. Ruth, as the Rabbis read her words, declares her acceptance of all the stringencies of Jewish law. Satisfied that her daughter-in-law is fully determined to become a Jew, Naomi "ceased to argue with her" (Ruth 1:18).

205   **"like a newborn child" . . . :** *B. Yevamot* 62a.

205   **they created *new lives* . . . :** *Genesis Rabbah* 39:14, on Gen. 12:5, and see Rashi to the verse.

205   **The Bible itself does not know of the institution of "conversion" . . . :** Some scholars have maintained that the term *ger* in the Bible undergoes an evolution of meaning so that, by the time the latest strata of biblical literature are composed, it carries a meaning quite similar to that of "proselyte"; see, for example, T.J. Meek, "The Translation of *Ger* in the Hexateuch and Its Bearing on the Documentary Hypothesis," *Journal of Biblical Literature* 49 (1930): 172–80. This view is now challenged: "Though (the *ger*) may have worshipped Israel's God . . . he was neither an *ezrach* [citizen] nor part of the *kahal* [community] but a *ger*"; Jacob Milgrom, "Religious Conversion and the Revolt Model for the Formation of Israel," *Journal of Biblical Literature* 101 (1982): 171.

205   **"resident alien" . . . :** See Gen. 15:13 and 23:4; Exod. 2:22; Lev. 25:23.

205   **the *ger* does take part to some extent . . . :** See, e.g., Num. 15:15. But the *ger* was not obliged to follow all the religious prescriptions incumbent upon his Israelite neighbors. If he is circumcised he may offer the Passover sacrifice (Exod. 12:47–48), but unlike Israelites he is not required to do so. The *ger* abstains from work on Yom

Kippur but is not required to fast (Lev. 16:29ff.). He must observe all the negative ("thou-shalt-not") commandments whose violation by anyone, citizen or alien, pollutes the land (Lev. 18:26–28), but he is not included in such positive commandments as that of *sukkah* (Lev. 23:42).

205   **justice . . . :** Deut. 1:16 and 24:17.

205   **economic protection . . . :** Exod. 22:20; Lev. 19:33.

206   **like the widow and the orphan . . . :** Deut. 24:19; Pss. 94:6 and 146:9.

206   **"strangers in the land of Egypt" . . . :** Exod. 22:20 and 23:9; Lev. 19:34; Deut. 10:19.

206   **By rabbinic times, however . . . :** The later biblical books do give some evidence of a new conception of the *ger*. The prophet Ezekiel declares that upon their return from Babylonian exile, the people shall allot portions of the land to the *gerim* and that "you shall treat them as Israelite citizens" (Ezek. 47:21–23). The Isaiah who lived during that period states that God will bring the "foreigners" who wish to adhere to the covenant "to My sacred mount and let them rejoice in My house of prayer ... for My house shall be called a house of prayer for all peoples" (Isa. 56:1–8).

206   **This citizenship requires that the proselyte undergo a formal ceremony . . . :** *B. Yevamot* 46a–b, and see below in this chapter.

206   **just as all generations of Israelites . . . :** *B. Shevu'ot* 39a.

206   **Traditional *halakhah* maintains . . . :** For example, the female proselyte may not marry a *Kohen*, a man of priestly lineage (*M. Kiddushin* 4:1, 7; *B. Kiddushin* 77a; *Yad, Isurei Bi'ah* 18:3), and a convert is disqualified from assuming many positions of authority within the community (*B. Yevamot* 45b and *B. Kiddushin* 76b; *Yad, Melakhim* 1:4). Reform Judaism disregards these prohibitions. We no longer observe the laws of priestly status (see Polish, *Rabbi's Manual*, 234), and we regard the disqualification from political office as an unnecessary discrimination. Moreover, some Orthodox halakhists suggest that this disqualification is limited to hereditary offices like that of king (cf. Deut. 17:15) and does not apply to officeholders chosen by the community; see *Resp. Mishpetei Ouziel* 3:6, and Yitzchak Halevy Herzog, *Techukah Leyisrael al pi Hatorah,* 1:95–101.

206   **a good deal of ambivalence:** See Bernard J. Bamberger, *Proselytism in the Talmudic Period,* 149ff., and Ilene L. Bogosian, "Ambivalence Towards Gerim in Jewish Law and Practice" (Rabbinic thesis, HUC-JIR, 1992).

206   **the *ger* is especially dear in God's sight . . . :** *Mekhilta* to Exod. 22:20. Note, however, that R. Eliezer cites the same proof texts as evidence that the *ger* is an evil influence among us.

206   **when one converts to Judaism he receives a reward . . . :** *Sifre,* ch. 354.

206   **The *ger* may recite the words . . . :** *M. Bikkurim* 1:4, *Y. Bikkurim* and Maimonides' *Commentary to the Mishnah* ad loc. See also *Resp. Rambam,* no. 293, the famous letter to Ovadyah the proselyte.

206   **"*gerim* delay the coming of the Messiah" . . . :** *B. Niddah* 13b.

206   **"misfortune upon misfortune . . . " :** *B. Yevamot* 109b.

206   **a literature of interpretation . . . :** For an example, see *Tosafot, Kiddushin* 70b, s.v. *kashim,* which offers various readings of R. Chelbo's description of *gerim* as a sore on the body of Israel.

207   **Some communities have recently gone so far . . . :** See Moshe Zemer, "Ambivalence in Proselytism" in Walter Jacob and Moshe Zemer, eds., *Conversion to Judaism in Jewish Law,* 83–101.

207   **The Reform movement has enthusiastically chosen this positive approach . . . :** See the many publications of the Commission on Outreach of the UAHC, especially Stephen J. Einstein and Lydia Kukoff, eds., *Introduction to Judaism: Instructor's Guide and Curriculum.*

207   **While the existence of such missionary activity is open to debate . . . :** The theory is severely challenged by, among others, Shaye J.D. Cohen, "Was Judaism in Antiquity a Missionary Religion?" and Martin Goodman, *Mission and Conversion.*

207   **while Jewish legal thought does not speak of a positive duty . . . :** See Freehof, *Recent Reform Responsa,* no. 15.

207   **"the Holy One exiled Israel among the nations . . . ":** *B. Pesachim* 87b.

207   **It is therefore a *mitzvah* . . . to welcome . . . :** Maslin, *Gates of Mitzvah,* 23–24, and 74, n. 31.

208   **The *Ger Toshav*:** See Bamberger, *Proselytism in the Talmudic Period,* 134–38, and Lawrence H. Schiffman, *Who Was a Jew? Rabbinic and Halakhic Perspectives on the Jewish-Christian Schism,* 37–38.

208   **The *halakhah* defines the *ger toshav* . . . :** *B. Avodah Zarah* 64b and elsewhere; *Yad, Avodat Kochavim* 10:6 and *Isurei Bi'ah* 14:7.

208   **the seven "Noachide Laws" . . . :** The most widely accepted version of these: 1) the prohibition against idolatry; 2) the prohibition against cursing God; 3) the prohibition against murder; 4) the prohibition against incest and adultery; 5) the prohibition against theft; 6) the obligation to establish courts of justice; 7) the prohibition against eating flesh torn from a living animal. See *B. Sanhedrin* 56b ff.; *Yad, Melakhim* 9:1.

208   **in the presence of a *beit din* . . . :** *B. Avodah Zarah* 64b; *Yad, Melakhim* 8:10.

208   **By the talmudic period . . . :** One indication of this is the opinion that the law of the *ger toshav* was observed only when the Jubilee year was practiced, that is, during the days of the First Temple, many centuries before the rabbinic era. See *B. Arakhin* 29a; *Yad, Isurei Bi'ah* 14:8. The contrary view is maintained by Rabad, *Hasagot* ad loc.

208   **it designates those Gentiles, in particular Muslims and Christians . . . :** Rambam (*Yad, Ma'akhalot Asurot* 11:7) identifies Muslims as a community whose legal status is quite similar to that of the *ger toshav.* See also Meiri, *Beit Habechirah* to *Avodah Zarah* 64b, and *Resp. Mishpat Kohen,* nos. 61 and 63.

208   **Reform responsa do not accept this suggestion . . . :** Jacob, *Contemporary American Reform Responsa,* no. 162.

209   **Course of Study:** Polish, *Rabbi's Manual,* 232–33; Maslin, *Gates of Mitzvah,* 23; Jacob, *Questions and Reform Jewish Answers,* no. 124.

209   **The content of the course . . . may vary:** A person who knows a great deal about Judaism and is well-acquainted with Jewish life may not require a lengthy period of formal instruction; Jacob, *American Reform Responsa,* no. 66; Freehof, *Modern Reform Responsa,* no. 27.

209   **Sincerity:** *B. Yevamot* 47a and Rashi ad loc., s.v. *ve'eini khedai.*

209   **with no reservations whatsoever:** *B. Bekhorot* 30b, although none of the great codifiers has cited this statement as authoritative *halakhah.*

209   **"ulterior" motives . . . :** Such a candidate should be turned away. However, should one convert for such reasons, the conversion is nonetheless valid. *B. Yevamot* 24b; *Yad, Isurei Bi'ah* 14:14–18; *Shulchan Arukh, Yore De'ah* 268:12. Although some recent authorities maintain that "insincere" conversions are by definition invalid (*Resp. Da'at Kohen*, nos. 154–55; *Resp. Heikhal Yitzchak, Even Ha'ezer* 1:1, nos. 19–21; *Resp. Chelkat Ya'akov*, no. 13), theirs remains a minority opinion. See, in general, David Ellenson, "Retroactive Annulment of a Conversion" in Jacob and Zemer, *Conversion to Judaism.*

210   **The Talmud itself presents examples . . . :** R. Chiya converts a woman who wants to marry one of his students (*B. Menachot* 44a), and Hillel accepts a Gentile who wants to convert to Judaism in order to become the High Priest (*B. Shabbat* 31a). Later tradition justified these decisions on the grounds that the Rabbis were convinced that the proselytes would ultimately develop a sincere attachment to God and to Torah; see *Tosafot, Yevamot* 24b, s.v. *lo.*

210   **the discretion of the rabbi . . . :** *Beit Yosef, Yore De'ah* 268; *Shakh, Yore De'ah* 268, no. 23; *Arukh Hashulchan, Yore De'ah* 268, par. 10. See, in general, Freehof, *Reform Responsa for Our Time*, no. 14.

210   **in the context of our culture and our time . . . :** Indeed, even a number of Orthodox authorities have ruled that "conversion for the sake of marriage" should not be rejected out of hand. *Resp. Tuv Ta'am Veda'at*, no. 230; *Resp. Melamed Leho'il* 2:83, 85; *Resp. Achiezer* 3:26; *Resp. Mishpetei Ouziel, Yore De'ah*, no. 14 and *Even Ha'ezer*, no. 18. See, in general, Mark Washofsky, "*Halakhah* and Ulterior Motives" and Bernard M. Zlotowitz, "Sincere Conversion and Ulterior Motive" in Jacob and Zemer, *Conversion to Judaism.*

210   **We insist that the convert . . . :** Polish, *Rabbi's Manual*, 201–2.

210   **agnosticism:** Jacob, *American Reform Responsa*, 65.

210   **an avowed atheist . . . :** Plaut and Washofsky, *Teshuvot for the Nineties*, 5754.15; Polish, *Rabbi's Manual*, 201–2. The service of *giyur* (the acceptance of proselytes) in *Rabbi's Manual* leaves no doubt as to the centrality of God in Judaism, whatever one's conception of God might be.

210   **a Christian . . . :** Jacob, *Contemporary American Reform Responsa*, no. 55. See also Jacob, *Questions and Reform Jewish Answers*, no. 130.

211   **When Family Members Do Not Join in the Decision to Convert:** Jacob, *Contemporary American Reform Responsa*, no. 54; Freehof, *Current Reform Responsa*, no. 53 (1).

211   **On the other hand . . . :** Jacob, *American Reform Responsa*, no. 70.

211   **The way in which . . . :** Polish, *Rabbi's Manual*, 232–33.

211   **Jewish law prescribes . . . :** *B. Yevamot* 46a–b; *Yad, Isurei Bi'ah* 13:4, 6; *Shulchan Arukh, Yore De'ah* 268:1ff..

211   **a drop of blood is taken . . . :** *B. Shabbat* 135a (but see below); *Yad, Isurei Bi'ah* 14:5; *Shulchan Arukh, Yore De'ah* 268:1.

211   **the candidate is a Jew in all respects:** *B. Yevamot* 47b; *Yad, Isurei Bi'ah* 13:17; *Shulchan Arukh, Yore De'ah* 268:2.

212 **"Just as your ancestors entered the covenant . . . "**: *B. Keritot* 9a. That these "conversion" rituals took place prior to or at Sinai is, of course, never stated in the Torah; they are derived by means of *midrash*, rabbinic interpretation of Scripture. See as well the discussion in *B. Yevamot* 46a–b and Rashi ad loc.

212 **the Rabbis did not wish to deny . . .** : *B. Keritot* 9a. Rambam (*Yad, Isurei Bi'ah* 13:5) holds that "when the Temple is rebuilt, the *ger* will be required to bring a sacrifice." This is his opinion; the Talmud does not explicitly mention such a requirement.

212 **the resolution adopted by the Central Conference of American Rabbis in 1893 . . .** : See Jacob, *American Reform Responsa*, no. 69; Polish, *Rabbi's Manual*, 232.

212 **Subsequent Reform responsa . . .** : See Freehof, *Reform Responsa for Our Time*, no. 15, and *Responsa Committee*, no. 5756.13. These criticisms may be summarized as follows: 1) The Pentateuch prescribes no initiatory rites for proselytes because "proselytism" did not exist until much later in Jewish history. The *ger* of the Torah is a resident alien, not a "Jew-by-choice". It was the rabbis who defined the biblical *ger* as a convert, and they definitely believed that initiatory rites were required. 2) Contrary to the report's assertions, the rabbis of the Mishnah and the Talmud did regard both *milah* and *tevilah* as Toraitic requirements for conversion. 3) The 1893 report misreads the medieval statements which it cites to prove that later authorities viewed these rites as dispensable. These statements in fact prove the contrary. 4) The 1893 report began with a statement of principle that the Pentateuch is the foundation of Judaism. Our attitude has changed since then. We view the entire tradition, not just the Bible, as a source of religious guidance. Thus, even if the traditional laws of conversion are "post-biblical," this fact is of less importance for us than it was for our predecessors.

213 **who are terrified of the prospect of circumcision:** Jacob, *American Reform Responsa*, no. 69; Freehof, *Today's Reform Responsa*, no. 21.

213 **"there are social, psychological, and religious values . . . "**: Polish, *Rabbi's Manual*, 232.

213 **Orthodox rabbinical authorities declare . . .** : Jacob, *Contemporary American Reform Responsa*, no. 44: we ought not to adopt these rites if our purpose in doing so is to elicit a recognition from the Orthodox that they simply will not give.

214 **they remain serious and relevant options for conversion under Reform auspices:** Jacob, *American Reform Responsa*, nos. 57 and 69; Jacob, *Contemporary American Reform Responsa*, nos. 44, 45, 47, and 49; Plaut and Washofsky, *Teshuvot*, 5752.2; *Responsa Committee* 5756.6, and 5756.13. The latter two responsa suggest that the traditional rites be viewed as the normal procedure for accepting *gerim*. This does not contradict the 1893 resolution, which merely declared that the initiatory rites are not *required*; it rather interprets that resolution in a narrower sense than previous generations have interpreted it: that is, while we do not *have* to adopt these rites, in most cases we *ought* to do so.

214 **Circumcision of Male Proselytes:** *B. Shabbat* 137b; *Shulchan Arukh, Yore De'ah* 268:5 and *Taz*, no. 12.

214 **When a circumcised male . . .** : *B. Shabbat* 135a; *Yad, Isurei Bi'ah* 14:5; *Shulchan Arukh, Yore De'ah* 268:1.

215 **No benediction is recited . . .** : Among those who do not require *hatafat dam berit* are *Sefer Hama'or, Shabbat, fol. 53b–54a, and Meiri, Beit Habechirah*, Shabbat, 530–

31. See, in general, Mark Washofsky, "Reinforcing Our Jewish Identity: Issues of Personal Status," *CCAR Yearbook* 104 (1994): 51–57.

215   **Many Reform rabbis . . . :** Jacob, *American Reform Responsa*, no. 69; Polish, *Rabbi's Manual*, 232–33.

215   *Mikveh* **and Immersion:** The rules are quite complex. For source material and discussion, see *Responsa Committee*, 5756.6 and Jacob, *Contemporary American Reform Responsa*, no. 45.

215   **a swimming pool built into the ground . . . :** *Responsa Committee*, 5756.6; R. Benjamin Z. Kreitman, "Ha'im Bereikhat Sechiyah Kesheirah Lemikveh?" *Proceedings of the Rabbinical Assembly* 33 (1969): 219–22, and R. Yitzchak Halevy Herzog, *Pesakim Ukhetavim* 4:64.

215   *'al hatevilah*: B. *Pesachim* 7b and *Otzar Hageonim* ad loc., no. 25; *Shulchan Arukh, Yore De'ah* 268:2. Most blessings are recited *over le'asia'tah*, prior to the act to which they are attached. This *berakhah*, however, must wait until after the immersion, since prior to that time the proselyte is not yet a Jew and the *mitzvot* do not yet apply to him or her.

215   **The Jew-by-Choice and the Community:** See B. *Bava Metzi'a* 59b and Rashi to Lev. 19:33–34; *Yad, Mekhirah* 14:13; *Shulchan Arukh, Choshen Mishpat* 228:4.

216   **The Torah commands us to love the proselyte . . . :** See *Yad, De'ot* 6:4.

216   **The Jewish Name:** Jacob, *Questions and Reform Jewish Answers*, no. 115; Freehof, *Modern Reform Responsa*, no. 26; *Nachalat Tzvi*, 1:124.

216   **a child who converts along with his or her parent(s) . . . :** Jacob, *Questions and Reform Jewish Answers*, no. 117; *Nachalat Tzvi*, 1:124.

216   **Non-Jewish Relatives:** See B. *Yevamot* 22a: a *ger* must not ignore those moral duties which he or she observed as a non-Jew, "lest it be said that [the *ger*] has descended from a higher degree of holiness to a lower one"; *Yad, Mamrim* 5:11; *Shulchan Arukh, Yore De'ah* 241:9.

217   **The Convert's Privacy:** Jacob, *Contemporary American Reform Responsa*, no. 46.

217   **a conversion requires the presence of a Jewish court . . . :** B. *Yevamot* 46b; *Yad, Isurei Bi'ah* 13:6; *Shulchan Arukh, Yore De'ah* 268:4.

217   **Conversion in Cases of Doubtful Jewish Status:** Jacob, *Questions and Reform Jewish Answers*, nos. 132 and 133.

217   **the fact that he or she has lived as a Jew in our midst . . . :** Jacob, *Questions and Reform Jewish Answers*, nos. 127 and 129; Freehof, *Recent Reform Responsa*, no. 17; see *Yad, Isurei Bi'ah* 13:9 and *Shulchan Arukh, Yore De'ah* 268:10.

218   **Incomplete Conversion:** Freehof, *Modern Reform Responsa*, no. 27; Freehof, *New Reform Responsa*, no. 18.

218   **Conversion of Children:** Jacob, *Contemporary American Reform Responsa*, nos. 47 and 48; B. *Ketubot* 11a; *Yad, Isurei Bi'ah* 13:7; *Shulchan Arukh, Yore De'ah* 268:7–8. The child who renounces conversion reverts to the status of Gentile. But once he or she lives as a Jew upon reaching the age of majority, the conversion is regarded as permanent, and should the young person then renounce Judaism he or she is considered an apostate Jew.

218   **Teenagers . . . :** Jacob, *Contemporary American Reform Responsa*, no. 50.

Chapter 6: Medical Ethics

220   **Healing and the Jewish Tradition:** See Plaut and Washofsky, *Teshuvot for the Nineties*, no. 5754.18.

220   **King Hezekiah . . . :** *B. Berakhot* 10b and Rashi, s.v. *sheganaz sefer refu'ot.*

221   **human beings committed a serious error . . . :** *B. Berakhot* 60a and Rashi, s.v. *she'ein darkan shel benei adam.*

221   **"the best physician is deserving of hell" . . . :** *M. Kiddushin* 4:14.

221   **the many rabbinic scholars . . . :** See N.Z. Friedman, *Otzar Harabbanim,* whose list counts eighty rabbis who were physicians.

221   **who wrote medical literature . . . :** Especially Maimonides. See Fred Rosner, *The Medical Aphorisms of Moses Maimonides,* Maimonides' Medical Writings, vol. 3; Fred Rosner, *Medicine in the Mishneh Torah of Maimonides;* U. Barzel, *The Art of Cure: Extracts from Galen,* Maimonides' Medical Writings, vol. 5; and J.O. Leibowitz and S. Marcus, *Moses Maimonides on the Causes of Symptoms.*

221   **But since the Torah does not require us to depend upon miracles . . . :** *B. Pesachim* 64b.

222   **King Asa's sin . . . :** *Bach, Yore De'ah* 336.

222   **If King Hezekiah put away a medical text . . . :** Maimonides, *Commentary to M. Pesachim* 4:9.

222   **one who injures or kills his patients . . . :** Maharsha, *Kiddushin* 82a, *chidushei aggadot.*

222   **one who refuses to treat . . . :** Rashi, *B. Kiddushin* 82a, s.v. *tov shebarof'im.*

222   **As for Nachmanides' essay . . . :** See R. Yitzchak Arama, *Akedat Yitzchak, Vayishlach.*

222   **while others note simply . . . :** *Taz, Yore De'ah* 336, no. 1; *Birkei Yosef, Yore De'ah* 336, no. 2.

222   **"one who is in pain should go to the physician" . . . :** *B. Bava Kama* 46b.

222   **forbids a scholar . . . :** *B. Sanhedrin* 17b.

222   ***pikuach nefesh* . . . :** The *midrash* is found in *B. Yoma* 85b; see Ramban, *Torat Ha'adam,* 41–42, and *Shulchan Arukh, Yore De'ah* 336:1.

222   **the duty to rescue . . . :** *B. Sanhedrin* 73a; Maimonides, Commentary to *M. Nedarim* 4:4.

222   **"whoever delays its performance . . . ":** *Torat Ha'adam* loc. cit.; *Tur Yore De'ah* 336.

223   **the act of a "pious fool" . . . :** *Resp. Radbaz* 1:1139.

224   ***Bikkur Cholim:*** Maslin, *Gates of Mitzvah,* 49. The tradition derives this commandment from Exod. 18:20; see *B. Bava Metzi'a* 30b and *Nedarim* 39b–40a; *Yad, Avel* 14:1; *Shulchan Arukh, Yore De'ah* 335:1. God, too, is said to practice this *mitzvah;* thus, *bikkur cholim* is a means by which we imitate God's ways in our own lives. See *B. Sotah* 14a and Rashi to Gen. 18:1.

224   **although it should be carried out . . . :** *B. Nedarim* 39b–40a; *Yad, Avel* 14:4; *Shulchan Arukh, Yore De'ah* 335:4, 8.

224   **The Physician: Status, Training, and Compensation:** *Torat Ha'adam*, 43; *Shulchan Arukh, Yore De'ah* 336:1. "Proper authorities" means the public body legally empowered to supervise the medical profession; *Arukh Hashulchan, Yore De'ah* 336, no. 2.

224   **The comparison . . . between . . . the physician and . . . Rabbi:** *Torat Ha'adam*, 41.

225   **it is unreasonable to require . . . :** *Torat Ha'adam*, 44–45; *Shulchan Arukh, Yore De'ah* 336:2.

225   **a rate competitive with . . . :** R. Shelomo Goren, "Shevitat Harof 'im Bahalakhah," *Assia* 5 (1986): 41–54; see Plaut and Washofsky, *Teshuvot*, no. 5754.18.

225   **The Physician's Right to Strike; Medical Treatment for the Indigent:** Plaut and Washofsky, *Teshuvot*, no. 5754.18.

225   **And since the duty to save life outweighs . . . :** *B. Sanhedrin* 74a; *Yad, Yesodei Hatorah* 5:1ff.; *Shulchan Arukh, Yore De'ah* 157:1.

225   **economic freedom . . . :** See *B. Bava Kama* 116b (on Lev. 25:55); *Yad, Sekhirut* 9:4; *Shulchan Arukh, Choshen Mishpat* 333:3.

225   **workers are allowed to organize . . . :** *B. Bava Batra* 8b; *Yad, Mekhirah* 14:9; *Shulchan Arukh, Choshen Mishpat* 231:27–28.

226   **the ultimate responsibility for the performance of the *mitzvah* . . . :** On this basis, R. Shelomo Goren ("Shevitat Harof 'im Bahalakhah") permitted doctors in Israel to strike against the government-run health care system, provided that they continued to offer medical treatment to all at a reasonable cost.

225   **Every member of the community enjoys the right to adequate medical care:** *CCAR Yearbook* 101 (1991): 32–34; Plaut and Washofsky, *Teshuvot*, no. 5754.18.

227   **Under what "extraordinary circumstances" . . . :** *Resp. Tzitz Eliezer* 16:4 and 13:81, sec. 2; *Resp. Chelkat Ya'akov* 3:136; *Resp. Yechaveh Da'at* 4:60; *Chofetz Chaim, Hilkhot Isurei Rekhilut* 9, *tziyur* 3, par. 4.

227   **forbidden "to stand idly by the blood" . . . :** Lev. 19:16; *B. Sanhedrin* 73a, *Yad, Rotzeach* 1:14, and *Shulchan Arukh, Choshen Mishpat* 425:1.

227   **placing a "stumbling-block before the blind" . . . :** Lev. 19:14 and *Sifra* ad loc.

227   **Even when the physician has sworn an oath . . . :** *B. Shevu'ot* 29a; *Yad, Shevu'ot* 5:14–15; *Resp. Tzitz Eliezer* 13:81, sec. 2.

227   **Reform responsa stress, however . . . :** Plaut and Washofsky, *Teshuvot*, no. 5750.3 and 5750.1; Jacob, *Contemporary American Reform Responsa*, no. 5.

228   ***dina demalkhuta dina* . . . :** See the discussion of this principle at p. 164.

228   **The majority view in the *halakhah* . . . :** Nachmanides, *Torat Ha'adam*, 46; *Shulchan Arukh, Yore De'ah* 338:1 and *Shakh* ad loc.; *Bach* to *Tur Yore De'ah* 338; R. Shelomo Aviner, "Ha'amadat Choleh Mesukan 'al Matzavo," *Assia* 3(1983): 336–40.

228   **in the medical profession as well . . . :** See *Journal of the American Medical Association* 175 (1961): 1120–28.

228   **Reform responsa, too . . . :** Jacob, *American Reform Responsa*, no. 74; Freehof, *Reform Responsa*, no. 28.

228   **even God "bends" the truth . . . :** *B. Yevamot* 65b; Jacob, *American Reform Responsa*, no. 74.

228   **This situation has changed radically ... :** See Dr. Shimeon Glueck, "Divu'ach Emet Lacholeh," *Assia* 11(1987): 8–15.

229   **Newer Reform responsa ... :** Plaut and Washofsky, *Teshuvot*, no. 5753.2.

229   **as well as some ... Orthodox community ... :** See R. Yigal Shafran, "Amirat Emet Lacholeh," *Assia* 11(1987): 16–23.

229   **Medical Malpractice; The Physician's Liability for Damages:** See *Tosefta Bava Kama* 6:6; *Torat Ha'adam*, 41–42; *Shulchan Arukh, Yore De'ah* 336:1; *Ramat Rachel*, ch. 23.

230   ***mipnei tikkun ha'olam* ... :** *Tosefta Gittin* 3:13; *Resp. Tashbetz* 3:82.

230   **A Reform responsum shows ... :** Plaut and Washofsky, *Teshuvot*, no. 5753.2.

233   **Artificial Insemination:** See Immanuel Jakobovits, *Jewish Medical Ethics*, 244.

233   **The earliest rabbinic discussions ... :** Talmudic tradition and Jewish folklore hold that a woman can become pregnant by absorbing semen from bath water or from bed sheets upon which a man has ejaculated (*B. Chagigah* 14b–15a; Eisenstein, *Otzar Hamidrashim*, 43; *Resp. Tashbetz* 3:263; *Bach* to *Tur, Yore De'ah* 195). Although we reject these as biological possibilities, traditional authorities accepted them and discussed the legal implications of conception by these means.

234   **Traditional authorities generally approve ... :** *Resp. Maharsham* 3:268; R. Zvi Pesach Frank, cited in *Otzar Haposkim* 23:1, no. 1; *Resp. Seridei Esh* 3:5; R. Shelomo Zalman Auerbach, "Hazra'ah Malakhutit," *No'am* 1 (1958): 157.

234   **to "be fruitful and multiply":** See the discussion in Chapter 4. In addition, the establishment of legal paternity determines whether the wife is obligated under the rules of levirate marriage (see Deut. 25:5ff.) in the event her husband should die without producing children by the "normal" means. If this child is legally *his*, then his wife may remarry without undergoing the ritual of *chalitzah* (ritual of release from a levirate marriage).

234   **"emitting seed for no purpose":** *B. Niddah* 13a; *Yad, Isurei Bi'ah* 21:18; *Shulchan Arukh, Even Ha'ezer* 23. See *Resp. Mishpetei Ouziel* 2:19.

234   **so long as the intention is to conceive a child ...** See *Resp. Minchat Yitzchak* 1:50, as well as the "approving" opinions cited above.

234   **only as a last resort ... :** *Resp. Tzitz Eliezer*, 9:51, sec. 4; *Resp. Yabi'a Omer, Even Ha'ezer* 2:1.

234   **prohibiting AID ... :** *Resp. Tzitz Eliezer* 9:51, end; R. S.Z. Auerbach, in *No'am* 1 (1958): 165; *Resp. Yabi'a Omer, Even Ha'ezer* 2:1, end ("Heaven forbid that we should permit such a thing"); *Resp. Seridei Esh* 3:5 ("this is an ugly act, one which resembles the abominations of Egypt"); *Resp. Chelkat Ya'akov* 3:45ff.

234   **tantamount to adultery:** *Resp. Ma'arakhei Lev*, no. 73; R. Ovadyah Hadayah, in *No'am* 1 (1958): 130–37; *Resp. Tzitz Eliezer* 9:51, sec. 4.

234   **Those who do not accept that idea ... :** *Resp. Igerot Moshe, Even Ha'ezer* 1:71 and *Even Ha'ezer* 2:11; *Resp. Yabi'a Omer, Even Ha'ezer* 2:1; *Resp. Chelkat Ya'akov* 3:46; *Resp. Zekan Aharon* 2:97.

234   **with but one notable exception ... :** R. Moshe Feinstein, in *Resp. Igerot Moshe, Even Ha'ezer* 1:10 and 71. His argument is that the prohibition against using a donor's semen is based upon the fear that the child "might marry his sister (i.e., his half-sister, the daughter of his biological father)." This concern does not apply if the

semen donor is a non-Jew, since the laws of incest and adultery apply only among
Jews; a Jew, as a matter of technical *halakhah*, cannot be a blood-relative of a Gentile.
Feinstein's opinion was rejected by a number of other *poskim*, and he later retreated
somewhat from it; see his letter reprinted in *Resp. Chelkat Ya'akov* 3:47, as well as the
discussion in Jakobovits, *Jewish Medical Ethics*, 273. On the implications of
Feinstein's ruling, see below.

235   **Reform responsa . . . :** Jacob, *American Reform Responsa*, nos. 157–59.

235   **to the wishes and desires of the women involved . . . :** Note that the one Orthodox
posek who treats the woman's desire to conceive as a relevant halakhic consideration
(R. Moshe Feinstein, *Resp. Igerot Moshe, Even Ha'ezer* 1:10 and 71) is also the one
who permits AID, provided the semen donor is a non-Jew to whom the halakhic rules
of incest do not apply.

235   **"to be fruitful and multiply" . . . incumbent upon males only:** B. *Yevamot* 65b;
Yad, Ishut 15:2; *Shulchan Arukh, Even Ha'ezer* 1:13.

235   **A Jewish woman . . . fulfills a *mitzvah* . . . :** Some traditional authorities hold that
women, though not obligated under the commandment to "be fruitful and multiply,"
do partake in the related requirement, derived from Isaiah 45:18, to populate the
world (*lashevet yetzarah*). See Magen Avraham, *Orach Chayim* 153, no. 9; *Beit Shmuel,
Even Ha'ezer* 1, no. 2; and *Resp. Tzitz Eliezer* 10:42.

236   **In Vitro Fertilization:** See *Responsa Committee*, 5758.3 and 5757.2; Jacob, *Contemporary American Reform Responsa*, nos. 18–19; David Ellenson, "Artificial Fertilization and Procreative Autonomy" in Jacob and Zemer, *The Fetus and Fertility in Jewish
Law*. The affirmative attitude taken toward IVF in Reform responsa is based upon
the presumption that the woman or the couple involved will receive sufficient counseling as to the physical and the emotional risks inherent in the procedure.

236   **Some traditional authorities . . . :** For an example of the more positive view, see the
ruling of R. Ovadyah Yosef cited in *Nishmat Avraham, Even Ha'ezer* 1, no. 3. The
negative position is well represented by R. Eliezer Y. Waldenberg, who prohibits IVF
in all cases as morally repugnant, warning that its unchecked use by "mad" scientists
will lead to terrifying consequences (*Resp. Tzitz Eliezer* 15:45).

236   **Since it does not entail unacceptable physical risks . . . :** But see *Responsa Committee* 5758.3: IVF does pose *some* risk to mother and child. This fact, along with others
(the great expense and difficulty involved with the procedure, along with its uncertain
prospects of success), leads us to conclude that no woman or couple should consider
themselves under any religious "obligation" to undertake IVF in order to fulfill the
mitzvah of childbearing.

237   **One particular difficulty . . . :** *Responsa Committee*, no. 5757.2. *Halakhah* prohibits
the destruction of the fetus without good reason, but this prohibition applies *only* to
the fetus and not to an embryo that, unless implanted in a womb, has no possibility
of further development.

237   **Surrogacy:** Jacob, *American Reform Responsa*, no. 159.

238   **In the Bible . . . :** Gen. 16 and 30. On concubinage see *Responsa Committee*, no.
5756.10.

239   **Sex Preselection:** See Daniel Schiff, "Developing *Halakhic* Attitudes to Sex Preselection" in Jacob and Zemer, *The Fetus and Fertility*.

239   **Talmudic literature contains . . . :** B. *Niddah* 31a–b and 70b–71a; B. *Berakhot* 5b;
B. *Shevu'ot* 18b.

239   **The existing Reform responsum . . . :** Jacob, *American Reform Responsa*, no. 160 (from 1941).

239   **one can raise several objections . . . :** Schiff, "Developing *Halakhic* Attitudes to Sex Preselection," 103–13.

241   **"laws of nature" . . . :** *B. Kiddushin* 39a: "the laws I have already decreed for you"; Rashi ad loc. and *Torah Temimah* to Lev. 19:19, no. 130–31, describe these as the laws of "creation" or of "nature."

241   **One who alters them suggests thereby . . . :** Nachmanides to Lev. 19:19.

241   **rabbinic authorities who have discussed this subject . . . :** R. S.Z. Auerbach, cited in *Nishmat Avraham* 4:215–17.

241   **understood as the granting of permission . . . :** Nachmanides to Gen. 1:28.

241   **we may be ready to accept . . . for medical purposes:** Jacob, *Questions and Reform Jewish Answers*, no. 154.

242   **it is a *mitzvah* . . . to have children:** See the discussion of "Birth and Childhood" in Chapter 4.

242   **when a couple might justifiably not be prepared . . . :** For example, when a woman is nursing a child (*B. Yevamot* 12b).

242   **Jewish law permits the use of birth control methods . . . :** Especially when the commandment to procreate (i.e., a son and a daughter) has been fulfilled; *Birkei Yosef, Even Ha'ezer* 1, no. 2; *Resp. Chelkat Ya'akov* 3:62; *Resp. Igerot Moshe, Even Ha'ezer* 3:24. On artificial contraceptives, see Jacob, *American Reform Responsa*, no. 156; *B. Yevamot* 12b, Rashi, s.v. *meshamsho bemokh,* and *Tosafot,* s.v. *veshalosh nashim; Yam shel Shelomo, Yevamot* 1:8.

242   **Reform Judaism respects the right . . . :** Maslin, *Gates of Mitzvah,* 11.

242   **sterilization and vasectomy . . . :** Jacob, *Contemporary American Reform Responsa,* no. 198; Jacob, *Questions and Reform Jewish Answers,* no. 150.

242   **Abortion:** See Plaut and Washofsky, *Teshuvot,* no. 5755.13; Jacob, *Questions and Reform Jewish Answers,* no. 155; Jacob, *Contemporary American Reform Responsa,* no. 16; Jacob, *American Reform Responsa,* no. 171.

242   **a statement in the Mishnah . . . :** *M. Ohalot* 7:6.

242   **A number of commentators . . . :** Most notably Rashi to *B. Sanhedrin* 72b, s.v. *yatza rosho.* See also *Chidushei Haramban, Niddah* 44b; *Beit Habechirah, Sanhedrin* 72b; *Tosafot Yom Tov* and *Tiferet Yisrael* to *M. Ohalot* 7:6.

243   **the fetus is compared to the "pursuer" . . . :** Chiefly Maimonides (*Yad, Rotzeach* 1:9) and after him *Shulchan Arukh, Choshen Mishpat* 425:2. This classification is based upon the talmudic discussion in *B. Sanhedrin* 72b, which uses the concept of "pursuer" to describe the fetus in the case of dangerous childbirth. See also *Y. Sanhedrin* 8:9: upon parturition, one may not touch the fetus, since at that point it is impossible to know "who is killing whom"; prior to that point, it is clear that the fetus is the aggressor. On the law of the *rodef,* see Exod. 22:1–2; *B. Sanhedrin* 73a; *Yad, Rotzeach* 1:10; and *Shulchan Arukh, Choshen Mishpat* 425:1.

243   **the mother's "healing" (*refu'ah*) . . . :** The earliest precedent is a ruling by R. Yosef Trani (d. 1639), *Resp. Maharit,* no. 99: the fetus is sacrificed on behalf of the mother's health (or "need," *tzorekh*) because it is not a *nefesh.* He does not cite Maimonides and does not mention the "pursuer" analogy. See also *Resp. She'elat Ya'avetz,* no. 43.

243 **grave physical or psychological consequences . . . :** See *Resp. Mishpetei Ouziel, Choshen Mishpat* 3:46, where abortion is permitted when childbirth would result in the mother's permanent deafness; *Resp. Seridei Esh* 3:127, which allows abortion when the mother contracts rubella during her first trimester; and *Resp. Tzitz Eliezer* 13:102, which sanctions the termination of pregnancy when the fetus is determined to be afflicted with Tay-Sachs disease. The latter two responsa argue that the prospect of severe psychological trauma and anguish for the mother is enough to warrant an abortion. See also *Resp. Shevet Halevy* 5:193.

243 **Those who believe . . . aggressor . . . :** *Resp. Chavat Ya'ir*, no. 31; R. Issar Y. Unterman in *No'am* 6 (1963): 1–11; *Resp. Igerot Moshe, Choshen Mishpat* 2:69; *Resp. Yabi'a Omer, Even Ha'ezer* 4:1. The term "lifesaving" may include a variety of circumstances; still, those who adopt the "aggressor" analogy tend to be more stringent than those who do not.

243 **most contemporary Orthodox authorities . . . :** See J. David Bleich, *Judaism and Healing: A Halakhic Perspective*, 96–103, and Fred Rosner and J. David Bleich, eds. *Jewish Bioethics*, 134–77.

243 **Reform responsa . . . :** Plaut and Washofsky, *Teshuvot*, no. 5755.13; Jacob, *Questions and Reform Jewish Answers*, no. 155; Jacob, *Contemporary American Reform Responsa*, no. 16; Jacob, *American Reform Responsa*, no. 171.

243 **We reject the comparison . . . :** as do a number of commentators. Some note the inconsistency of the theory: if the fetus is a *rodef* while *in utero* and therefore may be destroyed, why does it suddenly cease to be a pursuer once it emerges from the womb? (*Resp. Noda Biyehudah* 2:59; *Chidushei R. Akiva Eger, M. Ohalot* 7:6). Others suggest that it makes little sense to call the fetus a "pursuer" when its "pursuit" is entirely the result of natural causes (*Arukh Hashulchan, Choshen Mishpat* 425, no. 7; *Tiferet Yisrael, M. Ohalot* 7:6). Maimonides himself says that the emergent infant may not be touched, because "such is the natural order of things" for childbirth to pose a danger to the mother; if so, why is the danger posed prior to parturition a fundamentally different thing, to be understood as a case of "pursuit" (and see *Sefer Me'irat Einayim, Choshen Mishpat* 425, no. 8)? Rather, the fetus is not sacrificed because it is a *rodef* but because, until its emergence, it is not a *nefesh*. An ingenious (but, to us, unpersuasive) attempt to rehabilitate this analogy and to reconcile it with Rashi's understanding of *M. Ohalot* 7:6 is offered by R. Haim Soloveitchik in *Chidushei R. Chaim Halevy* to *Yad, Rotzeach* 1:9; see Mark Washofsky, "Abortion and the Halakhic Conversation: A Liberal Perspective" in Jacob and Zemer, *The Fetus and Fertility*, 48–51.

243 **better explained by the theory that the fetus is not yet a *nefesh* . . . :** The destruction of the fetus for no purpose, although prohibited, is not classified as "murder" under Jewish law, since only a person (*nefesh*) can be "murdered." See Exod. 21:22; *M. Niddah* 5:3; and *B. Niddah* 44b. See also *B. Arakhin* 7a: if a pregnant woman is sentenced to death, the execution is carried out even though it results in the death of the fetus. The fetus is not regarded as a person (*nefesh*) with a separate "right to life" but rather a limb of the mother's body (*B. Yevamot* 78a and parallels).

244 **"We do not encourage abortion . . . ":** Jacob, *Contemporary American Reform Responsa*, no. 16, end; Plaut and Washofsky, *Teshuvot*, no. 5755.13. Jewish law prohibits abortion in the absence of justifying reasons, though the authorities dispute the precise basis of the prohibition; see *Nishmat Avraham, Choshen Mishpat* 425:2, no. 1.

244   **the first forty days of pregnancy . . . :** See *Responsa Committee*, no. 5757.2 and Jacob, *Contemporary American Reform Responsa*, no. 16. *B. Yevamot* 69b; *Yad, Terumot* 8:3 and *Isurei Bi'ah* 10:1; *Resp. Achiezer* 3:65.

245   **An aborted or miscarried fetus . . . :** Jacob, *Contemporary American Reform Responsa*, no. 21; Jacob, *Questions and Reform Jewish Answers*, no. 163; *Responsa Committee*, no. 5757.2.

245   **Jewish tradition teaches . . . :** See the discussion on *pikuach nefesh* at p. 222.

245   **Preventive medicine . . . :** Maimonides codifies the rules for healthy and hygienic living—as understood in his time—in *Yad, De'ot* 4:1ff. He thus accords the status of *halakhah* to measures undertaken to prevent disease.

245   **vaccinations . . . :** *Responsa Committee*, no. 5759.9.

246   **The obligation to practice medicine . . . :** See Plaut and Washofsky, *Teshuvot*, no. 5754.14.

246   **a reasonable chance of success . . . :** See *Yad, Rotzeach* 1:14: whoever is *able to save* another's life but does not do so has violated the commandment of Lev. 19:16 ("do not stand idly by . . . "). See also Maimonides, Commentary to *M. Nedarim* 4:4: the duty to heal a sick person applies when one is *able* to save that person by means of one's medical knowledge.

246   **chavalah . . . :** *M. Bava Kama* 8:5; *B. Bava Kama* 91a–b; *Yad, Chovel* 5:1; *Shulchan Arukh, Choshen Mishpat* 420:31.

246   **which are tested and proven . . . :** R. Ya'akov Emden, *Mor Uketzi'ah* 328; *Resp. Beit Ya'akov*, no. 59; *Resp. Shevut Ya'akov, Orach Chayim*, no. 13.

247   **a number of Orthodox rabbinical authorities rule . . . :** *Resp. Netzer Mata'ai*, no. 30; *Resp. Tzitz Eliezer* 5, *Ramat Rachel*, no. 28. See also J.D. Bleich in Rosner and Bleich, *Jewish Bioethics*, 266–76.

248   **"Dangerous" Treatments and the Treatment of Severe Pain:** Jacob, *Contemporary American Reform Responsa*, no. 85.

248   **to undergo "dangerous" treatment . . . :** *B. Avodah Zarah* 27b; *Mor Uketzi'ah* 328; *Resp. Beit Ya'akov*, no. 59; *Resp. Shevut Ya'akov, Orach Chayim*, no. 13.

248   **survival rate . . . at least fifty percent . . . :** *Resp. Tzitz Eliezer* 10:25, ch. 5, sec. 5.

248   **even a slight chance of survival . . . :** *Resp. Igerot Moshe, Yore De'ah* 2:59.

249   **to relieve a patient's suffering and pain:** Plaut and Washofsky, *Teshuvot*, no. 5754.14; Jacob, *Questions and Reform Jewish Answers*, no. 151; Jacob, *American Reform Responsa*, no. 76; *Mor Uketzi'ah* 328; *Resp. Tzitz Eliezer* 13:87.

249   **Discontinuation of Treatment:** Plaut and Washofsky, *Teshuvot*, no. 5754.14; Jacob, *American Reform Responsa*, no. 77.

249   **Jewish tradition teaches . . . :** On the distinction between hastening death and removing an unnecessary impediment to death see *Shulchan Arukh, Yore De'ah* 339:1 and commentaries, as well as our discussion of euthanasia and assisted suicide, below. Those texts speak of the *goses*, the person in the very final stages of life, and not specifically of the terminally-ill patient whom we describe here. Given our understanding of the concept of therapeutic effectiveness, however, we think that the notion of "unnecessary impediments to death" can apply to the terminally ill as well as to the *goses*.

250   **the procedure may be discontinued . . . :** If a patient or (should the patient be mentally incapacitated) the patient's next-of-kin desire it, the procedure may be maintained; there is, however, no moral obligation to do so.

250   **Heroic Measures:** Plaut and Washofsky, *Teshuvot*, no. 5754.14.

251   **Rabbinic opinion . . . :** Those who prohibit the disconnecting of feeding tubes include *Resp. Igerot Moshe, Choshen Mishpat* 2:74, sec. 3; R. Immanuel Jakobovits in *Hapardes* 31:3 (1957): 18–19; and R. Avram Reisner in *Conservative Judaism* 43:3 (1991): 52ff. Those who permit discontinuation include R. Zev Shostak in *Journal of Medical Ethics* 20:2 (1994): 98, and R. Elliot N. Dorff in *Conservative Judaism* 43:3 (1991): 36–39.

251   **ethicists . . . :** For references, see Plaut and Washofsky, *Teshuvot*, no. 5754.14.

251   **Reform responsa . . . :** Jacob, *Questions and Reform Jewish Answers*, no. 159 and Jacob, *American Reform Responsa*, no. 77. See also Mark N. Staitman, "Withdrawing or Withholding Nutrition, Hydration or Oxygen from Patients" in Jacob and Zemer, *Death and Euthanasia in Jewish Law,* which discusses the issue in relation to patients in a persistent vegetative state (PVS).

251   **the most recent discussion . . . :** Plaut and Washofsky, *Teshuvot*, no. 5754.14.

251   **Treatment for Accompanying Illnesses:** Ibid., no. 5754.14; R. Immanuel Jakobovits in *Hapardes* 31:3 (1957).

252   **Jewish tradition prohibits suicide . . . :** *B. Bava Kama* 91b to Gen. 9:5; *Yad, Rotzeach* 1:4 and 2:2–3.

252   **"A dying person . . . is like a living person in all respects":** *Semachot* 1:1ff.; *Yad, Avel* 4:5; *Shulchan Arukh, Yore De'ah* 339:1.

252   **A Jew is obligated . . . :** *B. Sanhedrin* 74a–b and parallels; *Yad, Yesodei Hatorah* 5:1–4; *Shulchan Arukh, Yore De'ah* 157:1.

252   **Reform responsa literature . . . :** See Plaut and Washofsky, *Teshuvot*, no. 5754.14, for sources and argumentation.

253   **since tradition suggests that it is forbidden to delay unnecessarily . . . :** Isserles, *Yore De'ah* 339:1, from *Sefer Chassidim,* no. 723; *Darkei Moshe* to *Tur, Yore De'ah* 339; *Shiltei Giborim* to Alfasi, *Mo'ed Katan,* fol. 16b

254   **Cryonics:** Jacob, *American Reform Responsa*, no. 81.

255   **It is permissible to transplant organs from a corpse . . . :** Ibid., no. 86 and 85.

255   **repositories or "banks" . . . :** Jacob, *Contemporary American Reform Responsa*, no. 78.

255   **It is permissible and praiseworthy for a healthy individual . . . :** Freehof, *New Reform Responsa*, no. 15.

255   **placing one's own life in unnecessary danger . . . :** *B. Yoma* 85b on Lev. 18:5; Isserles, *Yore De'ah* 116:5. In general, see Mark Washofsky, "AIDS and Ethical Responsibility: Some Halakhic Considerations," *Journal of Reform Judaism* 36 (Winter, 1989): 53–65.

255   **While some authorities interpret it quite strictly . . . :** *Resp. Radbaz* 3:1052 (627); *Sefer Me'irat Einayim* to *Choshen Mishpat* 426; *Shulchan Arukh of R. Sheneur Zalman, Orach Chayim* 329:8; *Minchat Chinukh,* mitzvah 237, no. 2; *Ha'amek She'elah, Re'eh* 147:4. On this basis, some prohibit a healthy person from donating a kidney; *Resp. Minchat Yitzchak* 6:103.

255   **others conclude that we are permitted . . . :** *Resp. Igerot Moshe, Yore De'ah* 2:174, sec. 4; *Resp. Tzitz Eliezer* 10:25, sec. 7; and *Resp. Yechaveh Da'at* 3:84, which declares that it is a "*mitzvah*" to donate a kidney for transplant.

255   **the superior and compelling interpretation of Jewish moral teaching . . . :** Plaut and Washofsky, *Teshuvot*, no. 5755.11.

255   **the sale of human organs for transplant:** Jacob, *Contemporary American Reform Responsa*, no. 79.

256   **The definition of death in Jewish law . . . :** The classic statement is that of R. Moshe Sofer in the early nineteenth century; *Resp. Chatam Sofer, Yore De'ah* 338, based upon *M. Yoma* 8:5 and *B. Yoma* 85a.

256   **To remove a beating heart is therefore to kill the donor . . . :** and it is forbidden to kill one person to save another; *B. Sanhedrin* 74a ("who is to say that your blood is redder than that of your fellow?"); *Yad, Yesodei Hatorah* 5:1ff.; *Shulchan Arukh, Yore De'ah* 157:1. Self-defense is an exception to this rule: one is entitled to stop the aggressor (*rodef*) from committing murder, even at the cost of the aggressor's life (Exod. 22:1-2; *B. Sanhedrin* 73a; *Yad, Rotzeach* 1:10; *Shulchan Arukh, Choshen Mishpat* 425:1). In our instance, however, the potential donor can hardly be called an "aggressor." Nor can we say that, because the donor is dying in any case, it is permissible to take his or her life to save the potential recipient (*B. Sanhedrin* 87a; *Yad, Rotzeach* 2:7–8).

256   **the heart transplant operation would be absolutely forbidden . . . :** and a number of Orthodox authorities do indeed forbid it: *Resp. Tzitz Eliezer* 10:25, sec. 25; *Resp. Minchat Yitzchak* 5:7, 9; R. Shmuel Halevy Wasner, in *Hamodi'a*, 22 Cheshvan 5747 (1987); R. S.Z. Auerbach, cited in *Nishmat Avraham, Yore De'ah* 292:158, no. 24. That is to say, these authorities do not accept the standard of "brain death" as a sufficient criterion of death according to *halakhah*.

256   **Recently, however, some rabbinical authorities have come to accept . . . :** These include Rabbi Dr. Moshe Tendler, *Journal of the American Medical Association* 238 (1977): 1651–55, and the Chief Rabbinate of Israel, "Hashtalat Halev." In a letter dated July 5, 1986 and reprinted at the beginning of the statement by the Chief Rabbinate, Rabbi Tendler declares that his father-in-law, R. Moshe Feinstein has reversed his earlier opposition to heart transplantation (*Resp. Igerot Moshe, Yore De'ah* 2:146 and *Choshen Mishpat* 2:72). Some evidence of this change of mind is provided in *Resp. Igerot Moshe Yore De'ah* 3:132. This interpretation of Feinstein is strenuously challenged by R. J. David Bleich in *Time of Death in Jewish Law*, 171–76.

256   **Medical consensus now holds . . . :** See *Journal of the American Medical Association* 246 (1981): 2184–87, a statement signed by nearly all the leading American authorities in the field. The clinical tests to determine brain death are described by the Ad Hoc Committee of the Harvard Medical School, *Journal of the American Medical Association* 205 (1968): 337–40. It is important to remember that "brain death," as understood in a Jewish-legal context, means the cessation of *all* brain activity, including that of the brain stem, and not simply the irreversible loss of cerebral or "higher brain" function.

257   **Reform Judaism . . . :** Jacob, *Contemporary American Reform Responsa*, no. 78.

257   **Our sources understand . . . :** See *B. Yoma* 85a: the absence of respiration is not death itself but *evidence* that the person trapped under the rubble is dead.

257   **A person may volunteer . . . :** Plaut and Washofsky, *Teshuvot*, no. 5755.11.

257   **There are, however, limits . . .** Jacob, *Questions and Reform Jewish Answers*, no. 152.

258   **May experimental medical procedures be tested . . . :** Plaut and Washofsky, *Teshuvot*, no. 5755.11. Compare the discussion among secular ethicists on the subject of randomized clinical trials (RCTs) in Beauchamp and Childress, *Principles of Biomedical Ethics*, 351.

259   **causing physical injury (*chavalah*) . . . :** *M. Bava Kama* 8:5; *B. Bava Kama* 91a–b; *Shulchan Arukh, Choshen Mishpat* 426:31 (one is not permitted to inflict self-injury, but one is not punished for doing so).

259   **the precise definitions we give to this prohibition . . . :** Maimonides (*Yad, Chovel* 5:1) holds that self-injury is forbidden only when it is done out of an attitude of contempt for the body, when performed for harmful or pointless ends.

259   **Some assert . . . :** See *Resp. Igerot Moshe, Choshen Mishpat* 2:66, where a young woman is permitted cosmetic surgery in order to make herself more attractive and therefore more "marriageable."

259   **Others, however, argue . . . :** *Resp. Tzitz Eliezer* 11:41, end: purely cosmetic surgery is not "medicine" at all but rather willful damage to the body.

259   **Reform responsa . . . :** *Responsa Committee*, no. 5759.4; Plaut and Washofsky, *Teshuvot*, no. 5752.7; Jacob, *Contemporary American Reform Responsa*, no. 15. Compare, however, to Jacob, *American Reform Responsa*, no. 172, which concludes that "the cosmetic purpose is an honored one and an important one."

259   **piercing of the ear . . . :** Jacob, *Questions and Reform Jewish Answers*, no. 246; Jacob, *Contemporary American Reform Responsa*, no. 76.

260   **tattooing and more extreme forms of body piercing . . . :** *Responsa Committee*, no. 5759.4.

260   **Priorities in Medical Treatment:** Jacob, *American Reform Responsa*, no. 75; Mark Washofsky, "Is Old Age a Disease? The Elderly, the Medical System, and the Literature of the *Halakhah*" in Jacob and Zemer, *Age and Aging in Jewish Law*.

260   **"we do not dispose . . . ":** *M. Ohalot* 7:6; *Yad, Rotzeach* 1:9; *Shulchan Arukh, Choshen Mishpat* 425:2.

260   **"Who is to say . . . ":** *B. Pesachim* 25b and parallels.

261   **A *mishnah* declares . . . :** *M. Horayot* 3:7–8; *Yad, Matanot Aniyim* 8:15–17; *Shulchan Arukh, Yore De'ah* 252:8; *Shakh, Yore De'ah* 251, no. 13.

261   **The Talmud explains . . . :** *B. Horayot* 13a.

261   **"a *mamzer* . . . who is a Torah scholar . . . ":** *M. Horayot* 3:8. Compare *M. Bava Metzi'a* 2:11: if one has to return two lost objects, the first belonging to one's father and the second belonging to one's Torah teacher, the latter comes first, since "one's rabbi brings one to eternal life."

261   **Some rabbinic authorities . . . :** *Resp. Igerot Moshe, Choshen Mishpat* 2:75, sec. 2; R. Issar Yehudah Unterman, in *Hatorah Vehamedinah*, 4 (1952): 28.

262   **from our understanding of the *mitzvah* of medicine . . . :** See the discussion at the beginning of this chapter.

262   **A number of rabbis shared this opinion . . . :** *Mor Uketzi'ah*, chs. 210 and 511; *Penei Yehoshua*, Shabbat 39a. See, in general, Y.Z. Kahana, *Mechkarim Besifrut Hateshuvot*, 317–29.

262   **whether a blessing ought to be recited . . . :** See *Magen Avraham* 210, no. 9; *Resp. Ketav Sofer, Orach Chayim* 24.

263   **rabbinic opinion now condemns smoking . . . :** See Plaut and Washofsky, *Teshuvot,* 5753.23; *Resp. Tzitz Eliezer* 15:39; *Resp. Aseh Lekha Rav* 6:59; *Resp. Yechaveh Da'at* 5:39.

263   **As Judaism forbids us to endanger our lives needlessly . . . :** Deut. 4:9, 15; *Yad, Rotzeach* 11:4.

263   **Other intoxicants can serve . . . :** If these substitutes are considered *chamar medinah,* a choice beverage in that locality, worthy of serving as a proper symbol of joy and festivity; see Plaut and Washofsky, *Teshuvot,* no. 5755.16.

263   **in some (but not all) of these settings:** The Seder is an obvious exception, since most other intoxicants are *chametz.*

263   **including the Passover Seder:** This is a subject of some controversy, since the tradition emphasizes the importance of wine as a symbol of our liberation from bondage. "One who cannot drink wine because it causes him harm or because he loathes it should nonetheless force himself to drink the four cups"; *Shulchan Arukh, Orach Chayim* 472:10. Yet this requirement is waived if drinking wine causes one to "fall into the sickbed"; *Mishnah Berurah* ad loc., no. 35. One is permitted to use grape juice in place of wine at the Seder (*Sha'arim Metzuyanim Behalakhah* 118:1; *Chazon Ovadyah* 2:125, though some authorities disagree). "Local wine" (*chamar medinah*) may be used for the Seder, and this need not be an intoxicant; see *Mishnah Berurah* 472, no. 37 and Plaut and Washofsky, *Teshuvot,* no. 5755.16.

263   **drunkenness as an evil:** See Jacob, *Contemporary American Reform Responsa,* no. 73.

263   **is even forbidden to pray . . . :** *B. Eruvin* 64a; *Yad, Tefillah* 4:17; *Shulchan Arukh, Orach Chayim* 99.

263   **The clear implication of these sources . . . :** Plaut and Washofsky, *Teshuvot,* no. 5755.16; Jacob, *Contemporary American Reform Responsa,* no. 73.

264   **the "twelve-step" method . . . :** On the problem of the "Lord's Prayer," see Jacob, *Contemporary American Reform Responsa,* no. 171. On our relationship to non-Jewish religious practices, see the discussion in Chapter 7. For an example of a Jewish approach to this method, see Kerry M. Olitzky, *Twelve Jewish Steps to Recovery: A Personal Guide for Turning from Alcoholism and Other Addictions.*

264   **The same admonition . . . :** Jacob, *Contemporary American Reform Responsa,* no. 72, 73, 74.

264   **AIDS:** *CCAR Yearbook* 96 (1986): 222–23.

265   **The Community and the AIDS Carrier:** Jacob, *Questions and Reform Jewish Answers,* no. 161; Plaut and Washofsky, *Teshuvot,* no. 5750.1.

265   **Failure to reveal this information . . . :** See this chapter's discussion of medical confidentiality. The operative traditional categories are *pikuach nefesh,* the duty to save life, and the *rodef,* the "pursuer" who constitutes a mortal danger to another's life. One who sees a person threatening the life of another is obliged to take action to save the potential victim. If one has the ability to save the victim and does not do so, then one has violated the principle laid down in Lev. 19:16: "Do not stand idly by the blood of your neighbor" (*B. Sanhedrin* 73a; *Yad, Rotzeach* 1:10–14; *Shulchan Arukh, Choshen Mishpat* 425:1).

Chapter 7: Between Jews and Non-Jews

Tradition, for a "centrist" Orthodox perspective on the "encounter between an ancient faith and the basic assumptions of contemporary Western culture" (p. 1).

270   **Our borrowing has been much more an act of translation . . . :** See Harry Orlinsky, *Ancient Israel*, 21: "The Hebrews infused whatever concepts they did borrow with their own spirit and thinking, thus endowing them with a content of ethics and morals which lifted the primitive mythology of their Asiatic neighbors to a wholly new spiritual level."

270   **a *mitzvah* to say "no" . . . :** See Plaut and Washofsky, *Teshuvot for the Nineties*, no. 5751.3.

270   **The verse Leviticus 18:3 . . . :** See also Lev. 20:23, 26.

270   **The Rabbis understood this prohibition . . . :** *B. Sanhedrin* 52b and *Avodah Zarah* 11a. One authority (*Sefer Yere'im*, ch. 313), following the plain sense of the biblical text, restricts the prohibition to "all" nations which practice idolatry (*avodah zarah*). Most, however, apply its terms to "all Gentile nations" regardless of the nature of their religion; see *Resp. Rashba* 1:345, *Resp. Rivash*, no. 158, and *Resp. Tashbetz* 3:93.

270   **Maimonides states its rationale . . . :** *Yad, Avodat Kokhavim* 11:1.

270   **This does not mean . . . :** See *Sifra* to Lev. 18:3.

270   **the "statutes" (*chukkot*) . . . :** See, notably, *Resp. Maharik*, no. 88, cited in Isserles, *Yore De'ah* 178:1, who writes that Lev. 18:3 forbids two kinds of practice: 1) any sort of conduct which has no rational explanation and serves no practical purpose, so that a Jew would have no other reason for adopting it save a desire to imitate Gentile ways; 2) any action connected to lewd or licentious behavior.

270   **Jewish tradition never developed a litmus-paper test . . . :** See, for example, *Resp. Rivash*, no. 158: although the Jews of a particular community had adopted a particular mourning custom from the local Muslim community, this was no reason to demand that they change their practice: "If you say otherwise, we might as well forbid eulogies, on the grounds that Gentiles also eulogize their dead."

272   **Jewish doctrine . . . :** For a "history" of idolatry, written from a traditional Jewish perspective, see *Yad, Avodat Kokhavim* 1. A Jew who commits idolatry is considered as though he has rejected the entire Torah; *B. Chulin* 4b; *Yad, Avodat Kokhavim* 2:5. Idolatry is one of the three sins, along with murder and incestuous or adulterous sexual unions, which one must never commit even to save one's life; *B. Sanhedrin* 74a and parallels; *Yad, Yesodei Hatorah* 5:1ff.; *Shulchan Arukh, Yore De'ah* 157:1.

272   **lest "they turn your children away . . ." :** Deut. 7:4, interpreted by the Rabbis as referring to all idolatrous nations and not merely the Canaanites; *B. Kiddushin* 68b.

272   **the "children of Noah" . . . :** The prohibition of idolatry is one of the "Seven Noachide Commandments" which, according to rabbinic teaching, are incumbent upon all humankind; *B. Sanhedrin* 56a; *Yad, Melakhim* 9:1.

272   **to refrain from doing business . . . :** *M. Avodah Zarah* 1:1; *B. Avodah Zarah* 2a and following. To encourage or enable a Gentile to perform idolatrous service is to violate the commandment "do not place a stumbling-block before the blind" (Lev. 19:14), i.e., do not entice a person into committing an act which is forbidden to him or her; *B. Avodah Zarah* 6a–b.

273   **neither Christians nor Muslims could be considered idolaters:** This is a necessarily inadequate summary of a long and complex intellectual process. The Talmud already discusses the possibility that the laws restricting commercial contact may not apply

to individual Gentiles who do not practice idolatry (*B. Avodah Zarah* 64b–65a). And the *amora* R. Yochanan distinguishes between the Gentiles who live in the land of Israel, who are "true" idolaters, and those living outside it, who "merely continue the traditions of their ancestors" (*B. Chulin* 13b). Yet not all post-talmudic authorities applied this teaching to *all* Gentiles. Maimonides, for example, declares that Muslims are not idolaters, and places them in the category of *ger toshav* (*Yad, Ma'akhalot Asurot* 11:7; see the discussion of *ger toshav* in Chapter 5) since "they declare with complete sincerity the unity of God" (*Resp. Rambam*, no. 448). Yet he views Christianity as *avodah zarah* (*Yad, Ma'akhalot Asurot* 11:7 and *Avodat Kokhavim* 9:4 in the manuscript and the uncensored editions; these statements have long since been removed from most printed editions of the *Mishneh Torah* due to pressure from Christian censors. See also his *Commentary to the Mishnah, Chulin* 1:1, Kafich edition, p. 117. Again, his remarks are censored from the standard printed editions of the *Commentary*). This ruling may have reflected Maimonides' own perception of the nature of Christian dogma and worship; it may also stem from a talmudic statement that identifies Christianity with *avodah zarah* (*B. Avodah Zarah* 6a. Here, too, our printed texts have been censored under Christian pressure. At any rate, a number of medieval rabbinic scholars did have this version before them; see *Dikdukei Soferim* ad loc., no. 5). The rabbis of northern Europe, who lived in the midst of a Christian society, were more inclined toward leniency on this point, though they were hardly consistent. On the one hand, they could write that "the Gentiles in our day do not practice idolatry" (*Tosafot, Avodah Zarah* 2a, s.v. *asur; Hilkhot Harosh, Avodah Zarah* 1:1, in the name of Rashi); on the other hand, they could and did refer to contemporary non-Jews as "idolaters" (*Resp. Rashi*, no. 180). The single most consistent author on this subject was R. Menachem Hameiri (13th–14th century Provence), who defined Christians and Muslims as "peoples characterized by religious behavior"; i.e., nations who do not merely refrain from practicing idolatry but who, on account of their monotheism and ethical behavior, have attained to an essential measure of religious truth. Hameiri used this designation to argue that the Gentiles of his era were exempt from all the pejorative legislation that the tradition aimed at non-Jews. See *Beit Habechirah, Avodah Zarah*, 4, 39, 46, and 59, and *Bava Kama*, p. 320. On the connections between Hameiri and the thought of Maimonides (though he, as we have noted, did *not* extend these ideas to Christianity), see Jacob Katz, *Exclusiveness and Tolerance: Jewish-Gentile Relations in Medieval and Modern Times*, 114ff.

273   **None of the laws . . . applies:** Freehof, *Modern Reform Responsa*, no. 11: "This is too well-known a principle in Jewish law to need more than this mention" (at p. 71). See also Jacob, *Contemporary American Reform Responsa*, no. 167.

273   **Yet even though we find much of value . . . :** See Jacob, *Contemporary American Reform Responsa*, no. 167.

273   **the non-Jew is not entitled to formal membership . . . :** See the discussion in Chapter 2. On the role of the non-Jew in synagogue ritual, see the discussion in Chapter 1.

274   **Fraternal Orders; Meditation Groups:** Jacob, *American Reform Responsa*, nos. 91 and 92.

274   **purpose of meditation and spirituality . . . :** Jacob, *Contemporary American Reform Responsa*, no. 169.

274   **Joint Services:** See Freehof, *Modern Reform Responsa*, no. 11, and Plaut and Washofsky, *Teshuvot*, no. 5751.3.

275   **The participants should not be required . . . :** We insist that the liturgy of the service be neutral and non-Christological; Jacob, *Contemporary American Reform Responsa*, no. 167. For another example, see Plaut and Washofsky, *Teshuvot*, no. 5751.3, on the ritual of the "blessing of the fleet" practiced in communities where the fishing industry is a mainstay of the local economy. The ritual is a Christian one; Jews do not customarily "bless" objects such as boats. (For example, we do not "bless" the bread we eat; the blessing we recite is a statement of thanks to God for having given it to us.) The rabbi or other Jewish participant should not therefore bless the boats, but might recite a prayer for the success and safe return of the sailors.

275   **The "Civil Religion":** See Plaut and Washofsky, *Teshuvot*, no. 5751.3 and 5753.8.

275   **we have always expressed our concern . . . :** See Jer. 29:7 and *M. Avot* 3:2.

276   **Participation in Non-Jewish Religious Services:** Jacob, *Contemporary American Reform Responsa*, nos. 167 and 168.

276   **"there is no way in the law . . . ":** Jacob, *Reform Responsa*, no. 25.

276   **a Jewish child who attends . . . :** Ibid., no. 26.

276   **A Jew . . . should not perform a Christian sacrament . . . :** Plaut and Washofsky, *Teshuvot*, no. 5755.9. The responsum rejects the argument that a Jewish chaplain who performs a baptism "dispenses comfort, not salvation." The very power of these ritual acts to dispense comfort stems from their origin in systems of religious belief which run counter to our most basic theological affirmations. We surrender our religious integrity when we allow ourselves to become the tools by which others act out religious commitments that inescapably conflict with our own.

277   **Hinduism or the Native American religions . . . :** Jacob, *Questions and Reform Jewish Answers*, nos. 85 and 86.

277   **many of the so-called "Gentile" influences . . . :** See the discussions in Chapter 1 on prayer in the vernacular and on the use of instrumental music in worship.

278   **Non-Jewish Liturgy and Music:** Jacob, *Contemporary American Reform Responsa*, no. 195; Plaut and Washofsky, *Teshuvot*, no. 5752.11. This latter responsum discusses prayer texts as well as music. See *Resp. Bach*, no. 127: the only music forbidden to borrow from Gentiles is that which they explicitly use in their worship. On the "Lord's Prayer," see Jakob J. Petuchowski and Michael Brocke, eds., *The Lord's Prayer and Jewish Liturgy*. See also *Contemporary American Reform Responsa* no. 171: "Although its content is neutral...its origin with Jesus and its strong Christian overtones make its use unacceptable to Jews."

278   **songs and melodies composed by non-Jews:** Jacob, *Questions and Reform Jewish Answers*, no. 19.

278   **Should individuals or families request . . . :** Instructive here are the words of Solomon Schechter, *Studies in Judaism*, 136ff., cited in Plaut and Washofsky, *Teshuvot*, no. 5752.11: "A people that has produced the Psalmist, a Rabbi Judah Halevi, and other hymnologists and liturgists counted by hundreds, has no need to pass around the hat to all possible denominations begging for a prayer or a hymn."

279   **joint "Christmas-Chanukah" celebrations:** Jacob, *Contemporary American Reform Responsa*, no. 173 ("luminary displays").

279   **"season's greetings" . . . to exchange gifts . . . :** Ibid., no. 172. The tradition does not object to a Jew sending a holiday gift to a Gentile, "so long as there is no concern

that the gift will incite the Gentile to worship idolatry," a fear that does not exist with respect to Christians; *Resp. Terumat Hadeshen*, no. 195.

279   **holiday decorations in a place of business . . .** : Ibid., no. 174.

279   **Jewish children . . .** : See Freehof, *Reform Responsa*, no. 25 (Jewish children might attend a Christmas celebration at school, within strict limits: i.e., we should make sure that no worship or singing of carols occurs there) and Freehof, *Today's Reform Responsa*, no. 33 (a professional actor who is Jewish may act in a Christmas play, since that is his/her livelihood, *unless* the audience is composed largely of Jewish children).

279   **to substitute for Christian workers . . .** : Jacob, *American Reform Responsa*, no. 52. On the conflict between Shabbat and other *mitzvot*, such as *tzedakah*, see the discussion of Shabbat in Chapter 3.

280   **Incense:** Jacob, *Questions and Reform Jewish Answers*, no. 16.

280   **All-Night Vigils:** Ibid., 17.

280   **during the night of Yom Kippur . . .** : *Shulchan Arukh, Orach Chayim* 619:6, a custom linked to the practice in the days of the Temple, when the High Priest was forbidden to sleep that night and notables from Jerusalem would keep watch to insure he stayed awake; *B. Yoma* 19b.

280   **Carillon Music:** Jacob, *American Reform Responsa*, no. 25. See at p. 71: "Richly equipped as the synagogue is with adequate and satisfying symbols of its own, it stands to profit little from this glaring imitation of the church."

281   **Flowers:** Jacob, *Questions and Reform Jewish Answers*, no. 48.

281   **Concerts:** Ibid., no. 53.

Chapter 8: Reform Judaism and the Jewish Community

283   **"we all stood at Sinai" . . .** : See Deut. 29:9ff., and especially vss. 13–14, which the Rabbis (*B. Shevuot* 39a) understand as including all subsequent generations in the Sinai moment.

283   **"All that God has said we will faithfully do!":** Exod. 24:7.

284   **"a permanent annual festival . . .":** *CCAR Yearbook* 80 (1970): 39. See Chapter 3 for the discussion of Yom Ha'atzma'ut.

284   **The above sentence indicates . . .** : On Reform Judaism and Zionism, see David Polish, *Renew Our Days: The Zionist Issue in Reform Judaism*, and Meyer, *Response to Modernity*, 292–93, 326–34, and 383.

285   **"America is our Zion . . . ":** *Proceedings, Union of American Hebrew Congregations* 5 (1898–1903): 4002.

285   **In 1917 . . .** : *CCAR Yearbook* 28 (1918): 133–34.

286   **"Reform Judaism and Zionism: A Centenary Platform":** For the Hebrew and English texts of this platform, see *CCAR Yearbook* 106 (1997): 49–57.

287   **a number of rules or rules-of-thumb . . .** : For example, "A duty which is frequent takes precedence over one that is less frequent"; *M. Horayot* 3:6. The Rabbis derive this from their understanding that in the days of the Temple, the daily sacrifice was

always offered first, prior to the additional sacrifice (*musaf*) for Shabbat, Rosh Chodesh, and festivals. See *B. Horayot* 12b, based on Num. 28:23. The rule is applied to *Kiddush* in *B. Pesachim* 114a; thus, the more frequently-recited blessing over the wine, *borei peri hagafen*, is recited before the *Kiddush* proper (. . . *mekadesh hashabbat*). Similarly, *berit milah* takes precedence over Shabbat if that is the child's eighth day, because the Torah requires that the circumcision occur on *that* day. A *berit milah* that is delayed past the eighth day does not override the Shabbat and is put off until another day. Reform responsa have adopted this mode of thought in considering the propriety of conducting *tzedakah* projects on Shabbat; see the discussion on p. 85.

288   **In the first responsum . . . :** Freehof, *Contemporary Reform Responsa*, no. 15.

288   **a *mitzvah* . . . to settle in the land of Israel . . . :** See *M. Ketubot* 13:11 (the head of household can compel his entire family to move to the land of Israel); *Yad, Ishut* 13:19 and *Shulchan Arukh, Even Ha'ezer* 75:3. And see *Beit Shmuel* and *Chelkat Mechokek* ad loc.: the coercion can be applied upon the head of household as well, should the other family members decide to move to *Eretz Yisrael*.

288   **Others, however . . . :** See *Tosafot, Ketubot* 110b, s.v. *ha'omer*: the requirement to settle in the land of Israel is no longer in effect, due to the dangers of travel and the inability of those who live there to observe the agricultural commandments which are specific to *Eretz Yisrael*, such as the sabbatical year. See *Kenesset Hagedolah, Even Ha'ezer* 75, to *Beit Yosef,* and *Be'er Hetev, Even Ha'ezer* 75, no. 19: the dispute among the authorities is such that no one today can be required to move to Israel. A great deal of this controversy is based upon the fact that Maimonides, in his *Sefer Hamitzvot,* does *not* list the obligation to possess the land of Israel as one of the Torah's 613 commandments. Nachmanides criticizes this as a failure: he reads Num. 33:53 as a commandment to settle the land. See his "Omissions" to the List of Positive Commandments, no. 4, in *Sefer Hamitzvot.* See as well his commentary to Num. 33:53, although compare it to Rashi's comment on that verse. R. Yitzchak de Leon, in his commentary *Megillat Esther* to *Sefer Hamitzvot,* responds that Rambam omits the commandment to possess the land of Israel precisely because that *mitzvah* was incumbent only during the days "of Joshua and David." See *Resp. Rashbash,* no. 2: to live in the land of Israel is a great *mitzvah*; however, "this *mitzvah* does not apply to the entire Jewish nation." The argument is based principally upon a talmudic tradition, according to which God has required Israel to swear not to revolt against the other nations and not to attempt to seize Jerusalem by force; see *B. Ketubot* 111a.

288   **only with the coming of the Messiah . . . :** For a recent exposition of this view by the leader of the Satmar Chasidim, see *Vayo'el Moshe.*

288   **the Jewish people has "voted with its feet" . . . :** For example, *B. Ketubot* 111a states that the Jews swore an oath never to take Jerusalem by force without the consent of the nations of the world. To take this passage literally is to declare that the Jewish people is forbidden to exercise self-determination and national sovereignty. Yet these are "rights" which every nation claims; if we renounce them, we condemn ourselves to precisely that kind of political powerlessness which our own platform "Reform Judaism and Zionism" links with the Holocaust. Within halakhic literature, scholars favorably disposed to the Jewish national movement have questioned whether the tradition in *B. Ketubot* 111a is valid any longer, particularly in light of the 1947 resolution of the United Nations which allowed the Jews to form a state in Palestine. See R. Yitzchak Halevy Herzog in S.Z. Shragai and Yitzchak Rafael, *Sefer Hatziyonut Hadatit.* For discussion, see Mark Washofsky, "Halakhah and Political Theory: A

Study in Jewish Legal Response to Modernity," *Modern Judaism* (October, 1989): 289–310.

288   **the study of the world *is* the study of Torah . . . :** Cp. *Yad, Talmud Torah* 1:12 and *Yesodei Hatorah* 4:13. In general, see Lamm, *Torah Umadda.*

289   **In the second case . . . :** *Responsa Committee,* no. 5757.1.

289   ***dina demalkhuta dina* . . . :** See the discussion of civil marriage in Chapter 4. The theory that the law of the state is valid because all the citizens have agreed to it can be traced to Rashbam (R. Shmuel b. Meir, 12th-century France) in his commentary to *B. Bava Batra* 54b, s.v. *veha'amar shmuel dina demalkhuta dina.* Of the various theories which justify the validity of the law of the state, this is the most congenial to our democratic temperament.

289   **legitimate legislative power . . . :** To qualify as "legitimate," a law must apply equally to all and not discriminate (*Yad, Gezeilah* 5:14) and be generally accepted as falling within the constitutional authority of the legislature. See Shilo, *Dina Demalkhuta Dina,* 191ff. Laws prohibiting espionage do not violate such guidelines.

289   **when allocating funds for *tzedakah* . . . :** *B. Bava Metzi'a* 71a; *Yad, Matanot Aniyim* 7:13; *Shulchan Arukh, Yore De'ah* 251:3.

289   **immediate danger . . . :** *Peri Megadim, Mishbetzot Zahav,* 328, beginning.

290   **Jewish religious pluralism . . . :** See Jakob J. Petuchowski, "Plural Models Within the Halakhah," *Judaism* 19 (1970): 89: "We are not arguing for diversity in Jewish observance. There *is* diversity in Jewish observance. All we have tried to do was to outline some kind of conceptual framework by means of which we can bring light to the underlying unity in that diversity."

291   **This affirmation is not shared by many Orthodox Jews . . . :** We do not mean that Orthodox Jews never disagree among themselves on religious matters. Orthodox Judaism, as we know, tolerates a good deal of diversity in custom and observance from one community to the other. By "one correct way," rather, we mean that Orthodoxy regards the *only* proper path to Judaism to be the *halakhah* as interpreted and applied by Orthodox rabbis, particularly the *gedolei hador,* the outstanding rabbinic sages of the contemporary generation. All variations of Orthodox belief and observance exist within this framework. Reform Judaism does *not* exist within this framework, and therefore to an Orthodox Jew it is not simply "different" but *wrong.*

292   **moral conversation or religious argument:** On the subject of limits, see the Introduction to Plaut and Washofsky, *Teshuvot.* Members of the same religious community can disagree sharply about the right answers to any number of questions. What makes them a community is that they all accept a common set of standards by which to measure the validity or persuasiveness of their arguments. In the absence of these standards, no argument could ever be resolved. Someone belonging to another community would appeal to different standards. A Christian, for example, would "prove" a theological point by citing evidence that Jews *as Jews* do not find persuasive.

292   **Religious Pluralism in Israel:** *CCAR Yearbook* 104 (1994): 123–24; Jacob, *Questions and Reform Jewish Answers,* no. 92.

292   **Reform Support of Orthodox Institutions:** Jacob, *Questions and Reform Jewish Answers,* no. 92; Jacob, *Contemporary American Reform Responsa,* no. 25.

293   **A case of marriage and divorce . . . :** Plaut and Washofsky, *Teshuvot for the Nineties,* no. 5754.6. On divorce and the *agunah* in Jewish law and tradition, as well as the Reform position on divorce, see Chapter 4. The responsum advances an additional

argument: the couple in this case were married in an Orthodox setting, an act which involves their acceptance of the religious obligations that flow from the *halakhah*. One of these is the contractual obligation to follow the legal requirements determined by the Rabbis (*B. Ketubot* 3a: "all who marry do so with the implicit acceptance of rabbinic law"; and *B. Bava Batra* 48a: "it is a *mitzvah* to heed the instructions of the sages"). The husband in this case made a promise to his wife to act faithfully according to *halakhah* as interpreted by Orthodox rabbis and to issue her a divorce when required by them to do so. His refusal to issue the *get* constitutes a breach of promise, an unethical act. Our cooperation with the Orthodox rabbi is aimed at persuading the husband to keep his word, an ethical obligation which we as Reform Jews certainly recognize.

294　**the right to hold an Orthodox service . . . :** *Responsa Committee*, no. 5758.12. The talmudic precedent is *B. Eruvin* 13a–14a, dealing with the disputes between the schools of Hillel and Shamai.

294　**Hebrew Christians, Messianic Jews, Jews for Jesus:** See the discussion in Chapter 2.

295　**Humanistic Jews:** Plaut and Washofsky, *Teshuvot*, no. 5751.4. A minority of the Responsa Committee dissented: while the theology of the humanistic congregation is deplorable, our devotion to religious pluralism demands its acceptance into the UAHC. The Committee's majority held that this was a clear case of the limits of pluralism: if we admit a humanistic congregation on grounds of pluralism, on what principled basis could we deny admission to, for example, a congregation of Jews for Jesus, or one which denies religious equality to women? See the Introduction to *Teshuvot*. The Board of Trustees of the UAHC ultimately concurred with the majority of the Responsa Committee, voting overwhelmingly to deny admission to the humanistic congregation; see *Reform Judaism* (Winter, 1994): 25–27.

296　**"we ground our lives . . . ":** Centenary Perspective; cited in Plaut and Washofsky, *Teshuvot*, no. 5751.4, 12.

Chapter 9: Judaism And Society

297　**mending the world (*tikkun ha'olam*) . . . :** This expression originated in the rabbinic literature, where it denotes a legislative enactment adopted to correct an observed defect in the law, so that observance of the law need not lead to injustice or abuse. See *M. Gittin* 4:2, 4, 5, 6, 7, 9; 5:3; 9:4; and *M. Eduyot* 1:13.

297　**a number of books:** A decidedly incomplete list: Albert Vorspan, *Reform Judaism and Social Action;* Albert Vorspan and David Saperstein, *Jewish Dimensions of Social Justice: Tough Moral Choices of Our Times*; and Balfour Brickner and Albert Vorspan, *Searching the Prophets for Values.*

298　***tzedakah* is a *mitzvah* . . . :** *B. Ketubot* 68a, and see *Sifre* to Deut. 15:7–11; *Yad, Matanot Aniyim* 7:1 and 10:1; *Shulchan Arukh, Yore De'ah* 247:1. The Torah speaks of other monetary contributions that were to be made to the poor from the produce of the land of Israel. These include: a) the *ma'aser ani*, the "tithe to the poor," donated every third and sixth year of the sabbatical cycle in place of the "second tithe" (*ma'aser sheni*) which in other years was consumed by its owner in Jerusalem (Deut. 14:28–29; see *Yad, Matanot Aniyim* 6); b) the "corner" (*pe'ah*) of the field where the standing grain was not reaped (Lev. 19:9 and elsewhere; *Mishnah, Pe'ah*); c) the "gleanings" (*leket*), sheaves of grain that were left in the field and not collected during the harvest

(Lev. 19:9 and elsewhere; *M. Pe'ah* 4:10ff.); d) grapes not fully matured (*'olelot*) or fallen to the ground (*peret*) during harvesting (Lev. 19:10; *M. Pe'ah* 7:4); e) the "forgotten sheaf" (*shikhechah*), accidentally left in the field during harvest (Deut. 24:19; *M. Pe'ah* 5:7ff.). These contributions are obligatory only in the land of Israel and do not apply to land owned by Jews elsewhere. Still, they serve us as examples of the principle of stewardship, the perception that we do not own our property but hold it on loan from God, who is entitled to direct us in its proper disposition.

298   **It is more a tax . . . :** Like taxes, *tzedakah* could be collected from the individual who refused to contribute by means of coercion or the attachment of his or her property; *B. Ketubot* 47b; *Yad, Matanot Aniyim* 7:10; *Shulchan Arukh, Yore De'ah* 248:1.

298   **even the poor person who receives *tzedakah* . . . :** *B. Gittin* 7b; *Yad, Matanot Aniyim* 7:5; *Shulchan Arukh, Yore De'ah* 248:1.

298   ***tzedakah* ought not to exclude "charity":** See *Yad, Matanot Aniyim* 10:4 and 10:14: the lowest rung on Maimonides' eight-step "ladder of *tzedakah*" is occupied by the one who gives to the poor but does so unhappily.

299   **we must provide the poor with *whatever* they lack . . . :** See *B. Ketubot* 67b: "If an orphan wishes to marry, the community rents for him a home and all its furnishings; then it provides him a wife...it even provides him a horse on which to ride and a servant to run before him (if such was his standard of living prior to his becoming poor)." See also *Yad, Matanot Aniyim* 7:3. "How much should one give? If one can afford to do so, one should give as much as the poor need": *Shulchan Arukh, Yore De'ah* 249:1.

299   **or the provision of the tools . . . :** The highest rung on Maimonides' "ladder of *tzedakah*"; *Yad, Matanot Aniyim* 10:7.

299   **the word "lend" comes to tell us . . . :** *B. Ketubot* 67b; *Yad, Matanot Aniyim* 7:9.

299   **Priorities in *Tzedakah*:** Jacob, *Contemporary American Reform Responsa*, no. 24.

299   **"A member of one's family takes precedence . . . ":** *B. Bava Metzi'a* 71a; *Yad, Matanot Aniyim* 7:13; *Shulchan Arukh, Yore De'ah* 251:3. See also Isserles ad loc.: "One's own sustenance takes precedence over that of all others . . . Then comes the sustenance of one's parents, should they be poor, followed by the sustenance of one's children; followed by one's siblings; followed by one's other relatives; followed by one's neighbors; followed by the poor of one's city; followed by the poor elsewhere."

299   **the provision of nursing care . . . :** Jacob, *Questions and Reform Jewish Answers*, no. 91.

300   **one who contributes to a communal *tzedakah* campaign . . . :** *Mordekhai, Bava Batra* 486; *Shulchan Arukh* and Isserles, *Yore De'ah* 251:5; *Shakh, Yore De'ah* 251, no. 8.

300   **The sources, too, offer a powerful practical argument . . . :** *Arukh Hashulchan, Yore De'ah* 251, par. 4.

300   **The ancient Rabbis already instructed . . . :** *B. Gittin* 61a; *Yad, Avodat Kokhavim* 10:5; *Shulchan Arukh, Yore De'ah* 251:1.

301   **Gifts to Organizations Inimical to Reform Judaism:** Jacob, *Questions and Reform Jewish Answers*, no. 92; Jacob, *Contemporary American Reform Responsa*, no. 25.

301   **"one who intentionally violates . . . ":** *Shulchan Arukh, Yore De'ah* 251:1.

301   **The explanation given . . . :** *Beit Yosef, Yore De'ah* 251, beginning.

301   **whom the Torah calls our "brothers"** . . . : See Lev. 25:36 and Deut. 15:17.

302   **united, communal** *tzedakah* **campaigns** . . . : The Reform responsa which declare against giving to "organizations inimical to Reform Judaism" speak specifically to those organizations and *not* to Federations, the UJA, and other examples of communal campaigns. The responsa speak highly of the value of Jewish unity, a goal that lies at the foundation of communal campaigns.

302   **Support for Reform Jewish Organizations:** *Responsa Committee*, no. 5758.1; Jacob, *Contemporary American Reform Responsa*, no. 140.

302   **one-half shekel** . . . : Exod. 30:11–16 and *Mishnah, Shekalim*.

302   **In the Middle Ages** . . . : It is not at all clear in the earlier *halakhah* that communities possess such legislative and regulatory power. When the Talmud speaks of *takkanot* and other enactments, it refers to acts of a recognized *rabbinic* court or of particular trade groups, much like the guilds of later times. The notion that the citizens of a town may constitute themselves as a body politic and impose by majority vote all manner of obligations upon the entire community, as though they exercise all the power of a rabbinic *beit din*, is a development of medieval halakhic thought. On the theory and practice of Jewish self-government in the pre-Emancipation period, see Louis Finkelstein, *Jewish Self-Government in the Middle Ages;* Menachem Elon, *Jewish Law*, 678–779; Jacob Katz, *Tradition and Crisis: Jewish Society at the End of the Middle Ages*, trans. Bernard Dov Cooperman; and Mark Washofsky, "*Halakhah* and Political Theory: A Study in Jewish Legal Response to Modernity," *Modern Judaism* (October, 1989): 289–310.

302   **The rabbis** . . . : did not take a proactive role in developing a political theory which would justify the exercise of communal legislative power but rather sought to find after-the-fact legal justifications for actions that the communal authorities took in any event. See Jacob Katz, *Halakhah Vekabalah*, 237–51.

302   **individual Jews were bound to act** . . . : *Resp. Rashba* 3:408; *Resp. Maharil*, no. 12.

303   **Tzedakah on Shabbat and Festivals:** See the discussion of Shabbat on p. 85.

303   **given our movement's recent emphasis** . . . : Evident in a number of publications by the Central Conference of American Rabbis: Shapiro, *Gates of Shabbat*; Knobel, *Gates of the Seasons*, 15–33; and Plaut, *A Shabbat Manual*.

304   **Jewish law permits** . . . : *Responsa Committee*, 5756.4; Freehof, *Contemporary Reform Responsa*, no. 12; B. *Shabbat* 150a (on Isa. 58:13); *Yad, Shabbat* 24:5; *Shulchan Arukh, Orach Chayim* 306:6.

304   **before** *Kol Nidrei* **itself** . . . : Freehof, *Contemporary Reform Responsa*, no. 12. The traditional custom is to recite *Kol Nidrei* "while it is yet daylight," since the ceremony in some ways resembles a legal act (the annulment of vows) which requires a court (*beit din*), and the court does not convene on a Shabbat or a *yom tov*. The blessing *Shehechiyanu*, which follows *Kol Nidrei* (*Gates of Repentance*, 253) is seen as the official beginning of Yom Kippur (Isserles, *Orach Chayim* 619:1; Bach, *Orach Chayim* 619; *Mishnah Berurah* 619, nos. 4–5).

305   **Even the existence of a legal system** . . . : See *Sifrei* to Deut. 16:18.

305   **In the words of Maimonides** . . . : *Yad, Sanhedrin* 1:1.

306   **Economic Dignity; Fair Wages and Prices:** Plaut and Washofsky, *Teshuvot for the Nineties*, no. 5754.18.

306   **"and they are not the servants of servants":** B. *Bava Kama* 116b.

306 **One who seeks to serve God ... :** See the comment of Rabbi Yochanan (*B. Kiddushin* 22b) on Exod. 21:6, concerning the Hebrew slave who chooses continued servitude over the freedom to serve his true Master. We pierce his ear, for he has made himself deaf to God's instruction that "the people of Israel are *My* servants."

306 **the worker may quit ... :** *B. Bava Kama* 116b; *Yad, Sekhirut* 9:4; *Shulchan Arukh, Choshen Mishpat* 333:3.

306 **The Talmud already mentions ... :** *B. Bava Batra* 8b.

306 **Later *halakhah* ... :** *Resp. Rashba* 4:185; *Beit Habechirah, Bava Batra* 8b; *Hilkhot Harosh, Bava Batra* 1:33; *Yad, Mekhirah* 14:9–11; *Shulchan Arukh, Choshen Mishpat* 231:27–28 and Isserles ad loc.

306 **Recent authorities ... :** *Resp. Mishpetei Ouziel* 3, *Choshen Mishpat*, no. 42; *Resp. Aseh Lekha Rav* 2:64; *Resp. Yechaveh Da'at* 4:48; *Resp. Tzitz Eliezer* 2:23.

306 **Most halakhists ... :** See above note. The "relevant talmudic passage" is *B. Bava Batra* 9a.

306 **"has violated the terms of employment ... ":** *Resp. Tzitz Eliezer* 2:23, end. The concept here is the right of *any* individual to take action to secure justice for him- or herself when convinced that he or she is "in the right"; *B. Bava Kama* 27b; *Yad, Sanhedrin* 2:12; *Shulchan Arukh, Choshen Mishpat* 4. Clearly, the power to take the law into one's own hands, were it to become a common practice, would threaten the existence of a well-ordered legal system. There are times, however, when the interests of justice demand that the legal formalities be set aside. Thus, if the workers cannot secure justice in any other way, a strike is permissible in spite of the harm it causes others, although halakhists still may limit the right of workers in such vital sectors as medical care to strike. See Plaut and Washofsky, *Teshuvot*, no. 5754.18.

307 **Wages and salaries ... are set by the market:** As one author puts it, with respect to the salaries paid to physicians, income should match "the respect they are due and the level that is customary throughout the world": R. Shelomo Goren, "Shevitat Harof 'im Bahalakhah," 53. We must presume that "the world," in Rabbi Goren's phrase, means those economically-developed countries whose standards of living we would wish to emulate.

307 **inflation ... :** See Goren, loc. cit.

307 **price distortion ... *ona'ah* ... :** *M. Bava Metzi'a* 4:4ff.; *Yad, Mekhirah* 12; *Shulchan Arukh, Choshen Mishpat* 227.

308 **If, however, the seller discloses ... :** This is the case of "the one who does business in good faith" (*hanoseh venoten be'emunah*); *B. Bava Metzi'a* 51b; *Yad, Mekhirah* 14:1; *Shulchan Arukh, Choshen Mishpat* 227:27.

308 **communal price controls ... :** *B. Bava Batra* 89a; *Yad, Mekhirah* 14:1 and *Sanhedrin* 1:1; *Shulchan Arukh, Choshen Mishpat* 231:2. On price controls in Jewish history, see Meir Tamari, *With All Your Possessions: Jewish Ethics and Economic Life*, 94–96.

308 **deception ... *geneivat da'at* ... :** *M. Bava Metzi'a* 4:12; *Yad, Mekhirah* 18; *Shulchan Arukh, Choshen Mishpat* 228:6ff.

308 **A Reform responsum ... :** Jacob, *Questions and Reform Jewish Answers*, no. 91.

309 **Competition:** See ibid., no. 153; Freehof, *Modern Reform Responsa*, no. 50, and Freehof, *New Reform Responsa*, no. 38.

309 **The ancient sources dispute ... :** *M. Bava Metzi'a* 4:12.

309   **the accepted position of the *halakhah* . . . :** *Yad, Mekhirah* 18:4; *Shulchan Arukh, Choshen Mishpat* 228:18.

309   **the aggressive storekeeper does nothing wrong . . . :** *B. Bava Metzi'a* 60a–b.

309   **Another passage teaches . . . :** *B. Bava Batra* 21b; *Yad, Shekhenim* 6:8, 12; *Shulchan Arukh, Choshen Mishpat* 156:5. The residents may enact certain "zoning" regulations for environmental reasons, such as "we cannot sleep due to the noise your customers make; you must operate your business from the public marketplace"; but they cannot restrict the entry of new businesses once a similar business has been established in the neighborhood. See also *B. Bava Batra* 22a: an ancient enactment forbids communities from restricting access to wandering peddlers. Although the established businesses might be adversely affected by the peddlers' entry into the market, the needs of the consumers demanded that competition be encouraged.

309   **halakhic authorities have allowed communities . . . :** Many of these restrictions on competition are embodied in the enactments of medieval community councils; see Louis I. Rabinowitz, *Herem Hayishuv.*

309   **The rise of the professional rabbinate . . . :** This was by no means an uncontroversial decision. Some authorities held that an "outside" rabbi had the unlimited right to enter a community to teach Torah, even if this lessens the income of the current rabbi (*Resp. R. Ya'akov Weil,* no. 151; R. Yisrael Isserlein, *Pesakim,* no. 158). Others, however, recognized the power of communal custom (*minhag*) to protect the rabbi's income by forbidding another from serving as a rabbi in the community (*Shakh, Yore De'ah* 245, no. 15). See, in general, Jacob, *Questions and Reform Jewish Answers,* no. 153.

309   **copyright . . . :** The first to deal with the subject is the sixteenth-century R. Moshe Isserles (*Responsa,* no. 10), who approved of copyright for the reprinting of previously-published sacred texts. As R. Moshe Sofer explains, "were printing to cease, Torah would disappear. Yet it is impossible to print these works without incurring great expense, and no one would take this upon himself without first guaranteeing for himself an exclusive market... Therefore, our rabbis barred the door to competition in this case...not for the benefit of the publisher but rather for the increase of Torah study" (*Resp. Chatam Sofer, Choshen Mishpat,* no. 41). Here, too, there was opposition, as some authorities argued that the words of Torah do not belong to any one person and cannot be reserved to any individual's control; see *Resp. Beit Yitzchak, Yore De'ah* 2:75. Nonetheless, even the opponents of copyright under Jewish law acknowledge the binding quality of copyright under the law of the state (*dina demalkhuta*).

310   **One Reform responsum . . . :** Freehof, *New Reform Responsa,* no. 38. According to traditional *halakhah* certain *mitzvot* connected with burial can be performed only by Jews. It would pose a special hardship for Orthodox Jews, therefore, were this funeral director to be driven out of business. As the responsum notes, however, the best solution is for the Jewish funeral home, in the spirit of *M. Bava Metzi'a* 4:12, to find a way to match the lower price of its competitor.

310   **Gossip and Privacy:** Plaut and Washofsky, *Teshuvot,* 5750.1 and 5750.4.

310   **legal or human "rights" . . . :** For a full discussion, along with other examples of "rights" derivable from Jewish legal sources, see Haim Cohn, *Human Rights in Jewish Law,* 18–19. Modern Israeli jurists use the Hebrew word *zekhut* (pl. *zekhuyot*) to express the concept of "rights." In the traditional sources, however, *zekhut* does not carry that meaning. It refers rather to a means of acquisition. It also conveys "benefit," "merit," and "favor"; one who "wins" a court case or is acquitted of a crime is called *zaka'i,* which means "free of culpability."

311   **A home owner, too, may take action . . . :** *M. Bava Batra* 3:7; *Yad, Shekhenim* 5:6; *Shulchan Arukh, Choshen Mishpat* 154:3. The *halakhah* uses the language of tort law to express this idea: we seek to avoid "damages caused by seeing" (*hezek re'iyah*; see *B. Bava Batra* 59b). The duty to avoid such damage amounts to what we would consider a guarantee of the privacy of others.

311   **"One should not act like a peddler . . . ":** *Y. Pe'ah* 1:1 (16a).

311   *lashon hara* **. . . :** See *Yad, De'ot* 7:1–5 for the gradations in the offense of gossip and slander.

311   **compared to that of leprosy . . . :** The slanderer is called *motzi shem ra* (cf. Deut. 22:19), "one who damages reputation." The word for "leper" is *metzora*; the *midrash* is found in *B. Arakhin* 15b. The similarity in these Hebrew terms allows us to draw likenesses between the impurity spread by the leper and the social destruction engendered by the slanderer.

311   **equivalent to the sins of idolatry . . . :** *B. Arakhin* 15b; *Yad, De'ot* 7:3. The seriousness with which the tradition takes the prohibition of gossip can be measured by the widespread and lasting popularity of the book *Chafetz Chayim* (cf. Ps. 34:14), a treatise on the laws of *lashon hara* by R. Yisrael Meir Hakohen Kagan, the author of the *Mishnah Berurah*.

311   **Engaging in *lashon hara* is also held . . . :** *Chafetz Chayim*, Introduction.

311   **"My God, preserve my tongue from evil . . . ":** *B. Berakhot* 17a; *Gates of Prayer*, 47.

312   **compulsory testing for AIDS . . . :** Plaut and Washofsky, *Teshuvot*, 5750.1.

312   **Huntington's disease . . . :** *Responsa Committee*, no. 5756.2.

313   **domestic peace (*shalom bayit*) . . . :** See *B. Bava Metzi'a* 87a to Gen. 18:12–13 and Rashi to v. 13: household peace is such a worthy goal that even God "shades the truth" in order to preserve it.

313   **no relationship . . . suffices to justify:** See Lev. 19:3 and *B. Yevamot* 5b: the *mitzvah* to revere one's parent does not permit one to violate Shabbat if the parent requests this. See *Chafetz Chayim, Hilkhot Lashon Hara* 1:5: "Even if one's parent or teacher, whom one is required to honor and revere...were to request that one tell about so-and-so...it is forbidden to obey them."

313   *mitzvah haba'ah beaveirah* **. . . :** See *B. Sukkah* 29b and *Bava Kama* 94a. Does this mean that we say "the end *never* justifies the means"? Not necessarily; there may be cases whose conditions would demand that we act even against an explicit prohibition. But such cases are extreme and thankfully rare; we do not analogize from them to learn about how we should conduct our daily lives.

313   **Confidentiality:** Jacob, *Contemporary American Reform Responsa*, nos. 4, 5, and 6; Plaut and Washofsky, *Teshuvot*, no. 5750.3.

314   **legal status . . . determined by the law of the state:** See the discussion of *dina demalkhuta dina* at p. 163.

314   **a professional counselor is just as obligated . . . :** See Plaut and Washofsky, *Teshuvot*, no. 5750.3. One difficulty is that the counselor may have sworn a professional oath to keep secret all information revealed by clients or patients. That oath may impose a moral or religious obligation upon the counselor *not* to reveal the information, even in the most dire circumstances. To this, we might respond in two ways. First, an oath which obliges an individual to violate a *mitzvah* is generally invalid on its face. We all "took an oath" at Sinai to uphold the *mitzvot*, including that which

requires us to save life, and we cannot escape this responsibility by swearing an additional oath (*M. Shevu'ot* 3:8; *Yad, Shevu'ot* 5:14–15). Second, even if the new oath does take priority, we interpret its terms more narrowly than do some others. Thus, when a physician swears the professional oath, we hold that he or she does not intend thereby to oblige him- or herself to violate other overriding moral responsibilities (*Resp. Tzitz Eliezer* 13:81, sec. 2).

314   **when a physician knows . . . :** *Resp. Chelkat Ya'akov* 3:136. On the *rodef*, see B. *Sanhedrin* 73a; *Yad, Rotzeach* 1:14.

314   **Even when there is no physical danger . . . :** Jacob, *Contemporary American Reform Responsa*, no. 5; *Chafetz Chayim, Hilkhot Rekhilut*, no. 9.

314   **The physician or counselor . . . must weigh the advantages . . . :** Plaut and Washofsky, *Teshuvot*, no. 5750.3; Jacob, *Contemporary American Reform Responsa*, no. 5. If the patient or client threatens to commit suicide if the information is revealed, this is a strong argument in favor of maintaining confidentiality.

314   **The Disabled and the Community:** Plaut and Washofsky, *Teshuvot*, no. 5752.5.

315   **One might think that a blind person would indeed wish to be exempt . . . :** See B. *Bava Kama* 87a: "One who performs the act out of obligation is greater than the one who performs the act even though he is not obligated to do so." This sentiment may be puzzling to us, especially since we tend to regard the volunteer, the one who chooses to do the right thing out of the goodness of his or her heart, as more praiseworthy than the one who does the right thing out of "duty" or "obligation," terms we associate with coercion. The traditional point of view, of course, can be defended in Kantian terms: we do the right thing, not necessarily because we want to do it but because we *have* to do it. We cannot imagine the moral or religious life in any other way. Once we have determined that a particular action is "good" or "just," we really have no choice in the matter; it becomes our *duty* to take that action, for there is no justification in *not* taking it, in choosing to do wrong or evil. The point here is that Rav Yosef's community is one which defines itself through the language of obligation, duty, and *mitzvah*. These, says tradition, are the things we do because we cannot choose otherwise and yet remain "Israel" in any understanding of that term which makes sense to us. By "escaping" *mitzvah*, the Jew is separated from the rest of the community; "if you exempt the blind from all the *mitzvot*, they will be like Gentiles who do not walk in the ways of Israel" (*Tosafot, Bava Kama* 87a, s.v. *vekhen*).

315   **the blind *are* included . . . :** *Resp. Harosh* 4:21; *Yam shel Shelomo, Bava Kama* 8:20; *Beit Habechirah, Bava Kama* 87a. See *Shulchan Arukh, Orach Chayim* 53:14, along with *Be'er Hagolah* and *Bi'ur Hagra* ad loc.: the blind are obligated to perform any and all *mitzvot* which by their nature do not require eyesight.

315   **The deaf-mute (*cheresh*) . . . :** B. *Chagigah* 3a; *Yad, Chagigah* 2:4.

315   **the mentally disabled (*shoteh*) . . . :** Often translated as "imbecile," "idiot," or "insane," the term describes one whose behavior indicates that he/she lacks the mental capacity to act in a minimally-responsible manner. See B. *Chagigah* 3b: "Who is a *shoteh*? One who destroys all that is given to him." *Yad, Edut* 9:9; *Shulchan Arukh, Yore De'ah* 1:5. See *Responsa Committee*, no. 5758.7.

315   **one who has no arms . . . :** *Mishnah Berurah* 651, no. 22.

316   **"lest the people gaze at him":** *M. Megillah* 4:7; *Yad, Tefillah* 15:2.

316   **the Rabbis established a procedure . . . :** *M. Yevamot* 14:1; B. *Yevamot* 112b–113a.

316   **schools and languages for the deaf . . . :** See *Resp. Tzitz Eliezer* 15:46, sec. 1.

316   **the mentally retarded . . . :** The *peti*; see the essay by R. Moshe Feinstein in Paul Kahn, ed., *Behavioral Sciences and Mental Health.*

317   **the maximum inclusion of disabled persons . . . :** See the discussion of Bar/Bat Mitzvah ceremonies for "special needs" youngsters at p. 152: the "adjustment" made in Jewish ritual practice to allow the blind to be called to the Torah is best understood, we think, as a response to a real desire to include them within the circumference of Jewish ritual life.

317   **To the extent that sexual relations take place within a marital union . . . :** See *Yad, Isurei Bi'ah* 21:9ff. and *Ishut* 15.

317   **Maimonides . . . :** *Yad, Ishut* 1:1–4.

317   **Nachmanides . . . :** *Resp. Harashba Hameyuchasot Laramban,* no. 284. The position is also that of Rabad, *Hasagot* to *Yad, Ishut* 1:4. See Isserles, *Even Ha'ezer* 26:1.

317   **harlotry (*kedeishah*) . . . :** This word is commonly translated as "cult prostitute" rather than "harlot"; this would imply that common prostitution was not outlawed by the Torah. For a contrary view, which supports the traditional understanding of *kedeishah* as *any* prostitute, see Jeffrey Tigay, *The JPS Torah Commentary: Deuteronomy,* 480–81.

317   **concubine (*pilegesh*) . . . :** See Genesis 25:6. According to the rabbinic view of this institution, the concubine received neither *kiddushin* nor *ketubah*; thus, she could be sent away without benefit of a divorce proceeding, and she had no valid financial claim upon the man in the event their relationship dissolved; *B. Sanhedrin* 21a.

317   **only the king of Israel . . . :** *Yad, Melakhim* 4:4.

318   **we could adopt that institution . . . :** The eighteenth-century R. Ya'akov Emden suggested as much (*Resp. She'elat Ya'avetz* 2:15). As we shall see, however, his is very much a minority opinion.

318   **even those who, like Nachmanides . . . :** See *Kesef Mishneh* to *Yad, Ishut* 1:4, end.

318   **the predominant view . . . :** *Resp. Achiezer* 3:23; *Resp. Radbaz* 4:225 and 7:33; *Resp. Igerot Moshe, Even Ha'ezer* 1:55. Some worry that allowing a man to take a concubine will frustrate the Torah's true goal that he establish a marriage; see *Resp. Tzitz Eliezer* 1:27, sec. 18; *Yam Shel Shelomo, Yevamot* 2:11.

318   **This has been the approach of Reform responsa as well:** *Responsa Committee,* 5756.10; Jacob, *American Reform Responsa,* no. 154.

320   **Homosexuals in Society:** *CCAR Yearbook* 106 (1996): 330; idem, 100 (1990): 107ff.; idem, 87 (1977): 86.

320   **the rights and benefits . . . of civil marriage:** This is a broad endorsement of the goals of "domestic partner legislation," under which same-sex partnerships might qualify for the financial and social benefits (life and health insurance, tax exemptions, etc.) which society accords to married couples. This sentiment follows the traditional Jewish legal position that individuals and communities are permitted to make stipulations in matters of monetary law (*dinei mamonot*) which depart from the financial arrangements set forth in the Torah. See *B. Bava Metzi'a* 94a and *Yad, Ishut* 6:9; *Responsa Committee,* no. 5756.8.

320   **These sharp disagreements are explored . . . :** *Responsa Committee,* no. 5756.8. The brief summary in this volume cannot do justice to the process of argument that the responsum attempts. The reader is urged to consult the original source.

320   **The Torah explicitly prohibits . . . :** Lev. 18:23 and 20:13.

321   **defiles the land:** Lev. 18:24–30; Lev. 20:22.

321   **A people called to holiness . . . :** Lev. 18:5 and 20:7–8, 26.

321   **Female homosexual activity . . . :** *B. Shabbat* 65a–b; *B. Yevamot* 76a; *Yad, Isurei Bi'ah* 21:8; *Shulchan Arukh, Even Ha'ezer* 20:2.

321   **a breakdown in the institution of marriage . . . :** See *B. Sanhedrin* 58a on Gen. 2:24; *B. Nedarim* 51a (on *to'evah*) and the Commentary of R. Nissim Gerondi ad loc., s.v. *to'eh atta bah*; *Sefer Hachinukh*, mitzvah no. 209; *Torah Temimah* to Lev. 18:22, no. 70. See also *Genesis Rabbah* 26:5 and *Leviticus Rabbah* 23:9: the generation of the Flood was destroyed because they wrote wedding contracts for "marriages" between two men and between men and animals.

321   **punish individuals who *choose* of their own free will . . . :** The rule is *ones rachmana petarei*, "one is legally exempt for acts committed under duress"; *B. Bava Kama* 28a and parallels.

322   **a ceremony in which Jewish couples reaffirm . . . :** The wedding benedictions (*sheva berakhot*) recited under the *chupah* illustrate this point: at the moment of this couple's great private joy, we gather as a community to rehearse some of the great themes of Jewish sacred history.

323   ***kiddushin* . . . cannot be interpreted . . . :** *kiddushin* is a legal institution that assumes certain boundaries as conditions for its existence. For example, *kiddushin* is possible only between two Jews. Additionally—and of particular relevance to our discussion—"Jewish marriage" is impossible between two individuals whose union is prohibited as adultery or incest in Leviticus 18. That is to say, the structure of Jewish marriage incorporates two essential factors: 1) as a result of *kiddushin*, sexual relations between this man and this woman are permitted; 2) as a result of *kiddushin*, other sexual relations become forbidden, either on grounds of adultery or incest (the incest prohibitions are now widened to include many in-laws in addition to many of one's blood relatives). Homosexual relations involve neither adultery nor incest, which is another way of saying that they cannot be imagined as falling within the essential structure of Jewish marriage.

324   **ceremonies of mixed marriage . . . :** The analogy to mixed marriage is not perfect: while a Gentile partner can always convert to Judaism, we do not believe that a homosexual can "convert" to heterosexuality. Yet the similarities are close enough to warrant caution, especially on the practical level. Both are forms of "marriage" that Jewish tradition does not recognize. Many will wonder why some rabbis will officiate at one such variety of "non-Jewish marriage" but not at the other.

324   **all the rituals and ceremonies that pertain to the Jewish home . . . :** For example, a homosexual couple who are the legal parents of a child may celebrate the child's naming in exactly the same way as a heterosexual family would do so; *Responsa Committee*, no. 5758.2.

324   **an acceptance we do *not* offer to unmarried heterosexual couples . . . :** See *Responsa Committee*, no. 5756.10. Thus, an unmarried heterosexual couple may not join the synagogue as a "family" or "household." We do not afford them this recognition because marriage for them is a real possibility and the proper means by which they can establish a true Jewish home.

325   **The Environment:** Jacob, *Contemporary American Reform Responsa*, no. 12.

325   ***bal tashchit* . . . :** *B. Bava Kama* 91b–92a; *B. Shabbat* 105b; *B. Kiddushin* 32a; *Yad, Melakhim* 6:8–10.

325   **"This is the way of the truly pious . . . "**: *Sefer Chassidim,* no. 530.

326   **a source of pleasure or gain for the few . . .** : See Plaut and Washofsky, *Teshuvot,* no. 5753.3: Judaism has never approved of hunting for sport, even though the activity of hunting is a source of pleasure to hunters.

326   **the difficult task of balancing . . .** : See ibid., no. 5753.3, on protection of endangered species. There is no hard-and-fast Jewish requirement that all existing species of plant and animal life be preserved; see the discussion on genetic engineering in Chapter 6. The question we face is a more nuanced one: does the disappearance of a species serve an identifiable economic purpose that outweighs the disadvantages, those of which we know and those at which we can only speculate, that result from the disappearance?

326   **War:** Ibid., no. 5750.2.

327   **self-defense in a violent world . . .** : The principle of self-defense is derived from Exod. 22:1–2; see *B. Sanhedrin* 72a and *Yad, Geneivah* 9:9. The "burrowing thief" is likened to a pursuer (*rodef*) who may be stopped from endangering another, even if this means killing the pursuer; *B. Sanhedrin* 74a.

327   **within accepted ethical boundaries . . .** : The "Jewish ethics of warfare" are discussed by Maimonides in *Yad, Melakhim.* A recent, extensive treatment is provided by Rabbi Shelomo Goren, *Meshiv Milchamah,* as well as his *Mishnat Hamedinah.*

327   **On the Redemption of Captives:** Plaut and Washofsky, *Teshuvot,* no. 5753.5.

327   *pidyon shevuyim* **. . .** : *B. Bava Batra* 8a–b. See *Yad, Matanot Aniyim* 8:10: one who ignores the duty to redeem captives violates the commandments of Deut. 15:7 ("do not harden your heart...from your brother in need"); Lev. 19:16 ("do not stand idly by the blood of your neighbor"); Lev. 19:18 ("you shall love your neighbor as yourself"); and others. See also *Shulchan Arukh, Yore De'ah* 252:3, quoting *Resp. Maharik,* no. 7: "when one fails to redeem a captive when it is possible to do so, it as though one has shed blood."

327   **We are not to redeem captives . . .** : *M. Gittin* 4:6.

327   **"their monetary value" . . .** : This might be calculated according to the estimated price that this individual would fetch on the slave market (*Resp. Maharam Lublin,* no. 15), the "going rate" normally paid to kidnappers (*Resp. Radbaz Hachadashot,* no. 40), or the social status of the hostages (*Beit Habechirah, Ketubot* 52b).

328   **If we adopt this second explanation . . .** : See Rashi, *B. Gittin* 45a, s.v. *o dilma.*

328   **Halakhic authorities . . .** : *Shulchan Arukh, Yore De'ah* 252:4; *Bach* to *Tur, Yore De'ah* 252; *Shakh, Yore De'ah* 252, no. 4.

328   **One contemporary halakhist . . .** : R. Ovadyah Yosef, in *Torah shebe'al peh* 19 (1977): 9–39.

328   **We disagree . . .** : See our criticisms of R. Yosef's position in Plaut and Washofsky, *Teshuvot,* no. 5753.5. See also R. Shaul Yisraeli in *Torah Shebe'al Peh* 17 (1975):69–76; R. Yehudah Gershuni in *Hadarom* (1971):27-37; and R. Moshe Zemer, *Halakhah Shefuyah,* 202–5.

Halakhic Sources

The citations of Mishnah, Talmud, Tosefta, and the midrash collections follow the standard printed editions unless otherwise noted.

Halakhic Compendia

Alfasi. R. Yitzchak Alfasi. 11th century, North Africa/Spain
Arba'ah Turim. R. Ya'akov b. Asher. 14th century, Spain
Arukh Hashulchan. R. Yechiel M. Epstein. 19th–20th century, Lithuania
Ben Ish Chai. R. Yosef Chayim b. Eliyahu. 19th century, Iraq
Chafetz Chayim. R. Yisrael Meir Kagan. 19th–20th century, Lithuania
Chayei Adam. R. Avraham Danzig. 18th–19th century, Germany/Lithuania
Chiluf Minhagim. 9th–10th century, Babylonia (?)
Even Ha'ezer. R. Eliezer b. Natan (Raban). 12th century, Germany
Gesher Hachayim. R. Y.M. Tucatzinsky. 20th century, Palestine/Israel
Halakhot Gedolot. R. Shimeon Kayara. 8th century, Babylonia
Hanhagat Hagra. R. Eliyahu, Gaon of Vilna. 19th century
Hilkhot Harosh. R. Asher b. Yechiel. 14th century, Germany/Spain
Kitzur Shulchan Arukh. R. Shelomo Ganzfried. 19th century, Hungary
Kol Bo 'al Avelut. R. Y. Greenwald. 20th century, United States
Levush. R. Mordekhai Yaffe. 16th–17th century, Poland
Ma'aseh Rav. R. Eliyahu, Gaon of Vilna. 18th century, Lithuania
Machzor Vitry. R. Simchah of Vitry. 12th century, France
Maharil. R. Ya'akov Molin. 15th century, Germany
Mateh Efraim. R. Efraim Margoliot. 18th–19th century, Poland

Mishnah Berurah. R. Yisrael Meir Kagan. 19th–20th century, Lithuania
Mishneh Torah. R. Moshe b. Maimon (Maimonides). 12th century, Egypt
Mordekhai. R. Mordekhai b. Hillel. 13th century, Germany
Nachalat Tzvi. R. Gedaliah Felder. 20th century, Canada
Or Zaru'a. R. Yitzchak of Vienna. 13th century
Perushei Ibra. R. Eliyahu Henkin. 20th century, United States
Ra'abyah. R. Eliezer b. Yoel Halevy. 12th–13th century, Germany
Ramat Rachel. R. Eliezer Yehudah Waldenberg. 20th century, Israel
Sedei Chemed. R. Chayim Chizkiah Medini. 19th century, Eretz Yisrael
Sefer Abudarham. R. David b. Yosef Abudarham. 14th century, Spain
Sefer Chassidim. 12th–13th century, Germany
Sefer Hachinukh. R. Pinchas Halevi (?). 13th century, Spain
Sefer Hamanhig. R. Avaham b. Natan Hayarchi. 12th–13th century, Provence
Sefer Hamitzvot. R. Moshe b. Maimon (Maimonides). 12th century, Egypt
Sefer Ha'orah. 11th–12th century, France/Germany
Sefer Hapardes. 11th–12th century, France/Germany
Sefer Kol Bo. 13th–14th century, Provence (?)
Sefer Mitzvot Katan. R. Yitzchak of Corbeil. 13th century, France
Sefer Yere'im. R. Eliezer b. Shmuel of Metz. 12th century, France
Sha'arei Ouziel. R. Benzion Ouziel. 20th century, Israel
She'arim Metzuyanim Bahalakhah. R. S.Z. Braun. 20th century, United States
She'iltot. R. Acha Mishabecha. 8th century, Babylonia
Shevet Miyehudah. R. Issar Yehudah Unterman. 20th century, Israel
Shibolei Haleket. R. Zedkiyah b. Avraham Harofe. 13th century, Italy
Shulchan Arukh. R. Yosef Karo. 16th century, Balkans/Eretz Yisrael; R. Moshe Isserles. 16th century, Poland
Shulchan Arukh of R. Shneur Zalman of Liady. 18th–19th century, Russia
Siddur Rashi. 11th–12th century, France/Germany
Torat Ha'adam. R. Moshe b. Nachman (Nachmanides). 13th century, Spain.
Tur. See *Arba'ah Turim*
Yad. See *Mishneh Torah*
Yalkut Yosef. R. Ovadyah Yosef. 20th century, Israel
Yam shel Shelomo. R. Shelomo Luria. 16th century, Poland
Vayo'el Moshe. R. Yoel Teitelbaum. 20th century, United States

Halakhic Commentaries

Be'er Hagolah (to *Shulchan Arukh*). R. Moshe Rivkes. 17th century, Amsterdam

Be'er Hetev (to *Shulchan Arukh, Orach Chayim, Even Ha'ezer*). R. Yehudah Ashkenazi. 18th century, Lithuania

Beit Shmuel (to *Shulchan Arukh, Even Ha'ezer*). R. Shmuel Phoebus. 17th century, Poland

Beit Yosef (to *Tur*). R. Yosef Karo. 16th century, Balkans/Palestine

Birkei Yosef (to *Shulchan Arukh*). R. Chayim Y. D. Azulai. 18th century, Eretz Yisrael/ Amsterdam/ Italy

Bi'ur Hagra (to *Shulchan Arukh*). R. Eliyahu, Gaon of Vilna. 18th century

Bi'ur Halakhah (to *Mishnah Berurah*). R. Yisrael Meir Kagan. 19th–20th century, Lithuania

Chidushei R. Chayim Halevy (Soloveitchik) (to *Yad*). 19th–20th century, Lithuania

Ha'amek She'elah (to *She'iltot*). R. Naftali Zvi Yehudah Berlin. 19th century, Lithuania

Hagahot Maimoniot (to *Yad*). R. Meir Hakohen. 13th century, Germany

Kereti Ufeleiti (to *Shulchan Arukh, Yore De'ah*). R. Yonatan Eybeschuetz. 18th century, Prague

Magen Avraham (to *Shulchan Arukh, Orach Chayim*). R. Avraham Gumbiner. 17th century, Poland

Magid Mishneh (to *Yad*). R. Vidal de Tolosa. 14th century, Spain

Mor Uketzi'ah (to *Orach Chayim*). R. Ya'akov Emden. 17th century, Germany

Nimukei Yosef (to Alfasi). R. Yosef ibn Habiba. 14th century, Spain

Nishmat Avraham (to *Shulchan Arukh*). R. A.S. Avraham. 20th century, Israel

Otzar Haposkim (to *Shulchan Arukh, Even Ha'ezer*). 20th century, Israel

Pitchei Teshuvah (to *Shulchan Arukh*). R. Avraham Eisenstadt. 19th century, Lithuania

Rabad (notes to *Yad*). R. Avraham b. David. 12th century, Provence

Rabbeinu Nissim (to Alfasi). R. Nissim Gerondi. 14th century, Spain

Radbaz (to *Yad*). R. David ibn Zimra. 16th–17th century, Egypt

Sefer Hama'or (to Alfasi). R. Zerachyah Halevy. 12th century, Provence

Sefer Me'irat Einayim (to *Shulchan Arukh, Choshen Mishpat*). R. Yehoshua Falk Katz. 16th–17th century, Poland
Shakh. See *Siftei Kohen.*
Shiltei Giborim (to Alfasi). R. Yehoshua Boaz b. Barukh. 16th century, Italy
Siftei Kohen (to *Shulchan Arukh*). R. Shabbetai Kohen. 17th century, Lithuania
Taz. See *Turei Zahav.*
Torah Temimah (to the Torah). R. Barukh Halevi Epstein. 20th century, Lithuania
Turei Zahav (to *Shulchan Arukh*). R. David Halevy. 17th century, Lithuania

Talmudic Commentaries

Bartenura (Mishnah). R. Ovadyah of Bartenura. 15th century, Italy/Palestine
Beit Habechirah. R. Menachem Hameiri. 13th century, Provence
Chazon Ish. R. Avraham Y. Karelitz. 20th century, Palestine/Israel
Chidushei Haramban. R. Moshe b. Nachman (Nachmanides). 13th century, Spain
Chidushei Harashba. R. Shelomo b. Adret. 13th–14th century, Spain
Chidushei Haritva. R. Yom Tov b. Ishbili. 14th century, Spain
Chidushei R. Akiva Eger (Mishnah). 18th–19th century, Germany
Maharsha. R. Shmuel Edels. 16th–17th century, Poland
Meiri. See *Beit Habechirah.*
R. Nissim Gerondi (to *B. Nedarim*). 14th century, Spain
Otzar Hageonim, ed. B.M. Levin, Jerusalem, 1928–43. A compilation of geonic responsa and commentaries.
Rashbam. R. Shmuel b. Meir. 12th century, France
Rashi. R. Shelomo b. Yitzchak. 11th century, France
Tiferet Yisrael (Mishnah). R. Yisrael Lipschutz. 19th century, Germany
Tosafot. A style of talmudic commentary associated with the scholars of 12th–13th century, France and Germany. (When cited in this book, the term refers to the *tosafot* printed on the page of the standard editions of the Babylonian Talmud.)

Tosafot Yom Tov (Mishnah). R. Yom Tov Lipmann Heller. 16th–17th century, Moravia

Responsa

Achiezer. R. Chayim Ozer Grodzinsky. 20th century, Lithuania
Aseh Lekha Rav. R. Chayim David Halevy. 20th century, Israel
Avkat Rokhel. R. Yosef Karo. 16th century, Balkans/Palestine
Bach. See *Bayit Chadash.*
Bayit Chadash. R. Yoel Sirkes. 17th century, Poland
Be'er Yitzchak. R. Yitzchak Elchanan Spector. 19th century, Lithuania
Beit Ya'akov. R. Ya'akov b. Shmuel. 17th century, Germany
Beit Yitzchak. R. Yitzchak Schmelkes. 19th century, Galicia
Binyan Tziyon. R. Ya'akov Ettlinger. 19th century, Germany
Chakham Zvi. R. Zvi Ashkenazi. 18th century, Germany
Chatam Sofer. R. Moshe Sofer. 19th century, Hungary
Chavat Ya'ir. R. Ya'ir Bachrach. 17th century, Germany
Chelkat Ya'akov. R. Mordekhai Breisch. 20th century, Switzerland
Chesed Le'avraham. R. Avraham Zvi Brudna. 20th century, Palestine
Da'at Kohen. R. Avraham Yitzchak Hakohen Kook. 20th century, Palestine
Ha'elef Lekha Shelomo. R. Shelomo Kluger. 19th century, Galicia
Halakhot Ketanot. R. Ya'akov Hagiz. 17th century, Jerusalem
Harosh. R. Asher b. Yechiel. 14th century, Germany/Spain
Heikhal Yitzchak. R. Yitzchak Halevy Herzog. 20th century, Israel
Igerot Moshe. R. Moshe Feinstein. 20th century, United States
Kenesset Yechezkel. R. Yechezkel Katzenellenbogen. 18th century, Germany
Ketav Sofer. R. Avraham Sofer. 19th century, Hungary
Ma'arakhei Lev. R. Yehudah Lev Zirelsohn. 20th century, Russia
Mabit. R. Moshe Trani. 16th century, Palestine
Maharam Lublin. R. Meir b. Gedaliah. 16th–17th century, Poland
Maharam Padua. R. Meir Katznellenbogen. 16th century, Italy
Maharam Schick. R. Moshe Schick. 19th century, Hungary
Maharik. R. Yosef Kolon. 15th century, Italy
Maharshal. R. Shelomo Luria. 16th century, Poland
Maharsham. R. Shalom Schwadron. 19th century, Galicia
Mashat Binyamin. R. Binyamin Selonick. 16th century, Poland

Meir Azaryah of Fano. 16th–17th century, Italy
Melamed Leho'il. R. David Zvi Hoffman. 20th century, Germany
Meshiv Davar. R. Naftali Zvi Yehudah Berlin. 19th century, Lithuania
Mima'amakim. R. Efraim Oshry. 20th century, Lithuania/United
   States
Minchat Yitzchak. R. Yitzchak Ya'akov Weiss. 20th century, Israel
Mishpat Kohen. R. Avraham Yitzchak Hakohen Kook. 20th century,
   Palestine
Mishpetei Ouziel. R. Benzion Meir Hai Ouziel. 20th century, Israel
Miyam Hahalakhah. R. Yonah Metzger. 20th century, Israel
Netzer Mata'ai. R. Natan Zvi Friedman. 20th century, Israel
Noda Biyehudah. R. Yechezkel Landau. 18th century, Bohemia
Nogah Hatzedek. Various rabbis. 19th century, Central Europe
Panim Me'irot. R. Meir Eisenstadt. 18th century, Poland
Parashat Mordekhai. R. Mordekhai Benet. 19th century, Germany
Penei Yehoshua. R. Yeshoshua Falk. 17th century, Poland
Pesakim Ukhetavim. R. Yitzchak Halevy Herzog. 20th century, Israel
R. Ezriel Hildesheimer. 19th century, Germany
R. Moshe Isserles. 16th century, Poland
R. Ya'akov Weil. 15th century, Germany
Radbaz. R. David ibn Zimra. 16th–17th century, Egypt
Rambam. R. Moshe b. Maimon (Maimonides). 12th century, Egypt
Rashi. R. Shelomo b. Yitzchak. 11th century, France
Rashba. R. Shelomo b. Adret. 13th–14th century, Catalonia
Rashbash. R. Shelomo b. Shimeon Duran. 15th century, Algeria
Rivash. R. Yitzchak b. Sheshet. 14th–15th century, Spain/North Africa
She'elat Ya'avetz. R. Ya'akov Emden. 18th century, Germany
Seridei Esh. R. Yechiel Ya'akov Weinberg. 20th century, Germany
Shevet Halevy. R. Shmuel Helevy Wasner. 20th century, Israel
Shevut Ya'akov. R. Ya'akov Reischer. 18th century, Germany
Sho'el Umeshiv. R. Shaul Nathanson. 19th century, Galicia
Ta'alumot Lev. R. Eliahu Hazan. 19th century, Palestine
Tamim De'im. R. Avraham b. David (Rabad). 12th century, Provence
Tashbetz. R. Shimeon b. Tzemach Duran. 14th–15th century, North
   Africa
Terumat Hadeshen. R. Yisrael Isserlein. 15th century, Germany
Teshuvah Me'ahavah. R. Eliezer Fleckeles. 18th–19th century, Prague
Teshuvot Rashi. R. Shelomo b. Yitzchak. 11th century, France
Tuv Ta'am Veda'at. R. Shelomo Kluger. 19th century, Lithuania

Tzitz Eliezer. R. Eliezer Yehudah Waldenberg. 20th century, Israel
Tzofnat Paneach. R. Yosef Rosen. 19th–20th century, Belarus
Yabi'a Omer. R. Ovadyah Yosef. 20th century, Israel
Yad Halevi. R. Seligman Baer. 19th century, Germany
Yechaveh Da'at. R. Ovadyah Yosef. 20th century, Israel
Yehudah Ya'aleh. R. Yehudah Aszod. 19th century, Hungary
Zekan Aharon. R. Aharon Walkin. 20th century, Russia
Zera Emet. R. Ishmael Sacerdote (Cohen). 18th–19th century, Italy

Other Works

Akedat Yitzchak. Commentary to the Torah. R. Yitzchak Arama. 15th century, Spain
Meshekh Chokhmah. Commentary to the Torah. R. Meir Simchah Hakohen of Dvinsk. 19th–20th century, Russia
Moreh Nevukhim. Philosophical treatise. R. Moshe b. Maimon (Maimonides). 12th century, Egypt
Piskei Din Rabaniyim. Collected rulings of the rabbinical courts of the State of Israel.

Bibliography

Abramov, S.Z. *Perpetual Dilemma: Jewish Religion in the Jewish State.* Cranbury, NJ: Associated University Presses, 1976.

Abrams, Judith Z. *A Beginner's Guide to the Steinsaltz Talmud.* Northvale, NJ: Jason Aronson, 1999.

_____. *Judaism and Disability: Portrayals in Ancient Texts from the Tanach to the Bavli.* Washington DC: Gallaudet University Press, 1998.

_____. *Learn Talmud.* Northvale, NJ: Jason Aronson, 1995.

_____. *The Talmud for Beginners.* 3 vols. Vol. 1: *Prayer.* Vol. 2: *Text.* Vol. 3: *Living in a Non-Jewish World.* Northvale, NJ: Jason Aronson, 1994–97.

Albeck, Chanokh. *Shishah Sidrei Mishnah* (with commentary). 6 vols. Jerusalem/Tel Aviv: Mosad Bialik/Dvir, 1954.

Alon, Gedalyahu. *Jews, Judaism and the Classical World.* Jerusalem: Magnes Press, 1977.

Anderson, Bernhard W. *Understanding the Old Testament.* Edgewood Cliffs, NJ: Prentice-Hall, 1975.

Aviner, Shelomo. "Ha'amadat Choleh Mesukan 'al Matzavo." *Assia* 3 (1983): 336–40.

Avraham, A.S. *Nishmat Avraham.* 5 vols. Jerusalem: Makhon Schlesinger, 1984–87.

Baer, Seligmann. *Seder Avodat Yisrael.* Roedelheim, 1868.

Bamberger, Bernard J. "The Festival Calendar." In W.G. Plaut, ed., *The Torah: A Modern Commentary,* 919–23. New York: Union of American Hebrew Congregations, 1981.

_____. *Proselytism in the Talmudic Period.* New York: Ktav Publishing House, 1968.

Baron, Salo W. *The Jewish Community: Its History and Structure to the American Revolution.* 3 vols. Philadelphia: Jewish Publication Society of America, 1942.

Barth, Lewis M., ed., *Berit Milah in the Reform Context.* New York: Berit Milah Board of Reform Judaism, 1990.

Barzel, Uriel S. *The Art of Cure: Extracts from Galen.* Maimonides' Medical Writings, vol. 5. Haifa: The Maimonides Research Institute, 1992.

Beauchamp, Tom L. and James F. Childress, *Principles of Biomedical Ethics.* New York: Oxford University Press, 1989.

Berlin, Meir and S.Y. Zevin, eds. *Encyclopedia Talmudit.* Jerusalem: Talmudic Encyclopedia Institute, 1947–.

Bial, Morrison D. *Liberal Judaism at Home: The Practices of Modern Reform Judaism.* New York: Union of American Hebrew Congregations, 1971.

Birnbaum, Philip. *Hasiddur Hashalem. / Daily Prayer Book.* New York: Hebrew Publishing Company, 1949.

Bleich, J. David. *Contemporary Halakhic Problems*, 4 vols. New York: Ktav Publishing House, 1977–95.

_____. *Judaism and Healing: A Halakhic Perspective.* New York: Ktav Publishing House, 1981.

_____. *Time of Death in Jewish Law.* New York: Z. Berman, 1991.

Blidstein, Gerald J. "Menahem Meiri's Attitude Toward Gentiles: Apologetics or Worldview?" In Joseph Dan, ed., *Binah*, vol. 3: *Jewish Intellectual History in the Middle Ages,* 119–34. Westport, CT: Praeger, 1994.

Blumenkrantz, Avrohom. *The Laws of Pesach: A Digest.* New York: Beis Medrash Ateres Yisroel, 19– (published every year).

Bogosian, Ilene L. "Ambivalence Towards *Gerim* in Jewish Law and Practice." Rabbinic thesis, Hebrew Union College–Jewish Institute of Religion, 1992.

Bokser, Barukh M. *The Origins of the Seder: The Passover Rite and Early Rabbinic Judaism.* Berkeley: University of California Press, 1984.

Boraz, Edward S. *Understanding the Talmud: A Modern Reader's Guide for Study.* Northvale, NJ: Jason Aronson, 1996.

Borowitz, Eugene B. and Naomi Patz. *Explaining Reform Judaism.* New York: Behrman House, 1985.

_____. *Reform Judaism Today.* New York: Behrman House, 1983.

Breuer, Mordekhai. "Hasemikhah Ha'ashkenazit." *Zion* 33 (1968): 15–46.

Brickner, Balfour and Albert Vorspan. *Searching the Prophets for Values.* New York: Union of American Hebrew Congregations, 1981.

Brody, Robert. *The Geonim of Babylonia and the Shaping of Medieval Jewish Culture.* New Haven: Yale University Press, 1998.

Bronstein, Herbert, ed. *A Passover Haggadah: The New Union Haggadah.* New York: Central Conference of American Rabbis, 1974 and 1975.

Bronstein, Herbert and Albert H. Friedlander, eds. *The Five Scrolls: Hebrew Texts, English Translations, and New Liturgies.* New York: Central Conference of American Rabbis, 1984.

Bulka, Reuven. *The Coming Cataclysm.* Oakville, Ont.: Mosaic Press, 1984.

Bulka, Reuven, ed. *The RCA Lifecycle Madrikh.* New York: Rabbinical Council of America, 1995.

Chief Rabbinate of Israel. "Hashtalat Lalev." *Techumin* 7 (1986): 187–89.

Code of Ethics for Rabbis. CCAR Yearbook 103 (1993): 179–86.

Cohen, Jeffrey M. *1,001 Questions and Answers on Pesach.* Northvale, NJ: Jason Aronson, 1996.

Cohen, Sandra. "Mourning the Temple's Destruction: The Laws of Tisha B'Av and the Other Public Fasts in the *Arba'ah Turim* and the *Bet Yosef.*" Rabbinic thesis, Hebrew Union College–Jewish Institute of Religion, 1995.

Cohen, Shaye J.D., "The Origins of the Matrilineal Principle in Rabbinic Law." *AJS Review* 10 (1985): 19–53.

____. "Was Judaism in Antiquity a Missionary Religion?" In M. Mor, ed., *Jewish Assimilation, Acculturation, and Accommodation,* 14–23. Lanham MD: University Press of America, 1992.

Cohn, Haim M. *Human Rights in Jewish Law.* New York: Ktav Publishing House, 1984.

Daichovsky, Shelomo, "Kefiat Bedikah Vetipul." *Assia* 12 (1989): 28–33.

deVaux, Roland. *Ancient Israel.* New York: McGraw-Hill, 1961.

Diamant, Anita. *Choosing a Jewish Life: A Handbook for People Converting to Judaism and for Their Family and Friends.* New York: Schocken Books, 1997.

Dobrinsky, Herbert C. *A Treasury of Sephardic Laws and Customs*. New York: Ktav Publishing House/Yeshiva University Press, 1988.

Donin, Hayim Halevy. *To Be a Jew: A Guide to Jewish Observance*. New York: Basic Books, 1991.

_____. *To Pray as a Jew: A Guide to the Prayer Book and the Synagogue Service*. New York: Basic Books, 1991.

Doppelt, Frederic A. and David Polish. *A Guide for Reform Jews*. New York: Bloch Publishing Co., 1957.

Dorff, Elliot N. *Matters of Life and Death: A Jewish Approach to Modern Medical Ethics*. Philadelphia: Jewish Publication Society of America, 1998.

Einstein, Stephen J. and Lydia Kukoff, eds. *Introduction to Judaism: Instructor's Guide and Curriculum*. New York: Union of American Hebrew Congregations, 1999.

Eisenstein, Yehuda David. *Otzar Dinim Uminhagim*. New York: Hebrew Publishing Co., 1928.

_____. *Otzar Hamidrashim*. 2 vols. New York: Published by the Editor, 1915.

Elbogen, Ismar. *Jewish Liturgy: A Comprehensive History*. Trans. by Raymond Scheindlin. Philadelphia and New York: Jewish Publication Society and Jewish Theological Seminary, 1993.

Ellenson, David, "Artificial Fertilization and Procreative Autonomy." In W. Jacob and M. Zemer, eds., *The Fetus and Fertility in Jewish Law*, 19–38. Tel Aviv and Pittsburgh: Freehof Institute of Progressive Halakhah, 1995.

_____. "Retroactive Annulment of a Conversion." In W. Jacob and M. Zemer, eds., *Conversion to Judaism in Jewish Law*, 49–66. Tel Aviv and Pittsburgh: Freehof Institute of Progressive Halakhah, 1994.

Ellinson, Elyakim. *Nisu'in Shelo Kedat Moshe ve-Yisrael*. Tel Aviv: Dvir, 1975.

Elon, Menachem. *Jewish Law: History, Sources, Principles*. 4 vols. Philadelphia: Jewish Publication Society of America, 1994.

Epstein, Louis. *The Jewish Marriage Contract*. New York: Jewish Theological Seminary of America, 1927.

Felder, Aaron. *Yesodei Smochos*. New York, 1974.

Feldman, David M. *Health and Medicine in the Jewish Tradition*. New York: Crossroad Publishing Co., 1986.

_____. *Marital Relations, Birth Control, and Abortion in Jewish Law*. New York: Schocken Books, 1975.

Finkelstein, Louis. *Jewish Self-Government in the Middle Ages.* New York: Philipp Feldheim, 1964.

Fleischer, Ezra. "Lekadmoniyut Tefillot Hachova Be-Yisrael," *Tarbiz* 59 (1990): 397–441.

_____. *Shirat Hakodesh Ha'ivrit Bimei Habeinayim.* Jerusalem: Keter Publishing House, 1975.

Forst, Binyomin. *The Laws of Kashrus.* Brooklyn: Mesorah Publications, 1993.

Foster, Steven E., "The Community Rabbinic Conversion Board—The Denver Model." *Journal of Reform Judaism* 31 (1984): 25–32.

Frank, Yitzchak. *The Practical Talmud Dictionary.* Spring Valley, NY: Philipp Feldheim, 1991.

Freedman, David Noel, ed. *Anchor Bible Dictionary.* New York: Doubleday, 1992.

Freehof, Solomon B. *Contemporary Reform Responsa.* Cincinnati: Hebrew Union College Press, 1974.

_____. *Current Reform Responsa.* Cincinnati: Hebrew Union College Press, 1969.

_____. "Devotional Literature in the Vernacular," *CCAR Yearbook* 33 (1923): 375–415.

_____. *Modern Reform Responsa.* Cincinnati: Hebrew Union College Press, 1971.

_____. *New Reform Responsa.* Cincinnati: Hebrew Union College Press, 1980.

_____. *Recent Reform Responsa.* Cincinnati: Hebrew Union College Press, 1963.

_____. *Reform Jewish Practice and Its Rabbinic Background.* 2 vols. Combined edition (2 vols. in 1). New York: Union of American Hebrew Congregations, 1963.

_____. *Reform Responsa.* Cincinnati: Hebrew Union College Press, 1960.

_____. *Reform Responsa for Our Time.* Cincinnati: Hebrew Union College Press, 1977.

_____. *The Responsa Literature.* Philadelphia: Jewish Publication Society of America, 1955.

_____. *Today's Reform Responsa.* Cincinnati: Hebrew Union College Press, 1990.

_____. *A Treasury of Responsa.* Philadelphia: Jewish Publication Society of America, 1963.

Friedland, Eric L. *Were Our Mouths Filled With Song: Studies in Liberal Jewish Liturgy.* Cincinnati: Hebrew Union College Press, 1997.
Friedman, M.A. *Ribui Nashim Be-Yisrael.* Jerusalem: Mosad Bialik, 1986.
Friedman, N.Z. *Otzar Harabbanim.* Benei Berak: Otzar Harabbanim, 1975.
Ganzfried, Shelomo. *Code of Jewish Law.* Trans. by Hyman Goldin. New York: Hebrew Publishing Co., 1963.
_____. *The Metsudah Kitzur Shulchan Arukh.* Trans. by Avrohom Davis. New York: Metsudah Publications, 1987.
Gilat, Yitzchak. *Perakim Behishtalshelut Hahalakhah.* Ramat Gan: Bar-Ilan University Press, 1992.
Glueck, Shimeon. "Divu'ach Emet Lacholeh." *Assia* 11 (1987): 8–15.
Gold, Michael. *And Hannah Wept: Infertility, Adoption, and the Jewish Couple.* Philadelphia: Jewish Publication Society of America, 1988.
Goldberg, Chaim Binyamin. *Mourning in Halakhah: The Laws and Customs of the Year of Mourning.* Brooklyn NY: Mesorah Publications, 1991.
Goldenberg, Thomas, "Medical Issues and *Berit Milah.*" In L.M. Barth, ed., *Berit Milah in the Reform Context,* 193–205. New York: *Berit Milah* Board of Reform Judaism, 1990.
Goldin, Hyman E. *Hamadrikh: The Rabbi's Guide.* New York: Hebrew Publishing Co., 1956.
Goldschmidt, Ernst Daniel. *Haggadah shel Pesach.* Jerusalem: Mosad Bialik, 1969.
_____. *Seder Rav Amram Gaon.* Jerusalem: Mosad Harav Kook, 1971.
Goldstein, Jonathan, "Jewish Acceptance and Rejection of Hellenism." In E.P. Sanders, ed., *Jewish and Chrsistian Self-Definition,* 2:64–87. Philadelphia: Fortress Press, 1981.
Goldwurm, Hersh and Gedaliah Zlotowitz, eds. *Talmud Bavli: The Schottenstein Edition.* Brooklyn: Mesorah Publications, 1990–.
Goodman, Martin. *Mission and Conversion.* Oxford: Clarendon Press, 1994.
Goren, Shelomo. *Meshiv Milchamah.* Jerusalem: Ha'idra Rabbah, 1983.
_____. *Mishnat Hamedinah.* Jerusalem: Ha'idra Rabbah, 1999.
_____. "Shevitat Harof'im Bahalakhah." *Assia* 5 (1986): 41–54.
Greenberg, Irving. *Will There Be One Jewish People by the Year 2000?* New York: National Jewish Center for Learning and Leadership, 1986.

Greenberg, Simon, ed. *The Ordination of Women as Rabbis: Studies and Responsa.* New York: Jewish Theological Seminary of America, 1988.

Greenwald, Yekutiel Y. *Kol Bo 'al Avelut.* New York: Philipp Feldheim, 1947–51.

Grossman, Avraham. *Chakhmei Tzarfat Harishonim.* Jerusalem: Magnes Press, 1995.

Grunfeld, I. *The Jewish Dietary Laws.* 2 vols. London: Soncino Press, 1972.

Gurock, Jeffrey S. "Resisters and Accommodators: Varieties of Orthodox Rabbis in America, 1886–1983." *American Jewish Archives* 35:2 (1983): 100–187.

Gutmann, Joseph. *The Jewish Sanctuary.* Leiden: Brill, 1983.

Gutmann, Joseph, ed. *The Synagogue: Studies in Origins, Archaeology, and Architecture.* New York: Ktav Publishing House, 1975.

Guttmann, Alexander. "The Jewish Calendar." In Peter S. Knobel, ed., *Gates of the Seasons: A Guide to the Jewish Year,* 7–11. New York: Central Conference of American Rabbis, 1983.

_____. *The Struggle Over Reform in Rabbinic Literature.* New York: World Union for Progressive Judaism, 1977.

Haas, Peter J. *Responsa: Literary History of a Rabbinic Genre.* Atlanta: Scholars Press, 1996.

Hakohen, Mordekhai. *Mikdash Me'at.* Jerusalem: Yad Ramah, 1975.

_____. "Yom Ha'atzma'ut." In Y. Reppel, *Mo'adei Yisrael,* 174–75. Tel Aviv: Ministry of Defense, 1989.

Halivni, David Weiss. *Midrash, Mishnah, and Gemara: The Jewish Predilection for Justified Law.* Cambridge, MA: Harvard University Press, 1986.

Hammer, Reuven. *Entering the High Holy Days: A Guide to the Origins, Themes, and Prayers.* Philadelphia: Jewish Publication Society of America, 1998.

_____. *Entering Jewish Prayer: A Guide to Personal Devotion and the Worship Service.* New York: Schocken Books, 1994.

Harlow, Jules, ed. *Siddur Sim Shalom: A Prayerbook for Shabbat, Fesitivals, and Weekdays.* New York: Rabbinical Assembly of America, 1985.

Haut, Irwin H. *Divorce in Jewish Law and Life.* New York: Sepher-Hermon Press, 1983.

Hecht, Neil S., Bernard S. Jackson, Stephen M. Passamaneck, Daniela Piattelli, and Alfredo Mordechai Rabello., eds. *An Introduction to the*

History and Sources of Jewish Law. New York: Oxford University Press, 1996.

Heinemann, Joseph. "Hamachzor Ha'telat-shenati' Veluach Hashanah." *Tarbiz* 33 (1964): 362–68.

_____. *Prayer in the Talmud.* Trans. by Richard S. Sarason. Berlin and New York: de Gruyter, 1977.

Hertz, J.H. *The Authorised Daily Prayer Book of the United Hebrew Congregations of the British Commonwealth of Nations.* New York: Bloch Publishing Co., 1962.

Herzog, Yitzchak Halevy. *Techukah Le-Yisrael al pi Ha-Torah.* Jerusalem: Mosad Harav Kook, 1989.

Heschel, Abraham Joshua. "The Vocation of the Cantor." In *The Insecurity of Freedom,* 242–53. New York: Schocken Books, 1972.

Hoffman, Lawrence, A., ed. *Gates of Understanding.* 2 vols. Vol. 1: *Essays and Notes to Shaarei Tefillah.* New York: Central Conference of American Rabbis and Union of American Hebrew Congregations, 1977; Vol. 2: *Appreciating the Days of Awe.* New York: Central Conference of American Rabbis, 1984.

_____. "Historical Introduction," in Bronstein, Herbert, ed. *A Passover Haggadah,* 9–12. New York: Central Conference of American Rabbis, 1974 and 1975.

Holtz, Barry W., ed. *Back to the Sources: Reading the Classic Jewish Texts.* New York: Summit Books, 1984.

Idelsohn, A.Z. *Jewish Liturgy and Its Development.* New York: Schocken Books, 1932.

_____. *Jewish Music in Its Historical Development.* New York: Tudor, 1948.

Isaacs, Ronald H., ed. *The Jewish Sourcebook on the Environment and Ecology.* Northvale, NJ: Jason Aronson, 1998.

Isaacs, Ron H., and Kerry M. Olitzky, *A Jewish Mourner's Handbook.* Hoboken, NJ: Ktav Publishing House, 1991.

Jackson, Bernard S., "On the Problem of Roman Influence on the Halakhah and Normative Self-Definition in Judaism." In E.P. Sanders, ed., *Jewish and Christian Self-Definition,* 2:157–203. Philadelphia: Fortress Press, 1981.

Jacob, Walter, ed. *American Reform Responsa: Collected Responsa of the Central Conference of American Rabbis 1889–1983.* New York: Central Conference of American Rabbis, 1983.

_____. *The Changing World of Reform Judaism: The Pittsburgh Platform in Retrospect.* Pittsburgh: Rodef Shalom Press, 1985.

_____. *Contemporary American Reform Responsa*. New York: Central Conference of American Rabbis, 1987.

_____. *Liberal Judaism and Halakhah*. Pittsburgh: Rodef Shalom Press, 1988.

_____. *Questions and Reform Jewish Answers: New American Reform Responsa*. New York: Central Conference of American Rabbis, 1992.

Jacob, Walter and Moshe Zemer, eds. *Conversion to Judaism in Jewish Law*. Pittsburgh and Tel Aviv: The Freehof Institute of Progressive Halakhah / Rodef Shalom Press, 1994.

_____. *Death and Euthanasia in Jewish Law: Essays and Responsa*. Pittsburgh and Tel Aviv: The Freehof Institute of Progressive Halakhah, 1995.

_____. *Dynamic Jewish Law: Progressive Halakhah, Essence and Application*. Pittsburgh and Tel Aviv: The Freehof Institute of Progressive Halakhah / Rodef Shalom Press, 1991.

_____. *The Fetus and Fertility in Jewish Law: Essays and Responsa*. Pittsburgh and Tel Aviv: The Freehof Institute of Progressive Halakhah / Rodef Shalom Press, 1995.

_____. *Israel and the Diaspora in Jewish Law: Essays and Responsa*. Pittsburgh and Tel Aviv: The Freehof Institute of Progressive Halakhah, 1997.

_____. *Rabbinic-Lay Relations in Jewish Law*. Pittsburgh and Tel Aviv: The Freehof Institute of Progressive Halakhah / Rodef Shalom Press, 1993.

Jacobs, Louis. *A Tree of Life: Diversity, Flexibility, and Creativity in Jewish Law*. Oxford: Oxford University Press, 1984.

Jakobovits, Immanuel. "Bedin Im Mutar Lekarev Mitato Shel Choleh No'ash Hasovel Yisurim Kashim." *Hapardes* 31:3 (1956): 16–19.

_____. *Jewish Medical Ethics*. New York: Bloch Publishing Co., 1975.

Kahana, Y.Z. *Mechkarim Besifrut Hateshuvot*. Jerusalem: Mosad Harav Kook, 1973.

Kahn, Paul, ed. *Behavioral Sciences and Mental Health*. New York: Sepher Hermon Press, 1984.

Karp, Abraham J. "The Conservative Rabbi—'Dissatisfied But Not Unhappy'." *American Jewish Archives* 35:2 (1983): 188–262.

Kasher, Menachem. *Haggadah Sheleimah*. Jerusalem: Torah Sheleimah Institute, 1967.

Katz, Jacob. *Exclusiveness and Tolerance: Jewish-Gentile Relations in Medieval and Modern Times*. New York: Schocken Books, 1961.

____. *Hahalakhah Bameitzar*. Jerusalem: Magnes Press, 1992.

____. *Halakhah Vekabalah*. Jerusalem: Magnes Press, 1986.

____. *Tradition and Crisis: Jewish Society at the End of the Middle Ages*. Trans. by Bernard Dov Cooperman. New York: Schocken Books, 1994.

Kehati, Pinchas. *Mishnayot Mevo'arot*. Jerusalem: Heikhal Shelomo, 1966–. / *The Mishnah*. Jerusalem: World Zionist Organization, 1988–.

Kimelman, Reuven. *The Ethics of National Power: Government and War from the Sources of Judaism*. New York: National Jewish Center for Learning and Leadership, 1987.

Klein, Isaac. *A Guide to Jewish Religious Practice*. New York: Jewish Theological Seminary of America, 1979.

Klirs, Tracy Guren, comp. *The Merit of Our Mothers: A Bilingual Anthology of Jewish Women's Prayers*. Trans. by Tracy Guren Klirs, Ida Selavan, and Gella Schweid Fishman; annotated by Faedra Lazar Weiss and Barbara Selya. Cincinnati: Hebrew Union College Press, 1992.

Knobel, Peter S., ed. *Gates of the Seasons: A Guide to the Jewish Year*. New York: Central Conference of American Rabbis, 1983.

Kook, Avraham Yitzchak Hakohen. *Igerot HaRe'ayah*. 4 vols. Jerusalem: Mosad Harav Kook, 1984.

Korinaldi, Michael, "Leshe'elat Ma'amdam Ha'ishi shel Hakara'im Be-Yisrael." *Mahalakhim* 1 (1969): 7–18.

Kraemer, David. *The Mind of the Talmud: An Intellectual History of the Bavli*. New York: Oxford University Press, 1990.

Kreitman, Benjamin Z., "Ha'im Bereikhat Sechiyah Kesheirah Lemikveh?" *Proceedings of the Rabbinical Assembly* 33 (1969): 219–22.

Kukoff, Lydia. *Choosing Judaism*. New York: Union of American Hebrew Congregations, 1981.

Lamm, Maurice. *Becoming a Jew*. Middle Village, NY: Jonathan David Publishers, 1991.

____. *The Jewish Way in Death and Mourning*. New York: Jonathan David Publishers, 1969.

____. *The Jewish Way in Love and Marriage*. New York: Jonathan David Publishers, 1991.

Lamm, Norman. *Torah Umadda: The Encounter of Religious Learning and Worldly Knowledge in the Jewish Tradition*. Northvale, NJ: Jason Aronson, 1990.

Landman, Leo. *The Cantor: An Historic Perspective.* New York: Yeshiva University Press, 1972.

_____. "Jewish Attitudes Towards Gambling." *Jewish Quarterly Review* 58, n.s. (1967): 34–62.

Langer, Ruth. "The Impact of Custom, History, and Mysticism on the Shaping of Jewish Liturgical Law." Doctoral dissertation, Hebrew Union College–Jewish Institute of Religion, Cincinnati, 1994.

Lauterbach, J.Z., "The Ceremony of Breaking a Glass at Weddings." *Hebrew Union College Annual* 2 (1925): 351–80.

Lebeau, James M. *The Jewish Dietary Laws: Sanctify Life.* New York: United Synagogue of America, 1983.

Leibowitz, J.O. and S. Marcus. *Moses Maimonides on the Causes of Symptoms.* Berkeley: University of California Press, 1974.

Levine, Aaron. *Economics and Jewish Law.* Hoboken/New York: Ktav Publishing House/Yeshiva University Press, 1987.

Levy, Richard, "The Liturgy of *Berit Milah*." In L.M. Barth, ed., *Berit Milah in the Reform Context,* 3–15. New York: *Berit Milah* Board of Reform Judaism, 1990.

Lieberman, Saul. *Greek in Jewish Palestine.* New York: Jewish Theological Seminary of America, 1942.

_____. *Hellenism in Jewish Palestine.* New York: Jewish Theological Seminary of America, 1950.

Litvin, B. and S.H. Hoenig. *Jewish Identity.* New York: Philipp Feldheim, 1965.

Mann, Jacob. *The Bible as Read and Preached in the Old Synagogue.* New York: Ktav Publishing House, 1971.

Maier, David, "Ein Tzorekh Be'etikah Refu'it." *Assia* 1 (1976): 244–48.

Martin, Bernard, ed. *Contemporary Reform Jewish Thought.* Chicago: Quadrangle Books, 1968.

Maslin, Simeon J., ed. *Gates of Mitzvah: A Guide to the Jewish Life Cycle.* New York: Central Conference of American Rabbis, 1979.

Meek, Theophile J. "The Translation of *Ger* in the Hexateuch and Its Bearing on the Documentary Hypothesis." *Journal of Biblical Literature* 49 (1930): 172–80.

Meyer, Michael A. "*Berit Milah* Within the History of the Reform Movement," in L.M. Barth, ed., *Berit Milah in the Reform Context,* 141–51. New York: *Berit Milah* Board of Reform Judaism, 1990.

_____. *Response to Modernity: A History of the Reform Movement in Judaism.* New York: Oxford University Press, 1988.

Mielziner, Moses. *Introduction to the Talmud.* 1894; 4th ed. New York: Bloch Publishing Co., 1968.

_____. *The Jewish Law of Marriage and Divorce in Ancient and Modern Times.* Cincinnati: Bloch Publishing Co., 1884.

Milgrom, Jacob, "Religious Conversion and the Revolt Model for the Formation of Israel." *Journal of Biblical Literature* 101 (1982): 169–76.

Millgram, Abraham E. *Sabbath: The Day of Delight.* Philadelphia: Jewish Publication Society of America, 1965.

Munk, Elie. *The World of Prayer.* New York: Philipp Feldheim, 1998.

National Jewish Welfare Board: Commission on Jewish Chaplaincy, Responsa Committee. *Responsa in War Time.* New York: Division of Religious Activities, National Jewish Welfare Board, 1947.

Neusner, Jacob. *The Oral Torah: The Sacred Books of Judaism. An Introduction.* San Francisco: Harper and Row, 1986.

Noivirt, Yehoshua. *Shemirath Shabbath: A Guide to the Practical Observance of the Sabbath.* Jerusalem: Philipp Feldheim, 1989.

Novak, David. *The Image of the Non-Jew in Judaism.* New York: Edward Mellen Press, 1985.

Olitzky, Kerry M. *Twelve Jewish Steps to Recovery: A Personal Guide for Turning from Alcoholism and Other Addictions.* Woodstock, VT: Jewish Lights Publishing, 1991.

Orlinsky, Harry M. *Ancient Israel.* Ithaca, NY: Cornell University Press, 1960.

Petuchowski, Jakob J. "Plural Models Within the Halakhah." *Judaism* 19 (1970): 77–89.

_____. *Prayerbook Reform in Europe: The Liturgy of European Liberal and Reform Judaism.* New York: World Union for Progressive Judaism, 1968.

_____. *Theology and Poetry: Studies in the Medieval Piyut.* London: Henley; Boston: Routledge and Kegan Paul, 1978.

_____. "Toward Sectarianism." *Moment* 8 (September, 1983): 34–36.

Petuchowski, Jakob J. and Michael Brocke, eds., *The Lord's Prayer and Jewish Liturgy.* New York: Seabury Press, 1978.

Plaut, W. Gunther. *The Growth of Reform Judaism.* New York: World Union for Progressive Judaism, 1965.

_____. *The Rise of Reform Judaism.* New York: World Union for Progressive Judaism, 1963.

_____. *A Shabbat Manual.* New York: Central Conference of American Rabbis, 1972.

Plaut, W. Gunther, ed. *The Torah: A Modern Commentary.* New York: UAHC Press, 1981.

Plaut, W. Gunther and Mark Washofsky, eds. *Teshuvot for the Nineties.* New York: Central Conference of American Rabbis, 1997.

Polish, David. "The Changing and the Constant in the Reform Rabbinate." *American Jewish Archives* 35:2 (1983): 263–341.

Polish, David. *Renew Our Days: The Zionist Issue in Reform Judaism.* Jerusalem: World Zionist Organization, 1976.

Polish, David, ed. *Rabbi's Manual.* Historical and Halachic Notes by W. Gunther Plaut. New York: Central Conference of American Rabbis, 1988.

Rabbinovicz, Raphael N. *Dikdukei Soferim.* Munich, 1867–97.

Rabinowicz, Rachel Anne, ed. *Passover Haggadah: The Feast of Freedom.* New York: Rabbinical Assembly, 1982.

Rabinowitz, Louis I. *Herem Hayishuv.* London: Goldston, 1945.

Rakover, Nachum. *Hilkhot Yom Ha'atzma'ut ve-Yom Yerushalayim.* Jerusalem: Ministry of Religion and Ministry of Education and Culture, 1973.

Reif, Stefan C. *Judaism and Hebrew Prayer.* Cambridge: Cambridge University Press, 1993.

Report of the Committee on Patrilineal Descent on the Status of Children of Mixed Marriages. CCAR Yearbook 93 (1983): 157–60. (Included in W. Jacob, ed., *American Reform Responsa,* 547–50.)

Rheins, Richard. "The Development of the Professional Rabbinate as Evidenced in the Halakhic Sources." Rabbinic thesis, Hebrew Union College–Jewish Institute of Religion, 1989.

Riemer, Jack, and Nathaniel Stampfer, eds. *Ethical Wills: A Modern Jewish Treasury.* New York: Schocken Books, 1983.

Riskin, Shlomo. *The Passover Haggadah.* New York: Ktav Publishing House, 1983.

_____. *Women and Jewish Divorce.* Hoboken, NJ: Ktav Publishing House, 1989.

Romberg, Henry C. *Bris Milah.* New York: Philipp Feldheim, 1982.

Rosenberg, Aaron. *Divrei Benei Mitzvah.* New York: Central Conference of American Rabbis, 1990.

Rosner, Fred. *The Medical Aphorisms of Moses Maimonides.* Maimonides' Medical Writings, vol. 3. Haifa: The Maimonides Research Institute, 1989.

_____. *Medicine in the Mishneh Torah of Maimonides.* New York: Ktav Publishing House, 1984.

_____. *Modern Medicine and Jewish Ethics.* Hoboken, NJ: Ktav Publishing House, 1991.

Rosner, Fred, ed. *Medicine and Jewish Law.* Northvale, NJ: Jason Aronson, 1990.

Rosner, Fred, and J. David Bleich, eds. *Jewish Bioethics.* New York: Sanhedrin Press, 1979.

Sacks, Jonathan. *One People? Tradition, Modernity, and Jewish Unity.* London: Littman Library of Jewish Civilization, 1993.

Safrai, Shmuel, ed. *The Literature of the Sages.* Philadelphia: Fortress Press, 1987.

Salkin, Jeffrey K. *Putting God on the Guest List: How to Reclaim the Spiritual Meaning of Your Child's Bar or Bat Mitzvah.* Woodstock, VT: Jewish Lights Publishing, 1992.

Sarna, Nahum M. *Understanding Genesis: The Heritage of Biblical Israel.* New York: Schocken Books, 1970.

Schacter, Jacob, ed., *Jewish Tradition and the Non-Traditional Jew.* Northvale, NJ: Jason Aronson, 1992.

Schechter, Solomon. *Studies in Judaism.* New York: Meridian Books, 1958.

Schereschewsky, Benzion. *Dinei Mishpachah.* Jerusalem: Rubin Maas, 1992.

Scherman, Nosson. *The Complete Art Scroll Machzor for Rosh Hashanah.* New York: Mesorah Publications, 1985.

_____. *The Complete Art Scroll Machzor for Yom Kippur.* New York: Mesorah Publications, 1986.

_____. *The Complete Art Scroll Siddur.* New York: Mesorah Publications, 1984.

_____. *The Haggadah Treasury.* New York: Zeirei Agudath Israel of America, 1978.

Schiff, Daniel. "Developing *Halakhic* Attitudes to Sex Preselection." In W. Jacob and M. Zemer, eds., *The Fetus and Fertility in Jewish Law,* 91–117. Tel Aviv and Pittsburgh: Freehof Institute of Progressive Halakhah, 1995.

Schiffman, Lawrence H. *Who Was a Jew? Rabbinic and Halakhic Perspectives on the Jewish-Christian Schism.* Hoboken, NJ: Ktav Publishing House, 1985.

Schwarzfuchs, Simon. *A Concise History of the Rabbinate.* Oxford: Basil Blackwell, 1993.

Shafran, R. Yigal. "Amirat Emet Lacholeh." *Assia* 11 (1987): 16–23.

Shapiro, Mark Dov. *Gates of Shabbat: A Guide for Observing Shabbat.* New York: Central Conference of American Rabbis, 1991.

Sharlin, William, "Israel's Influence on American Liberal Synagogue Music." In L.A. Hoffman, ed., *Gates of Understanding,* 122–28. New York: Central Conference of American Rabbis and Union of American Hebrew Congregations, 1977.

Shaviv, Yehudah, ed. *Shanah Beshanah, 5756.* Jerusalem: Heikhal Shelomo, 1995.

Shilo, Shmuel. *Dina Demalkhuta Dina.* Jerusalem: Academic Press, 1975.

Shragai, S.Z. and Yitzchak Rafael. *Sefer Hatziyonut Hadatit.* Jerusalem: Mosad Harav Kook, 1977.

Sicker, Martin J. *The Judaic State: A Study in Rabbinic Political Theory.* Westport, CT: Praeger, 1988.

_____. *What Judaism Says About Politics: The Political Theology of the Torah.* Northvale, NJ: Jason Aronson, 1994.

Silberstein, Laurence J. and Robert L. Cohn, eds. *The Other in Jewish Thought and History.* New York: New York University Press, 1994.

Sirat, Colette. *A History of Jewish Philosophy in the Middle Ages.* Cambridge: Cambridge University Press, 1985.

Solomon, Norman. *The Analytic Movement: Hayyim Soloveitchik and His Circle.* Atlanta: Scholars Press, 1993.

Speiser, E.A. *Genesis.* The Anchor Bible. New York: Doubleday, 1981.

Sperber, Daniel. *Minhagei Yisrael.* 6 vols. Jerusalem: Mosad Harav Kook, 1989–.

Staitman, Mark N. "Withdrawing or Withholding Nutrition, Hydration or Oxygen from Patients." In W. Jacob and M. Zemer, eds., *Death and Euthanasia in Jewish Law,* 1–10. Pittsburgh and Tel Aviv: The Freehof Institute of Progressive Halakhah, 1995.

Steinberg, Avraham. *Jewish Medical Law.* Jerusalem: Mosad Harav Kook, 1978.

Steinsaltz, Adin, ed. *Talmud Bavli.* Jerusalem: Israeli Institute for Talmudic Publications, 1967–. / *The Talmud.* New York: Random House, 1989–.

Stern, Chaim, ed. *Gates of Prayer: The New Union Prayer Book.* New York: Central Conference of American Rabbis, 1975.

_____. *Gates of Repentance: The New Union Prayer Book for the Days of Awe.* New York: Central Conference of American Rabbis, 1978.

Stern, Chaim, ed., with Donna Berman, Edward Graham, and H. Leonard Poller. *On the Doorposts of Your House / Al Mezuzot Beitekha*. New York: Central Conference of American Rabbis, 1994.

Stevens, Elliot L., ed. *Rabbinic Authority*. New York: Central Conference of American Rabbis, 1982.

Strack, H. L. and G. Stemberger. *Introduction to the Talmud and Midrash*. Minneapolis: Fortress Press, 1992.

Suggested Constitution and By-Laws for Congregations. Joint Commission on Synagogue Administration, Union of American Hebrew Congregations and Central Conference of American Rabbis. April, 1984.

Tabory, Yosef. *Pesach Dorot*. Tel Aviv: Hakibbutz Hameuchad, 1996.

Tamari, Meir. *With All Your Possessions: Jewish Ethics and Economic Life*. New York: The Free Press, 1987.

Ta-Shema, Yisrael. *Minhag Ashkenaz Hakadmon*. Jerusalem: Magnes Press, 1995.

Tcherikover, Victor. *Hellenistic Civilization and the Jews*. Philadelphia: Jewish Publication Society of America, 1959.

Tigay, Jeffrey H. *The JPS Torah Commentary: Deuteronomy*. Philadelphia: Jewish Publication Society of America, 1996.

Twersky, Isadore. *Introduction to the Code of Maimonides*. New Haven: Yale University Press, 1980.

Urbach, Ephraim E. *Ba'alei Hatosafot*. Jerusalem: Mosad Bialik, 1980.

_____. *The Halakhah: Its Sources and Development*. Ramat Gan: Masada, 1986.

_____. *The Sages: Their Concepts and Beliefs*. 2 vols. Jerusalem: Magnes Press, 1975.

Vorspan, Albert. *Jewish Values and Social Crisis: A Casebook for Social Action*. New York: Union of American Hebrew Congregations, 1968.

_____. *Reform Judaism and Social Action*. New York: Union of American Hebrew Congregations, 1983.

Vorspan, Albert, and Eugene J. Lipman. *Justice and Judaism: The Work of Social Action*. New York: Union of American Hebrew Congregations, 1956.

Vorspan, Albert, and David Saperstein. *Jewish Dimensions of Social Justice: Tough Moral Choices of Our Time*. New York: Union of American Hebrew Congregations, 1998.

Wagner, Stanley M., "The *Meshumad* and *Mumar* in Talmudic Literature." In M. Katz, ed., *The Jacob Dolnitzky Memorial Volume,* 198-227. Skokie, IL: Hebrew Theological College, 1982.

Waldman, Menachem, "Nisu'in Vegerushin Bekerev Yehudei Ethiopia." *Techumin* 11 (1990): 214–40.

Washofsky, Mark, "Abortion and the Halakhic Conversation: A Liberal Perspective." In W. Jacob and M. Zemer, eds., *The Fetus and Fertility in Jewish Law,* 39–89. Tel Aviv and Pittsburgh: Freehof Institute of Progressive Halakhah, 1995.

_____. "AIDS and Ethical Responsibility: Some Halakhic Considerations." *Journal of Reform Judaism* 36:1 (Winter, 1989): 53–65.

_____. "Halakhah and Political Theory: A Study in Jewish Legal Response to Modernity." *Modern Judaism* (October, 1989): 289–310.

_____. "*Halakhah* and Ulterior Motives." In W. Jacob and M. Zemer, eds., *Conversion to Judaism in Jewish Law,* 1–47. Tel Aviv and Pittsburgh: Freehof Institute of Progressive Halakhah, 1994.

_____. "Is Old Age a Disease? The Elderly, The Medical System, and the Literature of the *Halakhah*." In W. Jacob and M. Zemer, eds., *Age and Aging in Jewish Law,* 43–82. Tel Aviv and Pittsburgh: Freehof Institute of Progressive Halakhah, 1997.

_____. "The Proposal for a National *Beit Din*: Is It Good for the Jews?" In M. Shapiro, ed., *Divisions Between Traditionalism and Liberalism in the American Jewish Community,* 35-54. Lewiston NY: Edwin Mellen Press, 1991.

_____. "The Recalcitrant Husband: The Problem of Definition." *Jewish Law Annual* 4 (1981): 144–66.

_____. "Reinforcing Our Jewish Identity: Issues of Personal Status." *CCAR Yearbook* 104 (1994): 51–57.

_____. "Responsa and Rhetoric: On Law, Literature, and the Rabbinic Decision." In John C. Reeves and John Kampen, eds. *Pursuing the Text: Studies in Honor of Ben Zion Wacholder,* 360–409. Sheffield: Sheffield Academic Press, 1994.

Weissler, Chava. "The *Tkhines* and Women's Prayer," *CCAR Journal* 39:4 (Fall, 1993): 75–88.

Werner, Eric. *The Sacred Bridge.* New York: Columbia University Press, 1959.

Wertheim, Aharon. *Halakhot Vehalikhot Bachasidut.* Jerusalem: Mosad Harav Kook, 1989 / *Law and Custom in Hasidism.* Hoboken, NJ: Ktav Publishing House, 1992.

Wiesenberg, E.J. "Calendar." In *Encyclopedia Judaica*, 5:43–50. Jerusalem: Keter Publishing House, 1972.

Wolfson, Ron. *The Shabbat Seder*. Woodstock, VT: Jewish Lights Publishing, 1995.

Zamek, Stanton M. "Even Though He Sins He Remains a Jew: The Repentance of the Returning Apostate." Rabbinic thesis, Hebrew Union College–Jewish Institute of Religion, Cincinnati, 1996.

Zemer, Moshe, "Ambivalence in Proselytism." In W. Jacob and M. Zemer, eds., *Conversion to Judaism in Jewish Law*, 83–101. Tel Aviv and Pittsburgh: Freehof Institute of Progressive Halakhah, 1994.

_____. *Halakhah Shefuyah*. Tel Aviv: Dvir, 1993. / *Evolving Halakhah: A Progressive Approach to Traditional Jewish Law*. Woodstock, VT: Jewish Lights Publishing, 1999.

_____. "Purifying *Mamzerim*." *Jewish Law Annual* 10 (1992): 99–114.

Zlotowitz, Bernard M., "Sincere Conversion and Ulterior Motives," in W. Jacob and M. Zemer, eds., *Conversion to Judaism in Jewish Law*, 67–82. Tel Aviv and Pittsburgh: Freehof Institute of Progressive Halakhah, 1994.

Zevin, S.Y. *The Festivals in Halachah*. New York: Mesorah Publications, 1981.

Zucker, David J. *American Rabbis*. Northvale, NJ: Jason Aronson, 1998.